THE MOST TRUSTED NAME IN TRAVEL

Frommer's®

LONDON

10th Edition

By Jason Cochran

FrommerMedia LLC

Frommer's London, 10th Edition

Published by:
FrommerMedia LLC

ISBN 978-1-62887-665-9 (paper), 978-1-62887-666-6 (e-book)

Editorial Director: Pauline Frommer
Editor: Elizabeth Heath
Production Editor: Kelly Henthorne
Cartographer: Andy Dolan
Photo Editor: Meghan Lamb
Indexer: Kelly Henthorne
Compositor: Lissa Auciello-Brogan
Cover Design: Dave Riedy

Front cover: Fuller's Churchill Arms is an historic and iconic pub located in Kensington.
Title page: Primrose Hill in Regent's Park offers panoramic views of London.

For information on our other products or services, see www.frommers.com.

Frommer Media LLC also publishes its books in a variety of electronic formats. Some content that appears in print may not be available in electronic formats.

Manufactured in Malaysia

5 4 3 2 1

HOW TO CONTACT US

In researching this book, we discovered many wonderful places—hotels, restaurants, shops, and more. We're sure you'll find others. Please tell us about them, so we can share the information with your fellow travelers in upcoming editions. If you were disappointed with a recommendation, we'd love to know that, too. Please write to: Support@FrommerMedia.com

FROMMER'S HEART RATINGS SYSTEM

Every hotel, restaurant, and attraction listed in this guide has been ranked for quality and value. Here's what the hearts mean:

♥ Recommended
♥♥ Highly Recommended
♥♥♥ A must! Don't miss!

AN IMPORTANT NOTE

The world is a dynamic place. Hotels change ownership, restaurants hike their prices, museums alter their opening hours, and busses and trains change their routings. And all of this can occur in the several months after our authors have visited, inspected, and written about these hotels, restaurants, museums and transportation services. Though we have made valiant efforts to keep all our information fresh and up-to-date, some few changes can inevitably occur in the periods before a revised edition of this guidebook is published. So please bear with us if a tiny number of the details in this book have changed. Please also note that we have no responsibility or liability for any inaccuracy or errors or omissions, or for inconvenience, loss, damage, or expenses suffered by anyone as a result of assertions in this guide.

CONTENTS

Piccadilly Circus
National Gallery
Charing Cross
Savoy Pier
Waterloo Bridge
River Thames
Festival Pier
Upper Ground
Duke St
Savoy Pl

LIST OF MAPS

ABOUT THE AUTHOR

Jason Cochran is the author of *Here Lies America.* He was twice awarded "Guide Book of the Year" by the Lowell Thomas Awards (Society of American Travel Writers) and once by the North American Travel Journalists Association for his books on London and Orlando. His voice has reached millions of travelers, from the mid-'90s, when as a long-term backpacker he wrote one of the world's first travel blogs, to his appearances as a commentator on CBS and for AOL, to his work at Frommers.com, which under his editorship won Silver for Travel Journalism Website in the 2021 Lowell Thomas Awards.

It was an honor to create this edition with the expertise and support Yhago Maia, Nina Hook-Zurlino, Tracy Temple, Robin Oakley, and others.

This book's research and writing are 100% AI-free.

ABOUT THE FROMMER TRAVEL GUIDES

For most of the past 65 years, Frommer's has been the leading series of travel guides in North America, accounting for as many as 24% of all guidebooks sold. I think I know why.

Though we hope our books are entertaining, we nevertheless deal with travel in a serious fashion. Our guidebooks have never looked on such journeys as a mere recreation, but as a far more important human function, a time of learning and introspection, an essential part of a civilized life. We stress the culture, lifestyle, history, and beliefs of the destinations we cover, and urge our readers to seek out people and new ideas as the chief rewards of travel.

We have never shied from controversy. We have, from the beginning, encouraged our authors to be intensely judgmental, critical—both pro and con—in their comments, and wholly independent. Our only clients are our readers, and we have triggered the ire of countless prominent sorts, from a tourist newspaper we called "practically worthless" (it unsuccessfully sued us) to the many rip-offs we've condemned.

And because we believe that travel should be available to everyone regardless of their incomes, we have always been cost-conscious at every level of expenditure. Though we have broadened our recommendations beyond the budget category, we insist that every lodging we include be sensibly priced. We use every form of media to assist our readers, and are particularly proud of our feisty daily website, the award-winning Frommers.com.

I have high hopes for the future of Frommer's. May these guidebooks, in all the years ahead, continue to reflect the joy of travel and the freedom that travel represents. May they always pursue a cost-conscious path, so that people of all incomes can enjoy the rewards of travel. And may they create, for both the traveler and the persons among whom we travel, a community of friends, where all human beings live in harmony and peace.

Arthur Frommer

THE BEST OF LONDON

1

Whether you realize it or not, London shaped your destiny. There's hardly a quarter of the globe that London, as the seat of England's government, hasn't changed. The United States was founded in reaction to London's edicts. Australia's first permanent European settlers were London's criminals. Modern Canada, South Africa, and New Zealand were cultivated from London. India's course was irrevocably changed by the aspirations of London businessmen, as were the lives of millions of Africans who were enslaved and shipped around the world while Londoners lined their pockets with profits. That you bought this book, written in English somewhere other than in England, is evidence of London's reach across time and distance. And London dominion continues to this day: The city is the world's most popular destination for foreign tourists.

London is inexhaustible—you could tour it for months and barely get to know it. Few cities support such a variety of people living in remarkable harmony. In 2016, this historically Christian country even elected a Muslim mayor, Sadiq Khan. That diversity makes London like a cut diamond: Approach it from a different angle each day, and it presents an entirely fresh shape and color. From famous stories to high style, London is many things in every moment to many people from all walks of life.

But at this moment, London is embattled by monumental shifts—the passing of its beloved Queen Elizabeth II in September 2022 and the ascension of King Charles III, the Covid-19 pandemic and subsequent economic uncertainty, and Britain's exit from its membership in the European Union (a messy move that people call Brexit). These shifts are molding this place into something new, but as yet undefined. Few can be confident about how these waves of change will alter the color of the city and the mood of the nation. London is already an extremely difficult place to live. Locals still pay the highest rate in the world for their public transit, and it's still a brutally expensive city for housing—the average monthly rent for a one-bedroom flat outside the center of the city is £2,220, but the average salary is just £60,921. Will the city squeeze out the young

Crowds wait to enter Westminster Abbey, a place of worship and ceremony for a millennium.

and the poor? Can small businesses survive the onslaught by moneyed brands? Are the high times coming to an end? For now, London waits.

LONDON'S best ATTRACTIONS

- **British Library** (p. 130): The finest and rarest books on the planet, plus the Magna Carta, are laid open for your eyes.
- **British Museum** (p. 135): Some of the most astounding treasures of the classical world are housed in one overwhelmingly glorious neoclassical building.
- **Churchill War Rooms** (p. 156): A time capsule of the tense days of World War II and the most advanced biographical museum in existence.
- **London Museum** (p. 201): This world-class compendium of the city's life and times is reborn in 2026 with a lavish new home in a sprawling Victorian food market. (p. 186)
- **National Gallery** (p. 146): Some 2,000 masterpieces, the cream of Western European art, reside at what may be the best fine art collection in the world, which got a glow-up for its 200th anniversary.
- **Natural History Museum** (p. 172): For kids, it's all about the dinosaurs, but this "cathedral of nature" has major chops as a research facility, too.
- **St Paul's Cathedral** (p. 188): Sir Christopher Wren's masterpiece is the icon of London and a shrine to historic events and people.
- **Tate Modern** (p. 160): Bankside's hymn to the "shock of the new," a former power station, makes an impression before you see a single artwork.

An interactive area in the Design Gallery at the Young V&A.

- **Tower of London** (p. 192): Britain's gruesome underbelly and its glittering Crown Jewels coexist in one sprawling city castle of stone.
- **Victoria & Albert Museum** (p. 176): Always evolving and growing, this is probably the world's finest collection of decorative arts, and in 2023 it reopened a learning-inflected play space for kids, now called **Young V&A**.
- **Westminster Abbey** (p. 161): Be awed by Britain's ancient spiritual heart, where nearly 1,000 years of monarchs have been crowned and many are buried.

LONDON'S essential EXPERIENCES

- **Promenading on South Bank:** In 1957, the Thames was declared "biologically dead." Today, it flows with life both in the water and on the banks. Alongside it, as restaurants, bars, and creative developments continue to pop up, a walk along the South Bank from Westminster Bridge to Tower Bridge is newly one of the world's great promenades. The ever-changing perspective from Parliament to the Tower is ceaselessly inspiring.
- **Following in Royal Footsteps:** London is where some of the most famous characters in history played their scenes. Nearly every British monarch

since 1066 was crowned in **Westminster Abbey** (p. 161). Henry VIII strutted around **Hampton Court Palace** (p. 211), and the life story of Queen Elizabeth II centers on **Buckingham Palace** (p. 155) and **Windsor Castle** (p. 333). And the story continues: The future King George VII and his siblings were diapered in **Kensington Palace** (p. 172). Sample the family's priceless art collection at **The King's Gallery** (p. 166).

- **Explore the Entire World at the British Museum:** This inexhaustible institution endeavors to preserve the cream of all epochs and places; find everything from remnants of formerly buried treasure, exquisite Roman craftsmanship, and survivors from the 7 Wonders of the Ancient World. See p. 135.
- **Climbing the Dome of St Paul's Cathedral:** Wren's baroque masterpiece stirs emotion in everyone who lays eyes on its lead-coated wooden dome. But it's the climb to the Golden Gallery for a 360° panorama that will stay with you forever. As for Wren, he was forced to add the balustrade for Queen Anne. "Ladies think nothing well without an edging," he complained. For city views without stairs (or fees), there's **Horizon 22** (p. 142), now London's highest observation deck. See p. 188.
- **Immersing Yourself in World War II:** More than 80 years later, the Blitz still isn't far from many Londoners' minds. Dig into the power of their resistance at the superlative time capsule of the **Churchill War Rooms**

The skyline of London as seen from the Golden Gallery at St Paul's Cathedral.

The British Tea Guild Council bestows awards for best afternoon teas, and the Goring has earned the top prize in years past.

(p. 156), the immersive **London Museum Docklands** (p. 201), the floating military museum **HMS *Belfast*** (p. 187), and the top-secret code-breaking headquarters of **Bletchley Park** (p. 345).

- **Taking Afternoon Tea:** Look smart at **Brown's Hotel,** the **Goring, Fortnum & Mason,** or the **Langham** (p. 102), where the traditional tea ritual carries on as it did in Britain's colonial heyday.
- **Spending an Evening at a West End Theatre:** London is the theatrical capital of the world. The live stages of **Theatreland** around Covent Garden and Soho offer a combination of variety, accessibility, and economy—but the shows of the Fringe are where the future can be found. See p. 265.

LONDON'S best FOOD

- **Tucking into Honest British Ingredients:** After many lost years of too much boiled cabbage and bread, the English have fallen back in love with farm-fresh ingredients. The gastropub movement, epitomized by its still-potent pioneer, the **Eagle** (p. 89), is just the beginning. Delectable English traditional cooking can be found from the oldest establishments (**Rules,** p. 98) to neighborhood holes-in-the-wall (**Andrew Edmunds,** p. 92; **10 Greek Street,** p. 92).
- **Sinking a Pint in a Traditional Pub:** From Tudor coaching inns to riverside taverns, London's pub culture spans the centuries. Raise a pint where Shakespeare did at **The George** (p. 123), raise one with Sir Ian McKellen at his pub **The Grapes** (p. 124), immerse yourself in an ale at Dr. Samuel

Candlelight sets the scene for consistently excellent cuisine set Soho's Andrew Edmunds.

A tempting selection of appetizers and mains at 10 Greek Street.

Johnson's local **Ye Olde Cheshire Cheese** (p. 129), and drink in a Victorian jewel box of etched glass at **The Princess Louise** (p. 126). Then repeat. See "22 Pubs You'll Love" on p. 121.

- **Mining the Stalls at Borough Market:** The top port of call for foodies is the market under the railway by London Bridge station—not least for the free samples dished out by vendors keen to market their wares. It's gourmet heaven. See p. 110.
- **Taste the World at the New Food Halls:** As a response to a tightening economy, many indoor markets for prepared dishes have opened across town, providing affordable hot dishes in a convivial community atmosphere, including a raising cocktails in a deconsecrated 200-year-old church at **Mercato Mayfair** (p. 120) and sampling cheese, street food, hot chai, and beers in a former banana warehouse at **Seven Dials Market** (p. 120).
- **Chowing Down on Farmhouse Cheese:** England produces hundreds of artisan cheeses. Check out the West Country cheddars, red Leicester, and goat cheeses at such cheesemongers as **Neal's Yard Dairy** (p. 111) or eat a gloppy, gooey plate of raclette at **Kappacasein** (p. 111). But get your fill while you're here: You can't get it back through Customs.
- **Tasting Britain's Fading Traditions:** As young English diners insist on trendy fare and healthy options, the older custom of restaurants as pillars of their neighborhoods becomes rarer. Whether it's the deep-fried goodness at the linoleum-lined "chippy" **Fryer's Delight** (p. 90), the family-run diner **E. Pellicci** (p. 115) in the East End; or the traditional "caff" of the **Regency Café** (p. 106), mid-century Britain is still steaming along—affordably.

LONDON'S best HOTELS

It's no exaggeration to say London has some of the world's best hotels.

- **Meet the Locals at a Family-Run B&B:** Mom-and-pop inns once ruled London. The new dominance of corporate hotels has all but extinguished the once-bright flame of local English hospitality. But you can still find some stellar homegrown homes where owners put you first, including the Valotis and Cabrals of the **Alhambra Hotel** in St Pancras (p. 47) and the Beynons of Bloomsbury's **Jesmond Hotel** (p. 48), and the Marazzi of the **Celtic Hotel** in near the British Museum (p. 48).
- **Lose Yourself in a Grande Dame:** The first all-service grand hotel in Europe, the **Langham** (p. 64) was built in 1865, and it's still extending top-flight hospitality to guests with taste—and cash. **Claridge's** (p. 62) and **The Savoy** (p. 67) have attracted royalty and creative misadventures since the late 1800s. Best of all, you can tour their ground floors without being a guest.
- **Make the River Your Base:** Throughout London's history, the riverfront was mostly an unsavory industrial zone worth avoiding, but we're luckier in our times. Excellent hotels like **Bankside** (p. 70), **Sea Containers** (p. 71), and a youth-skewing **Hoxton** (p. 73) have set up shop on the south end of Blackfriars Bridge, putting guests within quick reach of the Thames Path, Tate Modern, and St Paul's and the City.

Queen Victoria and Prince Albert visited Claridge's hotel in 1860, 4 years after its original building opened. It still feels regal today.

- **Pay Less Than $90:** You may not think it's possible, but with advance planning, you can get a new, impeccably maintained private room in the center of town. Book way ahead with the British chains **Premier Inn, Travelodge,** or **easyHotel,** or with the imported budget brands **Ibis** and **citizenM,** and London is yours, cheap. See p. 38.
- **Sleep Where History Happened:** Rather than tear it down, Londoners would rather revitalize it. Be party to the spy stories at **St. Ermin's Hotel** (p. 58); rest under the swoony spires of Gilbert Scott's neo-Gothic **St. Pancras**

Renaissance Hotel (p. 44); dine in a former church at the boutique charmer **L'Oscar** (p. 51); sleep where D-Day was planned at the new, ultra-luxury **Raffles London at the OWO** (p. 67); or relax in the onetime headquarters of the Ministry of Defence at the **Corinthia London** (p. 67).

- **Enjoy Style for Less:** A new mid-level style of European hotel gives you all you need in a stylish package without the dull corporate formula. At the **Resident** hotels (p. 55) and **Z Hotels** (p. 43), you'll surrender some space, but not the chic. Buzzy Dutch boutique **citizenM** (p. 40) has huge beds and a loopy personality, but a fair price.

A hip, comfortable and compact room typical of The Hoxton in Shoreditch.

LONDON'S best FOR FAMILIES

- **Cruising London's Waterways:** In addition to the grand River Thames, London has a working canal system that once kept goods flowing to and from the city's docks. The best value trips are on the **Thames Clipper** traversing the city's entire waterfront (p. 368) and on the **Regent's Canal** (p. 223).
- **Riding the Tiny Tube:** Climb aboard a segment of the miniature London Post Office Railway, which for 76 years shuttled mail under the capital's streets. It's part of the kid-oriented Mail Rail at the **Postal Museum** (p. 142).
- **Visiting Harry Potter:** Warner Bros.' deep dive into how it designed and made its blockbuster films, **The Making of Harry Potter** (p. 213), is one of the country's most popular family attractions, surpassing expectations. Potterheads could happily spend a whole day here.
- **Losing Your Way in the World's Most Famous Hedge Maze:** The green labyrinth at **Hampton Court** twists and turns for almost half a mile. When you manage to extricate yourself, stroll through centuries of architectural styles at this stunning palace, home of many an English monarch. Don't forget to pick up a kids' activity trail. See p. 211.
- **Going Botanic in Royal Kew:** The **Royal Botanic Gardens, Kew,** house more than 50,000 plants from across the planet, including Arctic and tropical varieties. Youngsters will love the 200m-high (656-ft.) Treetop Walkway, up in the Gardens' deciduous canopy. See p. 212.

- **Asking How, Where & Why:** Inside South Kensington's **Science Museum** (p. 175), interactive exhibits keep inquisitive minds occupied. Or pilot a simulated ship at the kid-centric **National Maritime Museum** (p. 206), or learn how to drive a Tube train at the **London Transport Museum** (p. 144).
- **Learning the Panto Lingo:** From November to early January, join one of Britain's most delightful holiday experiences: pantomimes, which are slapstick musical romps through famous stories, usually starring D-list celebrities. Hiss at villains, shout instructions for heroes, and giggle at good-natured drag performers, a traditional role called *the dame*. Try the **Theatre Royal Stratford** (www.stratfordeast.com), the **New Wimbledon** (www.atgtickets.com/venues/new-wimbledon-theatre), the **Hackney Empire** (p. 271), or the **Richmond Theatre** (www.atgtickets.com/venues/richmond-theatre).
- **Seeing Peter Pan in Kensington Gardens:** You'll feel like a character from a Victorian novel as you stand beneath Sir George Frampton's beloved 1912 statue of the boy who played the panpipe. There's no better way to admire and enjoy the "green lung"—the largest and most popular open space in the middle of a city that already holds the record for the most green space for a city of its size. See p. 222.

LONDON'S best FREE & DIRT CHEAP EXPERIENCES

- **Visiting the Great Museums:** London's best museums and galleries show off their permanent collections for free. Those include the **British Museum,**

Hands-on exhibits and a train ride make the Postal Museum & Mail Rail a hit with families.

Hidden London partners with the London Transport Museum to access secret or abandoned parts of the city's Underground.

London Museum, National Gallery, National Portrait Gallery, Tate Britain, Tate Modern, Natural History Museum, Science Museum, V&A, and the **British Library.** See chapter 5.

- **Taking in Fresh Air & a City View:** North of the River Thames, **Hampstead Heath** (p. 220) offers miles of woodland trails, historic pubs, and sumptuous mansions. In the southeast, the flower beds of **Greenwich Park** (p. 220) enjoy a panoramic sweep over the Thames.
- **Dining on the Cheap:** Away from the multi-starred hotspots, London is surprisingly well equipped with affordable, tasty places to enjoy a full meal for under £20. Among the most memorable is the West End's most venerable budget pit stop, **Café in the Crypt** at St Martin-in-the-Fields church (p. 94).
- **The King of Libraries:** The **British Library** (p. 130) started as the monarch's private stash but now its doors yawn wide to the public with free exhibitions and priceless manuscripts that must be seen to be believed.

Londoners and visitors alike flock to Hampstead Heath in warm weather.

The 85,000 volumes contained in The King's Library and assembled by King George III form the core collection of The British Library.

- **Catching a Free Event in the Center of the City:** From the **Lord Mayor's Show** to the **Notting Hill Carnival,** a large number of major public events cost nothing to attend. See "London Calendar of Events" (p. 372).

THE best HISTORIC EXPERIENCES

- **Meeting the Heroes & Villains of History:** Get face-to-face with a rogue's gallery from the past at the just-refurbished **National Portrait Gallery,** where faces seem to watch you across time with a sparkle in their eye. The gang's all here, from a supercilious Henry VIII to a pugnacious Hogarth to a sad-eyed Princess Diana, already fading into a memory. See p. 150.
- **Taking a Tour of Royal London:** From palaces and parks to the royal art collections, history, geography, and culture have been shaped—or owned—by centuries of aristocratic rule. You can see the best of it in a day, including the late Queen Elizabeth's favorite grocer, **Fortnum & Mason** (p. 239), plus any one of 800 other Royal Warrant holders (p. 247). Roam the very rooms used in daily life by kings and queens at **Buckingham Palace** (p. 155), **Hampton Court Palace** (p. 211), **Kensington Palace** (p. 172), and **Windsor Castle** (p. 333).
- **Peering into a Time Capsule:** Some museums preserve scenes that were frozen in time. No reconstructions or fakery here: You'll gaze upon authentic World War II military operations at the **Churchill War Rooms** (p. 156); admire the graves of great artists and the location of epic rituals at **Westminster Abbey** (p. 161); explore the secret cloisters of the **Charterhouse** campus (p. 196), founded in 1371 and only opened to tourists in 2017; see the home that made **Charles Darwin** want to stop traveling (p. 213); roam

Since 1856, the National Portrait Gallery has collected thousands of portraits of the famous and the lesser-known.

an intact battleship at the **HMS *Belfast*** (p. 187); and marvel at the treasure-crammed townhouse of a 19th-century collector (**Sir John Soane's Museum,** p. 152).

- **Shopping in the Grandest Department Stores of Them All:** And, no, it's not Harrods. **Liberty** (p. 241), founded in 1875 and moved to its current half-timbered, mock-Tudor home in 1924, and **Selfridges** (p. 242), both designed and built by Americans, redefined sales methods, liberated women from homebound drudgery, and played crucial roles in world history.
- **Imagining Domestic Life Through the Ages:** At the **V&A** (p. 176), gape at one of the finest collections of fine historic furniture in the world. But that's a museum—nothing immerses you in the past quite like the brain-bending role-playing of a night visit to **Dennis Severs' House** (p. 200).

Liberty department store recalls the style of Tudor Britain but was built in 1924 out of old ships.

SUGGESTED ITINERARIES & NEIGHBORHOODS

2

Few great modern cities are as multilayered, intricate, and unknowable as London, Western Europe's most populous city (9.8 million, the highest level since before World War II). Perhaps that's because history is knitted into its layout. London is mostly the haphazard product of blind evolution, which piled up over successive generations to produce a complicated metropolis.

As recently as the early 1800s, London—and by London, I mean what we now call the City of London, the area between St Paul's and the Tower, also called the City—was a frenzied cluster where many lives, birth to death, were carried out within the same few blocks. The main streets ran south to the river (not east or west, as they do now), the smoke of industry was banished downwind to the east, and kings lived near the Thames for easy transportation. All around the City were dozens of villages, many of which retain their names as modern neighborhoods—and, if you're lucky, a whiff of their original personalities, but not of their original pestilence.

Quickly, London swelled to swallow its current territory. Yet because of ancient echoes, neighborhoods remain surprisingly small—many are just minutes across by foot, and even crucial streets can change names several times. It's still possible to stroll along and sense sudden shifts in energy and character. In many ways, London is still a complex system of hamlets. It's one of the many delights that makes it so surprising. It also means it can take a lifetime to scratch its surface.

Addresses sometimes reflect this improvisation; a building numbered 75 may sit across the street from one numbered 32. Despite this, it's immensely difficult to get lost. The City maintains some 1,200 Legible London map **"Finger Posts"** on sidewalks throughout town.

London, as both the capital and the most populous city of its country, tends bask in the attentions of developers and investors even as many other parts of Britain are neglected. When you're in London, you're buffered somewhat from the rapid economic

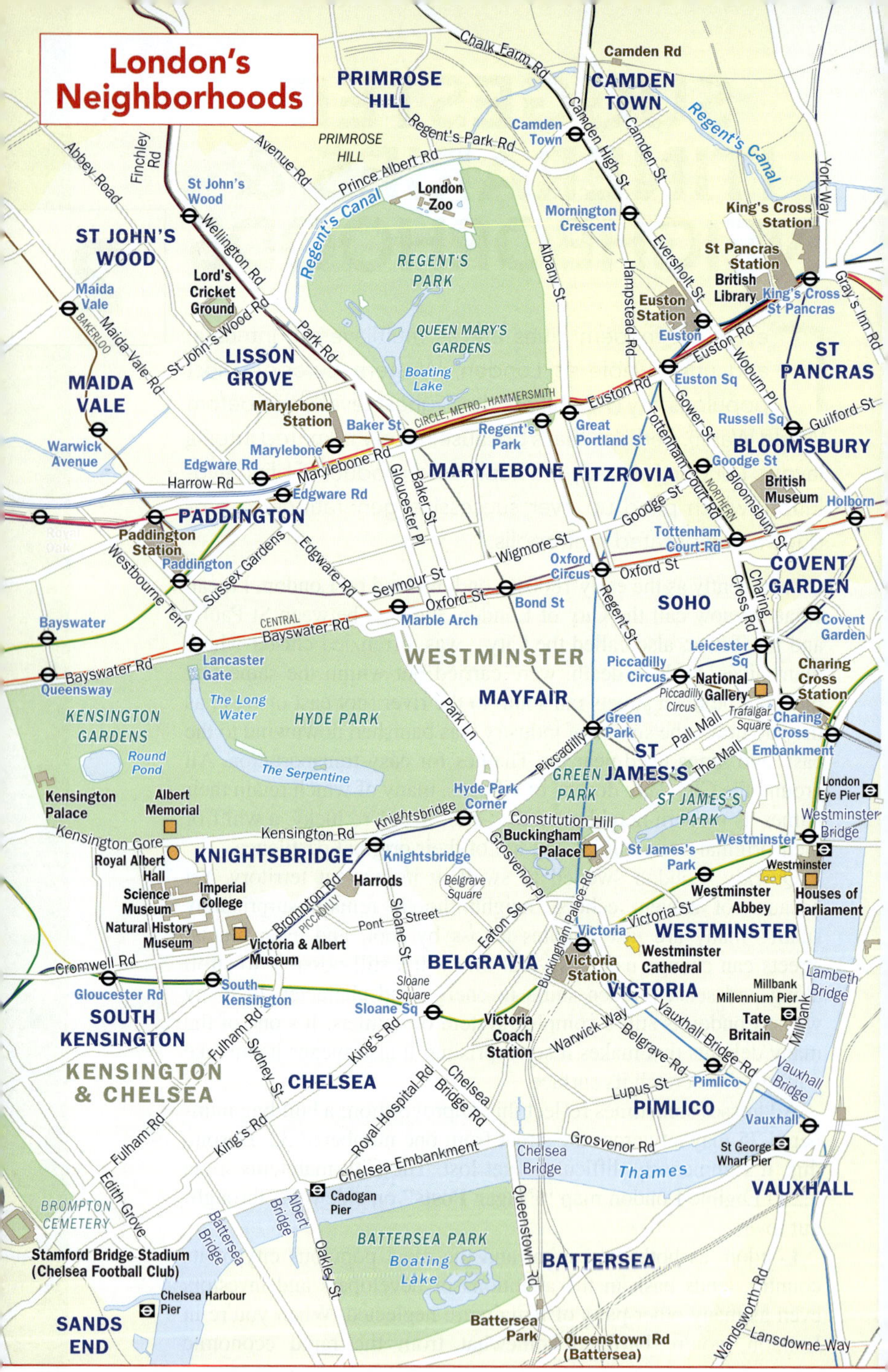
London's Neighborhoods
PRIMROSE HILL
CAMDEN TOWN
Camden Rd
Chalk Farm Rd
Regent's Canal
Camden Town
Camden High St
Camden St
Regent's Park Rd
PRIMROSE HILL
Prince Albert Rd
Avenue Rd
London Zoo
York Way
Finchley Rd
Abbey Road
St John's Wood
Wellington Rd
Mornington Crescent
King's Cross Station
St Pancras Station
British Library
King's Cross St Pancras
Gray's Inn Rd
ST JOHN'S WOOD
REGENT'S PARK
Albany St
Hampstead Rd
Eversholt St
Euston Station
Euston
Maida Vale
Lord's Cricket Ground
QUEEN MARY'S GARDENS
Boating Lake
St John's Wood Rd
Park Rd
Maida Vale Rd
LISSON GROVE
Euston Rd
Euston Sq
Woburn Pl
ST PANCRAS
MAIDA VALE
Marylebone Station
CIRCLE, METRO., HAMMERSMITH
Gower St
Russell Sq
Guilford St
Baker St
Regent's Park
Great Portland St
Tottenham Court Rd
BLOOMSBURY
Warwick Avenue
Marylebone
Edgware Rd
Marylebone Rd
Gloucester Pl
MARYLEBONE
FITZROVIA
Goodge St
British Museum
Harrow Rd
Holborn
PADDINGTON
Paddington Station
Paddington
Westbourne Terr
Sussex Gardens
Edgware Rd
Wigmore St
Tottenham Court Rd
Bloomsbury St
Oxford Circus
Oxford St
COVENT GARDEN
Seymour St
Oxford St
Bond St
Charing Cross Rd
Marble Arch
SOHO
Covent Garden
Bayswater
CENTRAL
Bayswater Rd
Regent St
Lancaster Gate
WESTMINSTER
Leicester Sq
Piccadilly Circus
National Gallery
Charing Cross Station
Queensway
The Long Water
MAYFAIR
Trafalgar Square
KENSINGTON GARDENS
HYDE PARK
Park Ln
Green Park
Pall Mall
Charing Cross
Round Pond
Piccadilly
ST JAMES'S
The Mall
Embankment
The Serpentine
GREEN PARK
ST JAMES'S PARK
London Eye Pier
Kensington Palace
Albert Memorial
Hyde Park Corner
Knightsbridge
Constitution Hill
Westminster Bridge
Kensington Gore
Kensington Rd
Buckingham Palace
Westminster
Royal Albert Hall
KNIGHTSBRIDGE
Knightsbridge
St James's Park
Grosvenor Pl
Science Museum
Imperial College
Harrods
Belgrave Square
Westminster Abbey
Houses of Parliament
Brompton Rd
Sloane St
Natural History Museum
Pont Street
Eaton Sq
Victoria St
Buckingham Palace Rd
Victoria
WESTMINSTER
Victoria & Albert Museum
Westminster Cathedral
Cromwell Rd
BELGRAVIA
Victoria Station
Lambeth Bridge
Gloucester Rd
South Kensington
Sloane Square
VICTORIA
Millbank Millennium Pier
Sloane Sq
SOUTH KENSINGTON
Victoria Coach Station
Vauxhall Bridge Rd
Tate Britain
Fulham Rd
Sydney St
King's Rd
Warwick Way
Belgrave Rd
Millbank
KENSINGTON & CHELSEA
CHELSEA
Pimlico
Vauxhall Bridge
Royal Hospital Rd
Chelsea Bridge Rd
Lupus St
PIMLICO
Vauxhall
Fulham Rd
King's Rd
Chelsea Bridge
Grosvenor Rd
St George Wharf Pier
Chelsea Embankment
Thames
Edith Grove
VAUXHALL
BROMPTON CEMETERY
Cadogan Pier
Albert Bridge
Battersea Bridge
Queenstown Rd
BATTERSEA PARK
Boating Lake
Stamford Bridge Stadium (Chelsea Football Club)
Oakley St
BATTERSEA
Chelsea Harbour Pier
Wandsworth Rd
SANDS END
Battersea Park
Queenstown Rd (Battersea)
Lansdowne Way

London Transportation
Underground Station
Rail Station
Docklands Light Rail
Underground Lines
Bakerloo
Central
Circle
District
Elizabeth Line
Hammersmith & City
Jubilee
Metropolitan
Northern
Overground
Piccadilly
Victoria
Waterloo & City
0
1 mi
1 km
BARNSBURY
DE BEAUVOIR TOWN
SOUTH HACKNEY
ISLINGTON
HOXTON
HAGGERSTON
VICTORIA PARK
Grand Union Canal
Cambridge Heath
SHOREDITCH
CLERKENWELL
FARRINGDON
BETHNAL GREEN
Bethnal Green
Shoreditch
Whitechapel
STEPNEY
CITY (LONDON)
The Barbican Centre
Liverpool St Station
HOLBORN
THE CITY
Bank of England
WHITECHAPEL
St Paul's Cathedral
Fenchurch St Station
Blackfriars Station
Cannon St Station
Shadwell
SHADWELL
Thames
Blackfriars Pier
Bankside Pier
Tower Millennium Pier
Tower of London
Tate Modern
National Theatre
London Bridge City Pier
HMS Belfast
St Katharine's Pier
WAPPING
Festival Pier
SOUTH BANK
BANKSIDE
London Bridge Station
Waterloo Station
SOUTHWARK
BOROUGH
BERMONDSEY
SOUTHWARK PARK
NEWINGTON
SOUTHWARK
LAMBETH
ELEPHANT & CASTLE
LAMBETH
WALWORTH
KENNINGTON
The Oval (Surrey County Cricket Ground)
BURGESS PARK
CAMBERWELL
PECKHAM
Angel
Old St
Farringdon
Barbican
Chancery Lane
Moorgate
Liverpool St
Aldgate East
Aldgate
St Paul's
Mansion House
Bank
Cannon St
Temple
Blackfriars
Monument
Tower Hill
Tower Gateway
London Bridge
Wapping
Rotherhithe
Southwark
Waterloo
Borough
Bermondsey
Lambeth North
Elephant & Castle
Kennington
Oval
Caledonian Rd
Liverpool Rd
Upper St
Canonbury Rd
Essex Rd
New North Rd
Shepherdess Walk
Kingsland Rd
Hackney Rd
Roman Rd
Pentonville Rd
City Rd
Rosebery Ave
Bethnal Green Rd
Cambridge Heath Rd
Farringdon Rd
St John St
Old St
City Road
Great Eastern St
Clerkenwell Rd
Hatton Gdn
Mile End Rd
High Holborn
Holborn Viaduct
Bishopsgate
Whitechapel Rd
Commercial Rd
Fleet St
Fenchurch St
Leman St
Royal Mint
Cable St
Cannon St
Waterloo Bridge
Southwark Bridge
London Bridge
Tower Bridge
Blackfriars Rd
Tooley St
Borough High St
Tower Bridge Rd
York Rd
Waterloo Rd
Long Lane
Great Dover St
Borough Rd
Grange Rd
Lambeth Rd
New Kent Rd
Old Kent Rd
Walworth Rd
Kennington Ln
Park Rd
Trafalgar Ave
Camberwell New Rd
Camberwell Rd
Clapham Rd
Peckham Rd

deterioration happening elsewhere, but many locals find it hard to make ends meet and you'll still encounter your share of empty storefronts.

If you want a handheld map, buy what locals have used for nearly a century. The most cherished paper map booklet is the ***London A–Z*** (www.az.co.uk), first compiled by the indefatigable Phyllis Pearsall, who is said to have walked every mile of the City for the 1936 debut edition and commanded the resulting cartography empire until her death 60 years later. Simply owning a *London A–Z Pocket Atlas* (£7) could make people think you live in London. Just be sure to call it the "A to Zed" or you'll get a funny look; in England, the last letter in the alphabet is, quite sensibly, pronounced so it will not rhyme with eight other letters.

LONDON IN 1 DAY

First of all, what were you thinking? If you're in town on a layover, didn't you know that many airlines will allow you to stick around for a few days at no charge? Never mind. What's done is done. Eat a huge breakfast and make your way to Tower Hill.

1 The Tower of London ♥♥♥

Start here (p. 192) because it usually opens an hour earlier (9am) than most attractions. Spend about 2 hours making stops at the **Crown Jewels** and the **White Tower,** and snap that requisite photo of the **Tower Bridge** (p. 191) from the quay. Grab a "meal deal" sandwich (the quintessential London lunch, p. 116).

The 1066 White Tower is the oldest building in the Tower of London complex.

Tube it west on the Circle or District lines to Westminster.

2 Westminster Abbey ♥♥♥

Allot a rushed 2 hours to see the effigies of kings and queens (p. 161). Of the **Chapel of Henry VII,** Washington Irving wrote: "Stone seems, by the cunning labor of the chisel, to have been robbed of its weight and density, suspended aloft as if by magic, and the fretted roof achieved with the wonderful minuteness and airy security of a cobweb." Outside, take in the **Houses of Parliament** (p. 157) and **Big Ben in Elizabeth Tower** from across the street. The latter recently completed its

The High Altar at Westminster Abbey, scene of royal coronations and funerals.

first full restoration since 1859, and its faces have been returned to their original Prussian blue and gold colors. Did you notice the peculiar symbol it uses instead of X for 10?

Walk up Whitehall, passing No. 10 Downing St. (the walking tour on p. 293 will guide you).

3 The National Gallery ♥♥♥

At **Trafalgar Square,** the symbolic heart of the city, you can finally see some of the world's most famous paintings in person (p. 146). Park guards ask tourists not to climb those famous bronze couchant lions, each of them 20 feet long, that surround Nelson's Column. Don't mount them—they're cracking.

From the Strand, head to the back of Charing Cross station and cross the Thames.

4 Covent Garden shopping ♥♥

There's time to stroll the many lanes around Covent Garden, where some of the city's most popular boutiques are hidden. (p. 239).

Finish just north of the National Gallery, around Leicester Square.

5 West End Show ♥♥♥

Most curtains go up at 7:30pm (p. 262). Enjoy an ice cream during interval (intermission)—it's a custom. Afterward, hurry to a **pub** and raise a

Julia and Hans Rausing Room at the National Gallery.

pint to a city where you've barely scratched the surface (see p. 121 for ideas).

LONDON ON A 2ND DAY

You're going to have to move fast, but you'll be able to see some highlights. Take the Tube to Mansion House, Blackfriar, or St Paul's.

1 St Paul's Cathedral ♥♥♥

As you appreciate the underside of the dome, also appreciate the grave fact that before the 1940s, its exterior flanks were crowded with buildings. Bombings wiped away the structures that once hemmed it in.

Cross the Thames on the Millennium Bridge (the walking tour on p. 306 will help).

2 Tate Modern ♥♥♥

Here's a museum (p. 185) in a colossal structure with river views that can be more memorable and accessible than what's on display inside it. If it's summer, catch a matinee at **Shakespeare's Globe** (p. 184), just a few yards east; an afternoon pint across the bridge at the Art Nouveau **The Blackfriar** (p. 122) will recharge you.

Take the Jubilee line from Southwark to Green Park.

3 Green Park ♥♥

Walk south through Green Park (p. 220) to behold the front of **Buckingham Palace** (p. 155); if you're here in March, you may be lucky enough

Looking up to the dome of St Paul's Cathedral.

Buckingham Palace viewed from The Mall, with the Victoria Memorial in front.

to see fields of daffodils in bloom. Return to Piccadilly to browse the classy shops lining it, particularly **Fortnum & Mason** (p. 239), **Hatchards** (p. 245), **Cordings** (p. 248), and the haberdasheries of **Jermyn Street** just south.

Take the Tube's Piccadilly line (notice the century-old tilework) to Russell Square.

4 The British Museum ♥♥♥

You'll spend the afternoon roaming its vast halls (p. 135), but you'll scarcely be able to wrap your brain around the age, rarity, and craftsmanship of what you see. Such aesthetic exertions may induce cravings for cream tea at its Great Court Restaurant or another pint at a Victorian valentine of a pub, **The Princess Louise** (p. 126).

Catch bus 55 toward Oxford Circus. Sit on the top level for the views!

5 Oxford Circus ♥♥

Wind up the afternoon with a dive into the bustling fitting rooms of the shops on **Oxford Street, Regent Street,** and **Carnaby Street** (p. 236), where you'll find a huge selection of cool clothes at what Londoners call "High Street" prices—meaning they're sane. After 4pm, book a cocktail at the 1940s-themed **Cahoots Underground** (book ahead; p. 289) or walk southeast for a few minutes in Soho and have dinner at **Andrew Edmunds** (p. 92), a neighborhood gem with a changing menu that charges prices far below its rank, and afterward, stroll past the lights of **Piccadilly Circus.**

If you still have juice left, walk down Haymarket, turn left on Cockspur, and follow it down the Strand to Aldwych.

6 South Bank ♥♥♥

Cross right using the Waterloo bridge and wander east along the popular promenade of **South Bank.** During the evening, couples stroll, theaters light, cafes buzz, and the water of the Thames glitters in the light reflected from the **Illuminated River** light installation (p. 284) and the ancient grey dome of St Paul's. It makes for an unforgettable evening.

The lively South Bank area is perfect for dinner, drinks, or just an evening stroll.

LONDON ON A 3RD DAY

Follow the itinerary for 2 days in London, but add in one of the South Kensington museums, preferably the **Victoria & Albert (V&A)** (p. 176), and follow that with a walk through **Hyde Park** (p. 222) and a tour of the public areas of Prince William's London home, **Kensington Palace** (p. 172), in adjoining **Kensington Gardens.** Take the Tube or a bus to Westminster and dive into the time capsule of the **Churchill War Rooms** (p. 156). Follow that with a stroll along the South Bank from Westminster to London Bridge, taking your pick among the pubs and restaurants you find along the path.

AN ITINERARY FOR FAMILIES

London is low-rise and manageable, so anywhere except the financial centers (the City, Canary Wharf) are good places to stay with kids. But make sure they're ready to climb lots of stairs if you're taking the Tube. Also ask for kids' "trails" at the big museums: London's museums work hard to create materials that cater to children—maybe too much, as it's often at the expense of adult minds. Every major museum, no exceptions, also has an on-site cafe for lunch or refreshment.

Day 1: Double-Deckers & Thames Clippers

Forget expensive open-top tours: Start your day seeing Piccadilly Circus, Trafalgar Square, St Paul's Cathedral, the Tower of London, and much more for the price of bus fare on an antique, **double-decker bus**. Take route 15, every 15 minutes. Board at an endpoint, Charing Cross or Tower Hill, or a stop along the route. After visiting the **Tower of London**

(p. 192), head to the ferry dock and see the city from the river on a **Thames Clipper** (p. 268). Disembark at **Tate Modern** (p. 185), which comes fully loaded for young exploration with family trails and some very cool video tablets for interpreting the art. Take the Tube to the West End for a **musical** (p. 262).

The formal gardens of Kensington Palace were installed by Queen Anne at the beginning of the 18th century.

Day 2: Covent Garden & Coram's Fields

Make your way to Covent Garden's **London Transport Museum** (p. 144), where kids can pretend to drive a bus and explore other eye-level exhibits. Then bring your brood on a 15-minute walk north to the **British Museum** (p. 135) and hook them up with crayons and pads, exploration backpacks, and the special object collections tour geared to young minds—Hands On presentations allow them to actually touch ancient artifacts. If they're the daring types, the mummies never fail to impress. Just east you'll find a

Once the site of a home for abandoned children, Coram's Fields is now a popular playground.

city park just for children: The 7-acre **Coram's Fields** (www.coramsfields.org), which was set aside in 1739 for an orphanage at a time when 75% of London kids died before the age of 5. Its southern gate is where mothers once abandoned their babies in desperation. Today, no adult may enter without a child, and this once sad spot is now the scene of daily family joy; there's a petting zoo, two playgrounds for all ages, sand pits, and a paddling pool.

Day 3: The Brompton Road Museums

Today is devoted to exploration of the Brompton Road museums, a trio of world's-bests for kids: Take the Piccadilly line to South Kensington, where the **V&A** (p. 176) has hundreds of hands-on exhibits for kids, such as trying on Victorian costumes or donning armor gauntlets. Next door, the plain-speaking signs and robotic dinosaurs of the **Natural History Museum** (p. 172) impress kids as much as the airplanes and space capsules over their heads at the **Science Museum** (p. 175)—both institutions furnish even more kids' trails and activities for free. Go east on the Circle or District Tube lines to Temple, and you're at the dancing water jets (transformed in winter to a skating rink) of the **Somerset House** courtyard (home of the Courtauld Gallery; p. 143). If the weather doesn't suit that, the **London Eye**'s capsules are safe, climate-controlled, and move imperceptibly—although it has become something of a tourist trap, the view will stimulate and inspire kids without terrifying them.

A DISCOVERY WEEKEND

The Frommer's guides are designed to give you a firm introduction to the sights, hotels, and restaurants that speak most to a visitor about what's going on in each destination. But authentic London doesn't begin and end with these pages, and if you dip into neighborhoods where more locals live, your visit will be immeasurably richer.

Day 1: Brixton & Bollywood

When Victoria was queen, families flocked to live near the incandescent lights of Brixton's Electric Avenue, which in 1888 became one of London's first shopping streets lit by electricity. Today, it's a boisterous immigrant community, timeworn and down-market but safe. By morning, explore the glazed awnings of its Brixton Village market (https://brixtonvillage.com), where to inhale the aroma of meat, spices, and casual brunch is to walk through a portal to Jamaica or India by way of modern South London—and to be reminded that London, like few others, is a truly worldly city. In the afternoon, experience London's huge South Asian community, who form a significant portion of the population. The lively Whitechapel neighborhood in East London has long been favored by immigrants—right now, by people born in East Pakistan or Bangladesh. The area, known for active markets and cheap cooked foods, was previously home to successive waves of Jewish, French, and Chinese arrivals.

Day 2: Go Football Mad or Cricket Crazy

The Adventure Display in the Imagine Gallery at Young V&A.

London hosts 17 professional football (soccer) teams, more than any other city on Earth. From mid-August to mid-May, catch matches at some of the best Premier League teams: **Chelsea** (www.chelseafc.com), **Arsenal** (London's first club; www.arsenal.com), **Tottenham Hotspur** (www.tottenhamhotspur.com), **Fulham** (www.fulhamfc.com), or **West Ham United** (www.whufc.com), which took up residence in London Stadium, the former Olympic Stadium at Stratford. Filling the gap from April to September, and less likely to pelt you in the skull with a beer bottle, is cricket. Attend "test matches" at Marylebone's **MCC Lord's Cricket Ground** (www.lords.org) or Oval's **Surrey County Cricket Club** (www.kiaoval.com). The relatively young **T20 Blast** league (www.ecb.co.uk/T20-Blast), currently sponsored as the **Vitality Blast!**, plays faster-paced "T20" versions of the game to appeal to fans who don't want a

Brixton Village and the surrounding neighborhood are a living reminder that London is a truly international city.

Use the Code

London is chopped into geographic parcels, and you'll see those postcodes on street signs. The heart of the City, in postcode terms, is near the Chancery Lane Tube stop. From there, areas are given a compass direction (N for north, SW for southwest, and so on) and a number (but ignore that, since a number greater than 1 doesn't mean the area is in the boonies). In the very heart of town, addresses get an extra C for "centre," as in WC1, which is where Covent Garden is located. Every address in this book includes its postcode, which corresponds to the neighborhood in which you'll find it. Don't worry—you won't need to memorize these because each listing in this book also includes the nearest Tube stop to help you quickly place locations on a map. Here are some of the most common postcodes:

WC1 Bloomsbury
WC2 Covent Garden, Holborn, Strand
W1 Fitzrovia, Marylebone, Mayfair, Soho
W2 Bayswater
W6 Hammersmith
W8 Kensington
W11 Notting Hill
SW1 Belgravia, St James's, Westminster
SW3 Chelsea
SW5 Earl's Court
SW7 Knightsbridge, South Kensington
SE1 Southwark
SE10 Greenwich
EC1 Clerkenwell
EC2 Bank, Barbican, Liverpool Street
EC3 Tower Hill
EC4 Fleet Street, St Paul's
E1 Spitalfields, Whitechapel
E2 Bethnal Green
E14 Canary Wharf/Isle of Dogs
N1 Islington
NW1 Camden Town
NW3 Hampstead

match to take all day. If you figure out how the game works, fill us in, won't you? It's a little like baseball—and a lot like watching grass grow.

Day 3: Ale, Yorkshire Pudding & Tough Questions

On Sunday afternoons, find a pub with an inviting garden for a traditional **Sunday Roast,** a spread of roasted meats with all the trimmings such as Yorkshire pudding (a popover-like pastry, not a dessert) and gravy, washed down with copious amounts of beer. It's the more leisurely equivalent of brunch: After a long week of working to keep their exorbitantly priced shared flats, Londoners hang out at roasts all day, so it's always smart to reserve a place ahead of time; try **The Mayflower** or one of the other pubs we highlight (p. 121). Some pubs also hold **quizzes,** another staple of British life. Form teams and answer trivia for lame prizes, but be warned: Foreigners tend to fold on the sports and politics questions.

Neighborhoods in Brief

London's neighborhoods were laid out during a period of wagon and foot traffic, when districts were defined in narrower terms than we define them today; indeed, for centuries people often lived complete lives without seeing the other side of town. Ironically, in our times, the Tube has done much to divide these districts from each other. Visitors are likely to hop a train between them and don't often realize how remarkably close they really are.

Are these the only areas of interest? Not even close. Literally hundreds of fascinating village clusters abound, many with names as cherishable as Ponders End, Tooting, and The

From Arthur Frommer's *Europe on $5 a Day* (1957)

"All you've heard to the contrary, Londoners are among the warmest people of Europe, and London is a friendly and inviting city. It has charm and a politeness of attitude that belie its big-city status. You'll want to extend your stay. . . . Can you live in London on $5 a day? There's nothing to it."

Wrythe. And considering that about 40% of Londoners now belong to an ethnic minority and more than 200 languages are spoken, the flavor of your experience shifts as you go. But visitors are likely to spend time in the zones below. All are considered safe to walk around day or night.

BLOOMSBURY & FITZROVIA

Best for: *Museums, affordable inns, residential streets, universities*

What you won't find: *Evening entertainment, nightclubs*

Bloomsbury's dark-brick, white-sashed residential buildings and leafy squares date mostly from the Georgian period, when the district became the first in a chaotic city to be planned—although it seems urban to us, it was an early version of the modern suburban development. The refined air attracted the intelligentsia nearly from the start, and its two universities are both 19th-century institutions. The British Museum settled here, too. Bloomsbury became a place of remembrance on July 7, 2005; of the 52 who died in terrorist bombings that day, 26 perished underground on a Piccadilly line train between King's Cross and Russell Square stations, and 13 were killed on a double-decker bus passing through Tavistock Square. Bloomsbury's cozier sister Fitzrovia, similar in character but devoid of major attractions, lies on the western side of Tottenham Court Road. Famous residents included George Bernard Shaw and Virginia Woolf, who both lived (at different times) at 29 Fitzroy Square.

KING'S CROSS

Best for: *Budget hotels, trains heading north (and south to Paris), alternative/down-and-dirty nightlife, student housing, boutique shopping and dining*

What you won't find: *Green space*

In 2010, the area around King's Cross station was an unsavory tenderloin of porn stores and warehouses. Change came, as it often has in English history, from France: The Eurostar train now hurtles from and to France (and beyond) from this neighborhood, and its arrival revolutionized the local vibe. King's Cross is now where London's digital industry lives. Behind the station, millions of pounds have just transformed once-derelict industrial infrastructure into Granary Square and the Coal Drops Yard, a canalside center for arts hotspots, restaurants, colleges, and tech HQs. Fans of Harry Potter know that the young wizard boards the Hogwarts Express at the (fictitious) Platform 9¾; the movie versions shot at Platforms 4 and 5 but used prettier St Pancras station, next door, as a stand-in facade. Legend (surely apocryphal) says the Celtic queen Boudicca rests somewhere near Platform 8 of King's Cross.

MARYLEBONE & MAYFAIR

Best for: *Luxe shopping, hotels, restaurants, small museums, strolling, embassies*

What you won't find: *Historic sites, savings*

The middle-class hubbub of Oxford Street west of Regent Street divides high-hat Marylebone from its snobbish southern neighbor, Mayfair. Both play host to upscale shopping and several fascinating, if overlooked, museums, but there the similarities end. World-famous Mayfair, typified by hyperluxe bauble shops and blue-blood heritage (Queen Elizabeth II was born at 17 Bruton St. in a building that is no longer there), has a high opinion of itself as a starchy enclave of wealth, much of it from other countries. Yet Mayfair has less to offer the casual tourist, although it is the city's hot zone for cushy hotels. (The title of the musical *My Fair Lady* is witty wordplay on how its Cockney heroine, Eliza, would have pronounced "Mayfair lady.") Marylebone (*Mar*-le-bun), on the other hand, benefits from convenient Tube and bus connections and lively sidewalks crowded with evening celebrants, particularly around James Street. Also, thanks to a territorial local authority, its main shopping drag (Marylebone High Street) remains one of the last important streets in London that isn't awash with the ubiquitous corporate chain stores. Oxford Street was once the city's flagship shopping corridor but is in a slow decline; the western half between Oxford Circus and Marble Arch is the classier end, with marquee department stores such as Selfridges and Marks & Spencer and the recently revived HMV.

SOHO, COVENT GARDEN & CENTRAL WEST END

Best for: *Shopping, restaurants, theater, cinema, nightlife, opera, free art (National Gallery and National Portrait Gallery), star sightings*

What you won't find: *Elbow room, silence*

London's undisputed center of nightlife, restaurants, and theater, the West End seethes with tourists and merrymakers. After work, Old Compton Street and Covent Garden overflow with people catching up with friends; by 7:30pm, the theaters and opera houses are pulsing; by midnight, the action has moved into the nightclubs of Leicester Square and lounges of Soho; and in the wee hours, you might find groups of partiers trawling Gerrard Street, in a teeny Cantonese Chinatown, drunkenly singing football-related shanties and hunting for snacks. Prim Trafalgar Square, dominated by the peerless National Gallery, has often been called London's focal point. On a sunny day, you'll find few places that exude such well-being.

WESTMINSTER, INCLUDING ST JAMES'S

Best for: *Historic and government sites, river strolls, St James's Park*

What you won't find: *Affordable hotels, a wide choice of restaurants*

Though it's near the West End, this area's energy is more staid. It's a district tourists mostly see by day. South of Trafalgar Square, you'll find regiments of robust government buildings but little in the way of hotels or food. Whitehall's severity doesn't

Make like Ted Lasso and attend a football match to see Londoners at their most rambunctious.

spread far: Just a block east, its impenetrable character gives way to the proud riverside promenade of Victoria Embankment overlooking the London Eye, and just a block west, to the greenery of St James's Park, which is, in effect, the king's front yard, since Buckingham Palace is at the western boundary of this area. North of the park, the tidy streets of St James's are even more exclusive than Mayfair's, if that's possible.

THE CITY

Best for: *Old streets with new skyscrapers, the Tower of London, St Paul's, financial concerns*

What you won't find: *Nightlife or weekend life, ancient atmosphere*

Technically, this is the only part of London that's London. Other bits, including the West End, are under the jurisdiction of different local governments, such as Westminster or Camden. The City, as it's called, is where most of London's history happened. It's where Romans cheered gladiators. It's where London Bridge—at least 12 versions—touched shore. It's where the Great Fire raged. And, more recently, it's where the Deutsche Luftwaffe focused many of its nocturnal bombing raids, which is why you'll find so little evidence of the aforementioned events. Outside of working hours, the main thing you'll see in the City is your own reflection in the facade of corporate fortresses; even most of the pubs close on weekends. Although it encompasses such priceless relics as the Tower of London, St Paul's Cathedral, the Tower Bridge, the Bank of England, and the Monument, many of the area's remnants are underfoot. The spiderweb of lanes and streets dates to the Roman period, with names that hint at their former lives (Walbrook is where the river Walbrook, now hidden underground along with Roman-era ruins on its shore, flowed down to the Thames; Honey Lane, Bread Street, Milk Street, and Poultry all once hosted food markets). Buildings have come and gone, but the veins of the City have pumped in situ for thousands of years.

THE SOUTH BANK, SOUTHWARK & BOROUGH

Best for: *Museums, memorable pubs, strolls, gourmet foods and wines*

What you won't find: *Shopping, parks*

During the recent rehabilitation of Southwark (*Suth*-urk) from a crumbling industrial district, its blighted power station became one of the world's greatest museums (the Tate Modern), a master playwright's theater was re-created (the Globe), and a sublime riverfront path replaced the coal lightermen's rotting piers. Now it's where London goes to fall in love. It's a 1-mile riverside stroll between the London Eye and the Tate Modern, and every step is a pleasure. Once-dank railway viaducts are now filled with cafes and reasonable restaurants; one of Western Europe's tallest skyscrapers, The Shard, lords over from above; and the nation's dramatic showpiece (the National Theatre) anchors them at South Bank. But it's gratifying to see that some things never change: Borough Market, which attracts gourmet foodies from around the world, is the descendant of a market that fed the denizens of that medieval skyscraper over the water, London Bridge.

VICTORIA & CHELSEA

Best for: *Boutiques, low-cost lodging, town homes, wealthy neighbors*

What you won't find: *Transit options, street life, museums*

Victoria isn't technically the name of the neighborhood around the eponymous train station—Belgravia (to the west) and Pimlico (south and east) take those honors—but the shorthand is common. Most of the area, which is residential or uninterestingly workaday, was developed starting in the 1820s in consistent patterns of white stucco-terraced homes. The area by the station was recently redeveloped with glass office buildings full of corporate food options, contains two outlier West End theaters, but little else. Just north, you'll face the brick walls of Buckingham Palace Gardens. Chelsea, to its south, has a history of well-heeled bohemianism—Oscar Wilde, James McNeill Whistler, and the Beatles all lived here—although it's known more as one of the city's most exclusive (and some would say insular) communities. A stroll past boutiques and pocket-squared residents on the King's Road, turning ever-more average and indistinct, is not the adventure it was in the '60s.

Spitalfields Market, part of the once-impoverished but now trending Spitalfields area.

KENSINGTON, KNIGHTSBRIDGE

Best for: *Museums, shopping, ultra-luxe boutiques, also-ran hotels*

What you won't find: *Historic sites*

Here, one expensive neighborhood genuflects to another, and barely anyone you meet was born in England. South Kensington and Brompton draw the most visitors to their grand museums; and Knightsbridge is where moneyed foreigners spend and show off—London now has, per capita, among the most billionaires in the world, nearly twice as many as New York or Moscow. They can't legally change most of the facades, so to satisfy their hunger for more space, the big trend among the rich is to burrow downward to build underground rooms—the "pleasure caves" of Kensington. Privilege has long had an address in Kensington—that's a reason those edifying institutions were located here to begin with, away from the grubby paws of the peasants—but it also is home to a core of French expats; you'll find the cafes catering to them on Bute Street. Kensington Palace, at Kensington Gardens' western end, is where Prince William and Princess Catherine live when they're in town. When you travel west to Earl's Court, you experience a considerable drop in voltage. It's a frumpy zone, with undistinguished eats and sleeps; the rise of King's Cross and Shoreditch for younger travelers has reduced it to near-negligible stature. Your parents may have stayed here once, but you shouldn't have to.

SHOREDITCH, SPITALFIELDS & HOXTON

Best for: *Nightclubs, music, food of all types, galleries, clothing*

What you won't find: *Museums, parks*

If Mayfair is London's champagne, the East End 'hoods used to be its hangover. For centuries it was an impoverished slum for poor immigrants and shifty souls. Now Spitalfields (*Spit*-all-fields), named for its

Fair weather draws patrons to a sidewalk cafe in Knightsbridge.

The Best Days to Go

Not all of London's best areas are active every day of the week. Some places might be deserted, others too crowded, so plan your time better by matching your adventures with the right day for each one.

Better on weekends: Notting Hill, Houses of Parliament tours (p. 157)
Worse on weekends: Camden, Covent Garden
Better on weekdays: Camden, the Kensington museums
Worse on weekdays: Notting Hill
Better on Monday: West End ticket availability
Better on Thursday: Borough Market
Better on Friday: British Museum, National Portrait Gallery, National Gallery, V&A, and Tate Modern (when there's a late closing scheduled), Windsor (p. 332)
Better on Sunday: Speakers' Corner (p. 169), Brick Lane and Shoreditch, Sunday roast at a pub

excellent covered market for bougie wares like tees with ironic designs (p. 260) is being consumed by an unstoppable cancer of soulless, open-plan office buildings from the City. It blends into Shoreditch, which was hipster heaven in 2015 but now wears a self-assured mask of counterculture for people with plenty of disposable income. Shopping, restaurants, bars—it's all here now. Dalston, youngish and bohemian, is north of these, the factories-cum-lofts of Stoke Newington just north of that. Every few years, the younger set moves another neighborhood north, where they can most afford the rising rents. Northeast of the Tower of London, in ancient homes that have long housed waves of immigrants (French, then Jewish, now South Asian), you'll find the famed restaurants of Brick Lane (p. 110), the cafes and dance clubs of the converted Old Truman Brewery, and the art-savvy neighborhood of Whitechapel. Prostitutes are out, £5 coffee is in—which may not be an improvement.

GREENWICH

Best for: *Museums, antique and food markets, river views, strolls, boats*
What you won't find: *Hotels, bustle*

Greenwich, on the south bank across from the Canary Wharf developments, retains the tranquility of a village, which it once was, before London enveloped it. The town has an illustrious pedigree as a royal getaway (it has the oldest royal park in London), as a scientific capital, and as one of the world's most crucial command centers. If it all sounds like a living museum, it is: On top of being a UNESCO World Heritage Site (Maritime Greenwich), the village is literally the center of time and space, since it inhabits the exact location of Greenwich Mean Time, and of longitude 0° 0' 0". Set away from Greenwich town there's the colossal O_2 dome, the skyline-defining concert venue.

Other Popular London Neighborhoods

Mostly because of iffy transit connections (for example, service by a single Tube line that, should it go on the blink, would derail your vacation), this book doesn't focus on these neighborhoods as prime places to stay, but they're still vital parts of town.

BAYSWATER & PADDINGTON

Best for: *Sub-par inns, international food, well-preserved Victorian thoroughfares*
What you won't find: *Attractions, non-chain stores, adorable Peruvian bears*

Its whitewashed, terraced houses were briefly the most fashionable in the city (Churchill and Dickens were erstwhile residents), yet today, the sizable transient population of this area deprives it of sustained energy. Its shops are on the dismal side, its food cheap and tawdry, and its hotels tend to be for itinerant and undiscerning guests. Crowning the muddle is Queensway, a

In this aerial shot of the Thames, historic and modern London are clearly juxtaposed.

shopping street containing Whiteleys, a 1911 department store edifice now converted into investment apartments for grotesquely wealthy tenants who will probably never be home. Although the interior of Paddington station is still one of London's most beautiful train hubs (it was built by the architect Isambard Kingdom Brunel in 1838), the facade is obscured by a hotel; *Paddington* (2014) used Marylebone Station's more atmospheric entrance instead. Paddington Station is inconvenient to walk to, though the Elizabeth Line (p. 357) now visits it, and Heathrow and Windsor trains go from it.

DOCKLANDS

Best for: *Development, ancient warehouses, super-cheap chain hotels*

What you won't find: *Street life, nightlife*

Most of far east London along the north side of the Thames is ignobly called by a single, sweeping name: Docklands. Captain Cook set off on his explorations from here, and its hand-dug basins teemed with ships bearing goods from around the planet. Docklands made colonial Britain successful—and thus America, Canada, Australia, and South Africa, too. After a fallow generation, East London's pools are under constant redevelopment by corporations in stacks of fluorescent-lit office cubes, and the Olympics settled here in 2012 near the Stratford Tube stop. Away from the river, in salt-of-the-earth neighborhoods like Bethnal Green, Stratford, and West Ham, the city's Pakistani and Indian populations flourish, with marvelous but unglamorous food and shops.

ISLINGTON

Best for: *Antiques, gastropubs, theater, street markets, cafes, strolls*

What you won't find: *Museums, hotels*

Few neighborhoods retain such a healthy balance between feisty bohemianism and groomed prosperity, and almost none retain streetscapes as defiantly mid–20th century as Chapel Market. Islington's leafy byways are dotted with antiques dealers, hoary pubs with backroom theater spaces, beer gardens, and most pleasingly on a sunny day, pedestrian towpaths overlooking Regent's Canal. Why more tourists don't flood Islington is a mystery—and a blessing—but that hasn't stopped its ascendancy as a choice neighborhood for those with money.

CAMDEN

Best for: *Alternative music, massive clothing markets, junk souvenirs, pubs*

Vibrant Camden Town is a destination for pleasant strolls, shopping and dining, plus a lively pub and music scene.

What you won't find: *Elbow room, hotels, upscale restaurants*

London's analogue to San Francisco's Haight-Ashbury District, it was big in the counterculture 1960s and '70s and is still grotty enough for Amy Winehouse to have expired in. The area's shoulder-to-shoulder markets, which hawk touristy hokum, cheap sunglasses, and £7 falafel in the former warehouses and stables serving Regent's Canal, can be overcrowded with bickering teens, and the sort of places where you feel compelled to carry your wallet in your front pocket. Tourists come more out of duty than for any true mission for commerce, and they cram the inadequate Tube stop on weekends. But I would endure it all for a bowl of hot fettuccine alfredo at The Cheese Wheel (West Yard, Camden Lock Place), where steaming fresh pasta is coated with cheesy richness by being tossed around in a giant 40kg (88-pound) wheel of Parmesan.

NOTTING HILL

Best for: *Markets, village vibes, restaurants, pubs, tourists, antiques*

What you won't find: *Well-priced shopping, museums, Hugh Grant in a bookstore*

Thanks partly to Hollywood, this westerly village-like nook that was once known to locals for race riots and, in 2017, the horrible Grenfell Tower fire, appears high on many checklists. Its Saturday Portobello Road market, the principal draw, is fiendishly crowded but short on truly wonderful wares. In fact, it's dead touristy. Like Camden, people go because they think they should. But if you feel compelled, Hugh Grant's blue door from *Notting Hill* (1999)—it actually belonged to screenwriter Richard Curtis—is at 280 Westbourne Park Rd.

WHERE TO STAY

Some cities are so great, they can't slow down. Despite the turmoil of Brexit and a drooping economy, London still attracts some of the most discerning hotel customers in the world—in fact, there are more than 11,000 five-star rooms in the city.

Through Brexit, the United Kingdom renounced its partnership with the E.U., and shortly afterward, there was a pandemic, a new revolution in work-from-home jobs, and a global economic slowdown. Yet through it all, London's status as Europe's power city seemed unshakable, and hotel inventory still grew by thousands of rooms. The city hosted 146 million overnight visits a year before the pandemic, and by 2024, that figure had rebounded to 154 million. And hotel rates didn't drop—if anything, they rose about 30% on many nights as pent-up demand swamped availability. Now a creaking economy threatens to reshape leisure travel. Worse, homelessness is on the rise—one 2024 study by London Councils found that 1 in 47 Londoners, a 10% increase year over year, has no home of their own or depends on the government to temporarily house them, sometimes in budget hotels.

It behooves you, the visitor, to use the rates in this book as a starting point and **check prices for yourself.** London's non-corporate hotels are good about sticking to their posted rates no matter the night; in fact, every property is required by law to post the *maximum* rate (almost never charged) in the lobby. But company-run hotels are unabashed about extracting high dynamic prices given any uptick in demand, so rates can fluctuate wildly. Beware dates around the London Marathon (Apr), bank holidays, Wimbledon (June or July), New Year's, and summer. In London, it's almost always high season, and even winter months can see peak rates. In the summer of 2025, the average rate in town was £235, a tariff that's is in the middle of our Moderate price range.

Some ground rules: First, don't get caught up in the star ratings that hotels promote. In Britain, a hotel can earn an extra star simply because it serves food. In fact, the more stars a place has, the more likely it is to charge for something you won't use, so focus instead on the location and the price. Second, to save the most cash, look for smaller hotels that have been carved out of historic buildings, even if that means irregular-size quarters with tiny bathrooms. The cheapest places are still family-run, and many family-run hotels are converted former family homes. Third, to secure the lowest rates possible (usually found only on each property's website), timing is

London-Wide Hotels
PRIMROSE HILL
Chalk Farm Rd
Camden Rd
CAMDEN TOWN
Camden Town
Regent's Park Rd
Camden High St
Camden St
Regent's Canal
York Way
Finchley Rd
Abbey Road
Avenue Rd
Prince Albert Rd
London Zoo
St John's Wood
Wellington Rd
ST JOHN'S WOOD
REGENT'S PARK
Mornington Crescent
Albany St
Eversholt St
King's Cross Station
St Pancras Station
British Library
King's Cross St Pancras
Gray's Inn Rd
Hampstead Rd
Euston Station
Euston
Euston Rd
ST PANCRAS
Maida Vale
Lord's Cricket Ground
St John's Wood Rd
Park Rd
Boating Lake
Maida Vale Rd
LISSON GROVE
MAIDA VALE
Marylebone Station
Regent's Park
Euston Sq
Gower St
Tottenham Court Rd
Russell Sq
Guilford St
Baker St
Great Portland St
MARYLEBONE
BLOOMSBURY
Warwick Avenue
Marylebone
Edgware Rd
Marylebone Rd
Harrow Rd
Goodge St
Bloomsbury St
British Museum
Holborn
Gloucester Pl.
Marylebone High
FITZROVIA
PADDINGTON
Paddington Station
Paddington
Westbourne Terr
Sussex Gardens
Edgware Rd
Wigmore St
Oxford Circus
Oxford St
Tottenham Court Rd
Charing Cross Rd
COVENT GARDEN
Seymour St
Bond St
SOHO
Regent St
Bayswater
Bayswater Rd
Marble Arch
Covent Garden
Leicester Sq
Lancaster Gate
Queensway
WESTMINSTER
Piccadilly Circus
National Gallery
Charing Cross Station
MAYFAIR
Park Ln
Trafalgar Square
Charing Cross
Green Park
Pall Mall
Embankment
KENSINGTON GARDENS
HYDE PARK
Round Pond
The Serpentine
Piccadilly
The Mall
ST JAMES'S
Kensington Palace
Hyde Park Corner
GREEN PARK
ST JAMES'S PARK
Constitution Hill
Westminster
Westminster Bridge
Kensington Gore
Kensington Rd
Buckingham Palace
Royal Albert Hall
KNIGHTSBRIDGE
Knightsbridge
Grosvenor Pl
St James's Park
Harrods
Belgrave Square
Westminster Abbey
Houses of Parliament
Victoria & Albert Museum
Brompton Rd
Sloane St
Natural History Museum
Eaton Sq
Victoria St
WESTMINSTER
Westminster Cathedral
Cromwell Rd
BELGRAVIA
Victoria
Victoria Station
VICTORIA
Lambeth Bridge
South Kensington
Gloucester Rd
Sloane Square
Sloane Sq
Victoria Coach Station
Vauxhall Bridge Rd
Tate Britain
Millbank
SOUTH KENSINGTON
Fulham Rd
Sydney St
King's Rd
Warwick Way
Belgrave Rd
KENSINGTON & CHELSEA
CHELSEA
Chelsea Bridge Rd
Royal Hospital Rd
Pimlico
Lupus St
Vauxhall Bridge
PIMLICO
Fulham Rd
King's Rd
Grosvenor Rd
Vauxhall
Chelsea Embankment
Chelsea Bridge
Thames
Edith Grove
VAUXHALL
Albert Bridge
Battersea Bridge
Oakley St
Queenstown Rd
BATTERSEA PARK
Boating Lake
BATTERSEA
Stamford Bridge Stadium (Chelsea Football Club)
SANDS END
Battersea Park
Queenstown Rd (Battersea)
Wandsworth Rd
Lansdowne Way
1
2
3
4
5
6
7
8
9
10
11
12
13
14
15
16
17
18
19
20
21
22

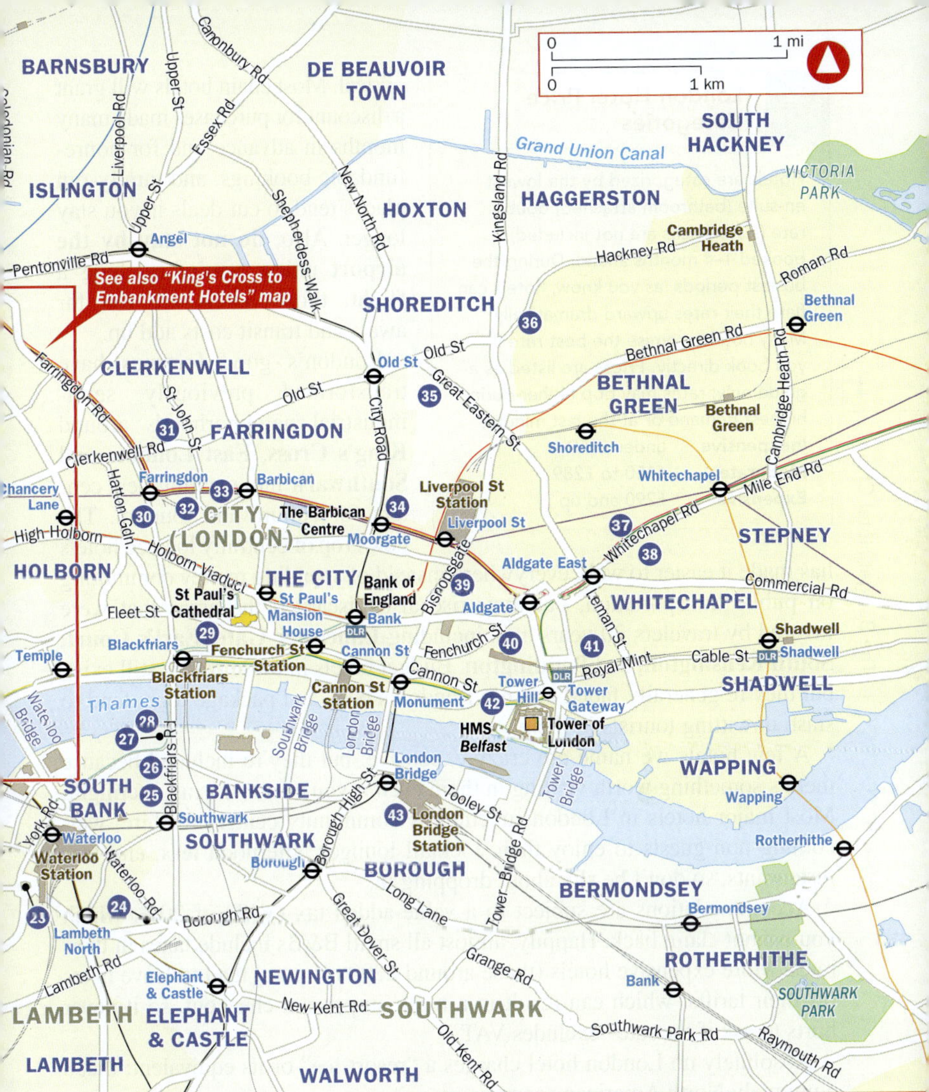

Apex City of London 42
Bankside 28
The Beaumont 8
Brown's Hotel 10
The Bull & The Hide 39
Canopy by Hilton London City 40
Claridge's 9
The Corner London City 38
Dukes Hotel 13
Fox & Anchor 33
The Goring 16
H10 London Waterloo 24
Hotel 41 18
The Hoxton, Shoreditch 35
The Hoxton, Southwark 25
Hyatt Place London City East 37
Hyatt Regency London—The Churchill 5
Inhabit, Queen's Gardens 1
Inhabit, Southwick Street 2
July London Victoria 21
The Lanesborough 14
The Langham 7
Leonardo Royal Hotel London Tower Bridge 41
Lime Tree Hotel 15
Lost Property 29
Luna Simone Hotel 22
Mad Hatter Hotel 26
Marrable's 31
The Mayfair Townhouse 11
Montcalm Mayfair 3
The One Tun 30
Park Plaza Westminster Bridge 23
Resident Hotel Victoria 17
The Rookery 32
Sanctuary House Hotel 20
Sea Containers London 27
Shangri-La Hotel at the Shard 43
Shoreditch Inn 36
South Place Hotel 34
St Ermin's Hotel 19
The Stafford London 12
The Welbeck Hotel 6
The Zetter Marylebone 4

London Hotel Price Categories

Hotels are categorized by the lowest en-suite (bathroom attached) double rate (suite prices are not included) booked 1–4 months ahead. During the busiest periods, as you know, hotels can flare their rates upward dramatically. Many hotels promise the best rate if you book directly. Prices are listed as a guide only; rates may pop higher during highest demand or at the last minute.

Inexpensive	under £150
Moderate	£150 to £289
Expensive	£290 and up

critical. Most chain hotels will grant a discount for purchases made many months in advance and for nonrefundable bookings, and family-run places tend to cut deals if you stay longer. Also, **do not stay by the airport** unless you're catching a flight; those hotels are too far away, and transit costs add up.

London's good fortunes have transformed previously semi-industrial neighborhoods around **King's Cross**, **East London,** and **Southwark** into exciting new centers for culture and tourism. The new crop of centrally located hotels has made it easier to walk everywhere instead of spending money commuting on public transportation, but their rise also discarded the areas that were favored by travelers 30 years ago, including **Lancaster Gate, Earl's Court, South Kensington,** and **Paddington**. Budget hotels in those places still exist, but they're generally faded and not London's best, and package tours tend to stash unwitting tourists in them.

A few hotels we name are crazy expensive, but they're included because there's something worth visiting in them even if you're not staying overnight. Most major hotels in London function as community centers for hire, welcoming non-guests to enjoy their cocktail lounges, afternoon teas, and fine restaurants, so don't be shy about dropping in.

Accommodations are subject to a value-added tax (VAT) of 20%, which you cannot claim back. Happily, almost all small B&Bs include taxes in their rates. More expensive hotels (those around £290 or more) tend to leave taxes off their tariffs, which can result in a nasty surprise at checkout, so it never hurts to ask if the rate "excludes VAT."

Absolutely no London hotel charges a "resort fee" or its equivalent; that's a uniquely North American scam.

THE BUDGET HOTEL CHAINS

Hotels chains are all over town. In a sad way, the proliferation of corporate hotels helped kill most of the family-run bed-and-breakfast that England used to be famous for. Local hospitality has been replaced by clock-punching staff who probably grew up elsewhere, but you can still expect reliable standards, decently sized rooms with private bathrooms, and unbeatable lead-in rates, especially for people who pay months ahead of time. Unfortunately, so many visitors habitually turn to these dominating brands that late-purchase prices usually rise far past the point of value. To stay at these places in central London for less, book well in advance.

King's Cross to Embankment Hotels
Alhambra Hotel 4
Apex Temple Court 31
Assembly Leicester Square 20
Celtic Hotel 9
The Clermont, Charing Cross 26
Corinthia Hotel London 25
The Fielding Hotel 15
Four Points Flex by Sheraton London Euston 7
The Haymarket Hotel 22
The Henrietta Experimental Hotel 28
Hotel Meridiana 3
The Hoxton, Holborn 12
Jesmond Hotel 8
Kaya Great Northern Hotel 1
L'Oscar 11
The Lincoln Suites 14
The Londoner Hotel 21
The Megaro 2
Middle Eight 13
The Montague on the Gardens 10
Montcalm Piccadilly Townhouse 18
Raffles London at The OWO 24
The Resident Covent Garden 27
The Resident Soho 17
The Savoy 29
Seven Dials Hotel 16
The Standard London 5
Strand Palace Hotel 30
St Pancras Renaissance Hotel 6
The Trafalgar St James London 23
Victory House Leicester Square 19
St Pancras Station
King's Cross Station
King's Cross St Pancras
KING'S CROSS
British Library
EUSTON
ST PANCRAS
WC1
Russell Sq
BLOOMSBURY
British Museum
Goodge St
Tottenham Court Rd
Holborn
HOLBORN
Chancery Lane
Sir John Soane's Museum
Lincoln's Inn Fields
COVENT GARDEN
Covent Garden
Covent Garden Market
SOHO
Leicester Sq
WC2
The Temple
Inner Temple Gardens
Temple
River Thames
Waterloo Bridge
Savoy Pier
Cleopatra's Needle
Embankment Pier
Embankment
Piccadilly Circus
National Gallery
Charing Cross
Nelson's Column
Charing Cross Station
National Theatre
Festival Pier
Royal Festival Hall
Hungerford Bridge
SOUTH BANK
Waterloo East
ST JAMES'S
St James's Palace
ST JAMES'S PARK
Jubilee Gardens
London Eye Millennium Pier
London Eye
Waterloo
0 1/4 mi
0 0.25 km

citizenM ♥♥♥ This excellent affordable chain that got its legs in London is actually Dutch, but it is now part of Marriott's Bonvoy network. Their glassy open-plan lobbies, where there's always a bar and lots of comfortable seating, are lined with shelves of unread orange-and-white Penguin classic paperbacks, which every self-conscious interior designer in London displays to denote postmodern intellectualism, and they churn day and night with people sipping fine coffee and telecommuting. Check-in is self-guided by kiosk, and rooms are compact—almost podlike at 14 sq. m (150 sq. ft.)—but arranged with genius. Expect king-size platform beds (and no other sizes) piled with super-seductive duvets, curvy unit bathrooms slotted into the space with calculated aplomb, and a bedside tablet that lets you control everything from motorized blinds to the color of the room's mood lighting. Ventilation can be laggy, and the frosted glass enclosing the bathroom units isn't ideal for modest bathers—better to share the room with someone who has already seen you naked. My favorite locations are Bankside (behind the Tate Modern) and Tower of London, where some rooms and the fab cloudM rooftop bar overlook that eternal fortress, which no other budget hotel does.

www.citizenm.com. 4 locations around London. Generally £135–£277. **Amenities:** Free movies; free Wi-Fi; bar; food served.

easyHotel ♥ Prefabricated room units differ only in how little space you're given—the smallest are 6 sq. m (65 sq. ft.), space only for a bed and a

The Tower of London branch of citizenM offers fantastic views from the CloudM rooftop bar.

shallow breath. No phone, no hair dryer, no frills at all. Bathrooms are just plastic cubicles combining a shower, toilet, and sink in one wet closet. The cheapest rooms don't even have windows (that's legal in London), and you cannot change the thermostat. Want your room serviced? You'll pay £15 each time. Want food? Pre-packaged. I find the no-nonsense atmosphere to be like camping inside a vending machine, but some visitors swear this is how you do London ultra-cheaply while avoiding hostels. Reservations typically cost £70 for double rooms if you book 6 months ahead, and around £110 if you procrastinate. The Victoria location is the nearest to major tourist sights and the most Tube lines.

www.easyhotel.com. No phone reservations. 4 locations in central London. Rooms £39–£160. **Amenities:** Free Wi-Fi.

Hub by Premier Inn ♥♥ Sleek, cannily designed rooms (just 11.4 sq. m/123 sq. ft.) are tight as air locks, packing in a platform bed for two with storage underneath, a bright and clean-lined shower/toilet module, well-located power outlets and USB charging ports, a fold-down desk, and a lime green chair. The staff won't do much for you, but using an app, you can dim or extinguish the lights, watch TV (all movies are free—the Wi-Fi is mercury-fast, too), or turn on the "do not disturb" light. ***Downsides:*** You may not get a mobile phone signal, and you won't be able to look out a window, but there's a cafe for breakfast (around £6 for continental—a bargain). The best rates (£70–100) sell out months in advance, and last-minute prices can be as high as a hotel that would give you much more space. Reservations must be done at the main Premier Inn website, so make sure you're booking a Hub location and not a standard Premier Inn. My favorite location: Covent Garden, steps from Trafalgar Square (in 2026, a 693 room location is under construction by Charing Cross station at 5 Strand); the Brick Lane location is unusual because so few hotels are directly on that market-and-nightlife street. Least favorite: West Brompton, which is too far west.

www.premierinn.com/hub. 15 locations around London. £71–£250 double. **Amenities:** Breakfast (charged); AC; free movies; free Wi-Fi.

Ibis Hotels ♥ This basic but 1,200-strong French chain by the Accor hotel giant is distinguished by utilitarian but cheerful decor. You'll get a double bed, bathroom with shower, climate control, a 24-hour kitchen, TV, phone, free Wi-Fi, at least one outlet, and a built-in desk. The breakfast charge varies per property (£12–£15 is typical), but food is usually served from 4am, making this a smart choice if you need to catch an early flight or train. The fresh-baked breakfast baguettes are delicious—hey, it's proudly French. My favorite location: Ibis London Blackfriars, which is usually a little cheaper than the others but still in walking distance to a lot. There's also **Ibis Styles,** the "all-inclusive" brand that is slightly less Spartan and includes breakfast and Wi-Fi; and **Ibis Budget,** a bare-bones, shower-only crash pad once known as Etap or Formule 1; rooms there are ultra-simple (though with flair), sleep up to three people, and have free Wi-Fi and TV, but practically nothing else. Buildings tend to have air cooling systems but not true A/C. Check the map before booking, as some of its locations are distant from central London.

ibis.accor.com. No English-reservations hotline. 24+ locations around London. Rooms in central London generally £72–£278, varying by season and location. **Amenities:** Free Wi-Fi.

Motel One London–Tower Hill ♥♥ The sole London branch of a German budget brand, Motel One is basic (no drawers, no closet, no phone, few hangers) and service can be machine-like, but the dignified design conforms to contemporary trends in architecture and interior decor, and the views of City buildings from many of the rooms can be splendid. Your quarters will be modest (16 sq. m/172 sq. ft.), soundproofed, and equipped with TV and A/C—amenities you often have to check for at this price point. The Tower of London, Whitechapel, and Spitalfields are short walks away, and there's a small bar in the lobby. London could use a few more locations of this value choice. Open more, please.

24–26 Minories, EC3; www.motel-one.com; ✆ **020/7481-6420;** doubles from £140–£225, often a 2-night minimum; Tube: Aldgate.

Point A Hotels ♥ This modern-budget brand provides everything you need in a compact room but nothing else: power shower, round-the-clock reception, A/C, bedside USB ports, a safe, a drop-down desk, hooks (but not a closet). Not all rooms have windows, and housekeeping comes every 3 nights. The a la carte model is no path to luxury, despite the higher-than-expected rates. Still, the facilities have AC and are designed with minimalist zip. Don't write off a windowless room's power to mediate jet lag. Join its free members' club for slight discounts. The "Westminster" branch (its most central one) is actually across the river by Waterloo, but it often sells out first.

www.pointahotels.com. No phone. 7 locations in the city. Rooms £140–£260. **Amenities:** AC; free continental breakfast; shared ironing rooms; free Wi-Fi.

Premier Inn ♥ The largest hotel chain in the country, Premier offers rooms (maximum of two adults) with a king-size bed, bathtub and shower with all-purpose shower gel, tea- and coffee-making facilities, TV, phone, iron, A/C (sometimes), at least three outlets, and a desk. Increasingly, it requires you to check in at a kiosk, eliminating human interaction, so if you need something, a pleasant stay can collapse into an instant fail. Prices rise and fall according to how much demand the company thinks there will be, so quotes fluctuate wildly. Final prices may be too high for such a standard room, so the key is early booking. ***Warning:*** The cheapest locations are deep in distant suburbs, so consult a map before taking the bait of a low price. Also, search results are mixed with its much barer Hub locations (see above). Favorite location: Southwark (Bankside), practically on the river.

www.premierinn.com. ✆ **0333/003-8101.** More than 60 locations around the city. Rooms generally £118–£210, depending on season and location. **Amenities:** A/C (some locations); bar/cafe; free slow Wi-Fi, £5/day for high-speed Wi-Fi.

Travelodge ♥ Rates for this economy brand, which has some two dozen properties in Central London, start around £77 for a non-flexible reservation if you book 11 months ahead, but if you book late, prices nudge the top of our Moderate price range. It's nicer than the American Travelodge brand, to which it isn't related. Expect king-size beds, bathtub and shower, TV (but no phone, hair dryer, or toiletries except hair/body wash), paid in-room movies, a wardrobe, at least one power outlet, and a desk. Breakfast, if your property offers it, costs from £10 more (kids 16 and under free). "Family rooms" have a pullout couch for two kids but cost the same as a double. "SuperRooms" have upgraded fittings and a coffeemaker, and PLUS locations have a simple cafe/bar. If you're willing to stay in a quiet suburban neighborhood with a bit of a rail commute, the deals can be extraordinarily cheap. The site's "Best Price Finder" shows the cheapest deals in the city for your dates—just be careful it doesn't seduce you into taking a room in a distant suburb. Favorite location: Covent Garden.

www.travelodge.co.uk. ✆ **08719/848-484.** More than 80 locations around the city. Rooms generally £72–£220, depending on season and location (lower if booked far in advance). **Amenities:** A/C (some locations); bar/cafe (often); Wi-Fi free for 30 min. daily, 24-hr. access £3/day.

Z Hotels ♥♥♥ Please say it "Zed," which rhymes with "bed." Now that you've got that down, here's the formula: ideal locations; extremely compact rooms, but lots of room under the duvets; glassy, sleek style; and a lobby that's always abuzz with breakfast, coffee, or free daily wine. The formula works because there are design smarts where they count: Shower nozzles swivel the way you need them to, towels are plump and copious, you can control your thermostat. They poured cash into the bedding and the 40-inch TVs but did without closets and drawers. The cheapest rooms may not have windows. Note that if you share a room with a platonic friend, bathrooms are enclosed only by panels of fogged glass. Book about 4 months ahead for prices around £100; late reservations can be three times that. My favorite locations, for convenience: Soho, Trafalgar, Covent Garden, and Piccadilly.

www.thezhotels.com. ✆ **020/3551-3700.** 12 locations around the city. Rooms £90–£369. **Amenities:** Cafe/bar; A/C; free evening wine and cheese; free Wi-Fi.

Is your booking up to date?

In North America, people tend to put the date after the month, as in *November 5, 1605.* But in the United Kingdom, and indeed in most of the world, the order is commonly written from smallest to largest increment of time: date *then* month *then* year—ergo, *5 November 1605.* That order is quite logical if you consider it. Avoid booking errors by putting the right numbers in the correct fields, i.e.: 5/11/1605.

KING'S CROSS & BLOOMSBURY

King's Cross was once known for small, down-market rooms run by widows and immigrants, but in the past 15 years, the area has gentrified. Ongoing development of Pancras Square and Granary Square in the old shipping yards behind the train stations has turned the area into London's tech neighborhood, and hotel offerings have expanded to attract moneyed young professionals. The location is easy to use: Six important Tube lines, the Eurostar to mainland Europe, and the Thameslink (which goes to Gatwick) all go from here. The rebirth of King's Cross essentially wiped Paddington and Earl's Court off the marketplace for cheap overnights. Just south, **Bloomsbury**'s chocolate-colored Georgian brick townhouses are more classically residential London and lie within a 20-minute walk of Soho and Covent Garden.

Expensive

The Montague on the Gardens ♥♥ It's not easy these days finding typically British mid-priced hotels that aren't mired in gloomy tour-group dinginess, but the conjoined townhouses of the Montague deliver intimate Englishness in demonstration as much as in word. Downstairs, a large staff (including porters and concierge) pays close attention to guest needs, and rooms, always tasteful and richly comfortable, are a mishmash of styles as if in a moneyed home. They're also an unpredictable mix of sizes (including singles) given the charming age of the buildings, but they're silent, plush, and otherwise appointed with more than you'll need. It's comfortable, dignified, and a homey bolt-hole for central London explorations, with the British Museum literally across the road. It's family friendly as well.

15 Montague St., WC1. www.montaguehotel.com. ✆ **020/7958-7731.** 100 units. Rooms £226–£356. Tube: Russell Square. **Amenities:** Restaurant; bar; A/C; free bottled water; free Wi-Fi.

St. Pancras Renaissance Hotel ♥ Behold one of London's architectural masterpieces: This Gothic redbrick palace, a terminal hotel for St Pancras railway station, was built as the Midland Grand Hotel in 1873 for £300 million in today's money. Palatial public spaces present a gilt-and-tile parade of self-important Victorian excess, from the marble Grand Staircase (seen in the Spice Girls's video for "Wannabe") to the lushly carved brasserie and the old wooden Booking Hall, now a classy place to get a drink. Hard to believe that in the 1960s, this glory was nearly torn down. The building was "too good for its purpose," lamented its architect, Gilbert Scott. It's worth a wander even if you're not staying here. As a hotel, service is distracted and rooms need some attention, so we currently recommend it more for tourist visits than for overnight stays. If you do choose it for Marriott-points reasons, the best premium rooms have an unforgettable view down the ribbed, cast-iron cavern of the train shed, and you can watch Eurostar arrive and depart in your bathrobe. Rooms in the modern Barlow wing are blandly corporate, lack those long

Many rooms at the St. Pancras Renaissance Hotel offer views of the glorious St Pancras station.

views (the ones in lower categories have small windows), and suit business travel tastes—for us, it's the original building or nothing.

Euston Rd., London, NW1. www.marriott.com. ✆ **020/7841-3540.** 245 units. £264–£391 double. Tube: King's Cross St Pancras. **Amenities:** Restaurant; 2 bars; indoor pool; 24-hr. fitness center; spa; A/C; free Wi-Fi.

The Standard London ♥♥ This concrete Brutalist core contains a knowing time warp to 1974. The Standard has been designed to eye-pleasing extremes—in this case, to evoke that bygone era in all its shag-carpeted, spherical-lamped, olive-and-beige glory. Everything takes its cues from its building, which used to house the local city government but now stylizes a groovier existence with a busy street-facing cocktail bar. It's an ideal addition for the consumerist dot-com overachievers who are moving into the new corporate offices around nearby Granary Square. The most affordable standard rooms are dubbed "Cosy," and at just 13 square meters (139 sq. ft.) and sometimes without windows, they're terrible rooms, so don't get suckered into one. But if you have the dosh, this is one place where an upgrade is worth it: The Terrace rooms (from £630) have outdoor spaces (with outdoor spa tubs) that overlook the ostentatious glory of St Pancras, which itself is an over-the-top representation of the design immoderation of the '70s—the 1870s, that is. Ask

HOW TO LOVE a historic townhouse hotel

Unfortunately, the once-famous English B&B is nearly extinct. Neighborhoods that were once dependable for cut-price lodging (Gloucester Place in Marylebone, Ebury Street in Victoria, Gower Street in Bloomsbury) have largely evicted B&B proprietors and sold out to luxury options. In London, the ultra-rich still own most of the land, and they chose higher returns over national tradition.

The B&Bs that survive usually occupy "listed" buildings. What does that mean? It means that it has historical or architectural importance—for example, it's an example of a fine Georgian townhouse or an original stately Victorian terrace home. To keep developers from knocking down a gem, "listed" buildings are protected. Changing anything requires permission, down to adding A/C or altering the color of the paint. American tourists who are unused to London's listed buildings often post huffy online reviews about the quirks that define townhouse hotels, penalizing London inns for being London inns. That hotel is not a dump! It's historic.

Rooms are small by American standards. Don't blame the current owners. Room subdivision happened on a wide scale after World War II, to fill a housing gap after so many buildings were bombed, and now even removing those slapped-up walls requires council (government) approval, which rarely comes. You are unlikely to have a closet. ***Tip:*** The largest rooms usually face the front.

Bathrooms are even smaller. In the old days, guests shared bathrooms. To suit changing tastes, landlords installed booths containing the staples (toilet, shower, sink) into rooms that weren't designed to have them. Would you rather go back to sharing?

Don't expect an elevator, or "lift." It's not that they're too cheap to install one. In these historic houses, they're not even allowed. Assume you'll have to use the stairs. They may be narrower than you're used to. Rooms on higher floors require climbing, but they also receive more light, less noise, and often cost less.

Ceilings get lower as you go higher. Until the 20th century, the floors of fashionable townhouses served distinct functions. The cellar was for kitchens and coal storage. The ground floor was usually used for living rooms. The first and second floors were reserved for bedrooms, and the top floor was for servants and for the children's nursery, which accounts for the slightly lower ceilings there.

Not all windows are double glazed. You think you hear traffic now? Imagine when horses and carriages clattered up the cobbles at all hours. If you're a light sleeper, simply ask for a room at the back. Rooms on back stairway landings often don't adjoin other rooms, either, which takes care of other ambient noises.

for a corner Deluxe Queen room, with a wraparound sofa under its curvy windows.

10 Argyle St., NW1. www.standardhotels.com/london. ✆ **020/3981-8888.** 266 units. From £199 single–£395 double. Tube: King's Cross St Pancras. **Amenities:** 2 restaurants; bar; 24-hr. fitness center; in-room A/C; free Wi-Fi.

Moderate

Kaya Great Northern Hotel ♥♥ Of all London's railway terminal hotels, from the outside the Great Northern seems the plainest—and the

The Great Northern Hotel at King's Cross Station opened in 1854.

smallest. Its crescent-shaped building went up quite early, in 1854, and as a consequence it isn't as bombastic as its brethren learned how to be. Rooms aren't huge, but they have a smart modern edge and they're part of the Bonvoy points network. The smallest rooms are called "Couchette" because the sled-style queen beds, attached at head and foot to the walls, are said to have been inspired by railway sleepers. (Don't worry—they have much more space for your luggage, although the result is less spacious than the higher-category Heritage and Victorian rooms.) Etched glass and cute little curved banquettes complete the allusions to trains. High-standard perks pack the other spaces—a good British restaurant and a cozy cocktail bar is another. ***Caveat:*** If you're quoted a rate over £300 for its Couchette category, you can do better elsewhere.

King's Cross St Pancras Station, Pancras Rd., N1. kayagnhlondon.com/. ✆ **020/3388-0800.** 91 units. From £240 double, max. occupancy 2. Tube: King's Cross St Pancras. **Amenities:** Restaurant; bar; snack bar; A/C; free Wi-Fi.

The Megaro ♥ This old office building has been tarted up with brassy colors and a cluttered exterior mural, but inside, the theme is spacious and Scandinavian-meets-steampunk, with open wood floors, unadorned paneling, poppy-colored lighting, smart slide-out makeup desks and workspaces, complimentary in-room snacks, and fresh tea leaves for your cuppa. Rooms on the main road have killer views of St Pancras and the plaza in front of King's Cross (no. 504, a corner, is the best for that), but if traffic noise irritates you, go for one facing the other way (no. 508, with a small balcony, picturesquely peeks over the pipe chimneys of nearby townhouses). If you're traveling with a platonic companion, ask for a room in which your bathroom isn't encased in glass walls; some are, some aren't. The staff can be overwhelmed at breakfast, but this hotel's common spaces and cocktail concoctions shine by night. It's fun but not five-star.

Belgrove St., WC1. themegaro.co.uk. ✆ **020/7843-2222.** 49 units. £190–£340, save 15% on website. Tube: King's Cross St Pancras. **Amenities:** Restaurant; bar; A/C; free Wi-Fi.

Inexpensive

Alhambra Hotel ♥♥♥ The comforting Alhambra is an inn with heart, and a top value in Frommer's ever since *Europe on $5 a Day*—an example of the long tradition of family-run establishments in London. Its proprietors, whose lineage has owned the land for decades and raised generations of children on this inn's income, take pride in the business, and they keep prices low. They have survived by converting the former breakfast area into three more rooms and lowering prices slightly. Picture simple, small, but dignified rooms (from singles to quad) squeezed into old spaces, but always spotless and freshened up with bright bedspreads, slate-grey carpeting, built-in desks with chairs, flat-screen TVs (but no phones), free fiber-optic Wi-Fi, and in-room safes, all rarities for this price point. If you share a bathroom, there are plenty to go around. In winter, it's easy to negotiate rates down by as much as 30%. Its simplicity is from another era.

17–19 Argyle St., WC1. www.alhambrahotel.com. ✆ **020/7837-9575.** 55 units. £63–£125 single, £65–£168 double, slight discount for nonrefundable rates. Tube: King's Cross St Pancras. **Amenities:** Free Wi-Fi.

Celtic Hotel ♥♥ A defiant and idiosyncratic throwback from the way British budget hospitality used to be, the Celtic is housed in an 18th-century building constructed from timber taken from ships from London's docks. This is the domain of the dedicated Marazzi family, who have been robust figures in London's affordable-travel scene for decades. For 56 years, the Marazzis owned a beloved place nearby, St Margaret's Hotel, before being forced out by gentrification, and their regulars followed them here. Their move to the Celtic retained the quirky features their fans love: Rooms don't have TVs or phones; furniture is endearingly mismatched; and the lounge is a hub for socializing with fellow guests. Add £5 to £23 if you don't want to share a shower or toilet. A full, cooked English breakfast is available, but **Fortitude Bakery**, mobbed for its fresh beignets (served at 11am daily), is literally around the corner. You must book the Celtic directly.

62 Guilford St., WC1. www.celtichotel.com. ✆ **020/7837-6737** or 020/7837-9258**.** 35 units. From £79 single, from £135 double. No lift. Tube: Russell Square. **Amenities:** 2 lounges; free Wi-Fi.

Hotel Meridiana ♥ This is what a value hotel should be: not lavish, but you happily get what you pay for. Walls can be thin, rooms truly teeny, and many share bathrooms, but everything is spotless and it's well-maintained. Heating and hot water are reliable, too, which isn't always the case in buildings of this age, and some rooms have drawers, another relative curiosity. If you just need a dead-cheap place to sleep where you'll have no regrets about hygiene, this no-frills B&B is a decent choice. You're unlikely to get as much value for the price elsewhere.

43–44 Argyle Sq., WC1. www.hotelmeridiana.co.uk. ✆ **020/7713-0144.** 27 units. From £79 single, from £100 double. No breakfast. No lift. Tube: King's Cross St Pancras. **Amenities:** Free Wi-Fi.

Jesmond Hotel ♥♥♥ It's easy to have a soft spot for this place near the British Library. This author even stayed here often when he was just out of

THE ENGLISH CHARM OF pub hotels

There was a time, not so long ago, when most people didn't travel much. Hotels were not the industry they are today. In most English villages, though, if strangers needed a bed, they only had to look as far as the local pub, many of which maintained a handful of clean and serviceable rooms upstairs as part of the business. Many still do, and the tradition continues in London, too, but now on the level of boutique hotels. Expect low-level service and old-fashioned charm mixed with modern conveniences (except lifts—most of these old buildings can't have one). Don't be worried about noise, because the pubs downstairs (where you'll have breakfast, and which have usually been upgraded, too) close by 11pm. These will feel like your own secret discoveries.

The Bull & The Hide There's nothing old and fusty about rooms here, and there's a free "pantry" for drinks and snacks. A winery owns the whole business, and it's amid a high-rise business district convenient to Spitalfields. 4 Devonshire Row, EC2. thebullandthehide.com. ✆ **020/7655-4805.** £149–£330. Tube: Liverpool Street.

Fox & Anchor The keyword is *plush*: Power showers, brass bathtubs, Hypnos mattresses. The Market Suite has a cute little terrace, too. The pub's frontage is a protected Art Nouveau masterpiece in tile. 115 Charterhouse St., EC1. www.foxandanchor.com. ✆ **020/7250-1300.** £204–£239,. Tube: Farringdon.

The Mad Hatter Hotel Mad Hatter offers big rooms, a high-quality pub below, and a winning location (a block from the Thames) for the price. Big enough (30 rooms) that it's run like a hotel. It's busier on weekends. 3–7 Stamford St., SE1. www.madhatterhotel.co.uk. ✆ **020/7401-9222.** £148–£216. Tube: Southwark or Blackfriars.

The One Tun Eight fully modern, light rooms with a whimsical dog-and-deer style motif are above a gastropub that does pan-Asian dishes. Dickens named it The Three Cripples when it played Bill Sikes' drinking den in *Oliver Twist*. It has A/C and nearby, a just-as-good sister pub hotel, The Clerk & Well (www.theclerkandwellpub.co.uk). 125 Saffron Hill, EC1. www.onetun.co.uk. ✆ **020/7405-1521.** £195–£252. Tube: Farringdon.

Also see the pub rooms of The Sanctuary House Hotel (p. 60).

college (in room no. 3, a cozy single on the rear landing—still there, still snug). Back then, the Beynon family had a young son, Glyn. Today, Glyn is a grown family man, and he's in charge—and he's doing a proud job of updating the family B&B in a 1780s townhouse (ask him about its history) far beyond the expectations of its tariff range. He installed new bathrooms with all-new piping, accounting for the larger-than-average showers; he soundproofed the front windows to keep out the roar of Gower Street's traffic. He also converted the former parlor, with its antique (nonworking) fireplace, into room no. 2, a spacious double. The Jesmond is a classic (four units share bathrooms) that still does a full, cooked breakfast as part of the rate, and in fact, has been a Frommer's selection ever since *Europe on $5 a Day* (when a room cost $3.20). Don't confuse this place with the Jesmond Dene, a B&B on Argyle Square—it's very good, too, but not as central.

63 Gower St., WC1. www.jesmondhotel.org.uk. ✆ **020/7636-3199.** 15 units. From £100 single, from £130 double, from £200 triple or quad, from £225 quint; discounts for advance reservationa; often a 2- or 3-night minimum. No lift. Rates include full breakfast. Tube: Goodge Street. **Amenities:** Free Wi-Fi.

Four Points Flex by Sheraton London Euston ♥ Let me tell you: These rooms are small. They're so small (the smallest are 8 sq. m/ 86 sq. ft.) that you'll wonder how they can be legal. There's barely leeway for one person: To open your luggage, you have to use up your free floor space. Sometimes it feels like the walls and the bed are in a death match for dominance, recalling the compactor scene in *Star Wars.* You won't get a closet; you'll get knobs with coat hangers. Your sink's wee size and shape will put you in the mind of an iPad. But there is a secure degree of comfort in this setup, like sleeping off jet lag in a giant's pocket. And this is why it makes our recommendations: This place is crazy affordable (most nights, in the low £100s) at a predictable corporate standard, with nominal nods to artful decoration (birds and ferns on two-tone wallpaper) instead of utilitarian walls. The shower in your baby bathroom is hot; the TV is large; and its Bloomsbury location is good for Tube connections and leafy strolls. Sure, the overworked staff is often addled, but their hotel is one of Central London's cheaper Marriott Bonvoy options, which matters to some people. If you don't need more, you can't find the equivalent for less.

8–11 Upper Woburn Pl., WC1. www.marriott.com. ✆ **020/7046-0043.** 201 units. From £88. Tube: Euston. **Amenities:** Bar; A/C; free Wi-Fi.

SOHO, COVENT GARDEN & WEST END

This is the middle of London. The part of town that offers everything you need outside your door. The area crawling with inebriated 20-year-olds singing shanties in full voice when the pubs close. You may not care, because staying centrally can save on Tube fare more than it costs in shoe leather. Sunday through Thursday are the cheapest nights here.

Expensive

The Haymarket Hotel ♥♥ Bubbly colored textures, mismatched but impeccably selected furniture, and exclusivity—this Firmdale Hotels property is like staying at the country house of a fabulous friend from the magazine design pages who has made a fortune in coffee-table books, because that's what its co-owner, Kit Kemp, has done. This elegant (but never stuffy) choice demands high prices and successfully collects them from her loyal style acolytes. It backs up her bright Modern English visuals with five-star features such as a sharp staff, indulgent showers, and an indoor swimming pool. It may be amid the West End action but it's serenely removed from its tumult—it's the one property in the Firmdale group not to be routinely mobbed with cocktail-swilling fashion chasers, which makes it a serenely central place to land and recharge after a long day as if you're in a style magazine spread.

1 Suffolk Pl., SW1. www.firmdalehotels.com. ✆ **020/7470-4000.** 50 units. Standard rooms £540–£750. Tube: Piccadilly Circus. **Amenities:** Bar/restaurant; fitness center; basement pool; A/C; free Wi-Fi.

The Townhouse Living Room at The Haymarket Hotel.

The Londoner Hotel ♥♥ Rising eight floors above Leicester Square and digging another eight below it, the newly built Londoner is quiet, beautifully designed for coziness, and ridiculously central. Standard rooms, in soothing putty-and-taupe tones, are less spacious than what Americans are used to for the price—what else is new, London?—but compensating for their size, they hit some luxury marks: wood paneling, inviting beds, marble bathrooms with heated robot toilets, plenty of charging ports. And if you're lucky enough to get a southern view, you can see the roof of the National Gallery and the Eye from your bed. Stay here, and you get access to a library-like lounge with nibbles and a bar for guests (The Residence) and a spa-connected indoor pool (free to use) ideal for melting away the stress from hours of treading city pavements or shouldering through the street life of the surrounding neighborhood on crazy weekend nights. You must make heavy use of those amenities to justify the cost.

38 Leicester Square, WC2. www.thelondoner.com. ✆ **020/7451-0101.** 350 units. From £375 double. Tube: Leicester Square. **Amenities:** 6 restaurants; cocktail bar; indoor pool; gym; spa; free bottled water; A/C; free Wi-Fi.

L'Oscar ♥♥♥ The owners of L'Oscar poured huge sums into refurbishing the once-abandoned seat of the Edwardian-era Baptist church, and the expenditure shows in sumptuousness: beds stuffed with Icelandic eiderdown, whimsical Arts and Crafts paintings, recessed carpeting that averts tripping, iridescent fabrics in rich purples and gold, and nearly 500 crystal bird sculptures scattered throughout. Hidden in back, the former chapel under an octagonal dome is now a magisterial setting for food and cocktails. Windows are triple-glazed against London traffic, creating silent private domains. All

The plush, elegant lobby of L'Oscar, a hotel set in a former church.

that said, the energy is cordial and not stuffy, in the best boutique style—with only 39 rooms to oversee, staff won't neglect you. As is often the case in government-protected buildings like this one, each room is differently shaped (the ones on lower floors, in former offices, are the most lavish, with elaborate architectural carvings and details), but almost all have king beds. Superior category ones, at the still-very-comfortable bottom rung of the price ladder, only have a shower and not a tub. A top candidate for honeymoons and marriage proposal vacations.

2–6 Southampton Row, WC1. www.loscarlondon.com. ✆ **020/7405-5555.** 39 units. Rooms £445–£697 double. Tube: Holborn. **Amenities:** Restaurant; cocktail bar; free gym passes; A/C; free Wi-Fi.

Middle Eight ♥ It's self-dubbed a "luxury lifestyle hotel," but that just means you'll find this midsized choice attractive and comfortable. Middle Eight, designed with care in golds, greys, and smoky yellow glass, is quiet and calming despite its situation on a popular road linking Holborn and Covent. Two typically thoughtful touches: Your key card (required to get beyond the lobby) is made of wood and your bathrobe from recycled plastic (although you wouldn't realize that if you weren't told). Most rooms don't have a desk, just a narrow counter, but there's an inviting settee for lounging. Bathroom floors are heated, and the minibars throw in a few free soft drinks. Despite the trappings, the hotel isn't much of a social scene; on our last visit, the bar struggled to stay open to its posted closing time, although it hardly mattered since there are hundreds of other bars to choose from in every direction around it. Comfortable, stylish without haughtiness, and an excellent place to snooze within steps of the action.

66 Great Queen St., WC2. www.middleeight.com. ✆ **020/7309-9300.** 168 units. Rooms £202–£484. Tube: Holborn. **Amenities:** Bar/restaurant; A/C; fitness center; free Wi-Fi.

The Trafalgar St. James London ♥♥ The Trafalgar St. James, part of the Hilton network, possesses so much that other hotels envy, including a golden location in the heart of town, a manageable size, and a rooftop bar overlooking Trafalgar Square that gets busy, but guests have priority. How lucky that it doesn't fumble the hidden details, either: Rooms have their own urban personality with cushioned headboards, settees, and ample bathrooms, some of which even have tubs in addition to shower booths. Furniture quality can be a touch Hiltonish (meaning mass-produced), and rooms on the upper floors trade unbeatable views for smaller windows than on the lower floors, but that's more than acceptable considering the reasonable price point and all the standout features. On the whole, there's a great deal to adore here, and more than enough to make it a primary choice for many.

2 Spring Gardens, Trafalgar Square, SW1. trafalgarstjames.com/. ✆ **020/7870-2900**. 137 units. Rooms from £284. Tube: Charing Cross. **Amenities:** 2 restaurant/bars, including on rooftop; A/C; fitness center; free Wi-Fi.

Moderate

The Clermont, Charing Cross ♥ The railway terminal hotel above Charing Cross Station opened a month after Lincoln's assassination and underwent many lives (and Blitz damage). Now the Charing Cross is a quiet, underrated hotel with spacious rooms that dips its toes into fancy trimmings (heated bathroom floors, walk-in showers, Nespresso coffee, free minibars that include beer and snacks). To top it off, there's a Tube stop (Bakerloo and Northern lines) underneath. Even without that, the location is spectacular and could command much higher rates: In fact, at the nexus of Trafalgar Square, Strand, the Covent Garden area, and the Embankment, you may feel spoiled. Breakfast (overcrowded) is taken with a view toward St Martin-in-the-Fields. Hints of a more genteel age at a good price.

The Strand, WC2. www.theclermont.co.uk/charing-cross. ✆ **020/7523-5052.** 239 units. Rooms £202–£382. Tube: Charing Cross or Embankment. **Amenities:** Restaurant; bar; business center; A/C; free Wi-Fi.

The Henrietta Experimental Hotel ♥♥ Don't mind the name—it's not an experiment; that's a reference to the Experimental Group, the hospitality outfit that runs it. The Henrietta's in a peerless location on a mostly pedestrianized Covent Garden street, above the Henri restaurant/bar, lively with customers. Upstairs and at an annex across the lane (there are lifts), you're happily ensconced in soundproofed quarters. Even if the rooms are all different sizes, their vibe consistently serves Comfy Modern Art Deco, nothing too flashy. Choose a unit with built-in seating by its huge front-facing windows (I prefer the namesake, The Henrietta, which has a tubbed bathroom that's larger than some whole hotel rooms in London), send down for cocktails and food, and you could spend many romantic hours people-watching and reading. Despite the small size, staff is on duty round the clock and is unusually attentive to welcoming service. This is a hotel where it's a relief to return

A modern Art Deco guestroom at The Henrietta Experimental Hotel

after a long day—not too big, not too fussy, but approachably inviting and personal-feeling.

14–15 Henrietta St., WC2. henriettahotel.com. ✆ **020/3794-5313.** 40 units. Doubles £264–£487. Tube: Covent Garden or Leicester Square. **Amenities:** Restaurant with cocktail bar; A/C; free Wi-Fi.

The Fielding Hotel ♥ The prime location, just steps from Covent Garden's food and shopping, is what makes it easy to overlook the cramped, liftless quarters at this family-owned hotel. In this early-19th-century warren of tight staircases and fire doors, the sometimes slightly airless rooms snuggle you with a certain throwaway charisma. Rooms no. 10, 20, and 30 are doubles with sitting areas that catch lots of afternoon light, thanks to their corner position and copious windows. Everything's en suite (mostly shower only, but three have tubs), and there are no common areas to speak of. Overall, the Fielding is a pleasant surprise, and if you don't demand tons of space, a certified value.

4 Broad Ct., Bow St., WC2. www.thefieldinghotel.co.uk. ✆ **020/7836-8305.** 27 units. Singles from £185, doubles from £300, a full flat (max. 6 guests) from £435. Tube: Covent Garden or Holborn. **Amenities:** Free Wi-Fi.

Montcalm Piccadilly Townhouse ♥♥♥ We have recommended this impossibly central hotel since it was known as The Piccadilly West End, and the service has only improved since it changed hands. If you're saddled with lots of bulky luggage, it's not the most spacious place you'll ever stay, but on balance it's solid, well-run, thoughtfully equipped, and a shining choice among the West End theatres. Slotted into a gorgeous old Victorian building in the heart of Shaftesbury Avenue (steps from Piccadilly Circus, you'd hustle right by it if you didn't know it was upstairs), this friendly independent hotel, smoothly buffered from the outside world (carpets, upholstered headboards), packs high-level room amenities (A/C, Nespresso coffee, safe) into moderately priced rooms. For being in the pounding heart of the city, the hotel feels calmly sealed away once you're inside. We'd classify this one as a find. Book at least 3 months ahead, and you'll find rates near £200—a price you could not improve upon for the high quality and unimpeachable central location.

65–73 Shaftesbury Ave., WC2. www.thepiccadillywestend.co.uk. ✆ **020/7871-6000.** 67 units. £189–£345 double. Tube: Piccadilly Circus or Leicester Square. **Amenities:** Restaurant/bar; spa; gym; A/C; free Wi-Fi.

The Resident Covent Garden ♥♥♥ An exterior that looks like just another Victorian office edifice in fact conceals an intelligently designed and carefully serviced oasis (charcoals, woods, gentle stripes). You get flat-screen TVs; free Internet; a free music library; some oversized showers; safes; very quiet rooms; lots of outlets; plenty of storage space; and, most helpfully, mini-kitchens with fridges, microwaves, and a kettle, so you can prepare simple meals. The location (on busy Strand) is solid because there's so much right out the door. The lift gets a little too busy, but you gain back time with the fantastic location. Frommer's started praising the brand early in 2013, but the secret is out, and this location books up quickly—last-minute rates can double, which cripples the value, so reserve at least a few months out. You'll find more good Resident hotels in Soho (great for nightlife) and near Buckingham Palace.

51 Bedford St. at Strand, WC2. www.residenthotels.com. ✆ **020/3146-1790.** 57 units. Rooms from £249. Tube: Charing Cross or Covent Garden. **Amenities:** In-room mini-kitchen; A/C; free Wi-Fi.

Strand Palace Hotel ♥ This dowager recently got wise to its stellar location—right across from the Savoy, beside Covent Garden—and it renovated itself out of the 1980s and back to the land of the living, but it's still at heart an aging grande dame dating to 1908. Service may be standard-issue because of its gargantuan size; rooms and their windows could be larger or provide more considerate views; but beds are comfortable; and the hotel has re-earned its place among budget tourists by keeping its quality in the game. The Strand Palace will never be intimate and personal, but it serves as a time-tested, acceptable last resort if you're dead-set on being able to walk to everything.

372 Strand, WC2. www.strandpalacehotel.co.uk. ✆ **020/7379-4737.** 785 units. Singles from £165, doubles from £200; 4th night free when booked on its website. Tube: Charing Cross or Temple. **Amenities:** 2 restaurants; 2 bars; business center; fitness center; free national calls; free minibar (deluxe rooms); A/C; free Wi-Fi.

Victory House Leicester Square ♥ The location is enviably central—behind a gorgeous 1898 French Renaissance facade on the north side of Leicester Square—so it gets noisy at night outside, but doubled-paned windows keep the clatter to a soothing murmur that satisfies most sleepers. The bathrooms are a higher grade than most with subway tile and heated towel bars, the beds large even if the ceilings are low, and the perks pleasing (like free bottled water). The major downsides, which won't be important to some travelers, is that the lobby is perilously small, so you'll have to seek breakfast elsewhere, and rooms can also be petite, which might be acceptable in a cozy way but only if you're not paying more than £300. Victory House lacks common areas to hang out in, but you only have to walk a few inches to be in pulsing heart of London. Think of it as the affordable analog to The Londoner, across the same square.

14 Leicester Place, WC2. www.victoryhouselondon.com. ✆ **020/3909-4100.** 86 units. Rooms £177–£381. Tube: Leicester Square. **Amenities:** Bistro; A/C; free Wi-Fi.

Inexpensive

Assembly Leicester Square ♥♥ Almost always reliable for a value-priced bed in the middle of the action, the Assembly is a secret that scrimping millennials won't want to share. Rooms are wee and sparse, to be sure, but they're modern (blonde wood, charcoal carpet, and subway-like tile in their little bathrooms) and clean, and because the Assembly inhabits a tower practically on top of the National Portrait Gallery, many of them have sublime views of the city. You won't get a phone, a desk, or even a lobby to speak of, but do you really need those? To compensate for the lack of TVs, the Wi-Fi is

SEVEN TRICKS FOR saving

To save money on guesthouses and inns, obey seven simple rules:

1. **Book early.** Even at the swankiest places, prices can more than halve if you commit at least six months ahead.
2. **Off-season is cheaper.** Many big hotels have two seasons: April through September vs. October through March (excluding holidays). Prices will be 10% to 25% cheaper in winter. Interestingly, very few family-owned B&Bs and inns bother with this system, pricing uniformly.
3. **Stay longer.** I haven't found a family-run hotel that wasn't willing to lower prices for anyone staying more than 5 or 6 nights.
4. **The days matter.** Any given hotel tends to be cheaper at one time of week over another: weekends in business zones like The City, weekdays in touristy Soho.
5. **Go mom-and-pop.** Their rates usually include taxes, but big hotels' rates don't.
6. **Book directly.** The chains now tend to give the best rates if you do that. (That said, in Frommer's' tests, Booking.com and HotelsCombined.com compare well to competitors, and Booking.com tends to include tax in its quotes, which helps.)
7. **Use the flexible date feature.** Some hotels will show you rates across days on a calendar so you can see if you'd save money by shifting your schedule.

Last-minute deals are rare but do exist. Routes for looking into deals within a week of travel are Hotwire.com, Priceline.com, and the app Hotel Tonight.

perfect, whip-quick, and free. You get a leafy rooftop bar/restaurant with a splendid east- and south-facing panorama that you won't find at luxury hotels five times the price. The evening pursuits of the West End are at your feet and the low price point creates some inevitable churn in a guest list full of younger folk. The very cheapest units might not have a window (you'll be warned), so pay another £20 to bump up with 30% more space; most rooms sleep 2 but "suite" rooms accept 3. Book direct for 10% off. Really, this is a crash pad extraordinaire.

27–31 Charing Cross Rd., WC2. www.assemblyhotels.com. ✆ **020/3953-4300.** 139 units. Windowless doubles from £127, standard doubles from £146. Tube: Leicester Square. **Amenities:** Bar/restaurant; A/C; free Wi-Fi.

Seven Dials Hotel ♥ Here, everything is wee, no-frills, and worn: the stairway, the rooms, the charm. And correspondingly, the rates. There's usually barely enough storage space, a TV mounted on an armature, a basic writing desk, teeny clean bathrooms, and firm beds, albeit ones covered with dowdy bedspreads. Basement rooms don't have windows. Forget the lack of a lift and all the ways it's dated and slipping year by year. Its footing on Monmouth Street, steps from a rainbow of pubs, boutiques, and food clustering around Covent Garden (light sleepers be warned), is without comparison. Most crucially, you can't pay less for a West End bed that doesn't charge by the hour. The target market for this old-school holdout is probably students traveling on a penny and a sense of adventure, but we value clean rudimentary hotels, too.

7 Monmouth St., WC2. www.sevendialshotel.com. ✆ **020/7240-0823.** 18 units. From £74 single, £90 double; occasionally there's a 3-night min. No breakfast. Tube: Covent Garden. **Amenities:** Free Wi-Fi.

BELGRAVIA, ST JAMES'S & VICTORIA

Restaurant choices and attractions thin out in the areas west of Westminster Abbey, where townhouses from a grander age hold court and areas shift to residential use. The center of London's hotel action shifted out of Victoria in the last few years as personality-free glass blocks and corporate food replaced many family-run B&Bs and restaurants. The area around Victoria Station, once a hub for budget visitors, now feels like any other city, but the transit links are strong. Guests who stay in these neighborhoods usually require Tube or bus rides to see most of the city's sights.

Expensive

Dukes Hotel ♥♥ Stashed in its own hidden lane in Buckingham-adjacent St James's, a neighborhood not wanting for Old World bolt-holes, Dukes, which emerges from a top-to-bottom renovation in 2026, sets itself apart for coziness and clubby service. It's virtually hidden near Green Park in a tight lane beside Spencer House (p. 159)—so no views—which makes this 1908 classic feel like it exists in a world of its own. Make a table reservation for the deservedly popular bar—Ian Fleming, creator of James Bond, is often said to have been a regular, so tourists flock to it. Potables are freshly mixed on a wooden trolley at your table, but do not order your martini "shaken, not stirred"—Bond's recipe is widely considered to be a way to ruin the vodka. Drinks in there are over £20 (and skimp on nothing), but the rooms upstairs are more affordable than many others in swanky St James's.

35 St James's Place, SW1. www.dukeshotel.com. ✆ **020/7491-4840.** 90 units. Rooms from £395. Tube: Green Park. **Amenities:** Restaurant; bar; fitness center; A/C; morning newspaper; free Wi-Fi.

The Goring ♥♥ The Goring famously hosted Kate Middleton, the wife of a future king and mother of another, for her final night as a single girl before she walked down the aisle of Westminster Abbey. Run by the same family since 1910, the Goring is classic but not self-importantly so, assiduously appropriate in style and rich in expensive fabrics, down to the Gainsborough silk on the walls, yet still goofy enough to put a stuffed sheep in every room. The fleet of doormen wears bowler hats, and the signature canary-yellow china at its hotly pursued afternoon tea (book months ahead) is made just for the hotel. The effect is something like an English country house, especially as you look out oversized windows at its blooming garden. When you're here, there's no mistaking you're steeping in London culture.

Beeston Place, SW1. www.thegoring.com. ✆ **020/7396-9000.** 69 units. Rooms from £462. Tube: Victoria. **Amenities:** Restaurant; bar; gym access; A/C; free Wi-Fi.

Hotel 41 ♥♥ A secret romantic nest only steps from Buckingham Palace, Hotel 41 is a London honeymooner's fantasy. You take a tiny private lift and tread a snug network of creaking corridors to reach its heart, a two-level, galleried conservatory bedecked like something to make Henry Higgins purr: mahogany shelves, inviting seating, sculptural busts and an oversized globe, and a yawning skylight to let the light in. There, staff makes the rounds, quietly addressing guests by name and filling glasses with champagne and plates with an endless flow of scones and hors d'oeuvres. People forget to go outside and see London. The rooms are equally individualized and top-flight: done nearly entirely in black-and-white and lacking nothing. There's no on-site restaurant or spa, and some rooms have no view to speak of—the focus is on intimacy, service, and discretion. The duplex Conservatory Suite, with a skylight over the bed, is favored by newlyweds and other nuzzlers.

41 Buckingham Palace Rd, SW1. www.41hotel.com. ✆ **020/7300-0041.** 30 units. Rooms from £333. Tube: Victoria. **Amenities:** Bar; free snacks; access to nearby gym; A/C; free Wi-Fi.

St. Ermin's Hotel ♥♥ No so long ago, it was a package-tourist misery locals nicknamed "St. Vermin's." But with a new owner, much investment, and a hookup to Marriott's points system, glory has been restored to this handsome 1889 Queen Anne structure, a hotel since 1899. The lobby's latticed riot of plasterwork and sweeping Art Nouveau stairs is enough to make a tourist

The entrance and terrace at St Ermin's Hotel, once a popular meeting place for spies.

drop one's baggage to rhapsodize about the London-ness of it all, but the history is just as rich: The premises were long used as a headquarters for British spy efforts—Ian Fleming, the creator of James Bond, worked here. Room sizes vary wildly, from puny to palatial, so you may need the guidance of a live person to get the right one, but they're all quiet and well-appointed—not five-star but solidly four. Children are emphatically welcomed (family rooms are available), and there's a pubby bar on premises; Westminster Abbey is a 5-minute stroll east. It could be closer to more sights, but precious Old World British vibrations such as these are to be protected and patronized.

2 Caxton St., SW1. www.sterminshotel.co.uk. ✆ **020/7222-7888.** 331 units. Rooms from £293. Tube: St James's Park. **Amenities:** 2 restaurants; bar; fitness center; A/C; free Wi-Fi.

The Stafford London ♥ When it opened in 1912, the intimate Stafford appealed to Americans on a European spree; it has a yacht-clubby cocktailerie known for a century as The American Bar. Today, renovated to expense-account standards (its Mews outbuilding is a particular romantic zone, but all areas are quiet and have super-soft beds), this rambling hideaway down a cul-de-sac in St James's, a short passageway from Green Park, is still popular with Americans who become repeat guests. Despite its classic affect and ensured traditional ambiance, it doesn't succumb to the arrogance rife in London's top-tier hotels. Having a subterranean wine cellar that's some 400 years old goes a long way toward attracting a discerning, but not stuck-up, clientele. A wonderful small hotel.

16–18 St James's Place, SW1. thestaffordlondon.com. ✆ **020/7493-0111.** 127 units. Rooms from £510. Tube: Green Park. **Amenities:** Restaurant; bar; fitness center; free Wi-Fi.

Moderate

Lime Tree Hotel ♥ This once-frumpy double Georgian guesthouse near Victoria Coach Station is now run by a moderate-priced Spanish chain, Room Mate Hotels, which amplifies the boutique, country-style hotel aspirations set by its previous owners but has removed the owner-operator attentiveness that made it successful. The conjoined brick townhouses are historic, so no lift is permitted, rooms are of various sizes, and stairs are plentiful (there's also no A/C, which most times is no issue), but everything is updated with slate-and-rose colors, safes, and touches such as bedside reading lights (but no tubs; only showers). If you have a first-floor room on the front, you'll have a small balcony over busy Ebury Street; in the quieter back, you'll overlook The Buttery, the house cafe in the cute flower garden. A basement room is larger than the others but has no view, and there are triples and singles available. Paying more than £300 would be too much, but around £200, which can be found 2–3 months ahead, is acceptable.

A meal in the garden of the family-owned Lime Tree Hotel.

135–137 Ebury St., London SW1. www.limetreehotel.co.uk. ✆ **020/7730-8191.** 26 units. Doubles from £200, 2- or 3-night minimum stay often required. Breakfast not included. Children 4 and under not permitted. Tube: Victoria or Sloane Square. **Amenities:** Free Wi-Fi.

The Sanctuary House Hotel ♥ Once, many pubs ran nondescript inns upstairs as sidelines. The pub here (a Fuller's, which is on the higher end of pubbery) is where you take breakfast, but the hotel upstairs accessed by lift is a creaking, well-tended reward unto itself for value and charm, and the staff is unusually responsive for such a small property on a road that's busy by day (don't worry—it's quiet at night and the windows block sound). The look plays up its Victorian origins with faux-antique telephones and plenty of handsome wood trim, but the modernized bathrooms and soft beds betray the fact that it's the beneficiary of some renovations by intelligent hoteliers. Even more miraculously, it's so near Big Ben that you can hear the bell peal. Walk west and you're connected to the transit options of Victoria.

33 Tothill St., SW1. www.sanctuaryhousehotel.co.uk. ✆ **020/7799-4044.** 34 units. From £212 double including full breakfast, cheaper Sat–Sun. Tube: St James's Park or Westminster. **Amenities:** A/C; free Wi-Fi.

Inexpensive

Luna Simone Hotel ♥ For many years, Luna Simone (also known as the Luna and Simone) has been an affordable and reliable staple in this guide. A protected townhouse building with old metalwork on the banisters and oddly sized guest rooms, it has kept up by way of inexpensive furniture and basic amenities, but it's the reliably thoughtful service that attracts many return guests. It's one of the last family-run inns in central London to still serve a

SHOULD I pack IT?

- Although all hotels include towels and linens, at family-run places you'll find for the most part that travelers are expected to bring their own washcloths.
- Many beds have duvets but not top sheets. It's just the style; Europeans would probably explain that the duvet cover *is* the top sheet.
- You may find that your bed is made each day, but your sheets aren't changed. This, too, is normal, and it saves on water, electricity, and detergent. If you want them changed, simply request it.
- In the budget category, nearly all rooms have TVs these days, but expect only four or five broadcast (or "terrestrial") channels.
- Ask for a loaner hair dryer or curling iron because your non-British one probably can't handle the voltage. New non-British hair curlers fare better, although they may get hotter than they do back home.
- Not every small hotel stocks in-room irons, sometimes for safety reasons.
- Family-run B&Bs can't afford a porter, but rare is the place that doesn't have at least one strong person to help with your baggage. But you must ask.
- Cheaper places don't have A/C because before climate change, London didn't get that hot. That's changing fast.

complimentary but simple English breakfast. There's no lift or A/C, but also no sharing of bathrooms. Cheap and cheerful, the way London used to do it—the owners have been at it since 1970.

47–49 Belgrave Rd., SW1. www.lunasimonehotel.com. ✆ **020/7834-5897.** From £149 single, £189 double. 10% discounts via its website. Rates include breakfast. Tube: Victoria or Pimlico. **Amenities:** Free Wi Fi.

MARYLEBONE, MAYFAIR & PADDINGTON

For visitors who want a balance of central location and private residential vibe, Marylebone's the place. A 10-minute walk takes you to the "smart" end of Oxford Street and Mayfair to the south, or the wide-open fields of Regent's Park to the north. The area around Paddington Station, to the west of that, has become shopworn, and aside from a few exceptions, doesn't have much to recommend it considering other neighborhoods are so much livelier and more appealing.

Expensive

The Beaumont ♥♥♥ Despite polished traditional appearances, this Art Deco beauty opened in modern times, which accounts for why its style keeps up with its luxurious substance. Its 1926 facade was once the garage of Selfridges department store nearby, but the interior is modern-built and diligently renovated to an unfailingly high standard. Its style may be luxurious but the vibe remains friendly, not stuffy, as a logical neighbor for Selfridge's, which was itself built in the model of vintage American high taste. Rooms were customized to be cutting-edge (free streaming movies, free minibar, heated bathroom floors), but the Beaumont is noted for Antony Gormley's geometric sculpture of a brooding man perched on one of its outcroppings—inside is an arty wooden suite you can stay in for a small fortune. You're more likely to go for a "Classic" room facing the courtyard or a "Superior" facing the quiet street and a pocket park.

The spa at The Beaumont offers a sauna, steam room, and plunge pool.

8 Balderton St., W1. www.thebeaumont.com. ✆ **020/7499-1001.** 73 units. King-bed rooms from £510. Tube: Bond Street. **Amenities:** Restaurant; bar; fitness center with hammam and spa; free local calls; free movies; limited use of chauffeured limo; free Wi-Fi.

Claridge's ♥♥♥ You won't find many people who don't like Claridge's, whether you know them from life or from the history books. The quintessential luxury Mayfair hotel proudly proclaims taste in discretion as administered through glittering Deco accents. The redbrick building dates to 1894 (when Gilbert & Sullivan's producer rebuilt it), but modern amenities are installed among the gilded plasterwork and (nonworking) fireplaces—neither antique floorboards nor exacting staff dare grumble. From the bathrooms (heated floors, high-tech toilet/bidets) to cavernous wardrobes and plump beds as wide as some studio apartments, there's not much to complain about. Its main lift is the last in central London to be operated by hand—there's a sofa inside should you tire during your five-level journey to the top floor—and its clubby cocktail bars (£30 martinis) and restaurant are favored by modern-day fashion icons (your Von Furstenbergs, your Jaggers, your Eltons) who detest the starched snobbery that can make the Ritz such a Thatcherized drag. Pedigreed unconventionality has always been a theme: In 1945, Winston Churchill declared suite 212 temporarily Yugoslavian territory so baby Prince Alexander II could claim to be born on home soil. Don't miss the lobby Christmas tree, designed each year by a luminary fashion house (in 2023, it was Louis Vuitton, and in 2025, Burberry).

Brook St., W1. www.claridges.co.uk. ✆ **020/7629-8860.** 203 units. Rooms from £790. Tube: Bond Street. **Amenities:** 3 restaurants; 2 bars; spa; fitness center; business center; A/C; free Wi-Fi.

Hyatt Regency London—The Churchill ♥♥ A strong choice for those with Hyatt points to redeem, it's a 2-minute walk from the back door of Selfridges department store, and many rooms have smart looks with completely fresh bathrooms (robot toilets!) and well-selected art. Hyatt gives the circa-1970 building plenty of attention with millions of pounds in investment. Now it offers everything a five-star should, like room service until 2am, and even if the location is a little off the main, it's still near the Tube, unquestionably comfortable, and run with snap for such a large place.

30 Portman Square, W1. http://londonchurchill.regency.hyatt.com. ✆ **020/7486-5800.** 440 units. Rooms from £344. Tube: Marble Arch. **Amenities:** 2 restaurants; bar; fitness center; tennis and jogging track in adjoining square; free Wi-Fi.

The Landmark London ♥♥ An excellent traditional experience in a glorious redbrick building topped by a clock tower, opened for guests in 1899 as a railway terminus hotel. Many tourists favor it for its top-level afternoon tea, taken in its elegant and palm tree-studded Winter Garden atrium, but the Landmark is under-appreciated for its larger-than-average rooms (average size of 55 sq. m/ 592 sq. ft for a standard room) with expensive fittings, assiduously maintained condition, and attentive service. Out your door, you'll find the tony residential district of Marylebone, full of bespoke boutiques and buzzy small restaurants, so you'll need short Tube rides for the major sights. The Landmark is that rarity in upscale travel: a hidden bargain that gives discriminating guests everything they expect from a luxury hotel, but at rates that are a fraction of its competitors.

222 Marylebone Road, NW1. www.landmarklondon.co.uk. ✆ **020/7631-8000.** 300 units. Rooms from £396. Tube: Marylebone. **Amenities:** 2 restaurants; 2 bars; fitness center; spa with indoor pool; A/C; free Wi-Fi.

The Lanesborough ♥♥ The 2023 debut of the custom-built Peninsula London next door has perhaps put the esteemed Lanesborough on its back foot, but there are longstanding reasons why discreet guests continue to choose this luxury landmark and not the new-money chain next door. Once, I sneezed in the Lanesborough's lobby. Moments later and without bidding, my butler—everyone has one here—delivered a silver tray of hot tea, fresh-cut ginger on a porcelain plate, and acacia honey. Here, guest needs are meticulously recorded, the cigar-and-Cognac salon entertains tycoons, the color palette favors Empire eggshell blues and lime greens, and anticipated and fresh-cut blooms are delivered to your bathroom counter the moment your back is turned. Every fixture was installed with made-to-measure finery—like a mansion of Wedgwood china, Corinthian leather, and canopy king beds. Previously a hospital building dating to 1844, it only became a hotel in the early 1990s, so this is technically a five-star pastiche for the one-percenters, but it's a pitch-perfect one, and it's also a honeymoon nirvana. Should the tariff at one of London's most expensive hotels understandably be out of your reach, at least stop by for the exquisite afternoon tea (p. 102) under the skylight of its magnificent Regency-style restaurant.

Hyde Park Corner, SW1. www.lanesborough.com. ✆ **020/7259-5599.** 93 units. Rooms from £860 including VAT. Tube: Hyde Park Corner. **Amenities:** Restaurant; bar; cigar lounge; fitness center; spa; fresh fruit and water daily; free landline calls to U.S., Canada, and Europe; A/C; free Wi-Fi.

The Langham ♥♥ The Langham has two claims to fame: It was the first grande dame hotel, in 1865, and it popularized afternoon tea. A lot has changed since then—the Luftwaffe hit it during the war and for a while it was even occupied by the BBC. It was fully rebuilt in the early 1990s, so although you'll see a scant few Victorian touches, rooms are sized to modern standards while the huge three-building complex (the Regent Tower is the most secluded and has great views down Regent Street) maintains that unmistakable grande dame feel. Americans have always felt at home here, partly because it's not off-puttingly fussy while being comfortable. The Wigmore, its on-site pub, serves meals with piquant flavors, and its cocktail bar, Artesian, puts a playful twist on serious mixology. If you can, spring for a Club Level access, where you can get all three meals and free cocktails. It's a few short blocks from Oxford Street's best shopping.

1c Portland Place, Regent St., W1. www.langhamhotels.com/london. ✆ **020/7636-1000.** 380 units. Rooms from £456. Tube: Oxford Circus. **Amenities:** 3 restaurants; 2 bars; indoor pool; spa; fitness center; business center; free Wi-Fi.

Montcalm Mayfair ♥♥♥ Approachably elegant with tactful service to match, this luxury newcomer in a crescent-shaped building (gut renovated for 2 years and reopened in 2025) is seductive. Although it's steps from the fray

The Parlour Suite at Montcalm Mayfair, a recently renovated luxury property that's worth the splurge.

of Oxford Street, the bespoke furniture done in creams, beiges, and fern greens put a guest in mind of a stylized garden sojourn. Rooms, which are well-lit and quiet, comprise their own inviting worlds that have clearly been designed by experienced hoteliers who know what makes a home away from home: Frette linens, bedside lamps that mimic brass flowers on the vine, big beds, plenty of space, robes and slippers, sparkling and distilled water, a scale, rain shower with Penhaligon's soaps, and a little sitting area with a table. The rest of the property is artfully designed and dignified, too. The lobby bar serves nobly conceived craft cocktails, the full restaurant by chef Akira Back is tended by career service staff that's amiable without sacrificing professionalism; and downstairs there's a spa with a plunge pool and steam room that guests may access as part of the tariff. And everything smells good—the gentle fragrance of rose and tobacco, apparently. The little touches make this well-run hotel swoon-worthy and give it more personality than many of its luxury competitors.

2 Wallenberg Place, W1. www.marriott.com. ✆ **020/9583-3200.** 150 units. Rooms from £298, although rates in £400s are more common. Tube: Marble Arch. **Amenities:** Restaurant; bar; spa; A/C; free Wi-Fi.

Moderate

The Mayfair Townhouse ♥♥ Despite the name, this 2021 newcomer is actually a string of 15 interconnected townhouses dating to the 1700s, and they line a one-block Mayfair street (a setting for Wilde's *The Importance of Being Earnest*) near the Green Park. Everything inside has been laboriously converted to comfortable luxury purposes and is overseen by a noticeably professional staff, including a doorman. Rooms may be of various sizes (there are a few especially for singles), but they're a high standard, with big bathrooms, walk-in showers, bathrobes and slippers and a special grey washcloth just for make-up, minibars stocked with free soft drinks, dark wood paneling, and modernized lighting and controls. The Dandy Bar, off the lobby, provides a sedate escape for evening cocktails, and there are even lifts, although you may have to negotiate the odd stair or two in corridors where two old townhouses connect at slightly different heights (typical at even the nicest hotels here). The Townhouse is favored by Americans searching for a taste of Mayfair without Mayfair extortion. While the Townhouse is walkable to many sites, including the charming boutiques and restaurants of Shepherd Market a block west, the clamor of the city is kept at bay by its quiet lane and excellent soundproofing.

27–41 Half Moon St., W1. www.themayfairtownhouse.com. ✆ **020/8138-3400.** 172 units. Standard rooms from £246, 15% discount for advance purchase online. Breakfast available. Tube: Green Park. **Amenities:** Bar; fitness center; free soft drinks in minibar; A/C; free Wi-Fi.

The Zetter Marylebone ♥♥♥ In nearly every way, it plays the part of the curious abode of an eccentric "wicked uncle" who collects oddities and likes to drink—each room has its own eclectic character of rich and heavy antique mismatched furniture, hand-hung wallpaper, vintage glass photographic slides embedded in bathroom walls, and expensive punchbowl-set glassware. Yet the essence of this Georgian townhouse near Hyde Park and Oxford Street is vigorous, down to strong showers. Downstairs, the dusky, parlor-style lounge bar (the Parlour) keeps pouring coffees and well-made cocktails deep into the night. This feels like a hotel in Oscar Wilde drag, and it's winkingly Londonish to a deliciously quirky extreme. There's another location in Clerkenwell, and it runs Marrable's Hotel, also in Clerkenwell, which was once the Zetter flagship but now charges as little as £138. ***Tip:*** The Studio Suite has a four-poster that could rival the Great Bed of Ware in the V&A, but the basement room has the least charm.

29–30 Seymour St., W1. www.thezetter.com. ✆ **020/7324-4544.** 24 units. Rooms from £296. Tube: Marble Arch. **Amenities:** Bar/restaurant; free Wi-Fi.

Inexpensive

Inhabit Southwick ♥♥ Inhabit offers a stay centered on sustainability and well-being without levying ludicrous prices to do it. Guests partake (optionally) of benefits such as in-room aromatherapy, an infrared sauna, egg-like meditation pods, regular guide yoga sessions, and a staff who has been trained to lead guests in mindfulness exercises. The concept is taken seriously, and it's as ambitious as it is generous: Places like 1 Hotel Mayfair skin guests for £600 a night for its bespoke wellness theme, but here, nightly rates are often merely in the mid-£100s. Inhabit is a townhouse hotel, which means it

A tranquil room at Inhabit Southwick a wellness-focused—and affordable—hotel.

AND BEAR IN mind

London attracts the world's most spendy visitors, so it has one of the world's biggest supplies of luxury hotels. The choices below are comfortable and time-tested, and if they didn't have so much high-end competition, they'd be more prominently featured.

Brown's Hotel The rambling Brown's, in Mayfair, holds history in every creak: The first-ever phone call was placed from its ground floor. While staying here, Agatha Christie devised murders, Rudyard Kipling finished *The Jungle Book*, and Stephen King started *Misery*. It's an ideal choice for someone who wants a fine London hotel without enduring classist snobbery. 30 Albemarle St., W1. www.roccofortehotels.com. ✆ **020/7493-6020.** Rooms from £790 double. Tube: Green Park.

Corinthia Hotel London This 1885 building near the river was first the Hôtel Métropole and then the Ministry of Defence, but today it's one of the most comfortable hotels in the city, right by the river and Trafalgar Square. You'll find a top jazz bar, one of the city's best spas, commodious quarters, and frequent stars. Whitehall Place, SW1. www.corinthia.com/london. ✆ **020/7930-8181.** Rooms from £720. Tube: Charing Cross.

Raffles London at the OWO London's most celebrated ultra-luxury hotel debut of recent times was this. It took 6 years and £1.5 billion to convert the Old War Office to the pinnacle of pampering, with 9 restaurants, a 20-meter pool, spa, and a bar that attracts the people who run the world. D-Day was planned in what's now the Churchill Suite (got £6,000 a night?). 52 Whitehall, SW1. theowo.london/. ✆ **020/3907-7500.** Rooms from £831. Tube: Embankment.

The Savoy There may be no more thrilling hotel entrance than the polished gleam of its porte cochere centered around a Lalique fountain. History happened here: Churchill puffing, Chaplin mugging, Wilde and Bosie dallying, Gilbert and Sullivan pattering in its theatre, Monet and Whistler painting the Thames from its windows. The Savoy now often feels like a corporate-run imitation of itself, but it's eternally a legend The Strand, WC2. www.fairmont.com/savoy-london. ✆ **888/265-0533** (U.S.), or 020/7836-4343 (London). 268 units. Rooms from £700. Tube: Embankment or Temple.

Shangri-La Hotel at the Shard Staying here, on the 36th to 52nd floors of a glass-sheathed skyscraper, means that your room will be encased with floor-to-ceiling windows overlooking the city. You're a bird singing in a flawless, gleaming cage. When you take a bath (in your marble-coated washroom with heated floors), you may feel as if you're flying over the Tower of London, and when you swim in the horizon pool in the sky above St Paul's, the vista is so surreal that you may wonder if it's all a dream. 31 St Thomas St., SE1. www.shangri-la.com/london/shangrila/. ✆ **020/7234-8000.** 202 units. King rooms from £510. Tube: London Bridge.

occupies conjoined 19th-century homes, so rooms are of different sizes and shapes. But they are comfortable and up-to-date, with large beds and easygoing taupe-and-grey décor (although if you're very tall, we suggest upgrading to a double because the singles are short). The townhouse setup is quintessentially London, and even though this audience is more likely to exercise by climbing stairs, there's a lift. Inhabit Southwick's sister property at Queen's

FINDING HOTELS online

If you contact the hotel directly, you'll usually not only get the lowest price, but you'll also have the power of negotiation.

Another danger of making a reservation through a third-party site: There are heaps of lousy budget options in London, particularly around Paddington and Earl's Court, that post misleading images, and it's easy to wind up in a seedy one. This is why you trust a book like Frommer's—we have been to every single place we recommend.

Most of the popular online travel agents have acquired each other to the point where the inventory doesn't change much between them. **Expedia** ate **Travelocity, Hotwire,** and **Orbitz. Priceline** ate **Agoda.com**, but for complex reasons, you could still find a bigger bargain on one, so check them all anyway, as well as **Hotels.com** and **Booking.com**. Remember that a deal on an expensive hotel may not be a steal; as luxury hotels add star levels, they also add extra charges beyond the rate.

HotelsCombined.com, Kayak.com, and **Google Hotels** are "aggregator" sites that scan dozens of sites for deals and pull results together. If you hit them, don't feel pressured to hit Expedia and the like, because they include them in the search.

Because apps that don't have a browser-based interface are privy to deeper negotiated discounts, you might sometimes see lower price quotes on services like **Hopper** or **Hotel Tonight**.

Gardens, a 15-minute walk west, also has a spa and delicious restaurant for vegan/vegetarian/sustainable cuisine; guests here can consider those an extended part of the property. The dignity afforded to budget travelers at Inhabit helps redeem the Paddington area; most of its other places to stay don't even try to be this thoughtful or curated.

25–27 Southwick St., W2. southwick.inhabithotels.com. ✆ **020/7479-2333.** 86 units. Rooms from £139. Tube: Paddington or Edgware Road. **Amenities:** Wellness amenities; library; breakfast restaurant; A/C; free Wi-Fi.

The Welbeck Hotel ♥♥ Recently renovated (2025) with a modern-moderate eclectic design that doesn't feel cheap, the Welbeck surprises by giving you a lot more than similar London hotels at the same price level. Think redone bathrooms with walk-in rain showers, robes and slippers, iron and hair dryer, coffee machine and tea kettle, cool hooded bedside lamps, and simple room-service options, not to mention plenty of outlets for U.S. plugs, European plugs, and USB-C (not always so common, even at the luxury level). Some north-facing rooms on high floors have terrific views over the rooftops, and the Elizabeth Line from Heathrow is a 3-minute walk from the front door, if that fits your plan. The lift is slightly overburdened by the number of guests, but that's not a dealbreaker—the staff is casual and chill, which rubs off and makes everything feel casual and homey. You get a lot for your money here, and I can see it becoming a firm favorite for many travelers.

57–59 Welbeck St., W1. thewelbeckhotel.com. ✆ **020/7935-4442.** 164 units. Doubles form £245; singles from £155. Tube: Bond Street. **Amenities:** Bar; in-room spa treatments; fitness center; free Wi-Fi.

The delightful Front Hall at Brown's Hotel.

THE SOUTH BANK & SOUTHWARK

From medieval times until the 1990s, "respectable" Londoners wanted nothing to do with this once-industrial area. They all wish they'd bought property now. It's a terrific place to dwell in good weather, when it comes alive with walkers, booksellers, pub-goers, and playgoers. Furthermore, moderate hotels are proliferating: Brands such as Hilton, Holiday Inn, and Mercure are all along Southwark's streets now.

Expensive

Bankside ♥♥♥ Bankside, part of the points-friendly Marriott Autograph Collection brand, is fresh and glassy and stylistically on-trend. Everything in this riverside tower has been thoughtfully but not pretentiously designed, with plenty of woods and natural fibers. Contemporary art is a focus, but as frisky as the stuff on the walls may be, it's nothing compared to the ribald nickname Londoners have given the bulbous building you'll be sleeping in. (We won't print it.) Bankside is forwarding thinking; not only can you refill your drinking water at stations in the corridors, but you can also buy champagne from a vending machine. The hotel's restaurant, Art Yard, is adventurous, too, but for better reasons like wicked clever cocktails (negronis that lilt with honey and truffles—wow) and a laid-back, airy personality. This neighborhood, just a few steps from the Thames Path at the southern foot of Blackfriars Bridge, is ideal area if you want a central location without cramped quarters.

The chic, minimalist lobby at Bankside Hotel.

2 Blackfriars Rd., SE1. www.banksidehotel.com. ✆ **020/3943-2201.** 161 units. Rooms from £246. Tube: Blackfriars or Southwark. **Amenities:** Restaurant; bar; spa; 24-hr. fitness center; A/C; free Wi-Fi.

Moderate

Park Plaza London Westminster Bridge ♥ This glassy mega-hotel looks like a carburetor abandoned on a median, but you won't believe the view from the "Big Ben View" rooms: straight down Westminster Bridge at the Houses of Parliament and Big Ben's tower, like a floor-to-ceiling wish come true. Otherwise it's a well-greased, impersonal formula (part of the Radisson network) that feels more like a convention center, and be warned that the cheapest "Atrium" no-view rooms (scrutinize the room description) are starved of natural light. Still, it has a lot of rooms to fill, which means discounts in low season. Studio rooms have microwaves, fridges, and pullout beds, and there's a dark and soothing indoor pool.

200 Westminster Bridge Rd., SE1. www.parkplaza.com/westminster. ✆ **333/400-6112,** 800/333-3333 in U.S. 1,019 units. Double rooms from £155, Big Ben or London Eye view from £240. Minimum stay in some periods. Tube: Waterloo or Westminster. **Amenities:** 2 restaurants; bar; indoor pool; fitness center; spa; free Wi-Fi.

Sea Containers London ♥ The hotel anchor of the South Bank riverwalk, Sea Containers (once a nerve center for oceangoing freight) is special because the vistas from its Thames-front units have no competition; book one and you'll feel like you're on a ship at water. That happens to be a theme here, coppery nautical motifs and all, some of which could use refreshing. There are plenty of appealing lifestyle embellishments (a basement first-run cinema, the rooftop 12th Knot bar, the Lyaness bar serving experimental no-ice cocktails that have been hailed as the best in the world), but although the hotel esteems itself in its ironic stylings, it's in fact at its best when you use it to simply welcome the skyline into your bedroom—the restaurant opens to the river, and the famous riverfront path literally runs beside it. Rooms that face the water, not the back, are the only ones you should consider. It's decent for families, too, because so many room types interconnect.

20 Upper Ground, SE1. www.seacontainerslondon.com. ✆ **020/3747-1000.** 359 units. Rooms from £183. Tube: Blackfriars or Southwark. **Amenities:** Restaurant; 3 bars; spa; fitness center; A/C; free Wi-Fi.

Inexpensive

H10 London Waterloo ♥♥♥ The sole London branch of a popular and well-run Spanish brand, the H10 is a recently built tower, so rooms are nicely sized and modern, with art that actually speaks of good taste, with a bonus of healthy floor-to-ceiling windows that let London in. Its flatiron shape means everyone enjoys lots of light, plus there's a fantastic eighth-floor terrace bar with London Eye views. The blocks nearby are slightly sleepy in a residential way, but there's much choice within a 5-minute walk in most directions. It sells out frequently because it's worth the strong price.

284–302 Waterloo Rd., SE1. www.h10hotels.com. ✆ **020/7928-4062.** 177 units. Double rooms from £144. Tube: Waterloo, Lambeth North, or Southwark. **Amenities:** Restaurant; 3 bars; spa; free Wi-Fi.

THE CITY & EAST LONDON

Not long ago, the City went to sleep at 7pm. Now, with Shoreditch and Spitalfields rapidly being developed, there are more reasons for creative types to linger by night. Some of London's prime party zones are, ideally, near hotels where rates bottom out on weekends. The Liverpool Street station area lacks character, but north of it, things get more lively. Just be wary of going *too* far east in East London: There are corporate choices in the Canary Wharf district and temptingly cheap rooms by the ExCeL convention center in the Docklands region, but they're intended for conference-goers; from there it will take you a tedious 45 minutes to reach Piccadilly Circus by the Tube and DLR. If sightseeing is your aim, make Shoreditch or Whitechapel your eastern cutoff.

Expensive

The Rookery Hotel ♥♥♥ In the 1990s, three derelict houses and shops were converted into a hotel that tells the story of England past: Georgian and 17th-century oak and four-poster beds, antique desks, era wood paneling and top-line attention and discretion. The owners fashioned this tucked-away realm of open fireplaces and polite staff that give a sense of what it must have been like to live with money in the 19th century. It's elegant, but not like a stuffy dowager aunt's parlor—more like an eccentric professor's study. Each huge room is a unique, characterful surprise of Persian rugs, gilt-framed mirrors, and oil paintings, but not neglectful of modern necessities. There's no restaurant, but you can get food brought to your room, as your breakfast will be. The Clerkenwell location used to be off the path for visitors, but the 2022 arrival of the Elizabeth Line changed that, and now it's a terrific home base from which you can zoom across town in mere minutes.

Peter's Lane, Cowcross Street, London EC1. ✆ **020/7336-0931.** www.rookeryhotel.com. 33 units. Rooms from £212. Tube: Farringdon. **Amenities:** Free Wi-Fi.

South Place Hotel ♥♥♥ Plugged-in, stylish, and sexy: That's the City crowd this hotel goes for, and you'll feel that way, too. Rooms are much larger than the London usual, every inch was run through the design filter (those push-button blackout blinds!), and much of the art was commissioned by celebrated contemporary artists. Rooms, charcoal-grey with wool carpets, are large (especially the showers) and hushed, and you'll find plenty of outlets, AV connections, and a huge bed you can flop around in. The two acclaimed restaurants and several bars, and the hotel's terraces with retractable roofs, lure lively professionals who work in the area. On Sundays, there's no food to be found for blocks, but the scenes of Old Street and Shoreditch are 10-minute walks away.

3 South Place, EC2. www.southplacehotel.com. ✆ **020/3503-0000.** 80 units. Rooms from £224. Tube: Moorgate or Liverpool Street. **Amenities:** 2 restaurants; 3 bars; guests' lounge; gym; spa; business center; free in-room movies; free Wi-Fi.

Moderate

Apex City of London ♥♥♥ An excellent contemporary boutique brand from Scotland that appeals to high standards for space and style, Apex is a friendly and peaceful urban retreat that actually looks like its website's pictures. You'll find it literally steps from the Tower of London, and a few rooms glimpse the Tower Bridge—if you score a room with a balcony, it's worth the slight price upgrade. It's handsomely designed in hardwood and walnut, with bathrooms larger than many B&B guest rooms, including walk-in power showers. The only downside is this part of the City is deader than Old Marley in the off hours, which is why it can be a steal on weekends.

The **Apex Temple Court,** near St Paul's Cathedral, is also tops (and closer to the West End).

1 Seething Lane, EC3. www.apexhotels.co.uk. ✆ **020/7702-2020.** 179 units. Rooms from £182, best prices Sat–Sun. Tube: Tower Hill. **Amenities:** Restaurant; bar; fitness center; free local calls; A/C; free Wi-Fi.

Canopy by Hilton London City ♥♥ A very good 2021 addition to the hotel landscape on the edge of East London, Canopy is much less corporate than a standard Hilton. This airy property was custom-built, not slotted into an ancient edifice, so it's able to give us rooms that are as spacious as we demand, including plenty of accessible facilities. It goes not for Business Travel Anonymous but for something closer to Tech Worker Loft Chic, with exposed concrete rafters, London-inflected art, furniture that evokes midcentury modern, an indoor/outdoor rooftop cafe with killer views, and sustainable sensibilities such as water refill stations instead of wasteful plastic water bottles. Walk 10 minutes north, and you're in the nightlife of Spitalfields; 10 minutes south, and you're at the flank of the Tower of London. It's a strong big-brand hotel that's more about style than conformity—but you can still use Hilton points to pay for it.

11–15 Minories St., EC3. www.hilton.com. ✆ **020/3988-7480** or 888/225-9644 in the U.S. 340 units. Double rooms from £150. Tube: Aldgate East, Aldgate, or Tower Hill. **Amenities:** 2 restaurants; cocktail bar; loaner bikes; fitness center; A/C; free Wi-Fi.

The Hoxton, Shoreditch ♥♥ The 2006 advent of "the Hox," which specializes in compact rooms that pack in style and cleverness, changed the way London thought of budget lodging, and now, international brands ranging like Marriott's Moxy steal its shtick. You sleep on a platform bed under exposed brick walls and you get pegs instead of a closet. You bathe under a rain shower that might be in a futuristic cylinder. Your continental breakfast is

A modern guest room at the Canopy by Hilton London City.

delivered each morning via a bag you hang on the door, which can make you feel like a monkey in a hipster zoo, and there's free water and milk for your little fridge and an hour of free telephone calls a day, even if you call internationally. The lobby is intended to be the chief social space: A grill, a bar, and coffee and free Wi-Fi flowing at all hours make it as much a gathering place for digital nomads as it is a way station for tourists. Just as good, but near the British Museum, is **The Hoxton, Holborn** (199–206 High Holborn, WC1; ✆ **020/7661-3000;** Tube: Holborn). New in 2019: **The Hoxton, Southwark,** in a purpose-built, loft-like tower a quick walk to the riverfront (40 Blackfriars Rd., SE1; ✆ **020/7903-3000;** Tube: Southwark). Book as far ahead as possible to keep the price down; £275 is too much for this indifferent treatment.

1 Austin St., E2. thehoxton.com/london/shoreditch/. ✆ **020/7550-1000.** 208 units. Rooms from £158. Tube: Aldgate or Tower Hill. **Amenities:** Restaurant; 1 hr. free calls; A/C; free Wi-Fi.

Lost Property ♥♥ This 2022 newcomer was an instant hit not only for its easygoing, comfortable style and sensible prices, but also for its location—practically on the steps of St Paul's Cathedral. It would be easy to get up at dawn to re-create "Feed the Birds" from *Mary Poppins* if only there were still pigeons around and you wouldn't get fined for feeding them (it's a £500 ticket in Trafalgar Square). Only rooms with numbers ending in -06 will catch a glimpse of the cathedral, and none are likely to hear the hourly gong of the 16-ton Great Paul bell because the hotel's soundproofing is just that good. Stay here and you can also dash across the Thames to South Bank via the nearby Blackfriars Bridge, but it might be hard tearing yourself away from the rooms, which are smallish (this was once an old office building) but not unkindly so, and well-appointed with Nespresso coffeemakers, Penhaligon's toiletries, a king or queen bed (only 5 rooms have twins), and if you're in a Deluxe room, robes. The restaurant, Found serves British French cuisine and

A guest room at Lost Property Hotel, located near St Paul's Cathedral and Tube station.

a good breakfast (look for the antique alley freight cranes through the windows), while its café/coffee bar fronts Ludgate Hill. It's simply a likeable place to stay (part of the Curio Collection by Hilton brand) that's near plenty of good things but unlike the West End, still gets quiet at night.

3–5 Ludgate Hill, EC4. lostpropertyhotel.com/. ✆ **020/4553-0555.** 145 units. Double rooms from £174. Tube: Blackfriars or St Paul's. **Amenities:** Restaurant with bar; coffee bar; fitness center; A/C; free Wi-Fi.

Inexpensive

The Corner London City ♥ This tiny Dutch-made budget design hotel, originally operated as Qbic, is a wacky antidote to other formula hotels. Everything you need—bed, outlets, bathroom with a rain shower, TV—is part of a prefabricated bed/bathroom structure that dominates the center of the room. The cheapest rooms, called "Snug," don't have a window—but you're not in prison, we promise. "Comfy" adds a desk, "Plush" adds a sofa. It's not a capsule hotel, just one that came up with a funky multipurpose bed unit: Your lamp is made out of petrified garden hose, your clothing rack a strange ladder/planter of some sort; it's freaky fun, and for every day you decline housekeeping, you get a free drink at the bar to make your stay freakier. There are free coffee and tea machines on every floor and a preposterously arty lobby where organic continental breakfast is served. You'll be within walking distance to Spitalfields/Shoreditch (15 min.) and the Tower of London (15 min.).

42 Adler St., E1. www.thecornerlondoncity.co.uk. ✆ **020/3021-1440.** 171 units. Rooms from £127, discounts on its website. Tube: Aldgate East. **Amenities:** Lounge; free coffee; free Wi-Fi.

Hyatt Place London City East ♥ Personality-free with catalog furnishings, but it's reliable and super cheap if you catch an early deal. Rooms have all the typical mod cons of a corporate-brand room, but top-floor ones also have balconies for admiring the City of London skyline from the east. You also won't sacrifice convenience; you can zip across town in mere minutes on the Elizabeth Line from the nearby Whitechapel station. So why is this place so inexpensive? Because it's at the leading edge of gentrification. Whitechapel, although safe, is scruffy, and some people don't favor the area because it has always been a home for London's recent immigrants. Today, that means a Bangladeshi community setting up a daily market on the road outside (the rooms are quiet), and the counterculture delights of Brick Lane start nearby. To me, those are bonuses.

45 Whitechapel Rd., E1. www.hyatt.com. ✆ **020/8159-1234.** 276 units. Rooms from £100, discounts for joining its free loyalty club. Rates include continental breakfast. Tube: Aldgate East or Whitechapel. **Amenities:** Bar/restaurant; terrace bar; grab-and-go kiosk; A/C; fitness center; free Wi-Fi.

Leonardo Royal Hotel London Tower Bridge ♥ There are people who want their British hotels to look and feel more like corporate American ones, and for them, this sprawling modern-built (2011) travelers' hive supplies just that while being kind on the pocketbook. The lobby at this busy hotel can be chaotic, but upstairs, rooms are as calm, spacious to an American standard, and as inoffensively designed as at any major business hotel, and the Tower of London and the draws of Spitalfields and Whitechapel are all a few minutes' walk away. What it lacks in distinctly London charm it makes up for in breadth of amenities, space, and a made-to-order group breakfast.

45 Prescot St., E1. www.leonardo-hotels.com/london/leonardo-royal-hotel-london-tower-bridge. ✆ **020/7959-5000.** 370 units. Rooms from £184, 10% discount online if you join its free loyalty club. Tube: Tower Hill or Aldgate East. **Amenities:** Restaurant; bar; spa; indoor pool; fitness center; A/C; free Wi-Fi.

Shoreditch Inn ♥ Look, we're not saying it's the pinnacle of hospitality—it's an affordable, clean crash pad in an economic environment that's increasingly hostile to those. Encumbered by none of the lifestyle obsessions that paralyze its navel-gazing neighbors, it's no-frills, tidy, and fit with little touches that distinguish it as a standout of its extremely low price class: double-glazed windows (to muffle Shoreditch revelry), quality toiletries, and roomy quarters. That it's in the middle of the action, especially on weekends, and that its front rooms overlook a church from 1740 have me wondering when the dream will end and the owners will put the price out of reach. They could ask for more money. Don't tell them. We need this place.

1 Austin St., E2. www.shoreditchinn.com. ✆ **020/3327-3910.** 14 units. Rooms from £95. Rates include continental breakfast. Tube: Shoreditch High Street or Hoxton. **Amenities:** A/C; free Wi-Fi.

RENT A PLACE

Long before Airbnb, England had a tradition of hosted accommodation. Partly because of the post-Blitz housing crunch, Londoners considered it normal to make a few pounds by welcoming strangers into their homes. This fast-fading tradition may work for you if you've got a car, because staying in Zone 3 or 4 may enable you to park it cheaply. What's included? At the minimum, a bed and breakfast. Everything else depends, because homestays are as unique as the hosts themselves. Some English people would still rather offer their place with a broker they trust than list it on a crowdsourced site. The sharing economy revolutionized what tourists demand, though, so most of the old B&B agencies have folded. There is still **The London Bed and Breakfast Agency** (www.londonbb.com; ✆ **01474/708-701**), though. It specializes in finding trustworthy hosts for single female travelers: between £55 and £180 in Zones 1 to 3. There's also **Homestay.com,** on which anyone in any place can post a listing for their spare rooms, but it's user-generated and hosts aren't vetted closely beforehand. It posts hundreds of options in London. To find safe and friendly options for LGBTQ+ travelers and renters, the **Mister B&B app** (www.misterbandb.com; download via Google Play or Apple App Store) has arranged rentals since 2013.

But if you want to rent your own flat in privacy, prices skyrocket. Because of London's deepening housing crisis, the city is cracking down on Airbnb and their ilk (like **Vrbo.com**), and the listings that are available are owned by

Londoners who know very well what their homes are worth on the rental market, so you'll find prices are comparable to—or often exceed—hotels. Most London home rentals no longer represent savings over hotels unless you're traveling with a group. You also have to watch out for fake listings and scams, a problem the big apps have had a hard time getting under control.

Because London apartments are in such high demand, there is little incentive for owners to upgrade facilities, so on the low end of the market, expect clean but scruffy places with well-used, cheap vacation-home furniture. For higher-quality results, we recommend booking through a London rental specialist—one who has vetted the unit and has a relationship with its owner. Large, well-appointed units go from around £125 to £490 a night—for places that sleep up to eight people. Discounts often kick in after 6 to 8 nights.

The recommended **New York Habitat** (www.nyhabitat.com; ✆ **212/255-8018** in U.S.) represents hundreds of flats and has a licensed, U.S.–based office. Units for two can start around £100 a night, but they come larger, too.

London Perfect (www.londonperfect.com; ✆ **888/520-2087** in the U.S.) has class and its flats, many of which feel like living spreads from lifestyle magazines, are extremely well maintained; owners who allow fittings to become dated are cut from the roster. Prices start around £240 a night for studios and one-bedrooms sleeping up to four people, largely in tony neighborhoods like South Kensington and Chelsea. There's usually a 7-night minimum.

A high-end renter, **One Fine Stay** (www.onefinestay.com; ✆ **800/808-5830** in the U.K., 855/553-4954 in the U.S.) shoots its flats as if it's photographing a fashion spread, which tells you something about its target market. Central London digs start around £350 a night, with impeccable design and service to match.

Now on to a few "aparthotel" companies that own their own units. One of the nicest (opened 2024) is the 114-unit **July London Victoria** (282 Vauxhall Bridge, Rd., SW1; www.thejuly.com; ✆ **020/4618-8200**), a well-executed Dutch concept located just east of Victoria Station. The July has been beautifully designed as if it's a contemporary upscale hotel but it's actually for short residential stays with all the trimmings—24-hour front desk and fitness center, sauna with cold plunge, a deli and an all-day diner serving British-Mediterranean food—and style-magazine-ready rooms that are fully outfitted for cooking your own meals. It's only missing a laundry room. Studios are about the size of a hotel room and start at £249. Another high-quality brand put together by professional interior designers: **Wilde Aparthotels** (www.wilde.com) has 4 outposts with studios and 1-bedrooms from £153 in easy-to-reach locations near Charing Cross (Covent Garden), Liverpool Street, Aldgate East, and Paddington. Wilde has fully equipped kitchens in each room, fitness rooms, breakfast and a bar, a staffed reception, and a laundry room.

Lincoln Suites (37–39 Kingsway, WC2; thelincolnsuites.com; ✆ **020/3995-0080**; from £179; Tube: Holborn), in a handsome five-story stone building close to Covent Garden, ranges from studio to one-bedroom apartments. It's well-appointed in an updated style, and you get unusual extras like free streaming movies, underfloor heating, and little kitchens including dishwashers. Rooms on the lower ground floor don't have windows, but they're cheapest.

More: **Citadines** (www.citadines.com; ✆ **0800/376-3898,** 833/443-2785 in the U.S.) runs corporate-style, personality-free hotel rooms fitted like little long-stay business apartments, and it has locations citywide. In order of centrality: Trafalgar Square, Holborn–Covent Garden, Barbican (cheapest, from £140), Islington (newest; built in 2019), and South Kensington.

Cheval Residences (www.chevalresidences.com; ✆ **020/7341-7052**) owns high-quality, fully serviced apartments with the poise and quality of a luxury hotel. It's in several neighborhoods in the city, but the most envy-inducing is the glassy Three Quays overlooking the Thames and the Tower of London. One-bedrooms there start at £300 a night, sliding up to three bedrooms sleeping six.

And here's an idea you might not have considered: comfortable, home-like houseboat barges tied up on the Regent's Canal. If you choose one between Little Venice, near Paddington, and Camden locks, you won't be any farther from the Tube than many hotels are. Rates are similar to a quality home rental. Find availability at **Book a Houseboat** (www.bookahouseboat.com), **Boutique Barges** (boutiquebarges.co.uk), **Coolstays** (www.coolstays.com), **Host Unusual** (hostunusual.com), and **Plum Guide**. (www.plumguide.com).

HOME EXCHANGES

You'd be surprised how many Londoners are dying to visit your own stomping grounds, and if you make contact with the right people, you can swap homes (sometimes simultaneously). It sounds strange, but nothing tends to get stolen because swappers often become good friends. Not just that, but neighbors will often pop by to check up on you, so you have a built-in source of insider advice.

All-day dining is just one of the perks at The July London Victoria, an upscale aparthotel.

So which club should you choose? Here are the biggies, in alphabetical order:

HomeExchange.com (sos@homeexchange.com): This slick service claims 200,000-plus homes in 145 nations. This is important because the more members, the more potential swaps. Results can be broken down by interest. It costs $235 a year for Americans to list.

HomeLink.org: Popular with British and Australian travelers (with reps in many countries) since 1953, this service costs Americans $118 per year.

Intervac (www.intervac-homeexchange.com): Intervac has been around since 1953 and its claim to fame is that some 80% of its listings are international (facilitating some 5,000 exchanges a year), which means (as it puts it), "you compete with fewer Americans for overseas properties." Access to all listings is US/CAD $130 a year, but you can take a limited 21-day trial for free.

Additional exchange sites include **SabbaticalHomes.com,** catering to academics. Or you could roll the dice with a website like **CouchSurfing.com,** on which folks (generally younger) offer spare space to visitors. That's free, but there is no vetting system, so consider the risks before taking an offer.

CHEAP COLLEGE ROOMS

Staying in college housing over holiday periods is an ideal budget saver for visitors of any age. Reservations are accepted starting in spring. At all of them, expect a wood-frame bed with linen, a desk, a dresser, an in-room sink, the possibility of an equipped kitchen (although it might be shared), an en suite bathroom (usually), laundry facilities, breakfast (often at a reasonable charge), Wi-Fi, and phones in the room or in the hall.

London School of Economics (stayatlse.co.uk/; ✆ **020/7405-7686**): Check these out first. Its five properties are in fine condition, with the dignity that you'd expect of a school that trains the world's power players in business. Rooms rent cheaply (under £100) for July, August, and the first chunk of September. A few rooms may be available at Christmas or Easter, too.

University College London (www.ucl.ac.uk/residences; guest-bookings@ucl.ac.uk; ✆ **020/3108-4455**): Its dorms, clustering in Bloomsbury, are less prestigious than LSE's, but they aren't depressing. From late June to September, 12 residences are available, but not all rooms have private bathrooms.

King's College (www.kcl.ac.uk/kingsvenues/summer-accommodation; ✆ **020/7848-1700**): Two halls are available near London Bridge and Waterloo for short rental from late June through mid-September. Kitchens but no utensils, no A/C. They rent for £75–£85 a night.

International Students House (229 Great Portland St., W1; www.ish.org.uk; ✆ **020/7631-8300;** Tube: Great Portland Street): Part dorm, part subdued hostel, rates start at £70 per night and not just in summer. Bathrooms are shared, female-only rooms are available, and some rooms are co-ed but partitioned. Other academic choices are more private.

4

WHERE TO DINE

In 1957, Arthur Frommer visited London for his seminal *Europe on $5 a Day.* His report was gloomy: "With great despair, this book recommends that you . . . save your money for the better meals available in France and Italy. Cooking is a lost art in Great Britain; your meat pie with cabbage will turn out just as tasteless for 40¢ in a chain restaurant as it will for $2 in a posh hotel." The report today is happily quite different: Bon appétit!

As it turns out, good cooking wasn't actually a lost art in London. If anything, it's meat pie with cabbage that became the lost art. Now that London swarms with people from across the world, you'll find nearly every style of dish. Ask any Londoner for their favorite restaurant and it's bound to serve a foreign cuisine.

In recent generations, British consumption of sugar, potatoes, and flour has halved. British eaters have become seasoned food consumers and now demand fresh seasonal ingredients from their country's farms. Even most of the major museums (listed starting on p. 130) run cafes that, surprisingly, more than pull their weight with balanced dishes using homegrown goods.

There is bad news. There's a huge price gap between a cheap meal of take-away sandwiches and the lowest-priced table-service meal, and many mid-priced restaurants are managing higher food costs by decreasing portion sizes slightly. When prices do go high in London, they're virtually insane. One restaurant in Knightsbridge, Nusr-Et, has a £500 Wagyu tomahawk steak on its menu. Meanwhile, affordable establishments are getting squeezed out. The most popular restaurants, unable to keep up given a labor market made weaker by Brexit (which made it harder for continental Europeans to work here), are often so slammed that it's increasingly important that you make reservations in advance by default.

London's greenie culture still thrives, and virtually every menu will have plenty of dishes for **vegetarians** to eat. The situation for **vegans** is nearly as promising; many kitchens understand those dietary requirements and mark menus accordingly. The news is also good for people with **food allergies:** A majority of potentially irritating ingredients are marked when you buy pre-made food at the major shops, and as part of a new modern routine, nearly every server you encounter will quiz you about your allergies when you order.

Advance **bookings** have become more essential than ever, even if it's for a last-minute lunch in an hour's time. You can sometimes find some meal deals on **OpenTable.co.uk** and **SquareMeal.co.uk**, the major reservations systems, but do not rely on them for accurate serving times.

Also, **late-night dining** culture is not universal here, so don't be surprised if a kitchen closes by 9:30 or 10pm (check ahead if you intend to eat late).

Do not rely on Google or Apple Maps for recommendations. Online inventory is often incomplete, opening hours are frequently totally wrong, and the results favor corporate chains and omit sublime holes in the wall.

We'll steer you clear of hyper-luxury places. We also skip the many flashy places where tourists won't know the right people to get a table or where the party dies after the star chef moves on. But in this book, every restaurant listed has demonstrated endurance, will welcome out-of-towners, and was chosen to say something about London of the moment—you'll taste what it's like to eat like a Londoner today.

At the end of this chapter, you'll find even more ideas for great places for meals: reviews of London's best pubs and food halls.

Tipping & Prices

Price categories are based on a typical main course.

- **Expensive** £27 and up
- **Moderate** £19 to £26
- **Inexpensive** under £19

Always check the bill to see if **service** is included. If it is, you don't have to tip. If not, 10% to 15% is customary. A minority of restaurants might charge a cover of a few pounds or the bill may list an "admin charge"—this goes to management and is not a tip for servers.

Most restaurants expect you to give up your table after 90 minutes to 2 hours.

BLOOMSBURY, FITZROVIA & KING'S CROSS

These areas north of the central tourist district are more residential and consequently less of a scene than other parts of town can be, but that the hip developments around Granary Square, north of King's Cross, have created a lively contradiction to that general rule.

Moderate

Clipstone ♥♥ MODERN BRITISH If you were to dream up the ideal neighborhood restaurant where you celebrate British ingredients in a bright space conducive to hanging out and chatting, you'd probably create the picture of Clipstone, a somewhat raw space on a glassy corner in mostly residential Fitzrovia a 10-minute stroll north of Oxford Circus. Aside from snacks and well-chosen wines (by the glass or by the bottle), meals are set-price, and you pick each course from a list of 4 or 5 inventive seasonal options such as pumpkin pappardelle, celery root fritters with Comté cheese and pickled red currant, or cow's curd and njuda ravioli with lemon butter. There's usually a fish choice, a chicken choice, and a third protein such a onglet (hangar steak), pork, or lamb, but the shifting options will always pull from the bountiful provisions of Britain's farms. Offering sophisticated, thoughtful cuisine in an

West End Restaurants & Pubs

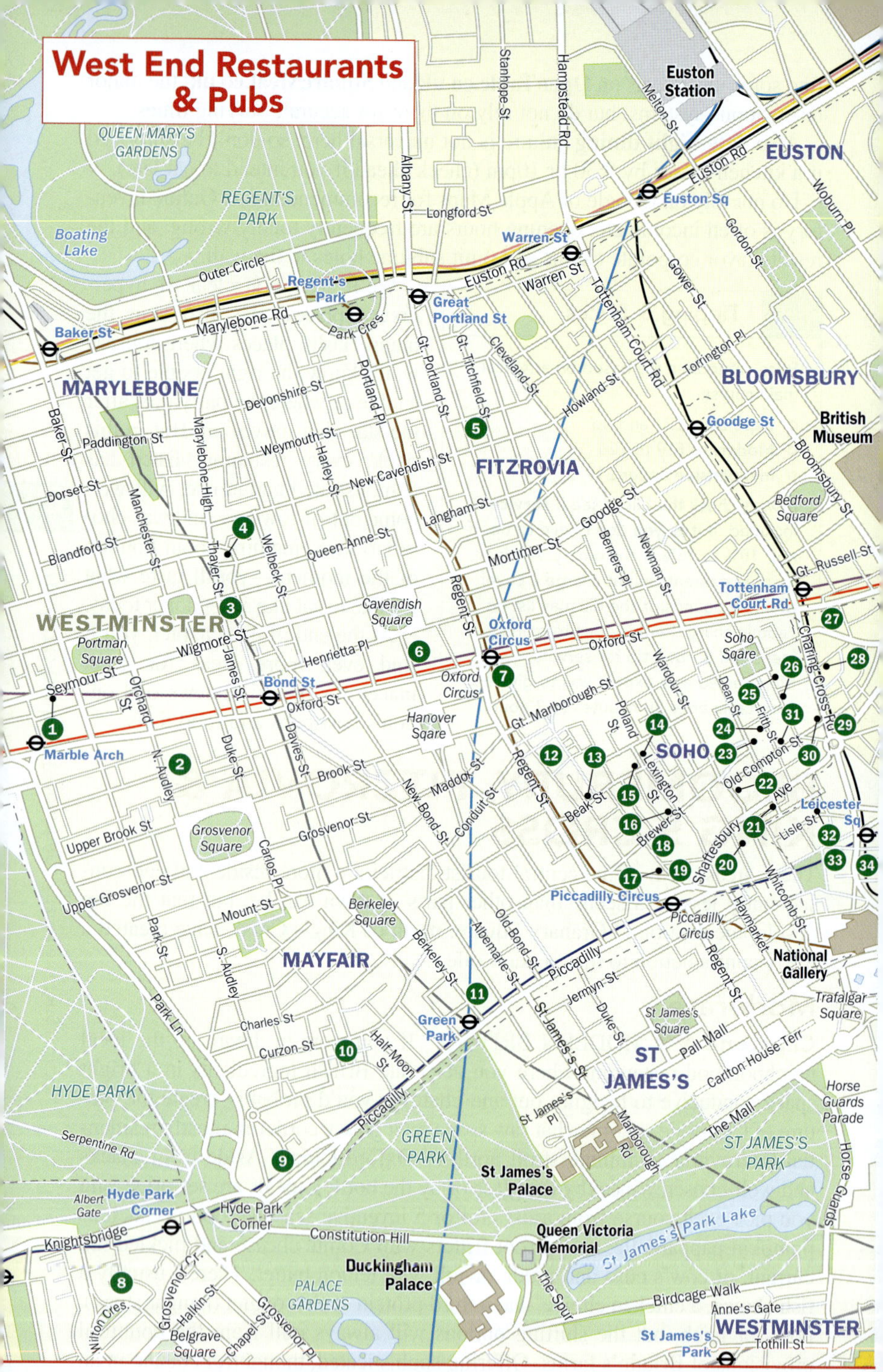

10 Greek Street **26**
Andrew Edmunds **14**
Arcade **27**
The Argyll Arms **7**
Ave Mario **44**
Bancone Covent Garden **39**
The Barbary **49**
Bar Italia **29**
Bill's **16, 47**
The Blackfriar **61**
Blacklock **40**
Blacklock Soho **18**
Brasserie Zédel **17**
Browns **42**
Bun House **32**
Café in the Crypt **35**
Clipstone **5**
The Coal Hole **38**
The Devonshire **19**
Dishoom **12, 46**
Dovetale **11**
Ducksoup **23**
The Eagle **58**
Flat Iron **13, 28, 44**
The Fryer's Delight **53**
Gordon's Wine Bar **37**
The Grenadier **8**
The Hard Rock Cafe **9**
Honey & Co. **55**
The Ivy **31**
J. Sheekey **34**
Kol Restaurant **1**
Koya Soho **24**
The Lamb **56**
The Lamb and Flag **43**
Market Hall Oxford Street **6**
Market Place Leicester Square **33**
Mercato Mayfair **2**
Mildreds **15**
Noble Rot **10, 25, 54**
Noodle Inn **30**
North Sea Fish **57**
Ottolenghi **4**
Paul Rothe & Son **3**
Poppies **22**
The Princess Louise **52**
Punjab Restaurant **50**
Rasa Sayang **21**
Rules **45**
The Salisbury **41**
Seven Dials Market **48**
Savoir Faire **51**
The Ship & Shovell **36**
Speedboat Bar **20**
Ye Olde Cheshire Cheese **60**
Ye Olde Mitre **59**

London-Wide Restaurants & Pubs

0 1 mi
0 1 km
BARNSBURY
DE BEAUVOIR TOWN
SOUTH HACKNEY
Grand Union Canal
VICTORIA PARK
ISLINGTON
HOXTON
HAGGERSTON
Cambridge Heath
Angel
See "East London Restaurants and Pubs" map
SHOREDITCH
Bethnal Green
CLERKENWELL
BETHNAL GREEN
FARRINGDON
Shoreditch
Chancery Lane
Farringdon
Barbican
Liverpool St Station
Whitechapel
CITY (LONDON)
The Barbican Centre
Moorgate
Liverpool St
STEPNEY
HOLBORN
THE CITY
Bank of England
Aldgate East
St Paul's
Aldgate
WHITECHAPEL
St Paul's Cathedral
Bank
Shadwell
Temple
Blackfriars
Fenchurch St Station
Cannon St
Shadwell
Blackfriars Station
Cannon St Station
Tower Hill
Tower Gateway
SHADWELL
Thames
Monument
HMS Belfast
Tower of London
SOUTH BANK
BANKSIDE
London Bridge
WAPPING
Wapping
Southwark
SOUTHWARK
Waterloo
Waterloo Station
Borough
BOROUGH
BERMONDSEY
Rotherhithe
Lambeth North
Bermondsey
ROTHERHITHE
Elephant & Castle
NEWINGTON
LAMBETH
ELEPHANT & CASTLE
SOUTHWARK
SOUTHWARK PARK
LAMBETH
Kennington
KENNINGTON
The Oval (Surrey County Cricket Ground)
Oval
CAMBERWELL
PECKHAM
The Anchor Bankside 16
Bill's 7, 17
Boisdale 5
Boro Bistro 21
Borough Market 20
Café Below 15
Camden Markets 2
Dishoom 3
Emilia's Crafted Pasta 1, 8
Flat Iron Square 18
The George Inn 22
Gong 23
The Grapes 28
The Jones Family Kitchen 4
Maltby Street Market 25
Market Hall Victoria 6
The Market Porter 20
The Marquis of Granby 10
The Mayflower 26
Mercato Metropolitano 14
OKAN South Bank 11
The Old Brewery 27
Oxo Tower 13
Padella 19
The Prospect of Whitby 28
Regency Café 9
Southbank Centre Food Market 12
Vinegar Yard 24

Convivial, casual Clipstone restaurant in Firzrovia.

unpretentious environment at affordable prices fills Clipstone with locals, so book ahead.

5 Clipstone St, W1. clipstonerestaurant.co.uk. ✆ **020/7637-0871.** 2-course lunch £34, 3-course lunch £39, dinner main courses £25–£33. Tues–Sat noon–2:45pm and 5:30–9:45pm, Sun noon-3pm and 5:30–8:45pm. Reservations recommended. Tube: Great Portland Street or Oxford Circus

Dishoom King's Cross ♥ INDIAN Dishoom, a boisterous collision of Irani and Indian foods, has been nothing less than a smash in Britain since its 2010 debut. Now it has seven locations in London, all popular as go-tos for a moderately priced meal. Far from being a standard curry slinger, its modern flavors bend expectation, and certainly back up the success. An accommodating range of dishes comes sweet and tangy, with ginger and garlic, grilled or green, from kebabs to tikkas to Bombay street food; many people order two or three. They're backed up by a smart cocktail list of original concoctions such as the Kohinoor Fizz (made of gin, gooseberry syrup with lime, and a kiss of Aperol). The Covent Garden location (12 Upper St., Martin's Lane, WC2; ✆ **020/7420-9320;** Tube: Leicester Square) often has an off-putting line, so I prefer this one, in an old train shed with a full cellar bar where you can wait for your table. This location also gives you a good excuse to explore the newly rehabbed and on-trend warehouses of Granary Square. The location just off Carnaby Street, near Regent Street shopping, is also prime (22 Kingly St., W1; ✆ **020/7420-9322**; Tube: Oxford Circus).

5 Stable St., N1. www.dishoom.com. ✆ **020/7420-9321.** Main courses £10–£20. Mon–Wed 8am–11pm; Thurs 8am–midnight; Sat 9am–midnight; Sun 9am–11pm. Reservations recommended, but most availability is for walk-ins. Tube: King's Cross St Pancras.

Honey & Co. Bloomsbury ♥♥ MIDDLE EASTERN It's packed for good reasons. First, the food on its changing menu brilliantly adapts Middle Eastern dishes to London palates. Spectacular lamb shawarma is tender as

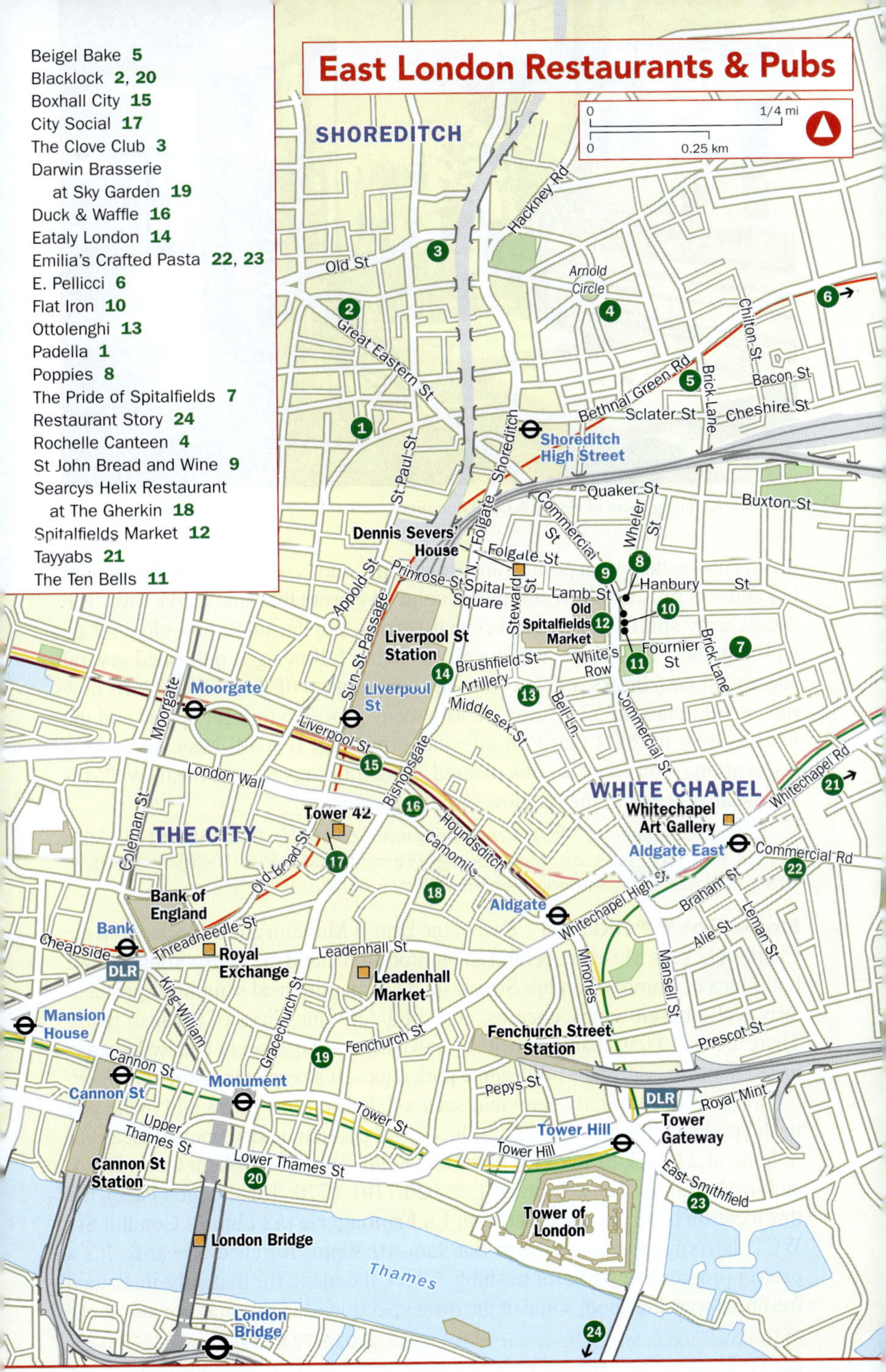
East London Restaurants & Pubs
Beigel Bake 5
Blacklock 2, 20
Boxhall City 15
City Social 17
The Clove Club 3
Darwin Brasserie at Sky Garden 19
Duck & Waffle 16
Eataly London 14
Emilia's Crafted Pasta 22, 23
E. Pellicci 6
Flat Iron 10
Ottolenghi 13
Padella 1
Poppies 8
The Pride of Spitalfields 7
Restaurant Story 24
Rochelle Canteen 4
St John Bread and Wine 9
Searcys Helix Restaurant at The Gherkin 18
Spitalfields Market 12
Tayyabs 21
The Ten Bells 11
0
1/4 mi
0
0.25 km
SHOREDITCH
THE CITY
WHITE CHAPEL
Hackney Rd
Old St
Arnold Circle
Great Eastern St
Chilton St
Bacon St
Bethnal Green Rd
Sclater St
Brick Lane
Cheshire St
Shoreditch High Street
Quaker St
Buxton St
Commercial St
Wheler St
St Paul St
Dennis Severs' House
Folgate St
Primrose St
Spital Square
Steward St
Lamb St
Hanbury St
Old Spitalfields Market
Fournier St
White's Row
Appold St
Sun St Passage
Liverpool St Station
Liverpool St
Brushfield St
Artillery
Middlesex St
Bell Ln.
Moorgate
Liverpool St
London Wall
Bishopsgate
Houndsditch
Camomile
Tower 42
Old Broad St
Coleman St
Whitechapel Art Gallery
Aldgate East
Whitechapel Rd
Commercial Rd
Braham St
Leman St
Alie St
Aldgate
Whitechapel High St
Bank of England
Bank
Cheapside
Threadneedle St
Royal Exchange
DLR
Leadenhall St
Leadenhall Market
Gracechurch St
King William
Minories
Mansell St
Mansion House
Fenchurch St
Fenchurch Street Station
Prescot St
Cannon St
Cannon St
Monument
Pepys St
Royal Mint
Tower St
Upper Thames St
Lower Thames St
Tower Hill
Tower Hill
Tower Gateway
Cannon St Station
East Smithfield
Tower of London
London Bridge
Thames
London Bridge

The cheerful dining room of Honey & Co. Bloomsbury.

brisket and spiked with pomegranate and mint, and is served in a little pot with hot and soft pita. Chicken dumplings come in a broth that smells like love. The "strawberry spliff" dessert proves that berries, phyllo, mint, and olive oil go well together. This place, which gained such a following it published several successful cookbooks, moved from the southern tip of Regent's Park (it now runs its old place at 52 Warren St. as a teeny grocery store for spices and the like) to here in 2022 partly to alleviate crowding. It's still busy, so make a reservation or miss out on this assured, sometimes revelatory, meal. Walk-ins are usually seated in the window or outside.

54 Lamb's Conduit St., WC1. www.honeyandco.co.uk. ✆ **020/7388-6175.** Main courses Mid-£20s. No cash. Mon noon–10:30pm, Tues–Fri 6am–10:30pm, Sat 9am–10:30pm. Reservations strongly recommended. Tube: Russell Square.

Noble Rot ♥♥ BRITISH East of the British Museum and 2 blocks from the Charles Dickens Museum, behind an old storefront amid the transporting upscale boutiques of Lamb's Conduit Street, spend a languid meal sampling spectacularly well-chosen wines, cheeses, and sublimely fine slices of Spanish hams. There are also a few changing British-drawn dishes like gnocchi with wild garlic, baked Scottish cod, and Middlewhite pork chops. It's perplexing how such *hunting lodge chic* simplicity can yield such a delightful few hours and make you wish you lived like this every day. Once it got popular, it also opened locations in Soho at 2 Greek St., W1 (✆ **020/7183-8190**; Tube: Tottenham Court Road) and in Mayfair (5 Trebeck St., W1; ✆ **020/7101-6770**; Tube: Green Park), but this location is across the street from **La Fromagerie** (52 Lamb's Conduit St., WC1; lafromagerie.co.uk; Mon–Sat 9am–10:30pm) for cheese boards; it's a perfect progressive party for noshing. Check the menu for that only-in-Britain freshness warning about some of the meat selections: "Game may contain shot."

51 Lamb's Conduit St., WC1. www.noblerot.co.uk. ✆ **020/7242-8963.** Set lunch menus £22 for 2 courses and £26 for 3 courses; plates £10–£40. Mon–Sat noon–2:30pm and 6–9:30pm. Reservations strongly suggested for dinner. Tube: Russell Square.

North Sea Fish ♥♥ SEAFOOD Suggested by pretty much every hotel manager within a walkable radius since it opened in 1977, North Sea Fish scratches the fish-and-chips itch in a table-serving setting. Expect a dignified fish market-cum-restaurant hidden on a lost-in-time side street. Portions are huge, and there's always a selection of 10 varieties of fresh fish (sole, salmon, halibut, and so on). If you need a healthier option, you can also get your dish grilled, and if someone in your group isn't so hooked on fish, the menu also has a few burgers of various types and meat pies. Try the terrific homemade tartar sauce, or, for fans of little fishies, sample grilled sardines with salad.

7–8 Leigh St., WC1. www.northseafishrestaurant.co.uk. ✆ **020/7387-5892.** Main courses £18–£35. Mon 5–9:30pm; Tues–Sat noon–9:30pm. Tube: King's Cross St Pancras or Russell Square.

Savoir Faire ♥♥ FRENCH/ITALIAN After braving the rummage sale of mediocre gastronomic clip joints around the British Museum, patrons are known to smugly proclaim this cozy French-and-Italian duplex their " discovery"—omitting the reality that it's been presenting what it correctly terms "affordable gourmet" since 1995. How could anyone have ignored this bistro-style traveler's gift, where nothing is processed and everything is made-to-order and served under hand-painted murals? Meals are more than reliable; in this area, they're miracles on plates. The menu might include ample portions of nimbly executed dishes like carbonara, bouillabaisse, pizza, or beef bourguignon so tender you wonder if they've got Julia Child's ghost back there. Sun-Fri noon–4pm, it does bottomless pasta or pizza brunch for £40.

42 New Oxford St., WC1. www.savoir.co.uk. ✆ **020/7436-0707.** Main courses £18–£25. Sun–Thurs noon–10pm; Fri–Sat noon–11pm. Tube: Holborn or Tottenham Court Road.

Inexpensive

Bill's ♥ INTERNATIONAL A 5 minute walk from the British Museum and handy for many uses—breakfast until 5pm, lunches, dinner, feeding kids, or downing cheap cocktails. In few other London establishments will you find mac-and-cheese, burgers, flatbreads, seafood linguine, and Caesar salad on the same menu. Two-course set menus, if you choose one, are £18, and three courses cost £22. Like American diners of yore, but with more farmhouse-style class, Bill's is a lifesaver when you're in need of drama-free, family-friendly grub served briskly, which is why you'll be glad to hear there are also locations near Piccadilly Circus (36–44 Brewer St., W1), in Southwark (Victor Wharf, Clink St., SE1) and not far south of Buckingham Palace (6 Cathedral Walk, SW1). Plus, there's free Wi-Fi.

St Martin's Courtyard, WC2. www.bills-website.co.uk. ✆ **020/2742-2981.** Main courses £15–£27. Mon–Thurs 8am–10pm, Fri 8am–11pm, Sat 8am–10pm, Sun 8am–9:30pm. Tube: Covent Garden.

The Eagle ♥♥ TRADITIONAL BRITISH By now, the word *gastropub* is so widespread that the term is virtually meaningless, but foodies note: That trend began here in 1991 (or so most agree), in an old pub in Clerkenwell, a then-ungentrified area between Bloomsbury and Islington. So old are this

KEEPING THE BILL low

If you're watching your money, bear in mind these cultural differences:

Avoid eating in By law, restaurants must charge you a higher tax rate if you eat on premises, so the take-away menu is always cheaper.

Avoid overtipping Credit card slips may have a line for a tip, even if the tip was already built in (if it is, it'll be about 12.5% and the description may be as subtle as "discretion"). Only tip (10%–20%) if the menu says "service not included" or similar.

Avoid soda It can cost more than £3.50, no refill, or even more now that the government taxes beverages with more than 50g of sugar per liter.

Avoid rice dishes It's customary to pay £2 to £3 for a side dish of plain rice, even if you think it should come with what you ordered.

Avoid water Well, avoid it bottled. If you just order "water," waiters may bring expensive bottled water, so if you want it for free, specify "tap water."

Avoid cocktails Mixed drinks can cost a dizzying £12 to £20, and because pours are standardized, they're usually of the same middling strength. If you do drink, stick to beer (£6–£8 a pint) or wine (around £9 a glass).

place's roots that it actually makes a cameo in the nursery rhyme "Pop Goes the Weasel": "Up and down the City Road/In and out of the Eagle/That's the way the money goes/Pop goes the weasel." Behind the bar of a bare-to-the-wood corner saloon, rebuilt in 1901, the often-surly staff prepares a changing selection of about a dozen flavorful dishes a day, from the likes of pork loin salad to pan-roasted sole to the house specialty, the insidiously spicy Bife Ana steak sandwich dripping with marinated garlic and onion. Tables are shared (it's bad for groups), menu delivered by blackboard only, service is best described as "survival of the fittest," furniture reassuringly shabby and mismatched. Order at the bar and relax with a beer, because here, the food's the thing, and it arrives on its own schedule, not much pomp about it.

159 Farringdon Rd., EC1. www.theeaglefarringdon.co.uk. ✆ **020/7837-1353.** Main courses £14–£24. Mon–Fri noon–3pm and 6:30–10:30pm; Sat noon–3pm and 6:30–10:30pm; Sun noon–3pm. Reservations required for parties of 5–10. Tube: Farringdon.

The Fryer's Delight ♥♥ TRADITIONAL BRITISH/TAKE-AWAY First-time visitors often wonder where all the famous fish-and-chips shops are. Unfortunately, most of them are gone. Our era has mostly rejected joints as hydrogenated as The Fryer's Delight. Fortunately, this joint is not of this era. Despite the fact it merits its own Wikipedia page now, it's a true old-world chippy, where the sputtering fry fat comes from beef drippings, chips come in paper wrappings, the orange formica tabletops and checkered floor come from the lean postwar years, and the men behind the counter are almost callously gruff. Prices are anachronistic, too. Order yours with mushy peas. It's a 10-minute walk east of the British Museum; look for the logo of a codfish tipping its bowler hat (seriously). Also respected: the more touristy **Rock & Sole Plaice** (47 Endell St.; ✆ **020/7836-3785**; www.rockandsoleplaice.com;

£20–£25; Tube: Covent Garden), which has operated under several names since 1871 and has been using the same recipe for 140 years. If you seek the best-reviewed fish-and-chips shops in the greater city, **The Golden Chippy,** is out east in Greenwich (p. 204), so plan to drop by if you're including those attractions in your visit (62 Greenwich High Rd., SE10; www.thegolden chippy.co.uk; ✆ **020/8692-4333;** Mon–Sat 11am–11pm, Sun noon–11pm; £12–£24; DLR/Rail: Greenwich).

19 Theobald's Rd., WC1. www.facebook.com/fishandchips.co.uk/ ✆ **020/7405-4114.** Main courses around £10. Mon–Sat 11am–9pm. Tube: Holborn or Chancery Lane.

SOHO & LEICESTER SQUARE

Visitors spend much time around here, in the dining-and-entertainment hub of London. Despite the miasma of culinary also-rans, from junky steam-table buffets to overpriced bistros, you'll still find a queue for nearly every affordable restaurant in the hours before showtimes. If you have theater plans, you should try to book an advance reservation. London's touristy (and pan-Asian) Chinatown sits between Shaftesbury Avenue and Leicester Square, but the neighborhood is more about feeding partying groups than about luxury dining. Find more clusters of good casual restaurants in Kingly Court and on Old Compton Street.

Expensive

The Ivy ♥ TRADITIONAL BRITISH A West End tent-pole since 1917, with guests ranging from Coward to Cumberbatch, this is where London thespians pretend to slum it, lifting hamburgers alongside cognac beneath its iconic wood paneling and harlequin mullioned windows. At its sumptuous flatiron bar, you may spot celebrities (try after 9pm), but you're more likely to be among tourists like yourself. The menu of Ivy classics (shepherd's pie, fish and chips) has been embellished with Asian-ish notions (crispy duck salad, Bang Bang chicken with peanut chili sauce), and the music might be the likes of Sisters Love or Candi Staton, which only accentuates the bohemian posture. There are licensed versions of The Ivy spreading around town, but this is where the original has been planted since World War I. Lunch and pre-theatre set menus are often available or around £30.

The classic Ivy restaurant on West Street in Covent Garden.

1–5 West St., WC1. www.the-ivy.co.uk. ✆ **020/7836-4751.** Main courses £20–£45. Mon–Fri noon–11pm; Sat 11:30am–11pm; Sun 11:30am–10:30pm. Reservations essential. Tube: Leicester Square or Covent Garden.

4

WHERE TO DINE | Soho & Leicester Square

LONDON food chains I RECOMMEND

London, like so many other cities, is experiencing an economic shift that squeezes out mom-and-pop establishments in favor of better-heeled chains; you'll see these mid-priced, kid-friendly names on storefronts wherever you go. They're delicious and most are English-owned, so rely on them as well:

- **Busaba:** Peppy noodles and Asian dishes at communal tables
- **Carluccio's:** New York–style Italian. Tile walls, pasta, fish, meats, coffees
- **Farmer J:** Affordable mixed bowls and 3-course food trays sourced mostly from British meat and veg farms
- **Franco Manca:** Well-priced pizza on soft sourdough crust. Its pies aren't frozen first, and it's better than **PizzaExpress**, which is prevalent but inferior
- **Giraffe:** Every kind of comfort food, extremely family-friendly, can get noisy
- **Leon:** Free-trade, organic alternative to fast food includes "hot boxes" of Moroccan meatballs, halloumi wraps, and "superfood" salads
- **M&S Simply Food:** Marks & Spencer's (p. 241) stand-alone shops for sandwiches, hit-or-miss ready-made dishes, and well-selected inexpensive wines
- **Tortilla:** Similar to Chipotle, but a few notches below it
- **Ugly Dumpling:** Asian-style dumplings with Western ingredients
- **Wagamama:** Hearty noodle bowls eaten at shared long tables
- **Wahaca:** Substantial Mexican approximated with British-grown ingredients

Moderate

10 Greek Street ♥♥♥ CONTEMPORARY EUROPEAN Sometimes, restaurants get it so right—from friendly and knowledgeable staff to unfussy surroundings to pure, clean, well-made food—that you wonder why they can't all be this way. The menu, all choices a top value for the money, changes but the impeccable standards don't: Frequent standouts include whole lemon sole with samphire (an edible coastal plant) and artichokes, lamb, Gloucester Old Spot pork, Dexter beef, Yorkshire lamb, elderflower sorbet, a continuous trickle of fresh-baked breads, and an affordable wine list chosen with as much care as the fish and meat cuts. If it seems full, just sit at the tiny bar.

10 Greek St., W1. www.10greekstreet.com. ✆ **020/7734-4677.** Main courses £14–£35. Tues–Thurs noon–10pm, Fri–Sat noon–10:30pm. Tube: Tottenham Court Road.

Andrew Edmunds ♥♥♥ BRITISH The relaxed, townhouse-style storefront, a study in natural woods and candlelit purity, has been going since 1985, enduring most likely because it hasn't caved to Soho trendiness and its stupendous wine list is priced fairly. Chairs don't match, staff isn't in uniform, and the menu is hand-scribbled daily with a haste that belies the effort the chef puts into sourcing farmhouse meats and preparing seasonal ingredients. Expect choices along the lines of skate wing with cauliflower and capers, free-range Aylesbury duck breast, and artichoke spaghetti with wild garlic and almond pesto, plus the occasional nose-to-tail adventure. Superb dessert cheeses are selected from area farms. It's very London.

46 Lexington St., W1. www.andrewedmunds.com. ✆ **020/7437-5708.** Main courses £17–£30. Mon–Fri noon–3:30pm and 5:30–10:30pm; Sat 12:30–3:30pm and 5:30–10:30pm; Sun 1–4pm and 6–10:30pm. Reservations essential; dinner accepted a month ahead, lunch accepted 3 weeks ahead. Tube: Piccadilly Circus or Oxford Circus.

Blacklock Soho ♥♥ MEATS Blacklock presents an existential challenge to American barbecue fans who think they're the world's best meat masters: The extravagant "meat mountain" roast (as *Food Insider* puts it) served here is piled precariously atop browned potatoes and Yorkshire pudding and walloped with gravy, a spectacle that made Blacklock a destination for unabashed carnivores. All the meat is raised sustainably in Britain, and the entire animal is used one way or another. Appetites won't sustain themselves for long in the face of such fresh-seared profligacy. Although you do get a lot of protein for your pound, there's not a lot for vegetarians other than a token dish, such as barbecued cauliflower. Make advance bookings for the Sunday roast. The formula works so well that further locations have been launched at 16a Bedford St., WC2 (✆ **020/3034-1394;** Tube: Covent Garden) and 28-30 Rivington St, EC2 (✆ **020/7739-2148;** Tube: Old Street) and in the City (13 Philpot Lane, EC2; ✆ **020/7998-7676;** Tube: Monument), but this is the location that's stashed in a former basement brothel, which in terms of indulgence seems fitting in a way I cannot articulate.

24 Great Windmill St., W1. theblacklock.com. ✆ **020/3441-6996.** Steaks £15–£23; Sunday roast £18–£28. Mon–Fri noon–3pm and 5–11pm; Sat noon–11pm; Sun 11:45am–8pm. Tube: Piccadilly Circus.

Brasserie Zédel ♥♥♥ FRENCH When you enter via its grand staircase, you'll feel like Toulouse-Lautrec in search of tonight's muse: The

The glamour of Belle Époque Paris at welcoming prices at Brasserie Zédel.

always-lively, gilt-and-marble cellar dining room, awash in *fin-de-siècle* statements like platter mirrors and vested waiters, is a perfect piece of Paris off Piccadilly. This is not a crusty survivor but a pitch-perfect modern scene that was crafted out of a huge space in what was once the Regent Palace, which in 1915 was the largest hotel in Europe. Menu choices are as authentic as Pernod, pastis, oysters, quiche Lorraine, and sublimely seasoned steak tartare (often, the first thing I eat upon arriving in town). The adjoining **Bar Américain,** a 1930s Art Deco treasure by an architect survivor of the *Lusitania,* does indulgently uptight cocktails and champagne, while its 80-seat cabaret, **Le Crazy Coqs/Live at Zédel** is an elegant venue that does matinees and evening shows. This *rêve* of London's historic connections to European high life is not nearly as expensive as it feels, and its Gallic poise only adds to the deliciousness.

20 Sherwood St., W1. www.brasseriezedel.com. ✆ **020/7734-4888.** Main courses £19–£32; 2 courses £17; 3 courses £20. Mon–Weds noon–10:30pm; Thurs–Sat 11:30am–11pm, Sun 11:30am–10pm. Reservations recommended. Tube: Piccadilly Circus.

Ducksoup ♥♥ INTERNATIONAL The sort of invisible hidey-hole you have to be told about, tiny little Ducksoup feels like "your" spot. The metal grille on the windows, world-weary checkerboard flooring, and life-beaten walls make it look like a greasy cafe that would sling a fry-up at you, but instead, there's a funky wine list and solid, whole-food selections, which change, such as grilled artichoke with lemon and capers, ricotta *gnudi* (cheese dumplings), and chargrilled bream. The owners invite you to browse the collection of vintage vinyl records and put on something you like. Ducksoup serves a version of London that went out with Thatcher, but the cuisine sits solidly within London's 21st-century gustatory passions.

41 Dean St., W1. www.ducksoupsoho.co.uk. ✆ **020/7287-4599.** Plates £14–£32. Mon 5–10pm; Tues–Sat noon–3pm and 5–10pm; bar open later. Tube: Tottenham Court Road.

Inexpensive

Bar Italia ♥♥ COFFEE/ITALIAN Italians settled Soho in the 1940s, and before they decamped for the suburbs, they installed a set of mod, gleaming coffee bars and cafes. This old-school straggler from 1946 is a haunt of slumming celebrities and artists who, we dare say, must not come for ingratiating service. While this institution is busy all day—making simple sandwiches, delivering pastries, grunting with effort—it swells with revelers after midnight. Even Rome doesn't have bars that steam, press, and shuffle coffee across the clock with such gusto. "Like everything in this city that Londoners really enjoy, it reminds us of being abroad," quipped the *Guardian.* Whatever; it practically leaks hipness.

22 Frith St., W1. No website. ✆ **020/7437-4520.** Coffee £3–£4; pizza £10–£11; panini £7. Mon–Sat 6:30am–4:30am; Sun 6:30am–2am. Tube: Leicester Square.

Café in the Crypt ♥ INTERNATIONAL Also marked as Crypt Café, it's super-central and unquestionably memorable—the tastiest graveyard in town! Under the sanctuary of the historic St Martin-in-the-Fields church at Trafalgar Square, atop the graves of 18th-century Londoners—fret not, the former occupants were moved elsewhere decades ago—one of the West End's sharpest bargains is served. The menu at this dependable 200-seat cafeteria changes monthly, but the large portions always include a few meat pies baked to perfection, a vegetarian choice, soups, salads topped with meats, and sweet apple crumble with custard; there's also fish-and-chips on Friday. The church keeps the draft beer and the wine (even by the bottle) flowing. This may be the only crypt you'll ever enter that's a lifesaver—at least for your budget.

Trafalgar Sq., WC2. www.smitf.org. ✆ **020/7766-1158.** Main courses £10–£20, kid's meal with 2 sides £6. No cash. Mon 10am–7pm; Tues 10am–5pm; Wed 10am–5pm; Thurs–Fri 10am–7pm Sat 10am–5pm;; Sun 11am–5pm. Tube: Charing Cross.

Gordon's Wine Bar ♥♥♥ INTERNATIONAL The atmosphere is matchless at this vaunted and vaulted casual wine bar, one of London's worst-kept secrets. It was established in 1890 (when Rudyard Kipling lived upstairs) and, thank goodness, hasn't been refurbished since—look in the front window and you'll see untouched champagne bottles intentionally left to grow furry with dust. These tight, candlelit cellars beneath Villiers Street are wallpapered with important newspaper front pages from the mid-20th century—the Crystal Palace blaze, the death of King George VI—and the wood barrels behind the bar are filled with port on tap (a *schooner* is small, a *beaker* is larger). Everything is suffused in a mustardy ochre from more than 42,000 past evenings of indoor tobacco smoke (no longer legal). Music is not played—not that you could hear it over the din of conversation. Pick a bottle of wine from the massive list in a binder and match it with a lavish selection of meats and cheeses for a personalized charcuterie board. In good weather, the event expands on Watergate Walk outside along Embankment Gardens. (The stone arch was built around 1625 as a palace gate on the Thames, but its mansion is long gone and the river moved 46m/150 ft. south.) Come down in midafternoon, well before offices let out, or waiting in line will be your fate.

Gordon's Wine Bar is a charming West End hiding place for a cheese plate and a good cabernet.

47 Villiers St., WC2. www.gordonswinebar.com. ✆ **020/7930-1408.** Plates £11–£20; shared plates £30–£46. Mon–Sat 11am–11pm; Sun noon–10pm, kitchen closes 1 hr. early. No reservations. Tube: Charing Cross or Embankment.

Koya Soho ♥♥ JAPANESE A queue for a quick and cheap bowl of noodle soup? That seems excessive, but this stuff is no plain soup. The Soho dining room, where transactional servers turn over trade quickly, is plain, supporting nothing more special than exposed ductwork, cheap chopsticks in cups, menu boards, and stacks of bowls. Even the menu of *donburi*, *udon* (wheat flour noodles), and Japanese small plates would appear to have no tricks. But then the finished product arrives in several parts for you to mix yourself, and the fog lifts. Noodles are made fresh each day using traditional methods. The tempura isn't too oily, the broth doesn't accost the palate with salt. By the time you taste the delectable walnut miso, though, you'll finally understand the line. You will then drink the dregs from the bowl.

The original Mildreds restaurant is in a townhouse from the 1700s.

50 Frith St., W1. www.koya.co.uk. ✆ **020/7434-4463.** Main courses £10–£20. Daily 10am–10pm. No reservations. Tube: Tottenham Court Road

Mildreds ♥ VEGETARIAN Packed since 1988, it's where vegetarians with palates go. The menu (all three meals) is ever-changing but always assembled with more care than the usual beans and tofu: Sri Lankan sweet potato and lime cashew curry, wood-roasted mushroom and ale pie, and green falafel with sour cherry and pistachio rice are three samples from its international menu. If you don't do onion or garlic, there's a thoughtful menu just for you. Big bowls and plates, appetizing presentation, and a vibe like home have secured Mildreds a following even among carnivores—it even had pretty cookbooks published. Save room for the cheesecakes or puddings—you won't believe they're gluten-free. You'll find another location near Trafalgar Square at 79 St Martin's Lane, WC2 (✆ **020/8066-8393;** Tube: Leicester Square) and just east of Victoria Station at 128 Wildon Rd., SW1 (✆ **020/8050-0164**), but this is the original, in a townhouse from the 1700s.

45 Lexington St., W1. www.mildreds.co.uk. ✆ **020/7494-1634.** Main courses around £17. Mon–Sat 9am–11pm; Sun 9am–10pm. Tube: Tottenham Court Road or Piccadilly Circus.

Digging into a spicy noodle laksa soup bowl at Rasa Sayang.

Rasa Sayang ♥♥ SINGAPORE/MALAYSIAN When you need something quick, flavorful, and filling before showtime in Chinatown or the Theatre District, this no-pretentions

An array of Thai/Chinese dishes at Speedboat Bar.

spot is superior to most of the other fast-casual Asian restaurants in Chinatown, and the service is more engaged. Rich and flavorful street food–inspired dishes abound like Malay *nasi lemak* with fragrant coconut rice, spicy/noodly *laksa* soup bowls, fluffy roti *canai* stringy flatbread, stir-fry noodles, and Singapore spicy crab. The Hainanese chicken is popular.

5 Macclesfield St., W1. www.rasasayangfood.com. ✆ **020/7734-1382.** Main courses around £16. Mon–Fri noon–10pm; Sat 11:30am–10pm; Sun 11:30am–9pm. Tube: Piccadilly Circus.

Speedboat Bar ♥♥ THAI/CHINESE Get your Chinatown late-night feed on (happy hour with a late-night menu is 10pm to closing) at this pastiche of the Bangkok street bars where Thai and Chinese food collide. Signature dishes involve punchy curries and noodles, zesty chicken skins with sweet-and-sour seasoning, crispy pork and black pepper curry, sweet corn fritters, and pineapple pie with taro ice cream that aren't like the milky Thai food you may know—it's Isaan-style spicy, each dish delivers its own unique unflinching flavors, and there's a menu for vegetarians. The campy '80s Thai sports theme, plus bespoke cocktails, make it a party, and the kind of place you want to head after you've already had a few in the pubs. Many customers agree, so, it's smart to book ahead.

30 Rupert St., W1. speedboatbar.co.uk. info@speedboatbar.co.uk. Main courses £10–£20. Mon–Thurs noon–midnight; Fri–Sat noon–1am; Sun noon–11pm. Reservation recommended via SevenRooms.com. Tube: Piccadilly Circus.

COVENT GARDEN

The streets surrounding Covent Garden are among the city's richest in terms of dining choices, from bistro discoveries to imported brands such as Shake Shack, Din Tai Fung, and Balthazar. The food within the market is

Delivery Apps

After a long day of trooping through museums and up and down stairs in the Tube, you're forgiven if you just want to put your feet up. These apps are favored by Londoners for finding nearby take-away or food delivery services, although look out for "ghost kitchens" (that aren't actual restaurants you can visit in person but exist only to pump out passable themed delivery meals) : **Deliveroo, Just Eat, Slerp, UberEATS,** and **Getir,** which delivers groceries like Instacart does in the U.S.

tourist-priced, but if you simply must eat there, head to the lower level where you'll find £10 *tartines* (open-faced sandwiches) at **Chez Antoinette** and good cheese at the **Crusting Pipe** wine bar.

Expensive

J. Sheekey ♥♥ SEAFOOD Smartly turned-out waiters prep you with so many specialized fish-eating utensils that your place setting starts to look like a workstation at Santa's workshop. Such presentational flourishes are appropriate to theatreland, where Sheekey has been a classic for years, and although prices aren't generous, portions and quality are. The least expensive main dish, fish pie, is fortunately its trademark, but there are plenty of other choices, from shrimp-and-scallop burgers to a delectable lemon sole, plus a changing slate of game and meats for the fish-averse. Despite all the fuss, children are welcomed.

28–35 St. Martin's Ct., WC2. www.j-sheekey.co.uk. ✆ **020/7240-2565.** Main courses £23–£50 , plus cover of £2 per person. Lunch and late-night set menu: 2 courses £36, 3 courses £42. Mon–Sat noon–10:45; Sun noon–8:45. Reservations recommended. Tube: Leicester Square.

The rock shrimp burger at J. Sheekey, which is known for its fish, shellfish, and oysters.

Rules ♥♥ TRADITIONAL BRITISH For a high-end kitchen that takes British cuisine seriously, go with an icon. Rules is London's oldest restaurant (est. 1798), and its patrons have included Graham Greene, Charles Dickens, Evelyn Waugh, and Edward VII, who regularly dined here with his paramour Lillie Langtry. (The management is less than discreet about it; the nook they used is named for him.) Being a major stop on the tourist trail lends force to its theatricality; beer comes in a "silver tankard," for example, and the landmarked rooms are an overdressed Georgian yard sale of yellowing etchings, antlers, and rich red fabrics. But what's on the table is indisputably high-class and perfectly prepared: fine reared meat, ideal English meat pies, whole roast squab or grouse (it serves 18,000 game birds annually), golden syrup sponge pudding, and cocktails like that famous one made of tonic, juniper, and quinine.

35 Maiden Lane, WC1. www.rules.co.uk. ✆ **020/7836-5314.** Main courses £26–£40. Tues–Thurs noon–10pm, Fri–Sat noon–11:30pm; Sun noon–10pm. Reservations recommended. Dress code: smart casual; no shorts. No children 9 and under admitted after 7pm. Tube: Covent Garden.

Moderate

Ave Mario ♥♥♥ ITALIAN One of the West End's most fun places to eat. In a high-ceilinged, bottle-festooned Covent Garden space best described as the collision between a Florentine mansion and Studio 54, conversation is loud and staff is overworked, but the family-friendly food is filling, high-spirited, and on point. Seated in circular booths, you'll eat airy warm focaccia, piquant cocktails, massive soft-doughed pizzas, lemon pies topped with head-turning towers of meringue, and best of all, La Gran Carbonara, which is homemade spaghetti alla chitarra for two basted tableside inside a giant wheel of pecorino cheese. Ave Mario is perpetually chaotic and popular for good reason, but if you fail to arrive with a booking, the crowd starts thinning out around 8:30 pm. Two-course lunch menus are £23 and 3-course pre-theatre menus are £34.

15 Henrietta St., WC2. www.bigmammagroup.com/italian-restaurants/ave-mario. Dishes £17–£30. Mon–Weds noon–10pm, Thurs–Fri noon–10:30pm, Sat 11:30am–10:30pm, Sun 11:30am–9:30pm. Reservations essential. Tube: Covent Garden

Cooks work at the robata charcoal grill at The Barbary.

The Barbary ♥♥ MEDITERRANEAN The aromatic spices of the Mediterranean and the Middle East are given life by award-winning chefs who care about clear and classic methods, using a bespoke robata charcoal grill and clay tandoor oven. Sit at the bar watching the cooks work, and feast on rich and savory tapas dishes. Most people order multiple dishes and send the bill high, which will be understandable once you've tasted its grilled octopus glazed in pomegranate molasses, prawns with a tropical zip, Jerusalem bagel with dip, and extraordinary homemade bread and hummus. It's small, hidden, and noisy, so it's probably best for parties of 4 or fewer, although solos tend to be seated swiftly.

16 Neal's Yard, WC2. thebarbary.co.uk/. ✆ **020/7870-5659.** Dishes £20–£30. Mon–Fri noon–2:30pm, 5–11pm, Sat noon–10pm, Sun noon–9pm. Tube: Covent Garden.

Browns ♥ TRADITIONAL BRITISH In London, there's a Browns for fashion and a Brown's Hotel, but Browns the spacious brasserie is the Browns you can afford. Installed in the former Westminster County Courts (check out the old proceedings chambers upstairs), this high-quality, Brighton-based English chain serves updated English food and imported beer. The globe lanterns, enormous mirrors, and staff buttoned into crisp white oxford shirts impart the sense of a Gilded Age chophouse. Expect lots of indulgently hearty dishes such as lobster risotto, steak and Guinness pie, fish-and-chips, or a nice fat

Steak is the specialty at Flat Iron.

burger with Irish cheddar. A sense of tradition—starchy, but the kind that's welcoming to tourists—is the main product here.

82–84 St Martins Lane, WC2. www.browns-restaurants.co.uk. ✆ **020/7497-5050.** Main courses £15–£29; Pre-theater meal (Mon–Fri 4–6:30pm) £20–£25. Mon–Wed 10am–11pm; Thurs–Fri 10am–midnight; Sat 9am–midnight; Sun 9am–10:30pm. Tube: Leicester Square.

Flat Iron ♥♥♥ STEAK For £15, you get an absolutely perfect 200g (7-oz.) steak cut by an in-house butcher from the tender shoulder of the cow, a cup of salad, a serving of beef-dripping popcorn, and on the way out the door, a cone of caramel ice cream topped with shavings from a block of dark chocolate. No wonder there's a queue. Specializing makes the cooking expert and the juicy meat is over-the-top delicious. Flat Iron owns a herd of cows in Yorkshire and serves the same ingenious concept at 15 London locations (others include one near the British Museum at 9 Denmark St., WC2, Tube: Tottenham Court Rd.; 17 Beak St., W1, off Carnaby St., Tube: Piccadilly Circus; and in the Royal Festival Hall in South Bank, Tube: Waterloo). This version by Covent Garden is the best for killing time before your table is ready—and it's also one of the few locations that serve the all-important ice cream.

17/18 Henrietta St., WC2. flatironsteak.co.uk. No phone. Main courses £15. Wed–Thurs 11:30am–11pm; Fri–Sat 11:30am–11:30pm; Sun–Tues 11:30am–10:30pm. Reservations recommended. Tube: Covent Garden or Leicester Square.

Inexpensive

Bancone Covent Garden ♥♥♥ ITALIAN A winning combination of perfect handmade pasta, an informally elegant space, and good value has made Bancone a big hit. The supple, star-shaped silk handkerchief pasta dish with walnut butter, nested with an unbroken egg yolk, is routinely photographed like a starlet upon arrival and has achieved local star status on social

Classic surf and turf at Browns Covent Garden.

media; *The Guardian* reviewed the dish as "casually orgasmic." But every option, served as small plates (get a few) makes the most of fresh ingredients and flavor accents, such as local burrata to a sublime cacio e pepe, a beautiful duck ragù, and a roasted pumpkin ravioli with oyster mushroom and sage brown butter. Only the cocktails disappoint (stylish giant ice cube but barely any liquid.

39 William IV St., WC2. www.bancone.co.uk. ✆ **020/7240-8786.** Dishes £10–£18. Mon–Weds 11:30am–10pm, Thurs–Sat 11:30am–10:30pm, Sun 11:30am–9:30pm. Reservations recommended. Tube: Charing Cross

Noodle Inn ♥ CHINESE This hole-in-the-wall has become virally famous in some circles for its wonderful hand-pulled noodles and handmade wontons, well-spiced and flavorful, spicy but not painful. Sit at the counter for a front-row seat watching the cooks make them with practiced precision. The "chilli oil spill noodles" (choose your protein topping) get a lot of customer attention. Expect a queue at all hours—it's best to be in line before opening. The staff is all business and moves customers along quickly. Is it worth all the fuss? Reviews are split, but I think it scores for high-value, high-flavor food served quickly. If you seek authentically powerful, tongue-numbing hand made Chongqing noodles that aren't mobbed by TikTok-influenced lemmings, go to **Liu Xiaomian** (www.liu-xiaomian.com), on a much quieter upper-level gallery at Kingly Court off Carnaby Street, a 10-minute walk away. And for TikTok-famous fresh-steamed buns that satisfy tamer palates and the smallest budgets, **Bun House Chinatown** (26–27 Lisle St., WC2; Tube: Leicester Square) can fill you up for £4 a bun from a takeaway window; it's a 5-minute walk south of Noodle Inn.

The star-shaped silk handkerchief pasta dish at Bancone Covent Garden has a cult following.

4–6 Old Compton St., W1. www.instagram.com/kungfunoodleuk. ✆ **020/7434-1627.** Dishes £8–£15. Daily noon–10pm. Tube: Leicester Square or Tottenham Court Road.

Punjab Restaurant ♥♥♥ INDIAN Do not be deceived by looks. This is not a hack kitchen sponging off the Covent Garden tourist trade—this comfort

STEEPED IN TRADITION: afternoon tea

Afternoon tea is an overpriced tourist's pursuit, to be sure, but that doesn't mean it's not delightful to pass the time by pretending to be fancy. Arrive hungry and you'll be served a never-ending banquet of scones, clotted cream, pastry, light sandwiches, and a bottomless brewed torrent. Dress up, if you please, and be discreet about photos. Hundreds of places throw teas (including some bus tours—fun, but not at all authentic), but these are among the most transporting, legendary, convenient, or best located. Most places will add champagne for a premium.

Brown's Hotel This Mayfair institution, open since 1837, offers exacting execution in the handsome paneled Drawing Room that Victoria loved having tea in, but it's not overly snooty. It veers trendy, mounting additional themed teas according to a posted schedule. www.roccofortehotels.com. ✆ **020/7518-4006.** Noon–4:30pm; £80. Tube: Green Park. Also see p. 67.

Fortnum & Mason The venerable department store on Piccadilly has sold tea for 3 centuries, so naturally in its Diamond Jubilee Tea Salon, nibbling off duck-egg-blue china and serenaded by grand piano, you choose from 150 tea types, many of which are supplied to the other hotels on this list. The crowd can be touristy. www.fortnumandmason.com. ✆ **020/7734-8040.** Tea served all day; £82. Tube: Green Park. Also see p. 239.

The Goring Near Buckingham Palace, it serves on its own bespoke canary-yellow china in your choice of the lounge, the airy conservatory, or the garden. So exacting that even the napkins are starched. You'll need to book far ahead, but you can sit as long as you want once you're there. www.thegoring.com. ✆ **020/7396-9000.** Mon–Sat noon–6pm; from £75. Tube: Victoria. Also see p. 58.

Great Court Restaurant, The British Museum Enjoy more sensibly priced scones under the courtyard's famed central glass canopy. It's casual and light on service, but a novel setting you're sure to be visiting anyway. www.britishmuseum.org. ✆ **020/7323-8990.** Daily 11:30am–5pm (last seating 4pm); £33. Tube: Russell Square. Also see p. 135.

The Lanesborough Dazzling in every way, from the delicacy of the pastry to the airy Regency frills of the conservatory glass overhead, this Knightsbridge hotel institution defeats the Ritz in warmth by a strong scone's throw. www.lanesborough.com. ✆ **020/7259-5599.** Mon–Thurs 2:30–4pm; Fri–Sat noon–4pm; Sun 3:30–4:30pm; £89. Tube: Hyde Park Corner. Also see p. 63.

The Langham The first London hotel to initiate the custom (in 1865) is still top quality, but it's also one of the most commercial, having branded itself with a Wedgwood partnership. There's a children's version with a literary theme. www.palm-court.co.uk. ✆ **020/7636-1000.** 5 seatings Wed–Sat 12:30–5pm; £85. Tube: Oxford Circus. Also see p. 64.

The Ritz The only way most of us can afford the formal gilding, mirrors, and boisterous floral arrangements of the Ritz, at 150 Piccadilly, is to submit to the machinelike attentions of the servile waiters in its gilded Palm Court (1906). They process 400 people daily over a range of hours the gentry would actually find unseemly for tea. The mood is hoity-toity and chilly. No jeans or sneakers, with jacket and tie required for men. Book 6 to 8 weeks ahead. www.theritzlondon.com. ✆ **020/7300-2345.** 5 seatings 11:30am–7:30pm; £81, £59 kids under 16 (no dress code for kids). Tube: Green Park.

Theatre Royal Drury Lane Not all afternoon teas are appropriate for restless kids, but this one is targeted to the whole family, and it's taken beneath the chandeliers of the Grand Saloon, recently restored to its 1812 opulence. thelane.co.uk/. ✆ **020/3925-2910.** Weds–Sun; £68 adults. Tube: Covent Garden.

food stalwart predates the recent curry trend, which is why it survived the crest of the popularity wave. Punjab has been cooking since 1946, when it was opened by Gurbachan Singh Maan, a wrestler, and moved to this location in 1951 to serve the bureaucrats of the India High Commission during a tumultuous political period. Now, his fourth generation runs it with striking professionalism. It proclaims itself the oldest North Indian restaurant in the U.K., and staff have worked here for decades. Cooking is light on the oil and *ghee.* Meats and tandoori (the oven was installed in 1962) are well marinated, and so they arrive tender. The menu is cheeky, too: "If you have any erotic activities planned for after you leave us, perhaps you should resist this sensational garlic *naan.*" It also runs the new casual, small-plate Punjabi Baithak next door on the corner.

80 Neal St., WC2. www.punjab.co.uk. ✆ **020/7836-9787.** Main courses £15–£23, min order of 1 main course. Mon–Sat noon–10:15pm (last orders); Sun noon–10pm. Tube: Covent Garden.

MAYFAIR & MARYLEBONE

It's hard to find a dining establishment in these high-toned hoods that isn't overpriced, swooning with self-importance, and wooing a clientele that's better-connected than you are. The "in" spots seem to change with the trends, but you may rely on—and be welcomed by—these stalwarts.

Expensive

Dovetale ♥♥♥ MODERN BRITISH Tom Sellers is one of London's most exciting young rock-star chefs, and after years of brilliant *trompe l'oeil* creativity at his boffo Restaurant Story (www.restaurantstory.co.uk) in Bermondsey, he's now expanding his brand by creating culinary destinations elsewhere. Here, in the sustainability-obsessed high-luxe 1 Hotel Mayfair (rooms, in which private gardens grow up the walls, usually cost £500 and up), he leads a bistro-style, midcentury-modern parlor with indoor/outdoor courtyard seating, where classical dishes are assiduously done by a huge team of chefs who rise to meet the potential of high-quality ingredients through accomplished feats—a must-order Wagyu carpaccio miraculously flat as a pizza, a triple-blind-baked tomato tart that could flush Paul Hollywood with envy, and just the right protein for the flame. Every element of a dish has a provenance and a logic that's carefully explained by the

The rolling ice cream sundae cart at Dovetale puts a posh Mayfair twist on an American classic dessert.

affably professional staff, but not in an off-putting way—showing off bright seasonal flavors is always the reason. Even something as simple as a burrata from Acton, of all places, is so knowledgably sourced that it melts in the mouth. Mayfair's snooty denizens get a semi-scandalized kick out of its Americanized dessert gimmick: a roving trolley that makes sundaes.

3 Berkeley St., W1. www.1hotels.com/mayfair/taste/dovetale. ✆ **020/3137-4983.** Main courses £12–£25 (breakfast), lunch and dinner £28–£68; set lunch menu £39 2 courses, £45 3 courses (without wine); Sunday roast £45–£55. Breakfast: Mon–Fri 7am–10:30am, Sat–Sun 8am–11am; Lunch and dinner: Mon–Fri noon–2:30pm and 6pm–10:30pm, Sat noon–4pm and 6pm–10:30pm, Sun noon–8pm; Reservations recommended. Dress code: smart. Tube: Green Park

KOL Restaurant ♥♥♥ CONTEMPORARY MEXICAN You may not think you came all the way to London for Mexican food, but you've almost certainly never had it prepared so experimentally and innovatively by a chef so laden with awards. Young Santiago Lastra has been laden with plaudits for rendering traditional Mexican dishes, but solely using British ingredients. The ideas are masterful, bursting with flavor, and repeated at no other restaurant: You might have a squid-and-rhubarb ceviche, a mole with blackcurrant, or langoustine tacos with sauerkraut, all tinged with a spicy kick grown right in the United Kingdom. KOL is a tiny place where cooking is performed amid the diners, and the experience is highly prized; reservations open early each month for timings two months hence (i.e., June 1 for August seatings). ***Warning***: If you don't cancel a booking within 72 hours, you're fully charged as if you'd gone.

9 Seymour St., W1. kolrestaurant.com. ✆ **020/3829-6888.** Set menus of 6 or 9 courses, lunch £95, dinner £181 with optional supplements. Seatings Tues 5:30pm–midnight; Wed–Sat noon–4pm and 5:30pm–midnight. Tube: Marble Arch.

Moderate

The Hard Rock Cafe ♥ AMERICAN We include the Hard Rock not because of life-changing food (it's good enough), but out of a grudging acknowledgment of authenticity—this is the original Hard Rock Cafe, opened here on June 14, 1971, long before you could find knockoff in every city from Key West to Kuwait. Its burgers nudge £20, it's cramped, and much of the so-called memorabilia consists of instruments played once and tossed aside. But you don't have to eat here or force down a sugary cocktail the color of toilet cleanser to take a free tour of its museum, **The Vault** (daily 1–8pm), packed with historic castoffs from the rock'n'roll trade. This is the original; the Hard Rock at 225–229 Piccadilly only opened in 2020.

150 Old Park Lane, W1. www.hardrock.com. ✆ **020/7514-1700.** Main courses £12–£19. Sun–Fri 11:30am–10:30pm; Sat 11:30–11pm. Reservations recommended. Tube: Hyde Park Corner.

Inexpensive

Paul Rothe & Son ♥ DELI You'd swear this shelf-lined wooden box is a modern pastiche built to flatter its upscale neighborhood just north of Oxford Street's shopping, but in fact, it opened in 1900, when this was a block

Deciphering the Menu

If you're used to an American food vocabulary, let us start you off with a few translations that will help you at mealtimes.

- Some people call dinner **tea**.
- If you need it to go, say it's for **take-away**.
- American-style appetizers are **starters**.
- What North Americans call entrées are **mains**.
- A sandwich is sometimes called a **sarnie** or **butty**
- French fries are sometimes called **chips**, but decreasingly so.
- A packet (such as for sugar) is a **sachet** ("sash-AY").
- baked potato = **jacket potato**
- beet = **beetroot**
- bell pepper = **capsicum**
- chicory = **endive**
- arugula = **rocket**
- cotton candy = **candy floss**
- eggplant = **aubergine**
- pickles = **gherkin**
- juice drink (from syrup, not fresh) = **squash**
- squash = can be called **marrow**
- lemon-flavored soda pop = **lemonade**
- potato chips = **crisps**
- sausages = **bangers**
- shrimp = **prawn**
- cilantro = **coriander**
- string beans = **French beans** or **runner beans**
- yellow corn = **sweetcorn**
- yellow raisin = **sultana**
- zucchini = **courgette** or **baby marrow**
- dessert = a **sweet**, or **pudding**, even if it's cake.
- molasses = essentially **treacle**
- Jell-O or gelatin = **jelly**
- jelly = **jam**
- cookie = **biscuit**
- popsicle = **ice lolly**
- To request your final check, ask for the **bill**.
- The tip = **service** or **service charge**

favored by German immigrants. The same family still runs it, doling out simple but classic British sandwiches like coronation chicken and cheese and piccalilli, but also a signature pastrami with Swiss, pickles, and mustard on quartered rye. One of the specialties is egg mayo with anchovies, but you can order whatever you want—if they have the ingredients, they'll make it—and then sit (tables are tight and shared; you'll make friends), or take away. But show up before noon unless you mind waiting in line with the local office workers who love this guileless throwback. Turns out the distant past was delicious, affordable, and adorable—why did we change? The shop doubles as a grocery for specialty chutneys, jams, and other goodies from around the world. 35 Marylebone Lane, W1. www.instagram.com/paulrotheandson; ✆ **020/7935-6783.** Sandwiches, baked potatoes and take-away salads £6–£10. Mon–Fri 8:30am–4pm, Sat 11:30am–4pm, last orders 1 hr. before closing. Tube: Bond Street

BELGRAVIA, KENSINGTON & WESTMINSTER

South Kensington near the museums is a particular disappointment; the museums offer insultingly overpriced food services while most nearby establishments are not a culinary credit to such fine institutions. If you must eat in South Ken, scout around the cafes at Exhibition Road around the Tube stop; look into frenetic local tapas chain **Casa Brindisa** (7–9 Exhibition Rd., SW7; www.brindisakitchens.com; ✆ **020/7590-0008**); or try **Carluccio's** (1 Old Brompton Rd., SW7; www.carluccios.com; ✆ **020/3907-8767**), a cheerful Italian chain. Otherwise, the pickings are ripe with the usual cheap take-aways.

Moderate

Boisdale ♥♥ SCOTTISH Richly done up in red and green like an all-year manifestation of the coziest Christmas, Boisdale makes a year-round gift of the best of Scottish cuisine, from whisky to neeps. It's big on brilliantly prepared fish (the delicately fried calamari with pickle and Tellicherry chili mayo is a starter standout), aged steaks, and oysters, but the accompaniments are compelling as well, even when they're as minor as the rich yellow table butter or the thrice-cooked chips with Bloody Mary ketchup. It's all served atop crisp tablecloths by heedful servers in rooms festooned with etchings and antlers—a masculine vibe, to be sure, and the setting for many a power lunch and cigar break on its terrace. There may be no finer place in the city to try properly prepared haggis—you can even get a vegetarian version of it as a burger. And surprise—it also supports an excellent jazz-and-standards cabaret (ticketed separately) that attracts excellent vocalists and musicians nearly nightly and for Saturday brunch.

15 Eccleston St., SW1. www.boisdale.co.uk. ✆ **020/7730-6922.** Main courses £16–£36. Mon 5–10:15pm; Tues–Fri noon–10:15pm; Sat 5pm–10:15pm; Sun noon–2:30pm, bar open until 1am Mon–Sat. Reservations recommended. Tube: Victoria.

The Jones Family Kitchen ♥♥ BRITISH This secluded courtyard bistro brings a groovy, convivial steakhouse vibe to the neighborhood near Victoria Station. If you love beef, the way JFK's grill can almost mystically seal in the flavors of its Yorkshire longhorn could blow your mind, but then again, the oxtail burger might do it instead. It's not just about beef, though; fish, duck, and pork knowingly prepared in generous portions. Many proteins come from The Ginger Pig, a network of principled farmers. Sides such as truffled mac-and-cheese and charred green beans fill out the traditional cuisine goals, and the lengthy list of creative cocktails, many of them gin-based or riffs on traditional English quaffs, seal the deal. Dining on the outdoor terrace, the ultimate choice to simulate the modern London lifestyle, only sweetens it.

7–8 Eccleston Yards, SW1. jonesfamilykitchen.co.uk. ✆ **020/3929-6000.** Mains £15–£40. Mon–Sat 11am–11:30pm, Sun noon–10pm, one-hour break daily from 3–4pm, last orders 1 hr. before closing. Tube: Victoria.

Inexpensive

Regency Café ♥♥♥ TRADITIONAL BRITISH/ DINER The mid-20th-century "caff" diner, once a staple of London life, is rapidly being swept into Formica heaven by trendy bistros. Among the few holdouts still doling out one of London's best English breakfasts all day is the 1940s Regency, a discount-Deco requiem to a lost age in yellowed white tiles and bolted-down plastic chairs. This isn't a gustatory treasure (the fryer is in heavy use, white bread heaped high, sausage a food group); it's an anthropological one. Big-value

Regency Café has been serving traditional English breakfasts since 1946.

food including £7 full breakfasts, £4 burgers, or homemade meat pie is prepared with lightning speed, and your order is jarringly bellowed so that you can come fetch it. London adores this place, and it was sold in 2025 to a new owner who told the press he aims to treat it like the city treasure it is. For another marvelous "caff," see E. Pellicci (p. 115).

17–19 Regency St., SW1. regencycafe.has.restaurant. ✆ **020/7821-6596.** Main courses £3–£8. Mon–Fri 7am–2:30pm and 4–7:15pm; Sat 7am–noon; closed Sun. Tube: Pimlico or Westminster.

THE SOUTH BANK & CITY

For a casual street-food meal, head behind the Southbank Centre for the Southbank Centre Food Market, a collection of changing food stalls cooking up curries, duck confit burgers, sausages, and other cheap and ready-to-eats. It runs Friday through Sunday, starting around noon and wrapping up by about 8pm (6pm Sunday).

If you're near St Paul's at lunchtime, St Mary Le Bow church operates a surprisingly elegant but inexpensive bistro (curries, roast meats, salad plates) in its crypt, **Café Below** (St Mary-le-Bow Church, Cheapside, WC2; www.cafebelow.co.uk; ✆ 020/7329-0789; Main dishes around £15; Tues–Thurs 7:30am–10am, Mon–Fri 11:30am–2:30pm; Tube; St Paul's)

Expensive

Restaurant Story ♥♥♥ MODERN BRITISH A meal here is hard to book and will take 3–4 hours, but this is how it might begin: Instead of handing

An edible candle of beef tallow and bone marrow is just one of the surprises at Restaurant Story.

TALL orders

London's skyscrapers are sprouting like bamboo, and with them, dining aeries. Top-floor restaurants are too sophisticated to bother with bottom-feeder grub—these places compete with terrific cuisine that's a pleasure to eat. The prices are higher because the views are. Reservations are suggested for all of them.

City Social *The scene:* The quintessential Special Occasion restaurant: ambience, style, exquisite plating by award-winning chef Jason Atherton, dizzying prices. *The view:* on the 24th floor among the City skyscrapers, with a clear view of the Shard and the Gherkin. It's also worth a trip for its bar. Tower 42, 25 Old Broad St., EC2. www.citysocial-london.com/. ✆ **020/7877-7703.** Mains £38–£85. Tues–Fri noon–2:30pm and 6pm–9:30pm; Sat 5–9:30pm. Tube: Liverpool Street.

Darwin Brasserie *The scene:* The atrium atop the "Walkie-Talkie", which welcomed its 10 millionth visit in 2023, is like an upscale mini-mall of evening pursuits, including thump-thump-thump beats at Sky Pod bar and a seafood place, **Fenchurch**. Our choice, Darwin, has an honest menu (lamb, chicken, pork, fish) on an elevated floor where some of the horizon may be obscured by the tower's drooping-eyelid roofline, but it's still pretty. (Soak in the panorama from elsewhere in the atrium after dinner.) *The view:* the Tower of London, the Thames, the Shard, and beyond. Sky Garden, 36th Floor, 20 Fenchurch St., EC3. skygarden.london/. ✆ **0333/772-0020.** Dinner main courses £17–£26. Mon–Tues noon–10pm; Wed–Thurs 9am–10pm; Fri–Sat 8:30am–10:30pm; Sun 8:30am–9:30pm. No cash. Reservations required. Tube: Monument or Bank.

Duck & Waffle *The scene:* All day and night—yes, it's 24 hours, and doubles as a skilled *cocktailerie*—it cycles through shared-plate menus that lean toward richness. *The view:* It's a little inland from the Thames, so the nearest views are of the Gherkin and the City. 40th Floor, 110

you a menu, your server lights a white taper on your table and begins serving you by that candlelight. A few courses in, as it burns down, comes the reveal: That candle was beef tallow and bone marrow that is now melted for dipping. You are actually amid a sensational parade of tricks of the tongue and deliberate gastronomic *trompe l'oeil*. The dramatic and whimsical flourishes are by chef talent Tom Sellers, who has been pelted with so many awards he practically has to collect them with a rake. Everyone receives a tasting menu formulated out of English ingredients and inspired by memories and moments from Sellers' upbringing. It sounds pretentious, and it's expensive, but it's also a gustatory event that continues to garner plaudits since its 2013 debut, and if you care about fine food it's one of the most sensational nights you may ever spend in a restaurant.

199 Tooley St., SE1. www.restaurantstory.co.uk. ✆ **020/7183-2117.** 8 courses £275. Mon 6:30–11pm; Tues–Sat noon–5pm and 6:30–11pm; in Dec, also Sun 6–11pm. Reservations essential. Tube: London Bridge or Bermondsey.

Moderate

Padella ♥♥♥ ITALIAN Eaters go wild for its succulent and savory pasta dishes—there's always a line curling out the front door into this one-room fishbowl alongside Borough Market. Once you're in, you mount a stool at a counter (facing the cooks is best, but it'll be too busy for you to be choosy)

Bishopsgate, EC2. www.duckandwaffle.com/london. ✆ **020/3640-7310.** Sharing plates £12–£50. Open 24 hrs. Tube: Liverpool Street.

Gong *The scene:* Take cocktails, small bites, and sashimi on the 52nd floor of the Shard in this tight little bar, and London's highest, atop the Shangri-La Hotel (p. 67). *The view:* sweeping eastern panorama from Southwark, including London Bridge Station, the Tower of London, and Tower Bridge. 35th floor, The Shard, 32 London Bridge St., SE1. www.gong-shangri-la.com. ✆ **020/7234-8208.** Small plates £8–£25, platters £35–£45. Mon–Tues 4pm–12:30am; Weds–Sun noon–1am. Tube: London Bridge.

The Oxo Tower *The scene:* Behold, a gratitude-inducing panorama over the Thames from an Art Deco landmark which, like Tate Modern, was once a power station. The associated bar, casual brasserie, and restaurant (pick one) are favorites for celebrating special occasions. *The view:* St Paul's and the City from South Bank, not too high up. 22 Barge House St., SE1. www.oxotowerrestaurant.com. ✆ **020/7803-3888.** Bar bites 6–£14; Brasserie mains £26–£40; Restaurant mains £29–£52. Sun–Fri noon–9:30pm, Sat noon–10pm. Reservations essential (none available Sat. at Bar). Tube: Blackfriars or Waterloo.

Searcys Helix Restaurant at The Gherkin *The scene:* Very James Bond. You provide ID, clear security, and ride a few lifts in The Gherkin to arrive at a former member's club duplex with floor-to-ceiling glass—a view forbidden to the public until 2018. The food is the freshest English fare, the wines immaculately chosen. *The view:* slowly being swallowed by a building boom. 39th floor, The Gherkin, 30 St Mary Axe, EC3. searcysatthegherkin.co.uk. ✆ **0330/107-0816.** 2 courses £49; 3 courses £57. Mon–Sat noon–2pm and 6–9pm; Sun 10am–4pm. Dress code: no sportswear. Tube: Liverpool Street.

and get busy delighting yourself from a brief list of small-plate superstars like creamy gnocchi with nutmeg butter, *pici cacio e pepe* (cheese-and-pepper pici noodles), and pappardelle with a ragù of 8-hour Dexter beef shin from Ireland, plus a few tap wines and beers. You'll be happier with two plates than with just one. For the best shot at quick seating, try daily around 9pm or Sundays before opening, or use the Dojo app to queue virtually. There's a just-as-busy but larger location at 1 Phipp St., EC2, in Shoreditch (Tube: Old Street).

6 Southwark St., SE1. www.padella.co. No public phone. Plates £10–£17. Mon–Sat lunch 11:30am–3:45pm; Mon–Weds dinner 5–10pm, Thurs–Sat dinner 5–10:30pm, Sun 11:30am–3:45pm and 5–9pm. Tube: London Bridge.

Inexpensive

Boro Bistro ♥♥ FRENCH/ALGERIAN If the aimlessly gawping hordes at Borough Market exhaust you, a relaxing chill-out spot can be found very near the grounds. Downstairs in the brick vaults between the Market and Borough High Street just east of Southwark Cathedral, this European-with-a-pubby-twist bistro is many visitors' fast favorite for Romanesque atmosphere. Lit by candles that have accumulated wax over countless nights, you dine at funky, weather-beaten wood tables on cocktails, wines, and craft beers; charcuterie platters (Corsican coppa, baked Camembert); burgers (the house version is draped with Comté cheese); and odds-and-ends alternatives (croque monsieur, spicy Parmesan chicken wings, orange salad with mint and red onion). In nice weather, the terrace is ideal for a drink, and in cold weather, there are heaters and fleece blankets.

Borough Market ♥♥♥ INTERNATIONAL There has been a market on this very spot since the 1100s. Welcome to its story. Countless visitors cite Borough Market as a highlight of their London vacations. This extremely popular indoor/outdoor complex beneath a railway viaduct, an outgrowth of a centuries-old commercial market, is alive with glorious, farm-fresh flavors, much of which is rendered as finished small dishes. A small city of vendors in **Three Crown Square** sells their country meats, cheeses, and vegetables beneath an ancient metal-and-glass canopy, fresh-cooked specialties fill the outdoor **Borough Market Kitchen** across Middle Road and spill beyond, and the **Green Market** across Bedale Street tends toward boutique items. The market is truly at its best Thursday through Saturday, when more than 100 additional traders unpack and the awe-inspiring scene hits its swing. The least crowded time is Thursday between 11am and noon or in the wind-down around 3pm; Saturdays are shoulder-to-shoulder. Most dishes are around £8 to £15—but you'll want several, and you'll keep spotting people eating things you want to try next. In peak hours, you'll probably have to eat standing up. Some don't-miss stops (you'll find more of your own):

- The **Black Pig** (www.theblackpigsandwiches.co.uk/), feeds a clamoring queue waiting for The Best One, divine roast pork sandwiches with truffle parm mayo, fennel apple slaw, pepperoncini, and aged parmesan shavings
- The **Brindisa Grill** booth (www.brindisa.com), facing Stoney Street, was an early staple at the Market for its grilled chorizo sandwich with oil-drizzled pequillo peppers from Spain.

Brick Lane: 24-Hour Playground

Brick Lane, named for its medieval status as a source for bricks, was once a Jewish area but has become so strongly identified with immigrants from the Indian subcontinent that its name has transcended geography to become a shorthand term for England's South Asian population. In the span of just a few blocks, most of which have signage in both English and Bengali, lines of Indian restaurants jockey for business. No discerning Londoner would claim that any serve the city's best Indian cuisine, and most of them are in fact run by Bangladeshi or Pakistani entrepreneurs catering to a milder English notion of northern curries. (If you want something more modernized, try **Gunpowder** (gunpowderrestaurants.com), a block west on Commercial Road at White's Row.) But it's nonetheless a fun place to leverage competition and sit down for a bargain meal in a happening hood. Bring your own wine, though, because many don't sell alcohol for cultural reasons. By day, the connecting Dray Walk is a short block of sophisticated boutiques and laid-back cafes. On weekends, it hosts blocks upon blocks of markets for vintage clothes, books, a food hall of world cuisines, and art—Sundays are good for hours of browsing and noshing (www.sundayupmarket.co.uk).

- In season, the **Turnips** under the railway churns out cups of fresh strawberries bathed in a fondue of warm milk chocolate; videos became the viral social media sensation that caused stomachs to grumble planetwide.
- Sample never-exported cheeses like melt-in-your-mouth **Bath soft cheese** (www.parkfarm.co.uk).
- **Shellseekers,** the fishmonger by the door to Roast, is known for hand-dived Dorset scallop, served in its own shell and topped with a bacon and sprout stir-fry; a bathtub-big pot of paella bubbles at its neighbor **Bomba.**
- **Roast** (www.roast-restaurant.com; mains £20–£40), which runs an expensive restaurant upstairs, has a stall for rich meats such as roast pork belly with crackling, or Bramley applesauce and beef with horseradish cream.
- **Brindisa Grill** booth (www.brindisa.com), facing Stoney Street, feeds a steady line of punters its grilled chorizo sandwich with oil-drizzled pequillo peppers from Spain.
- **The London Cider House**, tucked into a side space, offers a changing roster of (strong) British ciders on tap and a few stools to escape the crowds.
- **Humble Crumble**, among the Market Kitchen stalls near Winchester Walk, sells crumbles with and fresh hot custard in cups so overflowing they're served on a tray.
- Outside on Stoney and Park streets, by the well-stocked Market Porter pub (p. 125) and casual sit-down restaurant **Elliot's,** are more finds: **Kappacasein** dairy from Bermondsey (www.kappacasein.com), which melts great wheels of Ogleshield cheese into decadent *raclette*; **Monmouth Coffee Company** (www.monmouthcoffee.com), for 40 years one of London's most revered roasters, which sends tasters around the world to monitor the single-source growers of its beans (it no longer uses disposable paper, so bring your own cup or they'll rent you one); and **Neal's Yard Dairy** (www.nealsyarddairy.co.uk), the cream of the crop for English cheese, tended by clerks in caps and aprons.
- Amid it all, Bridget Jones lived above **The Globe Tavern** (8 Bedale St.) in her movies.
- There's a shop for souvenirs and cookbooks by vendors near the Southwark Street gate, and **Bedales** wine bar has a balcony overlooking the market floor.

It's best to explore on your own. Tours were popular, but overcrowding led management to crack down on them and on influencers. Food writer Celia Brooks leads one that's officially recommended by the Market (www.celiabrooks.com; 3 hrs.; £110), but other good ones are led by Eating London (£79; p. 228).

8 Southwark St., SE1. www.boroughmarket.org.uk. ✆ **020/7407-1002.** Tues–Fri 10am–5pm; Sat 9am–5pm, Sun 10am–4pm, closed Mon. Many vendors do not accept cash. Tube: London Bridge.

Emilia's Crafted Pasta ♥♥ ITALIAN There's not much good to eat around the Tower of London, so this marvel is most welcome. Just east over the approach to Tower Bridge is an atmospheric maritime enclave known as St Katharine Docks, dug by hand for cargo boats in the 1820s. Under cast-iron columns in a former goods vault, this speedy-service open kitchen makes succulent and indulgent pasta fresh daily with no preservatives. It's easy to love the truffled cacio e pepe, pancetta carbonara, green beans bathed in creamy green pesto, and ethereal tiramisu. Emilia's is ultra-casual but tiny (just a few tables that spill onto the waterfront in good weather, plus six bar seats), so make a booking in advance for your Tower trip. Its neighbors on the Docks include some other worthwhile cafes and premium coffee shops. Another useful location is a 5-minute walk southeast from Buckingham Palace (56 Victoria St., SW11; ✆ **020/3949-2777;** Tube: Victoria), and a third is near Madame Tussauds at 215 Baker Street, NW1; ✆ **020/3340-0694;** Tube: Baker Street).

Unit C3, Ivory House, St Katharine Docks, E1. www.emiliaspasta.com. ✆ **020/7481-2004.** Main courses £12–£17. Sun–Thurs noon–9:30pm; Fri–Sat noon–10pm. Reservations recommended. Tube: Tower Hill or Tower Gateway DLR.

OKAN South Bank ♥ JAPANESE In the tourist thicket around the London Eye and Westminster, you'll be grateful for an affordable lunch option that isn't pre-fab sandwiches or fried chips. Squeezed into a lobby space on the east side of County Hall (the opposite side from the London Eye booking hall) and fitting no more than 25 including 6 at a grill-facing counter, OKAN (slang for "mom" in Osaka) serves up hearty non-sushi Japanese that'll fuel you for more touring, including onigiri savory rice cakes, gyoza dumplings, fried noodles, donburi meat-and-rice bowls, teppanyaki, and the Osakan street-food delight *okonomiyaki*, an umami bomb of fried batter, vegetables, and stripes of a gorgeous Japanese mayo topping. It even serves simple, clean cocktails. A flavorful, non-touristy find hidden amid the heaviest tourist crush in town.

County Hall, Belvedere Rd., SE1. www.okanlondon.com/okan/south-bank/. ✆ **07746/025-394.** Main dishes £10–£14. Daily 11am–10pm. No cash. Reservations recommended (max. 5). Tube: Waterloo.

EAST END

Much of the city's most exciting cooking for a fun night out has migrated to Shoreditch and Spitalfields, leaving Mayfair to cater to the trust-fund gourmets and Soho to feed the beery hordes.

Expensive

The Clove Club ♥♥ BRITISH You wouldn't be the first rhapsodize about a set meal at The Clove Club, where the steady procession of impeccable proteins is exceeded only by the average customer's amazement at just how they were so cleverly prepared

A chilled salad of grilled aubergine, brown crab, and verbena at The Clove Club.

and plated. Scotland-born Chef Isaac McHale has pocketed many culinary stars for his gift for melding the fine details of complementary flavors, which he does with overlooked ingredients from his home isles, including smoked trout, venison, pork jowl, Scottish teal (duck), monkfish, and granita made from offbeat produce like fennel or grilled habanero. The plates keep coming in generous multitudes, but the tidy service intuits the moments you need your space, which is as it should be at this price level. The setting in the former Town Hall of Shoreditch (high ceilings, blue-tiled open kitchen) serves to imbue the wild creativity of this dining event with a commissary-style energy. London peddles many splurges to big spenders, but this one ranks as worth it.

Shoreditch Town Hall, 380 Old St., EC1. www.thecloveclub.com. ✆ **020/7729-6496.** Set menus £195. Tues–Sat noon–2:15pm and 6–9pm. Reservations recommended. Tube: Old Street or Shoreditch High Street.

Moderate

Ottolenghi ♥ MEDITERRANEAN Chef Yotam Ottolenghi, known for TV appearances, a food column in the papers, and popular books, runs a few casual spots to pick up his celebrated Middle East-inflected concoctions that lean on clean and sometimes surprising ingredient clashes like roasted cauliflower with mustard, cherry tomatoes and crispy capers or lamb kofta with caramelized black lime onions. It's higher-priced than most casual meals, but the flavor combinations are bright, succulent, and memorable, and you may very well be seduced into buying one of his cookbooks. This spot, hidden down a network of centuries-old narrow lanes south of Spitalfields Market, is the largest location; the Marylebone outpost (63–65 Marylebone Lane, W1; Tube: Bond Street) is a 10-minute stroll up from Oxford Street and geared more for take-aways.

50 Artillery Lane, E1. ottolenghi.co.uk/. ✆ **020/7257-1999.** Salads £20–£24, main dishes £24–£27. Mon–Sat 9–11:45am, noon–2:45pm, and 5:30–10:30pm, Sun 9–11:45am and noon–3:45pm. Tube: Liverpool Street

Rochelle Canteen ♥♥ BRITISH A sublime secret is hidden away, discovered only if you ring a doorbell beside a green door in a brick wall. You'll pass through the grassy yard of an 1880s school, and in the old bike shed, join a daytime garden party. The changing menu is rigorously British and fresh, yet without flourish: green pea soup, roast sirloin, leek and Wigmore cheese tart, fish-and-chips, chicken and wild garlic pie. Your companions will be high-functioning artists, designers, and professionals, many of whom now lease space in the former school, plus the occasional kid, if they behave as well as a Victorian child. In fine weather, it's easier to find a seat because dining spills outdoors, the better to enjoy jugs of rhubarb and ginger fizz.

Rochelle School, Arnold Circus, E2. www.rochelleschool.org. ✆ **020/7729-5677.** Main courses £15–£29. Lunch: Daily noon–2:45pm; dinner: Weds–Sat 6–7:30pm; closing changes seasonally. Reservations recommended. Tube: Shoreditch High Street.

St John Bread and Wine ♥♥ TRADITIONAL BRITISH Hand in hand with the gastropub trend is "nose-to-tail" eating. That's a polite way to say you'll be eating various animal body parts, resulting in tastes that are commonplace among English farmers (heart, cockscomb, marrow, whole pigeon) but perhaps daring for most North American tongues. Gross or not, St. John has reached institution status. Most places charge, um, an arm and a leg for this style of high-quality cooking, but you can sample it at this lower-priced offshoot of the influential St John restaurant (still running at 26 St. John St. in Smithfield), which in the 1990s revitalized British cooking in a big way. Walls are simple white, chairs are plain wood, the menu is posted afresh daily, and the kitchen staff is serious. Experience dishes like cold lamb with chicory and anchovy, smoked sprat (sardines) with horseradish, venison mince, and lamb's liver with mash. A meal here can be an adventure—ever eaten dandelion?

94–96 Commercial St., E1. stjohnrestaurant.com. ✆ **020/7251-0848.** Main courses £15–£40. Daily noon–3pm and 6–9:30pm. Reservations recommended. Tube: Aldgate East or Shoreditch High Street.

Inexpensive

Beigel Bake ♥♥♥ BAKERY The city's most famous take-away bakery, Jewish or otherwise, never closes but there's often a line hustling through. Watch the clerks, who are all business, slice juicy chunks of pink salt beef in the window, then slather it onto a beigel with pickle slices and some nostril-clearing mustard: It's an attraction unto itself, and a must-have meal for many devotées, rich or poor. The queue moves quickly even if time doesn't—the phone number on the sign out front still posts an area code that hasn't been active since 2000. The patronage is a microcosm of London, ranging from bikers to hipsters to arrogant yuppies to people just scraping by. Its beigels (*bi*-gulls) are more glutinous than the New York "bagel" variety. Its pastries

Savory beigels with salted beef, gherkin, and mustard at Beigel Bake.

Freshly prepared fish and chips at Poppies.

are gorgeous, too: The chocolatey fudge brownie could be nursed for hours but give you a grin for a lifetime.

159 Brick Lane, E1. bricklanebeigel.co.uk/. ✆ **020/7729-0616.** Most items around £2–3. Daily 24 hr. Tube: Shoreditch High Street.

E. Pellicci ♥♥♥ TRADITIONAL BRITISH London's tradition of mid-20th-century diners, or "caffs," is quickly being gentrified into nostalgia, but this fry-up on deeply authentic and unflashy Bethnal Green Road has been run by the same affable family since 1900. Some of them were born upstairs, and Maria Pellicci, matriarch of the family, has commanded the kitchen since 1966. The Deco interior, a greasy spoon fantasia of sunburst icons, chrome, and primrose, was carved by a regular in 1946 and is now protected by law. You may be boisterously welcomed with open arms and you'll spend a happy meal sharing a table with locals ("Where are you from?" "Looks like rain tomorrow"), sipping the best cuppa tea you ever had. In 2025, 85-year-old Maria was awarded one of Italy's highest honors for promoting friendship between Italy and the community. There's no more iconic "caff" in town, and certainly none happier.

332 Bethnal Green Rd., E2. epellicci.co.uk. ✆ **020/7739-4873.** Main courses £7–£17. Mon–Sat 8am–3pm. Tube: Shoreditch High Street or Bethnal Green.

Poppies ♥♥ SEAFOOD Big crispy portions flopping on big oval plates eaten with a big knife and fork to big 1950s sock-hop music: The franchise-ready Poppies does for British fish-and-chips what peppy jukebox diners have done for mid-20th-century American food. For all its plastic theatricality, it hews to authenticity: The chief dish, cooked to order, is sustainably caught and sourced. For those whose palates swerve differently, there's also chicken, the chance to try jellied eels (be afraid), wine, and strong drinks. Try the Soho

THE "MEAL DEAL": sandwiches

You'll go all day without crossing paths with a bobby or a Cockney, but you can't walk a block in London without passing a sandwich—everyone eats them, and they're the best way to save money on food. The cheapest ones are what I call **triangle sandwiches,** which are ready-made, sliced diagonally, and sealed into triangular containers. They are made fresh every day by the million, and even supermarkets like **Tesco** and **Sainsbury's** sell them in **Meal Deal** packages that come with a bag of crisps and a drink for a set cost less than £7.

A few ubiquitous chains in the triangle sandwich trade:

- **Gregg's** (www.greggs.co.uk): Its sandwiches are average in every way, but it also does hot meat pies. Some feel its sausage roll belongs on the national flag.
- **Marks & Spencer** (www.marksandspencer.com): Lots of cheap stuff, well done, and around dinnertime, markdowns up to 50%.
- **Pret,** a.k.a. Pret A Manger (www.pret.com): Ubiquitous chain with clever flavors, with gourmet fixings in snazzy combination. Pronounced *prett ah mahn-zjerr.*

location (55 Old Compton St., W1; ✆ **020/7734-4845;** same hours) for strolling the West End with chips.

6–8 Hanbury St., E1. www.poppiesfishandchips.co.uk. ✆ **020/7247-0892.** Main courses £12–£25. Sun–Wed 11am–10pm; Thurs–Sat 11am–11pm. Tube: Shoreditch High Street or Liverpool Street.

Tayyabs ♥ INDIAN Tayyabs, contemporary and brightly lit, is a London institution that has reliably served the Bangladesh-born residents and workers at The Royal London Hospital in Whitechapel since 1972. As soon as you sit down, old-school waiters automatically put pappadams on your table—they're fresh and good, but you'll be charged—and keep the water flowing from metal pitchers. Wednesdays, delicious pan-fried shami kebab is served, and the peshwari naan, served all the time, is the best I've had, but overall, I find Tayyab's flavors timid, a sign it aims to please the widest palates possible. Still, the reverence for Tayyabs (it even has merch and a counter for takeaway sweets) held by East Londoners prove it has value for potent comfort food. They get you in and out in no time.

83–89 Fieldgate St. E1. www.tayyabs.co.uk. ✆ **020/7247-9543.** Dishes £13–£27. Daily noon–11:30pm. Tube: Whitechapel

16+ AMAZING FOOD HALLS

Food halls have quickly blossomed as a market response to the over-gentrification of London's center city and the exclusion of budget-priced diners by high rents and taxes. In the past few years, London has suddenly grown new and vibrant communities of multiple vendors cooking specialized food to order for less than £15 a plate, usually inside disused buildings such as deconsecrated churches and failed department stores. You'll find at least one food hall option near most neighborhoods in the center of town—and some of them serve food later than many standard restaurants and pubs do, making them suited to post-theatre noshes.

Just as food courts at the mall served the masses 40 years ago, London's modern food halls attract people from all walks of life looking for affordable sustenance in a social setting—only now, the ingredients are of the best quality, recipes honor international cuisine traditions, and cocktails are served as part of the fun. Pretty much every working Londoner makes food halls part of their social routine; these places can be so jammed at mealtimes that you're bound to share a table with new friends. Aside from buying grim pre-packaged sandwiches from a corporate chain, working Londoners now power their affordable eating lives with food halls. And it makes sense—markets have played an integral role in English culture since before its history was recorded.

Arcade ♥ Arcade, which feels more like the lobby of a nice office building than a food court, presents food and cocktails from 6 or so from skilled vendors. Its central cocktail bar is elegant, which is why this place gets too rammed with bodies to be truly pleasurable during peak mealtimes. It has a second, less frenetic location at Battersea Power Station. 103–105 New Oxford St., WC1; www.arcadefoodhall.com; Mon–Sat 11:30pm–11pm, Sun 11:30am–9pm; Tube: Tottenham Court Road.

Borough Market ♥♥♥ The king of foodie meccas; the one all the others wish they were. See p. 110. Tube: London Bridge.

Boxhall City ♥ Geared to young professionals: 14 kitchens led by chefs pinned with high hopes, plus guest chefs and pop-ups, in a historic arcade space with added cocktail bars and DJs by evening. 1–27, The Arcade, Liverpool Street, EC2. www.boxhall.co.uk. Mon–Sat 7am–midnight, Sun 7am–10pm. Tube: Liverpool Street.

Camden Markets ♥♥ The down-market choice—mostly cheap and simple, like noodles and pizza—but bountiful. It's mostly outdoors. Star attractions: **Yorkshire Burrito** (yorkshireburrito.com), which packs the flavors of a Sunday roast in a wrap made of Yorkshire pudding, and **The Cheese Wheel** (www.cheesewheellondon.com; daily 11am–6pm) at Kerb Camden Market, where hand-rolled tagliatelle is tossed in a bowl made of a huge truckle of melting Parmesan. See p. 258. camdenmarket.com; Food stalls daily 11:30am–9pm; Tube: Camden Town.

Eataly ♥♥ Catered to an epicurian level of quality, this 42,000-square foot Italian eater's paradise feels especially sophisticated. In addition to a market that sells some the finest European meats and cheeses, you'll find about 10 lounges and counters serving everything from wood-fired pizza to pasta to a bruschetta-and-cocktails concept. 135 Bishopsgate, EC2. www.eataly.co.uk. Market: Mon–Fri 7am–11pm, Sat 9am–11pm, Sun 9am–10pm; last entry 1 hr. before closing. Tube: Liverpool Street.

Take a grand tour of Italian cuisine at Eataly.

Flat Iron Square ♥ A stone's throw from Borough Market, this small (a handful of vendors) but reliable spot (under brick arches and with a yard) is good for grubby pubby fare like fried chicken, barbecue, taproom beers. 45 Southwark St., SE1. www.flatironsquare.co.uk. Tues–Sat noon–11pm; Sun noon–8pm. Closed Mon. Tube: London Bridge.

Maltby Street Market ♥♥♥ Purveying gorgeous flavors such as "bad brownies" oozing salted caramel, duck confit over perfect fries, gooey grilled cheese toasties, and Ethiopian, Maltby's offerings are partly outdoors, partly in railway viaduct vaults, and suited to those with brunchy inclinations. Follow the railway vaults in either direction for more goodies, because they've become an ideal hive for London's brewery taproom scene, nicknamed the Bermondsey Beer Mile. Maltby St., SE1. www.maltby.st. ✆ **020/7394-8061.** Fri 5:30–9pm, Sat 10am–5pm; Sun 11am–4pm. Tube: London Bridge or Bermondsey.

Duck confit over fries is among the comfort foods on offer at Maltby Street Market.

Market Hall Victoria ♥♥ Some 8 restaurants (many open for breakfast), bars, and seating for 300 in an Edwardian baroque shopping arcade vacated by a nightclub. Don't miss the rooftop bar. Terminus Place, 191 Victoria St., SW1. www.markethalls.co.uk. Sun–Tues 8am–10pm; Wed–Sat 8am–11pm. Tube: Victoria.

Market Hall Oxford Street ♥ A onetime BHS department store off Oxford Street is now a cavernous food court, with 9 food stalls, 2 bars, a terrace with a retractable roof, live DJs in the evening, and—just to raise the game—proper forks, knives, and glassware. 9 Holles St., W1. www.markethalls.co.uk. Mon–Tues 11am–10pm; Wed–Sat 11am–11pm; Sun 11am–8pm. Tube: Oxford Circus.

Market Place Leicester Square ♥ Just opened in 2025: Sixteen vendors, three bars, and a comedy club. The same outfit also runs a food hall north of St Paul Cathedral's (9 vendors and 2 bars; 150 Cheapside, EC2; Tube: St Paul's) 21–21 Leicester Square, EC2. www.marketplacefoodhall.com. Tube: Leicester Square.

London Day for a Guinness

Guinness is Irish, but that didn't stop the brand from opening a new three-level, tourist-targeted **Guinness Open Gate Brewery** attraction (1 Mercer Walk, WC2; opengatelondon.guinness.com/) in December 2025. No, it doesn't brew its famous stout here—that's still made in Dublin—but the five-building complex between Mercer Street and Langley Street north of Covent Garden has historic roots as a brewery, so that's what the company is calling it. Mostly, this is a place for the tourist throng to drink, eat upscale food at two chef-led restaurants, down meat pies at its walk-in bar, learn how to pull a proper pint of it (it takes about 2 minutes to pour, in two stages), tour a showpiece micro-brewery, and most importantly, buy exclusive merch. For that, entry costs £30–£95, depending on the of day—the price is so high we feel you need to know they don't actually make Guinness here. My goodness!

Learn how to pull a proper pint at the Guinness Open Gate Brewery.

Mercato Mayfair ♥♥♥ To soothe your Oxford Street shopping breaks, the group behind the original Merato Metropolitano (see below) took over the Neo-Classical St Mark's church from the 1820s—sanctuary, balconies, and all, with wine and cheese now served in the crypt and an outdoor drinking terrace on the roof where worshipers once directed their prayers. With more than a dozen hot food vendors amid the stained glass and gilt altar, it's dazzling. If you can't go for a full meal, at least grab a cocktail on the balcony for the photo. Oddly, door staff confiscates all water bottles when you enter. North Audley Street, W1. mercatometropolitano.com. ✆ **020/7403-0930.** Mon–Thurs 8:30am–11pm; Fri–Sat 8:30am–midnight; Sun 8:30am–10pm. Tube: Bond Street.

Mercato Metropolitano ♥ Dedicated to small producers and emerging chefs, this former factory space was a smash from its 2016 opening, kicking off London's food hall craze, but it's slated to be replaced by the Borough Triangle development and only 12 of the original 40 vendors will remain during construction. The one that started it all is just a footnote now. 42 Newington Causeway, SE1. mercatometropolitano.com. ✆ **020/7403-0930.** Mon–Weds noon–11pm; Thurs noon-midnight, Fri noon–1am; Sat 11am–1am; Sun 11am–10pm. Tube: Elephant & Castle.

Seven Dials Market ♥♥ A 5-minute walk north of Covent Garden, this thriving multi-level hub wows palates in a complex of Victorian warehouses once used for bananas and cucumbers. Of the two bars and 20-odd vendors, do not miss **Pick & Cheese** (reservations recommended via www.thecheesebar.com), where cheese delicacies seduce gourmands from a slow-moving conveyor belt the way sushi does. 35 Earlham St., WC2. www.sevendialsmarket.com. Mon–Tues noon–10pm; Wed–Sat 11am–11pm; Sun 11am–9pm. Tube: Covent Garden or Leicester Square.

Southbank Centre Food Market ♥ This *al fresco* choice only sets up from Friday to Sunday, but that's perfect for weekend strolls by the Thames. It's also steps from the London Eye, BFI, and National Theatre. Eat Korean barbecue, saucy chicken katsu, Thai, curries, vegan Ethiopian, and more. Behind the Royal Festival Hall, SE1. www.southbankcentre.co.uk. Fri noon–8pm; Sat 11am–8pm; Sun noon–6pm. Tube: Waterloo or Embankment.

Spitalfields Market ♥♥ Street food, food trucks, and proper casual restaurants alongside the art-and-clothing Traders' Market in a Victorian-era structure that's also close to the vintage clothing markets of Brick Lane. 65 Brushfield St., E1. www.spitalfields.co.uk. ✆ **020/7377-1496.** Mon–Sat 10am–9:30pm; Sun 10am–5pm. Tube: Liverpool Street.

From gourmet pizza to food truck fare, the varied offerings at Spitalfields Market can satisfy most tastes and budgets.

Vinegar Yard ♥ Under the gleaming monolith of the Shard, Vinegar Yard is a friendly mix of top-level street food, local beers, art installations, and pop-up shops. There's a covered area for poor weather, and on weekends it adds a flea market. Last orders at 9pm. 72–82 St Thomas St., SE1. www.vinegaryard.london. Weds–Fri 5–10pm; Sun noon–8pm., last orders 1 hr. before closing Tube: London Bridge.

22 PUBS YOU'LL LOVE

Pubs are the beating heart of British life, as they have been for centuries. Your neighborhood hangout is called your "local," but many of the oldest premises have been so well-loved (or so well-bombed) that their original features are gone. Most are now company-owned and depressingly standardized, having stripped out ceilings and carpeting to expose ductwork and wood in a feeble attempt to look "modern." The situation for pub heritage is so dire that you will sometimes hear Londoners curse Wetherspoon, a cheap and low-class pub chain, the same way they might spit out the name of Beelzebub.

The following pubs, however, should do you right. All of them serve food of some kind (burgers, meat pies, and the like—but most take last food orders by 8:30pm) for at least part of the day; you usually order at the bar, where you receive a numbered tag for your table so that servers can find you.

Pubs in this city commonly charge around £7 for a pint of the favored serving size—about 20 American ounces—and the ABV percentage tends to be strong. A good cask ale is a specialty you must try while you're in England. Cask ale is not refrigerated because it's stored in the cellar, where the temperature is right for the fermentation process to continue until the drink hits your glass. Cask ale is drawn using stiff hand-pumped taps, and it only stays fresh for a short time, like bread or pastry—so don't be surprised if the one you select has already run out. To find pubs that persevere in the dying art of pouring old-fashioned cask ales, visit the **Campaign for Real Ale** (www.camra.org.uk). Basic mixed drinks like gin and tonic ("G&T") are also served, but mixers are charged extra, and don't expect a generous pour because measures are standardized—for true cocktail bars run by seriously skilled experts, see the list on p. 288. Pubs have bottled beer and cider, too. When the bell is rung, it's last call—as early as 11pm—and the landlord *will* turf you out.

The Anchor Bankside ♥♥ This Thames-side patio in sight of St Paul's dome is perhaps the most popular spot in London at which to sit on the water with a fresh-pulled pint. There's been a tavern here at least since the 1500s, when Londoners ferried to Southwark for bear baiting, gardens, brothels, and Shakespeare (the playwright surely would have known the place). Diarist and royal confidant Samuel Pepys is said to have watched London burn to the ground from the safety of this shore in 1666. The industrial Anchor brewery that subsumed it for 200 years was cleared away in the 1980s, and a spacious (but always crowded) riverside terrace was added. Beer snobs kvetch that it's become a tourist draw, particularly in fine weather, but that's all right with me;

pubs have always been hangouts for the hoi polloi, and few of them so perfectly meld abundant history with an enviable riverfront location.

34 Park St., SE1. www.greeneking-pubs.co.uk. ✆ **020/7407-1577.** Mon–Wed 11am–11pm; Thurs–Sun 11am–11:30pm; Sun noon–10:30pm; food served until 10pm (Mon-Sat), 9:30pm (Sun). Tube: London Bridge.

The Argyll Arms ♥♥ Having a beer in here can feel like drinking in a bejeweled red velvet box, thanks to the acid-etched glass screens that subdivide the busy bar into dignified drinking areas. Originally installed in 1895 to prevent brawls between the working and middle classes (at a time when even Underground rides were segregated), the screens somehow survived the 20th century. Drinks are £2 more than they should be, but it's one of the prettiest pubs in London, and its location southeast of Oxford Circus makes it an easy stop.

18 Argyll St., W1. www.nicholsonspubs.co.uk. ✆ **020/7734-6117.** Mon–Thurs 10am–11:30pm; Fri–Sat 10am–midnight; Sun 10am–11pm. Tube: Oxford Circus.

The Blackfriar ♥♥♥ Deservedly protected by landmark status, this 1904 Art Nouveau masterpiece (also spelled the Black Friar) is as jolly as the fat friars that bedeck it in bronze, wood, and glass. A short walk from St Paul's, it was once snuggled down a few dark alleys, but neighboring demolitions liberated it; now it's blessed with a noisy outdoor patio and walls of windows bathed in afternoon sunshine from over the Thames. The back saloon was designed for the upper classes, hence its exceptionally overbaked interior in marble and bronze; the undulating front bar, where pop music plays and pub crawls frequently pass through, is extraordinarily well-stocked with a range of cask ales and cider. Pricey food is shuttled from the upstairs kitchen via a hand-cranked dumbwaiter.

174 Queen Victoria St., EC4. www.nicholsonspubs.co.uk. ✆ **020/7236-5474.** Mon–Fri 10am–11pm; Sat 9am–11pm; Sun noon–10:30pm. Tube: Blackfriars.

The Coal Hole ♥ A onetime haunt of actor Edmund Kean, who drank himself to an early curtain, was rebuilt in 1904 in the Arts and Crafts style and is still a hangout for performers at the adjoining Savoy Theatre. Use the entrance in back, by the stage door, to access the clubbier lower level. The antique streetlamp in the lower passage off the Strand is a vestige of an experimental gaslight piping system that burned off sewage gases before the farty stink could overcome citizens. Bottoms up!

91–92 Strand, WC2. www.nicholsonspubs.co.uk/thecoalholestrandlondon. ✆ **020/7379-9883.** Sun–Wed 10am–11pm; Thurs 10am–11:30pm; Fri–Sat 10am–midnight. Tube: Charing Cross or Embankment.

The Devonshire ♥♥ So praised is its food that The Devonshire could just as easily have been a restaurant recommendation. Upstairs from the wood-paneled ground floor pub, a white-tablecloth grill-house restaurant reigns. Scottish beef, dry-aged and butchered on site, is served on a menu that prepares faultless, award winning, wood-fired proteins (mains £19–£50; restaurant bookings open at 10:30 am, 3 weeks ahead). But feats of meat aside, as

Pubgoers gather outside The Devonshire, which also offers fine dining on the upper floors.

a pub, this Piccadilly Circus modern success story basks in a distinction of its own—"The Dev" is said to dispense Guinness at a nitrogen-to-carbon dioxide ration closest to the bars in Ireland, which would make it Guinness pour more authentic than London's other pubs. Maybe that's why some 70% of its patrons order one, or so says *GQ*.

17 Denman St., W1. www.devonshiresoho.co.uk. Mon–Sat 11am–11pm; Sun 11am–10pm; restaurants seating starts 1 hr. after opening. Tube: Piccadilly Circus.

The George Inn ♥♥♥ Unquestionably one of the most important ancient pubs still standing, the George traces its lineage to at least 1542, when a map of Southwark first depicted it; the Tabard Inn, where Chaucer's pilgrims gathered in *Canterbury Tales,* was then a few doors south (it's gone now). Shakespeare knew it (check out Pete Brown's 2012 book *Shakespeare's Local*), and Dickens memorialized it in *Little Dorrit.* The oldest section, a galleried wood-and-brick longhouse, dates to 1677, built after a horrific fire swept the district. It later functioned as an 18th century transit hub, its courtyard encircled with a tavern, a hotel, stables, wagon repair bays, and warehouses; the rise of a railway nearly destroyed it, and only one side of the complex survives. (The National Trust now protects it.) Sip ale in the low-ceilinged timber-and plaster chambers, or sit in the cobbled courtyard, in the Shard's shadow, and soak up the fading echoes of history.

75–77 Borough High St., SE1. www.greeneking-pubs.co.uk ✆ **020/7407-2056.** Mon–Thurs 11am–11:30pm; Fri–Sat 11am–midnight; Sun noon–10:30pm; food until 10pm Mon–Sat, 9pm Sun. Tube: London Bridge.

Dating to the 1500s, The George Inn was once a stopover for long-distance carriage travelers.

The Grapes ♥♥ It's in every way a classic that is cherishable in that inimitable English way—Victorian wooden bar with stools, red carpeting, groaning plank floors, a blissful lack of clanging "fruit machines." That tiny back porch with a smashing riverfront panorama of a bend in the Thames and those stacks of board games waiting to be played all but waves a magic wand over it. If you find it all preposterously winsome, you wouldn't be alone—it's ridiculously narrow and jams at peak hours, but come at noon and it's a dream. Charles Dickens, who partied here, wrote about it in *Our Mutual Friend*, and the great actor Ian McKellen loved it so much (he lives nearby, so it's been his local for decades) that when it came up for sale, he and his ex-boyfriend teamed up to buy it and preserve it—look for the discreet sculpture of a wizard. Sir Ian is known to pull pints and host Monday's quiz night when he's not performing somewhere. In the toilets hang historic photos of long-gone people enjoying the same pub—you're now part of a long tradition.

76 Narrow St., E14. www.thegrapes.co.uk. ✆ **020/7987-4396.** Daily noon–11:30pm; food served until 9:30pm. Tube: Limehouse DLR or Westferry DLR.

The Grenadier ♥♥♥ They say this was the Duke of Wellington's local bar—his home, Apsley House (p. 167), is around the corner. It was also the unofficial clubhouse for his regiment, hence the battlefield artifacts on display; they also say someone was beaten to death here for cheating at cards, hence the routine ghost sightings. This plank-floored, currency-festooned pub/restaurant, tiny and pretty as a picture in a cobbled mews, comes off like a boozer in some upcountry village, with only 15 places at its pewter-topped island bar, but it's actually upscale for a pub—if you want to eat a Beef Wellington in the Duke of Wellington's actual favorite pub, it'll set you back £40, but beers are only a few quid more than usual. Once a haunt for servants of the surrounding townhouses, clientele these days can skews toward the rich and famous, who can seal off some of its coziest rooms with curtains.

18 Wilton Row, SW1. www.grenadierbelgravia.com. ✆ **07979/417-091.** Mon–Sat 11am–11:30pm; Sun noon–11:30pm; food served until 9:30pm. Tube: Hyde Park Corner.

The Lamb ♥ Quiet, not too touristy, with a small back garden in good weather, this east Bloomsbury choice (where Ted Hughes took Sylvia Plath on their early dates) is representative of a neighborhood local that still has some prime Victoriana from the old days. Check out the rare sunburst etched-glass snob screens obscuring the central bar, built so you don't have to look the help in the eye. Notice the polyphon in the corner—that's a musical metal disc that works like a music box and was the gramophone of a century ago. Floors are worn wood, the walls lined with sepia photographs of long-forgotten stage actresses, and the cask beers are out-of-the-ordinary enough to intrigue.

94 Lambs Conduit St., WC1. www.thelamblondon.com. ✆ **020/7405-0713.** Mon–Wed 11am–11pm; Thurs–Sun 11am–midnight; Sun noon–10:30pm; food served noon–9:30pm. Tube: Russell Square.

The Lamb and Flag ♥♥ Too tiny and thronged after work to supply much respite, it is nonetheless the epitome of a city pub, tucked down an atmospheric brick alley and blessed with an original fireplace. It has been known throughout the centuries as both the Coopers Arms and the Bucket of Blood (the latter because it hosted illegal prizefights in the early 1800s), and its building is said to be Tudor in origin. No one can prove it, because it was heavily rebuilt in the 1890s. You'll find the pub on a lane just east of the intersection of Floral and Garrick streets, near Covent Garden. But you probably won't find a place to sit unless you start drinking after lunch, which the regular patrons on its memorial wall surely did.

33 Rose St., WC2. www.lambandflagcoventgarden.co.uk. ✆ **020/7497-9504.** Mon–Sat 11am–11pm; Sun noon–10:30pm; food served until 9pm. Tube: Covent Garden or Leicester Square.

The Market Porter ♥ Amid the gastronomic mayhem of Borough Market, this lovely old timber-beamed boozer is a fine place to drink in any time of the week. In fact, more times than most pubs, because its location earned a special license to open at 6am when vendors are working. Sundays and off-hours are pleasant for sitting by a double-sided fire drinking one of its nine traditional ales (choices change) or eating upstairs—ingredients all come from the market. It can also act: It appeared as the Third Hand Book Emporium in the third Harry Potter film.

9 Stoney St., SE1. www.themarketporter.co.uk. ✆ **020/7407-2495.** Mon–Fri 6–8:30am and 11am–11pm; Sat noon–11pm; Sun noon–10:30pm; food served until 1 hr. before closing (until 5pm Sun). Tube: London Bridge.

The Marquis of Granby ♥ Amusingly, since the 1800s some pubs near the Houses of Parliament have been equipped with a "division bell," which rings—rather like a fire alarm—to warn socializing MPs they have only 8 minutes to scurry back to vote. The custom has been replaced by an app, which is disappointing. Other pubs that retain their division bells—St Stephens Tavern on Bridge Street across from Big Ben, the Red Lion on Whitehall—are cloyingly touristy, but not the Marquis. A single-room pub with bare floorboards and high wood walls, it's a hangout for government types (and their lobbyists) and prides itself on real hand-pumped ale.

41 Romney St., SW1. www.nicholsonspubs.co.uk. ✆ **020/7227-0941.** Mon–Fri noon–11pm; Sat noon–5:30pm. Tube: Westminster or Pimlico.

The Mayflower ♥ The story goes that in 1620, local resident and sea captain Christopher Jones was recruited by some dissenters, who boarded his ship the *Mayflower* alongside this pub (then it was the Shippe; the current building is from the 1700s) to set sail to Southampton and thence to the New World. It's hard to imagine, and otherwise it's a fairly traditional pub (oak beams, wood paneling) with real ales and a fire. Its extension dock over the Thames is a worthy place to raise a pint and survey your personal slice of the river on a summer day or for its popular Sunday roast (reserve ahead for that). Would the Pilgrims have called it a sin? Surely, but they were no fun.

117 Rotherhithe St., SW16. www.themayflowerrotherhithe.com. ✆ **020/7237-4088.** Mon–Sat 11am–11pm; Sun noon–10:30pm; food served until 10pm (Sun until 9pm). Tube: Rotherhithe.

The Old Brewery ♥♥ In 2010, a new microbrewery named Meantime took up residence in Sir Christopher Wren's palatial Old Royal Naval College (a stately UNESCO World Heritage site where the Paris scenes in 2012's *Les Misérables* were shot), which sits on the Thames in outlying Greenwich. It occupied the very brewery building that once furnished Napoleonic War veterans with their three daily pints. Now, the Old Brewery, run by respected British beermaker Young's, serves drinks on a large outdoor patio, and seasonal English fare inside. The beer selection isn't as rewarding as it once was, but on a sunny day, there are few places more dreamy for a pint in Maritime Greenwich (p. 32).

The Pepys Building, Old Royal Naval College, SE10. www.oldbrewerygreenwich.com. ✆ **020/3437-2222.** Mon–Sat 10am–11pm; Sun 10am–10:30pm; food served until 10pm. Tube: Cutty Sark DLR.

The Pride of Spitalfields ♥♥ Lovingly shabby, with a tired floral carpet and weary red upholstered banquettes, the backstreet boozer east of Brick Lane is the embodiment of a homey pub pulling pleasing pints. The upright piano is rarely played (recorded classic punk is preferred), the sewage system is finicky, the beer bottles are dusty, but the goings-on are lively and neighborly and the ale is real. Unlike in some neighborhood joints, they understand tourists, so if you're friendly, you'll have fun. Jack the Ripper suspect James Hardiman, a "cats meats vendor," drank here when it was called the Romford Arms. Your choice of victuals will be more mainstream; in the afternoon, you can get cheap salt beef for a few pounds.

3 Heneage St., E1. ✆ **020/7247-8933.** Mon–Tues and Thurs–Sat 11am–midnight; Wed 11am–11pm; Sun noon–10:30pm. Tube: Aldgate East.

The Princess Louise ♥♥♥ This Victorian fantasia just south of the British Museum is worth a visit even if you don't drink. Its lost-in-time feeling begins with the proud signage, a traditional marquee of gold lettering on black. The 1891 interior has been miraculously maintained in mint condition: Morris & Son etched glass, mirrors, mahogany privacy screens, cast-iron bar, Corinthian columns, Simpson & Son mosaic tile floor. Even the men's room marble urinals are legally protected from alteration. There's no music or TV, mobile phones are sternly discouraged, and all of the libations are by the resolutely old-fashioned Samuel Smith, which has been brewing since 1758 in Yorkshire and still draws its water from its original well.

208 High Holborn, WC1. ✆ **020/7405-8816.** Mon–Fri 11am–11pm; Sat noon–11pm; Sun noon–6:45pm; food served Mon–Thurs noon–2:30pm and 6–8:30pm, Fri noon–2:30pm. Tube: Holborn.

The Prospect of Whitby ♥♥ The oldest riverside pub in London has much to entice you: a pedigree that stretches back to 1520, during the reign of Henry VIII. A 400-year-old stone floor. A backstory that includes a seamy stretch as a den for river smugglers, thieves, bare-knuckle boxers, and cock fighters. The replica scaffold commemorating the hanging of infamous pirate

One of the oldest pubs on the Thames, The Prospect of Whitby dates back to 1520.

Captain Kidd beside the pub in 1701. A client list ranging from Charles Dickens (of course) to Richard Burton (of course), Princess Margaret (again, of course), and artists J. M. W. Turner and Whistler, who both captured the view from its confines. Not enough? If all of that doesn't convince you of its appeal, take note that it's fully reputable now, partly due to the popularity of its two creaky but spacious floors and its big side yard, where you can kick back with wide Thames views and great old-growth trees—look out for a replica scaffold that commemorates the many bankside executions that happened around here. Over weekends, it can get overly crowded, so to share the atmosphere with fewer souls, come on a weekday.

57 Wapping Wall, E1. www.greeneking-pubs.co.uk. ✆ **020/7481-1095.** Mon–Sat 11am–11pm; Sun noon–9pm; food served until 9pm. Tube: Shadwell DLR.

The Salisbury ♥ The Covent Garden/Leicester Square location is unbeatable, and the ornate exterior and interior are unmistakably Victorian—ostentatious, just-how-drunk-was-the-designer Victorian, to be precise. Thrill to the Grecian urns in the brilliant-cut glass, the pressed-copper tables, and the nymphs entwined in the bronze lamps. No wonder it was long a favored place for furtive meetings between gay men back when homosexuality was illegal, and then an actual gay pub when that archaic law was abolished. Now it's a haunt for all types of customers, including families but especially the city's theatrical community, and a suitable pit stop for any West End exploration. Fans of musicals should check out the cellar, which is papered with posters, many of them rare, from 1980s and '90s shows.

The ornate Victorian exterior of the Salisbury, a landmark pub near Covent Garden.

90 St Martin's Lane, WC2. www.greeneking-pubs.co.uk. ✆ **020/7836-5863.** Mon–Thurs 11am–11pm; Fri–Sat 11am–midnight; Sun 11am–10:30pm; food served until 10pm. Tube: Leicester Square.

Affable publicans at The Ten Bells, where Jack the Ripper's final victim drank her last pint.

The Ship & Shovell ♥♥ One of the most endearing configurations for any pub you'll ever see, it's cleft in two by an alley trod by commuters on their way to Charing Cross. On the north, there's a traditional Victorian-style space, and on the south, a cozier room with a languidly sloping floor and private snugs. A cellar corridor links the halves. The bewigged, tubby chap on the swinging sign is Admiral Cloudesley Shovell who, in 1707, wrecked his ship and drowned 800 sailors, which certainly gives the interior's nautical theme an ignoble context for drowning your own sorrows. It's special for another reason, too, being one of the few pubs in town to pour Badger Beers from Hall & Woodhouse, a Dorset brewer dating to 1777.

1–2 Craven Passage, WC2. www.shipandshovell.co.uk. ✆ **020/8391-1311.** Mon–Sat 11am–11pm; food served Mon–Fri noon–3:30pm, Sat noon–4pm. Tube: Charing Cross or Embankment.

The Ten Bells ♥ It's said that Annie Chapman, one of Jack the Ripper's victims, downed her last beer at this Spitalfields boozer, while another, Mary Kelly, picked up her clients outside. For an icky period in the 1970s, the pub capitalized on infamy by being renamed for their slayer. These days, the toilets are a bigger threat to health and safety than Jack the Ripper ever was. The pub's Victorian tilework has been restored, and now it's a busy waterhole where the clientele is young, the furniture casually mismatched, and the partying ever more intense as the evening advances. Nicholas Hawksmoor's Christ Church, which towers next door, silently observes the latest mortals at play.

84 Commercial St., E1. www.tenbells.com. ✆ **020/7247-7532.** Sun–Wed noon–midnight; Thurs–Sat noon–1am. Tube: Liverpool Street.

Ye Olde Cheshire Cheese ♥♥♥ Just the sort of rambling, low-ceilinged tavern you imagine London is full of (and was, once), it was built behind Fleet Street in the wake of the Great Fire in 1666; steady log fires and regularly strewn sawdust make it smell like it's still burning. In later generations, it played regular host to Dr. Samuel Johnson (who lived behind on Gough Square), Charles Dickens (who refers to it in *A Tale of Two Cities*), Yeats, Wilde, and Thackeray. You can get pretty well thackered yourself today: There are six drinking rooms, including a warren of cellar rooms that can feel particularly haunted and secluded, but the cozy front bar—of pallid light, candles in the fireplace, and antique paintings of dead fish—is the most magical. Observe the stuffed carcass of Polly the Parrot, enshrined above the bar since 1926: Her "adept use of profanity would have put any golfer to shame," according to her obituary in the *New York American*. ***Note:*** Don't confuse this place with the Victorian-era Cheshire Cheese pub at Temple.

Wine Office Ct., off 145 Fleet St., EC4; ye-olde-cheshire-cheese.co.uk. ✆ **020/7353-6170.** Mon–Sat 11am–11pm. Tube: Blackfriars, Temple, or Chancery Lane.

Ye Olde Mitre ♥♥♥ Suspended in a hidden courtyard and seemingly between centuries, this enchanter—no TVs, no music—was once part of a great palace mentioned by Shakespeare in *Richards II* and *III*. The medieval St Etheldreda's Chapel, its surviving place of worship, stands outside. This extremely tiny pub (established in 1546 but built in its present form in 1772) has two entrances that feed either side of the bar. The one on the left grants you access to "the Closet," a fine example of a semiprivate sitting area called a "snug"; the one on the right brings you face-to-face with a glass case containing a blackened stump said to be part of a cherry-tree maypole that Elizabeth I danced around. (Yeah, right, drink another one.) Suck down a house specialty: pickled or Scotch eggs. To find the pub, look for a little alley among the jewelry stores on Hatton Garden, between 8 and 9 Hatton Garden.

1 Ely Ct., off Ely Place, EC1. www.yeoldemitreholborn.co.uk. ✆ **020/7405-4751.** Mon–Fri noon–11pm. Tube: Farringdon or Chancery Lane.

EXPLORING LONDON

England was a top dog for 500 years, and London is where it kept its bark. Many of the world's finest treasures came here during the Empire and never left. Riches built this city. But the sheer abundance of accumulated wealth—layer upon layer of it—means that London boasts dozens of exciting smaller sights, too. You could spend a lifetime seeing it all, so you'd better get started.

The heavily promoted **London Pass** (https://londonpass.com) gets you into a bevy of attractions and a Golden Tours sightseeing bus for a fixed price (such as £89 a day or £124 for 2 days), but is unlikely to pay off in the small amount of time you're given to use it. The pass might say "one-day," but remember most attractions are only open for 8 hours of it. Only the version that lasts 6 days (£194 adult, £109 child, some discounts online) would potentially pay off, but still only *marginally* and only if you barely pause to eat.

Historic Royal Palaces operates Hampton Court (p. 211), Kensington Palace (p. 172), Kew Palace (p. 212), and the Tower of London (p. 192). An annual membership pass will possibly save you money if you plan to see several of them; do the math (www.hrp.org.uk; ✆ **0333/320-6000;** £60 one adult, £95 two adults, £75 for one adult plus up to six children, £115 two adults plus up to six children).

BLOOMSBURY, FITZROVIA & KING'S CROSS

In the same neighborhood, bear in mind **Queer Britain** (2 Granary Square, N1; https://queerbritain.org.uk; free admission; Wed–Sun noon–6pm; Tube: King's Cross St Pancras). This space, which is dedicated to the history of LGBTQ+ people, has no permanent collection on display, so whether you want to go will depend on whatever the temporary exhibition is.

The British Library ♥♥♥ MUSEUM One of the planet's most precious collections of books, maps, and manuscripts, the British Library holds approximately 170 million items and adds millions each year, so when it puts the cream (about 200 items) on display, you will be astounded. Until 2032, the library is undergoing a £1.1

Discounts Explained

Children's prices generally apply to those 15 and under. To qualify for a **senior discount** (often expressed as a **"concession"**), you usually must be 60 or older. **Students** require ID for discounts. Some places offer **Family Tickets** with discounts for up to three kids with adults.

Museums may also post prices that include a voluntary **"gift aid"** donation; British citizens get tax back for it but you don't, so no one will mind if you ask to have it removed.

In addition to closing on public holidays and on December 25 and 26 (Boxing Day), some heritage properties open only in the summer.

billion renovation, but its best attraction for visitors remains open: The **Treasures of the British Library,** at the Sir John Ritblat Gallery, displays priceless rarities in a cool, climate-controlled suite of black cases and rich purple carpeting. It ought to be mobbed, but isn't. The trove changes whenever something needs to be taken out of the light, but these artifacts have regularly been on view (other just-as-good things might be there when you go):

TOP DON'T-MISS EXHIBITS AT THE BRITISH LIBRARY

Delicate paper artifacts are frequently taken off display for preservation, but look for some of these holdings:

- Two of the four known copies of the **Magna Carta,** 800 years old in 2015
- The **Gutenberg Bible** from 1455
- The Beatles' first lyric doodles: "A Hard Day's Night" on Julian Lennon's first birthday card (with a choo-choo on it) and "Yesterday," which had the working title of "Scrambled Eggs"
- The **Diamond Sutra,** the oldest known printed book, which was found in a Chinese cave in 1907 and was probably made by woodblock nearly 600 years before Europeans developed similar technology

Sacred Texts on display in The British Library.

London-Wide Attractions

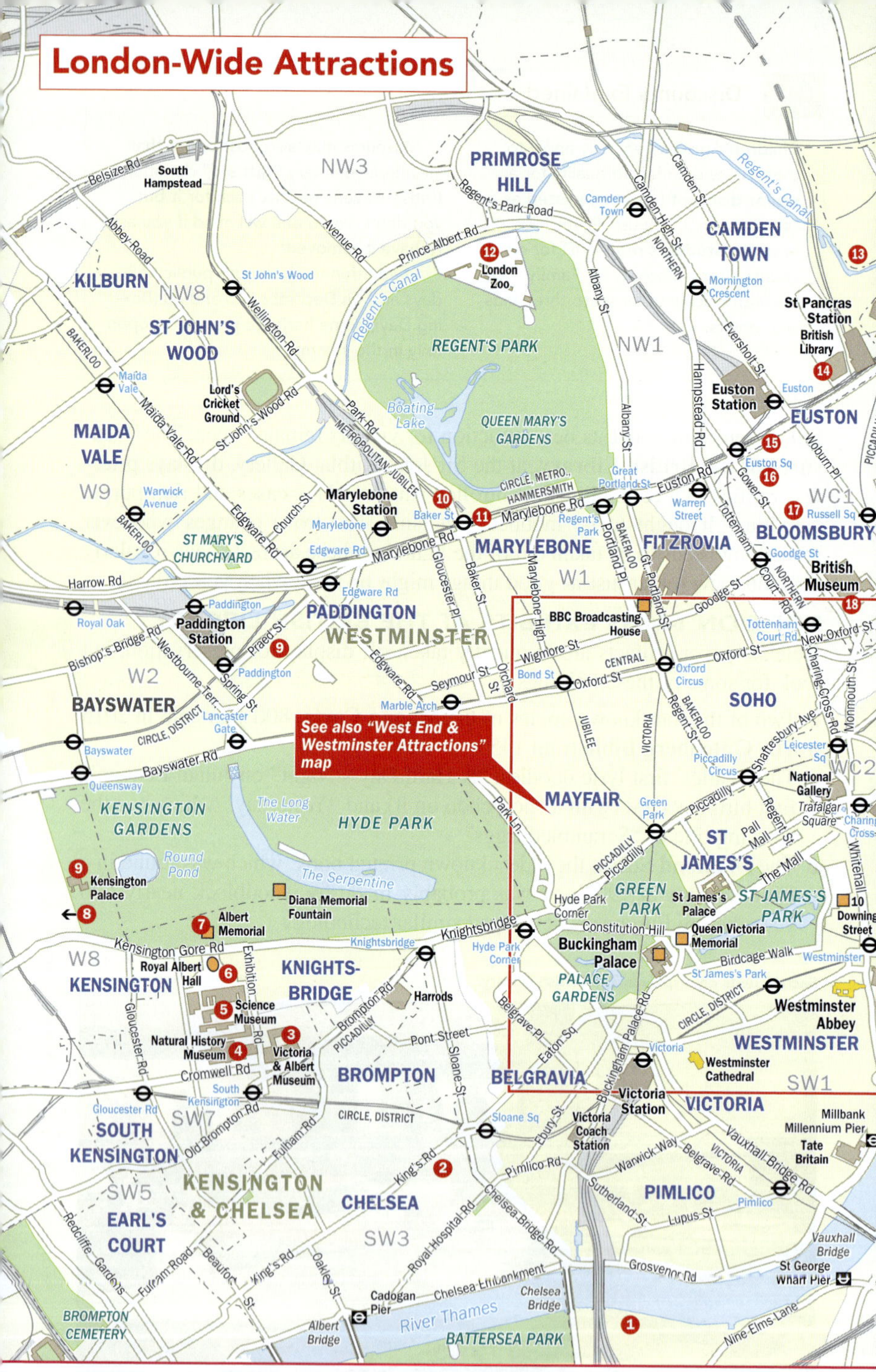

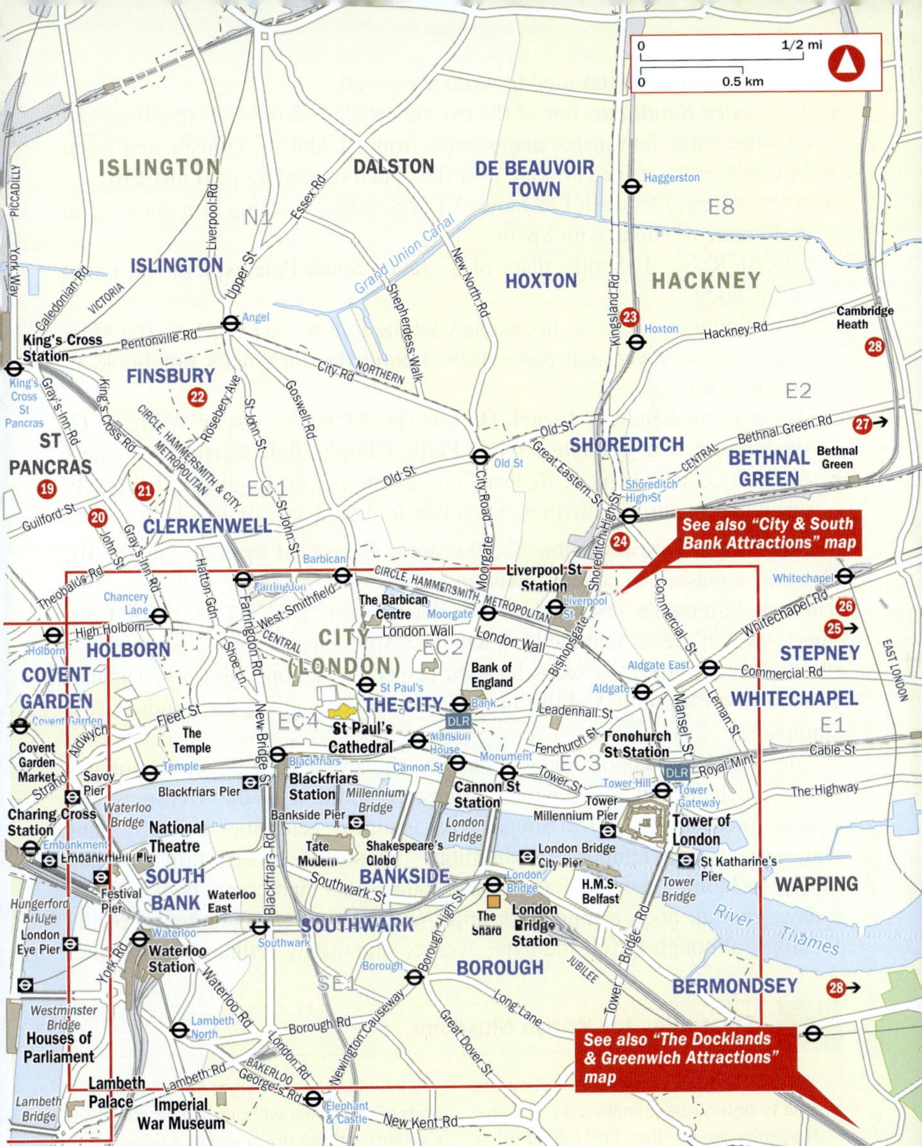

Albert Memorial **7**
Alexander Fleming Laboratory Museum **9**
The British Library **14**
The British Museum **18**
The Brunel Museum **27**
The Charles Dickens Museum **20**
The Chimney Lift **1**
Dennis Severs' House **24**
The Design Museum **8**
The Foundling Museum **19**
Jeremy Bentham's "Auto-Icon" **16**
Kensington Palace **9**
The London Zoo **12**
Madame Tussauds **11**
Museum of the Home **23**
Natural History Museum **4**
The Petrie Museum of Egyptian Archeology **17**
Postal Museum & Mail Rail **21**
Queer Britain **13**
Quentin Blake Centre for Illustration **22**
Ragged School Museum **25**
Royal Albert Hall **6**
The Royal London Hospital Museum **26**
Saatchi Gallery **2**
Science Museum **5**
The Sherlock Holmes Museum **10**
V&A **3**
The Vagina Museum **28**
Wellcome Collection **15**
Young V&A **27**

- The desk **Jane Austen** used to write her novels
- The ***Codex Sinaiticus,*** one of the two oldest Christian Bibles (the Pope has the other) and illuminated manuscripts from Buddhism, Jainism, and Islam
- Milton's contract for *Paradise Lost* (he ended up getting paid just £10)
- A letter from Elizabeth I to James VI of Scotland warning him not to open diplomatic relations with Spain
- Captain Robert F. Scott's diary of his failed South Pole exploration, found on his body
- **Michelangelo**'s letter to his nephew telling him he had finished *The Martyrdom of St. Peter,* and pages from **Leonardo da Vinci's notebook,** in mirror writing
- Works in the hand of **Mozart, Handel** (his *Messiah*), **Oscar Wilde, P. G. Wodehouse, Mary Shelley, Sylvia Plath, Chopin, Bela Bartók,** and others
- An 11th-century copy of ***Beowulf*** on vellum, in Old English; it's the only surviving manuscript, written when Ethelred the Unready was king.

The King's Library, some 85,000 tomes assembled by King George III, floats in a glassed-in central tower and forms the core of the collection, like Thomas Jefferson's library does for Washington, D.C.'s Library of Congress—which means that the king who lost America and a principal engineer of that loss provided the seeds for their respective nations' libraries. The hall contains the **Philatelic Exhibition,** 500 drawers containing thousands of rare stamps.

You can't handle books unless you're a scholar, but the Library encourages anyone to hang out in its public spaces. In addition to the Treasures, the Library presents about 150 annual talks featuring celebrities and historians and some strong temporary exhibitions (about £16; check https://events.bl.uk), including ones on Gothic horror, punk, gold, and comic books. Twice a day, you can book a tour (£10; https://events.bl.uk/whats-on/tours) of the facilities, although for all the hype over its supposedly brilliant architecture,

Strategies for British Museums

Many of London's biggest museums are free to enter, but to make up the cash they miss out on, they find lots of other revenue streams. Some institutions charge a few pounds for printed **maps** (to get around that, take a digital photograph of the posted floor plan in the lobby and use that as a guide). They also charge £16 or more for the most interesting **temporary exhibitions**. Often, the most exciting exhibitions sell out before travelers even know they're happening, but there's a sly workaround: If you **become a member** to that museum, you'll be able to walk right into exhibitions with a guest without paying admission and without pre-booking a ticket. This strategy works at the British Museum (annual membership: £74), the National Gallery (£68), the Tates (£120), and the V&A (£122), where exhibitions tend to be blockbusters. Fortunately, the British funding model also gives museums an incentive to operate superlative **shops,** publish wonderful keepsake guidebooks, and run gorgeous **cafes** that even attract people off the street—you'll never go hungry at the major museums.

the men's and women's washrooms are on opposite sides of the building and the whole place is riddled with little staircases.

96 Euston Rd., NW1. www.bl.uk. ✆ **01937/546-546.** Free admission. Mon–Thurs 9:30am–8pm; Fri 9:30am–6pm; Sat 9:30am–5pm; Sun 11am–5pm. 1-hr. tours, when available, are bookable at www.bl.uk/events. Tube: King's Cross St Pancras.

The British Museum ♥♥♥ MUSEUM Founded in 1753 and first opened in 1759 in a converted mansion, the British Museum is as much a monument to great craftsmanship as it is to the piracy carried out by 18th- and 19th-century Englishmen who, on their trips abroad, plundered whatever goodies they could find and then told the bereft that the thievery was for their own good. Although the backstory of each item is engrossing, most artifacts were, in fact, appropriated by imperial force, and in defending the change in ownership, the British have often claimed to be safeguarding the items from unstable governments abroad, neglecting to mention it was British misadventures that often caused those places to be unstable to begin with. Yet the exquisite taste of these English patriarchs is unquestionable, and now the British Museum may be the repository to beat all the rest. In fact, most years it's one of the top three attractions in the country—about 6.5 million people visit a year. Put on your walking shoes and steel yourself for crowds because it's not the king of museums for nothing.

You may only use the front entrance if you have pre-booked a ticket (do that at www.britishmuseum.org); walk-ins without them have walk all the way around the block to the rear entrance on Montague Place. Once you're inside, don't expect most museum staff to help you learn much. They're mostly concerned with whether you're touching things or misbehaving (even the people at the info desk just read off the website), so it's imperative that you do advance research and learn the background of the things you see. It helps to take advantage of the schedule of daily talks and exhibitions (at www.britishmuseum.org/visit/tours-and-talks and posted in the Great Court). These include a bevy of freebies: 15 daily **Eye-Openers** (40 min.), focused on particular rooms; 20-minute **Spotlight tours** about major holdings (the Reading Room Tues 11am and noon; other subjects Fri 5–7pm; 20 guests max.; first-come, first-served); and **Hands On,** which actually allows you to touch some ancient things (11am–4pm in rooms 1, 2, 24, 33, 42–43, 49, and 68).

Maps range from £2 to £6 depending on the level of guiding information you want, and even those are oversimplified. For a free and better one, scan the QR code at the info desk to bring up one on your phone (Wi-Fi is also free); another QR code brings you to an audio guide of highlights. Some loose touring plans are posted online (www.britishmuseum.org/visit/object-trails). Books from its gift shop may also help. A simpler path is to pay £6 to download the material on the British Museum Audio app, which details 250 of the most popular items for free and charges an add-on of £3 for themed walking tours. The app is less than ideal and books from the shop offer more detail.

Dominating the glass-roofed **Great Court** like a drum in a box, the cream-and-gold round **Reading Room,** completed in 1857, was once part of the

British Library containing King George III's exemplary book collection. Patrons had to apply for tickets, and they included Lenin and Karl Marx, who developed their political theories here; other habitués included Bram Stoker, Sir Arthur Conan Doyle, and Virginia Woolf, who wrote upon entering "one stood under the vast dome, as if one were a thought in the huge bald forehead which is so splendidly encircled by a band of famous names." You can't get inside unless you have a ticket to a tour, and those are snapped up months ahead. Beneath the Reading Room, you'll find one of the filthiest tourist restrooms in London. Above it, the **Great Court Restaurant** is a contrast in stylish luncheons (meals in the mid-£20s; last seatings at 4pm; reserve online or at ✆ **020/7323-8990**). To the right as you enter the Court, don't miss the paneled King's Library rooms (1827), now known as the **Enlightenment Gallery** and brimming with cabinets of curiosities retrieved from the ends of the earth by the likes of Captain James Cook himself.

The Great Court of the British Museum is a striking melding of classic and contemporary architecture.

Other holdings are grouped in numbered rooms by geography, with an emphasis on the Greek and Roman Empires, Europe, and Britain. Given the rarity and importance of this massive collection, it feels perverse to call anything a highlight, but these are some that the museum itself names as standouts.

Great Russell St., WC1. www.thebritishmuseum.org. ✆ **020/7323-8299.** Free admission. Sat–Thurs 10am–5pm; Fri 10am–8:30pm, last admission 15 min. before closing. No wheeled luggage, no checked items larger than 40cm x 50cm. Tube: Tottenham Court Road, Holborn, or Russell Square.

TOP DON'T-MISS EXHIBITS AT THE BRITISH MUSEUM

- The museum's most famous, and most controversial, possessions are the so-called **Elgin Marbles,** named after the nobleman who pinched them from Greece, but they are usually gingerly referred to as the **Sculptures of the Parthenon** (rooms 18 and 19) to disguise imperialist provenance. These slab sculptures (called friezes and metopes), plus some life-size weathered statuary, once lined the pediment of the famous Parthenon atop Athens' Acropolis. After being defaced (literally—the faces were hacked off) in the 500s by invading vandals (okay, not the East Germanic Vandal tribes—these guys were Persian), the sculptures suffered further indignities in a 1687 gunpowder explosion before being sawed off and carted away by Lord Elgin. Some of them sank in a shipwreck on the way over and had to be retrieved. They're laid out in the gallery in the approximate position in

The British Museum

1. Great Court
2. The Reading Room
3. Rosetta Stone
4. The Parthenon Sculptures ("Elgin Marbles")
5. Statues of the Nereid Monument
6. Mausoleum of Halikarnassos
7. Lindow Man
8. Treasures of Sutton Hoo
9. Clocks and Watches
10. Egyptian Rooms
11. Asia Galleries
12. Enlightenment Gallery

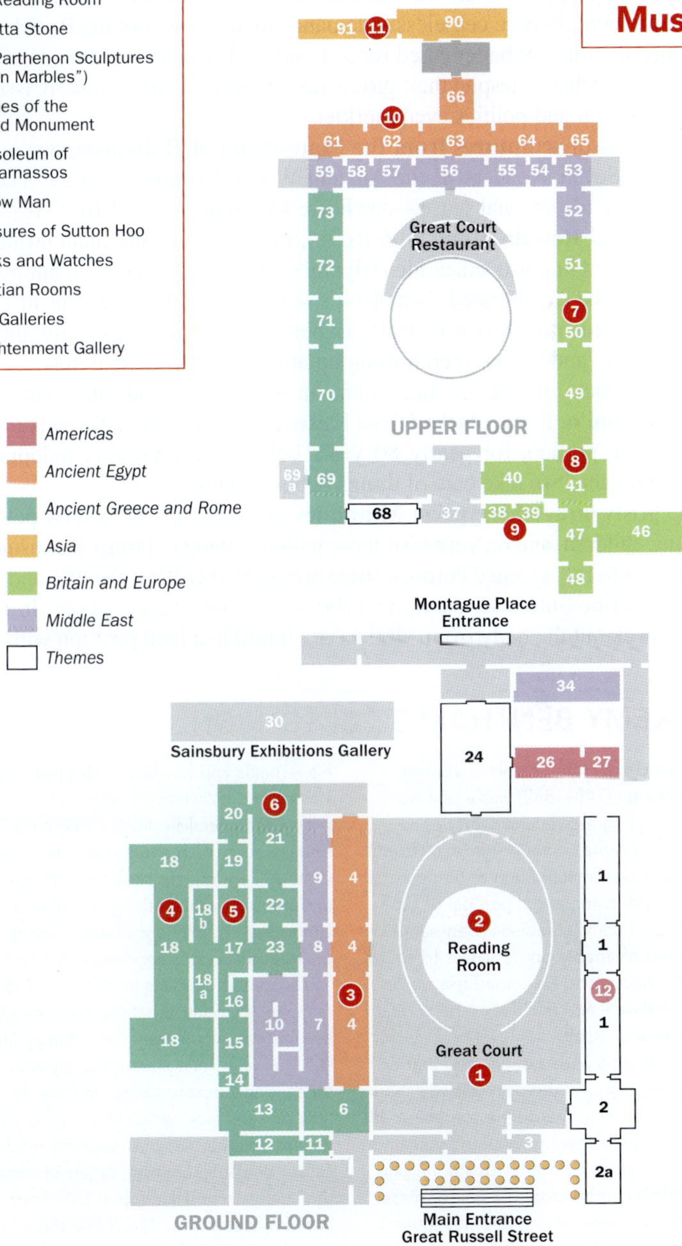

which they appeared on the Parthenon, only facing inward so you can admire them. Greece ceaselessly demands their return, but the British have argued that they're better cared for in London. The smog-burnt portions left behind in Athens, despite their glossy new galleries, make a muddy issue of conservation and politics even murkier.

- Fragments of **sculptures from the Mausoleum at Halikarnassos,** one of the lost Seven Wonders of the Ancient World, loom in room 21. They're colossal in the original sense—one horse's head measures 2.1m (7 ft.) long.
- The pivotal **Rosetta Stone** (196 B.C.E.), in room 4 off the main atrium, is what helped linguists crack hieroglyphics, and its importance to anthropology can't be exaggerated. Napoleon's soldiers found it in Egypt in 1799, but the British nabbed it in 1801. Experts think it was originally about 2 meters tall, and copies keep turning up at more archeological digs.
- At the back of the ground floor, in room 24, find the giant **Hoa Hakananai'a.** It was plucked from Easter Island in 1868 and stood outside, under the portico, for nearly 80 years before being brought indoors. So much for the "we take care of things better" argument.
- The grisly array of **Egyptian Mummies** in rooms 62, 63, and 64 petrifies living children, and on your visit these galleries will be thronged as usual. In addition to the wizened corpses, there are painted coffins; the hair and lung of the scribe Sutimose, dating to 1100 B.C.E.; and scarabs galore. In room 64, check out the body from 3400 B.C.E., found in a fetal position without a

JEREMY BENTHAM'S "auto icon"

England's own Ben Franklin, **Jeremy Bentham** (1748–1832) was a philosopher, a progressive, a subversive, a prison reformer, a supporter of suffrage and the decriminalization of homosexuality, an educator, and a pen pal of U.S. President James Madison. Bentham worked to enable equal access to courts and schools, and he coined the words *international* and *maximize*—he codified *codification* itself.

He was so ahead of his time that he refuses to stay in the past: His will stipulated eternal access to his corpse—a gift that keeps on giving, wouldn't you say? Starting years before his death, he purportedly carried around a pair of glass eyes that were intended for his future "Auto Icon" (auto = self, icon = image), which would represent him forever. After he expired, his body was dissected for students. In 1850, a colleague dressed his remains and Bentham's severed head was placed between his own feet on proud and ghoulish display. There his remains remain, in a lobby at University College London. His skeleton is hidden under his original clothing and gloves. Unfortunately, his noggin was clumsily preserved and kids kept swiping it (in 1975, some hooligans held it for a £10 ransom), so today it's stashed out of sight, and instead, you'll see a disturbingly lifelike waxwork head staring blankly with those long-pocketed blue eyeballs. His new doughy face, which looks quite a bit like his enlightened philosophical predecessor Benjamin Franklin, sagely observes the current scholarly crop at UCL from beneath a straw hat. You'll find this ghastly display attracting no attention whatsoever from the socializing scholars in the UCL Student Centre at 27–28 Gordon Square (Tube: Euston Square).

coffin, which was preserved by dry sand. Beside it is another one, 400 years younger, that rotted to soil because it was laid to rest in a basket.

- Kids stare moon-eyed at crumpled, leather-faced **Lindow Man** in room 50; he was discovered, throat slit, in a Cheshire bog nearly 2,000 years after his brutal demise. Preserved down to his hair and fingernails, he looks like he could spring to life and pound the glass of his case.
- Nearby (room 49) is the **Mildenhall Treasure,** a hoard of new-looking silver Roman tableware unearthed by Gordon Butcher, a Suffolk farmer, as he plowed fields in 1942; the saga of how he was cheated of his fortune was chronicled by writer Roald Dahl. (Yes, pillage is something of an underlying theme in this place.)
- The Anglo-Saxon treasures from the 600s unearthed in 1939 at the **Sutton Hoo** hoard, a discovery dramatized in the 2021 Ralph Fiennes film *The Dig,* are in room 41. Curators have learned their inlaid garnets were sourced from as far as modern-day Sri Lanka.
- The **Lewis Chessmen** (room 40), cartoonish and made from walrus ivory, are whimsical favorites dating from the 12th century. (Until July 2027, some of these, plus items from the Sutton Hoo treasure, will be temporarily exchanged with France for the world-famous **Bayeux Tapestry** while its own home is being renovated. The tapestry, which dates to the 11th century, depicts events leading up to the Norman conquest of England in 1066 through 58 scenes of 626 characters and 202 horses. The museum charges a separate entrance ticket for this blockbuster museum swap—it will sell out, so reserve ahead.)
- The **oldest known map** in the world, by the Babylonians, was carved on a clay tablet in the 6th century B.C.E. and now resides in room 55.
- Room 70, on Level 3, contains many remarkable holdings: the bronze **head of Roman Emperor Augustus,** found in the Sudan and unsettlingly lifelike

The Court Room in the Foundling Museum.

(it still has its eyeballs of glass and stone); the **Portland Vase,** a black, cameo-glass jug that would be very difficult to make even today; beside that, the historically important **Warren Cup,** a 1st-century silver chalice graphically depicting homosexual sex (and voyeurism of same) in relief; and a 3rd-century Roman **crocodile-skin suit of armor.**

Other Bloomsbury Area Attractions

Charles Dickens Museum ♥ MUSEUM Although Dickens moved around a lot, his last remaining London home, which he rented for £80 a year for less than 2 years when he was 30, is now his testament. A museum since 1925, and restored to a period look with a few family pieces, these five floors double as an education on what a stylish early Victorian home was like. This is where Dickens lived when his celebrity got a kick-start (*Oliver Twist* and *Nicholas Nickleby,* arguably his biggest hits, were written while he was in residence) and he experienced formative loss (his sister-in-law Mary Hogarth, age 17, died suddenly and mysteriously in his arms in the guest bedroom; 8 months later, he named his first daughter after her and later, he patterned Little Nell in *The Old Curiosity Shop* after her). As you inspect his desk from later in his life, his commode chair, and (incongruently in the middle of the nursery) window bars from a prison that housed his spendthrift dad, an unpleasant realization sets in: Charles Dickens was a brilliant storyteller, maybe the most gifted one in the history of the English language, but he was also kind of a jerk. Tough on his kids and publicly cruel to his wife. The museum doesn't sugarcoat a complicated life.

48 Doughty St., WC1. https://dickensmuseum.com. ✆ **020/7405-2127.** Admission £12.95 adults, £10.95 seniors and students, £7.95 children 6–16. Wed–Sun 10am–5pm; last admission 1 hr. before closing. Tube: Chancery Lane or Russell Square.

The Foundling Museum ♥♥ MUSEUM Small but devastating, it tracks the history of the Foundling Hospital, which took in thousands of orphans between 1739 and 1953. This was a period in which kids were treated like rubbish: For example, in 1802 a law was passed limiting the time children could work in mills—to 12 hours a day. By that measure, the benefactors were actually helping kids by locking them in this borderline prison—the kids were treated poorly to discourage mothers from giving them up. Don't miss the heartbreaking cases of tokens that mothers left at the doorstep with their babies. These tiny objects, into which a lifetime of hopes was imbued, never made it to their children lest they compromise anonymity. Also take the time to listen to the oral histories by some of the last kids to be raised by the Hospital; at the time of recording, they were elderly but still obviously quite shaken. Upstairs is the exquisitely rococo Court Room (1745) and a modest but respectable collection of 18th- and 19th century English works (Hogarth, Reynolds, Millais), which, because this was an institution that attracted well-positioned benefactors, was one of the first permanent art exhibitions in the world. Today, the museum also brings in temporary exhibitions exploring the relationship between adult artists and children. The composer Handel loved the Hospital: He frequently performed his *Messiah* as a benefit for the facility (a 1754 score is on display). The former exercise grounds, now called Coram's Fields, are still the domain of the child; adults are not permitted to enter without a kid in tow. Perhaps not at all coincidentally, J. M. Barrie's original *Peter Pan* play had 8 Grenville Street (demolished 1938), across Brunswick Square, as the Darling home, where the orphan Peter Pan flew into the nursery in search of his shadow.

40 Brunswick Sq., WC1. www.foundlingmuseum.org.uk. ✆ **020/7841-3600.** Admission £14.50 adults, £7.50 seniors, students 22+ £13, free for guests 21 and under; higher posted prices include a voluntary donation. Tues–Sat 10am–5pm; Sun 11am–5pm. Tube: Russell Square.

Hunterian Museum ♥ MUSEUM This ghoulish but respectfully curated exhibition at the Royal College of Surgeons, now 2 centuries old, chronicles the life's work of John Hunter (1728–93), who elevated surgery from something your barber dabbled in to something a saw-wielding, germ-spreading scientist would, ahem, undertake. It's a macabre scene, crowded with thousands of black-lidded jars of specimens, including extinct animals, all tastefully presented in a modern, gleaming facility rebuilt in 2023. Most of your time will be spent squeamishly perusing some 3,000 examples of human and animal pathology and anatomy (many originally obtained by grave-robbers, a common practice then), plus a bone-grinding collection of crude surgical instruments that could rattle even the steeliest physician, all of which paved the way to a better understanding of the human body and its treatments. Check out the cross-section of a chicken's head that Hunter grafted with a human tooth. Such Frankenstein projects were his stock in trade, and as creepy as they seem to us, they were crucial in helping mankind advance its understanding of our anatomy and how to heal it. The Hunterian is free to visit and takes an hour, max, but it does ask you to make a timed advance reservation. That can happen minutes ahead on your smartphone as long as there's space.

35-43 Lincoln's Inn Fields, WC2. https://hunterianmuseum.org. ✆ **020/7869-6560.** Free admission. Tues–Sat 10am–5pm. Tube: Holborn.

More than 80,000 artifacts are housed in the University College London's Petrie Museum of Egyptian Archeology.

The Petrie Museum of Egyptian Archeology ♥♥ MUSEUM Britain made a lot of mistakes when it comes to Egypt, and not just with Suez. Almost as soon as "explorers" could break into ancient tombs, they would lose track of thousands of things they discovered or leave poor information about how they found them. Since the 1800s, University College London has worked to properly collect, identify, and date more

RAISING the roof

Thirty years ago, if you wanted to scale a tall building to admire London, you had two main alternatives: dragging yourself up the stairs of The Monument (p. 199) or dragging yourself up the stairs of St Paul's (p. 188). Today, no self-respecting architect would design a new high-rise without an observation platform of some kind. In addition to a wide slate of great restaurants cooking on high (see p. 108), a bazillion rooftop cocktail spaces, and well-known tourist magnets like the London Eye (p. 217), The View from the Shard (p. 185), and the Level 10 deck at Tate Modern (p. 185), viewing floors are also proliferating. Among them:

Horizon 22 (22 Bishopsgate, EC2; https://horizon22.co.uk/; admission free, but timed reservation required; Mon–Fri 10am–6pm, Sat 10am–5pm, Sun 10am–4pm; Tube: Liverpool Street): London's second-tallest tower opened the city's highest observation platform in 2023—yes, even higher than The Shard's, which charges money. This 58th-floor perch dwarfs the other buildings in the City, and the double-height indoor viewing area makes you feel like you're soaring, although it could use some seating.

Roof Terrace (One New Change, EC4; https://onenewchange.com; admission free, no reservation required; Mon–Wed, Fri–Sat 10am–6pm, Thurs 10–8pm, Sun noon–6pm; Tube: St Paul's): It's not very high, but the straight-on view of the glory of St Paul's is worth the detour. There's a bar.

Sky Garden (1 Sky Garden Walk, EC3; https://skygarden.london; admission free, but reservation required; Mon 10am–6pm, Tues–Weds 10am–11pm, Thurs 10am–midnight, Fri 10am–2am, Sat 8:30am–2am, Sun 8:30am–11pm; Tube: Monument): An expansive view over the Thames (but not so much to the north) from the building locals call "the Walkie-Talkie." You can dine here, too, if you want, with obstructed views.

The Garden at 120 (120 Fenchurch St., EC3; www.thegardenat120.com; admission free, no reservation required; April–Sept Mon–Fri 10am–9pm, Sat–Sun 10am–5pm, Oct–March 10am–6:30pm, Sat–Sun 10am–5pm; Tube: Monument): More of a pleasant 15th-floor terrace than a long-distance panorama spot. Best part: Very few people will be around.

than 80,000 artifacts; roaming its treasure-crammed cases, some of which are stocked with items that still stump scholars, can be awe-inspiring. From the cotton Tarkhan dress last worn 5,000 years ago to Roman funerary portraits painted in beeswax, the things one finds in these stacks could blow a mind.

Malet Place, University College London, WC1. www.ucl.ac.uk/culture/petrie-museum. ✆ **020/3108-9000.** Free admission. Tues–Fri 1–5pm; Sat 11am–5pm. Tube: Goodge Street.

Postal Museum & Mail Rail ♥♥ MUSEUM In an industrial patch of central London no tourist usually wanders into, you can now find two well-done attractions in one, and both are perfect for kids. The first holds exhibits about the social history of mail delivery in the country, from origins (Henry VIII was once the only guy allowed to get mail) to antique vehicles to old "pillar" post boxes to Arnold Machin's sculptures of the young Queen Elizabeth II photographed to make stamps. There are lots of things for kids to press and bang, including a pneumatic tube that sends messages whizzing in an overhead tube across the hall, and there's a mail-themed play space, which costs a little extra. But the most memorable aspect of a visit will be a 20-minute loop on the Mail Rail, a little-seen 22-mile underground line that from 1927 to 2003 was used to deliver millions of letters a year. A short portion (with recorded narration and a plastic dome over the carriages, which are as tiny as the train in the kiddie section of a carnival, so please refrain from being tall) now carries curious tourists on a 1-mile looping journey 70 feet below the streets. (Claustrophobes can watch what they're missing on screens near the boarding platform.) To avoid noisy school field trips, go after 2:30pm.

15–20 Phoenix Place, WC1. www.postalmuseum.org. ✆ **0300/0300-700.** Admission £18.50 adults, £12.50 ages 16–24, £11 ages 3–15. Tues–Sat 10am–5pm. Tube: Farringdon or Chancery Lane.

Wellcome Collection ♥ MUSEUM Once upon a time, there was a strange Midwestern pharmacist named Henry Wellcome. Henry got very wealthy and developed a taste for hoarding medical oddities, such as Napoleon's toothbrush, hair from George III, oil paintings of childbirth, and Japanese sex toys. The offbeat gallery/ museum that still operates in his name always presents an offbeat temporary exhibit or two pertaining to the human body and its challenges—recent ones were on sex research, the psychology of magic tricks, how beauty standards differ across cultures, the cultural exclusion of Deaf people, and the search for fresh water. The shop is one of the best of London's museums, stocking unique science- and body-themed finds. The exhibits are not for sheltered children.

183 Euston Rd., NW1. www.wellcomecollection.org. ✆ **020/7611-2222.** Free admission. Tues–Wed and Fri–Sun 10am–6pm; Thurs 10am–8pm. Tube: Euston Square, Warren Street, or Euston.

SOHO, COVENT GARDEN & WEST END

The Courtauld Institute of Art Gallery ♥♥♥ MUSEUM Art historians consider the Courtauld one of the most prestigious collections on earth. Its two-level selection is small but supreme, with several masterpieces you will instantly recognize. Among the winners are an early version of Manet's scandalous *Le Déjeuner sur l'herbe,* depicting a naked woman picnicking with two clothed men, and the artist's *A Bar at the Folies-Bergère,* showing a melancholy barmaid standing in front of her disproportionate reflection. There are multiple Cézannes, Toulouse-Lautrecs, and Gauguins. Degas' *Two Dancers on a Stage* is popular, as is Van Gogh's *Self-Portrait with Bandaged Ear.* Especially rare is a completed Seurat, *Young Woman Powdering Herself,* which depicts his mistress in the act of dressing and initially included his own face in the frame on the wall—he painted over it with a vase of flowers to avoid ridicule. 2026 exhibitions include Seurat, Barbara Hepworth, and Salman Toor. **Somerset House,** the museum's home, is a beloved landmark, once a naval center and the city's main house of records. The

The Courtauld Gallery has an exceptional collection of Impressionist and other European art.

central courtyard has a grove of 55 ground-level fountains that delight small children, and it's the scene of both popular summer concerts and a winter ice rink. The terrace overlooking the Thames can be enjoyed for free.

Somerset House, Strand, WC2. www.courtauld.ac.uk. No public phone; email: galleryinfo@courtauld.ac.uk. Admission £12 adults, seniors and children 18 and under free. Advance booking recommended but not required. Daily 10am–6pm; last admission 5:15pm. Tube: Temple.

London Transport Museum ♥♥ MUSEUM Try to imagine London without its wheeled icons: the red double-decker bus, the black taxi, and the Tube. In Covent Garden's soaring cast-iron-and-glass 1871 flower-selling hall (Eliza Doolittle would have bought her flowers here), the transit systems' development and evolution are traced in affectionate detail (there are even fake horse apples beneath the antique carriages) with a fleet of intact landmark vehicles to climb aboard. You'll see Number 23, a steam locomotive that powered the Underground in its most unpleasant days ("a form of mild

Somerset House

Once a naval complex and later where Londoners came to settle taxes, **Somerset House** (Strand, WC2; www.somersethouse.org.uk; ✆ **0333/320-2836;** Tube: Temple) is now a favored cultural hangout and home of the Courtauld Institute of Art Gallery. The courtyard, beneath which lie the foundations of a Tudor palace, has a grove of 55 ground-level fountains that delight small children, and it's the scene of popular summer concerts, screenings, talks, and a winter ice rink. Guided 1-hr. tours (£12; book ahead online) go Tues & Sat at noon, 2pm, and 3:45pm from Seamen's Hall in the South Wing. Also look for changing exhibitions (either free or up to £20 adults, depending on what's on). The Victoria Embankment terrace overlooking the Thames (from across the street) can be enjoyed for free.

West End & Westminster Attractions

Climb aboard vintage vehicles at The London Transport Museum.

torture," wrote the *Times* then), historic trolleybuses (London once had the largest trolley system in the world), what city taxis looked like before the current black cab, and carriages with wooden floors and separate compartments for "ladies." Also on display are plenty of the system's famous Edwardian and Art Deco posters, many of which are art unto themselves. Designers will appreciate the background on Johnston, the distinctive typeface created in 1916 for the Underground, which could now be considered London's unofficial font. Along the way, you'll learn a great deal about shifts in London life and you may even feel a twinge of embarrassment about the state of your own town's public transportation. It's a must for fans of London history and a good place to entertain children, to whom it seems strongly geared—if you're childless, you'll need patience as kids run amok. Adult rail aficionados will find much deeper examinations available as books in the exemplary shop (open to 6:15pm), which doesn't require a ticket. That's full of fun stuff like hundreds of reproduction posters, Tube-themed clothing, and bags and furniture made from the Underground's signature seating upholstery (called *moquette*).

Covent Garden, WC2. www.ltmuseum.co.uk. ✆ **020/7565-7299.** Tickets are technically annual passes and cost £25 adults, £25 seniors and students, free for 17 and under; £22.50 entry weekdays after 2pm when schools are in session. Daily 10am–6pm; last admission 45 min. before closing. Tube: Covent Garden.

National Gallery ♥♥♥ MUSEUM When the bells of St Martin-in-the-Fields peal each morning at 10am, the doors promptly open on one of the world's greatest artistic fireworks shows—each famous picture follows an equally famous picture. Few museums can compete with the strongest, widest collection of Western European paintings in the world—one of every important style is on display, and it's almost always the best in that genre. There are 2,300 works, which is plenty to divert you for as long as you can manage, although most visitors just wander around without getting properly close to the brushwork. Be different.

National Gallery Highlights

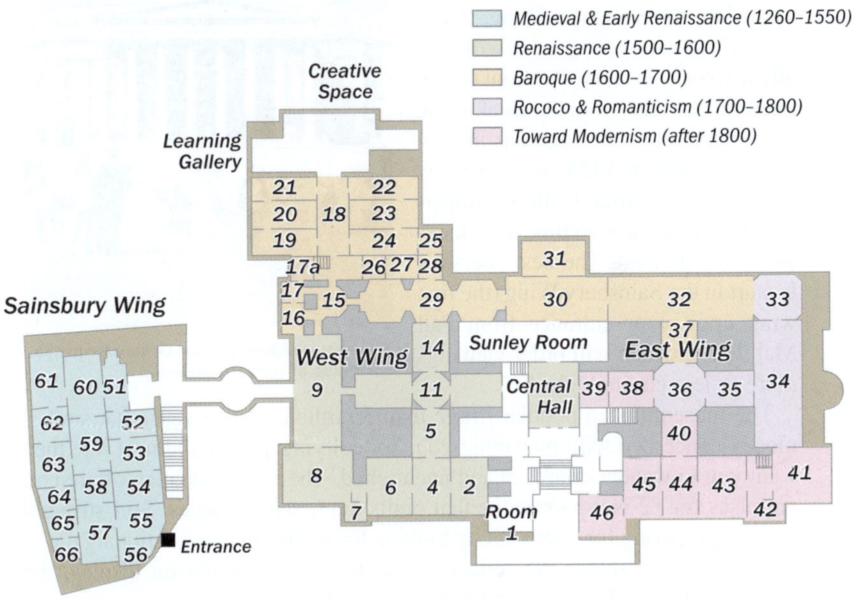

The Ambassadors, Hans Holbein the Younger ***4***

The Arnolfini Portrait, Jan Van Eyck ***52***

The Baptism of Christ, Piero della Francesca ***66***

Bathers at Asnières, Georges Seurat ***44***

Christina of Denmark, Duchess of Milan Hans Holbein the Younger ***11***

The Entombment, Michelangelo ***2***

The Execution of Maximilian, Edouard Manet ***41***

The Fighting Temeraire, J.M.W. Turner ***40***

Marriage à la Mode, William Hogarth ***34***

The Martyrdom of Saint Sebastian, Piero del Pollaiolo ***60***

An Old Woman, Quinten Massys ***54***

Samson and Delilah, Peter Paul Rubens ***18***

Self Portraits, Rembrandt ***15 and 22***

Sunflowers, Vincent van Gogh ***43***

Venus and Mars, Sandro Botticelli ***62***

Whistlejacket, George Stubbs ***34***

FINDING WORKS: Enter the complex through the bulky beige building to the left, the Sainsbury Wing. If you have a bag with you, guards will usually force you to carry it in front of you or pay £2 to check it in the cloakroom. This stupendous and palatial institution, founded in 1824, is marred by opaque presentation. Galleries imperceptibly surge through time in a clockwise arrangement. The best course is to start in the Sainsbury Wing (the first wing upon your entrance from Pall Mall East), which will order viewings more or less chronologically.

The treasure-filled National Gallery forms the north side of Trafalgar Square.

The museum is so popular (more than 3 million visits a year) that staff is mostly concerned with managing you, not edifying you. It's almost like they want you to wander confused and unenriched. The Art Guide map offered on premises for £2 is a poor value that omits many masterpieces. So I strongly suggest preparing for your visit by looking for works on www.nationalgallery.org.uk/paintings/search-the-collection on its website; if it's on display, the room number will appear under Key Facts>Location. Yet in the museum, directional signs lack room numbers, and the map signs post a QR code that just sends you to the map that's on the museum website—so you'd be smart to download the full map before you get here, too. The museum offers free Wi-Fi, but it may not work, and there's no place here for you to recharge your phone after you've done all that work.

LEARNING ABOUT WORKS: Posted descriptions are awfully straitlaced. You can glean a little more information if you download the Smartify app (free; bring earbuds) and point your phone at the limited number of works that participate in it. The Audio guide (£7; £5 if reserved ahead; device and headphones not included) covers 69 works in skimming detail. The Gallery's short spotlight videos on its YouTube channel (nationalgallerylondon) can help you appreciate a few works much more deeply, but your visit would be best illuminated by some expert input. Check the info desk or the website's What's On section for free perks such as the **10-Minute Talks** about a single work (Mon–Fri 4pm); 45-minute **Lunchtime Talks** (1pm) about a specific work or artist; storytelling for kids; or the few hour-long tours (Tues–Thurs at 3pm). Permanent displays are supplemented by temporary exhibitions, one free and one paid (£8–£25; if you can't get a ticket, buying a museum membership will get you in). The Gallery schedules most family activities for Sundays. The two restaurants are top-quality but overpriced, and besides, the view from the restaurant at the National Portrait Gallery next door (see below) is better. But don't miss the superlative gift shops—the online version (shop.nationalgallery.org.uk) will print you a color-matched custom copy of any of the 1,200 works or even mail a framed version home.

TOP DON'T-MISS EXHIBITS AT THE NATIONAL GALLERY

- Piero della Francesca, one of the most sought-after Renaissance painters, is represented by ***The Baptism of Christ*** (1450s, room 66 in the Sainsbury Wing). With its then-advanced use of light and foreshortening, its faces verge on bemusement, and the dove, representing the Holy Spirit, seems to fly straight at viewers.
- After Sandro Botticelli fell under the spell of the hardline reformer Savonarola, he burned many of his finest paintings in the Bonfire of the Vanities and changed to an inferior style, so his best works are rare. ***Venus and Mars*** (1485, room 62 in the Sainsbury Wing), depicting the lovers reclining, is one of them.
- Michelangelo's ***The Entombment*** (ca. 1500, room 2) is unfinished but powerful. The feminine figure in the red gown is now thought to be St John, but it's hard to know for sure, since the artist favored strong masculine traits.
- The subject of Sandro Botticelli's arresting ***Portrait of a Young Man*** (around 1480, room 51), watches you in an unassuming head-on pose that challenged the artistic conventions of its age. No one had done it before.
- King Henry VIII sent his trusted portrait painter, Hans Holbein the Younger, to Brussels to capture an honest likeness of 16-year-old ***Christina of Denmark, Duchess of Milan*** (1538, room 11), so he could decide if she was pretty enough to marry. She declined *his* proposal, and as a happy consequence, survived to 1590.
- Nearby, Holbein's ***The Ambassadors*** (1533, room 4) is full of symbolic riddles that refer to the French guy on the left, and famous for a stretched image of a skull that can only be viewed in proper perspective from the side. Get close; the fine brushwork extends even to the feathers on the shoes.
- Kids love Quinten Massys' grotesque, possibly satiric ***An Old Woman*** (*The Ugly Duchess;* 1513, room 54). It was recently restored, revealing the green glaze background and fine scratches in the paint of the veil that play with the light. Many artists have trouble rendering hands, but these are perfect.
- Among other works, Rembrandt van Rijn shows two self-portraits. One at age 34 (1637, room 15) is pridefully detailed to declare ego—he even gives himself a single name like the Renaissance masters. By age 63 (room 22), he's in simple clothes and broadly dolloping paint with a palette knife. The pair makes for a universal story of preening youth giving way to confident old age.
- Edouard Manet's ***The Execution of Maximilian*** (1867–68, room 41) was sliced into five sections after the artist's death, but Edgar Degas reassembled what he could find; the missing patches lend the firing-squad scene further tension.
- J. M. W. Turner's ***The Fighting Temeraire*** (1839, room 40), depicting a proud sailed battleship being towed for scrapping by a filthy steam-engine boat. As echoed by Q in *Skyfall* as he met James Bond in front of it, it's a national symbol for the decline of the Empire's glory days and the rise of industrialism.

- In room 34, George Stubbs' cryptic, life-size portrait of rearing stallion ***Whistlejacket*** stops everyone in their tracks; it was painted in 1762 for its proud owner.
- William Hogarth's lurid ***Marriage à la Mode*** (1743, room 34), is a lurid soap opera of marriage, infidelity, greed, disease, and poisoning told in six satirical paintings.
- The Gallery is rich in Peter Paul Rubens, with some 25 works attributed to him. His ***Samson and Delilah*** (1609–10, room 18) is known for Samson's muscular back and Delilah's crimson robe.

There's much more: George Seurat's not-quite-pointillist ***Bathers at Asnières*** (1884, room 44); Monet's ***The Water-Lily Pond*** (1899, room 46); Van Gogh's ***Sunflowers*** (1888, room 43); the Pollaiuolo brothers' altarpiece ***The Martyrdom of Saint Sebastian*** (1475, room 60); Jan van Eyck's instantly recognizable ***The Arnolfini Portrait*** (room 52), a mysterious but fabulously skillful depiction of light that dates to 1434 and looks years ahead of its time. **Brueghels** (rooms 27 and 54; bring your reading glasses to see the crazy details). **Cézannes. Uccellos.** There's so much good stuff here that you may want to go twice during your visit, and the Gallery is centrally located, so you can.

Trafalgar Square, WC2. www.nationalgallery.org.uk. ✆ **020/7747-2885.** Free admission. Mon–Thurs and Sat–Sun 10am–6pm; Fri 10am–9pm. Tube: Charing Cross or Leicester Square.

The National Portrait Gallery ♥♥♥ MUSEUM Many people are utterly seduced by how the best portraits here capture the sparkle of life behind these charismatic shapers of history. Here, the names from your high school textbook flower into flesh-and-blood people, and the accompanying biographies are so sublimely evocative that subjects come alive. Download the map (www.npg.org.uk/visit/floor-plans/) and the free Bloomberg Connects app (bring your own earbuds) for free access to more info than the signs tell you, plus a map. The galleries proceed chronologically from Level 3, so start by taking the long escalator up and then walk your way down. The descriptions of each work are remarkably astute at supplying a quick and easy-to-understand explanation of why each figure is important.

Know Before You Go

Your visit to London's major museums will be a lot better if you do these things *before* leaving home.

- **Check what temporary exhibitions are on.** You'll need a ticket, and they sell out.
- **Print maps from the website.** It costs £2 to £3 to pick one up, and they're not worth it because they lack detail.
- **Pick a few items you want to see.** Not just so you can find them (they often move around). Also, signage may be weak and curators unavailable. The more you know, the more you'll love what you see.
- **Check the times for talks and kids' events.** London's museums are generally abuzz with activities. Make sure you don't miss the good ones.

Modern portraits on display at The National Portrait Gallery.

One of the gallery's most instantly recognizable paintings is the **Darnley portrait of Elizabeth I** (1575; floor 3, room 1), in which the Virgin Queen's face is, as we all expected, a ghostly white—except conservators have recently discovered that in her time her skin was originally painted much rosier, almost normal, but the colors faded. Right away, it becomes clear that our perceptions of these once-breathing people are about to be reshaped. In the next room, the **Ditchley portrait of 1592** is a rare example of a portrait of Elizabeth I painted from an in-person sitting; she is depicted standing astride the globe and laden with precious stones. Also in Room 1, troublesome **Henry VIII** is shown in several likenesses. One is a delicate 1537 paper cartoon by Hans Holbein the Younger (for a mural at Whitehall—a rare survivor from that palace), in which the king suspiciously peers with flinty grey eyes—hinting at a shiftiness that His Majesty probably couldn't recognize in his own likeness, but that all who knew him feared. One painting of **King Edward VI,** painted when he was 9, is executed in a distorted perspective (called anamorphosis) that requires it to be viewed from a hole on the right side of its frame, which is original. In room 10, you'll also find **Benjamin Franklin** and **George Washington** (they were born Englishmen, after all) and one of the only authoritative images of **Captain James Cook,** who was so pivotal in colonial expansion. Look for the **Chevalier d'Eon** (room 18), a male diplomat and fencing champion who lived as a woman in the late 1700s; for the flamboyantly romantic, heartbreaking writers **Percy Bysshe Shelley**, **William Beckford**, **John Keats**, **John William Polidori, Mary Shelley,** and **Lord Byon** clustering like swoony emo teenagers at their own lunchroom table (room 17); and for the adorable nose of pugnacious **William Hogarth** (room 9) in his lifelike terra-cotta bust circa 1741. The genius of artist John Singer Sargent is immediately apparent in the 1913 likeness of writer and fellow American in England **Henry James** (room 19); you can no longer discern where activist Mary Wood hacked it with a meat cleaver the next year in protest for suffrage. When **Benjamin Disraeli**, the U.K.'s first Jewish prime minister, learned he was dying, he reluctantly allowed artist John Everett Millais to paint the likeness now hanging in room 19.

Fortunately, the portraits don't stop when cameras were invented, although the selections on display change more often as we get to present times. The ever-divisive **Margaret Thatcher** (room 28) is here in a not-very-affectionate depiction, imperiously glaring over the grey gunwale of a dais at a Conservative Party Conference in Brighton; Frederic Leighton's painting of **Richard Francis Burton** (room 23), has the arrogant explorer proudly displaying his scar and therefore his fearlessness; James Gunn's 1950 vision of the royal family sitting down to tea (room 28) makes the Windsors look as domestic as the Cleavers; **Kate Bush** gazes elusively in Patrick Lichfield's 1980 chromogenic print (room 28). Don't neglect the **Western Wing**, added in 2023 between floors 1 and 2, where you'll find more modern works, including a 2004 video of **David Beckham** sleeping, Alessandro Raho's 2004 masterpiece of **Judi Dench** in white, and a self-sculpture in blood by artist **Marc Quinn** that is preserved by its own freezer.

Just about everything can be photographed (never with flash). Late Shift evenings (Fri–Sat 6–9pm), with DJs, talks, live music, and dozens of people lounging on gallery floors in sketching sessions, are great fun and a smart way to free up daytime hours to see more attractions. Also consider the tony rooftop Portrait Restaurant (✆ **020/7312-2490**), which has a breathtaking view of Nelson's Column and Big Ben, although the farmhouse menu may be too rustic for some picky eaters. A better idea: Head down to the cellar, in the gallery's old vaults, for **Larry's**, a speakeasy-like hangout for cocktails, light bites, and live jazz Weds–Sun (closes at midnight Tues–Sat; 5:30pm Sun; 9pm Mon; kitchen closes at 10pm).

A free 30-minute Portrait of the Day talk leaves from the lobby daily at 11am and 2pm.

St Martin's Place, WC2. www.npg.org.uk. ✆ **020/7306-0055.** Free admission. Mon–Thurs 10:30am–6pm; Fri–Sat 10:30am–9pm; last admission 45 min. before closing. Tube: Leicester Square.

Sir John Soane's Museum ♥♥ MUSEUM These two town houses on the north side of Lincoln's Inn Fields are so overloaded with furniture, paintings, architectural decoration, and sculpture, that navigation is a challenge. The Georgian architect, noted for his influential but egotistic neoclassicism (the Bank of England) as much as for his aesthetic materialism, bequeathed his home and its contents as a museum for "amateurs and students." His oddball abode, which his will decreed must be left precisely as it was on the day he died (in 1837), so it's as if the well-connected eccentric had just popped out

It's Free!

All of the following attractions charge no admission fees for their permanent collections (temporary exhibitions excluded). Not a shabby lineup!

The Bank of England Museum, p. 196
The British Library, p. 130
The British Museum, p. 135
The Design Museum, p. 179
Hunterian Museum, p. 141
London Mithraeum, p. 198
London Museum Docklands, p. 201
The National Gallery, p. 146
The National Maritime Museum, p. 206
The National Portrait Gallery, p. 150
The Natural History Museum, p. 172
The Old Royal Naval College, p. 207
The Queen's House, Greenwich, p. 207
The Royal Observatory (partly), p. 208
The Science Museum, p. 175
Sir John Soane's Museum, p. 152
Tate Britain, p. 160
Tate Modern, p. 185
The V&A, p. 176
The Wallace Collection, p. 170
The Wellcome Collection, p. 143
Young V&A, p. 203

to purloin another Greek pilaster, leaving you to roam his groaning wood floors, sussing out the *objets d'art* from the certifiable treasures. It's a melee of art history, in which precious paintings and sculpture jostle for space like baubles in a junk shop. You have to wonder how Soane could legally acquire antiquities such as the sarcophagus of Seti I, carved from translucent limestone, and you won't know because almost nothing is marked. Ask to join a tour of the **Picture Room,** built in an 1823 expansion, so you can watch its false walls be opened, revealing layer upon buried layer of works (such as William Hogarth's eight-painting *A Rake's Progress,* a documentary of dissolution) filed inside false walls. Surf the simulated museum at http://explore.soane.org to get pre-acquainted, or, most helpfully, take a guided 1-hour tour (£25; noon; must book ahead). All in all, a visit reminds you of the unseemly way in which privileged Englishmen used to stuff their homes with pilfered art as a way of stocking up on a sense of superiority—but Soane's sticky fingers aside, the objects are still wondrous

13 Lincoln's Inn Fields, WC2. www.soane.org. ✆ **020/7405-2107.** Free admission. Wed–Sun 10am–5pm, last entry 4:30pm; tours at noon (book ahead online). Tube: Holborn.

Other West End Attractions

The Benjamin Franklin House ♥ HISTORIC HOME The only surviving residence of the portly politico is a sort of architectural preserve. Franklin lived as a colonial agent in this boardinghouse near the Thames for nearly 16 years, without his wife, Deborah—he lived here for the Boston Tea Party, the enactment of the Stamp Act, and his invention of the armonica. Although his friends warned him the separation was killing Deborah, it was only the Revolution (and a major international scandal that he helped cause) that forced him from his adopted home back to the Colonies, and by then she was dead. For much of his life Franklin was a fervent Loyalist who, even as late as 1775, felt the differences between Britain and the Colonies could be settled in "half an

The Benjamin Franklin House, where the colonial statesman lived for 16 years.

hour." Exhibits are sparse, so it's best not to come Weds–Thurs on a self-guided day but Fri–Sun, when there are tours. The "Historical" version of that is conducted by a young actress playing the landlady's daughter, Polly Hewson, who became such a dear friend to Ben that she moved to Philadelphia and was with him when he died. In empty rooms, Polly tells wistful tales as recordings chime in with voices from her memory. Rewards are mixed. It's humbling to see how this giant man made do with such small quarters. The worn wooden back staircase, on which he got his exercise when French trollops weren't available, is so well preserved it feels ghostly.

36 Craven St., WC2. www.benjaminfranklinhouse.org. ✆ **020/7839-2006.** Self-guided visits: Weds–Thurs 11am–3pm; Tours: Fri–Sun noon–5pm. Self-guided visits £8 adults, £6 seniors and students. "Architectural Tour" without performance £10 on Fridays, "Historical Tour" with performance £12 Sat–Sun, reservations required. Free for children 11 and under. Tube: Embankment or Charing Cross.

The Temple Church ♥♥ CHURCH/HISTORIC SITE For 900 years, this remarkable little sanctum has been a cradle for legal and religious liberties around the world. The oldest part, the Round, was built in 1185 by the Knights Templar from the Crusades. Back then, they were considered the good guys, so when befuddled King John ran afoul of his barons, he sought sanctuary here and, under protection of the Knights, hammered out the details of the Magna Carta, which gave common law rights to the people that they had never had before. America owes the basis of its Constitution to this building. You can see the stone effigies of nine of the Knights scattered in the Round. Horribly, on May 11, 1941, a Nazi incendiary bomb wrecked this precious place; many of the beautifully carved effigies are now as lumpen and faceless as corpses from Pompeii. The reconstruction of the Temple, which is still a working church serving the legal community in the surrounding Inner and Middle Temple Inns of Court (to which all English barristers must belong),

CLEOPATRA & "eros"

Two monuments in the West End have been enchanting visitors for years. When he finished his legendary fountain in the middle of Piccadilly Circus in 1893, sculptor Alfred Gilbert thought the playful, maritime-themed sculptures on its base would be celebrated. Audiences, however, have minds of their own: They responded instead to the scantily clad archer on top. But they got even that bit of admiration wrong—they thought he represented **Eros,** god of erotic love, when Gilbert had actually intended Anteros, god of requited love. Today, Piccadilly Circus isn't a "circus" roundabout anymore—it's an interchange—but the ceaseless tourist crowd photographing Gilbert's misunderstood masterpiece at least puts the circus back into Piccadilly. Gilbert's fabulous fountain is now dry and full of rubbish, but his misidentified god blesses the city as an icon. (Tube: Piccadilly Circus)

The original Cleopatra's Needles obelisks—which Cleopatra had nothing to do with—were erected in Heliopolis, Egypt, around 1450 B.C.E, and inscriptions were added 200 years later. The Romans moved the granite spires to Alexandria, where they toppled and were buried in the sand, which preserved them until the early 1800s. After a perilous delivery, London's 224-ton **Cleopatra's Needle** was erected here on the river in 1878 (New York City got one in 1881, and a third went to Paris). Two sphinxes were installed to guard it (some say backward, because they face the sculpture, not away from it). A century and a half in London wrecked what 20 Saharan centuries didn't: Pollution has rendered the hieroglyphs illegible. In 1917, German bombs scarred the western sphinx. Look closely; you'll find sphinxes and camels hidden in the armrests. (Tube: Embankment or Temple.)

was exacting. Notice how the Purbeck Marble columns, sourced from the same Dorset mine as the originals 700 years before, lean slightly according to the architect's plans from the 1200s. It also has world-famous acoustics, a sublime organ, and a top-notch choir, so if you come, time your visit to coincide with the music schedule.

Inner Temple, EC4 (in the quad south of the intersection of Fleet St. and Chancery Lane). www.templechurch.com. ✆ **020/7353-3470.** Admission £5 adults, £3 seniors and students, free for children 16 and under. Generally open Mon–Fri 10am–4pm, but check ahead because hours shift weekly. Tube: Temple or Blackfriars.

WESTMINSTER & ST JAMES'S

For information on the **Changing the Guard** ceremony, please see p. 218.

Buckingham Palace ♥♥ PALACE If you were to fall asleep tonight and wake up inside one of the **State Rooms,** you'd never guess where you were. Is it opulent? No question. But if gilding, teardrop chandeliers, 18th-century portraits, and ceremonial halls could ever be considered standard-issue, Buckingham Palace is your basic palace. The mild tastes of the late Queen Elizabeth II—call it respectable decadence of yellows and creams and pleasant floral arrangements, thank you very much—is partly the reason. The current Royal Family considers Windsor to be their real home. That's right:

Buckingham Palace is a mere *pied-à-terre*. All tickets are timed and include an audio tour that rushes you around too quickly (about 1 hr. 45 min.), and taking photographs is forbidden. The route threads through the public and ceremonial rooms at the back of the Palace—nowhere the Royal Family spends personal time (and besides, tours are held only when they're away). Highlights include the 50m-long (164-ft.) **Picture Gallery** filled mostly with works amassed by George IV, an obsessive collector; the 14m-high (46-ft.) **Ballroom,** where the king confers knighthoods; the parquet-floored **Music Room,** unaltered since John Nash decorated it in 1831, where the king's siblings were baptized in water brought from the River Jordan; and a stroll through the thick **Garden** in the back yard. It's definitely worth seeing—how often can you toddle around the spare rooms in a king's house, inspecting artwork given as gifts by some of history's most prominent names? Monarchists will simply lose their heads over the gift shop, full of premium products to which the Windsors have deigned to attach their approval, from tea sets to candy to ornaments to a house gin. If you're in London any time other than August or September and spot the standard of red, gold, and blue flying above, you'll at least know the king is home. If it's the Union Jack, he's gone—he much prefers Windsor (p. 324).

Buckingham Palace Rd., SW1. www.royalcollection.org.uk. ✆ **020/7766-7300.** Admission £37 adults, £24.50 age 18–24, £18.50 children 5–17, discounts when purchased ahead. Discounts online if you visit The King's Gallery and Royal Mews on the same day. Generally open for 10 weeks starting in late July. July–Aug daily 9:30am–7:30pm; Sept daily 9:30am–6:30pm; last admission 1 hr. 15 min. before closing. Occasional brief openings outside of summer; check website. Tube: Victoria or Green Park.

Churchill War Rooms ♥♥♥ MUSEUM/HISTORIC SITE One of London's most fascinating museums is the secret command center used by Winston Churchill and his staff during the most harrowing moments of World War II, when it looked like England might become German. We regard the period with nostalgia, but a staggering 30,000 civilians were killed by some 18,000 tons of bombs in London alone, and more than 65,000 innocent people were killed in Britain as a whole. Here, in the cellar of the Treasury building, practically next door to 10 Downing Street, the nucleus of the British government hunkered down in a place where one errant bomb could have incinerated the lot of them. When the War ended, the bunker was abandoned, but everything was left just as it was in August 1945, and when it was time to make it a museum, everything was intact—from pushpins tracing convoy movements on yellowed world maps to rationed sugar cubes hidden in the back of a desk drawer. Midway through, you disappear into the **Churchill Museum**. Exhaustively displaying every conceivable facet of his life (his bowtie, his bowler hat, and even the original front door to 10 Downing Street), it covers the exalted statesman's life from entitled birth through his antics as a journalist in South Africa (where he escaped a kidnapping and became a national hero), to, of course, his years as prime minister. The entire museum is atwitter with multimedia displays, but the centerpiece will blow you away: a 15m-long (50-ft.) Lifeline Interactive table, that looks like a long file cabinet and covers

Churchill's bedroom, part of the secret bunker complex at the Churchill War Rooms.

every month of Churchill's life. Touch a date, and a projected file "opens" with rare documents, photos, or, for critical dates in history, animated Easter eggs that temporarily consume the entire table (select the original Armistice Day or the *Titanic* sinking to see what we mean). Most people wish they had budgeted more time for this fascinating museum.

Clive Steps, King Charles St., SW1. www.iwm.org.uk. ✆ **020/7930-6961.** Admission £33 adults, £29.70 seniors 65 and over, £15.50 children 5–15, posted prices are higher and include a voluntary donation, discounts for entry after 3:30pm. Sept–June daily 9:30am–6pm; July–Aug daily 9:30am–7pm; last admission 1 hr. before closing. Tube: Westminster or St James's Park.

Houses of Parliament ♥♥ LANDMARK Luckily, the nation allows you to tour a dozen stately halls and even to wander through its vaunted House of Lords and House of Commons when they're not in session. In session, that could mean only Saturday availability. Choose a 100-minute guided group tour, which presents the usual issues of audibility, pace, and guides who don't know the answers. Or (our choice, having done both), take it easy with the 2-hour audio guide (and eavesdrop on groups whenever you want). Massive Westminster Hall, which was built in 1097 by William Rufus, son of William the Conqueror and is one of the most hallowed and historic spaces in the nation, if not *the* most. Richard II commissioned its oak hammer-beam ceiling before he was deposed in the 1390s. Charles I, William Wallace, Sir Thomas More, and Guy Fawkes were all condemned in it, and it's where a quarter of a million people paid respects to Queen Elizabeth II following her passing in September 2022. Look for the brass plaque in the floor.

For the Parliament tour, the rest of the Palace is roughly divided into three areas: those for the House of Lords (whose members inherit seats, done in rose with an unbelievable gilt sitting area where Queen Victoria would preside on designated occasions); the House of Commons (by far the most powerful,

The Houses of Parliament, viewed from the opposite bank of the Thames.

elected by the people, but plainer, with seats of blue-green under a hanging forest of microphones); and some flabbergasting lobbies, sitting rooms, and the "Robing Room" (golds, browns, burgundies), which the Sovereign flits through when he shows up once a year to kick off sessions. You walk right onto the floor of both Houses. Many delicious details are elucidated, from the knock-marks on the Commons door made by the Crown's emissary, the Black Rod, to the line in the carpet members may not cross when in the throes of vigorous debates. In the summer, the opulent **State Apartments of Speaker's House**, in which the Speaker of the House of Commons lives during their tenure, also opens for recommended 75-minute tours (£22), giving you a much more intimate inspection of the craftmanship of this complex and the intricacies of its history and functions. If you have any curiosity, tour these places while you can: The entire aged Parliament complex is in dire shape and will close in stages anytime now for a much-needed yearslong restoration.

Bridge St. and Parliament Sq., SW1. www.parliament.uk/visit. ✆ **020/7219-4114.** Guided tours £34 adults, £28 ages 16–24, £18 children 5–15, free for children 4 and under, add £2 if booked the same day. Audio tours £27 adults, £20 ages 16–24, £10 children 5–15, one free child for every paid adult ticket for audio tours. Tours: Mon–Sat during Parliamentary recesses; times vary; calendar on online ticket page. Reservations essential. Tube: Westminster.

Spencer House ♥♥ HISTORIC HOME Currently controlled by the Rothschild banking company, which hosts diplomatic and corporate events here, this lush home is the only surviving London mansion with an intact

Big Ben Up Close

Elizabeth Tower (1859), beside the House of Parliament, contains the 13½-ton bell known around the world as Big Ben, plus four smaller bells that collaborate to sound what's known as the Westminster Quarters. Until recently, the entire tower was forbidden to foreigners. (That was particularly unfair for Americans because Big Ben is actually a cousin of Philadelphia's Liberty Bell. Both were cast in the Whitechapel Bell Foundry in East London.) In July 2023, though, Parliament introduced a new bucket-list **Big Ben Tour** (£35 for adults, £20 kids 11–17, no kids 10 or younger, about 1 hr. 45 min.) that allows anyone to come, but you have to be fit, because you'll be climbing up 334 narrow, winding Victorian steps on the way; no lift exists. You'll be rewarded with the once-in-a-lifetime opportunity to squeeze behind the giant clock faces and even sit in the machine room to watch the enormous mechanism operate—before the clock went electric, it was wound by hand, and you can still see the divots in the floor where generations of operators planted their feet for leverage. At the tour's climax, you'll stand in the belfry, directly under the iconic bells as they automatically sound out the hour (earplugs are provided) and jitter your most interior organs. Book for before 12pm if you can, because its timing will ensure you are present for the maximum number of gongs at noon; later tours witness shorter bellringing. New tickets for the coming month or two are released at 10am London time on the second Wednesday of every month via www.parliament.uk/bigben.

The library at the Spencer House, London's only surviving 1700s mansion with an intact interior.

18th-century interior; tours let you see the ground floor and a portion of the first floor. The house was begun in 1756 as a love nest by Diana Spencer's ancestors (and, by extension, the future king's); its lavish gilt and carved decor repeatedly invoke the symbols of fidelity and virility. Great War damage spooked the Spencer clan, who moved out in the 1920s, and since then, they've gradually transferred the most precious elements to their estate at Althorp, 193km (120 miles) north of the city, and replaced them with equally fantastic facsimiles—the library fireplace, for instance, took 4,000 hours to carve. The original Painted Room suite was once at the V&A. Tours are limited to 20, so book ahead.

27 St James's Place, SW1. www.spencerhouse.co.uk. ✆ **020/7514-1958.** Tours £19.50 adults; £16.50 students, seniors, and children 15 and under; reservations essential. Sun 10am–4pm; closed Aug. Tube: Green Park.

Tate Britain ♥ MUSEUM Tourists often wonder about the difference between the Tate Modern and this, its sister upstream on the Thames. Well, the Modern is for contemporary art of any origin, and the Britain, besides its calmer and more civilized affect, is mostly for British-made art made after 1500. Shifting objectives consistently rotate beloved paintings into storage, a frustrating habit with Tate. A 2023 rehang did visitors few favors; many masterpieces are positioned without consideration of gallery traffic patterns or light glare, and while there are now two gift shops, there's only one bathroom, and it's in the cellar. But there's still much to appreciate and there's often an interesting (if separately ticketed) exhibition going on; big shows for 2026 and 2027 include James McNeill Whistler, Vanessa Bell and Duncan Grant, and a retrospective of the 1990s. In the river-facing lobby, look for a TV screen listing today's events, which usually include free tours on various topics on the hour between 11am and 3pm. To go chronologically, head down the building's center; see the oldest stuff in back and to the left, and then move anticlockwise around the central hall. Look for these: Turner's trenchant ***The Field of Waterloo*** (room 6) was painted in 1818, 3 years after the battle; its shadowy piles of corpses, and of bereaved family members searching them, is still considered a daring exposure of the true price of war. The oil-on-canvas ***Carnation, Lily, Lily, Rose*** (8) by John Singer Sargent depicts children holding paper lanterns so luminous that when it was first exhibited in 1887, its worth was instantly recognized and it was purchased for the nation. John Everett Millais' depiction of a drowning ***Ophelia*** (10) is also considered a treasure (and not just by Taylor Swift, who echoed the work in a 2025 video) for its phenomenally tricky depiction of water. Kids love the double vision of ***The Cholmondeley Ladies*** (1), two new mothers "born the same day, Married the same day, And brought to Bed the same day"; look closely and you'll realize they're not identical. Check out the sculptures, too, including forms by **Henry Moore** (22 & 23) and **Damien Hirst**'s *Away from the Flock* (26), which was part of a 1990s series that redefined contemporary art by preserving animals in tanks of formaldehyde. But the crowning attraction here is the **Turner Galleries** and their expansive collection of works by J. M. W. Turner (1775–1851). The son of a Covent Garden barber, Turner was a master of landscapes lit by gauzy, perpetual sunrise, and the dozens of paintings testify to both his undying popularity and his doggedly British tendency to convey information mostly by implication. Turner's works are atmospheric, if sleepy (the precise landscape painter John Constable called them "airy visions painted with tinted steam"), and they're best appreciated once you understand their profound influence on subsequent artists.

Millbank, SW1. www.tate.org.uk. ✆ **020/7887-8888.** Free admission. Daily 10am–6pm. Tube: Pimlico.

Westminster Abbey ♥♥♥ HISTORIC SITE/CHURCH If you have to pick just one church to see in London—nay, one church in the entire *world*—this is the one, making it one of the elite London attractions that's worth its high ticket price. The echoes of history are mind-blowing: The current building dates from the 1200s, but it was part of a monastery dating to at least 960. Every English monarch since 1066 has been crowned here (with three minor exceptions: Edward V, Edward VIII, and possibly Mary I). There are 17 monarchs interred here (deaths dating from 1066 to 1760—the crypts are overstuffed, so now they go to Windsor), as are dozens of great writers and artists. Even if England's tumultuous history and the thought of bodies lying underfoot don't stir your imagination, the interior—in places, as intricate as lace—will earn your appreciation. A visit should take about 3 hours and should begin early, since entry lines (some 1.4 million visits a year) can be excruciating. Tickets can sell out, so reserve ahead; also consider the optional special tours such as Abbey Unlocked, which gets you in before the official opening time and Hidden Highlights, which takes you behind the scenes.

Unlike St Paul's Cathedral (p. 188), which has an airy, stately beauty, the much smaller Westminster is more like time's attic, packed with artifacts, memorials, tombs, and virtuosic shrines—a confluence of God, art, and dense

The Coronation Chair display at Westminster Abbey.

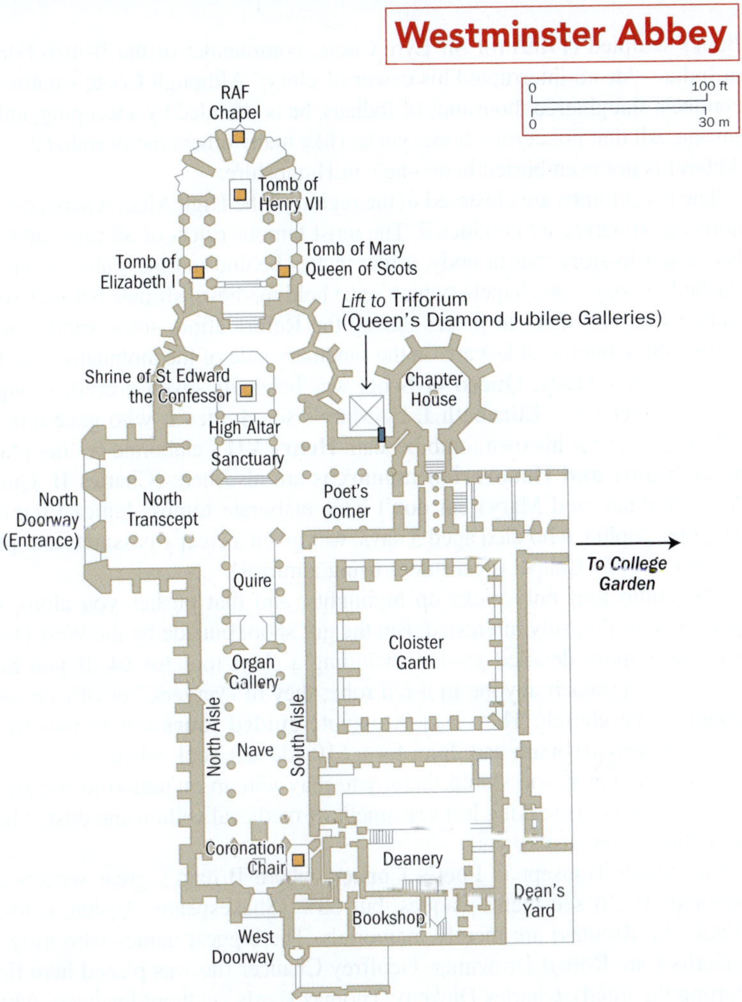

history. It's easy to feel overloaded after just a few minutes. Take your time and don't get swept along in the current of visitors. Let them pass. There are stories to be told in every square meter of this place—name another building where there is such a staggering continuity of a nation's heritage.

A visit is likely to start with a welcome from a volunteer; the Abbey follows the Benedictine tradition, which dictates a warm reception for everyone. It's also still a functioning Anglican spiritual center, so there may be calls for prayer or moments of silence as you tour. You'll be in the Nave, passing Darwin's resting place (just after the first blue gate), and it only accelerates from there. Bombastic tombs abound; take your time absorbing their colonialist self-importance. Google one and you'll unravel a tale, such as the one Thomas

Banks sculpted (1789) for Sir Eyre Coote, commander of the British Forces in India—"death interrupted his career of glory." Although Coote's battles of conquest slaughtered thousands of Indians, he is attended by a weeping, naked savage. All that ponderous stone, yet he (like many others memorialized in the Abbey) is not even buried here—he's in Hampshire.

The royal tombs are clustered in the region of the High Altar, where coronations and funerals are conducted. The most famous rulers of all time are truly *here*—not in story, but in body, a few inches behind marble slabs. Some are stashed in cozy side chapels (which once held medieval shrines before Cromwellians bashed them to pieces during the Reformation; some vandalism is still visible), but the oldest are on the sanctuary side of the ambulatory (aisle). The executed **Mary, Queen of Scots** was belatedly given a crypt of equal stature to her rival, **Elizabeth I,** by Mary's son **James I,** who gave himself only a marker for his own tomb beneath **Henry VII**'s elaborate resting place. Some **Stuart and Hanoverian monarchs** are also here (Charles II, Queen Anne, William and Mary) but don't have elaborate tombs. James I's infant daughter Sophia, who died aged 3 days, was given a creepy bassinet sarcophagus in the Lady Chapel (peer into it using a mirror).

The audio tour only picks up highlights, and that pushes you along too quickly if you're truly interested. But the gift shop (outside by the West Doorway) sells more detailed guides, including a short tour for £4. If you have questions, approach anyone in a red robe; they're "vergers," or officers who attend to the church. They lead 90-minute **guided tours** (up to four times daily between 10:30am and 2pm, for a £10 add-on; book when you arrive at the Abbey), and if you stump them, you may win an invitation to the atmospheric Library, a creaking loft that smells of medieval vellum and dust, where an archivist can answer you.

The South Transept is **Poet's Corner,** where Britain's great writers are honored. You'll see many plaques, but 60% (Shakespeare, Austen, Carroll, Wilde, the Brontës) are merely memorials. The biggest names who truly lie underfoot are Robert Browning, Geoffrey Chaucer (he was placed here first, starting the trend), Charles Dickens, Thomas Hardy (without his heart, which was buried in Dorset), John Gay, Rudyard Kipling, George Frideric Handel (who popularized the use of the Abbey as a concert venue), Dr. Samuel Johnson, Laurence Olivier, Edmund Spenser, and Alfred, Lord Tennyson. Ben Jonson is commemorated here, but is actually buried in the Nave near Isaac Newton, Charles Darwin, and the new genius on the block, Stephen Hawking. Also in the Nave, in the northwest corner, look out for a batch of prime ministers underfoot.

TOP DON'T-MISS EXHIBITS AT WESTMINSTER ABBEY

- That oak seat in the last niche before your exit is the **Coronation Chair.** Unbelievably, nearly every English monarch since 1308 has been crowned on this excruciating-looking throne. The slot under the seat is for the 152kg (336-lb.) Stone of Scone, said to have been used as a pillow by the Bible's Jacob, and a central part of Irish, Scottish, and English coronations since at least 700 B.C.E. After spending 7 centuries in the Abbey (except for when Scottish nationalists stole it for 4 months in late 1950), the Stone was returned to Scotland in 1996, where it's on view at Edinburgh Castle. It returns for every coronation, most recently for King Charles III in May 2023.

- **Oliver Cromwell,** who overthrew the monarchy and ran England as a republic, was buried with honors behind the High Altar in 1658. Three years later, after the monarchy was restored, his corpse was dug up, dragged to Tyburn (by the Marble Arch), hanged, and decapitated. The body was then tossed into a common grave, and its head put on display outside the Abbey. (Didn't they realize he was already dead?) Today his much-abused cranium is at Sidney Sussex College in Cambridge. Cromwell's daughter, who died young, was mercifully allowed to remain buried in the Abbey. In the window above the grave, look for a hole that was left after a 1940 Blitz bombing.
- The **High Altar,** with a mosaic floor laid in the year 1268, is where coronations take place. The actual event sounds glamorous, but it's actually excruciating for everyone involved: Some 8,500 spectators are packed into this small space, and the monarch's crown weighs a brutal 5.5 pounds.
- The **Quire** is where the choir sings; it comprises about 12 men and 30 or so boys who are educated at the adjoining Westminster Choir School, the last of its type in the U.K. The wooden stalls, in the Gothic style, are Victorian, and are so delicate they're dusted using vacuum cleaners.

A 2018 addition opened a very old space to the public for the first time. It's the 13th-century **Triforium,** a horseshoe-shaped attic 70 feet up with an astounding view down the length of the sanctuary—a lift tower was grafted to the venerable building just for it. This once-dusty aerie is now the mind-blowing (and lightly trafficked) **Queen's Diamond Jubilee Galleries** (sometimes closes by mid-afternoon or all day). You'll find such fascinating stuff as Prince William and Kate's marriage license and a crowd of the startlingly lifelike wax effigies used in centuries of notable funerals to show the masses what their heroes looked like—many, like Mary II, wearing their *original* garments. Back on the ground, look also for the panel concealing the **Chapter House,** which was made between 924 and 1030 and is Britain's oldest door. Time seems suspended in the **Cloister,** or courtyard. Writer Aphra Behn was buried in the East Cloister near the steps of the church when she "dyed" in 1689 (her wry inscription: "Here lies a Proof that Wit can never be Defence enough against Mortality."). Even better gardens are hidden away: Look for the fragrant and fountained **Little Cloister Garden,** blackened by 19th-century coal dust, and beyond that to the right, the wide **College Garden** (open Tues–Thurs), a tempting courtyard with daffodil beds, green lawns, and plane trees. It has been cultivated for over 900 years but is today discovered only by those in the know (now, that's you). The garden is thought to be Britain's longest-established one, having been cultivated for nearly a millennium. **Westminster School,** started by the abbey's monks in the 1300s, stands nearby; past students include Christopher Wren, Edward Gibbon, John Gielgud, and pop musicians Thomas Dolby and Gavin Rossdale. (Incidentally, there haven't been monks in this complex for 550 years, yet Londoners persist in calling it an "Abbey.")

Get a real sense of the majesty of the space at a service. Evening prayer services with choirs from around the world are at 5pm weekdays; sung Eucharist is on Sundays at 11am, plus a Sunday organ recital at 5:45pm and evening service with simple hymns at 6:30pm (but check ahead; services are sometimes shuffled to smaller, but equally historic, chapels). Holy Communion is daily at 8am, Matins are at 10am, and Evensong is Saturdays at 3pm. There's also a daily Eucharist at 12:30pm in the Nave. In the **Cellarium** cafe, a simple cream tea is £9.50 and starts at noon, full afternoon tea is £36.50, and cooked lunch is also served. Next door, pop into **St Margaret's Chapel** (free), which the monks built in 1523 so they'd be left alone in peace. The Germans didn't comply: Some southern windows were destroyed by a bomb and were replaced by plain glass, and in addition to damage to the north wall, Pew 3 remains charred.

Broad Sanctuary, SW1. www.westminster-abbey.org. ✆ **020/7222-5152.** Admission £31 adults, £28 seniors and students, £14 children 6–17, free for children 5 and under; price includes audio guide; access and prices may be reduced if portions of the Abbey are being used for official business. Queen's Diamond Jubilee Galleries £5 adults, free for young people 17 and under. Abbey may sell reduced-price tickets when some areas are inaccessible. Generally open Mon–Fri 9:30am–3:30pm; Sat 9am–3:30pm, but check the online calendar; last admission 1 hr. before closing. Closed Sun for worship. Summers only: Weds 4:30–6pm (£15, no multimedia guide). Check ahead for closures. Tube: Westminster.

Other Westminster & St James's Attractions

Jewel Tower ♥ HISTORIC SITE Built around 1365, it's one of only two remnants left from the 1834 fire that ravaged the Royal Palace of Westminster. Minor and easily overlooked, this three-level stone tower, once a moat-side storehouse for Edward III's treasures, has walls so thick it was later considered an ideal setting for taking accurate measurements. So, you'll see some explanation of weights-and-measures standards and some relics dug up from the moat (including a 1,200-year-old sword, and a bulbous bottle from the Sun, a 17th-c. tavern where Samuel Pepys drank).

Abingdon St., SW1. www.english-heritage.org.uk. ✆ **020/7222-2219.** Admission £5.90 adults, £5 seniors and students, £3.10 children 5–17; posted prices are higher and include voluntary donation. Apr–Sept Wed–Sun 10am–5pm; Oct–early Nov Sat–Sun 10am–5pm; Nov–Mar Sat–Sun 10am–4pm. Tube: Westminster.

The King's Gallery ♥ MUSEUM Every monarch inherits the mother of all art collections—one million items including 7,000 paintings, 30,000 watercolors, and half a million prints, to say nothing of sculpture, furniture, and jewelry—but it was the late Queen Elizabeth who decided she ought to show many of them to the public. This was her Queen's Gallery, which was renamed for the king in 2024. Only a tiny fraction is here; the booty is also in palaces such as Kensington and Hampton Court, and on loan. The few works (budget 1 hr.) are undoubtedly exceptional (one of the world's few Vermeers, a Rubens self-portrait given to Charles I, glittering ephemera by Fabergé), but depending on what temporary exhibition supplements them, they may not be the cream of what the crown owns, and it may bore kids.

Buckingham Palace Rd., SW1. www.rct.uk. ✆ **020/7766-7301.** Admission £22 adults, £14 young people 18–24, £11 children 5–17, under 5 free, discounts available for booking in advance online. Thurs–Mon (July–Aug daily) 10am–5:30pm; last admission 4:15pm. Tube: Victoria.

The Royal Mews ♥ MUSEUM Most visitors pop in to what amounts to the king's garage in about 15 minutes. You'll see stables fit for a you-know-who (they barely smell at all) and His Majesty's Rolls-Royces (many of which, at King Charles III's behest, run on green fuels). You'll also overdose on learning about regulations for when this set of harnesses may be used and when that leather must be polished.

Buckingham Palace Rd., SW1. www.rct.uk. ✆ **020/7766-7302.** Admission £18 adults, £12 students 18–24, £9 children 5–17, discounts available for booking in advance online. Thurs–Mon 10am–5pm; last admission 4pm. Tube: Victoria.

MARYLEBONE & MAYFAIR

Alexander Fleming Laboratory Museum ♥ HISTORIC SITE It was here in this room, in 1928, that a dashing young Scottish microbiologist, Alexander Fleming, came back from vacation to discover a wayward bacteria had contaminated a petri dish. This annoyance was fortunately recognized as a eureka moment, because that's when he realized what penicillin was and what it could do. Since World War II, it has saved millions of lives. Fleming's museum is super old school: crisp elderly volunteer docents, a clunky and barely audible film from decades ago, recalcitrant hours. But it's real, since it has never been renovated and the stuff in Fleming's lab was actually his. He moved out in 1933, but his equipment was kept and put back in 1993. In addition to his teeny lab, which preserves his microscope, you also visit a small exhibit explaining how the rescue of mankind went down—one fellow medical professional ate a little of the new mold to prove it was safe. "Tastes like Stilton!" he declared, and they're still not sure if the intruding bacterium flew in from Praed Street or fluttered up from the mold lab that was once where modern visitors enter. The museum is a part of the active maternity ward where Prince George, Princess Charlotte, and Prince Louis were born (for a while, Fleming's lab was for diaper storage and as a nap room for obstetricians). When you depart, you actually walk through it, past rushing nurses, beaming parents, and babies who will live long, healthy lives because of the accident that happened in the room you have just been in.

St Mary's Hospital, 135a Praed Street, W2. www.imperial.nhs.uk/about-us/what-we-do/fleming-museum. ✆ **020/7886-6528.** Admission free, but reservations required. Mon–Thurs 10am–1pm. Use of stairs required. Tube: Paddington.

Apsley House ♥♥ HISTORIC HOME This is how you'd be rewarded if you became a colonial war hero: You'd get Hyde Park as a backyard. In 1815, Arthur Wellesley defeated Napoleon and became the Duke of Wellington, and later prime minister. The mansion, still in the family (they maintain private rooms), was filled with splendid thank-you gifts showered upon him by grateful nations, including a thousand-piece silver set from the Portuguese court. Still, he never seemed to get his nemesis off his mind: Under the grand staircase stands a colossal nude statue of Napoleon that the little emperor despised; the Duke cherished it as a token of victory. Apsley's supreme art stash, which was largely looted by the French from the Spanish royal family and never went home, includes a few works by Jan Brueghel the Elder, Diego Velasquez's virtuosic *The Waterseller of Seville* (you can understand why it was the artist's favorite work—just looking at it makes you thirsty); and Correggio's *The Agony in the Garden,* in a case fitted with a keyhole so the Duke could open it and polish it with a silk hankie. The Duke and his best friend lived here together after their wives died, and the whiff of faded masculine glory pervades the place like cigar smoke. In other circumstances, the Duke and Napoleon, who both liked fancy finery and fancier egos, would have been buddies. If you're also visiting Wellington Arch (p. 171), a joint ticket will save a couple of pounds.

149 Piccadilly. www.english-heritage.org.uk. ✆ **020/7499-5676.** Admission around £10.40 adults, £9 seniors and students, £6.30 children 5–17 (including audio tour); posted prices are higher and include voluntary donation. Apr–Oct Wed–Sun 11am–5pm; Nov–Dec Thurs–Sun 11am–5pm, Jan–March Sat–Sun 11am–5pm. Check ahead for closures. Tube: Hyde Park Corner.

Handel Hendrix House ♥ HISTORIC HOME Here's a pleasant *Messiah* complex. This Mayfair building, the German-born composer's home for 36 years from 1723 (he was its first tenant) to his death here in 1759, has lived many lives—before the museum's 2001 opening, conservators chipped 28 layers of paint off the interior walls to uncover the original grey color. In its day, it was a factory for his celebrity: Handel would compose in one room (he wrote *Messiah* here in 24 days), debut his work in another (there are still

Jimi's bedroom, re-created as it was in 1968–69 at the Handel Hendrix House.

frequent performances, including on a resident double manual harpsichord; check the website), sleep in a third, and sell scores and tickets to the public from a ground-floor shop. (None of the furniture was his, but Handel fans can investigate the composer's collection at the Foundling Museum (p. 140), where he was a crucial patron.) In 2016, the museum expanded to encompass the top floors of a neighboring building, where legendary guitarist Jimi Hendrix lived in 1968 and 1969. Here, in a cozy flat above an office so he could loudly practice his guitar at night, his girlfriend Kathy Etchingham tried to give him his first stable home; here he made music and love, entertained, filmed interviews (which gave curators images to reconstruct it down to the last detail, and a couple items were really here then)—and played Handel records to absorb the genius of his neighbor across the centuries. But Etchingham's nurturing efforts were to no avail; soon after they broke up, he died at age 27 in Notting Hill. There are lots of tiny, uneven steps to navigate, but there's also a lift upon request.

25 Brook St., W1. https://handelhendrix.org. ✆ **020/7495-1685.** Admission £14.50 adults, £10.50 students, £5 kids 13–17, free for kids under 13; includes handheld tour device. Weds–Sun 10am–5pm; last admission 4pm. Tube: Bond Street.

Royal Academy of Arts ♥ MUSEUM Britain's first art school, founded in 1768, relocated here to Burlington House, a Palladian-style mansion away from Piccadilly's fumes. Although it's one of London's oldest arts institutions, or perhaps because it is, the Royal Academy is not the most rewarding of the creative palaces. Your interest in the topic of its current paid exhibition (£14–£20 tickets for those) will determine whether you want to visit. The biggest event, and always worth it, is the annual **Summer Exhibition,** which without fail since 1769 (even in 2020—just late) has displayed the best works from anonymous submissions; careers are made by it. The cafe to the left when you first enter is a secret place to charge your phone. Don't miss the wooden red "Phone Box No. 1" tucked behind the stone front gate—it was the 1924 prototype for what we now recognize as an international icon.

Burlington House, Piccadilly or 6 Burlington Gardens, W1. www.royalacademy.org.uk. ✆ **020/7300-8000.** Free admission. Tues–Sun 10am–6pm; last admission 30 min. before closing. Tube: Piccadilly Circus or Green Park.

Speakers' Corner ♥ LANDMARK Near the northeast corner of Hyde Park, where Edgware Road meets Bayswater Road, Londoners of yore congregated for public executions. By the early 1800s, the gathered crowds were jeering at hangings instead of cheering them, and the locale's reputation for public outcry became entrenched. An Act of Parliament in 1872 finally legitimized it as a place of free speech, and its tradition of well-intentioned protest has evolved into a quirky weekend attraction. Laborers and suffragettes fomented social change here, but these days, you're more likely to encounter a rogues' gallery of idealists and religious nutters. Anyone can show up, always on Sunday mornings after 7am, with a soapbox (or, these days, a stepladder), plus an axe to grind, and orate about anything from Muslim relations to the superiority of 1970s disco. If they don't have the debate skills to appease the crowd, they stand a good chance of being teased, or at the very least vigorously challenged. In true British style, most speakers refrain from profanity. Even the verbal volleys are usually polite. ("Communists, violent racists, vegetarians," reported Arthur Frommer in 1957. "They undergo the finest heckling in the world, a vicious repartee. . . .")

Tube: Marble Arch, exits 4, 5, 8, or 9.

The Wallace Collection ♥♥♥ MUSEUM A little bit V&A (decorative arts and furniture), a little bit National Gallery (paintings and portraits), but with a boutique French flair, the Wallace celebrates fine living in an extravagant 19th-century city mansion, the former Hertford House. Rooms drip with chandeliers, clocks, suits of armor, and furniture, usually of royal provenance, and there's not a clunker among the paintings. While other museums were stocking up on Renaissance works, this collection's originators, visionaries of sorts, were buying 17th- and 18th-century artists for cheap, and now its collection shines. You might recognize Jean-Honoré Fragonard's *The Swing* (Oval Drawing Room), showing a maiden kicking her slipper to her suitor below. Peter Paul Rubens' *The Rainbow Landscape* is also here (East Drawing Room), as is the world's most complete room of furniture belonging to Marie-Antoinette (Study; look for her initials hidden around a keyhole on one cabinet). Thomas Gainsborough's *Mrs. Mary Robinson "Perdita"* (West Room) depicts the sloe-eyed actress in mid-affair with the Prince of Wales; she holds a token of his love, a miniature portrait, in her right hand. If she exudes suspicion, it's for good reason—the Prince dumped her before the paint was dry. Don't miss the Great Gallery, a stupendous tour de force of world-class old master paintings. Red folders contain descriptions of pictures, and gold ones are for furniture—the information even tells who owned them before they got here. Be in the Ground Floor State Rooms at the top of the hour, when a chorus of golden musical clocks announce midday direct from the 1700s. Download the free Bloomberg Connects app (free Wi-Fi; bring earbuds) for an audio guide. The Wallace Restaurant, in the covered courtyard, has an exemplary atmosphere but stupidly high prices.

A young decorative arts admirer at the Wallace Collection.

Hertford House, Manchester Sq., W1. www.wallacecollection.org. ✆ **020/7563-9500.** Free admission. Daily 10am–5pm. Tube: Bond Street.

DEATH TAKES A holiday

If you're a major musical star, stay away from London! It seems a disproportionate number of singers have met untimely ends here (especially in the summer). These houses aren't open to the public, but their grim pasts make them music landmarks:

- **June 22, 1969, 4 Cadogan Lane, Belgravia** (Tube: Sloane Square): **Judy Garland** overdosed on barbiturates (Seconal) and expired in the bathroom of the two-room flat owned by her fifth husband of 3 months, Mickey Deans. The public outpouring of grief, and its suppression by police in New York City, is credited with starting, or at least fueling, the gay rights movement as we know it today.
- **September 18, 1970, 22 Lansdowne Crescent, Notting Hill** (Tube: Notting Hill Gate): In a basement flat of the Samarkand Hotel, **Jimi Hendrix** washed down nine Vesperax sleeping pills with alcohol. An ambulance was summoned, but arrived too late. The plot thickened 26 years later, when the last person to see him alive, girlfriend Monika Dannemann, was found asphyxiated in a car in Seaford, East Sussex, not long after being accused in court of keeping secrets about Hendrix's final moments.
- **July 29, 1974 and September 7, 1978, Flat 12, 9 Curzon Place, Mayfair** (Tube: Hyde Park Corner): **"Mama" Cass Elliot** of The Mamas and the Papas was found dead in between solo performances at the London Palladium in a flat owned by songwriter Harry Nilsson, who wasn't home. Contrary to lore, she didn't die by choking on a ham sandwich but from a heart attack in her sleep brought on by morbid obesity (she was 165cm/5'5" and weighed 108kg/238 lb.). Four years after Elliot's death, **Keith Moon,** drummer of The Who, died in the same flat. His undoing: chlormethiazole edisylate, a prescribed anti-alcohol drug. Horrified that two of his friends should die while borrowing his home, Nilsson quickly sold it to Moon's bandmate Pete Townshend.
- **July 23, 2011, 30 Camden Square, Camden** (Tube: Camden Town): After a period of abstinence, **Amy Winehouse** binged on vodka and succumbed to alcohol poisoning in her bedroom in this 2,500-square-foot townhouse, where she'd lived only a few months. Security guards were there but thought she was only sleeping. For years afterward, fans would leave bottles and cans of booze outside as a macabre tribute.

Wellington Arch ♥ LANDMARK When it was finished in 1830, it was intended as a triumphal entry to central London (Marble Arch, at Hyde Park's northern corner, was originally Queen Victoria's triumphal entry to Buckingham Palace), and in 2022, Queen Elizabeth II's funeral cortege passed through it on her final journey out of London. Minor anecdotes of its relocation and the switch from Wellington's original statue on top to a smaller statue (*Peace Descending upon War,* the largest bronze sculpture in Europe) are all this handsome landmark can muster in its little museum, which also discusses the period when the Arch served as a police station. If you buy a joint ticket with the Apsley House (p. 167), across Piccadilly, you'll save a couple of pounds; you can take an elevator up with the admission price.

Hyde Park Corner, Apsley Way, W1. www.english-heritage.org.uk. ✆ **020/7930-2726.** Admission around £5.90 adults, £5 seniors, £3.10 children 5–17; posted prices are higher and include voluntary donation. Apr–Oct Wed–Sun 10am–5pm; Nov–Mar Wed–Sun 10am–4pm. Tube: Hyde Park Corner.

KENSINGTON & KNIGHTSBRIDGE

Kensington Palace ♥ PALACE Most people know it as the place where Lady Diana raised Princes William and Harry with Prince Charles from 1984 to 1996, but it has been a royal domicile since 1689, when William and Mary took control of an existing home (then, this was in the country, far from town, to ease William's asthma) and made it theirs. Handsome and haughty, with little of the gilding and symmetry that defined later English tastes, the redbrick palace is not as ostentatious as you might expect. It has been constantly reused over time, so on your multimedia-led guide, you'll tour three areas grouped by three historical eras: the **King's State Apartments**, pegged to King George III and Queen Caroline and the early 1700s; the **Queen's State Apartments**, centered on Mary II and the turn of the 18th century; and **Victoria: A Royal Childhood**, which explores the room where the long-lived queen was born, raised, and groomed to rule before her ascension in 1837. (Victoria could use her own full museum, not just these spare rooms containing a few castoffs from her youth.) There's very little signage to tell you what you're looking at or even what time period you're meant to be considering, which is an issue since different sections have been restored to different eras, but each room has a red-bound Room Guide (sometimes it's hard to find) that briefly describes objects and art they did manage to bring in. Thankfully, the walk-through includes the magnificent King's Staircase, lined with delicate canvas panels whose perimeters are rigged with tissue paper slivers that will tear as a warning of shifting or swelling. The staircase is considered so precious that it wasn't opened to the public until 2004, 105 years after the rest of the palace first accepted sightseers. Outside in the Sunken Garden, there's a new statue of Diana (unveiled in 2021). Overall, though, if you're short on time, this Palace has seen better days, and heavy use over the centuries has stripped it down.

Kensington Gardens, W8. www.hrp.org.uk. ✆ **084/4482-7777.** Admission £24.70 adults, £20 seniors and students, £12.50 kids 5–15, including audio tour; posted prices are higher and include voluntary donation. Mar–Oct Wed–Sun 10am–6pm; Nov–Feb Wed–Sun 10am–4pm; last admission 1 hr. before closing. Tube: High Street Kensington or Queensway.

Natural History Museum ♥♥ MUSEUM The commodious NHM, which is the busiest attraction in Britain (around 6.3 million a year, mostly families, by far the most of the three big South Ken museums), is good for several hours' wander, but you'll have plenty of company. In all ways, it's a zoo. You

The Natural History Museum is filled with specimens collected in the Victorian era.

get a hall of dinosaur bones, a taxidermist's menagerie, racks of rocks, and case after case of stuffed stuff. Mostly, you'll encounter the wildest creatures of all: lurching, wailing, scampering children in all their varieties, because everything here, down to the simplified signage and touchable replicas, is pitched to kids on field trips. Most of the discussion here, and throughout the museum, is aimed at a child's mind, with signs answering such unasked questions as why we study nature. On weekends and school holidays, the outdoor queue can be an hour long, so go at opening.

Even if you don't give a hooey about remedial ecology, the main, cathedral-like Victorian building, started in 1873 and now called **Hintze Hall,** is unforgettable: Columns crawl with carved monkeys whimsically clinging to the terra cotta and plants creeping across 162 ceiling panels. (The museum throws a crazy New Year's bash in here.) The star gallery is probably the **Dinosaurs (Blue Zone),** where heavy crowds slog through one-way walkways past replicas including the 26m-long (85-ft.) **Dippy,** a 1905 plaster cast of a *Diplodocus carnegii* found in America. Some of the dinosaurs are robotic, which can scare small kids. More academic: At the top of the stairs, the **Treasures** gallery holds such historically meaningful stuff as a dodo skeleton and Britain's only moon rock. The pretend kitchen full of hiding places for insects and **Creepy Crawlies** (the **Green Zone**) are longtime visitor favorites, as is the **Red Zone** (the Earth Galleries), anchored by a toned-down, ride-along mock-up of a Japanese supermarket jolted by the 1995 Kobe earthquake. The **Darwin Centre**'s Cocoon looks like a seven-story egg laid in the back atrium; hidden inside are some 20 million bottled specimens (including those that came back on the *Beagle*) on 27km/17 miles of shelves, which you will not see unless you book a £28 "Spirit Collection" tour in advance (daily; 45 min.).

The museum's brainiacs even cultivate a wildlife garden and pond (the **Orange Zone**) that attract a range of English creatures and flowers. All that plus two requisite ceiling blue whales, one of which is a replica in the Mammals section and the other a genuine skeleton, strung up in Hintze Hall, from an animal that was grievously injured by whalers and washed up on an Irish beach to die in 1891. They named it "Hope."

Cromwell Rd., SW7. www.nhm.ac.uk. ✆ **020/7942-5000.** Free admission but £5 suggested donation, timed reservations suggested but not required. Daily 10am–5:50pm. Tube: South Kensington.

Royal Albert Hall ♥♥ CONCERT HALL In addition to being a great concert venue, the Royal Albert is also one of London's great landmarks, and

Royal Albert Hall opened in 1871 and honors Prince Albert, consort to Queen Victoria, and his commitment to the arts.

you don't need a seat to enjoy it. Conceived by Queen Victoria's husband Albert, it opened in 1871, a decade after his death from typhoid (Vicky was so distraught that she didn't speak at the opening ceremonies). Its crowning dome is an engineering achievement: 372 tons of iron installed with 1869 technology. If you don't mind stairs, you can take a 1-hour tour. The hall contains such oddities as Britain's longest single-weave carpet (in the corridors), the Queen's Box (still leased to the monarchy), and a spectacular glass dome (41m/135 ft. high and supported only at its rim). Only groups can go backstage, however: Some 320 performances a year are presented, many with less than 24 hours' set-up time, and a flow of sightseers would be in the way, but for some of those very rare quiet days (about 20 a year), true backstage tours may be bookable online.

Kensington Gore, SW7. www.royalalberthall.com. ✆ **020/7589-8212.** Free admission to lobby, tours £20 adults, £18 seniors and students, £12 children 5–16. Tours available most days; times vary, generally 10am–4pm. Tube: South Kensington.

Science Museum ♥♥ MUSEUM It's really two museums, one old-fashioned and one progressive, that have been grafted together and embellished with a few tacky gimmicks and blatant corporate propaganda, but it's a firm family favorite. Lines often form to enter, so it's smart to book a free reservation ahead. So many interesting exhibitions are on display here that you'll probably run out of time. The old-school section, which began collecting in 1857 and is split over six levels, is an embarrassment of riches from the artifact archives of science and technology. The hangarlike third floor, Flight, is a standout. Highlights there include a towering slice of a jumbo jet. The Mathematics gallery (second floor), one of the last projects overseen by the late architect Zaha Hadid, is full of lovely swooping forms inspired by the aerodynamic flow around its central object: an experimental Handley Page aircraft from 1929 that was only made possible by math (or as the English call it, "maths"). On level 1, Medicine is the largest medicines gallery in the world (3,000 objects). Of all the sections, Making the Modern World (currently under renovation to become "Ages of Invention" by 2028, but partially open) is the most consistently fascinating for its wealth of objects that helped our lives become so comfortable.

But not everything in the museum is enchanting. The gift shop (standard toys) and guidebook disappoint. And when you can see an actual Model T for free, you probably won't want to pay £12 more for a gimmicky IMAX 3D cinema, although spending £12 to play antique video games in Power Up may be more appealing. None of the maps show you where to find the highlights, so I've done some of the legwork for you:

TOP DON'T-MISS EXHIBITS AT THE SCIENCE MUSEUM

- "Puffing Billy" (1814), the world's oldest surviving steam locomotive, the first Daguerreotype camera from 1839, and the Leica M2 camera Nick Ut used in 1972 to take his iconic photos of the aftermath of a South Vietnamese strike on the village of Trang Bang. (Making the Modern World)

- A German V-2 rocket of the type that decimated many London neighborhoods in the late stages of World War II. These savage weapons claimed lives on both ends of their flights; prisoners of the Nazis assembled them. (Making the Modern World)
- A wooden telephone (1877) made by Alexander Graham Bell to show Queen Victoria how it worked. The earpiece was also the mouthpiece, so callers couldn't talk and listen at the same time. (Making the Modern World)
- A section of the first telegraph cable (1837), made even before the patent had been granted. The first message went between the station control rooms of Euston and Camden Town. It looks like a chunk of kindling; in the days before people realized rubber would be a better insulator, copper wires were threaded through a block of wood. (Information Age)
- The first sewing machine, brought to London in 1845 by the brother of its inventor, Elias Howe, to seduce investors. (Making the Modern World)
- 1969's *Apollo 10* command module. Between you and it, one of you has been to the moon. (Space)
- A porcelain bowl that was fused with sand and rocks in the 1945 atomic blast at Hiroshima. (Making the Modern World)
- The first color digital camera, a boxy thing from 1971. (Engineers)
- A modified Vickers Vimy bomber, the first plane to cross the Atlantic without stopping. It was flown by Arthur Whitten Brown, who promptly became the first person to report jet lag. He called it something much less catchy: the "difficulty of adjustment to the sudden change in time."
- A complete De Havilland Comet, which was the first jetliner. (1952, Flight)

Exhibition Rd., SW7. www.sciencemuseum.org.uk. ✆ **033/0058-0058.** Free admission, timed reservations recommended but not required. Daily 10am–6pm; last admission 5:15pm. Tube: South Kensington.

V&A ♥♥♥ MUSEUM If it was pretty, well-made, or valuable, the British Empire wanted to possess it. As a decorative arts repository, the V&A, or Victoria & Albert Museum, occupying a haughty High Victorian edifice (it was endowed by the proceeds from the first world's fair, the Great Exhibition of 1851, and still attracts 3.5 million visits a year), is about the eye candy of objects—not so much for paintings, but some—and if you're paying attention, it tells the story of mankind through the development of style and technique.

As for how to tour it, the ground floor, a jumbled grid of rooms, has lots of good stuff, but lots more bric-a-brac (Korean pots, 1,000-year-old rock crystal jugs from Egypt) that you'll probably walk past with polite but hasty appreciation. Rooms are arranged by country of origin or by medium (ironwork, tapestries, and the like) but you'll want to see the **20th Century** (rooms 74, 76; level 3), which surprises by including objects you may have once kept in your home (a Dyson vacuum cleaner, mobile phones); the U.K.'s only permanent **architecture** gallery (rooms 127–128a; level 4); the ever-popular **fashion** gallery (room 40) for looks both historic and haute; a recently expanded **Photography Centre** with some specimens dating to the 1850s (enter via rooms 100 & 101); original works by **Beatrix Potter** (the 90a

Vintage and historic fashion are among the countless decorative arts on display at the V&A.

corridor); and endless slices of **medieval stained glass** (rooms 83–84; level 3). Wherever you go, if you see a drawer beneath a display case, open it, because many treasures are stored out of the light.

TOP DON'T-MISS EXHIBITS AT THE V&A

- The **Europe 1600–1815 galleries,** to the left as you enter, are bright, rich, and instructive. They're crammed with 1,100 precious objects including 300 year-old furniture, 18th-century court clothing that looks like it was made yesterday, and even an entire bedchamber from the 1600s. Stream the audio guide from www.vam.ac.uk/europeaudio (there's free Wi-Fi).
- The seven **Raphael Cartoons** (room 48a), 500 years old in 2015, are probably the most priceless items. These giant paper paintings—yes, paper—were created by the hand of Raphael as templates for the weavers of his 10 tapestries for the Sistine Chapel. Before Queen Victoria moved them here, they hung for around 175 years in the purpose-built Cartoon Gallery at Hampton Court Palace (p. 211). The colors are fugitive, meaning they're fading: Christ's red robe, painted with plant-based madder lake, has turned white—his reflection in the water, painted with a different pigment, is still red. Look for the QR code that lets you explore the works layer by layer on your phone.
- None of the sculptures in the sky-lit **Cast Court** (rooms 46 and 46a) are original. They're plaster replicas of the greatest hits in Renaissance art, and they crowd the room like a yard sale. They were put here in 1873 for the poor, who could never hope to see the real articles for themselves. Now that's you! Find Ghiberti's doors to the baptistery at Florence's San Giovanni, whose design kicked off the artistic frenzy of the Renaissance, and Michelangelo's *David,* floppy puppy feet and all; he was fitted with a

fig leaf for royal visits (in a case behind David). Depressingly, many of these copies are now in better shape than the originals.

- Tipu Sultan of India hated imperialists. So, in the 1790s he commissioned an automaton of a tiger sinking its fangs into one. A crank on **Tippoo's Tiger** (room 41) activates a clockwork that makes an Englishman's hand flail while a hidden organ plays a death knell. To no avail; in the end, Tipu was killed by Europeans, and the English stole it as an ironic trophy. It has been a favorite since 1808, when it was part of the East India Company's trophy museum.
- The **Great Bed of Ware** (room 57), a 10×11-foot four-poster of carved oak that dates to about 1590, was once a tourist attraction at a country inn, renowned enough for Shakespeare to mention it in *Twelfth Night:* "big enough for the bed of Ware." As you admire it, consider that in those days, bed canopies were installed to protect sleepers from insects that might tumble out of thatched roofs and into mouths. Canopied beds, a mark of luxury today, were a sign of a humbler home requiring anti-insect measures. Nearby is James II's silver-embroidered wedding suit (1673, room 56).
- The **Ardabil carpet** (room 42), the world's oldest dated carpet (copies lay on the floors of 10 Downing St. and Hitler's Berlin office alike), is from 1539. To preserve its dyes, it's lit 10 minutes at a time on every half-hour.
- Implausibly well-preserved specimens of historic **fashion** (room 40), from pristine empire-waist dresses to mint-condition 18th-century silks.
- The **Hereford Screen** (1862, Ironworks balcony) is a liturgical riot by Gilbert Scott, the architect of the "Eros" (p. 155) and the St Pancras Renaissance (p. 44). It took 38 conservators 13 months to restore the 8-ton choir screen to its full golden, brassy Gothic Revival glory.
- The **Gilbert Collection** (rooms 70–73) of impossibly fine jewel boxes, cameos, silver, and mosaics was amassed by a rich enthusiast who originally gave them to LACMA in California, where he made his fortune. But in a museum-world scandal, he stripped them from it for not showing the whole collection at once. Despite that slap in the face, the V&A still displays only highlights.
- One volume of Da Vinci's legendary **notebooks** is on display in room 64 (Medieval and Renaissance).
- You can just imagine the kind of items it has on display in **Jewelry** (91–93). It's often busy.
- It's hard to forget the riotous figures and tilework of the **Ceramic Staircase** (1860s); originally, every staircase here was to look like this, but when the cost became apparent, even those excessive Victorians satisfied themselves with just one. To find it, turn left after coming through the Exhibition Road entrance.
- The second, third, and fourth levels have less space and therefore are easier to navigate. Look for the (always warm) **Theatre & Performance** collection (103–106b), which lends the spark of modern familiarity to the proceedings; you can see, for example, a Shakespeare Folio from 1623, Ingrid

Bergman's *Gaslight* dress by Irene, Fred Astaire's tux, Charlie Chaplin's hat and cane, Vivien Leigh's Oscar, Kylie Minogue's dressing room, and costumes from *The Lion King* and *Wicked*.

Questions about today's tours and how to find particular items will be referred to the information desk, which in turn may be referred to a search on the public website. Such is the sad reality of today's heavily touristed museum. That's why planning pays off: Consult the digital map (vam.ac.uk/map) or pay £6 for the official guide book, which is 150 pages of photos with maps. Also check to see what hot-ticket exhibitions are coming, many of them on topics that pander to a wide paying audience (David Bowie, Pink Floyd, and, in 2025, Cartier) or are blatantly influenced by sponsors (historic underwear); £25 is a typical upcharge for an exhibition here. Free 1-hour tours are given at 10:30am, 1pm, and 2pm (highlights), 12:30 (fashion), 1:30 (treasures of Europe), 2:30 (theater), and 3pm (Britain). Even the cafe (the world's first museum restaurant) is gorgeous; have a coffee in the extraordinary Gamble Room (1865–78), a visual feast in ceramic tile and enameled iron. Also visit the V&A's western exterior; scarred during the Blitz, the stonework was left unrepaired as a memorial.

Cromwell Rd., SW7. www.vam.ac.uk. ✆ **020/7942-2000.** Free admission. Sat–Thurs 10am–5:45pm; Fri 10am–10pm, with reduced gallery openings. Tube: South Kensington.

Other Kensington & Knightsbridge Attractions

Albert Memorial ♥ LANDMARK Albert, Queen Victoria's German-born husband (and, um, first cousin), was a passionate supporter of the arts who piloted Britain from one dazzling creative triumph to another. But when he died suddenly of typhoid (some say Crohn's disease) in 1861 at age 42, the devastated queen abruptly withdrew from the gaiety and remained in mourning until her death in 1901, shaping the Victorian mentality. She arranged for this astounding spire—part bombast, part elegy—to be erected in 1872 opposite the concert hall Albert spearheaded. Some of its nearly 200 figures represent the continents and the sciences, and some, higher up, represent angels and virtues. It's Victorian high-mindedness in stone. At the center, as if on an altar, is Albert himself, gleaming in gold.

Kensington Gardens. www.royalparks.org.uk. Tube: South Kensington.

The Design Museum ♥ MUSEUM The Design Museum is where you'll find the cool kids of current style and architecture waxing esoteric about their thought processes. The top-floor balcony celebrates everyday objects (typefaces, laptops) that have been designed well, but most of the space is given to temporary exhibitions. In point of fact, it's more of a contemporary art gallery than a museum, so the value of your visit depends on whether the temporary shows interest you. Everything is imbued with an awareness of how design can improve the lives of the less fortunate, a notion that's at best Victorian and at worst consumerist, and through changing exhibitions (in 2023, shows by Ai Weiwei and about rebellious fashion; in 2024, about director Tim Burton and

Barbie, in 2026, about director Wes Anderson and designer Nigo). The shop has some interesting finds, as you might suspect.

224–238 Kensington High St., W8. https://designmuseum.org. ✆ **020/3862-5900.** Permanent collection free, exhibitions charge £10–£25. Sun–Thurs 10am–6pm; Fri–Sat 10am–9pm. Tube: High Street Kensington.

THE SOUTH BANK, SOUTHWARK & BOROUGH

The Chimney Lift ♥ OBSERVATION TOWER Londoners are excited about the recent redevelopment of the Battersea Power Station because it's a giant, gorgeous landmark of industrial Art Deco on a prime riverfront lot, yet it was abandoned for most of their lifetimes. But it all turned out to be a big indoor mall surrounded by luxury flats. Its northwest chimney has been converted into an observation elevator tower, originally called Lift 109 which opened in 2022. After riding a standard elevator partway and then, curiously, being forced take some stairs, you enter a glass elevator that rises to 109 meters (358 feet) until it peeks out the top of the tower. There, you get to look out for a few minutes before descending again and exiting through the gift shop. It's a fun gimmick, but it's no substitute for the observation decks closer to the action—even Big Ben is a distant 2.4km (a mile and a half) away. Architecture nuts will find much to groove over in the Power Station, which also has an inviting Thames-facing park, but you don't need a ticket for those.

Battersea Power Station, Circus Road W, Nine Elms, SW8. https://thechimneylift.co.uk. ✆ **020/8208-1166.** Admission £24 adults, £17 kids 3–15, discounts up to £6 online. Sun–Thurs 10am–6pm, Fri–Sat 10am–8pm, advance booking recommended. Tube: Battersea Power Station.

Florence Nightingale Museum ♥ MUSEUM You probably don't know much about Florence Nightingale (1820–1910) now, but spend 45 minutes in this small and well-designed biographical museum (on the grounds of the hospital with which she worked) and you'll brim with newfound respect for this consequential person—as a founder of sensible nursing practices, as a leader who took no guff, and ultimately, as an all-around hard-core badass. It's broken into three sections, attractively presented and with kid-friendly elements: her headstrong youth, her fame-making work whipping the troop hospitals of the Crimean War into shape (another time events around Ukraine shaped the world), and her subsequent years of burned-out reclusiveness and ceaseless writing.

2 Lambeth Palace Rd., SE1. www.florence-nightingale.co.uk. ✆ **020/7188-4400.** Admission £12 adults, £10 seniors, £7 students, £6 children 15 and under. Tues–Sun 10am–5pm; last entry 4:30pm. Tube: Westminster, Waterloo, or Lambeth North.

Garden Museum ♥ MUSEUM Here, in a deconsecrated church (the tower, which you can climb, dates to 1377), you'll find artifacts and academic respect paid to the greatest gardeners of Britaindom, including John Tradescant the Elder, a green thumb and seed pioneer who himself was planted in the

City & South Bank Attractions
Bank of England Museum 10
The Charterhouse 5
Dr Johnson's House 4
Florence Nightingale Museum 25
The Garden at 120 14
Garden Museum 26
The Golden Hinde 21
Guildhall & Roman Amphitheatre 8
Hayward Gallery 32
HMS Belfast 20
Horizon 22 15
Hunterian Museum 2
Imperial War Museum London 26
The London Dungeon 30
London Eye 31
London Mithraeum 10
London Museum 5
The Monument 13
The Old Operating Theatre Museum & Herb Garret 22
Roof Terrace at One New Change 8
St Magnus the Martyr 12
St Paul's Cathedral 7
Sea Life London Aquarium 29
Shakespeare's Globe 24
Sir John Soane's Museum 1
Sky Garden 14
Tate Modern 25
The Temple Church 3
Tower Bridge Exhibition 19
The Tower of London 18
View from the Shard 21
Whitechapel Gallery 17
HOLBORN
CITY (LONDON)
EC2
EC3
EC4
THE CITY
BANKSIDE
SOUTHWARK
SOUTH BANK
River Thames
Barbican
Chancery Lane
Holborn
Moorgate
Liverpool St
Aldgate
St Paul's
Bank
DLR
Mansion House
Cannon St
Monument
Tower Gateway
Tower Hill
Blackfriars
Temple
Waterloo
Waterloo East
Southwark
London Bridge
The Barbican Centre
Smithfield Market
The Old Bailey
Law Courts
St Paul's Cathedral
The Temple
INNER TEMPLE GARDENS
Lincoln's Inn Fields
Fenchurch Station
Blackfriars Station
Cannon St Station
Tower of London
London Bridge Station
Borough Market
Waterloo Station
National Theatre
Royal Festival Hall
Cleopatra's Needle
JUBILEE GARDENS
Savoy Pier
Embankment Pier
Festival Pier
Blackfriars Millennium Pier
Bankside Pier
Tower Millennium Pier
London Bridge City Pier
St Katharine's Pier
Waterloo Bridge
Blackfriars Bridge
Millennium Bridge
Southwark Bridge
London Bridge
Tower Bridge
Hungerford Bridge
Westminster Bridge
Red Lion St
Procter St
High Holborn
Holborn Circus
Charterhouse St
Aldersgate St
London Wall
Coleman St
Old Broad St
Bishopsgate
Middlesex St
Commercial St
Whitechapel Rd
Houndsditch
Camomile St
Aldgate High St
Minories
Mansell St
Leman St
Gt. Queen St
Kingsway
Portugal St
Carey St
Bream's Bgs.
Chancery Ln
Fetter Ln
St Andrew St
Farringdon Rd
Holborn Viaduct
Newgate St
Gresham St
Cheapside
Threadneedle St
Leadenhall St
Gracechurch St
Fenchurch St
Pepys St
Drury Lane
Aldwych
Fleet St
Whitefriars St
St Bride St
New Bridge St
Ludgate Hill
Tudor St
Queen Victoria St
King William St
Cannon St
Great Tower St
Upper Thames St
Lower Thames St
Tower Hill
Queen St
Wellington St
Strand
Arundel St
Savoy Pl.
Victoria Embankment
Upper Ground
Stamford St
Hatfields
Blackfriars Rd
Sumner St
Southwark St
Tooley St
Roupell St
Belvedere Rd
Cornwall Rd
Waterloo Rd
The Cut
York Rd
Pocock St
0 1/4 mi
0 0.25 km

churchyard in 1638. You'll find an assortment of antique gardening implements, a collection of gardening-related art, plus a few curios such as an original 18th-century bronze season pass token for the Vauxhall Gardens—yes, only horticulture nerds need apply. The museum was set up in 1977 as a way to preserve the abandoned church of St Mary's, but—garden museum irony alert—no one thought to dig down. In 2016, workers discovered a vault containing a collapsing pile of 30 lead coffins topped with a rusted archbishop's miter cap—a picture of your nightmare's nightmare. Turned out the corpses included Richard Bancroft, who oversaw creation of the King James Bible, and as many as five Archbishops of Canterbury, who were like England's popes. You can find the clear, sealed panel leading to their chamber in The Ark. There are other graves to see: Captain Bligh of *Bounty* fame is in the yard. A more cheerful fact: Outside, at Lambeth Bridge, is the roundabout where Clark Griswold told his kids, "Big Ben! Parliament!" Ascend the old church tower for stupendous views of said buildings.

5 Lambeth Palace Rd., SE1. www.gardenmuseum.org.uk. ✆ **020/7401-8865.** Admission £16 adults, £13 seniors, £9 students, free for young people 17 and under. Church tower another £4. Daily 10am–5pm (but check ahead). Tube: Westminster, Waterloo, or Lambeth North.

Imperial War Museum London ♥♥ MUSEUM One of London's unexpectedly gripping museums has a deceptive name. It's not just for military buffs, and it's no gun-fondling armory, even if there is a Spitfire hanging from the rafters. Instead of merely showcasing heavy implements of death, which it does, this museum—the latest tenant of the commodious and palatial former mental hospital known as Bedlam—takes care to also convey the sensations, feelings, and motivations of soldiers and civilians caught in past conflicts. It is ultimately not about weapons but a museum about *people* at war. In addition to easy-to-grasp background on major conflicts, the museum

A section of the First World War Gallery at The Imperial War Museum London.

The hidden surgical theatre of The Old Operating Theatre Museum & Herb Garret.

intelligently balances tanks and planes with storytelling that unravels propaganda. While some exhibits are perhaps oversimplified, the First World War Galleries are the most advanced, best-stocked, most comprehensible, and most moving you'll ever see on the topic, followed by gut-punch segments on the Second World War and the Holocaust.

Lambeth Rd., SE1. www.iwm.org.uk. ✆ **020/7416-5000.** Free admission; timed reservations recommended but not required. Daily 10am–6pm; last admission 5:30pm. Tube: Lambeth North or Elephant & Castle.

The Old Operating Theatre Museum & Herb Garret ♥♥ MUSEUM In the mid-1800s, before general anesthesia, St Thomas' Hospital used the attic of a neighboring church as a space where surgeries, mostly amputations and other quick-hit procedures, could be conducted so that students could watch but other patients couldn't hear the agonized screams. When the hospital moved in 1862, the attic was abandoned, sealed away, and forgotten. It was considered lost until 1956, when an enterprising historian thought to look in the attic, and found the secret surgical stadium behind a wall. Creep up a tight, 52-step wooden spiral staircase (there's no lift) once used by the bell ringer and you'll find the theater, now the centerpiece of a ghoulish, but carefully educational, museum delving into medical methods of the early 1800s, from herbal remedies to leeches. Once a month on Saturdays (£12; book ahead), you can even sit where the surgical students once did and imagine what it would have been like to watch some unlucky sod lose a leg without anesthetics. What a white-knuckle reminder that in the old days, medicine was less about science and more about soldiering on. Which you might also have to do, as there are no toilets here.

9a St Thomas St., SE1. www.oldoperatingtheatre.com. ✆ **020/7188-2679.** Admission £9 adults, £7 seniors and students, £5.50 young people 17 and under. Thurs–Sun 10:30am–5pm; last entry at 4:15pm. Tube: London Bridge.

Shakespeare's Globe ♥ LANDMARK A painstaking re-creation of an outdoor Elizabethan theater, it tends to bewitch fans of history and drama. Opened in 1997, the open-air "Wooden O" was made using only Elizabethan technology such as saws, pillars made from solid oak trees, 17,000 bundles of Norfolk water reed, and plaster panels mixed with goat's hair (the original recipe called for cow's hair, but the breed they needed is now extinct). The first Globe burned down in 1613, aged just 14, when a cannon fired during a performance of *Henry VIII* caused its thatched roof to catch fire; it took a special act of Parliament, plus plenty of hidden sprinkler systems, to permit the construction of this, the first thatched roof in London since the Great Fire. The original theater was the same size (and stood 180m/591 ft. to the southeast), but it crammed in 3,000 luckless souls. Today, just 1,600 are admitted for performances. The Globe attracts so many curious tourists that it puts on interesting 50-minute **guided tours** covering the ancient backstories of the plays that are running, and, of course, the attributes of this magnificent Wooden O itself.

21 New Globe Walk, SE1. www.shakespearesglobe.com. ✆ **020/7401-9919.** Theater tours: daily 9:30am–4:30pm, £27 adults, £11.50 children 15 and under; reservations required; check ahead for schedule changes. Tube: London Bridge.

THE GREAT "lates"

When they are at full staffing levels, some attractions offer extended opening times for evening viewing in the main galleries. Often, extra inducements are tossed in, such as wine and sketch classes at the National Portrait Gallery or DJs at the V&A. They can really free up your daytime touring to include more sights:

ATTRACTION	LATE OPENING
Bank of England Museum (p. 196)	Third Thursday of month to 8pm
Barbican Art Centre (p. 265)	Thursday–Friday to 8pm
British Library (p. 130)	Tuesday–Thursday to 8pm
British Museum (p. 135)	Friday to 8:30pm
Design Museum (p. 179)	Friday–Sunday to 6pm
Hayward Gallery (p. 195)	Saturday to 8pm
London Mithraeum (p. 198)	8pm closing first Thursday of month
National Gallery (p. 146)	Friday to 9pm
Natural History Museum (p. 172)	occasional Fridays to 9:30pm, occasional ticketed events such as silent discos
National Portrait Gallery (p. 150)	Friday and Saturday to 9pm
Science Museum (p. 175)	Wednesday to 10pm (occasional; over-18s only)
Sir John Soane's Museum (p. 152)	once a month, announced online
Tate Modern (p. 185)	Friday–Saturday to 9pm
V&A Museum (p. 176)	Friday to 10pm (reduced galleries)
Whitechapel Gallery (p. 195)	Thursday to 9pm

The massive Turbine Hall at Tate Modern is the setting for visiting exhibitions, often of large-scale works.

Tate Modern ♥♥♥ MUSEUM In 2000, Bankside's chief eyesore, a goliath power station—was ingeniously converted into the national contemporary art collection and is now as integral to London as the Quire of Westminster Abbey or the Dome of St Paul's. The mammoth **Turbine Hall**, cleared of machinery to form a meadowlike expanse of concrete, often hosts gargantuan works by major artists for its periodic Hyundai Commission (usually Oct–Mar). People of every background frolic on the cement as if it were a park. The Turbine Hall connects the **Natalie Bell Building** on the left, which contains the **collection** and whatever blockbuster **temporary exhibitions** are currently on (as much as £25 for those; book ahead; big shows for 2026 and 2027 include Frida Kahlo, Tracey Emin, and Julio Le Parc), with a twisting 10-story tower on the right (the **Blavatnik Building**, named for a Soviet-born oligarch who gave cash), which stands above the power station's former oil tanks, now used as performance-and-video spaces (check online for what's on). take one of the daily free 45-minute guided tours at noon, 1pm, or 2pm (Level 2, Bell Building). One thing that doesn't miss is the surprising and well-stocked shop (on the lobby floor of the Blavatnik). Also carve out refreshment time: Kitchen and Bar on Level 6 (Bell; daily noon–6pm, for the best seats, queue about 20 min. ahead) is a city highlight. 30 first-come bar stools facing out over St Paul's and the Thames through floor-to-ceiling glass. (If you can't get a seat there, there's a free river-facing viewing platform, **Level 10**, in the Blavatnik building.) Even when the presentation confounds you, Tate Modern's facility is a star and will always merit a visit, and accordingly, it receives some 4.6 million visits a year.

Bankside, SE1. www.tate.org.uk/visit/tate-modern. ✆ **020/7887-8888.** Free admission. Sun–Thurs 10am–6pm; Fri–Sat 10am–9pm. Tube: Southwark.

The View from the Shard ♥ OBSERVATION DECK In 2013 the jagged 306m/1,016 ft.-tall Shard, one of the tallest buildings in Europe (but not even in the top 50 worldwide), added a pricey observation deck with timed tickets. After intense airport-style security and two ear-poppingly fast elevator rides, you'll emerge 244m/800 feet up to some weird angel-like choir music and vertiginous floor-to-ceiling windows far, far above the city—so high that, after the initial impression, if you don't know London well, you're not likely to figure out most of what you see. A few levels up (stairs lead to those last three floors), there's a patio shielded at body-level from the elements, but you won't find seating. Every step of the way, you'll be hustled to purchase souvenirs, cocktails, and champagne, etc. If the day turns cloudy, ask staff for a

View Guarantee voucher that will allow you to return for free. The Shard has been slicing its prices lately because the new **Horizon 22** (p. 142) in the City is actually higher—and free.

Joiner St., SE1. www.theviewfromtheshard.com. ✆ **0844/499-7111.** Admission varies by day and time, but is £22–£32 ages 4 and over, no ticket required for kids 3 and under; £19 Weds–Thurs when booked online. Hours change almost daily, so consult calendar online. Tube: London Bridge.

Other Bankside/Southwark Attractions

Brunel Museum ♥ MUSEUM/HISTORIC SITE The engineering contributions of Marc Brunel and his son Isambard Kingdom Brunel are too commonly taken for granted. Here they're given their due. With the help of a shield system they invented, these pioneers executed the first tunnel to be built under a navigable river. London's soft earth didn't make it easy, though—it took from 1825 to 1843. This redbrick building marked by a chimney was where steam engines pumped the seeping water out as diggers toiled. The tunnel, lined with arches and Doric capitals, was a commercial flop that deteriorated into a subterranean red-light district. It later found new purpose, however, as a part of the Overground Line, and it has gained new respect through this museum.

Railway Ave., SE16. https://thebrunelmuseum.com. ✆ **020/7231-3840.** Admission £9 adults, £6 seniors, students, and children. Fri–Mon 10:30am–3:30pm; Nov–Jan weekends only. Tube: Rotherhithe.

The Golden Hinde ♥ HISTORIC SHIP Tucked into one of the few remaining slips that enabled ships to unload in Southwark (another is Hay's Galleria, downstream by the HMS *Belfast* [see below], now a boutique shopping area) is a 1:1 replica of Sir Francis Drake's square-rigged Tudor galleon, which circumnavigated the world from 1577 to 1580. This 1973 version, which is so tiny you will forever feel pity for those old explorers, made its own

The London Museum: A Grand Opening for All Time

The Museum of London's repository's miraculous cache of rarities from the city's extraordinary history has been going in one form or another since 1823, and its collection would do credit to the greatest attractions of any land. But in December 2022, it left its home of 46 years at the Barbican in preparation for an upgrade to a lavish new facility in the former Smithfield meat traders' market, by the Farringdon Underground stop, where it reopens as **The London Museum** in 2026. The change is one of the largest cultural infrastructure projects in Europe. The move, which reportedly cost nearly a half a billion pounds, has given the institution the opportunity to modernize its displays as well as find new purposes for the 1963 Poultry Market and neighboring 1883 General Market buildings. If it has opened by the time of your visit, consider it unmissable. Until then, only its East London spinoff, London Museum Docklands (p. 201), is open. https://www.londonmuseum.org.uk

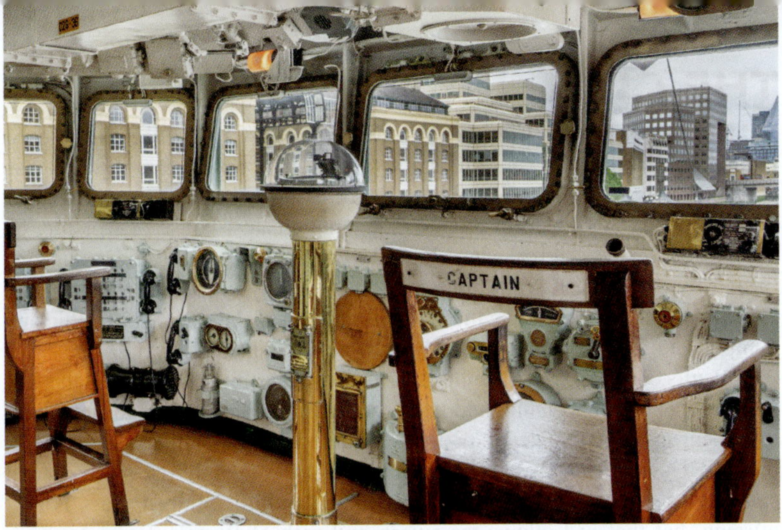

Moored near the Tower Bridge, the HMS *Belfast* is open to visitors.

circumnavigation in 1980. The schedule is full of events (like onboard escape room experiences), so maximize your visit by coordinating it with one.

St Mary Overie Dock, Cathedral St., SE1. www.goldenhinde.co.uk. ✆ **020/7403-0123.** Admission £6 including audio guide. Nov–March daily 10am–5pm, April–Oct daily 10am–6pm, last admission 30 min. before closing. Tube: London Bridge.

HMS *Belfast* ♥ HISTORIC SHIP It's as if the powerful 1938 warship, upon being retired from service in 1965, was motored straight to this dock and opened to visitors the next day. Nearly everything, down to the checked flooring and decaying cables, is exactly as it was, making the boat a fascinating snapshot of mid-20th-century maritime technology, and smart exhibits do a lot to make it come alive again. Authenticity also makes it a devil to navigate, especially if you have any bags with you—sorry, no cloakrooms, sailor. Getting around its labyrinth of decks, engine rooms, ladders, and hatches requires dexterity and a well-calibrated inner compass—it seems the Health and Safety rules that bedevil every aspect of British life do not apply here. You can roam as you wish, visiting every cubby of the ship from kitchen to bridge, touching nearly anything you want, while being thankful that it wasn't you who was chasing German cruisers (the *Belfast* sank the *Scharnhorst*) and backing up the D-Day invasion in this tough tin can. Admission includes an excellent audio guide, but privately, crew members tell me that they wish visitors would pause and ask them questions in person—there's so much more to point out to you.

Morgan's Lane, Tooley St., SE1. www.iwm.org.uk. ✆ **020/7940-6300.** Admission £26.35 adults, £23.70 seniors, £13.15 children 5–15; posted prices are higher and include a voluntary donation. Daily 10am–6pm (5pm closing in winter); last admission 1 hr. before closing. Tube: London Bridge.

THE CITY

St Paul's Cathedral ♥♥♥ HISTORIC SITE/CHURCH The old St Paul's, with its magnificent spire, stood on this site for 600 years before it was claimed by 1666's Great Fire. It was so beloved that when Sir Christopher Wren was commissioned to rebuild London's greatest house of worship, he tried to outdo the original, devoting 40 years to the project and going one further by crowning it with a mighty dome—highly unusual for the time. It was also stark and plain, like the Catholics did their churches, not Gothic and complicated like the Protestants. My, how people talked.

St Paul's cost £750,000 to build, an astronomical sum in 1697 when the first section opened for worship, and now, it costs £3 million a year to run. Wren overspent so badly that decoration was curtailed; the Byzantine-style mosaics over the Quire weren't added until Queen Victoria thought the place needed spiffing up (and some purists are still complaining). Stained glass is still missing, but that just allows the sweep and arch of Wren's design to shine cleanly through. Many of us were introduced to the front steps by "Feed the Birds" in *Mary Poppins* and to the sanctuary by the wedding of Prince Charles and Lady Diana Spencer in 1981, but the pulpit also saw a sermon by Martin Luther King, Jr. in 1964 and Churchill's funeral the next year. Frustratingly, you're not allowed to take photos on your tour.

The **Great West Doors,** which are largely unused unless you're important, are 27m high (90 ft.) and on their original hinges; they're so well-hung that even an infirm vicar can swing them open. In 2005, the cathedral completed a £10.8-million cleaning program; a stone panel beside the doors was left filthy to show just how gloomy centuries of candles had made it in here. The **High Altar** has a canopy supported by single tree trunks that were hollowed out and carved, and its 15th-century crucifix and candlesticks require two men to lift. (They're nailed down, anyway. As one docent, a half-century veteran of Cathedral tours, lamented, "You'd be surprised what people try to steal.") Behind it is the **American Memorial Chapel** to the 28,000 American soldiers who died while based in England in World War II; in a glass case, one leaf of a 500-page book containing their names is turned each day. The **organ,** with 7,000 pipes, was regularly played by Mendelssohn and Handel, and the **lectern** is original. Give special admiration to the impossibly fine limewood carvings in the Quire by Grinling Gibbons—dark wood is original and lighter wood has been replaced or restored. Nearby, there's a monument to pretty-boy poet and cleric **John Donne** that still bears on its urn the scorch marks it suffered in Old St Paul's during the Great Fire (it was the only thing that survived the conflagration).

Eight central pillars support the entire weight of the wood-framed dome; Wren filled them with loose rubble. In 1925, engineers broke them open to find the debris had settled to the bottom, and they filled them again with liquid concrete. If you're fit, you can mount the 259 steps (each just an awkward 13cm/5 in. tall, but double-wide with some spots to catch your breath) to the circular **Whispering Gallery**, 30m/98 feet above the floor. Famously, its

St Paul's Cathedral

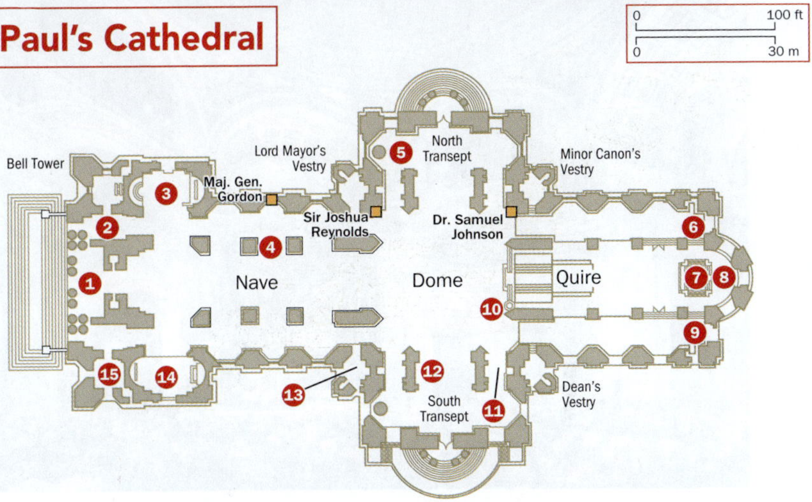

- All Souls' Chapel **2**
- American Memorial Chapter **8**
- Anglican Martyr's Chapel **6**
- Chapel of St Michael & St George **14**
- Dean's Staircase **15**
- Entrance to Crypt (Wren's grave) **11**
- Font **5**
- High Altar **7**
- Lady Chapel **9**
- Nelson Monument **12**
- Pulpit **10**
- St Dunstan's Chapel **3**
- Staircase to Library, Whispering Gallery & Dome **13**
- Wellington Monument **4**
- West Doorway **1**

acoustics are so fine that you can turn your head and mutter something that can be understood on the opposite side, 33m/108 feet away. Climb higher (you've gone 378 steps now, and now the stairs get tight) to the **Stone Gallery,** an outdoor terrace just beneath the dome. Catch your breath, if you choose, for the final 152-step push to the **Golden Gallery**—you'll be scaling the inner skin of the dome, past ancient oriel windows and along tight metal stairs. There are three domes, in fact—the inner skin with the monochrome paintings by Sir James Thornhill, the leaden outside, and in between, a brick one that holds it all together. That's what you traverse—look sharp for ancient carved graffiti by tourists who preceded you in the 1700s, and look for the strips of metal installed by Benjamin Franklin himself when he brought his newfangled lightning protection system to the cathedral. It's safe, but it's not for those with vertigo or claustrophobia. The spectacular 360-degree city view from the top (85m/279 ft. up), at the base of the Ball and Lantern (you can't go up farther), is so beautiful it defies full appreciation. For more than 250 years, this was the tallest structure in a city that itself was atop the world.

If you miss the **Crypt,** you'll have missed a lot. In addition to memorials to the famous dead (such as Florence Nightingale and plenty of obscure war heroes), you'll find tombs, such as composer Sir Arthur Sullivan's ebullient bronze plate and the tombs of two of Britain's greatest military demigods:

A concert under the dome of St Paul's Cathedral.

Admiral Horatio Nelson (whose body was preserved for the trip back to England by soaking in brandy and wine), and **Arthur, Duke of Wellington** (flanked by flags captured on the field of battle; they will hang there until they disintegrate). To the right of the OBE Chapel, in **Artists Corner,** you'll find the graves of the artists **J. M. W. Turner** and **Henry Moore,** plus, under a black slab by a window, **Christopher Wren** himself, who rests inside his masterpiece. "I build for eternity," he once said, and so far, so good: In 2010, the cathedral marked 300 years since its completion.

Volunteers, called "supers," lead a variety of free tours at various times between 11am and 3pm: 20-minute Highlights tours and 90-minute tours of the Crypt and Cathedral Floor (to join any of those, ask when you arrive). You can also secure a 1-hour tour of the high-level **Triforium** balcony, 141 steps up, where you'll behold stone remnants from the first cathedral, terrific views down, the gorgeous spiral **Geometric Staircase** (seen in the third Harry Potter film), the fascinating 1673 **Great Model** in wood of one of Wren's proposed cathedral designs, and terrific views down. Triforium tours (£12.50) must be booked along with your entry ticket. Listen closely, because the volunteers are the elder statesmen; many have been here for decades. Lest you forgot it's actually a cathedral, you can also worship here outside of sightseeing hours—for free (there's a service at 8am daily, but the Choral Evensong at 5pm on weekdays, after the tourists have gone, is atmospheric). When you're done inside, head just east to the **One New Change** shopping complex, where the free rooftop terrace has some spectacular close-up views of the dome—perfect for vacation snaps.

St Paul's Churchyard, EC4. www.stpauls.co.uk. ✆ **020/7246-8357.** Advance-purchase admission: £26 adults, £23.50 seniors and students 18+, £10 children 6–17, free for children 5 and under, family tickets £36–£62; includes multimedia guide. Mon–Sat 8:30am–4:30pm (Weds opening at 10am), last entry 4pm; Sun open for worship only. Tube: St Paul's.

The Forgotten Colosseum

Guildhall, a magnificent stone structure originally completed in 1440 but heavily rebuilt time and again, was once where Londoners went to pay taxes but today is used as the City's most regal events space. Partly due to World War II's wrath, the collection at its **Guildhall Art Gallery** is perhaps second-rate (for this city), although its works depicting London can be interesting. But the real reason to come is in the cellar: the foundations of the eastern entrance of **London's Roman Amphitheatre,** 2,000 years old, which were discovered when the gallery was being built in 1987. Once the largest in Britannia, the amphitheater could hold some 7,000 spectators at a time when the entire population of London was only about 25,000. Slots carved into one of the rooms suggest there was once a trap door that could release wild animals to fight in the arena. Sometimes it's hard to believe the Romans trod the same streets as you, but here in the darkness deep underground, the bones of their abandoned plaything provide an eerie reminder. (Gresham St., EC2; www.cityoflondon.gov.uk; ✆ **020/7332-1313;** free admission except for exhibitions; tours Tues–Sun 12:15pm and 1:15pm via www.cityoflondonguides.com/tours; open daily 10am–5pm; Tube: Moorgate or St Paul's.)

Tower Bridge Exhibition ♥♥ LANDMARK It took 8 years and unprecedented spunk and ingenuity to build this iconic bridge, and you may wonder: How did such a distinctive monument survive the Blitz when everything around it got flattened? Simple: The Luftwaffe needed its proud towers as a visual landmark.

It's always free to walk across the bridge on your own, but visiting this museum is like getting two attractions in one. The first one satisfies sightseers who dream of going up in the famous neo-Gothic towers and crossing its two high-level observation walkways—once you've been inside, you'll never look at a photo of the bridge the same way again. In a portion of both high-level indoor crossings, a glass floor was installed so visitors can get giddy to the sight of the river 42m (138 ft.) below their feet—the floor is frosted so weirdos can't take upskirt photos from below. The second fascinating aspect (which you'll encounter by leaving the towers, walking along the bridge, and entering the machine room on the southern shore) delves into the steam-driven machinery that so impressed the world in 1894. The bridge's boilers had to be fed and tweaked 24 hours a day, and those Victorian mega machines are still there, in fine condition despite being retired in favor of electricity in 1976. A

A tour of the Tower Bridge reveals its ingenious engineering.

visit here is even more fun if it's timed with the raising of the spans, which is controlled by joystick from a cabin in the north tower—since lifts must be scheduled at least a day in advance, the website's "Bridge Lift Times" can always give you a head's up. At the turn of the last century, it was opened some 9,000 times a year to accommodate bustling river trade. Now that freight ships are too big for the Thames, it only raises about 1,000 times a year, mostly for pleasure craft. ***Note:*** Tickets are discounted if you also buy entry to the Monument (p. 199).

A Beefeater leads a tour at the Tower of London.

Tower Bridge (on the Tower of London side), SE1. www.towerbridge.org.uk. ✆ **020/ 7403-3761.** Admission £16 adults, £12 students and seniors, £8 children 5–15, discounts available on low-season weekdays if booked ahead, scheduled guided tours £35. Daily 9:30am–6pm, last admission 5pm. Tube: Tower Hill or Tower Gateway DLR.

The Tower of London ♥♥♥ MUSEUM/HISTORIC SITE Every morning at 9am, a military guard escorts the keys to the Tower, and its huge wooden doors yawn open again for outsiders. It's the most famous castle in the world, a UNESCO World Heritage Site, and a symbol of not just London, but also of a millennium of English history. Less a tower than a fortified mini-town of stone and timber, its history could fill this book. Suffice it to say that its oldest building, the four-cornered White Tower, went up in 1078, and the compound that grew around it has served as palace, prison, treasury, mint, armory, zoo, and, now, a lovingly maintained tourist attraction that no visitor should neglect. Exploring its sprawl should take between 3 and 5 hours.

A Poignant Pocket Park

Little-known **Postman's Park** is beloved by those lucky enough to have stumbled across it. Hemmed in between buildings, its central feature is the moving **Watts Memorial,** a collection of plaques dedicated to ordinary people who died in acts of "heroic self-sacrifice." Have a seat on a bench and ponder John Clinton, 10, "who was drowned near London Bridge in trying to save a companion younger than himself" in July 1894. In 1893, William Freer Lucas tantalizingly "risked poison for himself rather than lessen any chance of saving a child's life and died." Alice Ayres saved three children from a burning house in 1885 "at the cost of her own young life." The commemorations mostly ceased in Edwardian times (poor Leigh Pitt squeaked in after saving a drowning child in 2009), making these forgotten faces obscure once again. (West side of St Martin's Le-Grand between St Paul's Cathedral and the Barbican Centre; daily 8am–dusk; Tube: St Paul's or Barbican.)

Tower of London

The key to touring the Tower is to arrive close to opening, since intimidating queues can form by lunchtime for the Crown Jewels, located in the Waterloo Block at the north wall (farthest from the Thames), and the White Tower, in the center. Tickets are sold outside the battlements. Hit the Welcome Centre, just past the Ticket Office, to jot down the times and locations of all the free talks, temporary exhibitions, and mini-performances. Plenty are offered—the Tower at times feels like a theme park with 1,000 years of history behind it. As soon as you're in, between the Middle and Byward towers, note the next time of the prime excursion: the 1-hour **Yeoman Warder Tour** (every 30 min.; from 10am Tues–Sat, 10:30am Sun–Mon; last tour 2 hrs. before close), led with theatrical aplomb by one of the Beefeaters—the nickname of the Yeoman Warders—who live in the Tower and preserve it. (There are about 100 Tower residents, including families, but only six Beefeaters in 500 years have been female.) The tour (don't arrive later than 2pm if you want one) is engaging, but juvenile—expect bellowing and histrionics, each reciting an identical script with a gleeful fetish for yarns about beheadings and torture. (In truth, you can count the people executed inside the Tower on your fingers and toes; it was considered an honor to be killed here, because it was private.) If you'd like your history delivered without vaudevillian shenanigans, head to the gift shop on the right after Middle Tower and grab an audio tour (£5), but do it early; headsets can run out. The official guidebooks (£5) here are pretty good, and they certainly help with orientation.

As you enter the **Crown Jewels** exhibition, you'll see archival film of the when the jewels were officially used at coronations. After passing into a vault, visitors glide via people-movers past cases of glittering, downlit crowns, scepters, and orbs worn (awkwardly—they're 2.3kg/5 lb. each) by generations of British monarchs. Check out the legendary 105-carat Koh-I-Noor diamond, once the largest in the world, which is fixed to the temple of the **Queen Mother's Crown** (1937), along with 2,000 other diamonds; the Indian government has sought to get the stone back. The 530-carat Cullinan I, the world's largest cut diamond, tops the Sovereign's **Sceptre with the Cross** (1661). The **Imperial State Crown**—ringed with emeralds, the 170-carat Black Prince's ruby, and diamonds aplenty—is the one used in the annual State Opening of Parliament; the solid gold **St Edward's Crown** is for coronations. After those come candlesticks that could support the roof of your house, trumpets, swords, and the inevitable traffic jam around the 1m-wide (3-ft.) **Grand Punch Bowl** (1829), an elaborate riot of lions, cherubs, and unicorns that holds 144 bottles' worth and shows what it would look like if punch bowls could go insane. Because Oliver Cromwell liquidated every royal artifact he could get his hands on, everything dates to after the Restoration (the 1660s or later). Clearly, the monarchy has more than made up for the loss.

The Ravens, Forevermore

Ravens probably visited the Tower in the 1200s to feast on the dripping corpses of the executed, who were taken from Tower Hill (the public execution ground, near the present-day Tube stop) and hung outside the battlements as a warning. You've probably heard the legend that if the ravens leave the Tower, England will fall, but it's a modern superstition. Nevertheless, six of the carnivorous birds are kept in cages north of Wakefield Tower. They are fed raw meat, blood-soaked cookies, and the occasional finger from a tourist dumb enough to get too close.

The four-sided **White Tower** (completed in 1098) is the heart of the fortress, and for more than 200 years, it was the tallest structure in London. Touring its four cavernous levels requires much circuitous stair-climbing, but takes in a wide span of history, including a fine stone chapel, Norman-era fireplaces and toilets, the gleaming **Line of Kings** collection of the **Royal Armoury** (even small children can't help but notice the exaggerated codpiece of King Henry VIII's intricately etched suit from 1540), and some models depicting the Tower's evolution (it's been much altered, but the six smallest arched windows on the White Tower's south side are original to the 11th c.). Try to time your arrival on the top floor to take one of three daily tours (10:45am, 12:45, or 2:15pm) of the nearly 1,000-year-old **Chapel of St John.** After you're finished in here, you'll have an excellent overview of how the whole complex worked.

Once you've got those two areas under your belt, take your time exploring the rest. I suggest a stop in the brick **Beauchamp Tower** (pronounced *beech*-um,

GREAT galleries

The Cartoon Museum ♥ The focus at this little gallery-style museum is British cartoonists, especially prominent political and cultural satirists, so it draws students of the United Kingdom's social history. Changing exhibitions (you would have loved the one on Wallace and Gromit) spice things up. 63 Wells St., W1. www.cartoonmuseum.org. ✆ **020/7580-8155.** Admission £12 adults, £8 seniors, £5 students, kids under 18 free. Tues–Sat 10:30am–5:30pm, Sun noon–4pm. Tube: Tottenham Court Road.

Hayward Gallery ♥ Hidden on a back rampart of the vital nonprofit Southbank Centre, the Hayward hosts terrific blockbuster shows, which have included Ansel Adams, Roy Lichtenstein, 1920s surrealism, and in 2026, Anish Kapoor. Always modern, never staid, regularly on London's art A List—make an advance booking. It also takes itself quite seriously, which can be good for a laugh. Southbank Centre, Belvedere Rd., SE1. www.southbankcentre.co.uk. ✆ **020/3879-9555.** Charge for exhibitions £22. Tues–Fri 10am–6pm; Sat 10am–8pm; Sun 10am–6pm. Tube: Waterloo.

Quentin Blake Centre for Illustration ♥ Founded by a major illustrator of Roald Dahl's children's books, its three galleries in a former Clerkenwell waterworks that was previously vacant for 70 years opens in 2026 for collections and temporary exhibitions about the genre. 1 Myddelton Passage, EC1. qbcentre.org.uk. ✆ **020/8150-7100.** Free admission. Tube: Angel or Farringdon.

Saatchi Gallery ♥ This landmark, the only resident in the three-story, 6,500-sq.-m (70,000-sq.-ft.) former Royal Military Asylum building (1801) in Chelsea, is generally a go-to for emerging avant-garde contemporary artists; sometimes exhibitions are just shills for luxury brands (Hermés, Rolls-Royce, Tiffany & Co.). Only commit if the current fare is a true artists' showcase. Duke of York Square, SW3. www.saatchigallery.com. ✆ **020/7811-3070.** Free admission; some exhibitions £10 admission. Daily 10am–6pm. Tube: Sloane Square.

Whitechapel Gallery ♥♥ Since 1901, the Whitechapel has reliably led the development of new artistic movements. In 1939, it brought to Britain Picasso's newly painted *Guernica* as part of an exhibition protesting the then-current Spanish Civil War. Later it introduced Jackson Pollock's abstracts. There's always a challenging exhibition, talk, or screening going on. 77–82 Whitechapel Rd., E1. www.whitechapelgallery.org. ✆ **020/7522-7888.** Admission £15 adults, £9.50 seniors and students, under 16 free. Tues–Wed and Fri–Sun 11am–6pm; Thurs 11am–9pm. Tube: Aldgate East.

built in 1280), where important political prisoners were held and where you can still glimpse graffiti testifying to their suffering. In front of it on Tower Green is the circular glass memorial designating the **Scaffold Site,** where the unlucky few (including sitting queens Anne Boleyn and Lady Jane Grey) are said to have lost their heads. In reality, we don't know exactly where they were killed, but Queen Victoria wanted a commemorative site set, and because of the evident dangers of displeasing the monarch, this spot was chosen.

The **St Thomas's Tower,** from the 13th century, is closest to the Thames and re-creates King Edward's bedchamber with authentic materials. Beneath it, **Traitor's Gate,** once called Water Gate, originally was used to ferry prisoners in secret from the Thames. Torture was never a part of English law, but it happened here anyway, and the **Bloody Tower** was where some of the worst stuff went down. In truth, there were only 48 recorded cases of torture in the Tower, but that doesn't stop curators from devoting an entire room to a display of (mostly replica) torture devices. Don't forget to climb the ramparts for that classic photo of the Tower Bridge. Skip the Royal Fusiliers Regimental Museum, a dreary hodgepodge of military memorabilia.

Daily at 2:50pm, the guards parade outside the Waterloo Block to the Byward Tower. On Sundays, your admission ticket allows you to attend services at the **Chapel Royal of St Peter ad Vincula,** the Tower's church with a Tudor-era Spanish chestnut ceiling, at 9:15 or 11am; otherwise, the only way to get in, and to see the marble slab beneath which Boleyn and Grey's decapitated bodies were entombed, is with a Yeoman Warder Tour—salacious tales of gory fates are spun virtually on top of the graves of the people who suffered them; Beefeaters are tacky for tourism. Then again, the goings-on of this ancient fortress have always terrorized outsiders with their melodrama.

Tower Hill, EC3. www.hrp.org.uk. ✆ **033/3320-6000.** Admission £35.80 adults 18–64, £28.50 seniors and students, £17.90 children 5–15. June–mid-Sept daily 9am–5:30pm; mid-Sept–May Tues–Sat 9am–5:30pm, Sun–Mon 10am–5:30pm; last admission 1 hr. before closing. Tube: Tower Hill or Tower Gateway DLR.

Other Attractions in the City

Bank of England Museum ♥ MUSEUM The intermittently compelling tale of the B of E is recounted in appealingly patronizing but generous detail in a disused section of the complex. The exhibition is guarded like a fortress (you'll go through metal detectors) and accompanied by plenty of antiques from the vaults. There's a lot to soak up if you understand finance, but most people lose the plot pretty quickly. Along the way are some fun oddities, including an explanation of how the current polymer banknotes are made and reimbursement claims from families of *Titanic* victims. There's also lots of expensive swag, such as a primitive safe from 1700, heaps of silver treasures, and a gold bar so pure (1 part in 10,000 impure) that it was given to Queen Elizabeth as a coronation gift. Guess she didn't need it. It's also fun to watch monarchs age on the money over the years. The most popular exhibit is a 28-lb. standard gold bar, encased in a clear plastic box, that you're challenged to lift. The rest of the bank isn't open.

Threadneedle St., EC2. www.bankofengland.co.uk/museum. ✆ **020/7601-5545.** Free admission. Mon–Fri 10am–5pm; last admission 4:30pm, third Thursday of the month until 8pm. Tube: Bank.

The Charterhouse ♥♥♥ HISTORIC SITE Once you enter this once-powerful vestige of medieval England, opened in 2017 after being off limits since 1348, it's hard to believe you're still in modern London. These ancient collected quads and halls have been a monastery (brutally and gorily crushed by Henry VIII), mansion, school, hospital, home for the poor, and burial ground—it's still the last four, and in fact, you'll meet the skeleton of one longtime resident, a victim of the Black Plague in the 1300s, discovered in the digging for the new Elizabeth Line. A journey so winding makes for a hodge-podge of ancient things to amaze you: gardens and cobbled courtyards,

More than 700 years of history are revealed at the Charterhouse.

slanted slots used by monks to receive food so they wouldn't have the disturbance of human contact, and a paneled Jacobean chapel (full of carvings of dogs and weapons, its patron's symbols) that miraculously survived the Blitz thanks to the protection of a mere wooden door that now hangs blackened on its hinges. The museum is free to see, but to truly get inside, you must be escorted. One of the 40 "Brothers" (even the women are called "Brothers") who have been lucky enough to be selected to retire here gives affectionate tours of what the last 700-odd years have left behind. On the afternoon tours, the smell of lunch still lingers in the great dining hall, for this time-stunned, one-of-a-kind hideaway is still in active use. On one tour I took, the Brother cocked his ear at the sound of church bells in the distance. "St Bartholomew's," he said. "The only set of bells to date from before the Dissolution. 1510, I think." At the Charterhouse, another miracle of survival, we can hear and see exactly what people did half a millennium ago.

Charterhouse Square, EC1. www.thecharterhouse.org. ✆ **020/3818-8873.** Free admission. Standard tours £15 and Brothers' Tours £20 (both 11am and 2:15pm); book ahead. Tues–Sat 10:30am–4:30pm. Tube: Barbican or Farringdon.

Dr Johnson's House ♥ HISTORIC HOME A rare surviving middle-class home from the 18th century (built in 1700), this slouching and brick-faced abode happens to be that of famous lexicographer Samuel Johnson, who lived here from 1748 to 1759. If you're hoping to learn a lot about him, you'll have to spring for a book in the gift shop. Little substance is provided in the house itself, which fortunately merits some mild interest on its own terms (the corkscrew latch on the front door, which prevented lock-picking from above, is an example). The rooftop garret in which Johnson and six helpers toiled to publish the first comprehensive English dictionary was burned out in the Blitz, ironically, by a barrel of burning ink that flew out of a bombed warehouse; you can still see some scorch marks on the ceiling timbers. Ink defined the house and nearly destroyed it, but it also saved it, because the printers who used the house in the intervening years boarded up the walls, preserving them. While you're here, pop round the corner to the wonderful Ye Olde Cheshire Cheese pub (p. 129). Dr Johnson sure liked to.

17 Gough Sq., EC4. www.drjohnsonshouse.org. ✆ **020/7353-3745.** Admission £10 adults, £9 seniors and students, £5 children 5–17, family ticket £20. Tues–Sat 10am–5pm, last entry 4:30pm. Tube: Blackfriars.

offbeat SIGHTS

Bow Street Museum of Crime and Justice ♥ For 266 years, this location was the intake court for many of London's most infamous "crimes," including Oscar Wilde's detainment for being homosexual and Emmeline Pankhurst's for demanding the vote. This small museum will show you the dock in which they stood for "justice," a few jail cells, and much praise for the police. They may have been the foot soldiers in the narrow-minded fight against equality, but the museum assures you they did throw lovely Christmas parties. 28 Bow St., WC2. bowstreetmuseum.org.uk. Admission £8 adults, £6 seniors and student, kids under 12 free. Fri–Sun 11am–4:30pm. Tube: Holborn.

London Mithraeum ♥ In the middle 3rd century, Romans built a temple to Mithraism, a male-only religion now lost to time. The foundational ruins of the temple were lost, too, until 1954, when construction unearthed them. Today you'll stand in the cellar of a modern building on a catwalk around the rocks, which are ingeniously lit with scrims of powerful light, and you hear voices that simulate what a ceremony to Mithras might have been like. It's an artful way to make a ruin interesting. In truth, we barely know a thing about what happened here. 12 Walbrook, EC4. www.londonmithraeum.com. Free admission. Reservations suggested. Tues–Sat 10am–6pm; Sun noon–5pm; first Thurs of month until 8pm. Tube: Bank or Cannon Street.

St Magnus the Martyr ♥♥ The London Bridge, completed in 1209 and the only Thames crossing in London proper until the 1700s, was a city unto itself; its span was stacked with homes, shops, and chapels, much like Florence's Ponte Vecchio is today. Until 1831, that teeming bridge touched down outside the west door of this church, making St Magnus the Martyr the gateway to London for centuries' worth of travelers. In 1987, a man named David T. Aggett built a 4.35-m (14.27-foot) 360-degree model of what the bridge looked like around the year 1400, complete with 900 painted figures crowding its jammed passageway. You can see this vivid evocation of how bad travel used to be in the church's sanctuary; leave a donation. Lower Thames Street, EC3. www.stmagnusmartyr.org.uk. Tues–Fri 10am–4pm. Tube: Monument.

The Vagina Museum ♥♥ Part education and part advocacy, this tiny museum, which is dedicated to destigmatizing "the vagina, vulva and gynaecological anatomy," exists thanks to the love of crowdfunding. The museum is handmade, but perspective-shifting: Did you know, for example, that the major behaviors people cited to accuse women of being witches matched the standard symptoms of menopause? The little gift shop sells amazing wares that hit the spot, too, including plushies of the star organ. Arches 275-276 Poyser St., E2. www.vaginamuseum.co.uk. Recommended donation £5. Weds–Sun 10am–6pm. Tube: Bethnal Green.

The Who Shop Museum ♥♥ A fan-run Doctor Who collector's emporium in East Ham, a 50-minute Tube ride east of Piccadilly Circus, also runs a mini-museum of some 120 screen-used props, costumes, and artifacts from the enduring British franchise. Make a booking, because it's not always open, and no photos are permitted, although you may take your picture with a genuine TARDIS. 39–41 Barking Rd., E6. www.thewhoshop.com and whoshopevents@gmail.com. ✆ **020/8471-2356.** Admission £5, cash only, reservations required. Thurs–Sat 11am–3pm. Tube: Upton Park.

A scale model of old London Bridge at St Magnus the Martyr church.

The Monument ♥ LANDMARK Back in 1677, it was the tallest thing (61m/200 ft.) in town and it made people gasp. Today, it's hemmed in by personality-free glass buildings. The Monument was erected to commemorate the destruction of the city by the Great Fire in 1666. Its height also represents the distance east from its base to the site of Thomas Farynor's bakery in Pudding Lane, where the conflagration began. There's only one thing to do in this fluted column of Portland stone: Climb it. The spiral staircase of 15cm (6-in.) steps, which has no landings, gradually narrows as it ascends to the outdoor observation platform. They'll tell you it's 311 steps to the top, but they're lying—it's 313, if you count the two steps before the box office. You'll get a certificate of accomplishment if you brave them. Check out the metal band snaking down the north side; it's a lightning rod, and it crosses along a Latin inscription blaming Catholics for starting the fire (the insult was chiseled off in 1831). Tickets are discounted in combo deals with the Tower Bridge Exhibition (p. 191). Go on a pleasant day (unless you'd like a good wind whipping) and be prepared to leave large bags downstairs.

Monument St. at Fish St. Hill, WC4. www.themonument.org.uk. ✆ **020/7403-3761.** Admission £6 adults, £4.50 seniors and students, £3 children 5–15. Daily 9:30am–1pm and 2–6pm; last admission 30 min. before each closing. Tube: Monument or Bank.

EAST LONDON & DOCKLANDS

The part of London east of the City encompasses many square miles and dozens of separate neighborhoods, but most visitors will only hear it referred to broadly as "East London." It starts around Shoreditch and Whitechapel and, as you go east, begins to incorporate rehabbed former industrial wastelands. **Docklands,** the area bordering the river, is rich in upscale condos and corporate offices. **Greenwich** is a gorgeous villagelike neighborhood on the southern bank of the Thames. And in Stratford, the biggest population center of East London, everything seems newly made, including the Queen Elizabeth Olympic Park.

Dennis Severs' House ♥♥♥ MUSEUM This 1724 town house was dragged down by a declining neighborhood until the 1970s, when eccentric Californian Dennis Severs purchased it for a pittance, dressed it with antiques, and created this amusingly pretentious imagination odyssey—he called it "Still Life Drama." Other museums are unrealistically tidy and cordoned off, but his house looks lived-in so the past feels as real as it truly was. As Severs, who died in 1999, put it, "In this house it is not what you *see,* but what you have only just *missed* and are being asked to imagine." You could go during the day ("Silent Visit"), but if you're in town during the winter, go after dark for "Silent Night." As you approach, the shutters are closed and a gas lamp burns. You're admitted by a manservant who speaks very little; he motions you to explore the premises, room by room, silently and at your own pace. Suddenly, you're in the parlor of a reasonably prosperous merchant in the 1700s. Candles burn, a fire pops in the hearth, and the smell of food wafts in the air. Room by dusky room, you silently explore corners overflowing with the implements of everyday life of past ages. It's as if the residents were just in the room, leaving toys on the stairs, beds rumpled, mulled wine freshly spilled, and tea growing cold. By the time you reach the last of ten rooms, the attic, you'll have accompanied the house and its occupants through its decay into a collapsing slum. "Silent Night" is one of London's most invigorating diversions.

18 Folgate St., E1. www.dennisseversheouse.co.uk. ✆ **020/7247-4013.** Silent Night (Fri–Sat evening) £25, Silent Visit (Sat–Sun afternoon) £16, day visit noon–3:15pm £16. Fri 5–9pm; Sat noon–9:30pm; Sun noon–4pm via timed entry. Reservations required. Tube: Liverpool Street.

Museum of the Home ♥♥ MUSEUM This exploration of the home was installed in a place originally constructed for people who didn't have one: a U-shaped line of 14 dignified brick houses built in 1714 to house indigent ironworkers. Inside is a walk-through of the history of domesticity, which the museum calls **Rooms Through Time**: re-creations and sundry artifacts form abodes from the 1600s to the present, artfully arranged and explained with plenty of interactive diversions for kids (like squashing digital bedbugs). You'll explore all sorts of historical ephemera we rarely think about. What did mass-produced chairs look like in the 19th century? When did servants stop eating alongside their employers at the same table? How long did it take for mirrors to be inexpensive enough for average people to have one in their own house? Outside in **Gardens Through Time**, you'll see live plantings that reflect the popular botanical trends you'd have found in yards in the Tudor, Stuart, Georgian, and Victorian eras. Make sure to take a minute to unwind and inhale in the fragrant **Herb Garden**, in the northernmost cloister—it's one of London's must idyllic secret spaces. You can also visit the museum's restored almshouse, where charity cases were allowed to live back in the day.

Docklands & Greenwich Attractions

People in the past were so cruel to the poor! They blamed them for their own poverty! Good thing we're not so mean to people without money now. 136 Kingsland Rd., E2. www.museumofthehome.org.uk ✆ **020/7739-9893.** Free admission. Tues–Sun 10am–5pm. Tube: Hoxton.

London Museum Docklands ♥ MUSEUM Most of the city's museums would have you believe that London was always a genteel bastion of refined gentlemen. The real story lies in working men who shortened their own lives to put teacups into more privileged, manicured hands. Housed in a brick rum-and-coffee warehouse from 1804, the three-floor museum, strong on plain-speaking explanations, traces the history of working on the Thames. The most trenchant and effective section by far is the one that fully confesses and explains the sin of slavery, the profits of which powered London for centuries, yet which is rarely acknowledged with such depth at its museums. You'll also roam Sailortown, a creepy warren of quayside alleys, all shanties and low doorways, meant to evoke the area's early-19th-century underworld. Finally, the spotlight shifts to the harrowing Blitz, when the East End, taking the brunt of the Reich, was obliterated by fire from the sky and forced to reinvent itself as a corporate citadel. The whole circuit takes about 90 minutes because there aren't many rare artifacts to tarry over. There's also an

London Museum Docklands retells stories of the past with a range of family-friendly interactive exhibits.

interactive, river-themed play area for kids, Mudlarks (arrive close to opening to book free tickets), and plenty of places to eat overlooking the old hand-dug shipping dock. ***Note:*** The main Museum of London, of which this is an offshoot, is closed until 2026.

No. 1 Warehouse, West India Quay, E14. www.londonmuseum.org.uk/docklands. ✆ **020/7001-9844.** Free admission. Daily 10am–5pm; galleries close 4:40pm. Tube: West India Quay DLR or Canary Wharf.

Ragged School Museum ♥ MUSEUM The Victorians weren't very nice people. Although in 1883 as many as 60,000 London families lived in a single room, church-run schools still charged a penny a week and had a dress code, and the many kids who couldn't afford to meet it ended up on the street. Thomas Bernardo was headed for missionary work abroad when he realized East London kids needed him more than foreigners did; he took in the "ragged" children who couldn't even muster shoes, gave them an education, and made them his "home kids," feeding and nurturing them. From 1877 (when one in four children who lived around here died before adulthood) to 1908, he used this canalside warehouse as a school—playground in the basement, classrooms (now re-created) up top—and he worked to help the most desperate kids emigrate for better lives. One in 11 Canadians can trace their ancestry to "home" children who went to ragged schools like this one.

46–50 Copperfield Rd., E3. www.raggedschoolmuseum.org.uk. ✆ **020/8980-6405.** Admission £5 adults, £2.50 seniors, students, and children. Wed–Sun 10am–5pm. Tube: Mile End or Limehouse DLR.

Up at the O_2 ♥♥ TOUR Built on a toxic peninsula wasteland on the Thames in the 1990s, the Millennium Dome was conceived as a showplace for what turned out to be a poorly attended turn-of-the-century exposition. It's supported by a dozen 100m-tall (328-ft.) yellow towers, one for each hour on the clock, in honor of the nearby Greenwich Prime Meridian—a preening and meaningless symbolism that cost £789 million, and then stood empty for half a decade. In 2007, however, it was finally reborn as the city's finest performance arena, with 20,000 seats (p. 283). Now, Londoners can stomp on it like they always wanted. Climbers, about 10 at a time, hook into a safety rigging system and follow a guide over a tensile fabric catwalk laid a few feet over the Dome's roof, to an observation platform at the zenith of the structure. There they pause for 15 minutes of photos of East London (the City is mostly hidden behind Canary Wharf's towers). Beneath them, humming like a ship at sea, is a Dome conquered. The excursion isn't for the height-averse—at your highest, you're 52m (171 ft.) above the ground. But it's also not scary, because you're tethered and the shoes they lend you grip well. If the weather's bad, you get matching jumpsuits like - Oompa Loompas. The climb, which is more like a stroll up a steep hill, takes 45 minutes; the rest of the 90-minute experience consists of getting harnessed and psyched up.

Peninsula Sq., SE10. www.theO2.co.uk. ✆ **020/8463-2680.** Climbs £37–£43, depending on weekday/weekend/holiday/sunset/twilight. Minimum age 8, minimum height 1.2m/47 inches, maximum weight 130kg/286 lb. Daily 10 or 11am to 6–8:30pm, depending on season. Tube: North Greenwich or North Greenwich ferry.

Young V&A ♥ MUSEUM Previously called the Museum of Childhood, this facility, an offshoot of design stalwart V&A (p. 176), reopened in 2023 after major renovations with a changed purpose. While it used to be a curated repository that was *about* children, it's now just a space *for* children, and local parents bring their brood here to run wild, like an indoor playground with a veneer of the past. There are a few cases of old toys behind glass, but signage won't teach anyone much about why artifacts were chosen. For example, all you'll learn about the 1985 Sesame Street playset selected for display is a sign reading "Nurseries and schools are an important part of every community." The double-galleried glass-and-steel hall, which turned 150 in 2022, is itself an artifact; it began its life in South Kensington as the home of the early V&A collection but was re-erected here in the 1860s—the fish-scale mosaic floor was assembled by female prisoners, many of whom (in an ugly irony) were forbidden to see their own kids. Now parents will find covered tables for drawing and wide spaces for scampering. In the context of this building's abusive history, perhaps that's beautiful, but don't expect an education. The shop, though, has smart toys.

Cambridge Heath Rd., E2. www.vam.ac.uk/young. ✆ **020/7942-2000.** Free admission. Daily 10am–5:45pm. Tube: Bethnal Green.

V&A East ♥ MUSEUM The venerable Victoria and Albert museum is world-famous for preserving art from other eras and cultures, but in April 2026, it cut the ribbon on this newly built facility, which spotlights the creative power of London's modern-day residents through changing exhibitions, events, and performances. Expect a deep dive into the backstory of contemporary art of all types, particularly as it relates to current British society in all its diversity, which this new attraction sims to serve. Curators previewed its two-level **Why We Make Galleries** featuring "over 500 objects from the V&A's

collections" that "offer a fresh look at contemporary culture through the V&A's collections" and **Breaking Boundaries**, which "reveals how making can challenge norms." The V&A is wonky, offbeat, and ever-changing in a way the main V&A in South Ken cannot be. A 15-minute walk northeast, you'll also find its new sister facility, V&A Storehouse (see below).

107 Carpenters Rd., E20. https://www.vam.ac.uk/east. ✆ **020/7942-2000.** Free admission. Daily 10am–6pm (10pm closing Thurs & Sat). Tube: Stratford.

V&A Storehouse ♥ MUSEUM The V&A's curators say that only 3% of its holdings can be displayed at one time, leaving some 97% to languish in storage. So in 2025, the applied arts institution opened its Storehouse, a warehouse/museum where 250,000 fine art objects (including books, furniture, clothing, paintings, and much more), 350,000 books, and 1,000 archives have been moved and catalogued in a delirious open-air jumble of beautiful artifacts from history—a collection of collections. The crammed multi-level shelves are overwhelming, like the final shot of *Raiders of the Lost Ark*, and although there are codes beside objects you can use to search for more information, most items are too far away from the walkways, so it's hard to get a bead on the provenance of everything in view. But visitors can also arrange to inspect most of the objects by hand through the Storehouse's recommended **Order an Object** program. In advance of a visit, anyone—and that means you—can go online to select up to five items marked as available for inspection on the collection pages of the V&A website. On the day of your visit, curators will be on hand to show you what you've requested, teach you how to handle the items correctly, and tell you about them. Appointments can book up weeks in advance, so make your plans as early as possible. The Storehouse is also home to the new but rather small **David Bowie Centre**, home to 90,000 objects from the artistic genius' archive including clothing, costumes, shoes, instruments, and awards. Like Order an Object, that requires an advance ticket, which are snapped up months in advance on the V&A Storehouse website.

2 Parkes Street, Queen Elizabeth Olympic Park, E20. https://www.vam.ac.uk/east. ✆ **020/7942-2000.** Free admission. Daily 10am–6pm (10pm closing Thurs & Sat). Tube: Hackney Wick.

A view of the Weston Collections Hall, which features more than 100 mini curated displays, at V&A East Storehouse.

Greenwich Attractions

Situated on a picturesque slope of the south bank of the Thames, Greenwich once was home to Greenwich Palace, where both Henry VIII and Elizabeth I were born. The last part of the palace to be constructed, the **Queen's House** (1616, Inigo Jones, p. 207), still stands, but most of the grounds were rebuilt in the late Georgian period as the equally palatial Royal Hospital, a convalescence haven for disabled and veteran sailors now known as the **Old Royal Naval College** (p. 207). High on the hill, in Greenwich Park, is the **Royal Observatory** (p. 208), and between them stands the **National Maritime Museum** (p. 206). Many of these treasures are owned by the state, so most entrance fees are waived; you can play the whole day without paying more than a few pounds. Most tourists come to get a photo straddling the **Prime Meridian,** the line that slices through the observatory and marks zero degrees longitude. Stop by the **Discover Greenwich visitor center,** alongside the *Cutty Sark,* for background information and to pick up a walking tour from the **Greenwich Tour Guides Association** (www.greenwichtours.co.uk; Mon, Thurs, Sat–Sun at 12:30pm). Tours cost £14 and last about 90 minutes.

Cutty Sark ♥♥ HISTORIC SHIP The only clipper ship left in the world was launched in 1869; by the end of its 52-year career, it had traveled the equivalent of to the moon and back, carrying cargos including tea, wool, and furniture. By the sunset of its sailing life, it was a decrepit old thing, renamed *Ferreira,* having survived hurricanes in America and the loss of its mast in Cape Town. It was eventually dry-docked in Greenwich to show off for tourists, but worse indignities were yet to come: A 2007 fire twisted its iron frame and devastated its hull planking (fortunately, sails, masts, prow, figurehead, and deckhouses had been safely stored for a restoration). As you tour its hold, climbing stairs and weaving across decks (and banging your head on low thresholds), note that the white-painted framework you see is original, while the grey is new. Restoration provided an opportunity for the present lavish presentation: Today, it's as gorgeous as when Britain dominated the seas, and instead of floating in the Thames, it floats 3.6m (11 ft.) over a dry dock skirted by a glass canopy. At the end of a full ship tour, visitors can peep beneath the streamlined brass keel. It's a slight cheat, because the hull originally was coated with Muntz metal, bitumen, and felt, but hey, it looks incredible. The ship will never be speedy again, but it's never looked hotter. Now you can also safely climb up its rigging partway on a tethered **Rig Climb** (up to £52, entry ticket

In Greenwich, visitors get a close-up view of the distinct shape of the hull that made the *Cutty Sark* such a speedy icon of world trade.

included). If you're also entering the Royal Observatory (p. 208), buy a Royal Museums Day Pass combo and save a few pounds.

King William Walk, SE10. www.rmg.co.uk/cutty-sark. ✆ **020/8312-6608.** Admission £22 adults, £16.50 student, £11 children 4–15, discounts when bought in conjunction with Royal Observatory ticket. Daily 10am–5pm; last admission 4:15pm. Free audio tour on Smartify app. Tube: Cutty Sark DLR, Greenwich river ferry, or Greenwich National Rail.

The Fan Museum ♥ MUSEUM This is as niche as museums get, but it's classy and it truly has the best of what it claims to honor—some 4,000 artful specimens, many of them precious, going back a millennium. Ladies are always fainting in English literature for a reason: In the centuries before air-conditioning, corsets severely restricted breathing and flames generated constant heat, so these tools were often the only things that helped fabric-swaddled women remain conscious. This charming collection of fans hosts regular exhibitions of the foldable lifesavers, such as collections of Christmas-themed imagery, Biblical themes, and so on.

12 Crooms Hill, SE10. www.thefanmuseum.org.uk. ✆ **020/8305-1441.** Admission £5 adults, £3 seniors and students 7–16. Tues–Sat 11am–5pm; last admission 4:30pm. Tube: Cutty Sark DLR, Greenwich river ferry, or Greenwich National Rail.

The National Maritime Museum ♥♥ MUSEUM Don't be put off by the topic: The world's largest maritime museum is extraordinarily kid-friendly, brimming with buzzy toys such as a giant play area that looks like a world map. So it's not as, ahem, dry as most would expect. Because so much of Britain's history from the 17th to 20th centuries was transacted via the high seas, there's a lot of meat. The facility has an endless supply of Smithsonian-worthy artifacts that would do any museum proud. In the Polar Worlds gallery, you see artifacts recovered from several ill-fated exploration attempts and hear by video from an Inuit man who explains how he survives the cold (the secret,

Appraising ship models at the National Maritime Museum in Greenwich.

surprisingly, is not wearing much clothing). Pacific Encounters comes to terms with British influence (islanders say missionaries were both "the coming of the light" and "one of the straightforward colonization tools"), and you'll see Fijian tattooing tools and a cannon thrown overboard from Captain James Cook's HMS *Endeavor* in 1770 to keep from sinking in the Great Barrier Reef; it was brought up 199 years later. The museum's crown jewels, ghoulishly, are probably the bloodstained breeches and bullet-punctured topcoat that Admiral Lord Nelson wore on the day he took his fatal shot (in a gallery devoted to the man). Also excellent is the Atlantic Worlds display, which plumbs the British role in the slave trade. The museum also presents the oft-ignored viewpoint that through the East India Company, England looted India—in fact, the English word *looted* has Hindi origins. It's not all so gloomy, though; there are big set pieces such as figureheads, models, antique instruments, entire wooden vessels, and a dark room just for J. M. W Turner's masterpiece *The Battle of Trafalgar* (1822–1824). Weekends are full of free kids' events (storytelling, treasure hunts) that bring suburban London families pouring into the gates, and the fun Greenwich Market is running nearby then, too.

Romney Rd., Greenwich, SE10. www.rmg.co.uk. ✆ **020/8858-4422.** Free admission. Daily 10am–5pm. Tube: Cutty Sark DLR, Greenwich river ferry, or Greenwich National Rail.

Old Royal Naval College ♥ HISTORIC SITE/LANDMARK This 1696 neoclassical complex, primarily the work of Christopher Wren, is mostly used by a university but offers two main sights: the Painted Hall and the Royal Chapel. The **Painted Hall** (daily 10am–5pm; £17.50 for a ticket good all year, £8.75 seniors and students; £5 first Sun of month) is adorned with 40,000 square feet of gob-smacking paintings by Sir James Thornhill that took nearly 2 decades (1707–26) to complete. It was the setting for the funeral of Admiral Nelson, but it may never have looked more glorious than today, following the 2019 removal of years of candle grime and crusty food splatters from rowdy pensioners' banquets. The **Royal Chapel,** in the Greek Revival style, is the work of James Stuart. If the ORNC's stately symmetry rings a bell, that's because it has been used in countless TV shows and movies such as *Les Misérables, Napoleon, Cruella,* and *Bridgerton,* and on Mon and Sat, you can take the Film Tour (£25; book ahead online) to show you more. It's also where you'll find the **Old Brewery** (p. 126), with plenty of garden space where you can kick back with very stiff pints.

Greenwich, SE10. www.ornc.org. ✆ **020/8269-4747.** Free admission. Grounds daily 8am–11pm; buildings daily 10am–5pm; Royal Chapel open Sun 11am for worship and Mon 7:30pm for Choral Evensong. Tube: Cutty Sark DLR, Greenwich river ferry, or Greenwich National Rail.

The Queen's House ♥ HISTORIC HOME Viewed from the river and framed by the newer Old Royal Naval College, the Queen's House enjoys as elegant a setting a building could wish for. Inigo Jones took 22 years to come up with a Palladian-style summer retreat for Charles I's wife, Henrietta Maria, and his daring style set new trends in architecture that we still follow today. It was completed only in 1638—just before the Civil Wars cut both Charles and his schemes off at the head, and Henrietta scurried off to France. The house now serves as a picturesque setting for paintings, most notably the instantly recognizable *The Armada Portrait of Elizabeth I* (supposedly commissioned for Sir Francis Drake in 1588) in the Queen's Presence Chamber. Elizabeth was born in Greenwich Palace, which once stood on these grounds, and the artwork was acquired for £10.3 million in 2016. The nautilus-shaped Tulip staircase, plus other rooms, are considered to be haunted by an unknown specter, so have a camera ready.

Romney Rd., SE10. www.rmg.co.uk. ✆ **020/8312-6565.** Free admission including multimedia tour. Daily 10am–5pm; last entry 4:15pm. Tube: Cutty Sark DLR, Greenwich river ferry, or Greenwich National Rail.

The Royal Observatory ♥ HISTORIC SITE/MUSEUM Commanding a terrific view from the hill in Greenwich Park, with the towers of Canary Wharf spread out in its lap, the Observatory is yet another creation of Christopher Wren (from 1675), and the place from which time zones emanate. Historically the Empire's most important house for celestial observation, it houses significant relics of star-peeping, but sadly, the paid areas are a tourist trap. Most of the good stuff is free, including a small Astronomy Centre and an exhibition on time. The only things admission get you is a planetarium (closed until 2027 for renovation anyway) and the bulk of the **Flamsteed House** by Wren, which includes a collection of clocks that cracked the mystery of measuring longitude, ushering the English Empire to worldwide dominance. Most people plunk down admission not because they care about those but to get access to the **Meridian Courtyard**. The **Prime Meridian** line, which crosses through the grounds, is meant to be located at precisely 0° longitude (the equator is 0° latitude), and tourists pay entry to wait an hour for

Chiswick House and Gardens evoke the Palladian architecture of Italy.

SUMPTUOUS HISTORIC HOMES

Chiswick House and Gardens ♥♥ In west London: The Earl of Burlington (1694-1753) was so into Italy that he commissioned a Palladian home to evoke the villas and gardens of Rome's suburbs. His abode has been restored for your pleasure, and the 65 acres of Italianate gardens are specked with classical statues of lions and the like. You'll spot it frequently in *Bridgerton*. 39–41 Barking Rd., E6. https://chiswickhouseandgardens.org.uk. ✆ **020/3141-3350.** House admission £12. Gardens open daily 7am–dusk. House open Thurs–Sun 10:30am–3:30pm, late May–early Oct. Tube: Chiswick.

Eltham Palace ♥ In southeast London: Eltham (*ell*-tum) was once a palace on the level of importance with Hampton Court or Greenwich—Henry VIII was a boy here. By the 1920s, Stephen and Virginia Courtauld, a wealthy couple with no children, bought the Tudor ruin to rebuild into an ocean liner–inspired mansion for entertaining their movie-industry friends. The guided tour provides a delightful peek into the eccentricity and insularity of the wealthy—Stephen was prone to sulking in public, and their obnoxious pet lemur, Mah-Jongg, had a thing for biting people so badly their lives were altered. The surrounding moat and 19 acres of greenery and gardens, however, still feel like they must have 400 years ago. Court Yard, Eltham, Greenwich, SE9. www.english-heritage.org.uk. ✆ **020/8294-2548**. Admission around £16.80 adults, £15 seniors and students, £10.40 children 5–17; posted prices are higher and include voluntary donation. Apr–Oct daily 10am–5pm; Nov–Mar Sat–Sun 10am–4pm. National Rail: Eltham from Charing Cross.

Kenwood ♥♥ In northwest London: Kenwood is a sublime 18th-century job by Robert Adam with a sigh-inducing view across Hampstead Heath within the green embrace of 112 acres. Inside, the walls are hung with paintings that would be the envy of the National Gallery, including Vermeer's *The Guitar Player*, a John Singer Sargent, and a Rembrandt self-portrait. The title character of the 2014 film *Belle* was raised by Lord Mansfield in this house, and the film was shot here. There's no better place to enjoy an English summer than on its acres of lawns or alongside its ornamental pond. Hampstead Lane, NW3. www.english-heritage.org.uk. ✆ **0370/333-1811.** Free admission. Guided tours Weds, Fri–Sat at 11:30am and 2:30pm, £10 adults, £5 seniors and students. House: daily 10am–5pm (summer until 6pm); grounds: daily 8am–dusk. Tube: East Finchley, then bus no. H3.

Syon House ♥♥ In southwest London: The family of the Duke of Northumberland has owned Syon for over 4 centuries and still lives here in the winter. A fortress-like exterior belies gorgeous historic interiors still full of family heirlooms. Young Queen Victoria spent 7 happy childhood summers here escaping her stultifying existence in Kensington Palace, and in its Long Gallery, Lady Jane Grey was told she would be queen. It's just across the river from Kew, but 200 acres of gardens make you feel like you're in the middle of the country. The 1826 Great Conservatory, built from gunmetal, Bath stone, and lots of glass, was a landmark in architecture. 39–41 Barking Rd., E6. https://syonpark.co.uk. ✆ **020/8471-2356.** Admission to house and gardens £16.50 adult, £15 seniors and students, £8.50 children, £1 discounts online, reservations required. Mid-March to mid-October, Thurs–Sat 11am–3pm. Tube: Ealing Broadway, then bus E2 or E8.

a silly social media moment of straddling the line with a foot in two hemispheres at once. They actually don't need to spend money to do that—the line continues north of the courtyard, where it's free and there's never a wait. Besides, your phone's GPS will reveal that even the line marked on the ground is actually wrong by about 330 feet. It was the best astronomers could do in their era, but modern GPS is pinpoint accurate.

Greenwich Park, Greenwich, SE10. www.rmg.co.uk. ✆ **020/8312-6565.** Free admission for most of grounds. Flamsteed House and Meridian Courtyard: Admission £24 adults, £18 students, £12 children 4–15, discounts when bought in conjunction with *Cutty Sark* ticket. Daily 10am–5pm; last admission 4:15pm. Free audio tour on Smartify app. Tube: Cutty Sark DLR, Greenwich river ferry, or Greenwich National Rail.

OUTER LONDON

Dulwich Picture Gallery ♥♥ MUSEUM A 15-minute train ride from Victoria and an 8-minute walk lands you in a pretty, villagelike enclave of South London, where a leafy stroll acclimates one to contemplation and appreciation. Here you'll find one of the world's most vital collections of old master paintings of the 1600s and 1700s, kept in just a few rooms. Magnanimous donors made it England's first public gallery (opened 1817), designed with a surplus of light by Sir John Soane (who also left us his own cramped museum; p. 152). A visit is almost indescribably serene, the better to stare into the Cheshire Cat face of one of its star masterpieces, Rembrandt's *A Girl at a Window*—how did he capture her bemusedly frank expression? A handheld video tour unspools fascinating backstories of a few works you might otherwise pass by, such as the portrait of young Venetia Stanley, which exists because she was discovered dead in bed and her distraught husband summoned Van Dyck to capture her beautiful corpse. Twist ending: Her beloved might have poisoned her. The airy cafe is reasonably priced.

Gallery Rd., Dulwich Village, SE21. www.dulwichpicturegallery.org.uk. ✆ **020/8693-5254.** Admission £10 adults, £5 seniors and students, free for young people 17 and under; special exhibitions cost more. Tues–Sun 10am–5pm; last entry 4:30pm. National Rail: West Dulwich Station.

The Dulwich Picture Gallery debuted in 1817 as the first purpose-built public art gallery in England.

The Freud Museum ♥ HISTORIC HOME In a hilly Hampstead neighborhood of spacious brick-faced homes, Sigmund Freud, having just fled the Nazis, spent the last year of his life here. His daughter Anna, herself a noted figure in psychoanalysis, lived on in the same house until her own death in

1982. Sigmund's study and library, which came from the doctor's famed offices at Berggasse 19, Vienna, were left precisely as they were on the day he died—which he did on a couch, of course.

20 Maresfield Gardens, NW3. www.freud.org.uk. ✆ **020/7435-2002.** Admission £14 adults, £12 seniors, £9 students 12–16, free for children 11 and under. Wed–Sun 10:30am–5pm. Tube: Hampstead.

Hampton Court Palace ♥♥ PALACE A 35-minute commuter train ride from the center of town, Hampton Court *looks* like the ideal palace because it *defined* the ideal. The rambling redbrick mansion was a center for royal life from 1525 to 1737, its forest of chimneys standing regally in 24 hectares (59 acres) of achingly pretty riverside gardens, now painstakingly restored to their 1702 appearance. Some people come seeking vibrations left by Henry VIII during the 811 days he spent here (yes, that's all; he had more than 60 houses, partly because his court devoured so much food it kept exhausting local resources). Others come because they've seen it on TV in *Bridgerton* as Queen Charlotte's abode, but in real life, she favored Buckingham Palace. The Crown still stocks precious art in many of the 70 public rooms, which start out Tudor and end up Georgian. It can take a whole day to see properly.

Historic reenactors at Hampton Court Palace.

The inflexibly programmed audio guide, which follows a handful of themed trails (Young Henry VIII's Story, Henry VIII's Apartments, and so on), is free, but it harps endlessly on the same old stories about King Henry's wives; if you're looking for deeper explanations, research beforehand. What you're told panders to Tudor scandals because curators apparently think it makes history more interesting. On a surface level it does, but ultimately, it reduces this famous location to little more than a stereotypical set of a tawdry bygone play. The staff can't even adequately describe the paintings on the walls because the Royal Collection, which loans them, keeps switching their locations at a whim. Days are full of live events, which may include reenactments of gossipy events by costumed actors; traditional cooking using bygone methods in the **Tudor Kitchens** (a popular stop); bizarre spoken-word performances in the hammer-beamed **Great Hall;** or ghost tours. Whatever you do, don't neglect the 26.7-hectare (66-acre) **gardens**—regally planted with historical accuracy (topiaries, sculpted yews, 300-year-old trees), they're half the reason to visit. Make time to lose yourself in the Northern Gardens' 500-year-old shrubbery

Maze, installed by William III; kids giggle their way through to the middle of this leafy labyrinth. The well-mannered **South Garden** has the Great Vine, the oldest and largest vine in the world, planted in 1768; its black grapes are sold in the gift shop in early September. Wear sturdy shoes because the grounds are cobbled. Knowing that this consumes at least half a day, if I had to choose between it and Windsor (p. 332) because of time, I'd choose Windsor.

East Molesey, Surrey. www.hrp.org.uk. ✆ **084/4482-7777.** Admission: Weekdays: £28 adults 18–64, £22.50 seniors, £14 children 5–15; weekends and holidays £30.90 adults 18–64, £24.70 seniors, £15.50 children 5–15. Sept–June Wed–Sun 10am–5:30pm; July–Aug daily 10am–5:30pm; last admission 4:30pm. Check ahead for unexpected closures. National Rail: Hampton Court from Waterloo Station.

Royal Botanic Gardens, Kew ♥♥ PARK/GARDEN The 121-hectare (300-acre) gardens, with many expansive lawns, earned a spot on the UNESCO list of World Heritage Sites in 2003. As you'd expect, the glasshouses are world-class—there are 2,000 varieties of plants, many descended from specimens collected in the earliest days of international sea trade. Of the seven conservatories, the domed **Palm House,** built from 1844 to 1848 and jungle-warm, is probably the world's most recognizable greenhouse, while the **Temperate House** is the world's largest glasshouse containing the world's largest indoor plant (the 17.7m-tall/58-ft. Chilean wine-palm, planted in 1843—and that's not a typo). In 2018 it completed a £41-million restoration, and it's full of some 1,500 species of incredible plants, some once thought lost, like the *Dombeya mauritiana*, and some, like the *Encephalartos woodii* cycad, extinct in the wild. Other attractions at Kew include a bamboo garden, a waterlily pond, **Treetop Walkway** (a tree-themed path 118 steps high in the branches), and, it must be said, a heartwarmingly charming village outside the gates. The gardeners are champs; in 1986, they coaxed a bloom from a portea that hadn't flowered in 160 years. Kew's contributions to botanical science are ongoing since 1759. George III, the dilettante ruler who lost the American colonies and went crazy from suspected porphyria, spent his childhood in **Kew Palace**, now part of the grounds, and later went insane there. You can tour a piece of his vanished palace, restored with scientific exactitude. It's only the size of a standard manor house and lacks interpretation except for some ill-advised histrionic audio enactments that no one pauses to endure. Across Kew Gardens, the little **Queen Charlotte's Cottage** is an imitation of a humble village home. Its Picnic Room is painted with vines across its vaulted ceiling—work attributed to King George's daughter, Princess Elizabeth. In late April, the cottage, which is at Kew's southwest end, is surrounded by bluebells in bloom. Many of the goodies at Kew, including the flowers, clamp down in winter, replaced with a holiday lights bonanza during for the end of the year.

Kew, Richmond, Surrey. www.kew.org. ✆ **020/8332-5655.** Admission Feb–Oct: £19–£27 adults, £17–£25 seniors, £10–£12 young people 16–29, £7–£8 children 4–15, lower price is Nov–Jan; £11 for entry after 4pm May–Oct; slight discounts on all tickets for booking online. Daily 10am–7pm (closes between 4–6pm in fall and 3pm in winter); last entry 1 hr. before closing. Tube: Kew Gardens.

Warner Bros. Studio Tour London—The Making of Harry Potter ♥♥♥ MUSEUM London's most popular family outing (about 7,500 people a day) deserves the acclaim; it's as gripping as the fine museums can be, but as eye-popping as a theme park. True, it costs a lot, but you can easily spend all day—you'll need at least 4 hours. On the very lot where the eight movies of history's most successful film franchise (and the 2027 HBO reboot) were shot, it seems that every set, prop, prosthetic, wig, and wand—and I mean every last thing—was lovingly saved for this polished, informative, and exhaustive walk-though feast. You'll spend hours grazing the bounty, from the students' Great Hall to Dumbledore's roost to Dolores Umbridge's den to the actual Diagon Alley to the massive Gringotts Wizarding Bank lobby. There's not much filler. The biggest mistake people make here is arriving too late in the day, so book your entry time for around opening time so you'll have time make a meal of it. Even if you care nothing about the Potterverse, you will be blown away by the craftsmanship of items that got barely 2 seconds of screen time. The finale, an astounding 1:24 scale model of Hogwarts Castle embedded with 2,500 fiber optic lights, is 15m (50 ft.) across and takes up an arena-size room, lit to simulate day and night. Midway through the tour, in an outdoor area containing 4 Privet Dr. and the actual Knight Bus, where you can buy Butterbeer and Butterbeer ice cream. And you won't *believe* the gift shop. Easy 15-minute trains (don't get on one that takes 40 min.) go three times an hour from Euston Station—but not, fans sigh, from Platform 9¾ at King's Cross, where London's official Harry Potter shop is. Wait just outside the Watford Junction station for the electric shuttle bus (included in admission).

Warner Bros. Studios Leavesden, Aerodrome Way, Leavesden, Hertfordshire. www.wbstudiotour.co.uk. ✆ **0345/084-0900.** Admission from £58.50 adults, £45 children 5–15, free for children 4 and under, £180 family of 4. Round-trip train ticket £10–£20. Reservations required. Daily 8:30am–10pm in summer and 9:30am–6pm in winter; check calendar ahead. First tours 9–10am, last tours 2:30–6:30pm depending on day. National Rail: Watford Junction, then a return shuttle bus (included in admission) that meets trains.

Other Outer London Attractions

Fuller's Brewery Tours ♥ FACTORY TOUR Beer has been made at Griffin Brewery, this Thameside property in West London, since the 1600s, and Fuller's has been in charge of the brewing since 1845. Now this steampunk-feeling brick complex supplies some 380 pubs with its products, particularly the popular London Pride. They refuse to move to cheaper digs because a new water supply would change the flavor. Its 2-hr. tour is professional and engaging, more educational than bacchanalian—these people are passionate about their heritage. Free samples once you're done!

Griffin Brewery, Chiswick Lane South. www.fullersbrewery.co.uk/brewery-tours. ✆ **020/8996-2662.** Tours £28. Tues–Sat hourly 11am–3pm; Sun hourly 1pm–3pm; Sun hourly 1–3pm. No one under age 18 admitted. Reservations required. Tube: Turnham Green, then a 20-min. walk.

Home of Charles Darwin—Down House ♥♥ HISTORIC HOME Charles Darwin made one of history's most important voyages, but once back

A 2-hour Fuller's Brewery Tour ends with free samples.

in England, he barely left his home here in the idyllic parish village of Downe. Upstairs you'll find out about the man and his life (did you know the scientist who theorized about mutation married his own first cousin?), and downstairs, guided by an audio tour narrated by Sir David Attenborough, you'll explore his study, his greenhouse, and his enchanting garden of lawns and breezy fields. No wonder Darwin never left again. There are two charming country pubs to enjoy while you wait for the bus back; your Oyster card will get you here.

Luxted Rd., Downe, Kent. www.english-heritage.org.uk. ✆ **01689/859-119.** Admission around £20 adults, £17.70 seniors, £12.80 children 5–17; posted prices are higher and include voluntary donation, discounts for buying online. Mar–Oct daily 10am–5pm; Nov–Feb Sat–Sun 10am–4pm. National Rail: Bromley South, then bus no. 122 and 7-min. walk.

Horniman Museum ♥ MUSEUM A rich Victorian dilettante collected crazy stuff from all over the world, and rather than let it gather dust, he built a museum in South London. This repository of some 350,000 items has since blossomed into a wild educational ride, with something for everyone, particularly children. To wit: a cherished collection of 7,000 musical instruments (Boosey & Hawkes, once the U.K.'s largest instrument maker, donated its archive) and a huge range of items regarding anthropology (masks, puppets, folk art) and natural history (stuffed creatures galore). There's even a modest aquarium, a cafe, and some gorgeous gardened grounds on a hill with a panorama of London 10km (6 miles) north.

100 London Rd., Forest Hill. www.horniman.ac.uk. ✆ **020/8699-1872.** Free admission. Daily 10am–5:30pm; last entry to Butterfly House (£9.75 adult, £6.50 child) 3:30pm. Tube: Forest Hill Overground.

Mandir ♥ TEMPLE The breathtakingly pretty, many-pinnacled Mandir in northwest London is the largest Hindu temple outside of India. This fabulous concoction was completed in 1995, after some 5,500 tons of Italian Carrara marble and Bulgarian limestone were carved in India and assembled by volunteers. Its dome was built without using steel or lead. The interior is as white and lavishly detailed as a doily—it's apt to amaze even people generally unimpressed by such virtuosity. Tourists are welcome—try to be there to witness the musical wick-lighting Arti ceremony at 11:45am. If you're entering, shorts or skirts must fall at least to the knee (although ankle-length is preferable and sarongs are available to borrow); visitors must also remove their shoes.

105–119 Brentfield Rd., NW10. https://londonmandir.baps.org. ✆ **020/8965-2651.** Free admission. Daily 9am–12:15pm and 4pm–6pm. Tube: Wembley Park, then bus no. 206, or Stonebridge Park, then bus no. 112.

Wimbledon Lawn Tennis Museum ♥♥ MUSEUM Most of us can't get into the tournament (see "Netting Wimbledon Tickets," below), and there's an 11-year waiting list to become a member of the All England Lawn Tennis & Croquet Club, the official name of Wimbledon. But for us, there's still something worth seeing the rest of the year. The museum is like a Hall of Fame, with an emphasis of course on Wimbledon, with artifacts going back to 1555. The climax, most times of year, is the hallowed room shimmering with the silver men's "Challenge-Cup" and women's "Challenge-Plate," which are the actual

Netting Wimbledon Tickets

It's easy watching the Wimbledon Championships on TV for 2 weeks in late June and early July, but seeing it in person is a trickier matter. High hotel prices are just the beginning. Because tickets for the final matches go to VIPs, you're more likely to catch famous players during the early rounds, when the club's 19 grass courts are all in use. For the price of a "ground pass" (£33 to start, less as days go by) you can get roaming access to all but three courts. Surcharges are levied for Centre, No. 1, and No. 2 courts, and while most of those tickets are distributed by lottery ("public ballot") the previous summer, 500 seats a day are sold to people who wait outside in what's called The Queue. Around 6,000 ground passes are distributed each morning to The Queue starting at 7:30am, so arrive many hours before that (by 5:30am at the latest) to camp in Wimbledon Park, Church Road side (no large luggage allowed). If you snag one, you'll probably be inside by noon, before matches begin. You can wander around to your heart's content, drinking Pimm's Cup and eating strawberries and cream, and watching matches on giant screens, but you'll still need to get into the three most important courts. You can try by online ballot, but that closes the autumn before the Championships. Meanwhile, Ticketmaster (and no one else; www.ticketmaster.co.uk) may release several hundred tickets for Centre Court and Court 3 the day before play. Another clever way to get in is to bum tickets off people as they get tired and leave for the day; just don't offer money—the organizers hate that because they sell unused tickets, too, for charity. Those are resold after 3pm to those already on the grounds (£5–£10). On weekdays and rainy days, your chances of getting unfilled seats for the best courts are better, because people are working or huddling indoors. And after 5pm, ground-pass rates dip to, at most, £18, which isn't such a bad deal because matches continue until 9pm. It's all ridiculously complicated—as the author of this book often laments, the English love arcane admittance schemes—so check ahead on www.wimbledon.com to ensure rules remain the same.

Championships trophies inscribed with every winner's name. There is no other museum in the world where a ghostly video apparition of John McEnroe appears in a locker room to vent about opponents. (He comes in peace. No need to duck.) Tennis fans should absolutely spring for the tour of the grounds, too, which is truly all-access, including entry into the Competitors' Complex reserved for players, a photo op in the press conference room where they meet the media, and the all-important Centre Court, where finals are always played, and always on grass. The guides are fantastic and challenge you to stump them.

Church Rd., SW19. www.wimbledon.com/museum. ✆ **020/8946-6131.** Museum admission £15 adults, £13 seniors and students, £10 children 5–16. Museum with grounds tour: £32 adults, £28 seniors and students, £22 children 5–16 (one free child for each paying adult). Apr–Sept daily 10am–5:30pm; Oct–Mar daily 10am–5pm. Tube: Southfields, then 15-min. walk or bus no. 493; or National Rail from Waterloo to Wimbledon Station, then bus no. 493.

OVERRATED ATTRACTIONS

In every city, you invariably find attractions that are heavily publicized but, once seen, are revealed to be time poorly spent. London provides a variety of overpriced pursuits catering to people who are ignorant of its true treasures. If these places lower their prices, maybe we'll reassess. Until then, take our advice: These are overhyped.

The Household Cavalry Museum MUSEUM Along Whitehall, where guards try mightily to ignore buffoonish tourists who try to get them to crack a smile, this tiny museum pays soporific tribute to the martial ceremonies of the King's Life Guard. You might see troopers groom horses through a glass partition or regard cases of uniforms and regalia with glazed eyes, but—nothing against these dedicated marchers—you won't get much back on your investment. On the hour, mounted dutymen change, and at 11am, the Life Guard changes, but you can see those outside for free.

Horse Guards, Whitehall, SW1. www.householdcavalrymuseum.co.uk. ✆ **020/7930-3070.** Admission £11 adults, £8 seniors and children 5–16. Apr–Oct Weds–Sun 10am–6pm; Nov–Mar Weds-Sun 10am–5pm; last entry 45 min before closing. Tube: Embankment.

IFS Cloud Cable Car OBSERVATION GONDOLA Opened for the Olympics as a Thames crossing between the ExCeL convention center and the O_2 dome, it's an enclosed, 10-person gondola with (barely audible) recorded commentary that shuttles between two places most tourists never go. It's too far from the City to be a panoramic substitute for the Eye or the Shard. The ride takes 5–10 minutes. Although they'll try to upsell you with unnecessary flimflam like champagne, a ride costs what a Tube ride does, and you can use Oyster for a lower fare.

Edmund Halley Way, E10, or Royal Docks side 27 Western Gateway, E16. tfl.gov.uk/modes/london-cable-car. ✆ **0343/222-1234.** One-way cash fare £7 adults, £3.50 children. Mon–Thurs 8am–9pm, Fri 9am–10pm, Sat 9am–11pm, Sun 9am–9pm. Tube: North Greenwich or Royal Victoria DLR.

London Eye OBSERVATION WHEEL When the Eye was erected in 1999 as a temporary vantage point known as the Millennium Wheel, it became such a sensation—and a money-spinner—that it was made permanent. Alas, the Eye has seen better days and is uproariously overpriced despite the fact many new places to see the city from on high have been opened, and for free (see p. 153). Also, it has curtailed its operating hours so severely that often, it's barely open past nightfall. Each of the 32 enclosed capsules, which accommodate up to 28 people (although there may be fewer with you), is climate-controlled and rotates so gradually over the 30-min. ride that it's easy to forget you're moving—which means this ride will upset only the desperately height-averse. This part of town is maddeningly gridlocked with tourists, so simply being here can drain your energy and your high spirits. The tourist trap proprietors do everything they can to confuse you into paying more than you have to. Basically, if you must, a Standard timed ticket will do.

Riverside Building, County Hall, SE1. www.londoneye.com. ✆ **020/7967-8021.** £39 adults, £35 children 2–15; slightly cheaper online, add-ons for shorter waits and champagne. Mon–Fri 10am or 11am–6pm, Sat–Sun 10am–8:30pm, daily closing at 8:30pm late May–late Aug. Tube: Waterloo or Westminster.

The London Dungeon ATTRACTION Avoid it like the plague. This expensive but sophomoric gross-out, with locations in 9 cities, sops up overflow from the London Eye. Costumed actors bray at you as you're led through darkness from set to set, each representing a period of English history as a 13-year-old boy might define them. The climax is a pair of indoor carnival rides. If you dread being picked on by bad stand-up comics, you're going to hate this place. Booking ahead may not save you having to queue. If you can't resist, at least bundle it with a ticket on the London Eye for a discount.

County Hall, Westminster Bridge Rd., SE1. www.thedungeons.com. ✆ **020/7967-8023.** Admission from £35 adults, £29 children 5–15; slightly cheaper online. Times change but roughly daily 10am–5pm. Tube: Westminster or Waterloo.

The London Zoo ZOO This is mostly an excellent zoo. It has an esteemed history going back to 1828 as a menagerie for members of the Zoological Society of London. It's just that it's ultimately only a zoo, and a smallish one at that. When they advertise it has 8,000 animals, they don't admit that's according to its own inventory list, that's counting creatures like 500 bluebottle flies and 600 Australian golden orb weaver spiders. Few of the animals are large, although the 7 lowland gorillas are incredible. Even the addition of Sumatran tigers, baby penguins, and a newly renovated monkey aviary are not enough to justify the high ticket price, especially for first-time London visitors who could be exploring the city instead.

Outer Circle Rd., Regent's Park, NW1. www.londonzoo.org. ✆ **0344/225-1826.** Admission £30.50–£37 depending on when you buy and when you visit. Daily 10am to 4–6pm, depending on the month. Tube: Camden Town, then bus no. 274.

Madame Tussauds ATTRACTION Have you ever heard of Mo Salah? Sachin Tendulkar? Cara Delevingne? No shade, but if you don't recognize

ritual **ABUSE**

I'm only telling you this because I love you: **Changing the Guard** (www.householddivision.org.uk/changing-the-guard; Mon, Weds, Fri, Sat at 11am; Tube: St James's Park, Victoria, or Green Park), sometimes called Guard Mounting, is an underwhelming use of your time, even though your friends back home tell you to go and admission is free. Arrive at Buckingham Palace at least 45 minutes early if you don't want to face the backs of other tourists. A marching band advances from Birdcage Walk (often, playing themes from *Star Wars, West Side Story*, or ABBA—so much for rich traditional English customs), then members of the King's Life Guard—two if the king's away, three or four if he's in—do a change around their sentry boxes behind a heavy fence. And that's it, give or take additional prancing. It gets canceled in heavy rain.

Guards patrol all day, without crowds, at both Buckingham Palace and at Horse Guards Arch on Whitehall (which does its own, uncrowded change daily at 11am, or 10am Sun). Or park yourself at **Wellington Barracks,** just east of the palace along Birdcage Walk, by 11am, and catch the Inspection of the Guard that happens before the same men march over to the palace for the main event. Then use the day's golden hours for something less touristy.

Ceremony of the Keys at the Tower of London (www.hrp.org.uk; Tube: Tower Hill, or Tower Gateway DLR) is held every night at 9:53pm as the Yeomen Warders lock up the Tower of London. It's been a routine for more than 700 years—not even German bombs canceled it. But it's an awful lot of work for not much payoff: You must enter the Tower at 9:30pm (several hours after closing time) and leave around 10:05pm, even though the whole show takes less than 7 minutes—plus, photos aren't allowed. As for the event, the Chief Yeoman Warder approaches the heavy wooden gate with keys and a lantern, is asked "Halt, who comes there?," passes muster, and locks up the gates to a bugle call. The end. If you want to see that, apply for tickets online (admission is £5, although some tour companies we shall not name resell them for as much as US $200), with a nightly maximum of six places April to October. Tickets for the following month are typically released on the first day of the month at 4pm London time.

them, you won't get much joy out of this ferociously priced, miserably crowded wax trap. The execution of its mannequin doppelgangers, which you can usually touch, comes in two ways, either superb or baffling. You'd never get this close to the real Harry Styles without consequences. But the focus of this world-famous waxworks is either on British celebrities or on *Star Wars* and Marvel characters. A 5-minute, Disney-esque ride, "The Spirit of London," invokes every painful London stereotype, from the Artful Dodger to plague victims. As you glide through, you'll suddenly wonder if you're the real dummy for being here.

Marylebone Rd., W1. www.madame-tussauds.com/london. ✆ **020/7487-0351.** Admission based on time of year and time of day, typically £39 adults, £35 children 3–15; discounts online. Daily 9am or 10am to 4–6pm, depending on the week, slightly longer Sat–Sun and holidays. Tours continue at least 45 min. past posted closing time. Tube: Baker Street.

Moco Museum ATTRACTION Splashy, hit-you-over-the-head artworks cranked out for mass consumption by the factories behind contemporary megastars like Warhol and Banksy, who mocked this kind of commercialized art theme park even as they raked in cash. It's terrific for kitschy Instagram and TikTok moments, and that's really what it's for. Don't mistake it for high art. Its neighbor, **Frameless** (6 Marble Arch; frameless.com) is a similar playground for smartphone photos, but this one animates famous paintings. Pretty, but not £28 pretty.

1–4 Marble Arch, W1. london.mocomuseum.com. No public phone. london@mocomuseum.com. Admission £22 adults, £18 senior and student, £17 children 4–17, discounts online. Sun–Thurs 10am–6pm, Fri–Sat 10am–9pm. Tube: Marble Arch.

Sea Life London Aquarium AQUARIUM Sure, it's fun to see sharks under your feet and penguins on a faux floe. But sorry, Charlie, the truth is there is nothing here you can't see at other fish zoos. There are more than three dozen other locations worldwide by Sea Life, the McDonald's of fish tanks, and this one feels as cramped as a 16th-century galleon. It's located on the most heinously overcrowded block in town, by the Eye.

County Hall, Westminster Bridge Rd., SE1. www.sealifelondon.co.uk. ✆ **0871/663-1678.** Admission £39 adults, £35 children 3–15, free for children 2 and under; discounts online. Times change but roughly daily 10am to 4–5pm; last admission 1 hr. before closing. Tube: Waterloo or Westminster.

The Sherlock Holmes Museum ATTRACTION Set up a house as if it were really the home of a fictional character, prop up some shabby mannequins, and then charge tourists to see it. That's the scheme, and it works so well there's often a line.

221b Baker St., NW1. www.sherlock-holmes.co.uk. ✆ **020/7224-3688.** Admission £19 adults, £17 seniors, £14 children 6–15. Daily 9:30am–6pm. Tube: Baker Street.

OUTDOOR LONDON

Buildings come and go, but London's open spaces have remained unchanged for centuries—they're the city's oldest places. There are often official walks and tours scheduled, so check websites to see what's coming.

Epping Forest ♥♥♥ PARK/GARDEN Mostly because its soil is unsuitable for farming, for a millennium this remained a semi-virgin woodland—it's the best place to get a feel for what Britain was like before humans denuded its land. It's the largest open space in London, 6,000 acres, 12 miles long by 2½ miles wide, and it contains a universe of diversity—650 plant species, 80 ponds where waterfowl splash, and even some 1,500 species of fungi. Getting lost in the woods is feasible, but not likely, because it stretches in a single direction. Henry VII built a timber-framed hunting lodge in 1542 that was inherited by his daughter Elizabeth and, astoundingly, still stands:

Epping Forest is the largest open space in London.

Queen Elizabeth's Hunting Lodge (reach that via the Chingford rail station).

Rangers Rd., Chingford, E4. www.cityoflondon.gov.uk/eppingforest. ✆ **020/8529-6681.** Free admission. Daily 6am–dusk. Lodge: daily 10am–5pm. Tube: Snaresbrook or Wood Street. National Rail: Chingford.

The Green Park ♥♥ PARK/GARDEN The area south of Mayfair between Hyde Park and St James's Park was once a burial ground for lepers, but now is a simple expanse of meadows and light copses of trees. It doesn't have much to offer except pastoral views, and most visitors find themselves crossing it instead of dawdling in it, although its springtime flower beds (which bloom brightest Mar–Apr) are marvelous. Don't sit in one of those picturesque striped deck chairs unless you've got a few quid to pay as rent.

Piccadilly, SW1. www.royalparks.org.uk. ✆ **030/0061-2350.** Free admission. Daily 24 hr. Tube: Green Park.

Greenwich Park ♥♥ PARK/GARDEN The top of its clean-swept main hill offers one of the more marvelous views in London (of the river and the Canary Wharf district), and the world-famous **Royal Observatory** (p. 208), commissioned in 1675 by Charles II, serves as the intersection point for the Prime Meridian, making it the center of Greenwich Mean Time. Decently sized (74 hectares/183 acres), it was once a deer preserve maintained for royal amusement; a herd of them still have 5 hectares (13 acres) at their disposal. It's been a Royal Park since the 15th century, although the boundary wasn't formally defined until the early 1600s when James I erected a brick wall around it, much of which still survives. Most people combine a visit here with the many other museums of Greenwich (p. 204).

Greenwich Park, SE10. www.royalparks.org.uk. ✆ **030/0061-2000.** Free admission. Daily 6am–9pm. National Rail: Greenwich or Maze Hill, or Cutty Sark DLR or Greenwich ferry.

Hampstead Heath ♥♥♥ PARK/GARDEN Some 7 million visitors a year come to the 320-hectare (791-acre) Heath, in northwest London, to walk on the grass, get enveloped by thick woods, and take in the view from the magnificent Pergola, a beguiling overgrown Edwardian garden and a true London secret. The Heath is a perennial locale for aimless strolls and (it must be confessed, George Michael) furtive trysts. The Heath has several sublime places to rest, including **Kenwood House** (p. 209), a neoclassical home dating from 1640 and redesigned in the 18th century; and the inviting and woody pub **The Spaniards Inn** (Spaniards Rd. at Spaniards End, NW3; www.thespaniardshampstead.co.uk; ✆ **020/8731-8406**). The Heath's hilltop is another favored lookout point. The Heath isn't considered a park by locals, but a green space. The difference is irrelevant. It's transporting.

www.cityoflondon.gov.uk. ✆ **020/7332-3505.** Daily 7:30am–dusk. Tube: Hampstead or Hampstead Heath Overground.

Highgate Cemetery ♥♥♥ CEMETERY/HISTORIC SITE For fans of spooky stuff and of history, this grand but decaying necropolis has no equal. The two-section, 37-acre cemetery was opened in 1839 to serve a booming city. Time passed, though, and the classical stone carvings and mausoleum terraces, once paragons of Victorian memorial architecture and design, succumbed to neglect and vandalism. They now quietly crack, crumble, and molder beneath ivy and gnarled branches. Self-guided tours of the East Cemetery, where you'll find Karl Marx and authors Douglas Adams and George Eliot among the 170,000 lives here, have been possible for a while, but only in 2021 did the deeply atmospheric West Cemetery begin allowing visitors

FAMOUS graves

London's top tombs don't just belong to royalty. Visit these historic area cemeteries for a tranquil day out and to say hello to some major figures.

Bunhill Fields (Tube: Old Street): *The Pilgrim's Progress*'s **John Bunyan,** poet **William Blake,** author **Daniel Defoe**

Golders Green Crematorium (Tube: Golders Green): Ashes of writers **Bram Stoker, Doris Lessing,** and **Seán O'Casey;** musician **Keith Moon;** dancer **Anna Pavlova;** actor **Peter Sellers; Sigmund Freud**

Highgate Cemetery (Tube: Archway; above): **Karl Marx,** pop star **George Michael**

Kensal Green Cemetery (Tube: Kensal Green, and National Rail Kensal Green): Writers **Terence Rattigan, Anthony Trollope, Harold Pinter, Wilkie Collins, J. G. Ballard, William Makepeace Thackeray;** engineers **Marc Isambard Brunel** and **Isambard Kingdom Brunel**

Royal Hospital Chelsea (Tube: Sloane Square): **Margaret Thatcher**

St Mary's Church, Battersea (Clapham Junction National Rail): Lapsed rebel **Benedict Arnold** (his crypt is now used as a kindergarten)

St Mary Magdalen Roman Catholic Church Mortlake (Mortlake National Rail): adventurer **Sir Richard Burton** (under a tent made of Carrara marble)

St Nicholas Church, Chiswick (Tube: Stamford Brook): Artists **William Hogarth** and **James McNeill Whistler**

St Nicholas Church, Deptford Green (Deptford National Rail): Writer **Christopher Marlowe**

again. There, among the moss and gloom of jumbled memorials, you'll find actor Jean Simmons, artist Lucian Freud, and singer George Michael. The 70-min. guided tour (£18 adults, £9 children 8–17; daily 10:30am, noon, and 2pm; reservations recommended) is unforgettable—it takes you through locked areas such as the shadowy tunnel of mausoleums of Egyptian Row and into the chilling Terrace Catacombs, where you'll stand in near darkness alongside actual coffins from the Victorian age. ***Warning:*** Wear sturdy shoes and stay on paths because it's frightfully easy to tumble into concealed open vaults and become a permanent resident.

Karl Marx's tomb at Highgate Cemetery, built in 1956 by his admirers.

Swain's Lane, N6. https://highgatecemetery.org. ✆ **020/8340-1834.** Self-guided visit £10 adults, £5 children 8–17; tours another £8. No cash. Daily 10am–5pm (until 4pm Nov–Feb), last entry 30 min. before closing. Tube: Archway.

Hyde Park & Kensington Gardens ♥♥♥ PARK/GARDEN Bordered by Mayfair, Bayswater, and Kensington, these two conjoined areas are the largest park in the middle of the city. Hyde Park is home to a meandering lake called the Serpentine, the famous **Speakers' Corner** (p. 169), and the **Diana Memorial Fountain,** a graceful, O-shaped fountain that undulates down a gentle slope, a lot like a water slide. The most famous promenade is Rotten Row, probably a corruption of "Route de Roi," or King's Way, which was laid out by William III as his private road to town; it runs along the southern edge of the park from Hyde Park Corner. Kensington Gardens, which flows seamlessly from Hyde Park, only opened to plebes like us in 1851, and it hasn't yet shed its country-manor quality. You'll also find the **Serpentine Galleries** (west of W. Carriage Dr. and north of Alexandra Gate; www.serpentinegalleries.org; ✆ **020/7402-6075;** free admission and free audio guide through the Bloomberg Connects app; Tues–Sun 10am–6pm; Tube: South Kensington), a venue popular for its modern art exhibitions and its excellent art bookshop. Each summer (mid-June to Oct), a leading architect creates a fanciful pavilion there. Volunteers sometimes run guided tours of the park's quirks; check the bulletin boards at each park entrance to see if one is upcoming. Borrow a Santander Cycle and cruise around this giant green playground, and don't forget to look for Sir George Frampton's marvelous bronze statue of Peter Pan (1912) near the west shore of the Long Water.

Hyde Park, W2. www.royalparks.org.uk. ✆ **0300/061-2000.** Free admission. Daily 5am–midnight. Tube: Hyde Park Corner, Marble Arch, or Lancaster Gate.

THE watery park

Sure, everybody knows about London's famous green spaces, but there's one recreation area, stretching from London's northwest to its east through gentrified lanes and industrial wasteland alike, that few tourists are told about. It's **The Regent's Canal,** which threads from Paddington through Camden, Islington, and East London before joining with the Thames (26m/86 ft. lower) just before Canary Wharf. It was completed in 1820 to link with canals all the way to Birmingham and feed the city's massive seagoing trade. In those days, barges were animal-drawn and the districts along the waterway were rat-infested and perilous, but today, it's one of the frontiers for development. Many of the horse tracks are leafy promenades, shadowy warehouses have become expensive loft condos. A new development north of King's Cross station is revealing even more glories. Along the shore, you'll pass docks where houseboat barges tie up; their owners can be found topside, making conversation with passersby. The most popular segment is probably the crescent just north of the Regent's Park. Set in a former icehouse, the **London Canal Museum** (12–13 New Wharf Rd., N1; www.canalmuseum.org.uk; ✆ **020/7713-0836;** admission £7.50; Tues–Sun 10am–4:30pm; Tube: King's Cross St Pancras) is devoted to the waterway and operates tours of its towpath and boat tours of the Islington Tunnel, which stretches for 1.2km (¾ mile) under the streets. April to early November, **London Waterbus** (www.londonwaterbus.com; ✆ **020/7482-2550**), **Walker's Quay** (www.walkersquay.com; ✆ **020/7485-4433**), and **Jason's Trip** (www.jasons.co.uk; no phone) ferry riders in longboats through the 82m (270-ft.) Maida Hill Tunnel and the glorious villas that line the canal between Little Venice (Tube: Warwick Ave.) and Camden's markets (Tube: Camden Town). Ferries run in either direction, year round; a ride costs around £18 for adults. There are no tourist boats that currently ferry riders east of the locks at Camden.

Queen Elizabeth Olympic Park ♥ PARK/GARDEN A dearth of trees and a usually bracing wind make this feel a lot like a theme park in which all of the attractions were torn down. Locals mostly love it because they remember when it was an industrial wasteland. The Pringle-shaped Aquatics Centre and Velopark make for striking architecture, but this park is mostly of interest if you want to see the place you saw on TV—the torch is gone, the stadium has been downgraded for a soccer team, and the ArcelorMittal Orbit observation is now mostly ignored because there's not much left to see from it. If you take the Underground there, Stratford station dumps into a mall (one of the nicest in the city); go up one level to exit.

Stratford, E20. www.queenelizabetholympicpark.co.uk. ✆ **020/3288-1800.** Free admission. Daily 24 hr. Tube: Stratford.

The Regent's Park ♥♥♥ PARK/GARDEN It's the people's park (195 hectares/487 acres), best for sunning, strolling grassy expanses—it can take a half-hour to cross it—and darting into the bohemian neighborhoods that fringe it. Once a hunting ground, it was very nearly turned into a development for the buddies of the Prince Regent (later King George IV), but only a few of the

In summertime, The Regent's Park hosts popular shows at its Open Air Theatre.

private terrace homes were built. You will notice Winfield House, on 5 hectares (12 acres) near the western border of the park, which has the largest garden in London after the king's; the American ambassador lives there—surprised? The most breathtaking entrance is from the south through John Nash's elegant Park Crescent development from the 1820s, by the Regent's Park and Great Portland Street Tube stations. Within walking distance from there, the **Open Air Theatre** (https://openairtheatre.com) mounts fully professional summer shows that are great fun to attend in good weather. North of the park, just over the Regent's Canal and Prince Albert Road, **Primrose Hill Park** (Tube: Chalk Farm or Camden Town) affords a panorama of the city from 62m (203 ft.) high.

The Regent's Park, NW1. www.royalparks.gov.uk. ✆ **030/0061-2300.** Free admission. Daily 5am–9pm. Tube: Baker Street, Great Portland Street, or Regent's Park.

Richmond Park ♥♥♥ PARK/GARDEN The biggest and wildest park, if you have the time, is 30 minutes from Waterloo station, in Richmond, which was once a distinct village but has been absorbed and yuppified by the greater city. It's more than a park—it's a habitat: 2,500 deliriously green acres brimming with herds of deer (since the 1600s!), 144 species of birds, and 11 of Britain's 17 bat species. Beeline to the Isabella Plantation, a 40-acre woodland garden, in May for a nearly pyrotechnic

The deer that roam Richmond Park are descended from the ones introduced by Charles I in 1637. Keep your distance—they're wild.

display of pink rhododendrons and azaleas. The visitor center is by the square in front of Pembroke Lodge, a Georgian mansion. Even if you don't have time to explore the whole park (no one does), you can follow the footpath on the south bank of the Thames for miles, starting by Richmond's waterside pubs and carrying on past ancient oaks (some nearly 800 years old) until you're ready to double back for a second pint.

Richmond-upon-Thames. www.royalparks.org.uk and www.visitrichmond.co.uk. ✆ **0300/061-2200.** Free admission. Daily 7am–7:30pm. Tube or National Rail: Richmond.

St James's Park ♥ PARK/GARDEN The easternmost segment of the contiguous quartet of parks that runs east from Kensington Gardens, it was laid out by James I in 1603 and Buckingham Palace redeveloped it a century later. Its little pond, St James's Park Lake, hosts ducks and other waterfowl. The Russian ambassador made a gift of pelicans to the park in 1667; a few still call it home, and are fed their 13kg (28 lb.) of whiting daily at 2:30pm at the Duck Island Cottage (when avian flu is circulating, feedings are done in private). The park has a fine view of Buckingham Palace's front facade, where royal couples smooch on balconies (but live in a section of the building you can't see). The real draw is people-watching; a cross-section of all London passes through here. It's not a place for picnics or ball throwing, and there's little in the way of amenities or activities—unless you count voyeurism, and why wouldn't you?

The Mall, SW1. www.royalparks.org.uk. ✆ **0300/061-2350.** Free admission. Daily 5am–midnight. Tube: St James's Park.

Victoria Park ♥♥ PARK/GARDEN This was the largest and finest open space in East London when it opened in 1845, the capital's first public park. Bordered by canals and divided in two by Grove Road, "Vicky Park" covers an area of just under 87 hectares (220 acres) and contains two lakes, formal gardens, sports facilities, and a bandstand. Other notable features include a Grade II–listed 1862 drinking fountain and two arches from the pre-1831 London Bridge—now turned into benches. In summer, big music events come here. The park also forms the central section of the **Jubilee Greenway Walk,** a route marked out in 2009 with glass paving slabs in honor of Queen Elizabeth's Diamond Jubilee (in 2012), and stretching for exactly 60km (37 miles)—1 kilometer for each year of her reign—from Buckingham Palace to the Olympic Park.

Grove Rd., E3. www.towerhamlets.gov.uk/victoriapark. ✆ **020/7364-7971.** Free admission. Daily 7am–dusk. Tube: Mile End/Overground, Hackney Wick, or Homerton.

Walking Tours

Good ones are led by government-accredited "Blue Badge" professionals who go through a rigorous historical training program, so always look for a Blue Badge (or, sometimes, Green Badge) guide—there are more than 500 in town, and their trade group has a website, **www.guidelondon.org.uk**, that can matchmake them to your interests and schedule. Plenty of other qualified operators cater to custom business (many only cater to groups), but these will let you

THE CABMAN'S shelter

As you roam, keep an eye out for curious timber-frame shacks, no bigger than a horse and cart, painted "Dulux Buckingham Paradise 1 Green." Wooden, shingled, and peaked, fringed in simple gingerbread latticework, topped by a wee cupola vent, they're as cute as a hobbit's outhouse. Some balance in the median overcrowded avenues, some hunker like newsstands along the pavements. These are **Cabman's Shelters**, built by a charity for £200 each between 1875 and 1914, when "respectable" classes fretted about cab drivers, who back then were carriage drivers exposed to the elements, seeking refuge in the pubs to "drink more than is good for their health or behaviour", per *Illustrated London News* of 1875. Inside these shelters, horsemen could obtain hot soup, tea, and other wholesome refreshments. Of the 61 original shelters, just 13 survive, and at a few of those, against the odds, modern cabbies can still pull over for a cuppa, cheap food, and to recharge their devices. Some shelters are closed for weeks on end, and hours are erratic, but when they're cooking, they're open from breakfast to mid-afternoon. Mostly, though, they're treasured relics of bygone London, and they're protected by the government.

Chelsea Embankment, near Albert Bridge (Tube: South Kensington)
Embankment Place at Northumberland Avenue (Tube: Embankment)
Grosvenor Gardens, west side (Tube: Victoria)
Hanover Square, north side (Tube: Oxford Circus)
Kensington Park Road, numbers 8-10 (Tube: Notting Hill Gate)
Kensington Road, north side by Queen's Gate (Tube: South Kensington)
Pont Street by Sloane Street (Tube: Knightsbridge)
Russell Square, west corner (Tube: Russell Square)
St George's Square, north side (Tube: Pimlico)
Temple Place near the river (Tube: Temple)
Thurloe Place, opposite the V&A (Tube: South Kensington)
Warwick Avenue at Clifton Gardens (Tube: Warwick Avenue)
Wellington Place at Wellington Road (Tube: St John's Wood)

join individually. Also check that online compendium of day tours, **Viator** (www.viator.com). You may also be interested in **London Greeters** (https://londongreeters.org; free), on which eager local volunteers will offer to show you around for 2 hours based on your interests—but there are many highly talented and specifically trained professional guides in the business now, too.

Bowl of Chalk ♥♥♥ Guide Jonnie Fielding leads about 11 rotating pay-what-you-want tours on weekends, and they're so good, satisfied customers ensure he makes a good living from them. He specializes in helping you dig into the neighborhoods you'll be hearing the most about, including Westminster, King's Cross, Bankside, and around St Paul's Cathedral. You can get to know his style before booking on Instagram at his popular account @bowlofchalk, but be quick about it because they can book up weeks ahead. The name, by the way, is Cockney rhyming slang for "walk."

www.bowlofchalk.net. Walking tours £15. Sat–Sun. Reservations essential.

Brit Movie Tours ♥♥ Most city tour companies try their hand at Harry Potter now, but this outfit specializes in movies, filming locations, and cinema history and hews in on entertainment icons like Bridget Jones, Doctor Who, *Downton Abbey,* and *Ted Lasso*—its excursion about romantic comedies like *Love Actually* and *Notting Hill* is a particular hoot.

www.britmovietours.com. ✆ **0844/247-1007.** Walking tours around £12–£35 adults and £10–£21 children 15 and under.

City of London Walks ♥♥ The government that oversees the Square Mile of the oldest part of London gives written and performance-based exams to the experts who lead its excellent tours, which have been running since 1983. The experience is less casual and denser with facts than what London Walks (see below) generally provides, and group sizes tend to be smaller, too. The list usually includes topics like a Thames river walk, Roman London, and Dickens. No need to book; just turn up at the starting point because tours go rain or shine. Between May and October, the City of London Guide Lecturers Association also runs a few themed **Garden Walks** in the City, including historic gardens, the hidden gardens of the legal quarters, and the atmospheric Bunhill Burial Ground (schedule and reservations: www.citygardenwalks.com; £12).

City Information Centre, St Paul's Churchyard, EC4. www.cityoflondonguides.com. Tours £15–£20 via eventbrite.co.uk. Early morning or midday hours. Tube: St Paul's.

The Classic Tour ♥ If you don't have all day, this summer-only, 75-minute whirlwind of the major sites gives you as much style as possible in a limited window of time: You ride on a modified double-decker 1960s Routemaster bus—for decades the standard for commuting Londoners—as a somewhat hammy guide gives you the quick lowdown on everything you pass, from Buckingham Palace to the famous Tower Bridge (which you'll cross).

www.theclassictour.com. ✆ **0844/318-7655.** Tours £25 adults, £19 seniors and students, £17 children 5–15. Three tours daily in summer. Tube: Embankment.

The Downton Abbey walking tour is one of the many tours offered by Brit Movie Tours.

Dotmaker Tours ♥♥ Dotmaker's clever weekend (mostly) walks delve into offbeat topics such as chimneys, tunnels, where geniuses have discovered inspiration, where the city dumps its rubbish, and the seats of London's power brokers. One tour is designed around taking moments to people-watch and observe the rhythms of the town.

www.dotmakertours.co.uk. ✆ **07985/464-314.** Tours generally £20 via eventbrite.co.uk. Most tours Sat–Sun; reservations required.

Eating London Tours ♥♥♥ Very well thought-out food-oriented tours that go from restaurant to bar to restaurant, sampling pre-arranged delights that have been selected to teach you something about London of this moment—all while getting a solid lay of the land from a young, entertaining guide. We haven't taken one we haven't enjoyed, and we've taken a few. It also does a more expensive evening tour of Soho (£109; no kids on that one). It also does a Borough Market tour. Locations vary.

www.eatingeurope.com. info@eatingeurope.com. Text WhatsApp: ✆ **+31-658/95-6001,** or 215/688-5571 in U.S. Tours £79–£110 adults, £50–£75 ages 13–17, £50–£70 ages 4–12.

Tour of Borough Market with Eating London Tours.

FlipsideLondon Tours ♥♥ Clever people lead clever tour concepts that explore the underbelly of Soho from several angles, from gangster yarns to David Bowie haunts to punk rock landmarks.

www.flipsidelondontours.com. Tours £22 via eventbrite.co.uk. Fri–Sat. Reservations recommended but not required.

Footprints of London ♥♥♥ For creative walks that aren't from canned scripts, tour with the truly passionate, accredited guides with a depth of knowledge who both own and operate this company; they come up with topics that are much more diverse and surprising than rivals': the docks and ports, ghost signs on the sides of buildings, the history of lawyers and legal affairs, Churchill's haunts, the Blitz, and even an exploration of spy hangouts. Great stuff! Have a look to see what they've concocted for when you visit.

www.footprintsoflondon.com. Tours £17.50 adults, £12.50 seniors and students. Reservations recommended but not required.

Greenwich Guides ♥ Like London, Greenwich operates its own official tours with carefully vetted guides. There is usually at least one basic 90-minute tour daily from the Greenwich Tourist Information Centre (Discover

Greenwich) that takes in the main sights plus the Royal Observatory and the Meridian Line. No booking is required.

www.greenwichtours.co.uk. Tours £14 adults, under 16 free. Tube: Cutty Sark DLR.

Hidden London ♥♥♥ Hidden London tours, which are partnered with the London Transport Museum, are the only way to access many secret or abandoned parts of the Underground system, such as Churchill's off-the-books wartime bunker in the disused Down Street stop (vacated with switchboards in place and old cooking grease still stuck to the tile walls), the out-of-service Aldwych stop (used in countless movies and shows), or the old air raid shelter remnants left behind in Clapham after the Blitz. These excursions are harder to come by—you'll need to snap up coveted reservations for the best tours months ahead (sign up for its free newsletter)—but are unquestionably worth the expense and effort. You must be able to manage stairs, and wear clothes you don't mind getting grubby, because it's filthy down there.

www.ltmuseum.co.uk/hidden-london. Tours £37–£90. Tube: varies by tour.

Finds from the Thames riverbed discovered during an In the Footsteps of Mudlarks tour.

In the Footsteps of Mudlarks ♥♥♥ For as long as London has been inhabited, people have used the Thames as their garbage dump, and as the water churns the riverbed with every tide, licensed explorers descend down to the river during low tide to find wondrous things poking out of the mud. Things like Roman roof tiles, medieval pottery, Elizabethan ferry tokens, Victorian beer bot tles, and clay smoking pipes by the thousand. Thames Explorer Trust is the only group that's legally permitted to bring visitors down with an archeological guide to look for treasures. It's absolutely wonderful.

thames-explorer.org.uk. ✆ **020/8742-0057**. Tours £28. 2 hr. Ages 8 and up. Reservations essential.

Karl Marx Walking Tour ♥♥ It's often forgotten that Karl Marx fled Prussia and lived in the U.K. for nearly 40 years, where dire conditions shaped everything he wrote, taught, and thought about revolution and the rights of man. The world changed because of what Marx did in London. This excursion, fine for beginning economists, runs you past the landmarks of his life, many of which are still standing (such as the Dean Street slum where one of his children died of malnutrition—and he lost three others, too), and culminates at the British Museum, where he studied. The guide who created the tour in 2012, Mick Brooks, passed in 2021 from Covid-19, but his acolytes continue his edifying legacy.

www.marxwalks.com. ✆ **077/2252-3629.** Tours £20 via eventbrite.co.uk. Sun 11am–1pm. Reservations required.

Liquid History ♥♥♥ Most of the also-ran tour companies peddle inferior pub tours, but they're actually Liquid History's specialty, and it's earned many fans for them. Over two miles of easy walking, they visit four well-chosen pubs and recount their fascinating histories will good humor and quirky high energy, with a maximum of 14 guests. When it's over, guides suggest more pubs you'll love to explore on your own.

www.liquidhistorytours.com. info@liquidhistorytours.com. Daily tours at 2pm and 7pm £29, drinks not included. Reservations essential. Tube: St Paul's.

London Walks ♥♥ London Walks's tour list is inspiring. On weekdays there can be more than a dozen choices from Oscar Wilde to Harry Potter, and on weekends, nearly 25, which means that if you ever find yourself with a few hours to kill, you can always find instant occupation. Every tour departs from a Tube stop, and none require reservations, which makes arrangements easy. On weekends, it unfurls a fun list of specialty themes (like a history of horses in the capital, Hampstead village, or the "Little Venice" area near the Regent's Canal). The marquee tour is probably "Jack the Ripper," which heads out to the streets of Whitechapel and, in the pursuit of ghoulish entertainment, employs considerably more grotesquerie than uncontested facts. Many of the group's other walks are more informative, including guided tours of the British Museum and Tate Modern. Tours are 2 hours; prices and locations vary.

Look Up London offers fun, fact-filled walking tours.

www.walks.com. ✆ **020/7624-3978.** Tours from £20 adults, £10 seniors/students, £5 kids 8–15.

Look Up London ♥♥♥ Guide Katie Wignall started this thriving entrant in the field in 2015. She now employs several Blue Badge guides, who lead a slate of witty weekend tours ("The Feminist Jack the Ripper Tour," "Sordid Soho," "Bankside Behaving Badly") with inclusion, professionalism, and a deeper fact-check of historical points than what some other guides can claim. Wignall also augments her tours with lively content on Instagram

Enjoy a hop-on-hop-off cruise through London with City Cruises.

(@Look_UpLondon), YouTube (LookUpLondon), and through affordable downloadable history books, which help you get to know her fun-loving, groovy-librarian vibe.

https://lookup.london. katie@lookup.london. Walking tours around £24. Sat–Sun. Reservations strongly recommended.

Take Walks ♥♥♥ This company operates in several cities worldwide, but in London, it shines via special access and innovative offerings on the major topics that make for an intelligent replacement for tour buses. These include an after hours exploration of the Crown Jewels with a Yeoman Warder at the Tower. It also sells passes that let you jump in on any of its scheduled tours and "London in a Day," a guided tour that takes care of admission to Westminster Abbey and the Tower of London (and you'll skip the entry lines), a Thames boat ride linking them, and the Changing the Guard.

www.takewalks.com/london-tours. ✆ **888/683-8670** in U.S., or 170/296-7516 in U.K. Tours £29–£185.

Tour for Muggles ♥♥ This well-assembled tour dispenses reams of Harry Potter trivia, from the books to the movies and locations from the movies. Groups of 20 start near the Monument Tube stop and wind up near Borough Market (p. 110). Because so much London history is folded in, there's enough for non-Potterheads. Book online. Tours are 2 hours.

www.tourformuggles.com. ✆ **020/4548-3535.** Tours £17 adults, £15 children 11 and under. No tours Mon. Tube: Monument.

Unseen Tours ♥♥♥ London is more than kings and queens, art, and canned tall tales. See it from a raw angle, and plumb its modern issues, on a walk guided by someone who has experienced homelessness here, someone who emigrated here, or someone on the autism spectrum—each guide has

RED-LETTER double-deckers

A few routes are truly world-class, linking legendary sights. With routes like these, you won't need to splurge on those tedious hop-on, hop-off tour buses.

- The **15 bus,** which crosses the city east-west, takes in Charing Cross, Fleet Street, St Paul's, and the Tower of London.
- The **8** connects Covent Garden with the liveliest part of East London via St Paul's, Spitalfields, Shoreditch, and Bethnal Green.
- The **9** goes to Royal Albert Hall, Kensington Gardens, Knightsbridge, Hyde Park Corner, Marble Arch, Green Park, Piccadilly Circus, Trafalgar Square, Charing Cross, and Somerset House.
- The **148** links Notting Hill, Marble Arch (Oxford Street), Hyde Park Corner, and Parliament Square (Westminster Abbey).
- The **139** hits Selfridges (Oxford Street), Regent Street, Piccadilly Circus, Trafalgar Square, Covent Garden, Somerset House, and Waterloo.

To see the stops and a map of any bus route, plug in the route number at this link on the TfL website: *https://tfl.gov.uk/bus/route/<route number>*.

their own special, illuminating perspective. Walks go around the major neighborhoods and last 2 hours; locations vary.

https://unseentours.org.uk. enquiries@sockmobevents.org.uk. Tours £15–£18.

Bus and River Tours

There are many reasons to avoid hop-on, hop-off bus tours. First, they're expensive. Second, when the weather is bad, the open top deck becomes unpleasant and customers sardine themselves into the lower cabin. Third, unlike the walking tours we recommend, which are owned by individuals who love London and know it intimately, these buses are owned and operated by multinational companies that are based overseas, and narration is often recorded. Fourth, your experience will depend on the quality of a poorly maintained amplification system, over which you have no control. Fifth, gridlock—if you're taking one just because you think it'll get you around quicker than the Tube, you're wrong.

Day tickets may come with a free walking tour (Changing the Guard, Jack the Ripper) and a hop-on, hop-off pass for the river shuttle boat (although paying customers may take priority over passholders like you). Unfortunately, those perks must often be used during the same 24-hour period of the bus ticket's validity, demolishing your ability to use them all. Because tickets are sometimes given a time stamp that begins your validity period, don't print out any vouchers until the moment you're ready to use them.

HOP-ON, HOP-OFF BUSES

These get you there but won't include attraction tickets. Although many advertise "24-hour" tickets, keep in mind buses generally only roll between around 9am and 5pm. If you're thinking of using these because they'll take care of transportation for you, think again. The city's public transportation is much quicker, more frequent, and obviously far cheaper. During the holidays, the big players do Christmas Lights tours (around £25).

We do not recommend **Tootbus,** which used to be known as **The Original Tour London Sightseeing.** In our experience, the audio portion is substandard.

Big Bus Tours ♥ Like its competition, it offers a couple of circuitous routes: Red (2 hr. 30 mins.), last departure 4:32pm and Blue (3hr. 30 mins.), last departure 3:43pm. are most useful for city overviews, and narration is frequently prerecorded with filler music (and even that is broken more than should be acceptable) with uninspired and out-of-date information. It doesn't matter at which of the 45-odd stops you get on, but because drivers often change by the Green Park Tube stop, you can avoid that wait by starting there. Most people get on at Marble Arch, Regent Street south of Piccadilly Circus, Charing Cross Road north of Trafalgar Square, or under the South Bank Lion at Westminster Bridge. Prices can be a few pounds higher if you don't book ahead. It asks you to download its app to aid you in locating its stops.

48 Buckingham Palace Rd., SW1. www.bigbustours.com. ✆ **020/7808-6753.** 24-hr. tours £50 adults, £40 children 5–15, discounts online and walk-up prices slightly higher.

Hop on Hop Off Plus ♥ One of the big tourist machines in town, offering every permutation of bus tour and day-trip excursion you can imagine. None are particularly special, but they get the job done at low-ish prices, which means crowds. Its main product is a system of three routes, although the cheapest tickets limit the routes you can use. Outside of summer, buses on its Red and Blue routes (for central attractions) come every 20 minutes, while you will have to wait an hour in between buses on its Orange route to the Natural History Museum, Science Museum and V&A. Buses can be shabby and communication spotty.

11a Charing Cross Rd., WC2; 156 Cromwell Rd., SW7; and 4 Fountain Sq., 123–151 Buckingham Palace Rd., SW1. www.hoponhopoffplus.com/london. ✆ **020/7630-2040** in U.K., and 800/509-2507 in North America. 24-hr. tickets £49 adults, £30 children 5–15, £127 for family of 2 adults and 2 children, discounts online. Daily 10am–5pm.

RIVER TOURS

After nearly a decade out of service, amphibious vehicles that travel both on land and the river are slated to return to the Thames in 2026, this time in all-electric versions. The company will be called **Big Duck Tours**, but they had not launched by our press time.

To save the most money on river sightseeing, use the **Thames Clipper** "River Bus" (p. 367), now branded as **Uber Boat**, which commuting Londoners themselves use. Clippers have no narrators but they do have snack bars and Oyster card payment capability (unfortunately, the fare does not count toward your daily price capping), and a lot more options for places to get on and off. See p. 367 for Thames Clipper. But if you want something more tailored to tourists, with narration, try these:

City Cruises ♥♥♥ When you take a standard trip on these generously glass-sided and -topped boats, live narrators point out details of interest. "Hop-on hop-off" tickets allow you use them for one price all day, which is a novel way to sightsee. Boats, which have cafe-bars, depart every 40 min., generally between 9am and 9pm, from four piers: Westminster, London Eye, the Tower, and Greenwich, which cover a lot of areas tourists like seeing. Using it to get to Greenwich and back costs a few pounds more than the unnarrated Clipper ferry service does for the same route.

www.cityexperiences.com. ✆ **020/774-0400.** Tours £14 single, £20 return. 24-hr. passes: £25 adults, £16.50 children 5–15, £49 for 2 adults and 3 children; online discounts available. Does not accept Oyster cards.

London Eye River Cruise ♥♥ It's river tourism on speed, but it may suit a tight schedule: This scenic whirlwind takes just 40 minutes with a live narrator. It goes round-trip from London Eye pier, has a top deck (something the commuter ferries don't), and can be packaged with tickets to the Eye (prepare for crowds), but ultimately, it's less of a value than other choices because you can't get off to explore.

www.londoneye.com. ✆ **020/7967-8021.** Tours £19.50 adults, £16.50 children 3–15; slight discount for booking ahead online. Does not accept Oyster cards.

Thames RIB Experience ♥ Touristy to the core and annoying to everyone except passengers, this outfit loads groups of about a dozen in semi-inflatable RIB speedboats with 740-horsepower engines and flits downriver to Canary Wharf, around the O_2, or Greenwich, from three far-flung piers. Try in vain to forge a lasting memory of Canary Wharf flying past, your eyes blurry from estuary spray. Tours are 50 to 75 min. Its competition, offering similar thrills: **Thames Rockets** (www.thamesrockets.com; ✆ **020/7928-8933;** £50–£60), which goes from close to the London Eye and from a pier near the Tower of London to Canary Wharf).

Victoria Embankment (weekends, also from Tower Pier and North Greenwich), WC2. www.thamesribexperience.com. ✆ **020/3245-1177.** Tours £35–£80 adults, £35–£65 children 15 and under; prices depend on tour length; max. 12 passengers per boat. Tube: Embankment or Charing Cross, Tower Hill, or North Greenwich.

LONDON SHOPPING

6

Blame Elizabeth I. Sure, the old girl loved her baubles and gold-embroidered bodices, but her biggest contribution to English consumerism was defeating the Spanish Armada. That established England as the dominant player on the high seas, which opened channels of international trade, and soon the Thames was more jammed with bounty than the parking lot of the mall on Christmas Eve. Ever since then, London has had a hankering for the finer things. Grease up your credit card!

Times have been tough for boutique store entrepreneurs, though. London is a shockingly expensive environment to operate in: shops must not only pay rent, but they also pay VAT on the rent, and beyond that, every premises is also assessed for "rates," which are taxes that could amount to hundreds of thousands of pounds a year for even a small shop. When people began working from home, pedestrian trade crashed, and when the United States' tariff rules became chaotic, mail order took a dive. Many small stores are still struggling to cling to life in the new economy. Even the corporate stalwarts on formerly great shopping thoroughfares like Oxford Street are pulling up stakes. For shoppers, finding that perfect purchase now requires more shoe leather and sharper eyes than ever—but despite all that, London still delivers some of the best shopping on Earth.

Stores across the city generally open at 9 or 10am daily and close at 7 or 8pm, although boutiques may close at 6pm and the department stores and Oxford Street shops are often open as late as 9pm. On Sunday, relatively new terrain for British shopping, 11am or noon to 6pm is common (although arcane laws mean some stores won't make a sale until noon); very few places stay open past then. Expect crowds on weekends, when people pour into town from the countryside.

Plastic bags are banned and shops charge a few pence for paper bags. Some of them are unsuitable for the purpose, so you might as well bring your own bag.

THE GREAT SHOPPING AREAS

Appropriately for a city obsessed with class, London's prime shopping streets aren't usually defined so much by what they sell as by how much you'll spend to bring home their booty. Most of these famous streets have groups that run a website that lists tenants you can currently find there.

The Arcades of Piccadilly & Old Bond Street

Tube: Green Park. Cameras ready! The area west of Piccadilly Circus is beautified by several iron-framed, skylighted "arcades" (many shops closed Sun), built by 19th-century blue bloods for shopping along these streets in any weather. The best include the longest one, Burlington Arcade, a block-long parallel to Old Bond Street at Piccadilly (watches, cashmere, handbags, Ladurée macarons); the Royal Arcade, south of Burlington Gardens (antiques, shoes, watches, and Budd Shirtmakers, in residence since the arcade's 1910 opening); and Piccadilly Arcade, across from Burlington Arcade (men's tailoring; it leads to Jermyn St. [see below], a harbor for haberdashery). burlingtonarcade.com; https://royalarcade.london; piccadilly-arcade.com.

Carnaby Street

Tube: Oxford Circus or Piccadilly Circus. Soho's famous street used to be for the mod crowd, but today its trendsetting looks are mostly found on Memory Lane. Instead, expect mainstream sporty choices such as North Face and Vans. Pause your hunt at **Kingly Court,** a former timber warehouse converted into a mini-mall for 21-odd restaurants, cafes, and bars. carnaby.co.uk. Soho: www.thisissoho.co.uk.

Cecil Court

Tube: Leicester Square. Distinguished by original glazed-tile Victorian storefronts, Cecil Court (it and St Martin's Court just north are said to have inspired Harry Potter's Diagon Alley) was once the cradle of British cinema, but today it's a holdout of the antiquarian book trade that used to dominate Charing Cross Road. Favorites are Marchpane, at 16, a trove of vintage children's literature; Storey's Ltd. for antique maps at 1 and 3; and Travis & Emery, at 17, specializing in music and books about music. www.cecilcourt.co.uk.

Coal Drops Yard

Tube: King's Cross St Pancras. The former freight-and-gas wasteland of Somers Town, north of King's Cross station, recently emerged from an upscale transformation, and major tech giants are gathering their offices in it. The brick arches and viaducts of the former horse stalls and coal warehouses (the Coal Drops Yard) are reborn as one of the most successful revitalizations of the city's industrial Victorian past, full of carefully chosen shops (often, unique twists on known designers and brands), pop-up boutiques, and buzzy restaurants for sophisticated urbanites with ready cash. Thurs–Sun it mounts a modest prepared foods market at Lower Stable Street Market. www.coaldropsyard.com.

Coal Drops Yard is another successful reclamation project of a former industrial area.

Jermyn Street

Tube: Piccadilly Circus or Green Park. The quintessential street for the natty man for more than a century. Try Harvie & Hudson, Hilditch & Key (since 1899), Hawes & Curtis (1913), and mahogany-lined Turnbull & Asser (1895)—dresser of Chaplin, Churchill, Charles, Ronald Reagan, William, Harry, and James Bond. There's also a growing number of shoemakers, such as Tricker's, which tend to be higher-quality as you move toward St James's Street. It connects to Piccadilly via Princes Arcade, which is also strong on shoes. https://jermynstreet.net.

King's Road

Tube: Sloane Square or South Kensington. The Chelsea avenue where affluent "Sloaneys" spend is where you go to dream—increasingly, about what King's Road used to be. Most of the unique stores have been elbowed aside by the same new names, but you'll find a few independent boutiques, high-end mommy wear, and some designer furnishings. The cafes on Sloane Square remain prime for watching rich kids. www.kingsroad.co.uk.

Lamb's Conduit Street

Tube: Russell Square. This Bloomsbury lane is the ideal respite after a trip to the British Museum, with dapper men's shoes (Grenson, since 1866), respected clothing names (Folk, Oliver Spencer), two Victorian pubs, a wine bar (Noble Rot; p. 88), a cheese palace (La Fromagerie), the well-loved restaurant Honey & Co. (p. 86)—and no corporate chains.

New Bond Street

Tube: Bond Street or Green Park. The ultimate high-end purchasing pantheon runs from Oxford Street to Piccadilly, partly as Old Bond Street. Real estate company Cushman & Wakefield calculates it's the most expensive shopping street in the world. Dare you to open your wallet at account-draining trinket dealers Sotheby's, Van Cleef & Arpels, Harry Winston, Chopard, and Boucheron. A short walk west, **South Molton Street** continues the luxury, but at a half-step down in expense. Check out Browns (https://brownsfashion.com), which gave Alexander McQueen and John Galliano early validation. www.bondstreet.co.uk.

Oxford Street

Tube: Marble Arch, Bond Street, or Oxford Circus. The onetime king of London shopping streets wears a tarnished crown. Once anchored by worthy department stores, Oxford Street over the last 20 years has been undermined by major closures, and now the thoroughfare supports only a few stragglers (like Selfridges and Marks & Spencer), international "fast fashion" (Bershka, Uniqlo, H&M, Primark), some brands tourists won't find helpful (IKEA, JD Sports), and a lot of empty storefronts and filler. Destination clothing shops and bookstores were replaced by fly-by-night businesses. You're advised to avoid the blight of "American candy" shops (American Sweet Dreams, Candy Surprise, and so on) that open and close overnight on Oxford Street and elsewhere before the local councils can shut them down; they have aroused legal suspicion by selling counterfeit products and raised accusations of money laundering. The city is actively working on attracting better vendors and removing car traffic to stimulate a rebirth of this once-great thoroughfare. For the most part, the shopping action has moved to smaller boutiques—and online. www.oxfordstreet.co.uk.

Redchurch Street

Tube: Shoreditch High Street. This 6-block Shoreditch stretch, once rammed with cabinetmakers, today is at the forefront for stylists. The 150-year-old menswear brand Sunspel opened its first retail shop here; Labour and Wait (p. 255) vends desirable kitchen toys; and the late Terence Conran's super-chic hotel/restaurant/cafe complex **Boundary** (https://boundary.london/), including the cafe Albion, seals the deal for scenesters. Around the corner, **Boxpark,** a hipster mall comprising five dozen rehabbed shipping containers, hosts both emerging names and slumming corporate brands (but its permanent closure is in the cards, so check ahead: https://boxpark.co.uk/shoreditch), while **Cheshire Street** is ideal for vintage discoveries.

The Royal Exchange and Leadenhall Market

Tube: Liverpool Street. There has been a commercial building on this site since Queen Elizabeth I opened it. The current version, from the 1840s, is centered on a palatial and galleried interior courtyard where moneyed workers from the banking district pick up mortgage-priced bibelots at Boodles, Tiffany & Co., and Hermès, and dine on delicacies from Ladurée and Fortnum and Mason (p. 239), which operates the central bar. Nothing here is priced for most of us, but it's a breathtaking setting. So is the painted wrought-iron-and-glass canopy of **Leadenhall Market**, a 5-minute walk east. That was once a poultry market but now it squanders its Victorian sumptuousness on a few pubs and pizza places catering to lager-swilling clock-punchers who work in the City. It's still sublimely photogenic. www.theroyalexchange.co.uk; https://leadenhallmarket.co.uk.

Seven Dials

Tube: Covent Garden. The pandemic and the drain of local office workers dimmed the party somewhat, but every lane around Covent Garden still has

Lively Leadenhall Market, dating to 1882, is an architectural marvel.

boutique shopping appeal. Check out **Neal Street** for shoes, **Long Acre** for big clothing stores, and **Floral Street** for designers. www.coventgarden.london.

Sloane Street

Tube: Knightsbridge. Offshore millionaires come here to feast at the top of the consumerist food chain: Bulgari, Valentino, Miu Miu, Prada, Chanel, and everything else haute and showy. And no farther than you can throw a chocolate truffle, Harvey Nichols and Harrods. www.sloanestreet.co.uk.

THE SHOPPING PALACES

Fortnum & Mason ♥♥♥ So venerable is this vendor, which began life in 1707 as the candlemaker to Queen Anne, that in 1922 archaeologist Howard Carter used empty F&M boxes to tote home the treasures of King Tut's tomb. The quintessentially British, modestly sized department store, which has a focus on gourmet foods, is renowned for its glamorous food hampers. These were first distributed in the days before World War I, when soldiers' families were responsible for feeding their men on the field. Picnic sets now come with bone china and can cost £300, but you can also pack your own. For the full experience, which will leave your heirs with no inheritance, head to the first floor to peruse its famous wicker hampers, which you can then fill with goodies from the ground-floor Food Hall and have shipped. Select from a cornucopia of such tongue-teasing triumphs as jarred black truffles and fresh Blue Stilton cheese in ceramic pots. In addition to a huge selection of truffles, sauces, and pickles, F&M makes its own "parlour ice" (ice creams), stocks countless types of honey in the comb and "royal game pie" (loaves of seasonal game meats layered with cheese), and presents varieties of tea that will surpass your understanding of the topic. Most wares are available in small, packable sizes but you can content yourself, as most do, with a wander

Entrance to Fortnum & Mason, a foodie department store renowned for its elegant picnic hampers.

through the carpeted upper-floor departments, which are lit by chandelier, serenaded by classical music, on a double-helix central stairway illuminated by a lotus-like atrium skylight. The fragrance department smells like a rose garden. High tea can be taken in the Tea Salon, since 1926 among the city's most sumptuous (reservations ✆ **020/7734-8040**), while lunching ladies can be found in the excellent corner brasserie called 45 Jermyn St., which in 2015 replaced the Fountain Restaurant after its 6-decade run. When the clock strikes the hour over the store's Piccadilly entrance, two modern mechanical representations of Mr. Fortnum and Mr. Mason emerge, bow to each other approvingly, and return to business inside. 181 Piccadilly, W1. www.fortnumandmason.com. ✆ **020/7734-8040.** Tube: Green Park or Piccadilly Circus.

Harrods ♥ Now owned by the Qatari royal family's financiers (Mohamed Al-Fayed owned it from 1985 to 2010), this miraculous holdover from the golden age of shopping has been retooled into a bombastic mall appealing largely to free-spending out-of-towners. Although it was once well-patronized by Londoners going about daily life (in 1921, one-year-old Christopher Robin received a stuffed bear purchased here, and named him Winnie-the-Pooh), in our age, few London-born people respect it, and its rabbit warren of rooms is too cramped for modern shopping preferences. Yet it thrives, proof of just how awash with foreign fortunes the city truly is. Its thronged but terrific Food Hall rooms are a glut of exorbitantly priced meats and cheeses, its ornate seven-floor facade emblazoned like a Christmas tree after dark, its jewelry hall attended by groveling staff plying spoiled spouses with champagne to grease sales. But much floor space, where too-loud rock music blares nonstop, is devoted either to brands you'd find for a third of the price at your local mall or to One-Percenter nonsense such as £150,000 sculptures. The artificial environment, from the overpriced razzmatazz to the clerks wearing straw hats, would be more authentic at Disneyland than in London of old. In the souvenir "emporium" on the second floor (£50 Harrods tote bags; £25 mugs; teddy bears aplenty), I sense the air has been pumped with the same scent you smell at Disney wherever the company wants to coax customers into purchasing (a trick called "olfactory coding"). If you crave a department store that's part of London's daily fabric, visit Fortnum & Mason or Selfridges; if you want to be flabbergasted by the pompous excesses of the jet set, Harrods is the overly shellacked circus for you, but don't be fooled into thinking it's real-life London. 87–135 Brompton Rd., SW1. www.harrods.com. ✆ **020/7730-1234.** Tube: Knightsbridge.

Harvey Nichols ♥ The shallow anti-heroines Patsy and Edina of *Absolutely Fabulous* spoke of it with the same breathless reverence most people reserve for deities. You'll need the resources of a god to afford a single thread of Harvey Nick's women's and men's fashions, and although the British-owned store isn't as popular as it used to be—it's been here since the 1880s—a stroll through this eight-floor spendthrift's heaven is entertaining. Note the lunching ladies on display in the fifth-floor restaurant—think of it as a zoo for old money. 109–125 Knightsbridge, SW1. www.harveynichols.com. ✆ **020/7235-5000.** Tube: Knightsbridge.

John Lewis ♥♥ Everyone English knows that if you want a sound deal, you go here, where there's a price guarantee; it employs an army of people to scout for the lowest prices in the area, which it matches. That may sound like the gimmick of a low-rent wannabe, but John Lewis, established in 1864, is in fact a respected cooperative owned by its employees. Still, times are changing and it's slowing down. In recent years, the company has investigated turning part of its Oxford Street flagship into offices. Art fans shouldn't miss the building's eastern face, upon which is mounted an abstract cast-aluminum sculpture, *The Winged Figure* (1960), by one of the most important artists of the 20th century, Dame Barbara Hepworth, whose work is in the Tate Britain (p. 160). Oxford St. at Holles St. www.johnlewis.com/oxfordstreet. ✆ **020/7629-7711.** Tube: Oxford Circus.

Liberty ♥♥ Founded in 1875, Liberty made its name (and earned some mockery) as an importer of Asian art, and as a major proponent of Art Nouveau style and of dresses that freed ladies from the tyranny of corsets. Now its focus is distinctly British. The timber-and-plaster wing looks Tudor, but it is actually a 1924 revival constructed from the salvaged timbers of two ships, HMS *Impregnable* and HMS *Hindustan;* the length of the latter ship equals the building's length along Great Marlborough Street. The store's stationery and scarf selections are deservedly celebrated, as are its fabrics. Much of what you see here is designed in-house and manufactured only once, so this beauty hall is one of the best and whatever you bring home is unlikely to be copied by anyone. The soft wooden spaces are creaky and seductive, while the staff service is so obsequious they evoke a bygone era. 210–220 Regent St., W1. www.libertylondon.com. ✆ **020/3893-3062.** Tube: Oxford Circus.

Marks & Spencer ♥♥♥ The beloved M&S is the country's favorite mid-level department store for good-looking clothing staples. Its own-brand looks, once shoddy and ill-fitting, have been re-envisioned as affordable riffs on well-tailored fashions, and it sells the go-to suit for many a young man starting out in life. M&S is particularly beloved for its underwear, socks, and casual wear. But its crowning achievement is its giant **food halls ♥♥♥** (usually tucked underneath the store but sometimes a stand-alone shop called **Simply Food**), which sell an astonishing array of prepared meals, soups and sandwiches, and well-selected yet inexpensive wines. M&S is a national middle-class treasure. Flagship: 458 Oxford St., W1. Tube: Marble Arch (currently being rebuilt) and 173 Oxford St. www.marksandspencer.co.uk. Tube: Oxford Circus

Selfridges ♥♥♥ Selfridges fills the real-life role in London life that many visitors think Harrods does; if you carry Harrods' olive drab sacks, you're a tourist, but if your shopping bag is a canary yellow screamer from Selfridges, you'll fit in like local. For casual spenders it's unquestionably the better of the two stores, since it's not merely a sprawling sensory treat, but also sells items you'd actually buy. Since its 1909 opening by Harry Gordon Selfridge, an immoderate American marketing genius from Marshall Field's in Chicago (the building was designed by Daniel Burnham, of Manhattan's Flatiron Building fame), Selfridges has pioneered many department store practices. Placing the perfumes near the front door, filling its 27 ground-floor windows with consumerist fantasias, coining the phrase "the customer is always right"—all Selfridges inventions. Some one million products are for sale, and the beauty department is Europe's largest. The thicket of food counters on the ground floor gets busy at lunchtime, and the rest of the store is just as popular at other times; some 17 million visits are recorded each year. Selfridges has traded in history, too; the first public demonstration of television was held on the first floor in 1925, and 3 years later, the store sold the world's first TV set. During much of the Blitz, Churchill's transatlantic conversations with FDR were encoded via a scrambler stashed in the cellar. 400 Oxford St., W1. www.selfridges.com. ✆ **0800/123-400** (U.K.) or 113/369-8040 (overseas). Tube: Bond Street or Marble Arch.

The 1931 Queen of Time decorates the clock at the entrance to Selfridges.

RECOMMENDED STORES

For a city world-famous for shopping, where people from around the world arrive with one fat wallet and leave with 10 stuffed suitcases, there's no way to give proper celebratory due to everything that is wonderful and for sale.

Some stores, though, are so original and site-specific that they can sweeten the experience of being in London, even if you don't buy a thing.

Art & Antiques

Alfies Antique Market ♥ You can't say you've hunted for antiques in London until you've explored this 35,000-square-foot stalwart, going since 1976 on the four floors of a former department store. When vendors succeed here, in London's largest indoor market, they sometimes spin off into their own shops along the same street. 13–25 Church St., NW8. alfiesantiques.com. ✆ **020/7723-6066.** Closed Sun–Mon. Tube: Marylebone.

Blue Mantle ♥ For dream renovations back home, the largest antique fireplace showroom in the world salvages the good stuff with warm English touches when developers knock down classic buildings—which is happening more than we like. 306–312 Old Kent Rd., SE1. www.bluemantle.co.uk. ✆ **020/7703-7437.** Tube: Borough.

Camden Passage ♥♥ Plenty of tourists swing through the booths, so bargains aren't always easy to come by. Still, shimmering examples of china, silverware, cocktail shakers, military medals, coins, and countless other hand-me-downs overflow the cases. Despite the name, it's in Islington. Off Upper St., N1. www.camdenpassageislington.co.uk. Market on Wed, Sat, smaller one Sun. Tube: Angel.

Grays ♥♥ Not the place to go if you're looking for the lowest deal (it's in Mayfair), but it's definitely a source for variety. Some 100 vendors, many experts registered in the official antiques societies, are split among two

The Best Museum Shops

Many London museums are free, which means they must get creative about making money in other ways. Some of their gift shops would be worth a visit even if there weren't priceless exhibits attached. All can be accessed for free.

- **The British Library** (p. 130): Literary totes, toys, and tomes
- **Churchill War Rooms** (p. 156): World War II posters, postcards, and novelties
- **The Design Museum** (p. 179): Selection of clever gadgets and conversation pieces actually better than the museum itself
- **London Transport Museum** (p. 144): Tube-themed bags, clothes, reproduction posters; items made from the same fabric ("moquette") as Underground seats; plus, a big selection of train toys and books
- **National Portrait Gallery** (p. 150): A 2023 renovation turned its wares away from books and toward lively lifestyle items styled to famous personalities.
- **Tate Modern** (p. 185): Gifts, books about art and London, prints, and the Tate Edit line of slick homewares
- **The V&A** (p. 176): Gorgeous fabrics, handbags, jewelry, stationery, and design glass—a mega-emporium of good taste.
- **The Wellcome Collection** (p. 143): Science-themed books and gifts so clever and well-edited they surpasses the quality of the museum upstairs

buildings, selling everything from Victorian jewelry to toys to strange bric-a-brac and collectible silverware. Weekdays are best. Head into the basement of the Mews building to see the River Tyburn, which was buried by 18th-century redevelopment but now feeds into Grays' goldfish trough. Grays is closed on weekends. 58 Davies St., W1. www.graysantiques.com. ✆ **020/7629-7034.** Tube: Bond Street.

Find something that will fit in your suitcase at LASSCO architectural salvage.

LASSCO ♥♥ From stained glass to paneling and faucets to wood flooring, you'll get an incredible selection of fittings and furniture rescued from museums, churches, pubs, and homes at LASSCO (the London Architectural Salvage and Supply Company). It's closed weekends. Brunswick House: 30 Wandsworth Rd., SW8. www.lassco.co.uk. ✆ **020/7394-2100.** Tube: Vauxhall.

Books & Music

The territorial nature of copyrights means that many books that are for sale in London won't be in print back home. Take time to trawl the dwindling used-book stores along **Charing Cross Road** and **Cecil Court** (p. 236), which runs to St Martin's Lane. The major art museums are strong on titles in their respective disciplines, especially **Tate Modern** (p. 185) and the **National Portrait Gallery** (p. 150). Performing artists turn to the scripts and theatrical ephemera at the **National Theatre** (Southbank, SE1; shop.nationaltheatre.org.uk; ✆ **020/7452-3456;** Tube: Waterloo), the **Barbican Shop** (Level G, Barbican Centre, Silk St., EC2; shop.barbican.org.uk; ✆ **020/7638-8891**; Tube: Barbican) and **Samuel French** (Lower Ground Floor, Royal Court Theatre, Sloane Square; www.royalcourttheatre.com; ✆ **020/7565-5024;** Tube: Sloane Square). For those, it's wise to shop *before* evening curtain, as the shops are apt to be closed by the final bows.

Daunt Books specializes in travel books but offers other genres as well.

Daunt Books ♥♥ Lined with oak galleries and lit by a long, central skylight, Daunt prides itself on its travel collection, which is located down a groaning wooden staircase. Everything is arranged by the country it's about—Third Reich histories under Germany, Tolstoy under Russia. It's no slouch in the general interest categories, either. Clerks seem to know what will interest the vaguest browser, and the cashier's desk is always piled with choice curiosities. There are other locations around the city. 83 Marylebone High St., W1. www.dauntbooks.co.uk. ✆ **020/7224-2295.** Tube: Baker Street.

Foyles ♥♥ In business since 1903, this institution's huge inventory of 200,000 titles straddles both popular and specialty topics. There are small outlets at Waterloo Station and the Royal Festival Hall on Southbank, but this beloved HQ is more like a theme park for readers, full of talks, events, and signings. 107 Charing Cross Rd., WC2. www.foyles.co.uk. ✆ **020/7437-5660.** Tube: Tottenham Court Road.

Gay's the Word ♥ Most English-speaking cities have lost their niche LGBTQ bookstores to Amazon and apathy, but London still has this venerable specialist, trading since 1979. 66 Marchmont St., WC1. Closed Mon. www.gaystheword.co.uk. ✆ **020/7278-7654.** Tube: Russell Square.

Hatchards ♥♥ Although the Duke of Wellington and Jane Austen have been counted among its customers, Hatchards, the oldest bookseller in the city (1797), is noted for its signed first editions, as well as for its famous shoplifters: An 18-year-old Noël Coward was apprehended as he stuffed a suitcase full of books. (Characteristically, he charmed his way out of trouble.) It has been trading since 1801 at its current location, which means it was selling books before Hardy, Dickens, or the Brontës were writing them. Virginia Woolf wrote about it, too, in *Mrs Dalloway.* 187 Piccadilly, W1. www.hatchards.co.uk. ✆ **020/7439-9921.** Tube: Piccadilly Circus.

The HMV Shop ♥ In November 2023, after a 4-year absence during which its store was occupied by a pitiful American candy shop, HMV triumphantly returned to the same storefront it first occupied in 1921, when it became the heartbeat of British entertainment culture. The music seller is drawing new power from young customers who prefer physical media to downloads, and they're drawn by the joy of perusing 8,000 vinyl albums, 12,000 CDs, plus tee-shirts, media tech, and live DJs. Browsing is finally back! 363 Oxford St., W1. hmv.com. ✆ **0843/221-0200.** Tube: Bond Street.

Housmans Booksellers ♥ London supports a vibrant protest community—don't forget this is where Karl Marx fashioned his views that changed the world—and since 1945, the city's preeminent store for radical books has been Housmans. You're not going to find most of the stuff here published back home. Wednesdays at 7pm, an author speaks. 5 Caledonian Rd., N1. www.housmans.com. ✆ **020/7837-4473.** Tube: King's Cross St Pancras.

Stanfords ♥♥♥ Marvelous since 1853, Stanfords trades in globe-trotting goodness, from guides to narratives to fiction with a worldview. There are reams of maps for purchase, especially for walking trails across Britain, and tons of travel-themed gifts. Leaner times forced it to leave its glorious Long

Acre flagship building in 2019, but it's still kicking and still superlative. 7 Mercer Walk. www.stanfords.co.uk. ✆ **020/7836-1321.** Tube: Covent Garden.

Feed your wanderlust with travel guides and maps from Stanfords.

Waterstones ♥♥♥ In a location opened in 1936 as Simpson's clothiers—the Art Deco model for Grace Brothers in the saucy Britcom *Are You Being Served?* (the show's creator was a clerk)—this branch of the giant chain is now Europe's largest bookshop. Even if Waterstones is a Big Gorilla of bookselling, it handles the stewardship of that dubious title with dignity; there are six sweeping floors, an enormous London section, plenty of easy chairs for freeloaders, and scads of discount offers. The top floor's panoramic cafe, 5th View, hops after work and into the evening. The Bloomsbury location at 82 Gower Street, WC1 (Tube: Goodge Street), once the famous bookstore called Dillons, benefits from its location by University College London be being particularly well-stocked in history, nonfiction, and biography titles. 203 Piccadilly. www.waterstones.com. ✆ **020/7851-2400.** Tube: Piccadilly Circus.

Clothing, Shoes & Accessories

The clothes you find in the U.K. will not be the same as in major stores elsewhere. Different markets, different tastes, different inventories. Sizes are probably different than at home, too, so make sure to consult a conversion chart.

Albam ♥♥ Unusually, this men's boutique seeks out well-constructed, honest clothing (most made in the U.K.), but doesn't mark it up by insane factors. Although its prices are similar to those of high-casual chain stores, the store has a following among guys because its clothing lasts so long. 23 Beak St., W1. www.albamclothing.com. ✆ **020/3157-7000.** Tube: Piccadilly Circus or Oxford Circus.

Arket ♥♥ Scandinavian-simple and ethically sourced, it aims a little higher in style and substance than its corporate cousin, H&M. This clean-and-casual newcomer does homewares, too. 224 Regent St., W1. www.arket.com. ✆ **020/3402-9150.** Tube: Oxford Circus. Also at 27–29 Long Acre, WC2. Tube: Covent Garden.

Article ♥♥ Everything a young urbanite needs to keep up: premium casual menswear from around the world, beautiful homewares from Scandinavia, great-looking bags and sunglasses. 61 Atlantic Rd., SW9. www.article-london.com. ✆ **020/7274-5714.** Tube: Brixton.

Atika ♥♥ Once called Blitz, Atika has crowned itself Europe's largest vintage shop, a boast I cannot authenticate, but it's true that within its 6,000 square feet, you'll be spoilt for choice. 55–59 Hanbury St., E1. www.atikalondon.co.uk. ✆ **020/7377-0730.** Tube: Shoreditch High Street.

Beyond Retro ♥♥ A one-stop shop for classic items (jeans, jackets, boots, and other casuals), it's a haunt of the poor and stylish, who can put together an off-margin look without overdrawing. 92–10 Stoke Newington Rd., N16. www.beyondretro.com. ✆ **020/7729-9001.** Tube: Dalston Kingsland. Also at 19-21 Argyll St., W1. Tube: Oxford Circus; and Unit 52–54 Coal Drops Yard, N1, Tube: King's Cross St Pancras.

Blackhorse Lane Atelier ♥ If you can't afford to cut a new suit on Savile Row, how about some bespoke jeans? Lifelong experts in the fabric industry set out to create the perfect manufacturer of custom jeans that are crafted from sustainable denims. Every step of the process is immaculately overseen (they even plant their own indigo in a garden nearby), and although the results aren't cheap (nudging £300), they'll fit your body perfectly and last for years. Unit 32, Lower Stable St., Coal Drops Yard, N1. www.blackhorselane.com. ✆ **020/3746-8303.** Tube: King's Cross St Pancras or 96 Berwick St., W1. ✆ 020/4618-5848. Tube: Oxford Circus

Browns ♥♥ Some 100 designers, all of them for higher-end purchasers, fill these five connected shops at the top of Mayfair. Since 1970, it's been a

The Royal Warrant

When you're snooping around the refined shops of St James's or Mayfair, keep an eye out for a royal crest near the store's sign. It's called a Royal Warrant, and the recognition has been around at least since Henry II made a deal with a weavers' trade guild in 1155. That insignia is a seal of approval—its presence means that the business counts a member of the royal family as a customer, has done so for at least 5 years, and may retain the symbol for 2 years after their death. Currently, only King Charles and Queen Camilla issue Royal Warrants, and the lion-and-unicorn design was selected to represent the sovereign. To earn the crest from Charles, stores must go the extra mile and abide by a sustainable environmental policy. Once a business wins one, seeing it withdrawn can be a shameful event. To its eternal humiliation, Harrods lost its seal in 2000; Rigby & Peller, which had made Queen Elizabeth's brassieres since 1960, was ejected in 2018 after its owner wrote a memoir that revealed too much; and Cadbury was dumped in 2024 not long after its now American owners cheapened its chocolate recipe. Which hotel receives the King's preference? **The Ritz** (p. 102), but only for banqueting and catering services, and it's not the sort of place where common tourists are made to feel that they belong. More distinguished retailers you may visit: **Anderson & Sheppard** (Charles's clothing), **Berry Bros. & Rudd** (wine; p. 252), **Charles Martell & Sons** (cheese), **Fortnum & Mason** (groceries; p. 239); **Hatchards** (books; p. 245); and **Philip Treacy** (hats and fascinators; p. 251). To learn which companies supply the throne, search the current warrant holders at www.royalwarrant.org.

Quintessentially British men's field clothing at Cordings.

marketplace for upscale women, but increasingly, it's pitching to a younger and more casual set. 39 Brook St., W1. www.brownsfashion.com. ✆ **020/7514-0016.** Closed Mon. Tube: Bond Street.

Cordings ♥♥ Britain's top manufacturer of Wellington boots, which were invented for the first Duke of Wellington, can be found at this well-heeled and very English emporium of field clothing, suits, waistcoats, tweeds, and knitwear that cost a pretty pound. It has traded here since 1877. 19 Piccadilly, W1. www.cordings.co.uk. ✆ **020/7734-0830.** Tube: Piccadilly Circus.

Diverse ♥ Diverse spotlights white-hot labels, many of which go on to greatness. Clothes tend toward arty, clientele tends toward obsessive. 148 Fortess Rd., NW5. www.diverseclothing.com. ✆ **020/7813-7425.** Tube: Tufnell Park.

Dover Street Market ♥ A long-running high-minded, multi-designer concept, heavy on pretentious industrial architecture, is supported by couture fused with multimedia art installations. 18–22 Haymarket, SW1. london.doverstreetmarket.com. ✆ **020/7518-0680.** Tube: Piccadilly Circus.

The Goodhood Store ♥♥ Consummately East End, the clothing and "life store" products sold in this popular, half-serious two-story emporium are all about what it means to feel cool. Don a faux-vintage T-shirt printed with inscrutable gibberish, carry home a "The Masses Are Asses" mug for your latte, and stock up on the latest on-trend grooming products. Independent, self-knowing—but it only *looks* secondhand. 15 Hanbury St., E1. www.goodhoodstore.com. ✆ **020/7729-3600.** Tube: Liverpool Street.

Herbert Johnson Hatters ♥♥ This hatter, in business since 1889, made Indiana Jones' famous fedora, called The Poet Hat, for Steven Spielberg in 1980. That's so awesome that not much more needs to be said, except that the shop can make a signature hat for you, too, if you're cool enough to pull it off. 18–19 Burlington Arcade, W1. www.herbertjohnson.co.uk. ✆ **020/7409-7277.** Closed Sun. Tube: Green Park or Piccadilly Circus.

The Hirst Collection ♥♥ A specialist in vintage jewelry—something you'll find in wondrous and ever-surprising bounty here in England—it usually has about 2,000 pieces to chose from, and it strives to offer something unique in every price range. 59 Pembridge Rd, W11. thehirstcollection.com. ✆ **020/7727-9364.** Tube: Notting Hill Gate.

James Smith & Sons ♥♥♥ This shop out of time, hung from the outside with old-style high Victorian lettering, is rattling the rafters inside with handmade umbrellas and walking sticks. That's all it makes, as it has done methodically since 1830, so you can imagine the wonders: handles of hazelnut wood, ebony, buffalo horn, and antler, from £25 to more than £300. Clerks can also fashion a box so you can get your purchase onto the plane. Hazlewood House, 53 New Oxford St., WC1. www.james-smith.co.uk. ✆ **020/7836-4731.** Closed Sun. Tube: Holborn or Tottenham Court Road.

Fine-gauge knitwear is the specialty at John Smedley.

John Smedley ♥♥ Specialists in the sort of fine-gauge, well-fitting knitwear that make many Londoners look so chic despite the damp, John Smedley can trace its manufacturing lineage back to 1784, yet its style feels a contemporary as tomorrow. King Charles gets clothes here. 24 Brook St., W1. www.johnsmedley.com. ✆ **020/7495-2222.** Tube: Bond Street.

KOTN ♥♥ Cute, cozy, casual, and sustainable wear. It's so careful about making sure its suppliers are responsible and pay fairly that it even knows the farmers in Egypt who grow the cotton that make its cloth. 113–115 Redchurch St., E2. kotn.com. ✆ **07476/913-444.** Tube: Shoreditch High Street.

Levisons ♥♥ In an old storefront with the vintage smell of bygone closets, find early-era men's jackets and suits you could only locate in England—Harris tweeds, school uniforms, tailored peacoats. The stock changes weekly. In fact, all of Cheshire Street hosts multiple boutiques for unusual vintage finds. 1 Cheshire St., E2. www.levisons.co.uk. ✆ **020/3609-2224.** Tube: Shoreditch High Street.

Lock & Co. ♥ Exquisitely crafted classic British hats (Panamas and bowlers, for men, women, and kids, too) are made by this hatter dating to 1765. Their hats have been favored by Wilde, Churchill, Chaplin, Oddjob from *Goldfinger,* Prince William, and Lord Nelson—it made his bicorne hat. 6 St James's St., SW1. www.lockhatters.com. ✆ **020/7930-8874.** Closed Sun. Tube: Green Park.

Luna & Curious ♥♥ Ebulliently colorful, peppy, and British-made by a collective of designers, this independent women-and-kids clothing store has a way of imbuing looks with cheerful positivity. 24–26 Calvert Ave., E2. lunaandcurious.com. ✆ **020/3222-0034.** Tube: Shoreditch High Street.

Women and kids clothing at Luna & Curious.

Mango ♥ Take the cream of high fashion and make it accessible for the typical English young woman—that's the formula at this slightly upmarket label, which does well when you want your look to be colorful, casual, and maybe even beachy. 229–235 Oxford St., W1. mango.com. ✆ **020/7534-3505.** Tube: Oxford Circus. Also at 8–12 Neal St., WC2. ✆ **020/7240-2935.** Tube: Covent Garden.

The Mercantile ♥♥ Founder Debra McCann, sorting through the work of some 150 international designers for her long-running and relaxed boutique, knows how to select looks that are appealing to women, fashion-forward enough to be eclectic but wearable, and relatively easy on the wallet. That's why she's been succeeding at this since 2012. 17a Lamb St., E1. www.themercantilelondon.com. ✆ **020/7377-8926.** Tube: Shoreditch High Street or Liverpool Street.

Misan Brothers ♥♥ If you sew, uncover a wealth of unique fabrics at this well-regarded Soho showcase and stock up on beautiful stuff you won't find imported at home. 3 Berwick St., W1. www.misan.co.uk. ✆ **020/3556-9806.** Closed Sun. Tube: Piccadilly Circus.

Monsoon ♥ One of the favored High Street brands for women and kids, Monsoon's outfits are for independent dressers who favor bright hues and aren't afraid of a few embellishments. It also does good evening wear. 290 Upper St., N1. monsoon.co.uk. ✆ **020/7354-2341.** Tube: Angel.

Office ♥♥ The H&M of footwear rips off designer styles cheaply but effectively. Office's major competition **Schuh,** found around town, mostly stocks other brands (although it has its own sub-line). 190 Oxford St. and 16 Carnaby St., W1. www.office.co.uk. ✆ **020/3410-6256.** Tube: Oxford Circus or Tottenham Court Road.

Pandora Dress Agency ♥♥ A used clothing store for women who would never dare use that term, Pandora is a "dress agency," thank you very much, that redistributes rarities by Dolce & Gabbana, Alexander McQueen, Gucci, Alexandre Vauthier, and such once their first owners have already been seen in them. You can save hundreds of pounds off a designer look—and you never have to tell anyone where you obtained it. 16–22 Cheval Pl., SW7. www.pandoradressagency.com. ✆ **020/7589-5289.** Tube: Knightsbridge.

Philip Treacy ♥♥ If you're invited to Ascot, it would be churlish not to be seen in one of Philip Treacy's world-famous designs in *haute couture* hats, bonnets, or fascinators. If you're not, you're welcome to go home with a £1,200 white elephant. 69 Elizabeth St., SW1. www.philiptreacy.co.uk. ✆ **020/7730-3992.** Closed Sun. Tube: Victoria or Sloane Square.

Primark ♥♥♥ The most intense, most crowded, most PTSD-invoking store on Oxford Street roils with young families stuffing baskets with cheap-as-chips outfits, shoes, luggage, and outrageously lowballed accessories. Unfortunately, we're also talking about a clientele that discards garments wherever they want, staff that deals with the rubble using big push brooms, no washrooms, long lines at checkout, and fast fashion products that look frayed after a year. But the bargains! Oh, the bargains—most stuff is less than £10, and £1 deals are common. You just can't help leaving with sacksful. "The devil wears Primark," mutter the snobs. 499 Oxford St., W1. www.primark.co.uk. ✆ **020/7495-0420.** Tube: Marble Arch. Also at 14–18 Oxford St., W1. ✆ **020/7580-5510.** Tube: Tottenham Court Road.

Rokit ♥♥ Because it's been cool for longer than many of its competitors have been in business, Rokit has a following. Probably the largest collection in the city, it sells retro and vintage threads, shoes, and accessories that are funky and hipster-prone, from 1950s industrial uniforms to tracksuits. 42 Shelton St., WC2. www.rokit.co.uk. ✆ **020/7836-6547.** Tube: Covent Garden. Also in Whitechapel (101 and 107 Brick Lane, E1; ✆ **020/7375-3864;** Tube: Shoreditch High Street) and Camden (225 Camden High St., NW1; ✆ **020/7267-3046;** Tube: Camden Town).

Vivienne Westwood Worlds End ♥ For a few years in the 1970s, the late Vivienne Westwood's shop was the coolest place on the planet. The clock at this guerilla boutique still runs backward, but London's punk heyday is long over. Never mind the bargains—her Anglomania label is fashion history itself, but it's not cheap. Still, the fanciful couture inventions, flowing with fabric,

WHAT CAN I bring home?

Although you should always claim foods when you pass through Customs, very few things will be confiscated. Most stuff, including baked goods, honeys, vinegars, condiments, roasted coffee, teas, candy bars, crisps, pickles, and homemade dishes are good to go. And Cadbury chocolate! Stores can't export the British-made version to the U.S. now, so grab all you can! Always check your country's requirements, but these things are certain to make the inspector dog's nose twitch:

- Meat and anything containing meat, be it dried, canned, or bouillon.
- Fresh fruit and vegetables.
- Runny cheeses, but not firm ones (rule of thumb: If you have to keep it chilled, leave it behind).
- Rice. As if you would import rice.
- Plants, soil, wood, and seeds (non-edible). Ask the nursery whether you need paperwork, because many varieties are permitted. And be warned that officers in Australia respond to wood like it's kryptonite.

are outlandish enough to enchant. 430 Kings Rd., SW10. www.viviennewestwood.com. ✆ **020/7352-6551.** Closed Sun. Tube: Fulham Broadway.

Food

Don't neglect the many fine foodie markets (p. 116) or the food halls of the shopping palaces (earlier in this chapter). ***One warning:*** Don't buy tea from a touristy shop. It'll be old and awful. You have a rare chance to patronize world-famous purveyors like **Twinings** (below) or **Fortnum & Mason** (p. 239), so plunder them instead.

Berry Bros. & Rudd ♥♥ If you think you don't have the need for a wine shop on your vacation, then you haven't been inside this institution, which has traded since 1698 (you can peek into its original wood-paneled shop around the corner at 3 St James's St.). It's true that its most devoted clients tend to be exclusive, but the staff still knows how to cater to anyone's budget and even pours single servings on premises. Centuries ago, famous people would come to its giant scales to find out what they weighed, and the results were marked in red books the shop still keeps. 63 Pall Mall, SW1. www.bbr.com. ✆ **020/7318-2075.** Closed Sun–Mon. Tube: Green Park.

Dark Sugars Cocoa House ♥♥ Sublime handmade chocolates and truffles (gin and lime, stem ginger and honey, and more) sourced from a family farm in Ghana are the addictive wares at this Brick Lane success story. The golden "pearl" orbs containing smooth hazelnut nougat are delicate and divine, and the shop makes incredible hot chocolates, piled with chocolate shavings that melt into the cup—try it with chili—and even vegan versions. 141 Brick Lane, E1. www.darksugars.co.uk. Tube: Shoreditch High Street. Also at Greenwich Market, 9 Nelson Rd., SW19, in Greenwich. Tube: Cutty Sark.

Prestat ♥♥ Here, in one of London's most exclusive arcades, is chocolate fit for a king, and here's proof: Charles gave it his royal warrant (he also likes

Berry Bros. & Rudd has been a premium wine merchant since 1698.

Bendicks for its chocolate mints), declaring it his favorite. Prestat has been meticulously preparing high-end confections since 1902; its cocoa-dusted Napoleon truffles are its most popular. 14 Princes Arcade, Piccadilly, W1. https://prestat.com. ✆ **020/7494-3372.** Tube: Piccadilly Circus.

Twinings ♥♥ Does this tea boutique rely on tourist traffic? Definitely. But it's still steeped in tradition, having taken over from a coffee shop in this narrow, portrait-lined location in 1706. Here you can sample, taste, mix-and-match, and savor the leaf in all its varieties—or just peruse its little tea museum. 216 Strand, WC2. www.twinings.co.uk. ✆ **020/7353-3511.** Tube: Temple.

Health & Beauty

Boots ♥ Something like 80% of fragrance sales in the U.K. are conducted at this chain, and its endless 3-for-2 promotions almost always include something worth taking home. Makeup costs a few pounds less than at most other stores. It's authentically British, too—its founder, John Campbell Boot, the second Baron Trent, has his picture in the National Portrait Gallery. Multiple locations. www.boots.co.uk.

Charlotte Tilbury ♥♥ The makeup mogul and beauty secret guru's flagship store, where you'll find her Pillow Talk and other formulations, is easy to find on a pedestrianized street opposite the Covent Garden Tube stop. 1 James St., WC2. www.charlottetilbury.com. ✆ **020/3961-7160.** Tube: Covent Garden

Floris ♥♥♥ In 1730, when this perfumery was established in this building using the dowry of young Juan Famenias Floris' bride, carrying a pleasant scent beneath your nose was crucial for drowning out the stink of the 18th-century city. Later on, Queen Victoria obtained her aromas here, Oscar Wilde favored the Malmaison Carnation variety, and Marilyn Monroe ordered some Rose Geranium (still sold) to be delivered to her at the Beverly Hills Hotel. Everything is historic; the shop's Spanish mahogany cabinets were purchased at the Great Exhibition of 1852 and there's a small Floris museum in back. You can hire them to create a bespoke fragrance to suit your own tastes, but that requires at least three meetings with you to get the details right. 89 Jermyn St., SW1. www.florislondon.com. ✆ **0330/134-0180.** Tube: Covent Garden.

Geo. F. Trumper ♥♥ Its Mayfair shop (est. 1875) is the picture of nineteenth-century mercantilism: glass-and-wood display cases, paisley carpet, and a responsive staff. Here, men may not only provision their morning ablutions with products from the pinnacle of grooming technique (including its own-brand nail buffers, shaving brushes, and soft cream in a pot), but they can also avail themselves of the services of a true shaving professional who begins a shave-and-trimming ritual with a hot towel and disturbs it with very little indiscreet banter. 9 Curzon St., W1. www.trumpers.com. ✆ **020/7499-1850.** Tube: Green Park.

Glossier London ♥ What started in 2014 with just four products (a moisturizer, a face mist, a lip balm, and a skin tint) and a marketing plan built around social media has found itself a dominant brand in a brick-and-mortar purchase palace that looks more like a venerable social club than a store. Young customers line up to snatch its makeup and skin care for their own looks. 43 King St., WC2. https://uk.glossier.com. ✆ **020/7173-4399.** No cash. Tube: Covent Garden.

Neal's Yard Remedies ♥♥♥ At the forefront of Britain's powerful green consumer goods movement, this shop supplies beauty aids, holistic treatments, massage oils, and even make-your-own-cosmetics ingredients, all cruelty-free, clear of toxins, and naturally formulated. Its products—London's answer to the New York beauty boutique Kiehl's—are respected for their quality. 15 Neal's Yard, W1. www.nealsyardremedies.com. ✆ **020/7379-7222.** Tube: Covent Garden.

Humidorable

Cigars are big business in London, and not just because the city was once the capital of the world tobacco trade. Many wealthy visitors from Arab countries are not permitted to drink alcohol by dint of their religion but they may enjoy a fine stogie, so most finer hotels offer humidors as well as cocktail bars. Dating to 1787, **James J. Fox** claims to be the oldest cigar merchant in the world, and its pedigree is peerless: Oscar Wilde indulged himself here, and Winston Churchill slouched in its weary brown leather armchair while he tasted the Coronas. Come to inhale the rich, musky aroma, to select one of its fine bowl pipes, or even to smoke—the city's public smoking ban does not apply here. (19 St James's St., SW1. www.jjfox.co.uk. ✆ **020/7930-3787.** Closed Sun. Tube: Green Park.)

Penhaligon's ♥♥♥ I don't enjoy the mental image of King Charles lighting a Lily of the Valley candle and anointing his body with English Fern eau de toilette, but the fact is that Penhaligon's, established in 1870, as a Royal Warrant as an official "manufacturer of toilet requisites" to Charles, so it could be happening right now. The company hand-squeezes and custom designs its own fragrances for both men and women—generally floral-based and gentle—and sidelines in luxury shaving and grooming products. Another picturesque location is at 16–17 Burlington Arcade (Tube: Green Park). 41 Wellington St., WC2. www.penhaligons.co.uk. ✆ **020/7629-1416.** Tube: Covent Garden.

Housewares

Conran Shop ♥♥ Gorgeous, contemporary, smartly selected pieces made Conran's name in housewares; its flagship store is a master class in elegant urban furnishings and desirable home accessories. Its building is just as worthy: the 1911 Art Nouveau headquarters of the Michelin Tire Company, coated with decorative tiles of the era's racing cars and the Michelin Man (aka Bibendum). 16 Sloane Square, SW1. www.conranshop.co.uk. ✆ **020/7589-7401.** Tube: Sloane Square.

Flying Tiger Copenhagen ♥♥ Huge in Europe, it's like a Scandinavian version of Japan's Daiso variety stores: scads of useful or funny sundries and gadgets for travel or the home at pound-shop prices. There are several locations around town, including in Spitalfields Market. This one is open until 10pm daily except Sun. 105-107 Oxford St., W1. flyingtiger.com. Tube: Tottenham Court Road

Heal's ♥♥ A stalwart since 1810, but not stuffy like one, Heal's (like Liberty; p. 241) was instrumental in forwarding the Arts and Crafts movement in England. Its furniture and housewares, which are usually defined by chic, up-to-date shapes, have proven so influential that in 1978 it donated its archive to the Victoria & Albert Museum. The kitchen department is popular. 196 Tottenham Court Rd., W1. www.heals.com. ✆ **020/7636-1666.** Tube: Goodge Street.

Natty housewares and other items you didn't know you needed at the carefully curated Labour and Wait.

Labour and Wait ♥♥ The most expensive dustpan you'll ever own will be the envy of dirt everywhere. This store's gorgeously designed kitchenware, bathroom items, gardening tools, and stationery—from vintage enamel to new sculptural metalwork—will put some chic into your chores. Even its location, an emerald-tiled former pub, is functionally fabulous, and its neighbors along Redchurch Street, selling clothes and interior items, are just as stylish. 85 Redchurch St., E2. www.labourandwait.co.uk. ✆ **020/7729-6253.** (Also: 48 Dorset St., W1, ✆ 020/7729-6253; Tube: Baker Street and 12 Dryden St., WC2; ✆ 020/7729-6253; Tube: Covent Garden). Tube: Shoreditch High Street.

Stationery

Choosing Keeping ♥♥ Truly beautiful stationery, gorgeous wrapping paper, artisan-made notebooks and sketchbooks, nib pens—this tidy boutique's throwback ethos, which appeals to anyone who loves a desk filled with quality things, celebrates the vibrancy of Victoriana. 21 Tower St., WC2. www.choosingkeeping.com. ✆ **020/7613-3842.** Tube: Leicester Square.

Present and Correct ♥ Well-designed, midcentury-modern wares for an organized and impeccably stylish desk. Even the Italian staplers and Japanese erasers ("made of natural rubber, for superior error removal") look like they've been approved by a museum curator when in fact, the owner was once a graphic designer for *Monocle*. 12 Bury Place, WC1. www.presentandcorrect.com. ✆ **020/7242-1421.** Closed Sun. Tube: Holborn.

Ryman Stationery ♥ If you're into office supplies (admit it—it's time to come out of the supply closet), the ubiquitous chain, which makes an appearance on almost every busy U.K. shopping street, is a good place to stock up on hard-to-find English-size A4 paper, clamp binders (not common in the U.S.), and convenient "box files" (also absent from other countries' stationers), available in a spectrum of sprightly colors. Multiple locations. www.ryman.co.uk.

Artisan-made notebooks and wrapping paper at Choosing Keeping.

Smythson of Bond Street ♥♥♥ In addition to a line of leather journals, organizers, and handbags, this firm, founded in 1887, does stationery impeccably. The late Queen Elizabeth II, a one-woman thank-you note industry, bought her paper here. The cotton-fiber content is probably higher than in your bedsheets. 131–132 New Bond St., W1. www.smythson.com. ✆ **020/3535-8009.** Closed Sun. Tube: Bond Street or Oxford Circus.

Søstrene Grene ♥♥ This affordable Danish lifestyle store stuffed with cute and sustainable gifts, decorations, hobby supplies, and homewares is sweeping the U.K. and opening locations at a fast pace. 12–14 Argyll St., W1. sostrenegrene.com. ✆ **020/7870-7698.** Tube: Oxford Circus.

Toys

Hamleys ♥♥♥ Remote-control helicopters in your hair, magicians at your elbow, rugrats at your knees. This high-octane toy store is run by a gaggle of cheerful young floor staff, themselves kids at heart, who giddily demonstrate the latest toys. The experience will send you into sensory overload. Seven floors are stuffed with amusements—the fifth floor is nothing but sweets. Depending on when you go, there may be free pirate face painting, a caricaturist, or even a beach party. It's one of the world's few department stores devoted just to children, and the only must-see toy store in London—even if you don't have kids. 188–196 Regent St., W1. www.hamleys.com. ✆ **020/7479-7398.** Tube: Oxford Circus.

Peppa Pig is one of the many animated stars at Hamleys, London's must-see toy store.

The Harry Potter Shop at Platform 9¾ ♥ On the western flank of King's Cross station, from which the storied Hogwarts Express is said to depart, there's an always-busy boutique where Warner Bros. cashes in on Pottermania. London has many imitators that sell off-brand wizardly gear, but this is the only official store, offering much of the same stuff you can find at the Wizarding World in Universal's theme parks: wands, school gear, collectibles, and even a carbonated version of Butterbeer that isn't sold in theme parks. Out front, you can pose for a souvenir photo as you appear to push a luggage cart through a brick wall to the legendary Platform 9¾—staff will throw a scarf on you and then fluff it when the shutter snaps to simulate racing speed. That cheesy photo op gets busy, so if that's why you're going, you're warned to come at least an hour before closing to get a place in the queue. Unfortunately, the train to the actual Harry Potter sets (p. 213) leaves from a different station, Euston, which is a 15-minute walk west. King's Cross Station, N1. www.harrypottershop.co.uk. Mon–Sat 8am–10pm; Sun 9am–8pm. Tube: King's Cross St Pancras.

LONDON'S GREATEST MARKETS

Unfortunately, with the inexorable spread of megastores, outdoor markets that have been feeding central Londoners since the Dark Ages are finding themselves extinguished. The following markets soldier on. Not every market sells something you can take home, unless you count memories: For example, the **Columbia Road Flower Market** (Sun at 8am, Tube: Old Street), is an Eden for English blooms, which get cheaper around 2pm, near closing time. **Borough Market,** which is fully described on p. 110, is all about prepared foods or things you can't get past Customs. Whether for gourmets, tourists, or locals, markets are a front-row seat to the ongoing opera of everyday life, and a taste of London as it once was.

Market Hours

Unless otherwise noted, markets are mostly outdoors and generally kick off around 8 or 9am and start packing up around 3pm.

Berwick Street Market ♥

Berwick St. around Broadwick St. Daily 9am–6pm except Sun. Tube: Piccadilly Circus.

Good for: The last daily street market in the West End, dating to the crowded days of the 1840s, is now being art directed by developers. Gone are the Cockney calls, in are the overpriced baked goods and Apple Pay—convenient, but false. I only mention it because it's historic.

Also check out: The gourmand-pleasing specialty shops lining the route.

Brick Lane Markets ♥♥♥

Brick Lane area, near Hanbury Street. ✆ **020/7770-6028.** Tube: Shoreditch High Street.

Good for: The Vintage Market (www.vintage-market.co.uk, clothes), Backyard Market (www.backyardmarket.co.uk, crafts), Boiler House (food), and Tea Rooms (www.bricklane-tearooms.co.uk, antiques). As you can see, Sundays are a banner

The arcaded "restaurant row" at Brixton Village.

day: UpMarket (www.sundayupmarket.co.uk) for trendy fashions, antiques, food stalls, and Spitalfields Market (www.spitalfields.co.uk) are also in full swing.

Also check out: The Beigel Bake (p. 114) for London's version of a bagel.

Brixton Market ♥

Electric Ave. at Pope's Rd. brixtonmarket.net. Mon–Sat. Tube: Brixton.

Good for: Global produce, spices, halal meats, music from soul to reggae and hip-hop. Expect real immigrant community vitality.

Also check out: Brixton Village (brixtonvillage.com), is one of the best places in London to grab Sunday brunch (after 11am) from a variety of restaurants serving affordable world food under the old double-height glass-topped arcades.

Camden Markets ♥♥

Camden High St. at Buck St. www.camdenlock.net. Daily (Sat–Sun busiest). Tube: Camden Town.

Good for: A rambling warren of 700 stalls for vintage wear, sunglasses, leather, goth gear, and fast foods, partly in a canal-side setting, and favored by tourists. Between the Lock Market, the Market Hall, the Horse Stables, and Camden Lock Village across the street, the crowds are utterly exhausting.

Also check out: Stables Market, on the other side of the railway off Chalk Farm Road, sells vintage clothes, antiques, and pop culture knickknacks, and it's where you'll find a beehive hairdo–bedecked statue of Amy Winehouse, who died in Camden in 2011; Electric Market (on Camden High St.) is an indoor fair of vinyl, programs, and film posters (Sat) and retro and punk clothes (Sun).

Chapel Market ♥

Penton St., Islington. Tues–Sun. Tube: Angel.

Good for: Cheese, dumplings, meat pies, toiletries—a real catch-all working-class market that actually feeds workaday Londoners.

Also check out: The antithesis of a market, the gleaming Angel Central mall dominates the eastern end of the street; it's New London versus Old London.

Greenwich Markets ♥

11a Greenwich Market. greenwichmarket.london. Daily 10am–5:30pm (Sat–Sun best). Tube: Cutty Sark DLR or Greenwich National Rail.

Good for: Antiques, crafts, jewelry, books, honeys, breads, and cakes under a historic market roof. It's worth a stop if you're already in Greenwich.

Also check out: The truffles, ice creams, and gifts at popular chocolatier Dark Sugars (p. 252), on Nelson Road at the Market's south end.

Leadenhall Market ♥♥

Gracechurch St., EC3. www.leadenhallmarket.co.uk. Space open 24 hr., businesses keep own hours. Tube: Monument.

Good for: The shops are thinning these days and the cafes always packed with suited City workers, but what a locale! The glorious wrought-iron-and-glass canopy (1882), once shelter for a meat market, is an architectural treasure. In the first Harry Potter film, this is where The Leaky Cauldron is found. The original heart of Roman London is also under your feet.

Also check out: The Monument (p. 199), two streets away.

Portobello Road Market ♥

Visitportobello.com. ✆ **020/7727-7684.** Daily 8am–7pm. Best on Sat. Tube: Notting Hill Gate or Westbourne Park.

Good for: Antiques, hot foods, jewelry, vintage clothes, tourist tat by the ton. Overcrowded and overrated, but thanks to its past reputation, it's not going anywhere.

Also check out: The packed pubs along the route; the galleries and antiques shops in the storefronts, where prices can be better than at the stalls.

Camden Market is a top place for new and vintage wear, including hats.

Queen's Market ♥

Green St. at Queen's Rd. www.newham.gov.uk. ✆ **020/8475-8971.** Tues and Thurs–Sat 9am–6pm. Tube: Upton Park.

Good for: 80 stalls and 60 local stores for ingredients from Asia, Africa, Russia, the Caribbean, and elsewhere; international clothes and rugs. Although it's not very posh, it is very Everyday London. Sunday is a quieter day.

Also check out: Its defenders' website, www.friendsofqueensmarket.org.uk, which has argued their market is half as expensive as Walmart.

South Bank Book Market ♥♥

Southbank under the Waterloo Bridge. www.southbankcentre.co.uk/shopping/south-bank-book-market. Daily noon–7pm in good weather. Tube: Waterloo.

Good for: Tables of used books, maps, lithographs, and wood engravings. Small, but the riverside setting is its own destination.

Also check out: Lower Marsh Market (www.lowermarshmarket.co.uk) on Lower Marsh between Westminster Bridge and Baylis roads (south of Waterloo station), a classic produce market.

Spitalfields Market ♥♥

Commercial St. between Brushfield St. and Lamb St. oldspitalfieldsmarket.com. Daily. Tube: Liverpool Street.

Good for: Prepared world food, handmade housewares, jewelry, vintage posters. It's the most gentrified market in town, and especially on Saturdays, there are one-of-a-kind clothing items. Sit-down restaurants surround it. The market's success was a linchpin in East London's revitalization.

Also check out: Visit the Style Market for fashions on Saturday afternoons.

The Southbank Centre Book Market is open every day of the week.

Indoor Spitalfields Market is part of a broader East London revitalization.

Walthamstow Market ♥

Walthamstow Market St. www.walthamforest.gov.uk. Tues–Sat. Tube: Walthamstow.

Good for: 450 non-touristy stalls selling everything from knockoff clothes to junky food to Chinese-made batteries—it's the longest market street in Europe, and it's been going since 1885.

Also check out: You may not have the energy to see much else in this multicultural neighborhood—the market itself is a kilometer (about half a mile) long.

YOU CAN'T HACK THE tax attack

When you see a price in England, that's the full price. Tax is always included.

That tax is usually charged at a rate of 20%. It's called VAT (Value-Added Tax), and it goes to enviable programs such as national health care, so that British citizens who get sick don't have to go bankrupt to get well.

Tourists used to have the option of stopping by a VAT refund airport desk on the way home to claim some of that money back on major purchases, but that privilege as we knew it is gone. Brexit ended it. Now you may only buy tax-free goods if they are delivered directly to an address outside the United Kingdom, but not if you carry them.

Business owners are pressuring the U.K. government to renew the system, which stimulates visitor spending, but at press time of this book, the bureaucrats have not relented. To check whether a replacement VAT refund scheme is in the works, look for updated information at **gov.uk/tax-on-shopping**.

7

LONDON NIGHTLIFE

Let no one tell you that London tucks itself into bed early. Perhaps that was true in your grandfather's day—not now. The Tube may shut down after midnight on weeknights, but now the main lines go all night on weekends, so for the intrepid, the entertainment can rollick until morning. With hundreds of theatres, nightclubs, cinemas, and bars, London offers more on a single night than many cities muster in an entire year.

That said, London's nights aren't perfect. The city's prevailing liquor laws force places to often unceremoniously evict their clientele in mid-toast. Whereas in Spain, Greece, and New York, the night rarely begins before 1am, that's usually when floors are being mopped in London, and Gen Z's general cultural shift away from alcohol and nightclubs has caused public nightlife options in Central London to shrink. If you require just one more cocktail to close the deal, a very few clubs will serve until 3am, and they come and go; ask your new friends at the bar which after-hours place is the cool one right now. Where the Night Tube doesn't go, the Night Bus system (p. 358) does, but it's a buzzkill to end a festive night of drinking with your legs crossed on an infrequent and slow-moving bus.

GETTING THE SCOOP Some information for weekly entertainment is published Saturdays in the London papers, but excellent online sources for things to do include **Resident Advisor** (ra.co/events/uk/london), **Londonist.com** and **TimeOut.com/London**.

THEATER

If you leave London without seeing at least one stage show, then you'll have missed one of this city's pillars: This is where Shakespeare defined great writing and Gilbert and Sullivan created the pattern for modern musicals. The great work continues to this day, and if you doubt it, look at the lists of Oscar, Emmy, and Tony winners.

Whenever you hear the phrase "West End" in relation to shows, think of the term as describing the 60 odd top-tier theatres in the middle of town. These are the shows that most tourists flock to see, but that doesn't mean they're always the best—the West End is increasingly clogged with mediocre dramas propped up by

Hollywood names and by so-called "jukebox" musicals that are intentionally simplified so tourists who don't speak English can have fun.

Many West End shows begin their lives at companies found elsewhere in town at "Off West End" or "Fringe" stages. We name some of the best ones here. For challenging work mounted by producers intent on taking artistic risks, head to the smaller theatres that have been designed expressly to incubate fresh projects. The stars perform Off West End, too—all at prices that are half what you'd shell out for a West End show that was mounted for maximum profits.

It's easy to make a night of a show. Most theatres have a bar, and even Off West End companies might have their own mid- to high-end restaurants so you can pre-show on the doorstep.

Curtain times range from 7 to 8pm for evening shows, with most starting at 7:30pm; matinees start anywhere between 2 and 4pm. Every theatre is different, so check your ticket. Most shows are closed, or "dark," on Sundays, but some of the family-oriented crowd-pleasers may go dark on Monday or Tuesday instead.

Theatre Tickets for Less

West End ticket prices are going up fast. Between 2024 and 2025, the cheapest seats rose 25%. But with plentiful discounts, West End shows cost dramatically less than Broadway's—the average top ticket price here is £161.61, while in New York, premium prices hit $825 or more. In London, you can easily find tickets for musicals for £30–£75 for musicals, so you might be able to afford to see a few. If you are desperate to see a specific show, book tickets directly with the production before you leave home to ensure you won't be left out. Check the **Society of London Theatre,** or SOLT (www.officiallondon theatre.co.uk), the trade association for theatre owners and producers (established in 1908), for a season rundown and discounts. Each year in late November, some shows launch a New Year's Sale on that site for deep discounts for shows early the next year. Keep in mind that many other websites will deliver you to third parties who charge a premium of as much as 20% for your booking. It's normal to be charged a booking fee and/or a "restoration fee" of a few pounds that goes to the city's ancient theatre buildings, the oldest of which opened in the 1800s.

The free app **TodayTix** is the one most West End producers use to sell "**rush tickets**" (a daily allotment of low-cost tickets). Each show has different rules, but most of their rush seats cost around £25 each and begin selling at 10am on the days when they're available. If worrying about rush seat timing is too much for you, TodayTix also sells advance tickets for fair prices. (See box, below, for more tips.) *Hamilton* uses its own system.

Many theatres post steep **student discounts,** but distribution methods vary—students are advised to check the websites of the major theatres and sign up ahead of time. And bring your student ID, or you will be denied.

Given a lead time of a few days or weeks, anyone can find some discounts on TodayTix or **LoveTheatre.com** (click "Deals").

saving ON THE STAGE

Apart from using TKTS, how can you save on a show?

- **Use the TodayTix app to find cheap same-day "rush" seats.** "Day seats," or "rush seats," are a daily allotment of cheap seats. Only a few theatres require you to queue in person anymore—you'll need to have a quick trigger finger on the TodayTix app, which handles the majority of shows.
- **Matinees are often cheaper than evening shows.** Unfortunately, they also cut into your daylight touring time.
- **Ask about standing room tickets and "day seats."** Many theatres sell standing room tickets (£15–£20).
- **Buy at the box office** to avoid paying booking fees. This method is increasingly falling out of favor, though.
- **In older theatres, you can settle for a discounted restricted-view seat.** You may have to crane your neck to see around the edge of a balcony or a pillar, but you'll be in the room. They cost about a third of top-price seats. **Theatremonkey.com** posts theatre-specific ratings, and **AViewFromMySeat.com** posts crowdsourced photos taken from specific seats in many houses—use it to determine whether the seat you're offered is worth it.

On the day of the show, **TKTS** (south side of Leicester Square; official londontheatre.com/todays-tickets; Mon–Sat 10:30am–6pm, Sun 11am–4pm; Tube: Leicester Square), operated by SOLT, has same-day seats for as much as half off—the best stuff is sold in the first hour of the booth's opening. Take note that unlike the TKTS booths in New York City's Times Square, London's booth sells its seats early in the day and will not remain open up to showtime. The white-hot tickets won't be found here, but about 80% of West End shows are—TKTS posts a list of going deals (but no show descriptions) on its website so you can know if it's worth the visit. Certain machinelike shows (*The Phantom of the Opera*, *Mamma Mia!*, *The Book of Mormon*, *Matilda*, *Wicked*) seemingly never die and can always be relied upon. In 2023, Agatha Christie's prototypical whodunit play *The Mousetrap* marked its 70th anniversary in London, setting a world record that's very unlikely to ever be slain, and it's still going, too.

The West End is also dotted with closet-size stalls hawking tickets to major shows and concerts. Don't deal with them. They are for audiences who simply *must* get tickets to their chosen show regardless of the fees—as high as 25% over cost. Reselling tickets for profit was outlawed in 2025. Before you give your money to any of these outfits, check the directory of the self-policing **Society of Ticket Agents and Retailers** (www.star.org.uk; ✆ **01904/234-737**) to find out who is reputable. Scalpers, called **touts** here, routinely issue counterfeit tickets or abscond with your money. Some sightseeing discount cards also brag about discounts, but their deals are mostly for the most touristy shows and they don't save you nearly as much as TKTS would—only around £20 off the top price. The website **Twickets** (twickets.live) is a marketplace where people can sell tickets they won't be using for at or below face value.

London's Landmark Performance Places

ABBA Voyage ♥♥♥ In 2022, the members of the '70s Swedish supergroup created a new concert show at their own custom-built arena in East London, where computer-generated "ABBA-tars" of their younger selves jam to the band's greatest hits in a party atmosphere. It's a technological wonder, it's a nonstop feat of cutting-edge lighting and staging, and it's a thousand times more fun than it sounds. ***Warning:*** The DLR stop outside gets swamped after performances; walk 20 minutes to Stratford instead or arrange a ride. ABBA Arena, Pudding Mill Lane, E15. abbavoyage.com. Shows Weds–Sun, extra shows for holiday weeks. Tube: Pudding Mill Lane DLR (arrival) and Stratford or Hackney Wick (departure).

The Barbican Centre ♥♥ In the 1950s, earnest but misguided city leaders turned their attentions toward redeveloping a bombed-out crater. The end result was a forbidding mixed-use concrete complex that took more than 20 years to finish. Today, it's considered a city landmark, if grudgingly so, and it's used as a filming location when a script calls for a dystopian seat of bureaucracy (*Andor*, *Quantum of Solace*). Architects consider the Barbican a crowning achievement in the Brutalist style—90-minute **Architectural Tours** are led daily at 11am (book ahead; £18). In addition to apartment towers, the grounds include a concert hall, two theatres, three cinemas, and two galleries, and together they host some of the most interesting arts events in London. It's nearly impossible to classify the Barbican's fare, since it hosts a wide range of the world's great orchestras (including the London Symphony Orchestra and the BBC Symphony Orchestra), short-run musicals and plays starring A-list talent, singers, and composers, plus a handful of banner festivals each year, particularly in the realm of contemporary music and experimental theater. Its cinemas also screen films fresh from major festival triumphs. Always

The Visitors at ABBA Voyage is a technological teat in a party atmosphere.

check what's on at the Barbican. Silk St., EC2. www.barbican.org.uk. ✆ **020/7638-8891.** Tube: Barbican.

The Bridge Theatre ♥ The bridge in the name of this hot young stage is none other than Tower Bridge, the southern foot of which is just outside the door, making for a sublime nighttime view as you emerge after a show. This venue, which was designed to enable the stage to be placed in a variety of configurations, puts an emphasis on well-produced new work and is unquestionably A-list, attracting heavy-hitters like Ben Whishaw, Ralph Fiennes, Laura Linney, and, in 2026, *Ivanov* starring Chris Pine. 3 Potters Fields Park, SE1. www.bridgetheatre.co.uk. ✆ **0333/320-0051.** Tube: London Bridge.

The Bush Theatre ♥♥♥ The Bush, which since 1972 has showcased a formidable output from a diverse group of new writers, started as a pub theatre. In 2011, thanks to a lifesaving campaign that rallied support from the likes of Judi Dench and Daniel Radcliffe, it got its own complex in a disused Victorian library. 7 Uxbridge Rd., W12. www.bushtheatre.co.uk. ✆ **020/8743-5050.** Tube: Shepherds Bush.

Actor Lenny Henry performs at The Bush Theatre.

Donmar Warehouse ♥♥♥ This 250-seat house mounts mostly limited runs of vividly reconceived shows, both new work and revivals. Past coups for this comfortably converted brewery warehouse include the *Cabaret* revival that introduced Alan Cumming to the world, as well as appearances by world-class performers such as Ian McKellen and Nicole Kidman. You can usually find standing room or cheap student tickets; check its website for the rules for the current show. 41 Earlham St., WC2. www.donmarwarehouse.com. ✆ **020/3282-3808.** Tube: Covent Garden.

Menier Chocolate Factory ♥♥ In an intimate setting among exposed beams and cast-iron columns, a converted you-know-what from the 1870s is where some of the city's hottest musical revivals have been mounted. Its *Merrily We Roll Along*, *Sunday in the Park with George,* and *A Little Night Music* transferred to the West End and later to Broadway. This company, which also does non-musical plays, is one of the few to do Sunday shows; it's usually dark on Mondays. 4 O'Meara St., SE1. www.menierchocolatefactory.com. ✆ **020/7378-1713.** Tube: London Bridge.

Old Vic ♥ There's always something worthwhile at the Old Vic. Nearly every great British actor of our times trod its boards when it was the home of

Aidan Kelly and Adrien Brody onstage at Donmar Warehouse.

the National Theatre, under the artistic direction of Laurence Olivier, before that organization built its own digs on the Thames in 1976. The not-for-profit house it left behind is pulling bigger crowds than ever and draws celebrities like, to take a recent few, Andrew Scott, Vanessa Redgrave, Sally Field, Rami Malek, Susan Sarandon, and *The Crown* couple Claire Foy and Matt Smith acting together again; acting legend Glenda Jackson was even coaxed back on stage here after a quarter century in Parliament. The place is known for mounting meat and potatoes drama—stuff actors love to sink their teeth into—as well as lively fare such as the musical *Groundhog Day,* which it exported to Broadway, and its annual production of *A Christmas Carol,* which is an institution of its own. The theatre dates to 1818 (the current interior to 1871) but has been given lots of love to make it a daytime hangout, too, including the recent addition of a café/bar, free script library, and outdoor terrace. The Cut at Waterloo Rd., SE1. www.oldvictheatre.com. ✆ **0844/871-7628.** Tube: Waterloo or Southwark.

Royal Court Theatre ♥♥ The preeminent writer's theatre (it also hosts the Samuel French theatre bookshop), the Royal Court, which marks its 70th season in 2026, has fought censorship and unveiled international brilliance for so long that it's now a preeminent actor's theatre as well (Tilda Swinton and Gary Oldman were announced for the 2026 season). On the east side of jaunty Sloane Square, it devotes a hefty portion of its schedule to important premieres by the likes of Bruce Norris and Caryl Churchill and performances from fierce actors. Among the plays it gave the world are *Look Back in Anger, The Rocky Horror Picture Show* (in its upstairs studio theatre), George

Bernard Shaw's *Major Barbara* and *Heartbreak House*, and Jez Butterworth's *The Ferryman*. Sloane Square, SW1. www.royalcourttheatre.com. ✆ **020/7565-5000.** Tube: Sloane Square.

Royal National Theatre ♥♥♥ The government-subsidized powerhouse people simply call the National is the country's, and possibly the world's, most noted showpiece for top-flight drama and classical acting. Laurence Olivier was its first director, and the tradition of world-class performances has been unerring: Judi Dench, Ralph Fiennes, Anthony Hopkins, Olivia Colman, and Benedict Cumberbatch have been regulars, plus every other British actor you have ever respected. In recent years, the National Theatre At Home service has broadcast screenings of live performances around the world, earning it wider acclaim than ever. The National always mounts a diverse repertoire of works in its three permanent theatres, spanning Shakespeare to classic musicals (the *Oklahoma!* that made Hugh Jackman a star) to emotional spectacles (*War Horse* began here) to world premieres of well-made plays by the world's best playwrights. The brutalist riverside complex is a pleasure to spend time in, with several pre-show places to eat, caffeinate, or tipple on picnic benches facing the Thames outside the Understudy, its craft beer bar. The fascinating (and free) Sherling High-Level Walkway allows anyone off the street to watch the activity backstage; there's even a periscope so kids can peer over railings into the on-site scenery shops. To find that, head down the eastern-side road toward the Dorfman, go inside, and take the lift to the second level. As the people's theatre, the National's pricing is populist. On Fridays between 12:30 and 1pm on its website, a bevy of £10 "Friday Rush" seats (nationaltheatre.org.uk/fridayrush) are released for the coming weeks' shows. Check the calendar for the 75-minute Guided Theatre Tours (£10–£20) showing off the inner workings or costume department, or shop in the terrific lobby store, a performing arts nirvana. South Bank, SE1. www.nationaltheatre.org.uk. ✆ **020/7452-3000.** Tube: Waterloo.

The riverfront Royal National Theatre complex stages simultaneous high-quality productions.

Sadler's Wells ♥ Sadler's Wells has been a part of the fabric of London life for so long (since 1683) that its current two-house home, dating to 1998, is actually the sixth. You can turn to this Islington establishment to catch some of the world's greatest companies in movement- or rhythm-based performances that transcend language. Its specialties are ballet (the English National Ballet performs here, and Matthew Bourne is a frequent guest artist), contemporary dance, and daring opera, although it dabbles in musicals as well. It also programs evening shows at the Peacock Theatre on Portugal Street near the Holborn Tube. Rosebery Ave., EC1. www.sadlerswells.com. ✆ **020/7863-8000.** Tube: Angel.

Shakespeare's Globe ♥♥♥ This reconstruction of an Elizabethan theatre on the Thames (see p. 184 for architectural details) attracts the best classically trained performers, thanks partly to its founding artistic director (1995–2005), Oscar-winning actor Mark Rylance. There are few finer settings in which to see a play, usually Shakespeare but always classic. The quality standard is high—in 2017, the artistic director was fired, in part, for the anachronistic sin of using artificial lighting—although selections can be startlingly progressive as well, as its female-performed *King Lear* proved. Groundling ("Yard") tickets to stand for the show have been £5 since the 1990s; in summer, it holds a Friday Rush at 11am for £5 spots (www.shakespearesglobe.com/5-pound-rush). In the outer ring, seats are also available, all of them so near the stage that the intimacy is palpable. The season at the open-air Globe is spring through fall, but in a 340-seat Jacobean indoor theatre, the Sam Wanamaker (named in honor of the American actor who fought to reconstruct the Globe), there's something happening year-round. The theatre also conducts daily 50-minute Guided Tours (p. 184). 21 New Globe Walk, Bankside, SE1. www.shakespearesglobe.com. ✆ **020/7401-9919.** Season: Apr–Oct. Tube: Southwark or Mansion House.

Southbank Centre ♥♥♥ Like the Barbican, this is a bleak, canvas-colored slab architects don't know quite how to fix. It was conceived as a postwar pick-me-up for a creativity-starved city, but age was not kind; despite a flawless Thames location, it's a forbidding architectural scowl, looking more like a pile of sidewalk curbs than an artistic capital. It's perkier on the inside, however. An ever-interesting hodgepodge of some 1,000 programs a

The Riverside Terrace Cafe at Royal Festival Hall in the Southbank complex.

THE QUIRKS OF LONDON theatregoing

London theatre can be a culturally strange experience for newcomers:

- Programs are not free; they cost from £5 (for plays) to £10 (for musicals). Big productions may only sell a glossy souvenir brochure, for £10 or more.
- What North American theatres call "orchestra" seats, London houses call the "stalls." And instead of a "mezzanine," they have a "Dress Circle," and above that, "Upper Circle" or "Royal Circle." If there happens to be a third, topmost level, that is the "balcony," or sometimes, the "gallery." And because many theatres were constructed in a class-obsessed era, there may be a separate street entrance for each area.
- The break between acts is called an "interval," not "intermission."
- The big snack? Ice cream, sold by ushers (or "attendants"). English people are nostalgic for ice cream at plays the way Americans link hot dogs with baseball.
- Most theatres allow you to preorder drinks and snacks before the show so you can pick them up quickly during the interval. Some even let you do it digitally from your mobile phone.
- During the bows, many musicals add a celebratory mini medley of the songs, and it's the only part of the show that you're allowed to video with your smartphone.
- Older theatres are required to deploy the "fire curtain," which seals the stage from the auditorium in the event of flames, once during every performance. It's usually done discreetly during the interval, and it's usually a true antique.
- Leave big bags at the hotel, not just because of security (they will be inspected), but also because these knee-knocking old seats were installed over a century ago for smaller people. And rethink short skirts, because in the Circles, your knees will likely be at head-level of the person sitting in front of you.

year go down at its three concert venues, as well as in its huge central hall, which has a cafe and is open to everybody. Dance, film, classical and contemporary music, and the London Jazz Festival fill the bill, which is prolific if self-important. But it also deals in more lively social events like craft and food markets, DJ holiday bars, gallery exhibitions, and much more. Don't miss the Undercroft, the hideous concrete negative space beneath the building along the Thames. When the Centre went up, this area was thought to be useless, so skateboarders and street artists claimed the architectural mistake. Years later, landlords tried to evict them for shops, but too late—the skaters proved too beloved, and they endure as a guerilla expression that found a home in this mix. Belvedere Rd., SE1. www.southbankcentre.co.uk. ✆ **020/3879-9555, WhatsApp:** 07931-730017. Tube: Waterloo.

London's Great Smaller Theatres

Almeida Theatre ♥♥ The inviting Almeida, which has its own contemporary pub, is gaining esteem by bounds. It regularly unveils new work by the likes of Jeremy O. Harris and *The Crown* auteur Peter Morgan, and its performers include the likes of Juliet Stevenson, Josh O'Connor, Saoirse Ronan, and Matt Smith. It also sticks to its guns, mounting intelligent and politically poignant plays (some new, some unfairly forgotten) without much regard for pushback. It has added *Ink*, *King Charles III*, and *American Psycho–The Musical* to the canon. Almeida St. off Upper St., N1. www.almeida.co.uk. ✆ **020/7359-4404.** Tube: Angel.

The Coronet Theatre ♥ This place was built as a small variety house in 1898, but for most of the 20th century it was a cinema—this is where Hugh Grant's character wistfully attended a space movie starring his estranged girlfriend (Julia Roberts) in *Notting Hill.* Now it's one of the up-and-coming Fringe theatres, specializing in international talents. 103 Notting Hill Gate, W11. www.thecoronettheatre.com. ✆ **020/3642-6606.** Tube: Notting Hill Gate.

Hackney Empire ♥ One of London's greatest and most ornate old houses (1901) was where, once upon a time, you could catch Charlie Chaplin as a vaudeville act. The ever-changing slate still presents the best of variety, but now with a multicultural twist that serves the community: kids' shows, opera, Christmas pantomime, hip-hop drama, and concerts. 291 Mare St., E8. www.hackneyempire.co.uk. ✆ **020/8985-2424.** Tube: Hackney Central Overground.

Lyric Hammersmith ♥ It may look like a fusty Victorian jewel-box theatre, but inside, you'll find spectacular stuff—a mix of multimedia-based works, avant-garde experiments, plays, celeb Q&As, and an annual Christmas show to write home about. Its kids' fare is its bread and butter. Lyric Square, King St., S6. www.lyric.co.uk. ✆ **020/8741-6850.** Tube: Hammersmith.

Roundhouse ♥♥ Located in a rehabbed 1846 locomotive shed, the Roundhouse picks up on the maverick spirit of neighboring Camden with a frisky, fast-changing lineup of innovative musical dramas and spectaculars, many of them given a crowd-pleasing, dance-inflected, shock-to-the-system twist. In the 1960s, it was one of London's most important stages, particularly for counterculture concerts. In more recent seasons, you're just as likely to see one-off comedy events, poetry slams, or concerts. Oscar-winning actor Daniel Kaluuya (*Get Out*) has launched Centre 59, a youth company, in an associate role; he was raised in the neighborhood and attended drama training here. Chalk Farm Rd., NW1. www.roundhouse.org.uk. ✆ **030/0678-9222.** Tube: Chalk Farm.

A concert at the Roundhouse, set in a 19th century locomotive shed.

Soho Theatre ♥ The Soho functions like a one-building arts festival; it casts a wide net in looking for the latest voices in theater, comedy, A-list drag, and cabaret. On weekend days, come for kids' shows. Its Theatre Bar is a fine hangout even sans tickets. In 2025, it expanded with a second location in a breathtaking 1929 Art Deco cinema in a neighborhood at the end of the Victoria Line. At the **Soho Theatre Walthamstow** (186 Hoe St., E17; Tube: Walthamstow Central), the roster of performances is just as wild and just as good. 21 Dean St., W1. www.sohotheatre.com. ✆ **020/7478-0100.** Tube: Tottenham Court Road.

The Unicorn Theatre ♥ A children's theater that caters to kids without suffering from a debilitating case of preciousness, the Unicorn runs at least two productions, one for each of its theatre spaces. Some are script-based and some sensory-based for younger kids and kids with autism. Many are designed to expose kids to other cultures, places, and classic stories. If only every city had a kids' facility as lush. 147 Tooley St., SE1. www.unicorntheatre.com. ✆ **020/7645-0560.** Tube: London Bridge.

OH, YES YOU CAN! how to panto

During each holiday season (Nov–early Jan), some large theatres mount a new pantomime, a madcap type of musical comedy for families that has its roots in Middle Age traditions, *commedia dell' Arte*, and other theatrical customs. Pantos are a beloved tradition, and they give some theatres their best sales of the year, but attending your first one can be hilariously bewildering. It seems like everyone in the audience, including the infants, knows exactly when to yell and what to say. Join their fun:

- Most pantos are from a list of about a dozen stories including "Jack and the Beanstalk," "Cinderella," "Aladdin," and "Peter Pan." The tale of Dick Whittington, about a poor boy (and his cat, portrayed by a human) finds his fortune in London, is not done often outside the city. Each company tinkers with the plot to suit the talents of that year's cast.
- The leading man, also called "principal boy," is played in drag by a woman pretending to be a man, usually by wearing revealing shorts or tights.
- The leading lady, or "dame," is a man dressed in drag as a woman, and the campy double entendres fly. Most of the time, you'll see a C-list TV celebrity.
- The villain should be vigorously hissed and booed.
- Whenever the good guy argues with the bad guy (or "the baddie"), the audience takes the side of the good guy and shouts along with the quarrel. Your exchange will go along the lines of "Oh, no, he isn't!" and, "Oh, yes he is!".
- Two performers in a single costume will portray a large animal, like a cow.
- Expect a slapstick "slosh" scene in which characters splatter each other with substances ranging from water to custard pies to slime.
- Whenever one character is being stalked by another (often a ghost), the audience must shout "They're behind you!"
- Before the finale comes the "Song Sheet," when the audience, especially children, is invited to sing along.

Young Vic ♥ Spry and defiant, this company programs a mixed bag of jarring plays, conversational touchstones (*Yerma*), edgy musicals (Daniel Fish's so-called "Sexy *Oklahoma!*," *The Scottsboro Boys*), and affordable opera, then stands back and hopes for frisson. It often achieves it, and if it fails, it doesn't dally long, since it has three theatres (seating 500, 160, and 80) to fill. There's nearly always something high-quality and new-to-you to plumb here. Some of its work is streaming on the National Theatre at Home app. 66 The Cut, SE1. www.youngvic.org. ✆ **020/7922-2922.** Tube: Waterloo or Southwark.

Pub Theatres

Pub theatres keep the lifeblood of London's performance culture flowing. In the early 1970s, this new form of alternative theater swept town, usually taking residence in a tatty back rooms of pubs where audiences could bring a beer from the scruffy front bar. Many a movie actor found their feet in pub spaces. They're still where some of the city's most affordable (£15 and under), idiosyncratic, balls-to-the-wall writing is found. And if you don't like the play, you didn't spend much and it won't be hard to find a drink to make it seem better.

The Etcetera Theatre ♥♥ Odd, challenging fare (sometimes multiple different shows a night) in a very small black box. 265 Camden High St., NW1. www.etceteratheatrecamden.com. ✆ **020/7482-4857.** Tube: Camden Town.

Hen & Chickens ♥ Frequent comedy bookings as well as strong writing are presented by the resident company, Unrestricted View. 109 St Paul's Rd., N1. www.thehenandchickenstheatrebar.co.uk. ✆ **020/7354-8246.** Tube: Highbury & Islington.

The King's Head ♥♥♥ Alums include Kenneth Branagh, Clive Owen, Joanna Lumley, Ben Kingsley, Juliet Stevenson, Hugh Grant, and John Hurt in their younger, braver, poorer days. After 53 years, its pub space was retired, in 2024, it finally graduated to its own purpose-built facility on the same block with 2 performance spaces. 116 Upper St., N1. www.kingsheadtheatre.com. ✆ **020/7226-8561.** Tube: Angel.

A comedy version of *Beowulf* at the King's Head, one of London's hilarious holiday pantos, or pantomimes.

Old Red Lion ♥ The very pubby ORL hires its 60-seat space to a variety of aspiring producers and hosts the occasional comedy night. 418 St John St., EC1. www.oldredliontheatre.co.uk. ✆ **0333/012-4963.** Tube: Angel.

White Bear Theatre ♥ Oscar nominee Emily Watson is an alum of this space, which has made a specialty of reviving forgotten plays. Its pub, here since 1780, has a spacious back garden. 138 Kennington Park Rd., SW11. www.whitebeartheatre.co.uk. ✆ **0333/012-4963.** Tube: Kennington.

OPERA

Opera can be a budget-breaker. Frugal travelers should try the street singers who perform daily at the **Covent Garden Piazza** (Tube: Covent Garden). That's not a joke: Performers are auditioned before being awarded buskers' licenses, so the caliber is high. Also check to see if there's a touring opera putting down stakes at Sadler's Wells (p. 268) or the Barbican (p. 265). Of course, nothing compares to these institutions:

English National Opera ♥♥ With the Royal Opera entrenched as the country's premium company, the ENO at the gorgeous London Coliseum (built in 1904; londoncoliseum.org/) is the progressive one that angles for younger audiences. Tightening purse strings have made it slimmer and more crowd-pleasing. The slate consists of both progressive choices and classics: A season usually includes one world premiere, a few revivals, and two new collaborations. Tickets start at just £15—although bear in mind that the balcony, where those cheapest seats are located, is remote indeed. More ways to find affordable seats are listed at www.eno.org/your-visit/ways-to-save-offers. St Martin's Lane, WC2. www.eno.org. ✆ **020/7845-9300.** Season: Sept–Apr. Tube: Leicester Square.

Royal Opera House ♥♥ Opera fans don't need to be reminded of the role the ROH plays on the world scene, but outsiders might be surprised at how inviting and attractive its terrace and cafe are. The main house, which is shared by the Royal Opera (conducted by Antonio Pappano until 2024) and the equally prestigious Royal Ballet (now past its 70th year here and now directed by Kevin O'Hare), is supplemented with two smaller spaces for chamber opera and studio dance. Surtitles appear on little screens or monitors. The Opera House has ended its tradition of cheap Friday Rush tickets; instead, it prices some seats at £50 or less and wishes audiences good luck in finding them. Daytime tours are available, too, of its architectural highlights or of backstage, the set and costume workshops, and its 2,256-seat, horseshoe-shaped auditorium (✆ **020/7304-4000;** £22–£30; 75 min.; recommended for kids 6 and over; must reserve days or weeks ahead with the online calendar). Bow St., Covent Garden, WC2. www.roh.org.uk. ✆ **020/7304-4000.** Tube: Covent Garden.

DANCE PERFORMANCE

London's dance scene has yet to achieve the vibrancy of New York's or Germany's, but that's not to say there's nothing to see; it's just that outside of Sadler's Wells (p. 268). some of the best terpsichorean productions are put on by visiting companies. The first thing to do is check the schedules at the Barbican (p. 265), Roundhouse (p. 271), and Southbank Centre (p. 269), which present a cornucopia of performance genres. The country's largest company,

Royal Ballet ♥♥, shares space with the Royal Opera (above). The adventurous **English National Ballet** ♥ tours Britain much of the time but finds itself in London often (www.ballet.org.uk; ✆ **020/7581-1245**), especially for its December *Nutcracker.*

The Place ♥♥♥ (17 Duke's Rd., WC1; www.theplace.org.uk; ✆ **020/7121-1100;** Tube: Euston) is known for contemporary dance and the host venue of companies from around the world. The lucky tenant of a gleaming translucent building by the same team that designed the Tate Modern, **Trinity Laban** ♥ (Creekside, Greenwich, SW8; www.trinitylaban.ac.uk; ✆ **020/8305-4444;** Cutty Sark DLR or Greenwich National Rail) trains artists but also puts on a mixed bill of works from around the world and by up-and-comers from its conservatory. Oscar winner A.R. Rahman (*Slumdog Millionaire*) is one of its leaders.

CLASSICAL MUSIC

Cadogan Hall ♥ This onetime Christian Scientist church (built 1907 in the Byzantine Revival style) with 950 seats and fine acoustics is now the home of the Royal Philharmonic Orchestra and the rest of its calendar is filled with high-level bookings by jazz artists, vocalists, chamber music, and more. 5 Sloane Terrace, SW1. www.cadoganhall.com. ✆ **020/7730-4500.** Tube: Sloane Square.

King's Place ♥♥ If you find yourself bored in London, it's not King's Place's fault. The relatively new development behind King's Cross (it shares a building with *The Guardian*) has become a versatile, exciting venue, with spaces for multiple galleries, chamber groups, choirs, and orchestras. Comedy, folk music, jazz, interviews with world notables—surprises abound. 90 York Way, N1. www.kingsplace.co.uk. ✆ **020/7520-1490.** Tube: King's Cross St Pancras.

The Aurora Orchestra at King's Place.

Royal Albert Hall ♥♥♥ Imposing, ornate, and adored by music lovers worldwide, the RAH is one of the few performance arenas on earth where, once they have performed there, artists can truly claim to have made it. During the summer, the storied BBC Promenade Concerts (the Proms) fill this historic, 5,200-seat circular hall with classical music, but the rest of the year, the space books a hodgepodge of movies with live music in concert (the house organ is 21m/69 ft. tall and has 10,000 pipes), arena-style musicals, the Olivier Awards, regular engagements by Cirque du Soleil, tours—even tennis matches. See p. 268 for

Royal Albert Hall hosts world-class musicians and performers.

tour information. Kensington Gore, SW7. www.royalalberthall.com. ✆ **0845/401-5034.** Tube: South Kensington.

St Martin-in-the-Fields ♥♥♥ Right in the thick of Trafalgar Square, this handsome church's evening candlelight concerts and lunchtime performances are London traditions. It's non-fussy with clean acoustics and has held a place of esteem among world musicians for many years. Trafalgar Square, WC2. www.smitf.org. ✆ **020/7766-1136.** Tube: Charing Cross or Leicester Square.

Wigmore Hall ♥♥ Opened in 1901 as a recital hall for the Bechstein piano showroom that was next door, it was seized (along with the company) as enemy property in World War I. A nasty start, but in time performers came to include Ravel, Saint-Saëns, Britten, and Artur Rubinstein. Today this intimate space, noted for chamber music and for a bombastic Arts and Crafts cupola over the stage, is known for ideal acoustics and a roster of some 450 concerts, mostly classical, each year. Some nights, there's free music in the bar. 36 Wigmore St., W1. www.wigmore-hall.org.uk. ✆ **020/7935-2141.** Tube: Bond St.

THE MUSIC SCENE

London's live music venues don't draw a heavy line between the genres they present, and no rigid division exists between gig venues and dance venues; in fact, many spaces switch from live music to dance in a single evening. That's one of the things that makes the city's nightlife so vibrant, but it's also why it's important to check programming in advance. Students can often get discounts on entry—as if you needed any more proof that education is valued in England. Bring your ID—under 18s aren't usually admitted.

Dice (dice.fm), which specializes in live music, offers smartphone ticketing plus an automated in-app waitlist for returns.

Live Music, Including Jazz, Pop, Folk & Rock

Dozens of theatres and arenas in town book concerts by recognizable names, but it would be fruitless to list them since they're almost all rented by promoters and don't always have something going on. The better advice is to stay on top of who's playing by checking **Secret London** (secretldn.com), ***Time Out*** (www.timeout.com/london) or ***New Musical Express*** (NME; "Gig Guide" at www.nme.com). Since big shows sell out months in advance, the best recourse is to book ahead via **See Tickets** (www.seetickets.com; ✆ **087/1220-0260**); **Ticketweb** (www.ticketweb.co.uk; ✆ **0333/321-9990**); or the latter's partner, the dreaded **Ticketmaster** (www.ticketmaster.co.uk; ✆ **0333/321-9999**), all of which levy fees but let you buy from abroad.

In the heart of town, it's tough to find a truly late-night venue since so many places that serve alcohol are required to stop by 11pm or so. Places in the outer neighborhoods are more likely to have been granted a late license, but the current crop of hotspots changes rapidly. London venues have also moved almost exclusively to online booking. I give you the phone numbers when I

the prince charles: THE MOVIE LOVER'S PALACE

The family-friendly "Sing-a-Long-a" *The Sound of Music*, a silly audience-participation screening of the 1965 classic, was born in 1999 at the eccentric **Prince Charles Cinema**, off Leicester Square (7 Leicester Place; www.princecharles cinema.com; ✆ **020/7494-3654;** Tube: Leicester Square). The concept swept the world thereafter, even reaching the Hollywood Bowl. Our campy movie favorites have shifted since then, and now, on weekend nights, other cult classics are given the call-and-response treatment, including *The Greatest Showman, Rocky Horror, Grease, The Muppet Christmas Carol*, and *Dirty Dancing* among them. But the Prince Charles, which occupies a failed 1962 theatre (named for a Stuart royal, not the current king) where Judy Garland once snag, is more than stunt screenings—it's a respected home for classic film and a necessary stop for our greatest living artists. Director Paul Thomas Anderson says visiting is "like tuning into your favorite radio station" and Quentin Tarantino says "for lovers of quality films, this is Mecca." The Prince Charles' packed daily schedule supplies a rare venue to screen 70mm projections of seminal cinematic masterpieces ranging from *Lawrence of Arabia, 2001: A Space Odyssey*, to *Die Hard.* It mounts daily revival screenings of landmark movies and marathons of beloved franchises like *Lord of the Rings*, the Burton *Batmans*, and Linklater's *Before* trilogy. It stages Q&As of world-renowned talent. So beloved is the Prince Charles, which receives no public funding and welcomes some 250,000 people a year, that when its landlord, which collects annual revenue over half a billion dollars, demanded increased rent that was beyond its curators' ability to pay, the venue sought protection from Westminster's council as an Asset of Community Value—and in late 2025, became only the 6th building to achieve it. The best way to keep the Prince Charles alive is to buy a ticket. That should be easy. As Anderson puts it, "You can close your eyes, press your finger to the program, and you'll hit something great."

have them, but if you call them, beware that you're most likely to connect with the void of a voicemail box that's never checked.

The 100 Club ♥♥ Many decades have passed since this venue, as the Feldman Swing Club, was a prime hangout for U.S. servicemen homesick for the jazzy sounds of Glenn Miller (who died serving in the U.K., you'll remember) and his colleagues. In 1976, after passing through an R&B and jazz period that had Louis Armstrong puckering up for audiences, it sponsored the world's first punk festival, and bands like the Sex Pistols, unsigned at the time, took the stage. This battered red-walled basement institution with good sightlines and expensive drinks still can't decide which era to honor, so it careens among punk, swing, R&B, jazz, and up-and-coming bands—but it never has lost the respect of the musicians' community. 100 Oxford St., W1. www.the100club.co.uk. ✆ **020/7636-0933.** Cover £15–£30, 25% discounts often available in advance. Music starts around 8:30pm. Tube: Tottenham Court Road.

Ain't Nothin' But ♥♥ Live blues 7 nights a week in the sort of tavern-like close cabaret quarters that Blues gods intended, although you might have to stand. Blues jams on Sunday afternoons and Monday evenings. 20 Kingly St., W1. www.aintnothinbut.co.uk. ✆ **020/7287-0514.** Tickets generally £15 or less. 2 performances weekdays, 3 on weekend days. Tube: Oxford Circus.

The Camden Assembly ♥ When it was known as Barfly, this dark, intimate bar/performance space in Camden was the launch pad for a thousand indie bands, some of which actually ended up soaring (Coldplay, Blur, Olivia Dean, and the like). Today it offers a good mix of club nights and concerts for students, musicians, and old-time locals. Gentrification has tamed the over-zealous moshers. When the bands wrap up, a house DJ spins for a few more hours while the audience chills. 49 Chalk Farm Rd., NW1. www.camdenassembly.com. ✆ **020/7424-0800.** Entry usually £8–£30. Tube: Chalk Farm.

The Gumbo blues band jams at Ain't Nothin' But.

The Crazy Coqs ♥♥ The stylish 1920s-style room is intimate and classy, making it a romantic setting for music, cabaret, and the occasional magic act, all accompanied by potent cocktails. It's part of the accessibly elegant Brasserie Zédel (p. 93) complex north of Piccadilly Circus. 20 Sherwood St., W1. www.brasseriezedel.com/crazy-coqs. ✆ **020/7734-4888.** Tickets £20–£35. Reservations required. Performances usually 7pm. Tube: Piccadilly Circus.

Dingwalls ♥♥ After 1973, when it started as a dance hall in a former industrial space by Camden Lock, Dingwalls evolved into an ever-popular house of rock, folk, and acoustic guitar. It was special for granting audiences (which usually number no more than 500) the dignity of sitting at tables to enjoy the music, and performers responded: The Sex Pistols, the Ramones, and Blondie in its U.K. debut were all artists who made the pilgrimage. The legendary Van Morrison came out of solitude to play it in 2021. Choose from a loft-like bar, a terrace bar, and one overlooking the Regent's Canal, where pub food is served all day. Middle Yard, NW1. dingwalls.com/. Daily 11am–3am. Tickets generally handled through AXS.com. Tube: Camden Town.

The Dublin Castle ♥ Any bar that proclaims itself the birthplace of the 1970s and '80s ditty band Madness would not, on the surface, seem to be a place you'd want to enter without prior insobriety. But it has street cred—it was the first bar in London to win a late liquor license from the government, so it became an important nightspot, and its legendary status was sealed in 1980 when AC/DC singer Bon Scott drank himself to death here. Really no more than a threadbare, greenish pub with a teeny backroom stage, it hosts acts struggling to make it—and a few (Blur, for one, and Madness, for two) that actually have. On weekends, late-night DJs spin after the band packs up. 94 Parkway, NW1. www.thedublincastle.com. ✆ **020/7485-1773.** Cover £10–£15. Tube: Camden Town.

Electric Ballroom ♥♥ One of those dicey, utilitarian halls (ca. 1938) that never loses the lingering smell of old beer, the Electric Ballroom has hosted the likes of Sid Vicious, The Clash, Prince, U2, and Pet Shop Boys. Steel yourself for a steady roster of punk, goth, industrial, glam, hardcore, metal, and other sensory abusers (like British pro wrestling and Kiefer Sutherland's band). Their aficionados could hardly inflict more architectural damage to the premises than what's already been done by the ravages of time and benign neglect. 184 Camden High St., NW1. www.electricballroom.co.uk. ✆ **020/7485-9007.** Entry £20–£40. Tube: Camden Town.

The Garage ♥♥ This 600-person concert space (once a billiard hall for teetotalers) has enough cred as a modern choice for indie and rock that Harry Styles once chose it for a surprise gig. Overpriced drinks in cans, intimate but loud; you know the drill. There's an all-day bar, too, but upstairs is better: **The Grace**, capacity of around 150, has a late license to serve alcohol till the wee hours (2am Mon–Thurs, 4am Fri–Sat) and tends to host grown-up gigs by singer-songwriters (over the years, Jeff Buckley, Sondre Lerche, and others). 20–22 Highbury Corner, N5. www.thegarage.london/. ✆ **0844/847-1578.** Tube and National Rail: Highbury & Islington.

Green Note ♥♥ This welcoming vegetarian cafe/bar books acoustic live gigs, from folk to jazz, roots to singer-songwriters. Softened by pillows and upholstered seating, it's a laid-back scene with no dancing. You can eat in the front room (tapas at sensible prices, no meat, all organic) and hear the music, or a cover charge will let you swing into the bar in the back room just for the show. 106 Parkway, NW1. www.greennote.co.uk. ✆ **020/7485-9899.** Cover £3–£18. Opens 7pm. Tube: Camden Town.

Jazz After Dark ♥ Trios, funk, and soul singers, all packed on a tiny stage (so tiny, it's wise to book a table). Amy Winehouse used to come—it's said she applied for a job but they gave her a gig instead. Who knows how true that is, but the cellar vibe is why visitors manage to overlook the grumpy owner and weak drinks. You know it's no good—but dammit, it has a certain charm. Much of its longevity is owed to the fact it serves later than most Soho pubs do. 9 Greek St., W1. www.jazzafterdark.co.uk. ✆ **020/7734-0545.** Cover: live music £10–£20. Until 2am. Tube: Tottenham Court Road.

Jazz Café ♥♥♥ A prime Camden venue for "names" keeps the music going nightly until 2am, usually in the form of acts (jazz, bluesy vocalists, funk, soul) seen up close. Converted from a bank and renovated with Deco touches in 2016, it has both cabaret tables and an upstairs gallery with food. Look for occasional club nights for EDM, house music gospel, and the like, so check the schedule. 5 Parkway, NW1. www.thejazzcafelondon.com. ✆ **020/7485-6834.** Cover: live music £10–£30. Doors open at 7pm, open until 3am Sat–Sun. Tube: Camden Town.

R&B artist Xavier Omar at the Jazz Café.

Koko ♥♥♥ Some time ago, Koko stopped being a mere joint for gigs and became an institution. It began its creative life in 1900 as the Camden Hippodrome and saw performances by Ellen Terry and Charlie Chaplin. By the 1970s and '80s, though, as it crumbled, its role as a global fixture was cemented when it rose as an epicenter for pop—Eurythmics, Boy George, and Wham! all played their earliest gigs here, and it's where Madonna made her U.K. debut. The name Koko brings respect, so when, amid the pandemic, its run-down building caught fire and nearly faced destruction from melted metal and water damage, you could almost hear the collective scream of horror from the music world. The close call prompted promoters to lavish Koko with all the love it's worth. In 2022, it came roaring back with a refurbishment befitting such an icon, adding an incredible rooftop terrace, a quirky bar in its crowning dome, a new performance space in the fly space of the old theatre, a speakeasy, a recording studio, a multimedia broadcast space, a shop, and a late-night pizzeria. None other than Arcade Fire opened the venue anew, and Koko also regularly sells out its weekend electronic club nights. The grubby old court jester now wears the vestments of a monarch. 1a Camden Rd., NW1. www.koko.co.uk. ✆ **087/0432-5527.** Cover £20–£50, student discounts before midnight. Entry until 3am on some weekend nights.Tube: Mornington Crescent.

The Piano Works ♥♥ A live band takes written requests while you eat, drink, and dance on a small dance floor, while its side room, **SingEasy** (SingEasy.bar), invites with an intimate, piano-and-mic cabaret vibe and singalong theme nights. The best is the You Can't Stop the Brunch party on Saturdays, when servers, many of them West End performers, join in as they tote bottomless mimosas and prosecco. Yes, of *course* someone will belt "Defying Gravity." There's a second Piano Works location at Farringdon (113–117 Farringdon Rd., WC1; Tube: Farringdon) without so many theater kids. Gillian Lynne Theatre, Parker Street, WC2. pianoworks.bar. ✆ **020/7889-1966.** Cover £5–£20. Closes at 3am (West End) and 2am (Farringdon). Tube: Holborn.

PizzaExpress Live ♥♥ Unlikely as it may seem, this so-so restaurant chain holds lunchtime and night concerts in jazz clubs at three of its locations—and unlike its food, they're widely respected. The cellar **PizzaExpress Live** in Soho (10 Dean St., W1; ✆ **020/7439-4962;** Tube: Tottenham Court Road) has seen acts such as Jamie Cullum, Norah Jones, and Roy Haynes. There's an upscale supper club for cabaret and talks at the Chelsea location, The Pheasantry (152 Kings Rd., SW3; Tube: Sloane Square), which also does a bottomless brunch on Saturdays. The newer Holborn location (99 High Holborn, WC1; Tube: Holborn) centers on acoustic, jazz, and vocals, and its Piano Lounge (80-81 St Martin's Lane, WC2; Tube: Leicester Square) spotlights up-and-coming keyboardists. www.pizzaexpresslive.com. Livemusic £15–£65.

Ronnie Scott's Jazz Club ♥ Since the 1960s, when it was first recommended in Frommer's, Ronnie Scott's has been London's standard bearer for stylish, American-style jazz—it even has its own house jazz orchestra, which puts on regular Big Band nights—and it honors a long tradition of pairing visiting U.S. greats with local acts. It's true that the club historically draws names, including John Legend, Patti Austin, Tom Waits, Cleo Laine, Chaka Khan, and George Clinton, and it's also true that, like its landmark neon sign promises, it's open until 3am, which is rare in these parts. Fridays and Saturdays, there's a Late Late Show for jazz-funk, soul, and more, starting at 11:15pm; there are tickets usually available at the door for that. In 2026, it reopens its cozy and stylish upstairs room, which has just 140 seats. 47 Frith St., W1. www.ronniescotts.co.uk. ✆ **020/7439-0747.** Tickets £25–£75. Kids 14–18 only permitted before midnight. Reservations recommended. Tube: Leicester Square.

Scala ♥♥ When it was a cinema, Stanley Kubrick got it shut down for screening *A Clockwork Orange* without permission. Good thing he did, or this 1920 theatre might not have been reborn as a pleasing place to catch an acoustic or lyrical band. Its three levels give nearly everyone a good view of the stage, fostering a sense of intimacy appropriate to its (standing) capacity of around 1,000 people. A warren of rooms confuses the drunk ones and conceals the shy ones. Weekdays, Scala hosts gigs by indie bands, and weekends, it turns to club nights (the long-running Face Down, every first Fri, is rock; the new Afro Spice is for "the very best Amapiano & Afrobeats with the sounds of the South Asian diaspora"). 275 Pentonville Rd., N1. www.scala.co.uk. ✆ **020/7833-2022.** Cover: £11–£30. Tube: King's Cross St Pancras.

Scottish synth-pop band CHVRCHES performs at Scala.

The Water Rats ♥♥ If you're not a headbanger, the modest singer-songwriters here may appeal more than Camden's squalling sets. Once it was a pub known as the Pindar of Wakefield; Bob Dylan made his U.K. debut on its back room stage in 1962, Oasis braved London audiences for the first time here in 1994, and Katy Perry played it before arenas—and returned for a nostalgia gig in 2017. The food is not for the faint of heart. 328 Grays Inn Rd., WC1. www.thewaterratsvenue.london. ✆ **020/7209-8747.** Cover from £8–£15 for several bands. Until midnight Mon–Fri, 1am Sat–Sun. Tube: King's Cross St Pancras.

Major Venues

If you want to get into the big-name gigs, you have to book ahead, before you arrive. Grittier, midsize venues, mostly repurposed century-old music halls, include **Bush Hall** (www.bushhallmusic.co.uk); the **O_2 Academy Brixton** (www.O2academybrixton.co.uk), good for metal and alt-rock; the **O_2 Academy**

BANGING festivals

Music festivals take over London's green spaces, making summer like one long Woodstock. Here are some highlights. Find more at Secret London (secretldn.com) and www.musicfestivalwizard.com.

- **All Points East.** Two days in Victoria Park. Past acts: Björk, The Chemical Brothers, Christine and the Queens, Nick Cave. www.allpointseastfestival.com.
- **BST Hyde Park.** Mainstream acts (2026: One Republic, Garth Brooks, Lewis Capaldi) take the stage in Hyde Park over three weeks. www.bst-hydepark.com.
- **Field Day.** Alternative acts and dance music (The Chemical Brothers, Floating Points, Aphex Twin, DJ Peggy Gou) in South London's Brockwell Park. Late May. www.fielddayfestivals.com.
- **Hampton Court Palace Festival.** High-end names (Lionel Richie, Van Morrison, George Benson, Tom Jones) in a temporary theater on palace grounds. June. www.hamptoncourtpalacefestival.com.
- **Lido.** Created in 2025 and still finding its feet, debut headliners included Charli XCX. June, Victoria Park. www.lidofestival.co.uk.
- **Mighty Hoopla.** Buoyant pop festival headlined by the likes of Lily Allen, Scissor Sisters, and Trixie Mattel. May, Brockwell Park. www.mightyhoopla.com/london.
- **Wireless Festival.** Held alfresco in Finsbury Park for 3 days. Recent years: Drake, Cardi B, Megan Thee Stallion, The Weeknd. https://wirelessfestival.co.uk.

Islington (www.O2academyislington.co.uk); the Art Deco **Eventim Apollo** in Hammersmith (www.eventimapollo.com); the **O_2 Empire Shepherds Bush** (www.O2shepherdsbushempire.co.uk); and the **Electric Ballroom** and **Koko** (see above). In 2026, the 3,800-capacity **British Airways ARC** (www.olympia.co.uk) has been announced to open above the West Exhibition Hall in Olympia, an entertainment complex dating to the 1880s. The most massive venues—where your favorite artist will look like a tiny, bouncing smudge on the far side of an ocean of sweaty fans—include the **London Stadium** (www.london-stadium.com), originally the main Olympics stadium but now an occasional concert venue. **OVO Arena Wembley** (www.ovoarena.co.uk), which began life in 1935 as the Empire Pool, is the city's second-largest indoor arena and has hosted everyone from ABBA to Led Zeppelin to the Beatles. Finally, there's **Wembley Stadium** (www.wembleystadium.com) the site of many an iconic event in its several incarnations, from speeches by the Pope and Nelson Mandela to Live Aid to tell-your-grandchildren concerts by Queen, the Spice Girls, Madonna, Adele, and Taylor Swift.

The O_2 The £789-million boondoggle on the Thames in East London is a dome 10 times the volume of St Paul's. It's where gargantuan acts from Dolly to Gaga to Kylie to Monty Python appear, packing in their own religious followings, in a 20,000-place arena (ladies, there are 550 toilets for you, too) fringed by a mall for food and clubs. Michael Jackson was in rehearsal for a concert series for the O_2 when he died. For those not keen to see their favorite artist reduced to a speck on a distant platform, there's O_2's "intimate" performance space, **Indigo at the O_2** (✆ **020/8463-2700**), although even that is still plenty big, with 2,800 places. An acoustically superior, contemporary room, it has four bars, and attracts comics and talent (the late Prince, Black Eyed Peas) and specialty acts. If you aren't carrying a ticket for a show, there's not much eat that isn't from chains—there are some boring "outlet" shops and kitschy diversions like bowling and indoor skydiving—but if you need something more jolting, you can climb above it, at the **Up at the O_2** roof-walking attraction (p. 202). Thames Clippers (p. 367) docks here, too. Peninsula Square, London, SE10. www.theo2.co.uk. ✆ **020/8463-2000.** Tube and ferry: North Greenwich.

The O_2 arena can hold up to 20,000 concertgoers.

Clubs

The city's dance scene, being embedded in the style scene, is various and shifting, and by the time you read this, the variety will have shifted again. Sadly, this is not down to shifting cultural trends of self-expression, but to runaway real estate investment. Spaces are discovered, celebrated, and then redeveloped in the space of a few short years. The social distancing demands of Covid-19 crippled the club scene, its recovery could not fully reclaim old glories, and some of the best nightlife venues are still being picked off one by one—goodbye Printworks, farewell Corsica Studios; we'll see you in the old memes. Aside from club nights at the venues listed above (see "Live Music," p. 277), the best source for tips on remaining parties is ***Time Out*** (www.timeout.com/london/clubs). The clubs around Shoreditch, Old Street, and King's Cross were until recently the markers of cool, but gentrification squeezed

THE illuminated RIVER

In London, even the river views have been taught to perform. In 2021, private donors sank more than £31 million into a project called **The Illuminated River** (illuminatedriver.london/), which lights up the bridges in central London, from Lambeth to St Paul's, with an atmospheric and slow-changing light show by New York–based artist Leo Villareal. It's not the kind of display that prances and dazzles, but one that changes gradually over the hours, inviting you to stop, pay attention to the slow-rolling sequence, and come away with a sense of beauty and gratitude that someone cared enough to bring beauty to your nighttime promenade.

some of the scene northeast to Dalston, which makes getting home in the middle of the night expensive—freelance cabbies charge double. Covers nudge toward £20. Most other places in this section are accessible to the Night Tube.

The king of clubs remains **Fabric** (77a Charterhouse St., EC1; www.fabriclondon.com; ✆ **020/7336-8898;** Tube: Farringdon or Barbican), a former butchery that sets a world standard. Its all-weekend parties (from Sat 10pm 'til the cock crows on Mon) are engineered to drill teeth-chattering bass frequencies into the souls of those who dare to submit. Buy early to pay as little as £10. The City is not lost to the nerds yet; the pedigreed managers of **XOYO** (32–37 Cowper St., EC2; www.xoyo.co.uk; ✆ **020/7729-5959;** Tube: Old Street) turned a former printworks into a stripped-down sound tank, and succeeded. The **Ministry of Sound** (103 Gaunt St., SE1; www.ministryofsound.com; ✆ **020/7740-8600;** Tube: Elephant & Castle), which began spinning in 1991, when cavernous and humanity-stuffed dance spaces were the vogue, is known around the planet for its top-notch sound system, upper-crust DJs, and extreme cover charges in the low £30s if you wait until the door. The 15,000-capacity **Drumsheds** (6 Glover Dr., N18; drumshedslondon.com; ✆ 020/3834-3416; National Rail: Meridian Water) mounts titanic light shows with organ-shifting beats in the vast warehouses of a disused IKEA, and **Exhibition White City** (Ariel Way, W12; exhibitionwhitecity.com/; ✆ **020/8498-4937;** Tube: Wood Lane or White City) brings 2,800 bodies together in a Victorian power house for semi-regular event club nights and EDM events. In 2026, a former Jones and Higgins department store from 1867 will reopen as the **Peckham Palace** (1A Rye Lane, SE15; palais.co.uk; Tube: Peckham Rye) for South London house and techno nights as well as nostalgia throwback nights.

93 Feet East (150 Brick Lane, E1; www.93feeteast.co.uk; ✆ **020/7770-6006;** Tube: Liverpool Street or Shoreditch High Street) was one of the first pioneers to reclaim disused industrial space in Spitalfields; it mounts a mix of experimental electronic music, live bands, house, and day parties. World-class DJs head to **Phonox** (418 Brixton Rd., SW9; www.phonox.co.uk; ✆ **020/7095-9411;** Tube: Brixton), which starts as a bar but opens into an all-night event. It's so carefully produced that smartphone use is banned on the dance floor. **The Social** (5 Little Portland St. ✆ **07939/651-255**. thesocial.com. Tickets free–£15. Tube: Oxford Circus), a tiny bar/club with an easygoing, age-mixed clientele, is more about a good time than innovative sounds. Otherwise, wander Dalston and its environs for cutting-edge venues and basement clubs. The **Dalston Superstore** (117 Kingsland High St., E8; www.dalstonsuperstore.com; ✆ **020/7254-2273;** Dalston Kingsland Overground) is a pansexual party mix of DJs, disco, and ravey go-go boys.

COMEDY CLUBS

You may be surprised to learn that London's comedy scene is dominated by Edinburgh's. Each August in the Scottish capital, seemingly all of Britain attends the city's famous festival season, where sharp minds vie for awards, audiences, and perversely, that shiniest of brass rings, a major London booking. The rest of the year, it seems that half the stages in town are either helping artists groom material for Edinburgh (June and July schedules are packed with new shows) or cashing in on past successes in Scotland. The fevered competition has created a comedy scene that has less in common with the stand-and-discuss neuroses of New York clubs and more to do with brittle high concepts that tickle university graduates. You may miss a few local references, but you're sure to appreciate the wit.

All comedy venues serve food and alcohol (so kids 17 and under may not be allowed), and tickets are almost always under £10 unless it's a big name or a very central location. Main shows are usually at 7:30 or 8pm. The tiny **Angel Comedy Club** (2 Camden Walk, N1; www.angelcomedy.co.uk; no phone; Tube: Angel), even though it's in the back of the Camden Head pub, is (legit) one of the best places in town to catch smart up-and-comers, and it's (legit) free to enter; just get there by 7pm on weekends (shows start daily at 8pm; no parties larger than 4 people) to avoid being shut out. It's on the upswing and, as a consequence, added a second space nearby, which it named **The Bill Murray** (39 Queen's Head St., N1). The cluttered, 60-seat **Canal Café Theatre** (The Bridge House, Delamere Terrace, W2; www.canalcafetheatre.com; ✆ **020/7289-6054;** Tube: Warwick Avenue) puts on a dozen shows a week; its biggest draw is "NewsRevue" (Thurs–Sat), a weekly send-up of current events running since 1979, which gives it a Guinness World Record for longest theatrical run of a comedy. And it's funny—comedy news commentary being a booming genre in U.K. television.

The unassuming entrance to Pleasance Theatre Islington, which is located in a former wood warehouse.

The 400-seat **Comedy Store** (1a Oxendon St., SW1; www.thecomedystore.co.uk; ✆ **0844/871-7699;** £18–£25; Tube: Leicester Square or Piccadilly Circus) was created in 1979 in imitation of clubs popular in New York; it launched both Eddie Izzard and Jennifer Saunders. Today it presents improv on Sunday, a rough-and-tumble open mic night on the last Monday of the month, and mainstream stand-up sets the other nights of the week.

In a former wood warehouse 20 minutes from the center of town, **Pleasance Theatre Islington** (Carpenters Mews, North Rd., N7; www.pleasance.co.uk; ✆ **020/7609-1800;**

Tube: Caledonian Road) has stronger ties than most venues have to Edinburgh; it operates the Scottish festival's chief comedy hub, and it starts previewing entrants in the spring for as little as £5. This is where a headline-making satirical show about Gwyneth Paltrow's ski accident played in late 2023.

The monumental **Clapham Grand** (21–25 St John's Hill, SW11. clapham grand.com. ✆ **020/7223-6523.** National rail: Clapham Junction) opened as a multi-tiered variety hall in 1900 and it's still one of London's best venues for variety. Bookings skew young, from drag superstars to club nights to "drink-alongs" of cult movies like *Love, Actually* to comedy bookings of well-known British talent.

CINEMA

Because so many handsome old cinemas have survived around town, movie-going can still feel like a grand event. In most, you can enjoy a beer and even select your seats when you buy your ticket—London was doing that long before America was. For quality revival screenings, don't miss the landmark **Prince Charles Cinema** (p. 277).

Major movie premieres attended by major movie stars are routinely held at a handful of giant cinemas around Leicester Square. Chief among them is the **Odeon Luxe** (24–26 Leicester Square, WC2; www.odeon.co.uk; ✆ **087/1224-4007;** Tube: Leicester Square), opened in 1937 and intensely renovated to replace the traditional setup with push-button recliners and top-form audio systems. It's the largest cinema in the country. **The Odeon Luxe West End** is an overflow house of 168 seats in a soundproofed box in the basement of the Londoner hotel, on the south side of Leicester Square. But tickets for Leicester Square theatres can cost over £20 at peak times (it's cheaper in the afternoon). The **Everyman** chain (www.everymancinema.com; multiple locations around London) serves food and drink and schedules a mix of new films, revivals, and live broadcast events in screening room-sized cinemas. More London cinema chains for mostly first-run film: **Curzon** (www.curzon.com) and **Picturehouse** (www.picturehouses.com), both of which often screen in revitalized vintage theatres.

BFI Southbank ♥♥♥ The programming of the British Film Institute (BFI)—a world leader in film restoration, preservation, and exhibition—is mind-bogglingly broad and savvy, from classics to mainstream to historic—more than 1,000 titles a year, many of them treasures selected from its deep archives. On a single day, its four main screens might unspool a retrospective of Indian director Satyajit Ray, Alfred Hitchcock's *Dial M for Murder* in 3D, a mid-20th-century series from the largely forgotten Boulting brothers, and outdoor screenings of Gothic monster schlock. The BFI can handle nearly every type of print in existence; it's the only place in the country equipped to project historic nitrate stock prints, and to fortify its consequential position in the cinematic art form, it programs plenty of talks, special previews, and the occasional free screening. The on-premises **Mediatheque** (Tues–Sun 11am–9pm) is a free video arcade for on-demand viewing of the BFI archive, including tons of titles you'd never see abroad because of rights issues. The shop (daily noon–8pm) stocks an incomparable list of rare films, including many treasures the BFI has restored and re-released ones you can only find here. Or just hang out at its two popular bars, one in the lobby and one on the water. Belvedere Rd., South Bank, SE1. whatson.bfi.org.uk. ✆ **020/7255-1444.** Tube: Waterloo.

Each seat at The Electric Cinema comes with a footstool, table, and a wine basket.

The Electric Cinema ♥♥♥ It's one of the world's great screens: Leather seats are softer and deeper than anything you have at home, and each one is equipped with a footstool, table, and a wine basket—it's a luxurious, romantic way to pass a few hours. The bar in the back of the house sells everything from crudités to booze, and downstairs is a barrel-roofed diner. Meanwhile, films, which change daily, hop between first-run and well-received art house movies—nothing too obscure. Shockingly, this place stood derelict from 1993 to 2001, and only a fierce campaign saved it. Now it's run by the exclusive Soho House, which opened a private club here and replaced some seats with bookable beds and sofas. 191 Portobello Rd., W11. www.electriccinema.co.uk. ✆ **020/7908-9696.** Tube: Ladbroke Grove or Notting Hill Gate. No cash.

Phoenix Cinema ♥ Thought to be the oldest purpose-built cinema in the U.K., the Phoenix was constructed as the Premier Electric Theatre in 1910; by 1985, despite its handsome Edwardian barrel-vault ceiling, it was nose-to-nose with the wrecker's ball until fans (including director Mike Leigh) rallied. It screens an immense range of films from across eras and borders, plus frequent transmissions of live performances. It also has a liquor license. 52 High Rd., East Finchley, N2. www.phoenixcinema.co.uk. ✆ **020/8444-6789.** Tube: East Finchley.

COCKTAIL LOUNGES

London is no longer dominated by ales. The cocktailing is so spectacular that you could happily remain tipsy for your entire stay—if only most bars didn't kick everyone out before midnight. You'll find some of the best and most famous hotel bars on earth here, be it **The American Bar** at the Savoy (p. 67); or the bar said to have inspired James Bond's beverage choice at **Dukes** (p. 57); an Art Deco jewel box at **Claridges** (p. 62); or the bar at Mayfair's **The Connaught** hotel (Carlos Place, W1; www.the-connaught.co.uk;

Mon–Sat 4pm–1am; Tube: Bond Street), which routinely scales the heights of the World's 50 Best Bars list. To participate in an especially long tipple tradition, **Donovan Bar** at Brown's Hotel (p. 67), has been serving since the 1830s, and Victoria used to have tea in the adjoining paneled room. A good martini can easily scrape £30 at those world-class institutions, but it'll be *damn* good. Foolishly, the London Hilton on Park Lane recently tore out Trader Vic's, one of the world's largest and most celebrated tiki bars, after an iconic 60-year run.

But there are plenty of other bars playing at a modern world-class level. The workshop-bare **Tayēr + Elementary** (152 Old Street, EC1; tayer-elementary.com; Thurs–Sat 8pm–1am; walk-ins only; Tube: Old Street) has consistently ranked among the planet's top achievers in mixology (although in our view, its signature One Sip Martini, just 63 calories, does more to spotlight the olive farmer than mixing prowess). Some critics have called **Lyaness** (lyaness.com; ✆ **020/3747-1063;** Tube: Blackfriars or Southwark), facing St Paul's Cathedral across the river in the Sea Containers hotel (p. 71), the best bar in the world. That's also been said about the Italian-themed **Bar Termini** (http://bar-termini-soho.com; ✆ **078/6094-5018;** Tube: Leicester Square) and the moody **Swift** (www.barswift.com; ✆ **020/7437-7820;** Tube: Leicester Square), which are just doors away from each other at 7 and 12 Old Compton St., W1, respectively. Swift also opened locations in Shoreditch (91–93 Great Eastern St., EC2; Tube: Old Street) and near Borough Market (66 Borough High St., SE1; Tube: London Bridge). For a reserved and mellow environment, book ahead at the speakeasy-style **Discount Suit Company** (29A Wentworth St., E1; discountsuitcompany.co.uk ✆ **020/7247-8755**; Tube: Aldgate East), in former tailor's stockroom, where the menu is classic and well-conceived and the award-winning drinks are affordable (around £10).

You don't have to take your imbibing so seriously, though. First, there are fun bars atop skyscrapers with a view (see "Tall Orders," p. 108). **Calloo Callay** (65 Rivington St., EC2; www.calloohcallaybar.com; ✆ **020/7739-4781**; Tube: Old Street) has been serving high-quality but adventurous quaffs to Shoreditch's younger crowd in its cheerfully mismatched drinking warren since 2008. And what could be more local than a love of football (soccer)? **Bar Kick** (127 Shoreditch High St., E1; www.urbanpubsandbars.com; ✆ 020/7739-8700; Tube: Shoreditch High Street) brings cocktails and footy together, and is a great place to catch matches on its multitude of screens.

Novelty cocktail bars, which celebrate the analog proficiency of a handmade cocktail by pretending the bar is set in another era, have also risen to become an important category. Drink prices are in the upper teens. My favorite is **Cahoots Underground** (13 Kingly Court, W1; www.cahoots-london.com; ✆ **020/7352-6200;** reservations essential Tube: Oxford Circus), a cocktail bar themed to the London Underground that opens at 4pm on most days. In the 1940s, and during the Blitz, from the looks of it. It's amusingly detailed (the menu is a newspaper, there are announcements in the toilets), and every concoction comes with a unique presentation such as a collectible mug shaped like Queen Elizabeth's head. Book ahead, and if possible, get a seat in the vintage Tube carriage. (If you can't get in, **Cahoots Ticket Hall**, steps away, is easier to get into and it's open for lunch, and its **Cahoots Postal Office** (18 Stoney St., SE1; Tube: London Bridge) near Borough Market does a similarly transporting schtick on a wartime postal theme.

There are also 11 variations of the Victoriana/steampunk cocktailerie **Mr Fogg's** (www.mr-foggs.com), and while some of them only open after 4pm, all of them are meticulously detailed evocations of the various haunts of a fictional Victorian explorer named Phileas J. Fogg, who has a complex backstory that informs each space a little differently. Each is embellished with 19th-century-inspired cocktails served in rococo and arcane settings of antique furniture, scientific collections, staff in waistcoats and the occasional top hat, and sepia-toned decor Jules Verne might have loved—but the music and lively customers are more current. You can imbibe in his elegant Mayfair townhouse (**Mr Fogg's Residence**, 15 Bruton Lane, W1; Tube: Green Park), in his half-brother's hock shop (**Mr Fogg's Pawnbrokers**, 50 Dean St., W1; Tube: Leicester Square), or his cozy upstairs **Gin Parlour** (1 New Row, WC2; Tube: Leicester Square). Probably my favorite is **Mr Fogg's Society of Exploration** (1a Bedford St., WC2; Mon–Fri 4:01pm–12:01am, Sat 1:01pm–12:01am, Sun 4:01–11:01pm; Tube: Charing Cross), which is set apart by a giant, rotating cocktail-making contraption that mixes Negronis on command.

GAY & LESBIAN

London's gay and lesbian bar scene is contracting. In 2015 came the unthinkable closure of Camden's half-century-old drag landmark The Black Cap (a rebirth is planned for 2026), and several important Soho bars including Madame Jojo's, Molly Moggs, and G-A-Y have been forced out or have been sold. Nevertheless, the city still has one of the more varied scenes in the world. The music seems to crank a few notches louder when the jolly and outrageous **Pride London** (www.prideinlondon.org) season rolls along, in early summer.

Daily gay-oriented pursuits were traditionally centered around Soho, where the bars and clubs took on a festive, anyone-is-welcome flair, and after work, guys spilled into the streets. But as a mark of a truly integrated city, now nearly every neighborhood has its own pubs and gay nights. Where you spend an evening depends on your proclivities and willingness to commute. At most places, there aren't usually cover charges unless an event or show is on, when they're about £5 at bars and £11 for clubs. Lesbians who want to go out at night must usually plan a little because most girls' events take the form of weekly scheduled nights in bars that might cater to other niches during the rest of the week.

DirtyBoyz (dirtyboyz.org/) and **QX Magazine** (www.qxmagazine.com) publish schedules that favor club events. *Time Out* also has a weekly "Gay and Lesbian" section that dwells more on clubbing than on well-rounded pursuits, and **Nonchalant** (www.nonchalantmagazine.com) is a lesbian publication that dips into London nightlife and lifestyle stories alike. **Lick** (www.everythinglick.com) schedules nightlife events for a lesbian and nonbinary crowd at a variety of venues.

There are many smaller venues, but these standouts in every flavor are welcoming to tourists and will provide a good overview of the culture.

Comptons is one of Soho's oldest gay bars.

Comptons ♥♥ This old two-level pub (built in 1890 as The Swiss Hotel) wears the tatty garb of a bygone saloon but it's one of Soho's oldest hangouts for men who are well out of their bubble-gum years. **Admiral Duncan,** across the street, and the **Duke of Wellington** ("Duke of Welly's"), where Old Compton Street T-bones into Wardour Street a few steps west, cater to the same professional age group, and it's not uncommon for punters to careen between all three. 51–53 Old Compton St., W1. www.comptonsofsoho.co.uk. ✆ **020/7096-5470.** Tube: Piccadilly Circus.

Bethnal Green Working Men's Club ♥♥ Serving drag, quiz nights, and cabaret hosted by an unmoored Mariah Carey spoof performer—that's the sort of louche and camp mayhem this straight-friendly joint presents. It varies per night (check the theme ahead of time) but it's always perfectly messy, yet the crowd is respectful to all kinds of guests. 42–44 Pollard Row, E2. www.workersplaytime.net. ✆ **020/7739-7170.** Cover £10. Tube: Bethnal Green.

Eagle ♥ No longer sullied by the dank cruise bar status it once shared with other Eagles worldwide, it's been brightened up and scrubbed down, and now it's a club with a beer garden that's more about celebrating queerness than worshipping leather. Sunday night's Horse Meat Disco is long-running, fun, and welcoming. 349 Kennington Lane, SE11. www.eaglelondon.com. ✆ **020/7793-0903.** Wed–Sun. Tube: Vauxhall.

Heaven ♥♥ Heaven came to Earth in 1979, when this history-making club took over an old roller disco near Charing Cross Station. Ambient house music was born here, London's modern LGBT+ culture was formed in its crucible, and no other dance club in Europe, gay or straight, can touch it for attracting such a pantheon of legendary live performances: Kylie, Miley, the Spice Girls, Adele, Bjork, Lady Gaga, and, of course, Madge, all made pilgrimages here and have been known to return impromptu. Mondays are Popcorn (student night); Tuesdays are for current pop; Thursdays are Porn Idol, a long-running and tongue-in-cheek amateur strip contest judged in part by a major drag queen who returns to perform on Saturday; Fridays are Camp Attack, a dance night institution. Kids aren't drinking and drugging the way Freddie Mercury used to do here, and rumors persist that the end is near for this relic from the heyday of megaclubs, but the city has acknowledged its value and it does what it can to help it endure. Put on your wings and fly here while you still can. Under the Arches, Villiers St., WC2. g-a-yandheaven.co.uk/. 7 nights a week. Ages 14 and over. Tube: Charing Cross or Embankment.

Ku Bar ♥♥ A manageably sized, young-skewing, three-level lounge is the place you go when you don't want a scene but you wouldn't mind being served by shirtless boys. It has a later license: until 3am Monday to Saturday, and on Fridays, it hosts She Soho, a lesbian night that made a home here after giving up its regular space nearby. 30 Lisle and 25 Frith sts., WC2. www.ku-bar.co.uk. ✆ **020/7437-4303.** Tube: Leicester Square.

Retro Bar ♥♥ Tucked down a side alley off Strand, this cozy boozer, which is festooned with '80s-derived pop culture posters and plays a nostalgic poppy soundtrack to match, is a low-key place to sit and chat with friends, including straight friends. 2 George Court, WC2. www.retrobarlondon.co.uk/london. ✆ **020/7839-8760.** Tube: Charing Cross.

Royal Vauxhall Tavern ♥♥♥ A 2013 biography revealed that Diana, Princess of Wales, once secretly attended this gay drag landmark dressed as a man. Two years later, it became the first U.K. building to gain protection for its status as an LGBTQ landmark. Inside, anything still goes. Whether it's club nights, cabaret nights, drag nights, or just dancing, when the party's thumping, this little brick building from the 1860s literally leaks dance-floor fog. 372 Kennington Lane, SE11. www.vauxhalltavern.com. ✆ **020/7820-1222.** Tube: Vauxhall.

The Two Brewers ♥♥ As drag rises in global popularity, the role of this casual, friendly High Street pub as a major hub for mainstream cabaret acts has likewise strengthened. But its weekend dance parties also bring the boys. It has been a mainstay since 1981. 114 Clapham High St., SW4. www.the2brewers.com. ✆ **020/7819-9539.** Tube: Clapham Common.

The Yard ♥♥ On weekends, all the cute jock types are here, cramming the pretty courtyard-like duplex space. Weekdays, it's more subdued and a place for the after-work crowd, but it's always straight-friendly. Developers are licking their chops over the space. 57 Rupert St., W1 www.yardbar.co.uk. ✆ **020/7437-2652.** Tube: Piccadilly Circus.

WALKING TOURS OF LONDON

8

Paying for a bus tour might seem smart in principle, but you'll glimpse monuments only briefly and hear only one or two eye-glazing facts about them as you whiz past. No coach tour convinces you that the things you're seeing are quite real, or allows you to mull over what's before you, or lets you breathe in the atmosphere. Get close to London. Don't pass it. Touch it—so that it can touch you.

WALKING TOUR 1: WESTMINSTER, WHITEHALL & TRAFALGAR SQUARE

START:	**Westminster Tube station**
FINISH:	**Trafalgar Square**
TIME:	**Allow 60 minutes, not including time spent in attractions**
BEST TIME:	**Be at the starting line just before noon to hear Big Ben deliver its longest chime of the day**
WORST TIME:	**After working hours, when energy drains out of the area**

When most people hear the word "London," this is the area they picture: the Houses of Parliament, the wash of the Thames, the gong of Big Ben, and the Georgian facade of No. 10 Downing St. Kings and queens, prime ministers and executioners, despots and assassins—this is where they converged to shape a millennium of events, at the command center for England and the British Empire. History buffs, lace up.

1 Westminster Tube Station

The best train to take here is the Jubilee line, which was added at great expense in 1999. The station's concrete-grey, 36m-deep (118-ft.) cavern, ascended by escalators from the Jubilee's platforms, is one of the city's finest newer spaces, providing a modern-day analog to the majestic space of Westminster Abbey nearby. Portcullis House, where many MPs (Members of Parliament) keep offices, is overhead.

Find your way to the Westminster Underground station, Exit 1, and walk outside.

2 Victoria Embankment at Westminster Bridge

Once you're outside, you'll see the River Thames. If you stood here in 1858, in the midst of what came to be known as The Great Stink, you'd have choked on the fumes rising from the fetid effluvia floating in the river below. Until then, the city had no sewers to speak of—only pipes that dumped into the water. The solution was the Victoria Embankment, a daring engineering project, completed in 1870, that saved engineers from having to dig up the whole city. They simply built a new riverbank, laid sewers along it, paired that with new Underground railway tracks, and topped the unattractive additions with a garden and a road. Destructive, but effective—how Victorian.

Today, the Embankment has benches that are raised to allow a good view of the water, and it's dotted with triumphant statuary like Boudicca in her bladed chariot, which you can also see from here. This tribal queen rose up against the Romans; she failed politically but, as you see, succeeded aesthetically.

The London Eye, spinning on the opposite bank, had a tricky birth in 1999; it was constructed lying flat over the river, resting on pontoons, and then it was laboriously hoisted upright and into place. The mock-baroque building behind it is County Hall—it looks old, but it only dates to the early 20th century—which was once the seat of the London city government.

At the bridge's opposite landing, you can see the South Bank Lion. Weighing 14 tons, 3.6m (12 ft.) tall, and as eager-eyed and floppy-pawed as a puppy, he was carved in 1837 by the Coade Stone Factory, which once stood where County Hall stands today. Made of a durable, synthetic ceramic stone formulated by a mother-daughter team, the lion stood proudly for over a century, painted red, atop the Red Lion Brewery that was located past the London Eye. Blitz bomb damage destroyed his

The Victoria Embankment, a historic engineering feat, is a place for gardens, strolling, and glorious Thames views.

Walking Tour 1: Westminster, Whitehall & Trafalgar Square

roost, but at the request of King George VI, he was saved and placed just feet from his birthplace.

Go back into Westminster station, head down the corridor, and turn left before the set of four stairs. Leave the station via Exit 3, marked Houses of Parliament.

3 The Palace of Westminster

You're now standing under the iconic Elizabeth Tower of the Houses of Parliament, once called St Stephen's Tower but renamed in 2012 in honor of QE2's Diamond Jubilee. This is as close as you can get to it—it stands in a restricted area. Look up: Assorted crowns, kings, and crests are carved into the facade. These buildings may look like they're from the Gothic period, but in fact they date to 1859, when they rose from the ashes of the old Parliament House, destroyed by a nightmarish fire in 1834. Big Ben, the name of the largest of four bells inside (2.7m/9 ft. in diameter, 13 tons), was named for the portly commissioner of works who oversaw its installation. (There's actually a bigger bell in town: Great Paul at St Paul's is 2 tons heavier.) Each side of the Clock Tower's four faces is 6.9m (23 ft.) long. Since 1923, the very earliest days of wireless, the BBC has broadcast the 16-note prelude (called "Westminster Quarters" and replicated in doorbells around the world) of Big Ben before its news summaries. Thanks to a crack that developed in the 1860s, the bell is now slightly off from its original note—E above middle C. This Big Ben is truly a ringer; the first Big Ben actually cracked within 3 months after being struck by bad hammers. A slightly smaller version was recast by the Whitechapel Bell Foundry which, 107 years earlier, made America's Liberty Bell, which also cracked. Apparently, that happened a lot to big bells and it didn't affect business. But what cracked bells couldn't kill, gentrification did: After 450 years of bell-making and 250 years in Whitechapel, the foundry finally shuttered forever in May 2017.

This plot of land has been used by royals since 1050, when Edward the Confessor built a palace here, away from the hubbub of the walled city. Kings ceased living on this block as of Henry VIII, when nearby Whitehall became his main London pad, followed in later reigns by St James's and, then, Buckingham palaces. But Parliament's land is nationally owned, so technically it meets in Westminster Palace.

Head away from the river to:

4 Parliament Square

The heavy metal bars on the spiked fence that distances you from this building are not there out of mere paranoia; as far back as the thwarted Gunpowder Plot of 1605, the Houses of Parliament have been a target for would-be revolutionaries. Prime Minister Spencer Perceval was fatally shot on the steps of the House of Commons by a former convict on May 11, 1812, and in the Blitz, the buildings were smashed on more than a dozen occasions, including one (May 10, 1941) that caused the near-total destruction of the House of Commons.

Few panoramas are as iconic as that of Big Ben's tower and the Palace of Westminster.

The section of the Houses that juts into the yards, behind the statue of Oliver Cromwell, is Westminster Hall, from 1097, one of the only survivors from the 1834 fire. Charles I, Sir Thomas More, and Guy Fawkes were all condemned to death in the Hall. Big Ben's tower completed a renovation in 2022; the entire Parliament complex has been called a firetrap and is commencing a massive refurbishment.

For more on visiting the **Houses of Parliament,** see p. 157.

Turn left and walk in front of the Houses of Parliament. Use the first crosswalk to your right, heading toward the church. At the far side of the church, enter the gate to see:

5 St Margaret's Church

The little side church by Westminster Abbey (p. 161), the one with the four sundials on its tower, is the Church of Saint Margaret, dating to the early 1500s and much changed over the years. Sir Walter Raleigh, who was executed outside the Palace of Westminster, is buried inside, and both the poet Milton and Winston Churchill married their wives here.

You can see the statues of Parliament Square better from here. Probably the most famous one is that of American president Abraham Lincoln, at the western end; it's a copy of one in Chicago by Augustus Saint-Gaudens. During the anti-capitalist protests of 2000, the statue of Winston Churchill that stands here received a temporary Mohawk made of grassy turf. This square has always attracted well-intentioned goofs: In 1868, the world's first traffic light was erected here. Gas powered, it blew up.

Follow the footpath to the front of:

6 Westminster Abbey

The lawn beside the abbey—yes, the one you just walked across—is in fact a disused graveyard. In a city this old, you simply can't avoid treading on final resting places. There are an unknown number of plague pits scattered through the city, into which thousands of victims were hastily dumped to avoid the spread of disease, and several city parks likely had the germ of their beginnings, so to speak, as potter's fields—group graves for paupers.

Although most of the Abbey is in the Early English style, the stern western towers above you now were the 18th-century work of Nicholas Hawksmoor, a protégé of Christopher Wren. Hawksmoor's designs are famous for emphasizing the forbidding, angry side of God; some critics accuse him of using architecture to frighten people into piety. Most of the time the people who use this main entrance in an official capacity do so in a crown, a gown, or a coffin. For more on visiting **Westminster Abbey,** see p. 161.

If you peer down Broad Sanctuary, which becomes Victoria Street, you can see the Italianate tower of Westminster Cathedral, the primary Roman Catholic cathedral of England. Good news, Catholics: The English don't execute you anymore!

Cross the street to your right (Broad Sanctuary), and cross again. You should be a block west of Parliament Square on Storey's Gate now. Walk straight until you find yourself at the corner of St James's Park. You're at:

7 Birdcage Walk

You've just walked past a variety of government offices; the proximity to the Houses of Parliament has appealed to paper-pushers for centuries. The military has a presence here, too. The road that heads to the left, Birdcage Walk, leads to the front of Buckingham Palace. Halfway down, you'll find the Wellington Barracks, the headquarters of the Guards Division, where a battalion of one of the king's five regiments of foot guards (Grenadier, Coldstream, Scots, Irish, and Welsh) bunks down. There's also a small, curio-packed Guards Museum (www.theguardsmuseum.com; ✆ **020/7414-3271;** daily 10am–4pm; £10), where you learn that their tall "busby" helmets are made of Canadian brown bearskin. Who knew?

Storey's Gate, the street you just walked, was named for the keeper of Charles II's aviary. Birdcage Walk, the street you're now on, was named after a royal aviary that stood in St James's Park; until 1928, only the Hereditary Royal Falconer was permitted to drive on Birdcage Walk. The park continues its tradition of hosting bird menageries; the pond is a haven for ducks and geese, and a small flock of pelicans has been in residence since the 1600s. They are fed fresh fish daily at 2:30pm (when avian flu is circulating, it happens out of view).

Cross Birdcage Walk and walk 1 block up Horse Guards Road, passing the Treasury Building on your right, until you reach Clive Steps at King Charles Street on the right. On your left, peek into:

8 St James's Park

See if you can spot the lake in the park. The body of water was originally a formal canal belonging to St James's Palace, the official royal residence from the burning of Whitehall in 1698 to the time Victoria moved into Buckingham Palace in 1837. The old canal was prim and straight in the

Hardly a saint, King Henry VIII gets a stained-glass window in Westminster Abbey for being a founder of the Church of England.

French style and outfitted with gondolas, a gift of the Doge of Venice. In winter, as Samuel Pepys described in the 1600s, it would freeze over, and people would frolic upon it using skates made of bone. It was later sculpted into something calculated to appear more random and thus more English. St James's Palace, which is not open to the public, is located on the north (far) side of the park. You might be able to make out a rustic-looking shack just inside the park. That's Duck Island Cottage, built in 1840 as a dwelling for the bird keeper. Not shabby for a servant's quarters.

You'd think that if London were under attack from flying bombers that you'd be much safer if you were a little farther from the Houses of Parliament. Yet in the basement of the sturdy 1907 Treasury Building, Britain's leaders orchestrated their country's "finest hour." Unbeknownst to the world, it was the hideout of Winston Churchill and his cabinet, known as the Cabinet War Rooms. Famously, but hardly wisely, that daredevil Churchill went onto the roof of the building so he could watch one of Goering's air raids slam the city. The cellar, preserved down to its typing pool and pushpins, is now the **Churchill War Rooms** (p. 156), a superlative museum paying homage to the bulldoggy prime minister.

Who is Robert Clive, the cutlass-wielding subject of this statue on the steps? He was the general who helped the East India Company conquer India and Bengal, partly through a series of underhanded bribes, thus delivering the region into the control of the British Empire for nearly 2 centuries. Don't be too hard on this hardened colonialist; the opium-addicted fellow committed suicide by stabbing himself with a penknife.

Walk down King Charles Street and through the arches at the end. You are now on Parliament Street. Look into the center of it. The somber stone column in the traffic island is:

9 The Cenotaph

The Cenotaph (from the Greek words for "empty" and "tomb") is a simple but elegiac memorial to those killed in the two World Wars and later conflicts. A 1919 plaster parade prop that was made permanent in stone by Edwin Lutyens the next year, it was executed with inconceivable restraint when you consider that nearly a million British subjects died in the Great War alone. Its inscription to the "Glorious Dead," coined by Rudyard Kipling, is repeated on other memorials in Commonwealth nations; the Cenotaphs in Auckland, New Zealand, and in London, Canada,

The Cenotaph war memorial and landmark near Downing Street in Whitehall.

are replicas. Uniformed servicemen and -women will always salute it as they pass, and on the Sunday closest to November 11, Britain's Remembrance Day, the sovereign lays the first wreath while other members of the Royal Family observe from the balcony of the Foreign Office. You may see flowers around it, or possibly silk poppies, the national symbol of remembrance.

Walk left up Parliament Street, which becomes Whitehall. In about 30m (98 ft.) on the left, you reach a black fence with glass lanterns. Look inside the gates. This is:

10 Downing Street

On the right, by the tree and tough to make out, is No. 10, the official home of the prime minister. It's famous for its lion's head knocker—although to be frank, if you have to knock, you aren't welcome. Once, you could walk around in there, but Margaret Thatcher made many enemies, so you'll have to make do with peering down the lane through metal bars. Such security was a long time coming. In 1842, a lunatic shot and killed the secretary to the prime minister, mistaking him for the big man; and in 1912, suffragette Emmeline Pankhurst and friends pelted the house with stones, breaking four windows, in one of many acts of civil disobedience in the fight for voting rights for women. If sentries prevent you from approaching, then the prime minister might be on the move. Prepare for the black gates to burst open, spew forth an armada of cars, and watch the prime minister's vehicle blast onto Whitehall as if fleeing a bank heist.

The lane was laid out by George Downing, the second man to graduate from Harvard University in America and by all accounts a shady individual, a turncoat, and a slumlord. He's one of history's great scoundrels; his underhanded dealings resulted in Dutch-held Manhattan being swiped by the British and the slave trade multiplying in the Colonies. Strange that the most important street in British politics should bear his name.

Downing built No. 10 (then, no. 5) as part of a row of terraced houses in the late 1600s, fully intending for it to fall apart after a few years (instead of actually laying bricks, he just painted on lines with mortar). Yet George II had his eye on the house, and he kicked out a man with the tantalizing name of Mr. Chicken—further information about him, to our eternal despair, is lost to the mists of time—to give it as a gift to the first prime minister, Robert Walpole, in 1730. Walpole insisted that the house be used by future First Lords of the Treasury, his official capacity. He also connected it to a grand home behind it on Horse Guards, now nicknamed The House at the Back—this deceptive Georgian facade actually conceals 160 rooms. No. 10 is also connected with nos. 11 and 12, and it's even linked to Buckingham Palace and Q-Whitehall, a sprawling war bunker, by long underground tunnels. Many prime ministers elected to live in their own homes, using No. 10 for meetings, but not William Pitt, who moved in upon becoming prime minister at the virtually pubescent age of 24 in 1783. He lived here for more than 20 years, longer than any other prime minister, until his death at 46. Whitehall became a slum in the mid-1800s, and the house fell out of fashion, but then it served as the nerve center for the two World Wars and became indispensable to the British spirit. You can see the original front door, now replaced by a stronger one, on display at the Churchill Museum at the Churchill War Rooms (p. 156), two stops back.

A little up Whitehall from Downing Street, look for the bronze monument to "The Women of World War II," which depicts no women, but rather their uniforms and hats, hanging on pegs as if they'd been put away after a job well done. The implication of this 6.6m-tall (22-ft.) tableau is, of course, that the women went back to the kitchen after briefly filling a more robust societal role. This sly bit of statuary-as-commentary was unveiled by Queen Elizabeth in 2005. Some 80% of the cost of the memorial was raised by a baroness who won money on ITV's *Who Wants to Be a Millionaire?*

Continue up Whitehall, past the monumental government buildings. In about 60m (200 ft.), you will reach another black gate broken by two stone guardhouses. Head inside the yard to view:

11 Horse Guards

Built in the Palladian style between 1750 and 1758 on a former jousting field of Whitehall Palace, the Horse Guards is the official (but little-used) entrance to the grounds of St James's Palace and Buckingham Palace. Two mounted cavalry troops are posted in the guardhouses every day from 10am to 4pm, and they're changed hourly. At 11am Monday to Saturday and 10am Sunday, the guard on duty is relieved by a dozen members who march in from The Mall behind, accompanied (when the king is in town) by a trumpeter, a standard bearer, and an officer. Don't try to crack up guards with your shenanigans. You'll look boorish and rude—and they still won't react.

If you think the clock tower arch looks small, you're right. Its designer made it that way so that its proportions would match the rest of the building. Walk through the clock tower arch to reach the graveled Horse Guards Parade, the city's largest non-park gathering space, which you may recognize as the setting for volleyball during the 2012 Olympic Games.

Return from the yard to Whitehall. Across the street you'll see:

12 The Banqueting House

Built by Inigo Jones, this is not a home but it is the last remaining portion of the great Whitehall Palace. The Banqueting House closed to daily tourists in 2020, but you can occasionally join scheduled tours (check www.hrp.org.uk/banqueting-house).

Inside is a bombastic ceiling by Rubens depicting the king as a god, commissioned by King Charles I. That vainglorious expenditure, and the king's grabs for more power, led to the gory event that happened on this spot on January 30, 1649. If you were standing here then, you would have been in the crowd that watched King Charles I mount the scaffold (wearing two shirts so that he wouldn't shiver—he was no true god, after all), place his head on the block, and be decapitated, delivering the country to a military dictatorship led by Oliver Cromwell. When the executioner held the head aloft, one witness said there was a queasy silence, followed by "such a groan by the thousands then present, as I never heard before and I desire I may never hear again." Charles I was buried privately at Windsor, not at Westminster Abbey, to avoid more unpleasant scenes. If you want to see what poor Charles looked like alive, hang on for the next stop. The regicide was somewhat for naught; by 1660, the country grew weary of its new leadership and Charles I's son, the hedonistic spendthrift Charles II, was back on daddy's throne. In revenge, the second Charles chose the Banqueting House as the site for his restoration party, and then had the nerve to show up late. England was royal again—and how.

Continue up Whitehall. Take the next right, Great Scotland Yard (the corner of Scotland Place was the "visitor's entrance" of the Ministry of Magic in the Harry Potter movies), and then cross Northumberland Avenue, veer slightly left, and head into Craven Passage.

The Sherlock Holmes

Time for a pint and maybe some traditional English pub grub, so head to **The Sherlock Holmes** (10–11 Northumberland St.). In 1957, a collection of Arthur Conan Doyle memorabilia was assembled as a tourist attraction for the huge Festival of Britain that gave London the Southbank Centre, and it became the centerpiece of this pub. It's nowhere near 221b Baker St., but it has a roof garden and a terrace.

Stop for a pint at the Sherlock Holmes pub near Charing Cross.

Return to Northumberland Avenue and turn right. When you reach Trafalgar Square, cross the street so you're in the oval traffic island.

13 Statue of Charles I

That this bronze statue stands here is a miracle. It's of Charles I, preheadectomy, and is a precious Carolinian original from 1633. When the king was beheaded in 1649, the Royal Family was deposed (permanently, so people thought). The owner of this statue was commanded to destroy it, but he was clever enough to bury it instead. A man named Rivet, a scrapper by both trade and character, made a tidy fortune selling knives and forks that he pretended were made from its metal, but after the Restoration, the statue was dug up and placed here, in about 1675. By then, his customers were too tired to demand refunds. All that happened even before Trafalgar Square existed (the zone was, as an equestrian statue suggests, used as stables). Charles wasn't a tall man, and boosting him with a horse went some way toward making the luckless fellow seem imposing. Someone stole his sword in 1867, and he went into hiding again during the Blitz, but otherwise, this is one of the oldest things in this part of London that remains in its original place. Its pedestal, unloved and weathered, could use a restoration, too.

This is a good spot, free of traffic and obstructions, to survey your surroundings and take some photos. Look back down Whitehall, from where you just came, and you'll see Big Ben's tower. To the right, the vista through Admiralty Arch concludes in the distance with the grand Victoria Memorial and Buckingham Palace. Important buildings for two Commonwealth nations stand astride Trafalgar Square: Canada House to the left (west) and South Africa House to the right (east; its country's name is inscribed in Afrikaans as Suid-Afrika).

Cross again so that you're on the south side of:

14 Nelson's Column & Trafalgar Square

Why is Lord Nelson atop that column? Money. The admiral sacrificed his life in 1805 to defeat Napoleon Bonaparte's naval aspirations at the Battle of Trafalgar, thus securing Britain's dominance over the oceans—and pumping untold wealth into London. In the late 1800s, lightning struck Lord Nelson—or at any rate his statue—damaging his left arm. It took until 2006 for the city to finally eliminate the bronze bands that held him together, repairing him with the same Craigleith sandstone with which he was constructed in 1843. During the work, they realized that the monument is actually 4.8m (16 ft.) shorter than guidebooks had been claiming for generations—it's 51m (167 ft.) from the street to the crown of Nelson's hat. The man himself is 5.5m (18 ft.) tall. The column's base is lined with four bronze reliefs that were said to be cast using metal from French cannon captured at the battle that each one depicts. All are guarded by four huge lions (installed in 1867), the mascots of the square, by Queen Victoria's favorite painter, Edwin Landseer. You might think such animals don't belong here, but in the 1950s, under their noses,

The landmark Nelson's Column in Trafalgar Square.

archaeologists found prehistoric deposits with remains of rhinos, elephants, hippos, and yes, cave lions. Landseer was onto something.

Edwin Lutyens, who did the Cenotaph (p. 300), also designed the plaza's two fountains (from 1845 originals), which were ostensibly for beautification but conveniently prevented citizens from gathering in numbers. Trafalgar Square has long been the setting for demonstrations that have turned from complaint to unrestful, such as infamous riots over poll taxes and unemployment. The English gather here for happy things, too, as they did for the announcement of V-E Day (May 8, 1945), and as they still do for festivals and free summer performances. In the southeast corner, you'll see a stone booth big enough for a single person, built in 1926. Once a closet for a phone that was used to summon backup, now it's used mostly to store chemicals for the fountains.

You may have heard about Trafalgar Square's famous pigeons. So where did they go? Until the early 1990s, the square swarmed with them—vendors sold bird feed and the incessantly excreting flock was estimated to peak at 35,000. Eventually, the GLC, London's government, grew tired of shoveling streaky poo off the statues and decided to return the square to its original function as a great public space to edify its great museum, the National Gallery. They began feeding the pigeons themselves first thing in the morning, and then hired a team of hawks (from the superhero-sounding Hawkforce, tended by a leather-gloved keeper) to patrol the square. The pigeons learned to clear out; anyone who feeds the birds today is subject to a £500 fine.

Head to the other side of the fountains to:

15 North Trafalgar Square

At night when landmarks are picked out by lights, the views down Whitehall are sublime. Most of the statues dotting the square are of forgotten military men and nobles: James II (1686; in front of the National Gallery) is finely crafted, but he looks ridiculous, pointing limply in those Roman robes. He was deposed in the Glorious Revolution just 2 years after the statue was cast. It used to stand outside the Banqueting House; for years, detractors joked he was pointing in the direction he planned to flee. (And yes, that's George Washington, who wrested the Colonies from the Crown, standing nearby. Feelings are no longer hard—he was a gift from Virginia in 1921. Urban legend has it the pedestal contains a layer of Virginia earth so he can be said to remain on American soil.) The northwestern plinth of Trafalgar Square was designed for an equestrian statue of its own, but money ran out and it stood empty from 1841. More than 150 years later, the naked spot was named the Fourth Plinth and filled by works commissioned by a subversive panel of top artists. It has become one of the most prestigious commissions in the art world. Sculptures show for 12 to 18 months, and they get the city talking. Marc Quinn's *Alison Lapper Pregnant* (2005) depicted a snow-white, nude woman born with limb deformities and heavy with child, and *Hahn/Cock* (2013) was Katharina Fritsch's two-story, ultramarine rooster, a sly send-up of the pompous military iconography elsewhere in the square. 2024's entry was Teresa Margolles's white box comprising slowly degrading plaster life masks of the faces of 850 transgender people. 2026 sees the arrival of American sculptor Tschabalala Self's striding bronze everywoman *Lady in Blue*, painted in rare lapis lazuli; and in 2028, Andra Ursuta's eerie shrouded green equestrian statue *Urntitled* takes up residence among the square's other swaggering tributes as a comment on our fragmented and paranoid era.

Along the north terrace, by the Café on the Square, look for the Imperial Standards of Length, which were set into the wall in 1876 and moved in 2003 when the central stairs were installed. They are the literal yardsticks against which all other British yardsticks are measured, showing inches, feet, and yards, plus mostly obsolete measures such as links, chains, perches, and poles.

And now, reward yourself with a visit to the loo, left of the stairs, and a spot of tea in the cafe. Or, if you crave some more substantial victuals, head over to the street east of the square to St Martin-in-the-Fields church, finished in 1724. Its combination of spire and classical portico was controversial at the time, but today, it pleases people of all persuasions with its excellent Café in the Crypt (p. 94). And, of course, two of the city's greatest museums, the National Gallery (p. 146) and the National Portrait Gallery (p. 150), share the same block and tower above you now.

WALKING TOUR 2: ST PAUL'S & SOUTHWARK

START:	**St Paul's Tube station**
FINISH:	**The George Inn, near London Bridge Tube station**
TIME:	**2 hours, not including restaurant breaks or attractions**
BEST TIMES:	**Weekend days in good weather, when the area is abuzz; Borough Market is most vital from Thursday to Saturday**
WORST TIMES:	**After dark, when cobbled streets are too dark to see well**

It was the best of advertisements, it was the worst of advertisements. Charles Dickens' novels, largely social protests wearing the cloak of entertainment, made readers feel as if they'd traveled to London when they never left their own armchairs. Trouble is, the city that Dickens has primed visitors to expect—the foggy, coal-smudged metropolis teeming with pickpockets and virtuous orphans—is nowhere to be found. Partly thanks to Dickens' work, London reformed itself. On this tour, you'll explore what's left of its darker side—from the libertine London of Shakespeare's day to the desperate one Dickens sought to solve with his pen. Along the way, you'll enjoy gourmet food and a beer on the Thames, which conceals a body count of its own.

Walking Tour 2: St Paul's & Southwark

1. St Paul's Tube Station
2. Panyer Alley
3. St Paul's Cathedral
4. St Paul's Churchyard
5. Peter's Hill/Sermon Lane
6. Millennium Bridge
7. Bankside
8. Southwark Bridge

- The Anchor

9. Clink Street
10. Borough Market
11. Southwark Cathedral
12. Nancy's Steps
13. London Bridge
14. Pool of London
15. The George Inn

1 St Paul's Tube Station

If you just took the Central Line here, you rode what was once called the Central Railway. In the first 75 years of the Underground, train lines were independently owned, and separate tickets were required each time a passenger changed trains. Fares were cumbersome, calculated according to the distance traveled and the class of carriage chosen. When the Central Railway held its grand opening in 1900, in the presence of American wit Mark Twain (who lived in London at the time), it soared above its competitors by dint of several innovations, the most important of which was it charged everyone a flat fare. The so-called "Twopenny Tube" had just one class of carriage like today's Tube trains, and it was a sensation. Gilbert and Sullivan, swept along, amended a line in their operetta *Patience* from a reference to the threepenny bus to "the very delectable, highly respectable Twopenny Tube." The Central Railway helped democratize public transit and accelerated expansion into the suburbs—even if London's authorities eventually went back to the old format of charging passengers by distance. The St Paul's station opened on July 30, 1900, as Post Office station—the city's main post office was then across the street (hence the name of Postman's Park just north; p. 192).

Exit the St Paul's Underground station and turn left, toward:

2 Panyer Alley

Panyer Alley, where you're standing, was named for the basket makers, or panyers, who once traded here. Look for a plaque on the wall depicting a child sitting on a basket. This plaque, the so-called Panyer Stone, is dated "August the 27, 1688," and reads, "When you have sought / the citty round / yet still this is / the highest ground." The artists behind this stone surely knew that Ludgate is not the highest point in the City; that's Cornhill, which is about 30cm (12 in.) higher. But the sign has been here so long that it would quite literally be a crime to take it down.

The famous inscription and relief sculpture at Panyer Alley, near St Paul's Cathedral, dates to 1688.

Head left, toward St Paul's, and make a right through the pedestrian alley, Paternoster Row, to Paternoster Square. Go through the ornate arch at the far left:

3 St Paul's Cathedral

The area you've just walked through, Paternoster Row, ranks among the most sacred in London. There have been major houses of worship on the

This statue of Queen Anne was placed at St Paul's Cathedral in 1714, shortly before she died at age 49.

plot of St Paul's as far back as 604, and for centuries these narrow surrounding streets have teemed with ecclesiastical scribes and clergy, as well as untold hordes of supplicants desperate for a handout from the merciful church. Paternoster Row was later known as the center of literary London, first for its publishers—who replaced the scribes—and later for its book market. This is where Shakespeare bought the historical texts that inspired him to write his plays. Yet what you'll see today is modern; even the 23m-tall (75-ft.) column in Paternoster Square was created to appear older than it is. Why would planners permit the wholesale demolition of such a rich heritage? They didn't. This was Ground Zero of the Blitz in 1940. The Germans, recognizing that the destruction of St Paul's would demoralize the nation, focused their power on it, and the spillover devastated everything around it. Every firefighter was called to the cathedral, saving it at the expense of just about everything else.

The ornate stone archway that you pass through, however, is a true antique. It's Temple Gate, one of eight ancient gateways to The City of London, which originally stood where Strand becomes Fleet Street from 1672. Charles Dickens described it in *Bleak House* as "a leaden-headed old obstruction." It was dismantled in 1878 and was destined for a dump somewhere when a visionary stepped in and brought the stones home. After spending more than a century in the hinterland of his family's Hertfordshire estate (and being spared the Blitz), the gate, possibly designed by Christopher Wren, was restored and re-erected here in 2004. The seven other gates, including Aldgate and Moorgate, were all lost over time.

In front of the cathedral (you might know the steps from "Feed the Birds" in *Mary Poppins*), a statue of Queen Anne, who ruled England when St Paul's was completed, looks down Ludgate Hill. In attendance are ladies symbolizing England, France, Ireland, and North America, which she considered her subjects. The statue is an 1886 copy of the 1712 original, which (like Temple Gate once did) now resides, in scabby condition, in the countryside.

Herbert Mason's iconic photograph of St Paul's dome, snapped during the mighty conflagration that engulfed London after air raids on December 29 and 30, 1940, was taken from Ludgate Hill. Next time you see that picture, note that it's lit only by firelight. (To take a photo that feels nearly as good, follow this detour. Continue on the main road, St Paul's Churchyard, down the length of the cathedral; across New Change, a small garden with a smooth-rimmed reflecting pool helps you line up drop-dead romantic images of the world-famous dome. Better yet, walk up New Change to the glassy One New Change building and take the lift to the top floor, where there's a free observation deck with a bar overlooking St Paul's.)

Return toward the cathedral along the busy street called:

4 St Paul's Churchyard

At the crossing below the dome, go over the street. Now's a good time to duck into the City of London Information Centre, located inside the origami-style, wing-roofed building, and stock up on free tourist brochures and timetables. It also runs daily guided walks on many afternoons. Check current options by visiting www.thecityofldn.com/directory/city-of-london-information-centre.

If you don't need information, turn left. If you do use the office, when you come out again, turn right. After the patch of grass, turn right again. You can see down Peter's Hill to a white pedestrian bridge over the river. Stroll down:

5 Peter's Hill/Sermon Lane

On the right is the Firefighters National Memorial, which depicts a young man gesturing wildly toward St Paul's as two others grapple desperately with a hose. It's impossible to exaggerate the devastation caused by the Blitz, both in property and in lives. The superheated firestorms created damage greater in area than those of the Great Fire of 1666. More than 20,000 people were killed, and 1.4 million left homeless. The names of some 1,000 victims, all volunteer firefighters defeated by the wild blaze and collapsing buildings, are inscribed on the octagonal base. Winston Churchill dubbed this monument "The Heroes with Grimy Faces." For their families, the survival of St Paul's Cathedral amid utter devastation remains a testament to their sacrifice. Keep going toward the river.

Designed by Sir Christopher Wren and completed in 1711, the majestic St Paul's Cathedral is a national icon.

Go onto the:

6 Millennium Bridge

You're now on the steel, pedestrian-only Millennium Bridge, the central city's first new crossing over the Thames since the Tower Bridge in 1894. Its design, which features side-located suspension cables that sag about six times shallower than a conventional suspension bridge's supports do, was a little too advanced for its own good. When the bridge opened in 2000, it was discovered that the shifting weight of pedestrians caused it to sway, and people had to grasp the rails for support. (At the start of *Harry Potter and the Half-Blood Prince,* Death Eaters attack the bridge and make it wobble—that scene was an inside joke for Londoners.) Engineers closed the 325m (1,066-ft.) span, poured in another £5.2 million to solve the issue, and reopened it in 2002. Now locals (and visitors) love it because it has transformed accessibility to the river's southern bank. It's still not perfect—it's plagued by joggers with little regard for idle strollers—but crossing the river here, in view of many of the city's landmarks, young and old, makes for some stirring photos.

Straight ahead is the monumental Tate Modern (p. 185), signaled by its factory-like "campanile" smokestack, which from 1952 to 1981 belched exhaust from the Bankside Power Station. Energy has been a fundamental part of the district's character for generations. The power station replaced an earlier one that dusted everything near it with a coating of soot, and that plant, too, supplanted a foul gasworks. Before that, the district was the domain of a legion of coal merchants who shuttled their filthy wares around town in shallow boats. These "lightermen" worked from docks that lined the entire southern shore, where land was cheaper than it was in the City on the northern side. The building you see before you is a direct descendant of the way of life that prevailed on the bank in the 1700s.

The pedestrian-only Millennium Bridge links the City with Bankside.

The near-exact replica of the Shakespeare-era Globe is both a museum and a working theater.

How deep is the Thames? The river fluctuates greatly with tides (so it's dangerous for swimming—in fact, that's illegal between Putney and the Thames Barrier), but depending on when you measure around here, it's generally 8.9m (29 ft.) deep at highest tide and 1.8m (6 ft.) at low tide. The Thames' moodiness is the main reason Southwark, the side of the river where the Tate Modern sits, was written off for so many centuries. Until medieval times, the low-lying southern bank was boggy and mostly uninhabitable, so it was instead thought of as part of Surrey, the county south of London. Londoners made use of the waterlogged land by turning it into gardens for secret trysts and fish farms (the Pike Garden, or Pye Garden, stood pretty much in front of you around the Tate's eastern flank). It wasn't until the latter part of the 1700s that people figured out how to drain the water and settle the area fully. Southwark was where you went for a rowdy time—that is, until the Puritans quashed the fun in 1642.

Before you completely cross the river, turn back for a stupendous view of St Paul's Dome symmetrically rising from the center of the bridge.

Once you're on the opposite bank, with the river in front of you, turn right. Stand midway between the cluster of houses and the building with the thatched roof. You're on:

7 Bankside

This river promenade also continues west, past the Tate Modern, to the London Eye and the Houses of Parliament. In *Four Weddings and a Funeral,* when Hugh Grant told Andie MacDowell he loved her (in the words of David Cassidy), he did it farther along this walkway by the

National Film Theatre, the building now known as the BFI. There's no better place to stroll, people-watch, and appreciate the sweep of the city.

As late as the 1960s, much of the path you're on, which at this place is called Bankside, was a vehicular street bearing two-way traffic, as it had been since the 1600s. Each building on the street owned rights to the docks or water-stairs on the river opposite it, so tenants were usually people who needed access to the water, such as ferrymen or sailors. The four-story white house at the left of the blind Cardinal Cap Alley, no. 49, was built around 1710 on the foundations of a pub, the Cardinal's Cap, which itself was built in 1547 to entertain the people who came to Southwark to carouse. No. 49 was home to successive generations of coal merchants, but not, as its plaque purports, to Sir Christopher Wren as he built St Paul's. The poorer tour guides in London will tell you that Wren lived here. Despite the plaque, he didn't. Wren did live nearby, but in a building that was torn down when the power station needed land. This plaque once hung on that vanished home, but it was moved by a D.I.Y. revisionist in the mid–20th century. No. 49 has received its own biography, *The House by the Thames* by Gillian Tindall.

To the left of where you stand is Shakespeare's Globe (p. 184), a theatre that made a premature exit in its own era, only to be rebuilt in ours. The circular Globe's stage is even at the same compass point as the 1599 original's. Interestingly, the city's theatrical life was centered on this riverbank from about 1587 to 1642, when it was illegal to operate a theater in the City proper. Once the laws relaxed, the entertainment venues moved back into town, where they've been ever since.

Southwark was the Tudor version of a multiplex, and the biggest blockbuster was bear-baiting—the spectacle of vicious dogs let loose upon tethered bears. Even Henry VIII and Elizabeth I were huge fans; he had a bear pit installed at Whitehall Palace, and she barred Parliament from banning the pursuit on Sundays. One and a half blocks past the Globe, squeeze between modern buildings down an alley called Bear Gardens. Three-quarters of the way down the lane is the rough location of the Davies Amphitheatre, one of the most popular bear pits. Samuel Pepys wrote in his diary in 1666 of attending one such slaughter where he "saw some good sport of the bull's tossing the dogs—one into the very boxes. But it is a very rude and nasty pleasure."

Under a modern office building in the next street, Rose Alley, lie the foundations of another theater known to have premiered plays by Shakespeare, the Rose. It lasted from 1587 to about 1606. The Swan stood nearby, too, although we may never find the footprint. The Rose's footprint gave us vital clues about what Elizabethan theaters looked like—architects also studied sketches made of it by a Dutch tourist in 1596. (Are you sketching your trip?)

Historians also know where the original Globe stood. If you'd like to see it, detour down Bear Gardens (between two modern buildings) one block to Park Street, turn left and go under the bridge, and just after it, past the buildings on the right, you'll find a fenced-off area. On the ground, slightly red cobbles show locations of fragments that archaeologists found in 1989. Digging to find more is impossible for now because housing has been built on top of part of the site. In 1949, this area was much drearier. It lay behind the gate of the decrepit Anchor Brewery, and when American actor Sam Wanamaker (father of Zoë, who played Madam Hooch in the Harry Potter movies) dropped by to pay pilgrimage, the indignity of the meager plaque so enraged him that he resolved to rebuild the Globe as a living home for England's great theatrical tradition—which is what came to pass, albeit 4 years after his 1993 death. Wanamaker's dream has now lasted longer than the original theatre did.

Continue along the river, keeping it to your left. You'll go through a pedestrian tunnel under:

8 Southwark Bridge

On the wall of the tunnel, you'll see illustrations of skaters and revelers at the bygone "Frost Fairs" that, starting in 1564, were regularly held on the icy Thames. No matter how many winters you spend in London, you'll never see the Thames freeze over. But back then, they had the London Bridge, a few hundred yards downstream. Its 19 arches were so narrow, and its supports so thick, that the river's flow became sluggish, allowing water (and the outhouse filth that churned within it) to freeze. By contrast, during outgoing tides the rush was so fierce that boats capsized and passengers (few of whom knew how to swim since there was nowhere sanitary to practice) drowned. When the bridge was dismantled in 1814, the Frost Fairs melted into history.

Take a look underneath Southwark Bridge where it meets the shore. You can still discern the remains of some water stairs, dating to before the construction of the first bridge here in 1819. Back then, getting across the river usually required boatmen, the taxi drivers of their day; you'd board via these. Ferrymen would court business by shouting destinations to theatergoers after their plays: "Eastward ho!" or "Westward ho!"

In 1912, this bridge's central 72m (236-ft.) span was the largest ever attempted in cast iron.

The Anchor

Few pubs are more lively than the **Anchor** (p. 121), situated where Bankside meets the railway viaduct. The riverside patio is open in good weather; otherwise, the interior is charming. This pub was once controlled, as nearly all pubs once were, by a brewery; it was Barclay Perkins, located just behind it from 1790 until about 1980. Even before that, it was a fixture; in 1666, Samuel Pepys watched the Great Fire rage from here before coming to his senses and hurrying across the river to rescue his possessions from his home in Seething Lane, near the Tower of London. In the 1950s, the Anchor was considered a slum and nearly was demolished. In our time, Tom Cruise had a drink here with Ving Rhames at the end of *Mission: Impossible* (1996).

After the Anchor, the path jogs inland. Take the first left onto:

9 Clink Street

Pass under the railway arch. In a few moments, you've gone from Elizabethan Southwark (theaters, bear-baiting) to Georgian Southwark (coal merchants, breweries). Now you're in Victorian Southwark, a claustrophobic underworld teeming with fetid-smelling industry and river rats. You can almost hear distant reverberations on this narrow wharfside street. If you called the sensation Dickensian, you wouldn't be wrong. When the writer was 12 years old, his father was thrown into a debtor's prison near where you're standing, off the Borough High Street.

Prisons were something of a cottage industry for the area; the Clink Street Prison stood here from 1127, when the Bishop of Winchester built it as a lockup for his Winchester Palace, until 1780, when the anti-Catholic Gordon Riots saw the dismal hole destroyed. Although the Clink gave its name as slang to all prisons that came after it, no one knows for sure how it got the name to begin with—Flemish or Middle English words for latch are likely the origin. Suffice to say it was awful—and so is the "museum" here that purports to tell its story. Avoid it.

In the 1800s, warehousing goods instead of people became this street's stock-in-trade. You'll still see hints of the street's past maritime uses, such as wooden loft windows and cranes used to hoist crates into upper floors. Today, these spaces house media companies and architects. During the week, you'll see professionals in their fashionable clothes, strutting in their Italian shoes across pavers that until recently were the original rounded cobbles salvaged from ballast. On weekends, you'll follow a current of tourists.

The latter Bishops of Winchester were not nice guys. Henry II (1133–89) gave them control of this neighborhood, and because it was outside the jurisdiction of the city, they could pretty much get away with whatever they wanted to. Principally, they cultivated countless brothels and skimmed the profits for themselves—which is how Southwark got its rep as a den of vice. Anyone who annoyed them (heretics, troublemakers) wound up in the Clink, where no one was likely to find them again. As you continue down Clink Street, past the modern building with the rounded grid of windows, on your right you'll see all that's left of the Bishops' palace: a fragment of old stone wall, dating to the 1300s, with a round panel of stone tracery at the top. That tracery once held a rose window, which lit the palace's great hall. This fragment was forgotten behind a wall until a warehouse fire exposed it again.

Even the most eagle-eyed movie fans may not recognize this gentrified lane as the godforsaken alley where the main character of *An American Werewolf in London* (1981) encountered his final showdown (albeit in front of a false brick wall). Double back to Stoney Street.

Turn down Stoney Street and walk under the railway. On your left, you'll see:

10 Borough Market

Stop at the frilly grey portico.

The mood of the neighborhood has changed drastically again. To your left, behind the portico, is Borough Market, a fantasy for the tongue (described in gastronomic detail on p. 110) and the oldest fruit and vegetable market in the city. A market has been held around here since C.E. 43, when Roman soldiers noted passing a market on their way to sack the City. More reliable records date it to 1014, when it served the denizens on the old London Bridge, the city's only river crossing. The cream-grey portico is not original to this place; it's the cast-iron Flower Hall of Covent Garden, rescued when the Royal Opera House was renovated in 2003. If it seems to blend seamlessly, it's because it was made around the same time as the rest of the Borough Market structure (1859–60). You are standing very near the spot, outside the Wheatsheaf pub, where police guns swiftly put an end to a ghastly Saturday night terrorist attack by knife-wielding attackers in June 2017.

The market is best known for gourmet supplies. Park Street, which runs into Stoney Street, looks as quaint as a movie-set version of old England; in fact, it was used in *Harry Potter and the Prisoner of Azkaban,* and no. 7a was the entrance of The Leaky Cauldron. The market itself has appeared in films including *Howard's End* and *Bridget Jones's* Diary (she lived at 8 Bedale St.). The city's first railway, a 6.4km (4-mile) run to Greenwich, plowed its route .8km (½ mile) east of here in 1836. Even after tunneling technology improved, railway tycoons kept barricading thriving neighborhoods with massive brick viaducts, cutting them off from each other and creating slums, all because it was cheaper than digging. On your tour, you have crossed under a number of railway viaducts built that way, and shortly, you'll see how narrowly one of England's most historic churches averted its own destruction.

Enter the market to the right of the portico and walk straight. Cross the next street and enter the brick arch marked Green Market. Before you is:

11 Southwark Cathedral

(If for some reason the Green Market arch is closed, turn left down railway-covered Bedale Street until you see a church appear on your right.)

Before you stands the oldest Gothic church in the city, and the oldest building in Southwark. In Roman times, it was the site of a villa. You'll see its tower appear in every medieval drawing of the city. Its Christian chapter was begun by the daughter of a ferryman in the 7th century; it was rebuilt in the 850s and again 300 years later. There was once a monastery and a chapel in this yard, where office workers now lunch on gourmet items from Borough Market, but those came and went, too. Southwark teemed with the poor, with factory workers, and with grubby river men. One such blue-collar child was John Harvard, one of nine kids of a man who owned a tavern and butcher shop just northeast of here.

John was baptized in this church in the early 1600s, but when he grew up and became a minister, he fled this slum for the Massachusetts Bay Colony, where Harvard University was later named for him. In time this place was limping along as a humble parish church called St Saviour's and dissolving into dilapidation. The rerouting of London Bridge Road sheared away several small chapels, and in 1863, the rumbling railway forced its way alongside the yard. But by 1905, its fortunes reversed when it was elevated to a cathedral, and now it's so well cared for that it's hard to discern its true age and sordid past.

The cathedral has some beautiful painted monuments, including one of England's oldest wooden effigies (1280). Shakespeare's brother Edmond was buried here in 1607, as was Philip Henslowe, who built the Rose theater, in an unmarked grave. Other worthwhile sights include Edwardian stained-glass tributes to the Bard's plays, the Harvard Chapel with masonry from the Norman period, and some of the original ceiling bosses, carved in 1469 and saved when things got bad. How bad? During Elizabeth I's reign, the retro-choir (the part behind the altar) was walled off and rented to a baker. Later on, vestrymen discovered the baker was also raising swine in there. Yes, inside the church. Things were rough.

Keeping the cathedral on your right, walk toward the Thames on Montague Close, which bends right to follow the north side of the cathedral. Just before the overpass, look left for:

12 Nancy's Steps

These are popularly held to be the location, in the Dickens novel *Oliver Twist,* where Noah Claypole eavesdrops on a conversation that leads to Nancy's murder by Bill Sikes. In the book, those steps faced the Thames; in fact, these steps are a rare surviving remnant of the New London Bridge, built here in 1821 as a replacement for the 600-year-old, overcrowded London Bridge. (The steps that Dickens wrote about were sold in 1968 to an American oilman. Locals superciliously quip he was duped, but, in fact, he knew exactly what he was doing and preserved what the English wouldn't. He had most of the New London Bridge shipped, stone by stone, to Lake Havasu, Arizona, to form a tourist attraction, and there it remains today, standing near a marina on a desert lake.) These steps were left behind and attached to the existing London Bridge, a featureless 1973 replacement.

Just so you know, the modern London Bridge was not the source of the nursery rhyme "London Bridge Is Falling Down"—that either referred to the burning of a wooden version in 1013, during a skirmish between Danes and Norwegians; or to Henry III's "fair lady" Queen Eleanor, who skimmed the tolls of the medieval bridge for her own purse, leaving its maintenance in a parlous state.

Climb the stairs to the road above. You're now on:

13 London Bridge

At the top of the stairs, you'll see a pedestal topped by a dragon, the symbol of the city, holding London's crest. You'll see these dragons at several of the city's medieval borders. About 30m (98 ft.) east of here, under modern buildings, is where you would have entered the Stone Gateway, the entry to the disaster-prone medieval London Bridge. For more than 3 centuries, tar-dipped heads of executed criminals were impaled on pikes and stuck atop the Gateway as a vivid warning to would-be ne'er-do-wells.

Potters Fields Park offers great views of the Tower Bridge.

Turn to the right to use the crosswalk. Go to the opposite side of the street and walk onto London Bridge, over the river. Don't cross the river—just enjoy the view of the:

14 Pool of London

This section of the Thames between London Bridge and the Tower Bridge is known as the Pool of London. It may be quiet now, but for nearly 2,000 years, it was the heart of international trade. So many goods passed through here that warehouses along the southern bank became known as "London's Larder." The water was so overcrowded with boats that developers kept having to carve new basins throughout East London where vessels could pull in and unload (you can see the mini-lakes forming a honeycomb of waterways on the maps), but ships eventually became so giant that now they have to unload downstream, closer to the sea. The part of river in front of you, parallel to this bridge, is where the medieval London Bridge stood.

Across the river from the Tower, you'll just make out an egg-shaped glass building on a riverside open space. From 2002 to 2022, that was London's City Hall, designed by Norman Foster (who also did the Millennium Bridge) to be ergonomic, with a huge spiral staircase curling around its atrium and "smart" windows that open on hot days. Just like a politician, it has no edge and you can't tell if it's coming or going. Now the city's offices are way out at the Royal Docks in East London, near London City Airport, but the riverside open space they left behind, Potters Fields Park, will be where you can take some of the best possible photographs of the Tower Bridge.

Turn around and keep London Bridge to your back, keeping on the left side of the road. This street becomes Borough High Street. You will pass under a railway arch. Just after you pass Southwark Street forking off to the right, look for "The George" sign. It marks:

15 The George Inn

Because the London Bridge was the only crossing to the city from the south for so many centuries, this area became the equivalent of a train depot, and it was dotted with inns, stables, coach yards, and pubs. Everyone going to or coming from southern England or Europe stopped here, often spending the night before pushing into the shoulder-to-shoulder crowds of London Bridge. If you've ever read *The Canterbury Tales,* you'll recall that in 1386, the pilgrims began their journey to the shrine of Thomas à Becket from the Tabard Inn. Until 1873, that was located a short walk farther down Borough High Street, on the left. The George, described on p. 123, is the last survivor from this bustling coaching era. Although the wooden building, which once encircled the entire yard, dates to 1677, the inn was here for at least another 130 years before that, if not longer. We know it was typical of the time because John Stow, in *A Survey of London* (1598), termed it "a common hostelry for travelers." A drink here makes a fitting end to your journey through time. Look up and you'll see the jagged glass spire of the Shard (p. 185), one of Europe's tallest buildings, peering down as you sit where people have lifted beer for nearly half a millennium.

WALKING TOUR 3: SOHO & ST GILES: POP, SHOP & MARX

START:	**Oxford Circus Tube station**
FINISH:	**British Museum**
TIME:	**2 hours, not including shopping or restaurant breaks**
BEST TIMES:	**Weekdays, when Berwick Street's market is on and Oxford Street is slightly less crowded**
WORST TIMES:	**Evening rush hour, when Oxford Circus Tube stop is positively rammed, and after dark, when stores and the museum close**

All churched out? London is more than stories about dead queens and bloody uprisings. It's always been cosmopolitan, too, and the flash point for trends that ripple out to the rest of the world. Songs first sung at the clubs of Soho soon caused toes to tap on the other side of the planet, and fashion trends born on Carnaby Street in the '60s remain internationally iconic all these years later. Bring along your credit cards as we roam some of the city's best shopping streets and touch upon a few leftovers from London's recent past, including forgotten air-raid shelters and the settings for some good, old-fashioned sex scandals. This is the London you found out about from the radio and the runways, not from your social studies teacher.

Walking Tour 3: Soho & St Giles: Pop, Shop & Marx

1. Oxford Circus
2. Marks & Spencer
3. Great Marlborough Street Magistrate's Court
4. Foubert's Court
5. Carnaby Street
6. Kingly Court

☕ John Snow Pub

7. Berwick Street
8. Berwick Street Market
9. Brewer Street
10. Old Compton Street
11. Frith Street

☕ The Dog & Duck

12. Denmark Street
13. St Giles
14. Shaftesbury Theatre
15. The British Museum

☕ "Take a Break" stop

0 — 1/8 mi
0 — 100 meters

1 Oxford Circus

Leave the Tube station using Exit 2. Position yourself out of the fray.

You are in the thick of mile-long **Regent Street,** which to the right is punctuated by the witches-hat steeple of All Souls Church and to the left curves toward Piccadilly Circus. When the Prince Regent, later George IV, was planning his new pet project, Regent's Park, he decided he also wanted a road to connect his house to it. He chose this particular location because, in his mind, it would provide a suitable demarcation line between the gentry of Mayfair, to the west, and the rabble of the traders who lived in Soho, to the east. George tapped John Nash to do the job, completed in 1825. Originally, the sidewalks were covered by stone colonnades, but when those attracted prostitutes, they were removed, and most of the original buildings were later rebuilt—the only Nash original is now All Souls. Even if most of the facades you see now mask more modern buildings, few streets in London impart such a sweeping, uplifting feeling, though few are also as congested with the hoi polloi George would have spurned.

The other avenue intersecting before you is Oxford Street, following the same line as a Roman road. George's class-centered definition of the landscape has more or less held: The exclusive shops of Oxford Street still lie west of Regent Street, and the downmarket stores tend to be east of it. Having a presence on Oxford Street is considered crucial for brands with mass appeal.

Head right, east on Oxford Street. You will pass Argyll Street on the right. When you pass Ramillies Street, prepare to stop in front of:

2 Marks & Spencer

London has a love-hate relationship with Oxford Street. People come here to shop by the thousands, but they often despair of the crush of the

The famous intersection of streets, shopping, transport and humanity known as Oxford Circus.

experience. Charles Dickens, Jr., described the street thusly in 1888: "It ought to be the finest thoroughfare in the world. As a matter of fact it is not by any means, and though it is, like all the other thoroughfares, improving, it still contains many houses which even in a third-rate street would be considered mean." We're only going to walk down a sample of Oxford Street. It's usually so crowded, that's as much as you can probably handle if you're keeping one eye on this book.

Marks & Spencer (p. 241), or M&S, dates to 1894 and is the favored British department store for staples. Perhaps proof of its appeal is that the chain can afford to run two giant frontages on Oxford Street; its flagship store is remarkably near here, between Bond Street and Marble Arch Tube stations. Its Food Halls are well known as an ideal place to pick up prepared foods, sandwiches, and inexpensive but well-selected wines.

Turn right at Poland Street, walk 1 block, and turn right again onto Great Marlborough Street. Soon on your right, at nos. 19–21, you'll see a stout white building. That's the:

3 Great Marlborough Street Magistrate's Court

Charles Dickens worked here as a reporter just before hitting it big as a novelist, and a variety of other big names appeared before the judges here, including the Marquess of Queensbury (defending himself from Oscar Wilde's libel charge). When this neighborhood turned bohemian in the Swinging '60s, the court began trying a string of drug charges against the likes of Mick Jagger, Johnny Rotten, Keith Richards, Francis Bacon, and, curiously (and coming full circle), the guy who wrote the musical *Oliver!,* Lionel Bart. It's now a hotel, but I suggest you go inside briefly to see some of the old judicial fittings, which were left intact. You can have a cocktail in one of the old jail cells—now converted into private booths—or even peek into a restaurant slotted into the authoritative Number One court, which still has its witness stand, bench, wood paneling, and vaulted glass ceiling.

Beyond the Courthouse Hotel on the left, you'll see a Tudor-style building of black beams and white plaster. This is Liberty (p. 241), famous for its haute fabrics. It's also famous for its building—it was made in 1924 using wood recycled from junked ships.

Great Marlborough Street runs into Regent Street. Turn left there and walk the short distance to:

4 Foubert's Court

Times have been better on Regent Street. Walmart-style box stores in the suburbs have put the screws on the destination shops of the city, and this avenue has seen long-termers lose their sizzle. Dickins & Jones, a department store at the corner you just turned, closed its doors in 2006 after nearly 170 years, and the same old shopping mall brands have been moving in.

Two doors farther from Foubert's Court, though, at nos. 188–196, is a well-loved holdover from the street's glory days. It's Hamleys (p. 256), one of the largest toy stores in the world. Some 5 million customers pour

More than 20 restaurants and shops fill the Kingly Court food hub near Carnaby Street.

through its doors every year, but since the sales force is famous for putting on a nonstop show on every floor, it's understandable if many of those customers come to gawp and not to buy. If you go into Hamleys, when and if you come out again, turn right and go back to Foubert's Court.

Walk down the very short Foubert's Court for 1 block; you'll see "Carnaby" on a metal arch. Go under it and head 1 block. Go right, and now you'll see a larger arch on:

5 Carnaby Street

Yes, those obnoxious arches proclaim your location with a self-promotion that proves this street is no longer the super-cool, forward-trending street of the kids in the know. It's more of a mall with an edge. The days of Swinging London, when men could cruise from store to store trying on hip-hugging black trousers and frilly shirts, are behind it. *Time* magazine spilled the secret of Carnaby Street in 1966, and by the 1970s, it was pedestrianized as a shopping street, making hipness a matter of retrospect.

Just after you cross Ganton Street, where Broadwick Street hits Carnaby Street, duck into the passageway on the right:

6 Kingly Court

Clever entrepreneurs led Carnaby Street's rebirth with this development, a lively gathering of bars and restaurants in a former timber warehouse.

Slip out the back door of Kingly Court, opposite its front door, and hang a left on Kingly Street. No. 9 was the Bag 'O Nails pub, where future Wings-mates Paul McCartney and Linda Eastman first clapped eyes on each other—and also where in 1961 John Profumo met Christine Keeler, kicking off the Profumo Affair, a notorious national security scandal. It's also where Fleetwood Mac's John McVie proposed to Christine. (The free audio touring app Carnaby Echoes dives into the music history of the neighborhood.)

Return to Kingly Court. Retrace your steps out of it, cross Carnaby Street, and head down Broadwick Street. You'll stop around:

John Snow Pub

So grateful were Dr. Snow's neighbors that they renamed their pub for him, albeit a century later. It stands at no. 39, at Lexington Street, on the site of his practice. Raise a pint in his honor here, as we read the words of Dr. Snow himself: "I feel it my duty to endeavor to convince you of the physical evils sustained to your health by using intoxicating liquors even in the greatest moderation." (Oops.)

Continue on Broadwick Street to:

7 Berwick Street

In the mid-1800s, this block was a foul slum. French, Greek, and Italian immigrants fled hard times and revolutions by cramming into these tight streets, and by the 1850s, cholera was storming through the overstuffed city. An 1854 outbreak killed 500 people in barely 10 days. Common wisdom at the time held that the disease was spread through the air—a reasonable conclusion, given how terrible the sewage-smeared city smelled—but a local anesthetist, John Snow (for whom the pub you just visited was named) had a different theory. Suspecting polluted water was the cause, he got permission to inspect the public pump at Broad Street, now Broadwick Street (in the block before Berwick St.) and found that it was being contaminated with sewage leaking from no. 40, at the corner of Broadwick and Poland streets. The saga was retold in the book *The Ghost Map* by Steven Johnson, and in 2015 the site of no. 40 was dug up to build this new building.

When you reach Berwick Street, look left. Think of this location as the modern-day Abbey Road. It's where, in 1995, Oasis photographed the cover of *(What's the Story) Morning Glory?*, one of the seminal CDs of the age. The photographer shot from farther down the street, aiming south, toward where you're standing. (Noel Gallagher, with characteristic tact, said he thought the album cover was "s**t.")

And here's another slice of rock history: One miniblock farther down Broadwick Street at no. 7, the corner shop covered in striking rust-colored tiles (now Sounds of the Universe record store, a local landmark for world music) was the Bricklayers Arms pub. Brian Jones auditioned the Rolling Stones here in 1962, and they held formative rehearsals upstairs. The word

"Soho" is probably derived from a hunting cry used when this area was parkland—it's nice to see that some folks around here are still on the hunt.

Turn south on Berwick Street. Walk down it to:

8 Berwick Street Market

This is the vestige of the last great weekday market in the center of the city—it's been in operation at least since the 1840s (vestry records indicate some illicit trading was going on as far back as 1778). London's first publicly available grapefruit was sold here in 1890. Now that the produce sellers have been mostly elbowed aside for gourmet nibbles, the market again caters to those with exotic, expensive tastes. It ends by mid-afternoon.

Pass over Peter Street and under Maurice House, going under the crossover and winding up on:

9 Brewer Street

From the late 1700s to the 1950s, it was impossible for a single gentleman to pass unpropositioned through Soho. A 1959 act chased the open salesmanship indoors, to be replaced by drinking joints where men could buy lap time with a lady, and by the 1970s, even those were forced to seek a lower profile. By law, today's displays are not permitted to titillate, complying with the British reputation (inaccurate in my book) for sexual modesty.

It was in this fleshy carnival that Laura Henderson bought a theater near Great Windmill and Archer streets (across the intersection from no. 20, where Karl Marx's *The Communist Manifesto* was commissioned in 1847, by the way). She got around indecency laws by ensuring that the performers in her naughty entertainment, the Revudeville, never moved a muscle. Famously, her Windmill Theatre never closed, not even during the Blitz. You might have seen it in the film *Mrs Henderson Presents* (2005). By the 1950s, Soho was a den of gang warfare and prostitution, full of craftsmen of every sort—costumers, ostrich feather trimmers, gun makers—until the Conservative government re-zoned the neighborhoods to admit offices, and the old ways were priced out.

Go left to Wardour Street, make a right and then a quick left. You'll be at the head of:

10 Old Compton Street

First, note the church of St Anne's, a few yards down Wardour Street, on the left. It was built in 1685, possibly by Wren (which ones weren't?), 2.5m (8 ft.) higher than the street because it went on top of a graveyard for 60,000 bodies (until 1853, when burials stopped, the neighborhood reeked from it). Everything save the church's tower was creamed by the Nazis.

Walk down Old Compton Street, Soho's de facto main street, which is busy round the clock and a center of gay life. No. 54 is the Admiral Duncan, where Dylan Thomas once drank (then again, where didn't he?). It was here, in 1999, that Nazi sympathizer David Copeland planted a bomb stuffed with 500 nails, which killed three people and injured many more.

Fun for shopping and dining by day, Old Compton Street is also a major party place come nightfall.

Copeland, an obvious madman, also bombed the South Asian population of Brick Lane and Black people in Brixton, but his only fatalities were here.

On the corner of Dean Street, look right. Down the block on the left, at no. 49, is the French House, more commonly called the French Pub. During World War II, it was the drinking haunt of Charles de Gaulle; here the exiled leader formed the Free French government and army. The street beyond the French House is Shaftesbury Avenue, the famous theatrical thoroughfare; many of the side streets between Old Compton and Shaftesbury contain the stage doors for the major playhouses, where famous actors report to work. Now look left, north up Dean Street. In no. 28, Karl Marx dwelled in abject poverty with his wife and several kids, but no running water or toilet. Three of his kids died while he was in residence in Soho in the early 1850s, and he had to borrow £2 for a coffin for one baby. No wonder he thought Marxism would be better.

Turn left at:

11 Frith Street

Bar Italia, the stylish cafe at no. 22, is a nightlife landmark of its own (p. 94). Upstairs is where, in 1925, John Logie Baird privately tested a homemade invention he called "noctovision," using his grocer's delivery boy as a test subject. The next year, he unveiled an improved model for the science nerds of the Royal Institution upstairs in this building. (Unsatisfied, he made another attempt in 1928 that involved hooking up a fresh human eyeball he'd rushed by taxicab from Charing Cross Ophthalmic Hospital. It created a mess.) Baird's system, which used a spinning disc, was eventually discarded, but it debuted ahead of American Philo T. Farnsworth's more famous electronic version. Within a decade, the BBC was broadcasting "television"—its new name—regularly. In the 1940s, Baird invented the first color picture tube.

Walk up three doors. For 10 months starting in September 1764, the 8-year-old Mozart lived with his father and sister at a house at no. 20 (the building was replaced in 1858). While he was in London, the prodigy amused King George III, wrote his first two symphonies, and befriended fellow composer J. C. Bach, who mentored him. By the 1800s, Soho's Wardour Street was the violin-making center of Europe. Music history of another kind happened at no. 47, which in 1969 hosted the first public performance of The Who's *Tommy,* and then Jimi Hendrix's last performance, in 1970.

The Dog & Duck

You should totally stop at another pub now. I mean, how often are you in London? This one, at 18 Bateman Street, is a beauty, rich with Victorian tilework and mahogany paneling. If it puts you in a literary frame of mind, perhaps you're sensing vibrations. It was a favorite of George Orwell's—he toasted with absinthe here when he learned he'd sold *Animal Farm* to a publisher. In May 2023, Prince William and Catherine showed up here as part of the pre-Coronation festivities for King Charles III. William himself pulled his pint of Kingmaker, a Warwickshire ale, for the cameras.

Turn right into Bateman Street (pub behind you), go 1 block, then left at Greek Street. Take the first right, the alley of Manette Street, and continue to Charing Cross Road. Cross using the crosswalk on your left and keep going straight along Denmark Street.

The Dog & Duck pub on Firth Street was a favorite of George Orwell.

12 Denmark Street

Look up, and you'll see the 35-story Centre Point development. Built in 1964 with government concessions, it was kept empty for years by its greedy owner, Harry Hyams, partly to hold out for astronomical rents and partly to get off the tax hook even as the city struggled through a crisis of homelessness. In 1974, a hundred squatters occupied it to make a point. The charity Centrepoint, which started in the basement of St Anne's Church in Soho and grew into a force, derisively took its name from the waste.

Denmark Street, recently decimated by development and lined with a now-paltry scattering of specialists in musical instruments, is just a hundred yards long, but it's dense with stories. This is London's version of New York's Tin Pan Alley—a nucleus for the British popular music industry. At no. 4, the Rolling Stones recorded their first album at Regent Sounds Studios (now The Alley Cat Club). Atop no. 20, Bernie Taupin wrote the lyric for "Your Song" (1970), his first hit with Elton John, during a break from work, which is why the words reference sitting on a roof. Charlie Chaplin wrote the tune of the iconic "Smile" in 2 hours on this street. David Bowie, The Kinks, Jimi Hendrix, Bob Marley, the Sex Pistols, and Black Sabbath all had countless formative moments—buying guitars, hiring bands, recording albums—along Denmark Street. It's mostly in the past now; the present lane is more consumerist than bohemian.

Keep following this road. It hangs slightly right, then is renamed St Giles High Street.

13 St Giles

You are standing in the worst slum in London. In the middle 1800s, the census counted more than 50,000 paupers within a few hundred squalid square feet. One eight-room house was stuffed with 107 luckless souls. People called poor neighborhoods "rookeries" because inhabitants were packed, shoeless and shivering, into single rooms like birds in nests. This is the London of *Oliver Twist*'s Fagin and his haggard gang of orphan pickpockets, of William Hogarth's "Gin Lane" prints warning of the villainy of drink among the destitute. This is the lawless labyrinth teeming with penniless immigrants, sex workers, drug addicts, thieves, orphans, and rats. This spot is so far gone that in World War II, even Hitler didn't bother to bomb it.

Except it's not. Not anymore. The new toybox-colorful development by Renzo Piano tells you nothing of the depravity that shocked and reformed the heartlessness of English society. Most of the remnants of poverty were bulldozed aside by development. But the church on the right, St Giles-in-the-Fields, has origins back to Saxon times (1101); this one was built in the 1730s because the architectural integrity of the previous one had been compromised by the huge number of plague victims buried all around it. The interior is fairly standard as churches go, but note The Angel pub (on St Giles High Street) just past it.

Until the late 1700s, St Giles was the last church on the wagon route from Newgate Prison to the gallows at the village of Tyburn a mile away (now near Marble Arch). The convoys of doomed criminals rolled by as many as eight times a year, and it was the equivalent of a major sporting event. Thousands of people would line the route to watch the condemned

The British Museum was first chartered by King George II in 1753.

be dispatched to their maker, and as they passed taverns, they would be offered one last draught of ale. The pub that stood here (in the past, called The Bowl) is recorded as being where many prisoners drank their last beer on this mortal plane. The phrase "on the wagon" may stem from this grisly ritual.

Continue straight to the Shaftesbury Theatre.

14 Shaftesbury Theatre

The Shaftesbury was built in 1911 as the New Prince's Theatre, and it has been one of the most important independent houses ever since. In 1923, the sibling dance team of Fred and Adele Astaire cemented their international stardom with *Stop Flirting*; Prince Edward, future abdicator and a man fatefully obsessed with Americans, attended almost nightly. Adele was soon swept off her feet by a duke, leaving Fred with the (then) unlikely prospect of forging a career alone. It was widely assumed his stardom was over. We know how all that turned out. Other past tenants: Peter O'Toole, Anthony Hopkins, the London premieres of *Pal Joey* (1954), *How to Succeed in Business Without Really Trying* (1963), *Hair* (1968), *Follies* (1987), *Rent* (1998), and *Hairspray* (2007).

Two short blocks later, you'll be where Museum Street and Drury Lane both cross High Holborn (the road you're on). Turn left onto Museum Street. In 3 blocks, one of them pedestrianized, you will find yourself standing before the world-famous British Museum (fully explained on p. 135).

15 The British Museum

When it received its charter from George II, in 1753, the idea was revolutionary: A museum not owned by either the king or a church, free for the masses to use, and dedicated to the advancement of a broad range of disciplines. It was called the National Museum, and as you've just learned, at the time, acres of slums rolled just outside its doorstep. But, in a miracle of liberal-leaning benevolence, the country was determined to improve itself. Even the filthy souls who inhabited mid-19th-century Soho and St Giles were welcomed here. And now, so are you. Go inside and discover the world.

DAY TRIPS FROM LONDON

9

You've flown all the way to England. It would be a shame to miss seeing some of the other sights that make it special—the rolling countryside, the stately mansions, the ageless villages built on slow-flowing rivers. An excursion enriches you with two experiences for the price of one: You'll taste everyday English life while you immerse yourself in world-famous landmarks.

Britain has comprehensive transport, but it's not quick as mercury. Because of traffic and a dearth of superhighways, you can expect a 48km (30-mile) trip to take an hour, so a spot that's 129 to 161km (80–100 miles) each way, such as Stonehenge or Bath, will require you to rise at dawn if you want to buy yourself much touring time at all. Going by bus is often less expensive than by rail, but the inefficient journey will involve narrow roads.

For in-depth coverage of everything outside of London, bring a copy of ***Frommer's England & Scotland***. For casual day-trippers, though, here's what you need to know to dash out of the city and see the best of these destinations.

WINDSOR & ETON

Buckingham Palace is a mere *pied-à-terre.* King Charles actually prefers this great castle, which dominates the skyline of Windsor like a cloud of stone. Windsor Castle (32km/20 miles west of London) has been the home of the Royal Family for some 900 years, far longer than anything in London. Prince William and Princess Catherine live with their children at Forest Lodge Windsor, 3.5 miles south of the castle. Queen Victoria is buried in the backyard, although they don't phrase it quite that way. Despite the inevitable crowds, this is unmissable.

Essentials

GETTING THERE The price difference between transport options is negligible. Riding the rails is quicker, so it's got the edge. **Trains** (www.nationalrail.co.uk; ✆ **03457/48-49-50,** or 020/7278-5240 from overseas; 38–56 min.; £12–£24) go directly from Waterloo station to Windsor & Eton Riverside or from Paddington to Windsor & Eton Central with a change at Slough. Both Windsor stations are a

3-minute walk from the castle. Trains requiring no changes leave twice an hour; trains requiring a change leave a little more frequently. Or take London Line 702 by **Reading Buses** (https://www.reading-buses.co.uk/windsor-express; ✆ **0118/959-4000;** 1 hr. 45 min.; £3 single. The bus goes 4 times an hour from Buckingham Palace Road by Victoria Coach Station, south of Victoria Station.

VISITOR INFORMATION Stop by Windsor Guildhall for the **Royal Windsor Information Centre** (Indelibly Windsor, 29–30 High St.; www.windsor.gov.uk; Wed–Sat 9am–6:30pm).

TOURS The most appealing way to see the area is by **boat,** departing from Windsor Promenade, Barry Avenue, for a 40-minute round-trip with fine views of the castle. Tours are operated by **French Brothers,** Clewer Boathouse, Clewer Court Rd., Windsor (www.frenchbrothers.co.uk; ✆ **01753/851-900;** 40-min. trip at 10am £13 adults, £11.70 seniors, £8.70 children 3–13, cheaper online; 2-hr. trip in afternoon £22 adults, £20.25 seniors, £14.70 children 3–13).

Exploring Windsor

Legoland Windsor (www.legoland.co.uk; ✆ **0871/222-2001;** tickets £34–£68, cheaper in advance online; Mar–Oct), 2 miles from town, has top-notch rides catering to small children and some impressive Lego constructions. London Line 702 by Reading Buses from London goes there, as do shuttles from Windsor's railway stations. The tourist office sells discounted tickets for late-afternoon entry.

Windsor Castle ♥♥ You may have had your fill of palaces in London proper, but you haven't seen the best. A fortress and a royal home for more than 900 years, it was expanded by each successive monarch who dwelled in

St George's Chapel at Windsor Castle, final resting place of Queen Elizabeth II and several other monarchs.

it—adding more battlements for the warlike ones, more finery for the aesthetes. The resulting sprawl, which dominates the town from nearly every angle, is the favorite residence of the royal family and its history is far richer than that of Buckingham Palace. American colonists spilled blood to escape the excesses of the Crown, but here is where their descendants queue up to bask in them in huge numbers. Even the gift shops have a prescribed traffic flow.

Absolutely do not neglect **St George's Chapel** (closed Sun), a delicately vaulted Gothic spectacle opened by Henry VIII. Because it often closes at 2:30pm and most tourists wait to see it after the main castle, you'd be wise to visit here first. Along with Westminster Abbey, this is the country's most important resting place for monarchs. Here are laid Henry and ten others, including Elizabeth II's father (George VI), Prince Philip, and Elizabeth herself. Elizabeth II's mother (the Queen Mum) and sister (Princess Margaret) are with them in a side chapel. It's also where Prince Harry married Meghan Markle in 2018. You may attend services here as a worshiper most days at 5:15 with a grounds ticket, but you may not take photos inside or in the main castle.

The castle's ceremonial **State Apartments**, which share a quadrangle with the part of the castle King Charles actually lives in, are sumptuous enough to be daunting, with architectural carvings on top of carvings, gilt, and marble. A tour through them—available unless there's a state visit—includes entrance to some mind-bogglingly historic rooms. Around a million people file through every year, so sharpen your elbows.

The palace has a cache of priceless furniture (some of it solid silver), paintings, ephemera, and weaponry, and the multimedia guide only describes one or two items per room (make sure to exhaust all the menu options for each chamber), so pepper staff with questions. In 1992, one-fifth of the castle area was engulfed by an accidental fire that started in the Lantern Lobby; Elizabeth recounted her despair over that, plus the breakup of two of her children's marriages, in her now-famous "annus horribilis" Christmas speech to the nation, and much effort and funding went into returning everything to the way it was before. In fact, Elizabeth originally opened Buckingham Palace to tourists to fund the restoration.

St George's Hall, one of the repaired areas, is the monarch's chosen room for banquets; investitures are bestowed in the **Waterloo Chamber**. Depending on official events, the tour may also include the Historic Route through the **Semi-State Rooms,** George IV's private area, considered by many to be among the best-preserved Georgian interiors in England, packed with an absurdly opulent collection of tapestries, cabinets of ebony and pewter and tortoiseshell, a disturbing masterwork by Peter Bruegel the Elder (in which animals were painted over depictions of children being slaughtered; in the King's Closet), several explosively detailed 17th-century sculptural bonanzas by Grinling Gibbons that go completely unremarked by the guide, and more. In the cases at the tour's end, look for exquisite banquet dish sets used by George III, Wiliam I, George IV, and Queen Victoria's coronation.

There's also **Queen Mary's Doll's House,** a preposterously extravagant toy mansion built for the allegedly grown-up Queen Mary in the 1920s to boast about British craftsmanship. It's got working electricity, plumbing, specially written library books, functional rotary lawn mowers, tiny tins of mustard, wine selected by Berry Bros. (p. 252), and other details so exorbitant you may struggle with the decadence. To see it, you'll join a separate queue, an often wicked one exposed to the rain, so visit it early or late in the day for the quickest wait. In August and September, you can also climb the **Round Tower** for views, and sometimes in January and midsummer, the castle's ancient **Great Kitchen** is open. There's also a **Changing the Guard** ceremony at 11am (generally Mon–Sat, but alternate days Aug–Mar, so check the website ahead).

The castle is the superstar here, but supporting roles are played by the succinctly named **Great Park** adjoining it, and the 4.8km (3-mile) pin-straight **Long Walk** that culminates with an equestrian statue of George III. **Frogmore,** rarely open, is the house where Victoria and Albert share their mausoleum. Just south of the castle is the **Guildhall,** where then-Prince Charles and Camilla Parker-Bowles had a quiet civil marriage ceremony in April 2005; it's no St Paul's, where in 1981 Charles wed his first wife, what's-her-name, but it is also the work of Christopher Wren (note its delicate arches). The building was apparently designed without the center columns, which made councilors nervous; Wren threw up some columns but left them an inch shy of the ceiling, just to prove that his architecture was sound.

Castle Hill. https://www.rct.uk. ✆ **0303/123-7300.** Admission £35 adults, £23 young people 18–24, £17.50 children 5–17 and people with disabilities, free for children 4 and under, all including multimedia guide device rental; discounts for advance booking, cheaper if the State Apartments are closed. Mar–Oct Thurs–Mon 10am–5:15pm, last admission 4pm; Nov–Feb Thurs–Mon daily 10am–4:15pm, last admission 3pm. Closed for special events or when the royal family is in residence; closures are posted online. National Rail: Windsor Central or Windsor & Eton Riverside.

Eton College ♥ A 15 minute walk over a footbridge on the Thames (narrow at this western remove), you're in a world served by snooty stationers and haberdashers. Eton is probably the most exclusive boys' school on Earth.

Saving on Your Excursion's Rail Ticket

Train fares listed in this section are provided as a guideline; National Rail pricing schemes are complicated and unpredictable. The good news is that for all of the destinations served by trains, if you return to London on the same day that you leave it, you can pay just a little more than the price of the usual one-way (single) ticket. Rail clerks call this a "day return." More tips:

- Do not wait until the day of travel to purchase a ticket. Last-minute fares are outrageous.
- Tickets tend to be most costly on Fridays, when Londoners head out of town.
- You can find incredible deals (up to 70% off) if you happen to be among the first customers to get tickets for a given departure. Book starting 12 weeks out.
- Prices are highest for "open" tickets with no restrictions, so opt for the restricted fare since you probably won't need to change your plans.

Aerial view of Eton College, a 15-minute walk from Windsor.

Princes Harry and William are alums, known as Old Etonians, as are kings and princes from around the world. There's a museum in its wine cellars—and the fact this school has a wine cellar tells you what kind of rich these kids are. Be nice to them. They're tomorrow's dictators.

Keats Lane, Eton, Windsor. https://collections.etoncollege.com/whats-on/heritage-tours. ✆ **01753/370-611** or email admissions@etoncollege.org.uk. Admission £15. 90-min. tours May–early Sept, Fri at 2 and 4pm; museum and gallery free Sun 1:30pm–4pm. No groups larger than 6, no kids under 7. Reservations required.

BATH

Easily roamed on foot, Bath, about 161km (100 miles) west of London, is revered as a splendid example of Georgian architecture—to tourists, Bath is resolutely stuck in that past. The pleasing sandstone hue of its buildings set against the slate-grey British sky, the assiduously planned symmetry of its streets, the newfound popularity brought to it by its *Bridgerton* locations, the illusion that Jane Austen (who lived here in 1800–1805) is taking tea within one of its 18th-century Palladian town houses—Bath's magic comes from its consistent and regal design. No wonder the upper crust of the 1700s found it so fashionable, and no wonder their descendants have not dared to alter it. And no wonder UNESCO inscribed it as a World Heritage Site—a rarity for an entire city.

Essentials

GETTING THERE The fastest **trains** (www.nationalrail.co.uk; ✆ **08457/48-49-50;** 90 min., twice an hour; £40 return with advance purchase) leave from Paddington and let you off in Bath Spa, an ugly section of town about 5 minutes' walk from the good stuff. Because buses take twice as long, I don't recommend buses by National Express (www.nationalexpress.com; ✆ **08705/80-80-80;** 3 hr.; £9 single). Most of the major tour bus companies (see box on p. 349) come here, combining it with Stonehenge (p. 348) for about £75.

TOURS Since 1934, the mayor's office has furnished professionally guided, free 2-hr. **The Mayor of Bath's Honorary Guides** (www.bathguides.org.uk; Sun–Fri 10:30am and 2pm, Sat 10:30am; May–Aug also Tues and Thurs 6pm). Meet outside the Roman Baths near Bath Abbey. Look for sign "free walking tour starts here"; no reservation required.

Exploring Bath

Begin your tour of Georgian Bath at **Queen Square** for some of the famous streets laid out by John Wood the Elder (1704–1754). Walk up to the **Circus,** three Palladian crescents (a row of attached houses built on a curve) arranged in a circle, with 524 different carved emblems above the doors. His son designed the **Royal Crescent,** an elegant half-moon row of townhouses. Robert Adam put up **Pulteney Bridge,** a shop-lined crossing of the River Avon, in 1773, just as a similar bridge in the same medieval style, London Bridge, was crumbling.

Roman Baths ♥♥♥ The Romans (ca. C.E. 60) were the first to recognize the tourism potential of the natural hot springs, which bubble at a rate of 250,000 gallons a day. Springs were redeveloped or rebored every few centuries; the current buildings are mostly from the 1800s, but Roman artifacts are occasionally found, and the restoration and accompanying museum are excellent. The Victorians mounted a proud colonnade around the excavation, and water has long been drawn in the adjoining **Pump Room**; you can drink a glass of the sulfuric stuff if you like, or settle down for a pricey lunch in neoclassical style. It's been the must-do thing in Bath since your great-great-great-grandma was in bloomers.

Bath Abbey Church Yard, Stall St. www.romanbaths.co.uk. ✆ **01225/477-785.** Admission £25.50 adults, £24.50 seniors and students, £18.50 children 6–18, £3 discounts for weekday bookings; higher prices are for weekends. June–late July daily 9am–6pm; late July–Aug daily 9am–10pm; Sept–Oct and Mar–June daily 9am–5pm; Nov–Feb daily 9:30am–5pm; last entry 1 hr. before closing.

Up close with Roman artifacts in the Roman Baths Museum.

Taking Tea in Bath

Yes, it's super-touristy—just go with it. The Regency stiffness of Bath is bound to give you a craving for that quintessentially English tradition of afternoon tea served with jam, clotted cream, and scones. Try the **Pump Room** at the Roman Baths (p. 337), which serves "Bath buns" (sweet buns sprinkled with sugar), or **Sally Lunn's** at 4 North Parade Passage (www.sallylunns.co.uk; ✆ **01225/461-634**), which makes such a big deal of its light Sally Lunn buns you'd swear you'd even heard of them before, which you haven't. The latter's building itself is one of the oldest in Bath, dating from 1482, and shows little hint of any changes with its crooked floors and low ceilings. For £10 to £20, you can sample a range of cream teas, which include toasted and buttered buns served with strawberry jam and clotted cream. The **Regency Tea Rooms** at the Jane Austen Centre offer "Mr. Darcy's Afternoon Tea" sets (Colin Firth not included) for £30, and basic cream tea from £13.

Bath Assembly Rooms ♥♥ The grand **Assembly Rooms,** designed by the younger John Wood and completed in 1771, once played host to dances, recitals, and tea parties. Damaged in World War II, the elegant rooms have been restored and look much as they did when Jane Austen and Thomas Gainsborough attended events here. The National Trust is restoring this site until 2027.

Bennett Street. www.nationaltrust.org.uk. ✆ **01225/466-414.** Assembly Rooms: free admission. Opening time varies (check site), generally 10am–6am. Guided tours Tues & Thurs.

Jane Austen Centre ♥ This small homage to Britain's favorite 19th-century writer isn't in her house, but Miss Austen did live up the hill (at no. 25) for a few months in 1805. Exhibits and a video convey a sense of what life was like when Austen lived in Bath between 1801 and 1806 (reader, she didn't particularly care for it). Visitors can try dressing up in Regency garb and ladies can learn the esoteric skill of using a fan to attract an admirer. Wholesome, corny fun. Allow at least 45 minutes. The tearoom is worth a visit (see "Taking Tea in Bath," below).

40 Gay St. www.janeausten.co.uk. ✆ **01225/443-000.** Admission £17 adults, £15.50 seniors and students, £9.50 children 6–16; £39 family ticket. Summer daily 10am–5:30pm, winter Sun–Fri 10am–4:30pm; Sat 10am–5:30pm.

1 Royal Crescent ♥♥ First-time visitors are blown away by the sweep and elegance of the Royal Crescent, a dazzling 30-house development that

The curving townhouses of the Royal Crescent, one of Bath's most regal examples of Georgian architecture.

Afternoon tea at The Pump Room at the Roman Baths.

took some 8 years to complete, from 1767 to 1775. Its first house, which absorbed the old servants' quarters in a massive restoration that religiously presents daily life in those days, is worth a swing-by if you want the full effect of learning how people lived during the Regency period.

1 Royal Crescent. www.no1royalcrescent.org.uk. ✆ **01225/428-126.** Admission £16 adults, £14.50 students and seniors, £9.50 children 5–15, family ticket £31. Tues–Sun 10am–5:30pm; last admission 4:30pm.

OXFORD

Whereas the face of London, 92km (57 miles) east, has been forcibly reshaped by the pressures of war, disaster, and commerce, Oxford was made stronger by them. When plague killed townspeople, the colleges snapped up their houses, and when the Reformation cleaned out the churches, the colleges took their land, too. Academies used the extra space to carve out some of the most beautiful college buildings in the world. Here, the reverence for education borders on the ecclesiastical. Yet Oxford is no cloister; it's a decidedly modern city—thriving, sophisticated, and busy.

Essentials

GETTING THERE The least expensive, easiest method is by coach, because companies compete for students with regular buses rolling round the clock. The so-called **Oxford Tube** bus (www.oxfordtube.com; ✆ **01865/772-250;** 100 min. with no traffic; £16 adults, £15 seniors over 60 or students age 16–26, £7 children 5–15; with Wi-Fi and power sockets) leaves every 10–20 min. at all hours. Every 10 minutes it picks passengers up near the Tube stations at Victoria, Marble Arch, and Notting Hill Gate. Give rush hours wide berth. **Trains** (www.nationalrail.co.uk; ✆ **08457/48-49-50;** 1 hr.; £15–£27 single with advance purchase) go from Paddington or Marylebone stations to

Oxford, sometimes via Reading. You could also take the Elizabeth Line to Reading and a 25-minute connection (3–4 per hr.) from there.

TOURS **Experience Oxfordshire** offers daily walking tours (www.experienceoxfordshire.org; ✆ **01865/686-441;** 10:30am and 1pm most days; £ 28; reservations required) using accredited guides. Themes include "Oxford on Screen," C. S. Lewis and J.R.R. Tolkien, and ghosts. **Oxford River Cruises** (www.oxfordrivercruises.com; ✆ **01865/987-147**) runs several boat tours along the River Thames; the tranquil 45-minute Oxford Experience (cheaper online: £19 adults, £13 children 11 and under; reservations suggested) is popular. **City Sightseeing** runs hop-on, hop-off bus tours with prerecorded audio (https://city-sightseeing.com; ✆ **01789/299-123;** from £20; 10am–6pm daily).

Exploring Oxford

Wandering Oxford's cobbled streets and ducking into its colleges to soak up their hidden loveliness makes for a happy afternoon, particularly for fans of architecture. Many of the most iconic building clusters in this city of 140,000 (30,000 of whom are students) are collected together in the center of town. Oxford, like Cambridge (p. 344), comprises individual colleges that feed off a central university system. Each of the 39 colleges has its own campus, tradition, character, and disciplines—and each has finicky hours, so always check ahead before planning a day. Unfortunately, many close their grassy inner sanctums to visitors. During the school terms (mid-Jan to mid-Mar, late Apr to mid-June, Oct to early Dec), some university buildings required for study (libraries, residence halls) are closed to the public, or only open on Saturdays. At all times of year, watch out for zooming cyclists; an unwritten law appears to grant them ownership of the city.

To get the most out of Oxford, poke around, looking inside cloisters and above rooftops. The doors between the inner and outer quadrangles of **Balliol College** (Broad St. and St Giles; www.balliol.ox.ac.uk; ✆ **01865/27-77-77;** £6 adults, £3 seniors and students; daily 10am–5pm) still bear scorch marks from where Bloody Mary burned two Protestants alive for refusing to recant. Viewpoints are popular attractions in Oxford: The 22m (72-ft.) rectangular **Carfax Tower** (£4 adults, £3 children 15 and under; Apr–Sept daily 10am–5:30pm, Oct–Mar daily 10am–4:30pm) is the last remaining chunk of the 13th-century St Martin's Church; it has only 99 steps, so it's not too taxing. It's located by the crossroads of the city center. Other popular panoramas are from the octagonal cupola above Sir Christopher Wren's **Sheldonian Theatre** (Broad St.; www.sheldonian.ox.ac.uk; ✆ **01865/277-299;** £8, £14 with guided tour; hours change daily with many closings, so check ahead, but opening tends to be at 10am). Perhaps the top view is from the **University Church of St Mary the Virgin** (www.university-church.ox.ac.uk; ✆ **01865/279-113;** £6; Mon–Sat 9.30am–5pm, Sun noon–5pm, last tower admission 30 min. before closing).

The Ashmolean Museum ♥♥ Offering more than just a pretty facade, the Ashmolean was founded way back in 1683, literally before anyone knew what the word "museum" meant. It houses an important hodgepodge of antiquities and art on par with (but on a smaller scale than) the British Museum, including a lantern carried by Guy Fawkes during the foiled Gunpowder Plot; the Anglo-Saxon Alfred Jewel of gold, enamel, and rock crystal; a Stradivarius violin; and assorted Old Masters paintings. Oh, and you know, minor stuff by Raphael and Michelangelo.

Beaumont St. at St Giles. www.ashmolean.org. ✆ **01865/278-000.** Free admission. Daily 10am–5pm. Closed Dec 24–26.

Christ Church ♥♥♥ The largest, most beautiful, and most popular college to visit looms large in children's literature: It was copied for Hogwarts School in the Harry Potter films, and it was where Lewis Carroll (aka mathematician Charles Dodgson) befriended the little girl for whom he wrote *Alice in Wonderland.* The college chapel, which dates from the 12th century, also serves as Oxford Cathedral for the local diocese. Bowler-hatted "custodians" still patrol the pristine lawns, and Christ Church Meadow, still grazed by cattle, is a delightful place to watch punters on the rivers Isis and Cherwell. Just being here makes you feel smarter. Tours come in many flavors: college, cathedral, both of them, architecture, monuments, and lantern-led in evening.

St Aldate's. www.chch.ox.ac.uk. ✆ **01865/276-492.** Multimedia tours £24 adults, £23 seniors and students, guided tours £22–£26, no kids under 11 on tours; slight discount for weekday visits. Mon–Sat 9am–5pm; Sun 2–5pm; last admission 4:30pm. Closed for week around Christmas and New Year's.

Magdalen College ♥♥ Pronounced "*Maud*-lin," it is one of the largest and most peaceful colleges here; its tower is the city's highest point, and its chapel is carved with breathtaking detail. Its site has a virtual tour to prep you on your explorations. Retired U.S. Supreme Court justice Stephen Breyer attended.

High St. www.magd.ox.ac.uk. ✆ **01865/276-000.** Admission £10 adults, £9 seniors, students, and children. July–Sept daily noon 7pm; Oct–June daily 1–6pm or dusk (whichever is earlier). Closed around Christmas and New Year's.

Christ Church college's dining hall was an inspiration for the one in the Harry Potter films and books.

Oxford students stroll by the Radcliffe Camera, a library on campus.

Old Bodleian Library ♥♥ The main research library in a town that made its name in research, "the Bod" opened in 1602 and has been burrowing under the streets of Oxford, trying to find new places to store its multiplying collection (11 million tomes and counting) ever since. See it by tour. The round **Radcliffe Camera** ("Rad Cam"; open via guided tours at the Bodleian) was built in the 1740s to house scientific books. It stands on the north side of Radcliffe Square.

Catte St. visit.bodleian.ox.ac.uk. ✆ **01865/287-400.** Divinity school tour £2.50; library tours 30-min. £10 (daily), 60-min. £15 (daily), 90-min. £20 (Sat–Sun). Library tour including Radcliffe Camera £30 (Sat–Sun). Reservations suggested; check current tour times online. Mon–Fri 9am–5pm; Sat 9am–4:30pm; Sun 11am–5pm. Closed for week around Christmas and New Year's.

The Pitt Rivers Museum ♥ An imposing 1886 cast-iron cathedral-like building, not unlike a railway station, houses a blend of folk art and anthropology—think African headdresses, masks, and bundles of poisoned arrows. Most of the collection was brought back by plundering British explorers over hundreds of years and so curators struggle with about how to display it sensitively.

Parks Rd. www.prm.ox.ac.uk. ✆ **01865/270-927.** Free admission. Mon noon–5pm; Tues–Sun 10am–5pm.

OUTSIDE OXFORD

Blenheim Palace ♥♥♥ Before Winston Churchill was famously born here in a makeshift cloakroom during a party, this eye-popping pile (in the rare English baroque style) was commissioned in 1705 as a reward for his triumphant military ancestor, John Churchill, the first Duke of Marlborough.

The birthplace of Winston Churchill, Blenheim Palace has about 200 rooms and 2,000 acres of gardens.

Winston, who wasn't in line to inherit it, would nevertheless try to impress girls by bringing them to visit, a tactic that finally paid off when he proposed to Clementine Hozier in its garden's Temple of Diana.

There's an artifact-packed biographical museum about Winston in the cellar, but mostly, the audio guide of the lavish Palace State Rooms of this rightful UNESCO World Heritage Site is obsessed with the intricacies of lineage and noble titles. You could spend all day (there's a cafe for lunch) gawping at bygone English indulgence by ambling through the glorious 2,000-acre gardens, both formal and falsely naturalistic, which were designed with such extravagance that they helped ruin the reputation of playwright-cum-architect John Vanbrugh (when he died, the wry poet Abel Evans wrote an epitaph for him: "Lie heavy on him, Earth! for he Laid many heavy loads on thee!"). The British rarely remind you that the oh-so-English savior of World War II was, in fact, half American: Winston's mom, Jennie, was from Brooklyn and married an English lord, *Downton Abbey*-style. A few decades later, the home was saved from financial ruin when the 9th Duke of Marlborough married another wealthy American, Consuelo Vanderbilt; their descendants still live here for part of the year, which may account for the family-obsessed audio tour.

Hensington Rd., Woodstock, Oxfordshire. www.blenheimpalace.com. ✆ **01993/810-530.** Admission palace and grounds £41 adults, £24 kids 3–16, £110 family ticket; about £10 less for grounds only. Daily 10:30am–5:30pm; last admission 4:45pm. Take half-hourly S3 bus (www.stagecoachbus.com; 30 min.; £3) from the Oxford train station or Gloucester Green to Hensington Road, Woodstock.

CAMBRIDGE

Oxford is a city in its own right, but Cambridge, in the marshes 79km (49 miles) northeast of London, would barely have a pulse without its university. That makes Cambridge manageable—it's also cheaper to visit. It feels in some ways like a typical English town, with a daily market for crafts and food on its central square, Market Hill. Its best rewards come when you wander through randomly chosen iron gates or along a river path—that's when the inviting little town really opens up.

Essentials

GETTING THERE Nonstop **coaches** from National Express (www.nationalexpress.com; ✆ **08705/80-80-80;** 2½ hr.; £7–£8 single) leave hourly from

Punting the River Cherwell

Punting on the River Cherwell is an essential if slightly eccentric Oxford pastime. From mid-March to October at the **Cherwell Boathouse,** Bardwell Road (www.cherwellboathouse.co.uk; ✆ **01865/515-978**), you can rent a punt (a flat-bottomed boat for up to five people, maneuvered by a long pole and a small oar) for £24–£26 per hour. **Magdalen Bridge Boathouse,** the Old Horse Ford, High Street (www.oxfordpunting.co.uk; ✆ **01865/202-643**), charges £32 per hour for up to 5 people, daily 10am until dusk. Both outfits offer basic training.

BLETCHLEY PARK: ENIGMA no more

For decades, it was top secret. Few people realized what had happened here during World War II in these rotting temporary wooden huts, so they were nearly bulldozed for a housing development. But in time, we learned what codebreaker Alan Turing and his brilliant team accomplished at **Bletchley Park** (https://bletchleypark.org.uk; ✆ **01908/640-404**), hidden from the world on a former estate 88km (55 miles) northwest of London. Here they cracked the Enigma machine code, breaking the German blockade that threatened to starve an entire country.

In 2014, the year a film about their story, *The Imitation Game*, was released, the fully restored Bletchley Park campus was opened as a fascinating large scale day out. A visit is like a spy novel set in a park, suffused with the urgency, intrigue, and excitement of those terrifying years when computers were born and Nazis were a few chess moves away from storming England. You can tour more than a dozen buildings around its soothing central pond, exploring the methods, experiments, and lucky breaks that enabled round-the clock workers—including many gifted women—to translate a jumble of meaningless letters into life-saving intercepted secrets.

The cramped, rudimentary Huts 3, 6, and 8, dressed to look like they probably did then (no one is sure—photographs were forbidden), were the heart of the operation, but you can also tour the ground floor of the mansion that served as its command post and outbuildings that housed the computers, which were later dismantled down to the rivets to prevent anyone from duplicating them. Head to the basement of Block B, where modern fans have rebuilt one. The number of Enigma-related artifacts and the level of codebreaking detail can be head-spinning, so children may tire quickly, but interested adults could spend 3 or 4 absorbed hours wrapping their heads around it, a pursuit made easier by the three cafes spread around its grassy acres. Admission is £28 adults, £25.50 seniors and students, £19.50 children 12–17, and £48.50–£76.50 family ticket. It's open daily, from 9:30am to 5pm, March to October (9:30am–4pm Nov–Feb); last admission 2 hours before closing.

Trains to Bletchley leave Euston a few times an hour (50 min.; £17 return in advance), and the gates are only 182m (200 yards) from the station; sit on the left of the carriage for good views of the Grand Union Canal as you go. If you fancy a country drive, Avis, Enterprise, and Budget are clustered near the Bletchley train station.

Victoria Coach Station; don't get off at Trumpington, but wait for the city center stop. There are **trains** from Liverpool Street or King's Cross, but be warned that Cambridge's station is far from the city center; coaches are the smarter way to travel. If you insist, though, note that some trains take about 45 minutes and some take twice that, so ask about journey times (www.nationalrail.co.uk; ✆ **08457/48-49-50;** 45–90 min.; £10–£23).

VISITOR INFORMATION Download a free map from **Visit Cambridge** (www.visitcambridge.org; info@visitcambridge.org); sometimes Cambridge City Ambassadors are on hand at the railway station to distribute info and maps.

TOURS **Cantab Tours** runs 90-minute walking tours of the city (www.cantabtours.com; daily 11:30am and 2pm, advance booking required; £20 adults, and up to £12 for children 15 and under). **City Sightseeing** runs

You can rent a punting boat on the River Cam, or take a guided ride and let someone else navigate.

hop-on, hop-off bus tours with prerecorded audio (https://city-sightseeing.com; ✆ **01789-299-123;** from £19; daily 10am–6pm).

Exploring Cambridge

Like Oxford, Cambridge's glory is the elaborate and ancient architecture of its colleges. However, unlike in Oxford, it's easy to venture into the cloistered grounds of many of Cambridge's colleges, though doing so usually requires a few quid. (Cambridge took shape in the early 13th c., after a squabble in Oxford drove several scholars to leave there and establish a second educational capital. The oldest Cambridge College, Peterhouse, was founded in 1284.) Mill Lane leads to the River Cam, where you can rent a punting boat for £6 or sit at The Mill pub overlooking the water. (If you want to seem savvy to Cambridge traditions, punt from the back of the boat. In Oxford, they punt from the front.) The meadows along the Cam, known as the **Backs,** make for idyllic walks.

The head of Oliver Cromwell, which was impaled outside Westminster Hall in London as a warning against regicide (albeit 3 years after the man died of natural causes), was finally buried within an antechapel (not open to visitors) at Sidney Sussex College in 1960. It's in an unmarked grave to keep pranksters from pinching the much-abused thing. That's Cambridge in a nutshell: It has many secrets, but since it's still a working university town, marvels won't be handed to you. You have to wander, wonder, and ask questions. Outside of term (terms run mid-Jan to mid-Mar, late Apr to mid-June, and Oct to early Dec), colleges aren't open, and street life is at a minimum.

Queens' College (www.queens.cam.ac.uk; daily 10am–4:30pm outside of examination periods; £5 adults, kids 12 and under free) has as its most famous calling card its wooden **Mathematical Bridge** linking the so-called Dark Side and Light Side of the grounds. You will hear an apocryphal story about it being assembled without bolts and later confounding some students who took it apart and couldn't put it back together again. You should be smarter than believe everything you learn at Cambridge. The tale is false, but the bridge is still a fascinating structure without it.

Egyptian antiques in the Fitzwilliam Museum, a vast collection of art and artifacts in Cambridge.

Fitzwilliam Museum ♥♥♥ Cambridge's most storied attraction is a first-rate neoclassical building full of applied arts and Old Masters that a city 10 times Cambridge's size (population 118,000) would covet. If a colonial Englishman could carry it home on a ship, it's here: precious antiquities from Rome, Greece, Egypt, and Asia, and paintings by every famous name under the European sun.

Trumpington St., near Peterhouse. www.fitzmuseum.cam.ac.uk. ✆ **01223/332-900.** Free admission, but booking timed admission is requested. Tues–Sat 10am–5pm; Sun and bank holidays noon–5pm.

King's College Chapel ♥♥ For some reason, the marauding Puritans neglected to smash the 16th-century stained-glass windows of this chapel—they probably thought they were too divine to destroy, just as you will. The chapel's fanned and vaulted ceiling, a work of craftsmanship that stuns even those who care little for such things, was completed at the behest of Henry VII. Its famous choristers sing at services during term time.

King's Parade. www.kings.cam.ac.uk. ✆ **01223/331-100.** Admission £17.50 adults, £15 students and young people 6–17, free for children 5 and under. Generally weekends 9:30am–4:30pm, last entry to chapel 3pm, but check website calendar in advance for frequent closures and changes.

Pembroke College ♥♥ The third-oldest college in town is one of the best, distinguished by the oldest gatehouse in Cambridge and by a chapel with an ornate plaster ceiling, which was the first completed work by Christopher Wren (after finishing this, the man seemed never to rest again). Unlike many of the colleges, Pembroke never charges visitors to poke around its common areas.

Trumpington St. www.pem.cam.ac.uk. ✆ **01223/33-81-00.** Free admission, building interiors not open. Daily 9:30am–4pm, except mid-May to mid-June when closed for exams.

Trinity College ♥♥ Trinity is the largest and most endowed of Cambridge's 31 colleges. Sir Isaac Newton first calculated the speed of sound here, at Neville's Court, and Lord Byron used to bathe naked in the Great Court's fountain with his pet bear. (The university forbade students from having dogs, but there was no rule against bears.) In *Chariots of Fire,* sprinters tried to get

The soaring interior of King's College Chapel, Cambridge.

around the .8-hectare (2-acre) yard in the time it took for its clock to strike 12. Your attempts at re-creating that will not be appreciated.

Trinity St. www.trin.cam.ac.uk. ✆ **01223/338-400.** Free admission. Grounds: daily 9:30am–5pm. The Wren Library: Mon–Fri noon–2pm; Sat 10:30am–12:30pm, but check website calendar in advance for frequent closures and changes.

STONEHENGE & SALISBURY

Stonehenge is a circle of rocks. If it's raining, it's a damned circle of rocks. But people without an interest in prehistory still ask to go, and if that's their dream, then they should do it. Just understand that it's an anthropological site.

Most coach tours offer an itinerary that combines Stonehenge with Bath (p. 336); bus and train connections make it difficult to do that if you're traveling independently. However, it's quite doable to combine Stonehenge with a visit to Salisbury, a lovely and relatively well-preserved cathedral town.

Essentials

GETTING THERE Trains don't go directly to Stonehenge; the nearest station is in Salisbury, nearly 16km (10 miles) south. So the easiest way to get here is to catch a group tour (see box, above) or drive. The rocks are located 3.2km (2 miles) west of Amesbury in Wiltshire on the junction of A303 and A344/360. If you must do public transportation, take a half-hourly **train** (www.nationalrail.co.uk; ✆ **08457/48-49-50;** 90 min.; £25 return with advance purchase) from Waterloo station to Salisbury station. There used to be a cheap public bus to the rocks from there, but it says a lot about the greed of local tourism authorities that they replaced that route entirely with the expensive but convenient **Stonehenge Tour Bus** (1 hr. 10 min. for return transportation; www.thestonehengetour.info; ✆ **01202/338-420;** bus only: £20 adults, £13.50 children 5–15; add tours of Salisbury Cathedral and Old Sarum for more; buy online or in cash from driver), which leaves from Salisbury station seven times a day between 10am and 4pm. Many tour companies offer round-trip all-day coach tours from London that take about 7 hours. One of them is **Premium Tours** (see above) for £72 adults, £62 seniors, including entry. Whirlwind versions that somehow include Bath start at £85.

VISITOR INFORMATION **Salisbury Information Centre** (Fish Row, Salisbury; www.visitwiltshire.co.uk; ✆ **01722/342-860**) provides info on both Stonehenge and Salisbury.

TOURS You can easily see Salisbury on foot, either on your own or by taking a guided daytime or evening walk, run by **Salisbury City Guides** (www.salisburycityguides.co.uk; ✆ **07873/212-941;** Fri Apr–Oct). Tickets are £12 for adults, £6 for students and children 12–18, and free for kids 11 and under.

Exploring Stonehenge & Salisbury

Stonehenge ♥ Construction on this bucket-list site began about 5,000 years ago; the first recorded day trips to the megalith were in 1562—just think, your day trip dates to Elizabethan times! Arranged in such a way that it

THE TRADE-OFF WITH escorted tours

With so many tour options, renting a car for day trips is a lousy idea. Arranging your own day trips using public transportation will almost always be the most cost-effective method, but there are cogent reasons for choosing a guided coach tour. It's simply quicker to allow someone else to drive you around, making sure you cram a laundry list of major sights into a short time span and consume spoon-fed nuggets of information about each place. At least you'll have been there. And some sights have a cache of tickets not accessible to the public—places like Highclere Castle (p. 352) may be easier to do as part of a coach tour.

Most tours cost about £70 to £130 for 6–11 hours out of London. You get a richer experience (and one that doesn't have you waiting for other tour members to catch up) when you do it yourself. But some people desperately want to soak up as many sights as they can, even if it means viewing sights as a blur from the motorway. For them, here are the major players in the coach-tour biz, sold aggressively through concierges at expensive hotels (who love getting the commissions). Most tours depart from Victoria Coach Station.

- **Evan Evans Tours** (www.evanevanstours.co.uk; ✆ **020/7932-8385** in the U.K., 800/422-9022 in the U.S.)
- **Gray Line's Golden Tours** (www.goldentours.com; ✆ **020/7630-2028** in the U.K., 800/509-2507 in the U.S.)
- **Premium Tours** (www.premiumtours.co.uk; ✆ **020/7713-1311** in the U.K., 800/815-4003 in the U.S.)
- **Rabbie's** (www.rabbies.com; ✆ **0131/226-3133** in the U.K.) tends to use small-group vans more than large coaches, and tends to be a little less expensive.

aligns with the rising of the sun during the midsummer solstice, this Neolithic circle of stones is certainly Britain's most important ancient wonder, and it's a UNESCO World Heritage Site (together with Avebury, a far less interesting, but still important, line of rocks 39km/24 miles north). Whether its builders, who remain anonymous despite growing theories, worshiped the sun or merely appreciated astronomy is only the beginning of the mystery. We also can only make educated guesses as to how these prehistoric people, using only rudimentary tools, managed to hoist these slabs from Wales to here, and then into place. Even if you don't salivate over such long-ago feats of ingenuity, the distinctive profile of the stones, surrounded by empty plains, "henge" earthworks, and hundreds of lumpen burial mounds, will surely feel iconic.

Tourists have been visiting the enigmatic stone circle at Stonehenge since at least the 1500s.

You're not allowed to walk among the rocks the way visitors once were. You have to stick to a footpath that curves near the circle but keeps the formation at a safe distance, good for pretty photographs but tough on curiosity. Most tourists like you and me are kept at arm's length (exception: Clark Griswold, who managed to topple them like dominoes in *National Lampoon's European Vacation*), but you can apply in advance for a 1-hour Stone Circle Experience pass to stroll with about 51 others among the rocks—no touching—timed in the very early morning or after it closes for the day. The application is at the English Heritage website (see below). Otherwise, you'll have a limited experience—a disappointment for many who trudge 129km/80 miles west of London to have it. Alternatively, climb **Amesbury Hill,** clearly visible 2.4km (1½ miles) up the A303. From here, you'll get a free panoramic view. Check opening times before heading out; closings are occasional.

At the junction of A303 and A344. www.english-heritage.org.uk/stonehenge. ✆ **08703/331-181.** Admission £27.20 adults, £23.60 seniors and students with ID, £17.20 children 5–15, £44.40–£71.60 family ticket; Stone Circle Experience £70 adults, £40 children 5–17. June–Aug daily 9am–8pm; Apr–May and Sept–mid-Oct daily 9:30am–7pm; mid-Oct–Mar daily 9:30am–5pm; last admission 2 hr. before closing. Train: Salisbury, then Stonehenge Tour Bus.

Old Sarum ♥ Believed to have been an Iron Age fortification, Old Sarum was used again by the Saxons and flourished as a walled town into the Middle Ages. The Normans built a cathedral; parts of that were taken down to build the city of "New Sarum," later known as Salisbury, leaving behind dramatically sited remains with unforgettable views of Salisbury and rolling green hills, not to mention the opportunity to commune with grazing sheep.

2 miles north of Salisbury, off A345. Castle Rd. www.english-heritage.org.uk/oldsarum. ✆ **01722/335-398.** Admission £6.80 adults, £5.90 seniors and students, £3.60 children 5–17; higher posted prices include a "voluntary donation." Apr–Sept daily 10am–6pm; Mar and Oct daily 10am–5pm; Nov–Feb daily 10am–4pm. Bus: X5, 8, or 501, every 30 min. during the day, from Salisbury bus station.

Salisbury Cathedral's spire is 404 feet tall—the tallest such structure in the U.K.

Salisbury Cathedral ♥♥ Built with uncommon efficiency between 1220 and 1258 and barely touched since, this early English Gothic masterpiece is considered by many to be the most breathtaking church in the world. The cathedral complex's octagonal Chapter House shelters one of four surviving copies of the Magna Carta signed by King John in 1215. (Two more are in London at the British Library; p. 130.) After you've seen the cathedral, and lost yourself in gazing at it and sighing, the rest of your time in Salisbury will be contentedly spent walking medieval streets, which were laid in a loose grid and give the city an airy character.

The Close. www.salisburycathedral.org.uk. ✆ **01722/555-120.** Admission £13 adults, £9.50 students 17 and up, £8.50 students 13–16, free for children 12 and under; discounts for booking in advance. Mon–Sat 9am–5pm; Sun 12:30–4pm; last entry 1 hr. before closing.

CANTERBURY

The ecclesiastical capital of England, Canterbury (62 miles southeast of London) feels like a seat of English charm itself, with the squared spire of its great Gothic cathedral rising from the cobbled cluster of its village. You can still find traces of the original city walls and punt on the calm water that meanders through town. It's also easy to explore on foot; start your explorations at The Goods Shed, a market for luscious English dairy, meat, and alcohol (with its own gourmet restaurant; www.thegoodsshed.co.uk), beside the Canterbury West railway station.

Essentials

GETTING THERE Two National Rail stations, Canterbury East and Canterbury West, are both conveniently just outside the city walls. High-speed

HIGHCLERE CASTLE, THE *real* DOWNTON ABBEY

The 8th Earl and Countess of Carnarvon still dwell under the sandstone turrets of **Highclere Castle** (Highclere Park, Newbury; www.highclerecastle.co.uk; ✆ **01635/253-204;** admission £32 adults, £30 students and seniors, £17.50 children 4–16; last admission at 3:30pm, grounds close at 5:30pm), known to TV viewers as the idyllic and stately Downton Abbey. Time and spendthrift earls took their toll on this historic home, and as recently as 2009, more than 50 rooms were uninhabitable due to mold and leaks. The current Earl faced repair bills running around £12 million, so he welcomes visitors to spend the day exploring the estate's 1,000 acres of private rolling Berkshire countryside.

He also rents out to film production: The upstairs scenes of TV series and films of *Downton Abbey* were shot on the ground floor and first floor using the house's actual furniture, though downstairs scenes were shot on a soundstage in Ealing, West London. That's partly because at Highclere, the basement is full not of kitchens but of mummy stuff: The 5th Earl was the guy who bankrolled Howard Carter's 1923 emptying of King Tut's tomb in Luxor, so unseen beneath Lord Grantham's feet lie items taken from the tombs of Egypt. The grounds are generally accessible, but Highclere house is open only on predetermined days (so buy tickets online in advance to ensure you're going on an open day), and they're scattered all over the calendar—typically Easter Week, bank holiday weekends, and from July to mid-September (closed Fri and Sat).

Taking a group tour guarantees a ticket, but those can sell out months ahead and herd you along. If you show up independently at 10am or by 2pm at the latest, you can usually get a walk-up ticket even though advance tickets are sold out. Only once you have a ticket can you also sign up for the afternoon tea (from £60 for two) in its Coach House (no children for that). Getting here on your own involves taking a 52-minute train from Paddington to the adorable town of Newbury (in town, admire the longboats on the Kennet and Avon canal and peruse the century-old village department store, Camp Hopson) and then a £25-ish taxi (try www.cabco33333.com, ✆ **01635/33333;** or www.gogreentaxisltd.co.uk, order by app). The coach tour companies make it a lot easier, and Premium Tours (p. 349) throws in a copy of one of Lady Carnarvon's books.

trains from Charing Cross, St Pancras, and Victoria take 60 to 90 minutes (www.nationalrail.co.uk; ✆ **08457/48-49-50;** £38 return in advance). Buses are not recommended for a day trip; trains are quick and deliver you right to the town.

VISITOR INFORMATION **Canterbury Visitor Information** is at the Beaney House of Art and Knowledge, 18 High Street (www.canterbury.co.uk; ✆ **01227/862-162**).

TOURS The popular **Canterbury Punting Company** (Water Lane; www.canterburypunting.co.uk; ✆ **07786/332-666;** £12.50–£35) lets you ply the River Stour on a wide, flat boat past medieval buildings under hanging bowers—an ideal outing.

Exploring Canterbury

Canterbury Cathedral ♥♥♥ The original modern tourist attraction, it's where the pilgrims were headed in Chaucer's *The Canterbury Tales* (1478). They were going to pay their respects to Archbishop Thomas Becket, who was assassinated in the northwest transept, next to what is now the Chapel of Our Lady Martyrdom. Henry VIII tore down that shrine in a typical fit of pique, but this transporting place is still one of the most visited sites in Britain. The cathedral, along with **St Augustine's Abbey** and **St Martin's Church** (the oldest still-functioning church in the English-speaking world; both were founded around 597), form a World Heritage Site. Look for the medieval tombs of King Henry IV and Edward the Black Prince; Becket lies in the Trinity Chapel, near the high altar. The stained glass depicting his reported miracles is regarded as some of England's finest; fortunately, the cathedral's windows survived Hitler's bombs by being removed and hidden away.

The Precincts. www.canterbury-cathedral.org. ✆ **01227/762-862.** Admission £21 adults, free children under 18, free for ages 6 and under, slight discounts for weekdays. Mon–Sat 9am–5pm; Sun 11:30am–5pm; last admission 1 hr. before closing.

A guided tour of Canterbury Cathedral, still one of the most visited sights in Britain.

PLANNING YOUR TRIP TO LONDON

10

Some 21 million tourists journey to London in a normal year, so it can't be that hard to do. London hospitality and tourist industries know a thing or two about helping foreigners. Finding airfare isn't much harder than finding a cross-country flight, and for most people, communicating is as easy as opening your mouth to speak. Being ready for the rest (money, transportation) is simply a matter of having the facts.

GETTING THERE

By Plane

Transatlantic flights usually land at **Heathrow,** Europe's busiest international airport (LHR; 17 miles west of London), or **Gatwick,** perhaps the most disliked (LGW; 31 miles south). With a few minor exceptions, the other four airports—**Stansted** (STN; 37 miles northeast), **Luton** (LTN; 34 miles northwest), **London City** (LCY; in London's Docklands area), and **Southend** (SEN; 42 miles east)—serve flights from Europe; they're where cut-rate flyers and executive jets tend to go.

FINDING THE LOWEST AIRFARE

The central question here is *when* are they? London is such a popular destination (it's served by more flights from the United States than any other European city) that plenty of airlines vie to carry you across—although the ones that are not American-run may be of higher in-flight quality. And partly because international routes are prized among crew with seniority, flights across the ocean are usually less likely to be canceled than domestic routes back home. To minimize the chances of your schedule being ruined by delays or cancellations, try to stick to nonstop flights. If you're not redeeming frequent-flier miles (book very far ahead if you are), there are six rules to finding bargains:

1. **Fly on days when traffic is lightest.** Some airlines post calendars that show you when their best prices are, or test fare trends on a site such as **Hopper.com** or by using a flexible flight search calendar.

The Cashless Revolution

You can no longer rely on cash in London. Even simple items like cups of coffee and theater programs may only be available if you pay by tapping credit cards. In London, it's now possible to conduct an entire vacation without using cash or coins a single time—in fact, many vendors won't even accept loose change anymore. You can pay by card swipe, but your life will be much easier if you're set up for tap-and-go. Before leaving home, ensure your cards can be used for contactless transactions: A little Wi-Fi symbol on the card usually denotes the capability, but you may have to ask your bank for a contactless version of a card. You can also use smartphone-centric payment such as Apple Pay or Google Pay (even for the Tube—but set it up in your phone before leaving home) as long as your associated credit cards work internationally.

2. **Depart after dinner.** This saves you from paying another hotel night, since you'll arrive in the morning. You're also likely to find lower fares, because business travelers, who spend more, like day flights.
3. **Go off-season.** London's weather isn't extreme, so there's really not a no-go month. November through March yield the lowest airfares and hotel rates, although the late-December holidays and the last week of November (Thanksgiving in U.S.) can be busy, too. Summer prices (June–Sept) soar well over a grand.
4. **Search for fares for or on a weekend.** Many major airlines post lower prices to fly then. You might also save money by flight shopping at 3am. That's because unpaid-for reservations are flushed out of the system at midnight, and prices often sink when the system becomes aware of an increase in supply.
5. **Try a bargain airline.** Norse Atlantic Airways (flynorse.com) and Icelandair (www.icelandair.com) are worth checking.
6. **Don't buy last-minute.** Desperation has a price.

Monitor airline emails, sale pages, Twitter accounts, and sites for sales. Sign up with a flight tracker notification service (there are plenty online, such as Skyscanner or Google Flights) that will spit out emails when airfare drops.

Primary websites that collect quotes from a variety of sources (whether they be airlines or other websites) include **Momondo.com** and **Skyscanner.com,** which consistently deliver the best price results in Frommer's tests, and the app **Hopper.** Always canvass multiple sites, because each has odd gaps in coverage because of how they obtain quotes. Always compare your best price with what the airline is offering, because that price might be lowest of all. Many sites force you to accept nonrefundable tickets with no luggage allowance for the cheapest prices, so be prepared for the extra fees to make those flights workable. If you hit a wall, search for transatlantic itineraries that allow for one or two stops, since routes that include stops in Reykjavik or Frankfurt (on Icelandair or Lufthansa, respectively) can produce hidden bargains. No matter which airline you go with, prepare yourself for added

Traveling to & from London's Airports

AIRPORT	COST/AVG. TIME USING NATIONAL RAIL	HOURS OF RAIL SERVICE
Heathrow (LHR), www.Heathrow.com	**Heathrow Express** (www.heathrowexpress.com): £10 (advance)–£25 single, £20 (advance)–£42 return, kids 15 and under free*/15 min.	5:12am to 11:57
Gatwick (LGW), www.GatwickAirport.com	Gatwick Express (www.gatwickexpress.com): £24.10 single (£21.50 online)/£47.90 return (£42.70 online), kids 5–15 £12.05 (£10/75 online)/£23.95 (£21.35 online)/30 min. OR ThamesLink (www.thameslinkrailway.com): adults £15.10 single, £26.90 return, kids £7.55 single, £13.45 return /44–63 min.	Several times hourly ~5am to ~12:30am
Luton (LTN), www.London-Luton.co.uk	ThamesLink from Luton Airport Parkway (www.thameslinkrailway.com): adult £7.60 single/£15.20 return, kids £3.80 single, £7.60 return, including 4-min. shuttle train, 24–41 min.	Several times hourly 5am to midnight; hourly midnight to 5am
Stansted (STN), www.StanstedAirport.com	Stansted Express (www.stanstedexpress.com). From adult £19 single, £35 return, kids £9.50 single, £17.50 return /47 min.	Every 30 min. 4:40am to 12:30am (also a 3:40am train)
London City (LCY), www.LondonCityAirport.com	N/A	DLR: 5:30am to midnight
London Southend (SEN), londonsouthendairport.com	Greater Anglia: About £21.90 single/43–52 min.	4am to midnight

* *Discounts for purchasing online in advance and avoiding rush hour departures.*

taxes and fees, which are usually $500 or higher round-trip from the U.S.—London's airport fees are truly noxious.

As of 2025, everyone visiting the United Kingdom must obtain pre-clearance in advance by applying for a £16 **Electronic Travel Authorisation (ETA)** on an official app. See Visas, p. 385.

AIRPORT TRANSPORTATION OPTIONS

Fares and trip duration can be found in the chart, above.

BY TRAIN Always take the train if you can. This is how nearly everyone does it here. Every airport offers some kind of rail connection to the central city. Tickets can be bought at kiosks in the arrivals halls, at machines before the platform, or online or via an official app ahead of time (almost always the cheapest way, when you'll get a discount). Don't wait until you board to buy a ticket—that costs the most. You'll rarely have to wait more than 20 minutes for the next train, and you don't have to pre-book, although advance purchases do frequently come with discounts.

TO MAJOR STATION	TUBE OR DLR: COST/TIME	TAXI OR HIRE CAR: COST/TIME
Paddington	£7 cash or £5.80 Oyster on **Piccadilly Line** (75 min.) £13.90 on **Elizabeth Line** (28 min.)	£64–£120 (+£1.60 from airport or £6 to airport)/70 min.
Gatwick Express: Victoria; ThamesLink: St Pancras, Farringdon, Blackfriars, or London Bridge	N/A	£100/70 min.
St Pancras, Blackfriars, Farringdon, or City ThamesLink	N/A	£110/80 min.**
Liverpool Street	N/A	£100/80 min.**
N/A	£7 cash, £3.80 Oyster/25 min. via **Docklands Light Railway**	£25–£40/20–40 min.
Liverpool Street or Stratford	N/A	£80–£110 (£30 shared)/60 to 80 min.**

*** Check www.london-luton.co.uk, www.stanstedairport.com, and www.southend airport.com for list of the latest approved car hire companies. Addison Lee (www.addisonlee.com) is an established cab giant we can recommend, and Heathrow has a partnership with WeKnow London (U.K.: ✆ **0800/310-0442;** www.weknowlondon.com). All services offer discounted prices for children.*

Opened in 2022, the **Elizabeth Line** takes you from Heathrow to Paddington Station in 7 stops and 28 minutes (£13.90) using the same Oyster card (p. 363) you'll be using to ride the Tube and buses during your trip anyway. You can remain on the Elizabeth Line to continue at any other station it calls on in central London, including Bond Street (for Marylebone and Mayfair), Tottenham Court Road (for Covent Garden and the West End), Farringdon, Liverpool Street (for the City), Whitechapel (for East London), and the Canary Wharf business district. All Elizabeth Line cars have A/C and all stops have lifts, although in some cases you'll have to navigate a maze of several of them.

Heathrow Express trains (www.heathrowexpress.com; ✆ **0345/600-1515**) zoom to Paddington in 15 minutes every quarter-hour. This used to be the dominant method, but now that the Elizabeth Line is available, Heathrow Express has had to be much more aggressive in its sales pitches to arriving passengers. The trip is so quick that paying for Business First Class is a waste of money; book at least 30 days ahead on its app for the cheapest prices for its Standard class. There are also vending machines at the stations, but the rates will be higher because you waited. It uses comfortable commuter-style carriages and departs every 15 minutes, but it also dumps you out at Paddington, where have to hop the Tube system or a taxi to continue. The Elizabeth line, on the other hand, goes to Paddington, too, but then proceeds to more stations across the heart of London, plus it's cheaper. During peak times such in the early morning hours when transatlantic flight arrivals and rush hour commuters collide, Elizabeth Line carriages may, at first, be standing room only, but Heathrow Express never is.

The slowest but cheapest train from LHR is the **Piccadilly Line** (£7 cash or £5.80 Oyster/contactless, which is explained on p. 363), which takes a slow 75 minutes to plod to the West End in an old-fashioned Tube carriage with very little luggage space. ***Night bus option:*** If you need to go in the middle of the night and the trains aren't running (they tend to shut down after midnight and return before dawn), Night Bus N9 goes to and from Trafalgar Square, Piccadilly Circus, Green Park, and Heathrow, taking about 75 minutes.

Gatwick Express trains (www.gatwickexpress.com; ✆ **0345/850-1530**) run from Victoria, although there are rumblings about discontinuing this service and putting all passengers on the other option, **ThamesLink** (www.thameslinkrailway.com; ✆ **0345/026-4700**). With that, you can get to Gatwick via Blackfriars, London Bridge, City Thameslink (near St Paul's), Farringdon, or St Pancras stations five times an hour—service usually ends just after midnight, but check ahead, because timings change.

Stansted Express (www.stanstedexpress.com; ✆ **085/600-7245**) runs from Liverpool Street station. **Luton** has rail service from St Pancras, Farringdon, City ThamesLink, and Blackfriars stations by **ThamesLink** (www.thameslinkrailway.com; ✆ **0345/026-4700**). The correct stop is Luton Airport, linked by a 5-minute train (5am–midnight and included in your train fare) to the terminals.

City Airport doesn't support heavy rail or coach service, but right out its front door, it has its own Docklands Light Railway stop that connects to the Tube. **London Southend** (www.southendairport.com) is so well-connected to a shiny new station by **Greater Anglia** rail from Liverpool Street that buses don't bother to go there.

BY BUS There's not enough of a speed or price advantage to take a bus into London. Still, if you adore fumes and traffic, **National Express** (www.nationalexpress.com; ✆ **0871/781-8181**) buses will take you from all airports (except Southend or City) from £10–£13.10. With extreme advance purchase, **easyBus** (www.easybus.com) can be a few pounds cheaper (from Gatwick, Stansted, Luton, and Heathrow). Most services deposit you at Victoria Coach Station, which is as appealing as it sounds and is a 10-minute walk to the Victoria Tube stop.

BY TAXI OR CAR SERVICE Because of traffic and price, taking a metered **taxi** (£64–£120) to the city the way you might do at home does not have our hearty recommendation. **Uber** drivers can only be hailed once you leave the terminal, and then they pick you up at the pickup point indicated on the app.

driving IN LONDON?

Don't! Roads are clogged. In bad traffic, a trip from Heathrow to the western fringe of London can take 2 hours. And once you're in the city, just about every technology is deployed against you. There's a hefty £18 fee just to drive to the city center. Roads are confusingly one-way. Cameras capture and automatically ticket the most honest driving errors. Parking is a fantasy when you're looking for it and a nightmare when you pay for it. The only time to *maybe* drive a car is if you're on a cross-country tour—but in cities, it won't be easy for you.

The cheapest coach and van services usually drop you off at standardized stops such as major train stations. For Gatwick, Heathrow, Stansted, and Luton, in addition to the usual National Express coach options, there's the no-frills **easyBus** (www.easybus.com). Unless you book far in advance, it may not be much cheaper.

If you insist upon wheels (don't!), reserving ahead from home yields the best prices. Try to return your car outside the congestion-charge zone to avoid charges and aggravation. You will find similar rates among **Auto Europe** (www.autoeurope.com), **Europcar** (www.europcar.com), and **Holiday Autos** (www.holidayautos.com). Also check the major names like Avis, Hertz, and Budget, in case they can do better. Air-conditioning, something you won't need, adds about £5 to the daily bill. Fuel, or *petrol,* is priced like liquid gold, and although most rentals include unlimited mileage, not all do. It's smart to have your own GPS unit because your mobile phone's roaming data is likely to be so throttled that maps won't render fast enough, and it's also smart to familiarize yourself with the particular rules of driving in English bus lanes and roundabouts. Do not add anything to a reservation once you're at the rental counter or you may negate that great deal you thought you had. ***Be prepared:*** Some rental cars are stick-shift models, which means you'll be driving on the left in a foreign land with a stick shift. Don't!

Heathrow makes drivers charge an extra £1.60 to catch a ride at the Heathrow taxi rank and an extra £6 to be dropped off at a terminal. All other road transport should be booked at least a day ahead, if possible. Door-to-door **car service** (£60–£80) is cheaper than a metered taxi and can take 45 minutes to 2 hours. The train-taxi or train-Tube combo is usually faster (although on trains you'll have to contend with your luggage). You can book taxis ahead, which often saves about 25%: Check each airport's website for a current list of the latest approved companies. **Addison Lee** (www.addisonlee.com; ✆ **020/7387-8888;** book via its app) is an established minicab company you can also use to request rides around town; the website **Minicabit.com** surveys companies for the best prices. Also try sustainable **Green Tomato Cars** (www.greentomatocars.com; book via its app); **Chaufferit** (www.chauffeurit.com); and **Carrot Cars** (www.carrotcars.co.uk; ✆ **020/7005-0557**), which serve all airports.

By Long-Distance Rail

For trips from northwestern Europe, the train is the dignified way to go. Train stations are right in the middle of town. We're living in marvelous times: The Channel Tunnel opened in 1994 (although they *still* seem to be working out the kinks), so you can reach the heart of London in an incredible 2 hours and 20 minutes from Paris. You can literally ride both the Tube and the Métro before lunch. In fact, you can ride both a black taxi and Space Mountain before lunch, because one Eurostar route alights in the middle of Disneyland Paris Resort (with a change). **Eurostar** links London's St Pancras station with Paris, Brussels (less than 2 hr.), Lille, and Calais, and from there, you can go just about anywhere using other trains. In 2018, after decades of dreams, it finally finished the line to Amsterdam, too (4–5 hr.), although that route might require a change in Brussels. **Virgin Trains** has been in talks to create a competitor to Eurostar using the same rails, but not until 2030 or so.

Book via **Eurostar** (www.eurostar.co.uk; ✆ **03432/186-186** in the U.K., or ✆ **646/934-6454** in the U.S.; phone bookings incur a surcharge) itself or the U.S.–based **Rail Europe** (www.raileurope.com; no telephone customer support), which also sells European rail passes. Check both sites, since prices can differ, but do it early, because rates boom as availability decreases. Advance-purchase deals to Paris regularly go as low as £39 each way, but last-minutes bookings cost in the middle £100s.

By Bus

A few coach companies also travel between the U.K. and the continent, usually crossing the English Channel with a ferry. Because of the pressure put on the market by mushrooming no-frills airlines, rates are extremely low, but because the ferry industry is in disarray and delays are common, **we don't currently recommend this method. Flixbus** goes from Victoria to multiple destinations around Europe (say, Antwerp from 50€). The trade-off: It can take all day, sunrise to sunset, to reach Paris by this method. Discouraged? The website **CheckMyBus.com** searches all the available carriers.

Some other companies arrange full-on organized tours of Europe's greatest hits—but never for less than you could do independently; choose one only because you'd enjoy having company: **Contiki** (www.contiki.com; WhatsApp: **+44 330/912-1140**) is geared toward a party-hearty under-35 crowd, and **Fanatics** (www.thefanatics.com; ✆ **+61-02/9071-4541**) is for followers of organized sports.

Keep Up-to-Date

Americans and Canadians often write dates as month / day / year, as in June 1, 1957. But the default way to express a date in the U.K. is day / month / year, à la 1 June 1957—which, honestly, makes more sense because the units of time are ordered by increasing size. When you make reservations for anything online, don't accidentally swap the day and month—if you can, select the day from a calendar grid to ensure you've got it right.

By Boat

Ferry travel was already nearly obsolete—and then pandemic woes made it even more unreliable. We don't think you should rely on them unless you have a very loose travel schedule. Besides, no ferry to Europe or Ireland sails directly to London. You'll have to get down to the southern coast (for France),

Portsmouth (for Spain), or Liverpool or Wales (Ireland). Fares are around £56 each way with a car and including taxes (150 min.) on **P&O Ferries** (www.poferries.com; ✆ **01304/44-88-88**) or **DFDS** (www.dfds.com; ✆ **0208/127-8303**), both of which do Dover–Calais. Ferries between Wales and Ireland are operated by **Irish Ferries** (www.irishferries.ie; ✆ **0818/300-400** in the Republic of Ireland, or ✆ **353/818-300-400** in Northern Ireland/U.K.). The aggregator **DirectFerries.co.uk** sells European routes from a diminishing roster of offers.

If you despise flying but love champagne, one ocean liner still makes the storied 7-day trip between New York City and Southampton, which connects by rail to London in an hour. That's the ***Queen Mary 2*** (www.cunard.com; ✆ **800/728-6273**), intermittently scheduled. Fares start around $1,200 per person one-way, including all your meals. Pack your tuxedos and gowns for the formal nights.

GETTING AROUND LONDON

There are three practical methods for taming London's sprawl: by Tube (historic and enchanting, but expensive and stair-ridden); by bus (less expensive and less glamorous, but more edifying and often quicker); and by foot (the best method, but not always possible). Taxis are priced like the professional service they are, and driving a car is lunacy.

Tube trains go shockingly slowly (34kmph/21 mph is the *average* and has been for more than 100 years); in the center of town, stops can be remarkably close together. In fact, if your journey is only two or three stations, you'll often find it less strenuous to simply walk.

The Underground

Londoners call their 400km (250-mile) metro system the Underground, its official name, or just as commonly, "the Tube." Its elegant, distinctive logo—a red "roundel" bisected by a blue bar—debuted in 1913 as one of the world's first corporate symbols, and it remains one of the city's most ubiquitous sights. The Tube is much more dignified than most American systems. In fact, seats are upholstered—because the British know how to take care of nice things. And yet there's no older subway system—the first section opened in 1863 while America was fighting its Civil War. The Tube often acts its age, lobbing frequent delays and shutdowns at travelers. Check posters and whiteboards in the ticket hall to see what "engineering works" are scheduled.

The Tube is an attraction unto itself. It's fun to seek out vestiges of the early system (1907 tilework on the Piccadilly Line; the fake house facades built at 23–24 Leinster Gardens to hide exposed tracks; abandoned stations like the one at Strand and Surrey Street). If such "urban archaeology" fascinates you, visit the London Transport Museum in Covent Garden (p. 144) and especially pre-book one of its Hidden London tours.

There are 13 named **Tube lines** serving nearly 300 stations, but the system includes more. There's the newer **Elizabeth Line**, which bisects the center city and has the best step-free access; the **Docklands Light Railway** (DLR), which serves East London; 6 **Overground** lines that have revived disused outdoor viaducts in outer neighborhoods; and a **tram** line in South London. Lines are color-coded: The Piccadilly is a peacock purple, the Bakerloo could be considered Sherlock Holmes brown, and so on.

In May 2022, after a controversial five-year delay, the newly dug £15-billion **Elizabeth Line** created a quick train line linking East London to West London. Before its opening, most commuters had to laboriously hop various Tube lines to get across the city. Now, if you stay near the new route, you're connected to all of the train stations that serve nearly all of London's airports. What's more, every Elizabeth Line stop in central London has step-free access, something many Tube stops can't claim.

Find "Mind the Gap"

As you gloss through London's tackier souvenir stands, you'll see a peculiar catch phrase repeated on tourist tat: MIND THE GAP. That's the warning you'll hear at some London Underground stops when Tube trains pull into curved stations and leave a chasm between carriage and platform. To hear it for yourself (and lap the tourists who merely bought the T-shirt), try these stations:

- **Bank** (Central Line)
- **Embankment** (northbound Northern Line)
- **Piccadilly Circus** (Bakerloo Line)

The Tube shuts down nightly from Sunday to Thursday. Exact times for first and final trains are posted in each station (using the 24-hr. clock), but the Tube generally operates from 5:30am (0530) to just after midnight (0000), and Sundays 7am (0700) to 11:30pm (2330). On Friday and Saturday nights, many lines in Central London run every 10 minutes all night long: **"Night Tube"** trains are the Victoria, Central, Piccadilly, and Jubilee lines, plus the Charing Cross branch of the Northern line and a slice of the Overground between Islington and New Cross Gate. (The Elizabeth line closes around midnight.) If you need to travel after midnight, always check the Night Tube map and schedule (tfl.gov.uk/modes/tube/night-tube) beforehand. **Transport for London** (TfL) offers 24-hour information at ✆ **0343/222-1234.**

What happens if you miss the last train? Don't worry—you're not stranded, although your trip may take longer or cost more. Just turn to the city's network of 24-hour and Night Bus routes, which start with N (p. 358).

NAVIGATING THE TUBE

It's easy once you grasp the concept. If you know the name/color of the line you want, as well as the direction of your destination, progressively more detailed signs will march you, anthill-like, to the platform you need. Nearly every station is combed with staircases. You'll shuffle through warrens of cylindrical tunnels, many of them faced in custard-yellow tiles and overly full of commuters, and you'll scale stairways and alpine escalators lined with ads. **Always stand to the right so "climbers" can pass you on the left**.

On the DLR, the Overground, and trains that stop outdoors, the carriage doors may not automatically open. Push the illuminated button and they will.

Electronic signs on platforms tell you how long it'll be until the next train. A 24-hour information service is also available at ✆ **0343/222-1234.** You can use the TfL Journey Planner online at **tfl.gov.uk/plan-a-journey**, but the best resource is the free app **Citymapper,** which tells you which Tube, bus, or train to use and how long it takes. It also includes mapped walking directions to the appropriate stop. Transport for London has its own free app, **TfL Go,** that's good for determining which lines are working (or closed). The **UK Bus Checker** app shows 3D maps of routes and where the next bus is.

The most confusing lines for tourists are the Northern line (black on the maps) and the District line (green). Owing mostly to the petty backbiting of the developers who built these lines as individual businesses, those lines split into several paths, but there are places to jump off and change course in case you mess up. Platform displays and signs on the front of the trains tell you its final destination before you board, so you can figure out which path it'll take. If you ride the DLR (and you should—it provides a lovely rooftop-level glide through the brickwork of the old East End and the monolithic towers of Canary Wharf), those lines split variously, too, but there are lots of chances to rectify mistakes.

The **Underground's website** provides the downloadable "London's Rail and Tube Services" map at tfl.gov.uk/maps/track/national-rail. It's a truer picture of *all* the places your fare card can take you by rail—the Tube is just a part of the picture. The Bus network is on separate maps, but the TfL site also has terrific simplified bus maps for any neighborhood.

FARES, PASSES & TICKETS

London Underground (**tfl.gov.uk/tickets**) provides some 1.1 billion rides in a normal year—and seemingly every passenger pays a different fare. Rates usually go up every March (these rates were current at press time and will give you a sense of proportion). Britain's system is so complicated that it's accused of having been engineered to bewilder travelers into paying more than they have to.

Zones determine cost: The center of town—basically everything the Circle line envelops, plus a wee bit of padding—is zone 1. Heading outside of town, in a concentric pattern, come zones 2 through 6. Most tourists stick to zones 1 and 2; very few major sights are outside those (Wimbledon, Hampton Court, and Kew being the main exceptions). Your fare is calculated by how many zones you go through, and the lower the zone number, the less you pay. If a station appears to straddle zones, you'll pay the cheaper zone's rate. One-way tickets are called "singles" and round-trips are "return."

Astonishingly, **kids 10 and under travel for free** when accompanied by an adult. Adults must buy their own ticket and then ask the staff to wave their kid through the entry gate. Ask an agent about the going discounts for kids.

There are three major methods tourists use to pay for a ride:

***Method 1:* Oyster cards, a debit system**. The system keeps track of your fare money on a card called Oyster, which you tap on a sensor as you enter and leave stations. Oyster cards can be purchased and refilled at vending machines when you enter Tube stations—ticket windows staffed by human

frustrations OF THE TUBE

The Tube lists everything about itself in exhaustive detail at **tfl.gov.uk**, which contains more maps, planners, and FAQs than a normal person can handle. As endearing as the Tube is, it is not perfect. In fact, it can be so dehumanizing that it has had to put up signs begging people not to abuse its staff. Be prepared for a few things:

1. **Stairs.** Many stations have been shaped by more than a century of changes and are consequently intricate. Passengers are sadistically corralled up staircases, around platforms, down more staircases, and through still more staircases. Even stations equipped with extremely long escalators (Angel has the longest one in the system—59m/194 ft.) perversely require passengers to climb a final flight to reach the street. So, if you bring luggage into the Tube, be able to hoist your stuff for at least 15 stairs at a time. (This is where backpacks make sense—but don't be the person who keeps it on while riding a crowded carriage.) For a list of which stations are step-free—about a third of Tube stops, but all of the DLR and the Elizabeth Line in the central city—check **Transport for London Access & Mobility** (tfl.gov.uk/accessibility; ✆ **0343/222-1234**), which offers free maps and services, or consult the TfL Go app.
2. **Delays.** The TfL Go app will tell you if anything is amiss. Or, when you enter a station, look for a standing sign before the fare gates. You'll see status bars reading "Good service," "Severe delays," or the like. If you note "Minor delays," don't worry. *Do* worry about labor strikes—they're unpleasantly common. Strikes are forewarned at tfl.gov.uk/campaign/strikes.
3. **Heat.** The network can be stuffy. In summer, health advisories are issued to passengers. The worst lines: Bakerloo, Central, and Northern. The best: Elizabeth, Circle, and District. Air-conditioning is being added—slowly.
4. **Hellish rush hours.** Shoulder-to-shoulder, silently shuffling through airless underground cylinders. It's memorable in the wrong way. It's nicer off-peak.
5. **Tough weekends.** Unlike modern systems, which generally have two sets of rails in each direction, London's ancient system has one set, so entire lines have to shut down when maintenance is required. Weekends are when this happens. This is a major reason why it's smart to stay in central London, where you won't depend on a single Tube line. Check in the ticket hall to see what "engineering works" are scheduled.

beings are a thing of the past. Oyster is valid on the Tube, buses, Thames Clipper ferries, and trains within the city, too. Oyster cards usually requires a £5 deposit. Oyster cards won't get erased if you keep them beside your mobile phone. If you accidentally overspend the cash you have stored on your Oyster by traveling too far on a ride, the exit turnstile will deduct the overage from your deposit. And if you don't use up all the money you put on it by the end of your trip, you can get a refund from a vending machine, too, as long as there's less than £10 value left on your card.

Method 2: **Pay As You Go (PAYG) by putting charges on your contactless credit card.** This is what locals do, and you can, too. Tap your own contactless-enabled credit card, including American Express, on the big sensor dots at the turnstiles and you'll pay the same price as Oyster fares, but without having to fuss with the Oyster deposit. Contactless credit cards are charged only when they're used: a max of £2.90 per ride in zone 1—that's a lot better than the £7 you'd pay with cash—and £1.75 for a bus (you can't pay cash on a bus). Using this method, the maximum total charge in a single day will always peak at £8.90 for anytime travel in the center city (£5.25 if you only took buses). You could ride all day long with your credit card and never pay more than £8.90 total that day, is called "price capping," and it resets daily at 4:30am. **Apple Pay** and **Google Pay** also work in lieu of a physical credit card, but if you use your phone to pay, complete your fingerprint or facial recognition steps before you approach the turnstiles or you'll hold everyone else up. Frankly, a tap with a standard credit card or an Oyster card is faster.

The system also sells archaic unlimited passes called Travelcards, but they don't make financial sense anymore. A one-day Travelcard valid for rides in the center city costs £16.60, but if you use Oyster or tap your credit cards, your daily costs will max out at £8.90. Although TfL will mail you Oysters or Travelcards ahead of time, that's a waste of money. You can easily purchase them at any Tube stop, including at airports, without shipping fees.

Everyone in your party must use their own card, whether it's Oyster or a contactless card. Parents cannot use their own credit cards for their kids as well; they'll need an Oyster for everyone else.

***Method 3:* In cash, per ride.** You could (except on buses, which are cashless), but don't. To travel a mile in zone 1 on the Underground, the cash fare is £7 (more than $9.22), while using PAYG would have been just £2.90. I did the math: It costs far more to pay cash to go a mile on the Tube than to fly a mile in transatlantic First Class.

> **From *Europe on $5 a Day*, 1969–1970**
>
> "For those who have played the sardine in New York's subway, the London 'underground' is a revelation. Quiet, clean, comfortable; the normal fare ranges from 6 to 18¢, depending on the length of the ride, but your average trip should cost no more than around 9¢."

How to use tickets: Since pricing always depends on how far you've gone, you **must** touch your card to the big yellow reader dot both before you board ***and*** after your trip—even if there are no turnstiles and even if turnstiles are wide open (so don't forget). On the DLR, the dot may be at the bottom of the stairs to the street. The same goes if you have a paper ticket for a major train; keep it handy because you'll need it to get back out at the end. If you can't find it or if you forget to touch out, you'll pay the maximum rate as if you had ridden to the end of the line. Inspectors regularly check passengers' tickets and they won't hesitate to fine you. They feast on the power.

How to pay at a vending machine: If you are using a credit card to buy tickets from a vending machine, don't pull your card out of the vending machine until you're told to, or it will falsely tell you it's declined. (Underground machines never hesitate to claim something is wrong with your card, fostering undue panic in many a tourist. Don't believe it. Try a few times.) Vending machines usually accept cash and coins. Cards embedded with a SIM make transactions infinitely easier in London, so make sure yours are.

Buses

The Tube and buses are seen as one piece, so the same payment systems work on both. Buses are what smart Londoners use. The buses in your city may not come often, but London's are frequent (every 5 min. or so on weekdays), plentiful (some 100 routes in central London and 700 in the wider city), and surprisingly fast (many zoom in dedicated lanes). Sitting on the second level of a candy-apple red double-decker, watching the big landmarks roll past, is one of London's priceless pleasures. Best of all, the bus is cheaper than the Tube.

Single trips are just £1.75. The most you can possibly spend in a day on bus travel using Oyster PAYG is £5.25, no matter the zone. (If you mix bus and Tube travel in the same day, you'll max out at £8.90.) You can make **free transfers** between as many buses as you want within a 1-hour window. Don't ride without tapping in on that yellow disc (on buses, you don't have to tap *out* when you leave): Surprise card inspections are common. Bus passes and Travelcards expire at 4:30am the day after you buy them. The TfL supplies 24-hour information at ✆ **0343/222-1234.**

Bus drivers do not accept money. You **must** have a contactless credit card or Oyster card (get one in any Tube stop; bus stops with vending machines are super rare). Major intersections might have multiple stops named with letters, and each stop will service different routes. Tube station lobbies have easy-to-read poster maps that tell you where to catch the buses going to your destination and where the routes go, but many Londoners simply use a free app like Citymapper, Apple Maps, or Google Maps to get directions that include the correct stop. Many bus shelters even have electronic boards that approximate the arrival time of the next bus.

When the bus you want approaches, always signal so the driver knows it has a passenger to pick up. Board in the front only and be careful not to sit in a seat prioritized for someone who needs it more. Once you're aboard, an automated voice announces stops with plenty of warning. Press a button on a handrail to request a halt before the next one. Get off via the door at the middle. A few buses have reinstated a rear-door design, those, you can leap off that back entrance and break your neck whenever you like.

Routes that start with N are Night Buses, which tote punters home after the Tube stops around midnight; many connect tediously in Trafalgar Square, so pee before setting off.

London once had Europe's largest tram network, but today, trams only exist in outlying areas where tourists are unlikely to go. They're charged like buses.

National Rail

These are the rail lines that aren't operated by the Underground but they can be as useful as the Tube within the city—for example a train from Charing Cross to London Bridge dramatically slashes transit time compared to the

Tube. These comfortable, standard-size trains wind up in suburbs and distant cities, and they operate on a regular, reliable, published timetable—on maps, they are denoted by two red parallel lines with a zigzag line connecting them. As you remain in the zone system, these trains can be paid for just like the Tube. (The major stations have information desks if you're unsure about Oyster's validity on any journey.) You must tap Oyster at the start *and* at the completion of each journey or you'll be charged as if you took the train to the end of the line. If you accidentally tap in for a wrong or missed train, alert staff. They can ensure you aren't penalized.

There are many termini for national rail, and many service operators, but you don't have to hunt by trial and error. Check **TheTrainLine.com** website or app, call the 24-hour operators at **National Rail Enquiries** (www.nationalrail.co.uk; ✆ **08457/48-49-50**), or plug your journey into your favorite directions app such as the free **Citymapper,** which will enlighten you.

National Rail stations (not Eurostar or the Underground) accept discount cards for certain folks. Each card requires proof of eligibility (passport, ISIC student ID), but since they can be used for trips to distant cities, they pay for themselves quickly if you're doing lots of rail-riding. Get them at rail stations:

- The **Senior Railcard** (www.senior-railcard.co.uk; £30 a year): Discounts of about 33% for those 60 or over.
- The **16–25 Railcard** (www.16-25railcard.co.uk; £30 a year): Discounts of 33% for those 16 to 25, plus full-time students of any age. It requires a passport-size photo, which may be uploaded from a computer. If you're applying in the U.K., bring a passport photo for that purpose.
- The **Family & Friends Railcard** (www.family-railcard.co.uk; £30 a year) is for at least one adult and one child age 5 to 15, with a maximum of three adults and four kids on one ticket; at least one child must travel at all times. It awards adults 33% off and kids 60% off. But know that two kids age 4 and under can travel with an adult for free at all times, even without this card.

Ferries

Partly thanks to the dedication of a series of mayors, London's river ferry services are now one of the most pleasurable ways to get around—and because they're intended for commuters, a ride comes at a fraction of the price of a sightseeing boat. The Clipper boats, nicknamed River Bus or Uber Boats, cover a surprising amount of terrain quickly. The most useful stops of its 23 piers include the London Eye, the Tate Modern, the Tower of London, Greenwich, and the O_2. Getting from Greenwich to Embankment takes all of 45 idyllic minutes. You'll sail right under the famous Tower Bridge.

Fares depend on how far you're going, but for a trip from Westminster to Greenwich, expect a one-way fare around £5.90 with Oyster or contactless credit card, your fare will not count toward your daily price cap; cash is £7. If you're paying cash, you will always save money if you buy a return trip instead of two one-ways. The fast catamarans of **Thames Clippers,** now branded as **Uber Boat** (www.thamesclippers.com; ✆ **020/7930-2062;** generally 6:30am–10:30pm; bookable via its app), go every 20 minutes during the day and are much cheaper and plentiful than the narrated tour boats. The RB1 route is particularly useful, hitting most of the major tourist stops plus Greenwich and the O_2. ***One snag:*** On weekends, the queue to return from Greenwich can be 40 minutes to an hour long.

Hop-on, hop-off **River Roamer** passes, which allow you to take as many trips as you want on a single day after 9am, cost £28.20 for adults, £14.10 kids, £56.40 for a family of two adults and up to three kids; they cost a few pounds less when pre-booked on the Thames Clippers Tickets app, downloadable via www.thamesclippers.com/commuters/download-the-tickets-app.

Thames River Sightseeing (thamesriversightseeing.com/; ✆ **020/3778-0700**; no Oyster cards) is an independently run, touristy version of the Clippers (it looks similar, but this one has a roof deck for passengers) and offers a £16.50 adult/£10.90 child ride (£21.70/£14.60 return) from Westminster to Greenwich. It calls these "sightseeing" trips but note that it's not fully guided. Clippers are just as good.

Bikes

Scattered in some 800 places throughout town, you'll see racks of identical red bikes in racks. They're in London's main bikeshare system. They're called **Santander Cycles** (www.tfl.gov.uk/modes/cycling/santander-cycles), but Londoners still call them **Boris Bikes,** after the blowsy former mayor-cum-ousted prime minister who brought them here, and they provide more than 800,000 rides a month. Bikeshare is ubiquitous today, but in 2010, London was one of the first cities to try it.

It works like this: You choose a bike (1 in 6 will be an e-bike at slightly higher rates) and pull it out of the rack by lifting the seat. You ride it to any other docking station in the city with a free space, and you park it by slotting the front wheel in until a green light appears on the dock. When you're ready to ride somewhere else, just get another bike. The idea is for you to use a bike as you need it, not to keep it with you all day. Paying £1.65 (£3 for e-bikes) gets you 30 minutes (payments are on your credit card) every time you pull a bike out of the rack. You can also buy a daily pass for £3.50 (+£1 per journey for e-bikes) that gets you unlimited 60-minute rides. You are required to follow the same traffic rules that cars do, which won't be easy, although the city's huge parks are safer places to cycle. Locations of nearby docks are listed on every pylon. Use the free **Santander Cycles** app to pay and find nearby stations with available docks.

Taxis

Even Londoners think taxis are crazy expensive. It's not the fault of the cabbies. They're the best in the world. Before they're given their wheels, every London taxi driver (there are some 16,000 of them—but Uber is reducing their ranks) must go through a grueling training period so comprehensive that it's dubbed, simply, "The Knowledge." On Sundays, you'll see trainees zipping around on mopeds with clipboards affixed above their dashboards. Cabbies arrive inculcated with directions to every alley, mews, avenue, shortcut, and square in the city, and if they don't know, they'll find the answer so discreetly you won't catch the gaffe. They're even trained in first aid, childbirth, and assisting after an acid attack—so breathe easy. And then there are those adorable vehicles: bulbous as old jalopies, roomy as a studio apartment (fitting up to 6), yet able to do complete U-turns within a single lane of traffic.

But for this admittedly peerless carriage, you'll pay a £4.20 minimum. Trips of up to 1.6km (1 mile) cost £8.40 to £12.80 during working hours; 3.2km (2-mile) trips are £12.40 to £19.80; 6.4km (4-mile) trips are £21 to £30; and trips of around 9.6km (6 miles) hit you for a painful £32 to £41. Rates rise when you're most likely to need a taxi: by about 10% from 8 to 10pm or all day on weekends, and roughly another 20% from 10pm until dawn. Trips that start at Heathrow cost an extra £1.60 and ones that end there cost an extra £6, and trips around Christmas and New Year's Day tack on £4. Mercifully, there is no charge for extra passengers or for luggage. It has become customary to tip 10%, but most people just round up to the nearest pound. Taxis are required to accept credit cards, but some drivers grumble about that and are some of last remaining professionals in London who will tell you they prefer cash.

Technically, if a car doesn't have a meter, it's not a taxi but actually a cab or hire car. **Minicabs,** which are hire cars that operate separately from the traditional black cab system, are easy to find using apps. Don't accept a ride from an unsolicited one. Among the top free apps that can hail the nearest ride: **Gett** (www.gett.com); **FreeNow** (www.free-now.com/uk); and London's reigning power minicab operator, **Addison Lee** (www.addisonlee.com). It's wise to set up your chosen apps with your credit card ahead of time.

Lyft does not operate in London, but ride-share service **Uber** does. Hailing a taxi on the street is often cheaper than taking an Uber, especially outside of rush hour. Do not trust the taxi prices quoted by the Uber app; they are not accurate because they include service charges you won't pay hailing a taxi yourself. If you are traveling internationally, Uber pre-selects your Wallet to "pay in preferred currency," but you will pay a better exchange rate if you reset the payment to British pounds.

CAN I do that?

Some things that are considered sins back home may lead to legal pleasures in London. Which means they're not sinful as long as you're on British soil! To wit:

- The drinking age is 18. But if you're having your first legit night out, take it easy, because beers here have higher alcohol content than in many countries.
- There are no open container laws. That means you can drink beer in public. The one exception is on public transportation, where, ironically, you need a drink the most.
- You may smoke Cuban cigars. Get them at any tobacconist and puff away. If you're American, though, don't try smuggling them home.
- Absinthe, the brutal quaff nicknamed "The Green Fairy," is available here. Drink up because American Customs frowns on many versions of it.
- The age of consent is 16 no matter the sexual preference.

Scooters maintained by **Lime** (www.li.me/locations/london; ✆ **0800/808-5223**) and **Voi** (www.voi.com/city/london; ✆ **0808/501-5724**) can be found for about 20p a minute, but for safety reasons they are not recommended for people without experience on this type of vehicle, and people under 18 may not use them. **Waymo** self-driving cars are slated to enter London service in 2026.

If You Need to Fake a British Postcode

When you're online in the U.K., such as when you sign up for free Wi-Fi, you may be asked for a mobile number and a postcode before you access a signal. Of course, you don't have those things—you're visiting! Bulldoze through this shortsightedness by giving a fake email address and a fake number you can invent at fakenumber.org. As for a postcode, use your hotel's. Better yet, use the following code: SW1A 1AA. After all, if that postcode is good enough for Buckingham Palace, it's good enough for you!

Renting a Car

Are you insane? Rare is the local who drives in central London, where there's a mandatory weekday "congestion charge" of £18 (Don't believe me? See **www.cclondon.com**.), and where parking prices look like your monthly rent back home. Streets were cramped enough when people rode horses, and now they're dogged with one-way rules and police cameras that will ticket you for even honest errors, which you'll definitely make since you're just visiting. You'll go crazy and broke, so why do it? If you're driving out of the city for a tour of the country, fine, pick up a rental on the outskirts, but *do not* rent a car for a central London vacation.

GETTING AROUND THE U.K.

By Train

The original railway tycoons plowed their stations into every town of size, making it easy to see the highlights of the United Kingdom without getting near a car. The British whine about the declining quality of the service, but Americans, Canadians, and Australians will be blown away by the speed (and the cost, unfortunately, if they don't book ahead) of the system. Find tickets to all destinations through **National Rail** (www.nationalrail.co.uk; ✆ **08457/48-49-50**) or the indispensable **TheTrainLine.com.** Early-bird bookings of 9–12 weeks can yield some marvelous deals, such as £26 for a 4-hour trip to Scotland (£125 last-minute is common). When hunting for tickets, always search for "off-peak" (non-rush hour) trips going or coming from London in general, not a specific London station, because each London terminal serves various cities. **SplitTicketing.com** also searches the rail companies' byzantine fare schedules to tell you journey configurations that can save you many pounds. Trainline accepts international credit cards.

Tickets bought reasonably well in advance will still be cheaper than what you'd pay for the same trips on a **BritRail pass** (www.britrail.com; must purchase outside the U.K.), good on long-distance trains but not on local London transport. Few tourists ride rails with the near-daily regularity that would make a timed pass pay for itself. Check prices against the U.S. seller **Rail Europe** (www.raileurope.com; ✆ **800/622-8600**), as quotes vary.

By Bus

National Express (www.nationalexpress.com; ✆ **0871/781-8181**) is the least expensive way to get from city to city in Britain (but not the fastest—that's usually the train). Because the country is not very big, it rarely takes more than a few hours to reach anyplace by bus. Even Scotland is only 5 hours away. A major carrier with scads of departures, **Megabus** (uk.megabus.com; ✆ **090/0160-0900,** or 44-141-352-4444), which serves more than 100 cities across Europe, charges in the zone of £45 for a popular city like Edinburgh. It accepts bookings 2 months ahead; book online to avoid phone fees. Both coach services depart from the miserable Victoria Coach Station, located behind Victoria railway station (www.tfl.gov.uk/coaches).

What's the best place to hear about inexpensive ground tours? Hostels. Drop into one; most of their lobbies are papered with brochures. Don't neglect their bulletin boards, either, because you may catch wind of a shared-ride situation that'll often cost you no more than your share of the gasoline (in Britain, *petrol*).

By Car

The only reason you might want to rent a car is if you're headed out of town (see "Driving in London?" on p. 359 for car rental tips).

WHEN TO GO

CLIMATE It's always time to visit London. It doesn't rain as much as they say and it hasn't been foggy since they got rid of coal. Even though it's approximately at the same latitude of Edmonton, Alberta, weather patterns keep the environment from being extreme. It gets cold in the winter, but rarely snowed in. It gets warm in the summer, occasionally blisteringly so (although many buildings don't have air-conditioning), although climate change is reducing rainfall and raising temperatures. The winter months experience only slightly more rain; the month with the least precipitation is March and the most is November. Locals use the free, reliable **Met Office Weather Forecast app,** by the U.K.'s national weather service, to pinpoint forecasts by GPS.

London's Average Daytime Temperatures & Rainfall

	JAN	FEB	MAR	APR	MAY	JUNE	JULY	AUG	SEPT	OCT	NOV	DEC
TEMP. (°F)	41	45	48	52	57	61	66	66	63	55	50	45
TEMP. (°C)	3	7	9	11	14	16	19	19	17	13	10	7
RAINFALL (in.)	1.6	1.4	1.6	1.6	1.7	1.8	1.3	2.1	2	2.4	2.2	1.9
RAINFALL (mm)	41	36	41	41	45	47	34	54	51	61	57	48

SEASONAL CONSIDERATIONS The principal indoor arts season (for theater, concerts, art shows) falls between September and May, leaving the summer months for festivals and park-going. A few royal attractions, such as the state rooms of Buckingham Palace, are only open in the summer when the

Royal Family decamps to Scotland. In summer, when the weather is warmest, the sun sets after 10pm, and half of Europe takes its annual holiday, when airfares are higher, as are hotel rates. Summertime queues for most tourist attractions, such as the London Eye and the Tower of London, might make you wish you'd come in March. For decent prices and lighter crowds, go in spring or fall—April and October seem to have the best confluence of mild weather, pretty plantings, and tolerable crowds. Prices are lowest in midwinter, but a number of minor sights, such as historic houses, sometimes close from November to March, and the biggest annual events take place during the warmer months.

London's Public Holidays

England observes **eight public holidays** (also known as "bank holidays"): New Year's Day (Jan 1); Good Friday and Easter Monday (usually Apr); May Bank Holiday (first Mon in May); Spring Bank Holiday (usually last Mon in May, but occasionally the first in June); August Bank Holiday (last Mon in Aug); Christmas Day (Dec 25) followed by Boxing Day (Dec 26)—you'll find it hard to do anything or even get around on those last two dates. If a date falls on a weekend, the holiday rolls over to the following Monday.

London Calendar of Events

Special events are an integral part of London's calendar, and many regular happenings draw tourists from around the world. Find even more events at London's **city website** (www.london.gov.uk/events), at the **official tourism site** (www.visitlondon.com), the blogs **Londonist** (www.londonist.com) and **IanVisits** (www.ianvisits.co.uk), and ***Time Out* magazine** (www.timeout.com/london).

JANUARY

London New Year's Day Parade. As many as 10,000 dancers, acrobats, musicians, and performers (heavy on the marching bands) promenade from Piccadilly to Parliament Square for 500,000 spectators and TV audiences. www.lnydp.com, ✆ **020/3275-0190.** January 1.

Chinese New Year Festival. In conjunction with the Chinese New Year, the streets around Leicester Square come alive with dragon and lion dances, children's parades, performances, screenings, and fireworks displays. 2027: Early February.

MARCH

St Patrick's Festival. When you're this close to Dublin and you consider England's long rivalry with the Emerald Isle, you can expect several days of raging Irish pride—parades, music, and food stalls around Trafalgar Square, where the fountains gush green. The city also sponsors concerts and craft fairs promoting Irish culture and heritage. It's not just about drinking—it only looks that way. www.london.gov.uk, ✆ **020/7983-4000.** Weekend around March 17.

Oxford and Cambridge Boat Race. This popular annual event (since 1829), held on the Thames in Hammersmith, takes less than 30 minutes, but the after-party rollicks into the night and the good-natured rivalry is undying. www.theboatrace.org. Late March or early April.

The Other Art Fair. Up-and-coming artists who are often left out of the cliquey big-ticket art world festivals are hand-selected by Saatchi Art to show and sell at this three-day event at the Truman Brewery on Brick Lane. www.theotherartfair.com/london; info@theotherartfair.com. March.

APRIL

London Marathon. Although it draws some 35,000 runners, the marathon is also a kick for spectators, so hotels tend to fill up ahead of it. The starter pistol fires in Blackheath; the home stretch is along Birdcage Walk near Buckingham Palace. If you want to run, apply by the previous October. www.londonmarathonevents.co.uk. Late April.

MAY

Regent's Park Open Air Theatre. Forget stuffy auditoriums. There's little shelter from sudden downpours, but in good weather the four-show season of high drama, crowd-pleasing musicals, and Shakespeare sparkles under a canopy of blue skies, towering trees, and natural beauty. www.openairtheatre.com, ✆ **0333/400-3562.** Mid-May to September.

Chelsea Flower Show. The Royal Horticultural Society, which calls itself a "leading gardening charity dedicated to advancing horticulture and promoting good gardening" (don't you just love the English?), mounts this esteemed show for 5 days on the grounds of the Royal Hospital in Chelsea. The plants, all raised by champion green thumbs, are sold to attendees on the final day, but sadly, foreigners aren't usually able to get their plants past Customs. Tickets go on sale in November for this lilypalooza, and they're snapped up quickly. The event is so celebrated that it is covered on nightly prime-time TV. Really. www.rhs.org.uk, ✆ **020/3176-5800.** Late May.

JUNE

Beating Retreat. Drum corps, pipes, and plenty of bugle calls. This anachronistic twilight ceremony, held for two evenings at Horse Guards Parade by St James's Park, involves the salute of the monarch and the appearance of many red-clad marchers. Scholars trace its origins to 1554—so for tradition's sake, it's deeply meaningful. It's the nearest relative to the better-known Trooping the Colour, but without the crowds. Watch along the route or reserve seating ahead starting in mid-December. www.householddivision.org.uk, ✆ **020/7839-5323.** Early June.

London Open Gardens. Green spaces and private gardens across the city that are normally closed to the public open their gates to be admired in full bloom. londongardenstrust.org. First weekend of June.

The Royal Academy Summer Exhibition. Artists have been in a frenzy to win entry to this blind competition since 1768. Paintings, sculpture, drawings, architecture—if you can dream it, you can enter it, and if you're one of the most talented, your piece is anointed as the best that year. The show is what the Royal Academy is known for, and although it's not envelope-pushing, it's a seminal event in British art culture and shouldn't be missed if you're in town. www.royalacademy.org.uk. Late June to late Aug.

Trooping the Colour. Never mind that the king was born in November. Since 1748, this is the "official" birthday of the British sovereign, and as a present, they get the same thing every year: soldiers with big hats. A sea of redcoats and cavalry swarm over Horse Guards Parade, 41 guns salute, and a flight of Royal Air Force jets slam through the sky overhead. Until her latter years, Queen Elizabeth herself led the charge, waving politely to her subjects before they lost themselves in a hearty display of marching band prowess. Try for grandstand seats instead of standing in the free-for-all along the route, where you'll only get a fast glimpse of passing royalty. Tickets are only sold by random draw, which closes at the end of February. www.householddivision.org.uk/trooping-the-colour, ✆ **020/7414-2479.** Mid-June.

Taste of London Festival. The city's top chefs and the region's finest farmers convene in Regent's Park for 5 days of belly-stuffing. london.tastefestivals.com, ✆ **087/1230-7132.** Mid-June.

Pride London. A signature event on the world's LGBTQ calendar, in a good year London Pride can pull nearly a million revelers, many of them heterosexual, with a buoyant roster of concerts and performances by famous names plus a parade (the U.K.'s largest) in the center of the city. The gay pride week, co-sponsored by the mayor's office, also makes an excellent excuse for some blowout dance parties. prideinlondon.org. Late June or early July.

Wimbledon Championships. Why watch on television yet again? Check p. 215 for how to be one of the 500,000 to witness it in person. www.wimbledon.org, ✆ **020/8944-1066.** June or July.

Greenwich+Docklands International Festival (GDIF). An ambitious program of free theatrical and musical pieces, many of them developed by artists expressly for the spaces they're performed in. festival.org. Late June and early July.

Meltdown. A compendium of hip prestige arts held at the Southbank Centre, curated in the past by such notables as Patti Smith, David Bowie, Grace Jones, and Yoko Ono. www.southbankcentre.co.uk/meltdown, ✆ **020/3879-9555.** Summer.

London Design Biennale. At Somerset House, catch up on the best in up-and-coming design through nearly a month of installations, talks, events, and performances. londondesignbiennale.com, ✆ **020/4551-2105**.

The Lambeth Country Show. A free, old-fashioned farm show overtakes Brixton's Brockwell Park (for a single weekend, anyway) with farm animals, jam-making contests, a fun fair, tractor demonstrations, and Punch and Judy puppet shows. Very English stuff. Free. www.lambethcountryshow.co.uk, ✆ **020/7926-7085.**

JULY

BBC Promenade Concerts. The biggest classical music festival of the year, held primarily at the Royal Albert Hall, "the Proms" consists of orchestral concerts for every taste, many of which are broadcast on prime-time television. Plenty of places are available starting at £10. www.bbc.co.uk/proms, ✆ **020/7070-4441.** July to September.

AUGUST

London T100 (London Triathlon). Some 11,000 participants cycle through the city from Westminster, sprint around the ExCeL center in Docklands, and swim in Royal Victoria Dock in this annual event. Sir Richard Branson often attends. t100triathlon.com/london/participate. Late July or early August.

Notting Hill Carnival. In August 1958, roving bands of white racists combed the slums of Notting Hill in search of Caribbean-owned businesses to destroy. Resulting community outrage and newly rediscovered cultural pride led to the formation of this festival, now Europe's largest street parade, attracting some 2 million people. It's a smorgasbord of cultures spanning the Caribbean, Eastern Europe, South America, and the Indian subcontinent. Sunday is kids' day, with scrubbed-down events and activities, but on Monday, the adults take over, costumes get skimpy, floats weave through small streets, and rowdy hordes celebrate into the wee hours. nhcarnival.org. August Bank Holiday weekend.

SEPTEMBER

The Great River Race. Always over too soon, the race is the aquatic version of the London Marathon, with rowers vying to beat out 300 other vessels—Chinese dragon boats, Canadian canoes, Viking longboats, and even Hawaiian outriggers—on a morning jaunt upriver from the Docklands to Richmond. www.greatriverrace.org.uk, ✆ **020/8398-8141.** Saturday in mid-September.

Totally Thames. In conjunction with the Great River Race (above), nearly half a million souls attend London's largest free open-air arts festival, with more than 150 events. Southwark Bridge is closed for a giant feast, and there's a flotilla of working river boats, circus performers, and antique fireboats, tugs, and sailboats. Sunday sees the Night Carnival, a lavish procession of thousands of lantern-bearing musicians and dancers crawling along the water. Everything is topped off with barge-launched fireworks. thamesfestivaltrust.org, ✆ **020/7928-8998.** September.

London Fashion Week. Collections are unveiled for press and buyers. It's tough to get a runway show ticket, but there's a raft of slick events and parties across the city. There's often an additional event in late winter. londonfashionweek.co.uk.

Open House Festival. For history nuts, Open House is worth traveling for. Hundreds of buildings, all of them important but normally closed to the public, yawn wide for free tours on a single, hotly anticipated event. Past participants have included the skyscraper headquarters of Lloyd's, the BT Tower, the new U.S. embassy, and even No. 10 Downing St. The list of open buildings comes out in August. Some require timed tickets, but for most, the line forms at dawn. open-city.org.uk, ✆ **020/7383-2131.**

OCTOBER

Dance Umbrella. Since 1978, one of the world's best contemporary dance festivals, with plenty of standing-room seats for as little as £10. danceumbrella.co.uk, ✆ **020/7257-9380.** October.

Frieze Art Fair. More than 160 galleries vie for big money from collectors in a colossal 4-day tent show in Regent's Park. It has become influential in the contemporary art world. www.frieze.com, ✆ **020/3372-6111.** Early October.

Diwali. One advantage of visiting a multicultural city like London is that it affords you the chance to sample major international holidays in an English-speaking environment. One such treat is Diwali, the Indian "festival of light," when Trafalgar Square is transformed with lights, floating lanterns, massive models of the elephant god Ganesh, music, dance, and DJs. It's free. Mid- to late October.

BFI London Film Festival. An important stop on the cinema circuit, this event, sponsored by the British Film Institute, is geared toward media exposure for more than 200 features, but there are plenty of tickets for the public, too. whatson.bfi.org.uk/lff, ✆ **020/7928-3232.** Mid-October.

NOVEMBER

Guy Fawkes Night. In 1605, silly old Guy Fawkes tried to assassinate James I and the entire Parliament by blowing them to smithereens in the Gunpowder Plot. Joke's on him: To this day, the Brits celebrate his failure by blowing up *him.* His effigy is thrown on bonfires across the country, fireworks displays rage in the autumn night sky, and more than a few tykes light their first sparklers in honor of the would-be assassin's gruesome execution. Although displays are scattered around town, including at Battersea Park and Alexandra Palace, get out of the city for the weekend nearest November 5, also called **Bonfire Night**—the countryside is perfumed with the woody aroma of burning leaves on this holiday. Mount Primrose Hill or Hampstead Heath for a view of the fireworks around the city. November 5.

Lord Mayor's Show. What sounds like the world's dullest public access program is actually a delightfully pompous procession, about 800 years old, involving some 140 charity floats and 6,000 participants to ostensibly show off the newly elected Lord or Lady Mayor to the king or his representatives. The centerpiece is the preposterously carved and gilt Lord Mayor's Coach, built in 1757—a carriage so extravagant it makes Cinderella's ride look like a Toyota Corolla. That's a lot of hubbub for a city official whose role is essentially ceremonial; the real Mayor of London (currently Sadiq Khan) wields the true power. All that highfalutin' strutting is followed by a good old-fashioned fireworks show over the Thames between the Blackfriars and Waterloo bridges. lordmayorsshow.london. Second Saturday in November.

EFG London Jazz Festival. Some 165 mid-November events attract around 60,000 music fans for 10 days. Many performances are free, and tickets are distributed by the venues. www.efglondonjazzfestival.org.uk, ✆ **020/7324-1880.** Mid-November.

Remembrance Sunday. Another chance to glimpse a monarch. The prime minister and the monarch, as well as many royals, attend a ceremony at the Cenotaph, in the middle of Whitehall, to honor the war dead and wounded, of which Britain has borne more than its share. Those red flowers you'll see everywhere—red petals, black centers—are poppies, the symbol of remembrance in Britain. Sunday nearest November 11.

DECEMBER

Carols at the Royal Albert Hall. Royal Albert Hall's annual evening of candlelight Christmas carols, readings from Dickens, and music by Handel, Bach, Mozart, and Corelli played by the Mozart Festival Orchestra—in period costume. www.royalalberthall.com, ✆ **020/7589-8212.** Late December.

New Year's Eve Fireworks. As Big Ben strikes midnight, London usually rings in the New Year with 12 minutes of fireworks over the Thames and the Eye. Tickets usually released via www.london.gov.uk/nye starting a few months ahead, and all are gone by early December.

[FastFACTS] LONDON

Accessible Travel London can't seem to strike the balance between preserving old buildings and making sure they're accessible to all. With the laudable exception of the Docklands Light Railway, only a few Tube stations have lifts (although the new Elizabeth Line is widely accessible), and those with plenty of escalators still require passengers to climb flights of stairs. Research your options and access free services at **AccessAble** (www.accessable.co.uk) and **Transport for London** (www.tfl.gov.uk/accessibility; ✆ **0343/222-1234**). In the map section of its **TfL Go** app, you can tap the wheelchair icons to show you only the stations that offer step-free access—sadly, the West End is pretty poorly served by lifts. The website **UpDownLondon.com** keeps tabs on step-free access at Tube stations, including temporary maintenance obstacles.

Many London hotels, museums, restaurants, and sightseeing attractions have dedicated wheelchair access, all taxis and buses do, and persons with disabilities often get admission discounts. Generally speaking, the more expensive a hotel is, the more likely it is to be wheelchair accessible, but not always, because in London, where buildings are often grafted together and changed over time, otherwise step-free surfaces may be broken by one or two stairs.

Travelers who are blind or partially sighted will find useful advice from the **Royal National Institute of Blind People** (www.rnib.org.uk; ✆ **0303/123-9999**). **Tourism for All** (www.tourismforall.org.uk; ✆ **084/5124-9971**) has accessibility information for older travelers as well as travelers with disabilities.

Area Codes The country telephone code for Great Britain is **44.** The area code for London is **020.** The full telephone number is usually 8 digits long. Businesses and homes in central London usually have numbers beginning with a **7;** those that are farther out begin with an **8.** For more info, see "Telephones," p. 384.

ATMs/Banks See "Money," p. 381. ***One quirk to note:*** Retrieve your card immediately from ATM slots; many machines suck them in within 10 to 15 seconds, for security. Cards that are thicker than the norm, lack raised numbers, or are not made of standard plastic may also be gobbled up by confused ATMs. Should that happen, you'll have to petition the operating bank to have it returned to you.

Business Hours Businesses are generally open weekdays between 9 or 10am and 5 or 6pm. Some remain open a few hours longer on Thursdays and Fridays. Saturday hours for stores are the same; Sunday store hours are generally noon to 5 or 6pm. Banks are usually open from 9:30am to 4 or 5pm, with some larger branches open later on Thursdays or for a few hours on Saturday mornings. Stores and restaurants are more likely to close on Sundays, Mondays, or both.

Cellphones See "Mobile Phones," p. 380.

Credit Cards Many places only accept cards now (see p. 355). Credit cards are accepted nearly everywhere, but if you can, bring **Visa** or **Mastercard,** because **American Express** is accepted less widely. (If you try to use it at a place that doesn't accept it, you may be mistakenly told your card has a problem or you've been declined; don't panic.)

Many credit card issuers levy an annoying international transaction fee on top of your purchase—many **American Express** cards have dropped that fee, as have **Capital One Venture** (www.capitalone.com; ✆ **800/695-5500**) and several options from **Chase** (www.chase.com).

If you are given a choice between being charged in British pounds or your home currency, always choose GBP (pounds); this is also known as Dynamic Currency Conversion (DCC). As long as your card has no international fee, the exchange rate for pounds will likely be better.

Try not to use credit cards to withdraw cash—you'll pay a currency exchange fee, and worse, you'll be charged interest from the moment your money leaves the slot.

It is now illegal for vendors to charge you a transaction fee to defray the cost of dealing with the card companies. Minimum purchases and clearly labeled service fees, however, remain legal.

The fastest way to pay is with a card that can make contactless payments. If yours doesn't, you may have to take extra steps when you buy things. Europeans use **"chip and PIN" cards** requiring a code number. Some vending machines won't accept swipe-only cards and may incorrectly inform you that you were declined. Most U.S. cards now come with such a chip, but if yours doesn't, ask your lender to send you one for free. If you do not normally use a PIN to make credit card purchases, inform clerks you're using a "Signature card," as they will usually have to scramble around for a pen (Europeans don't sign anymore). Using mobile payment such as Google Pay or Apple Pay speeds up transactions to a mere tap of your phone, no signature required for most purchases—I strongly urge you to set yours up with a Visa or Mastercard before leaving home. Restaurants will usually process your payment at your table wirelessly—the British consider it standard security practice not to let your card out of your sight and sometimes, to check ID along with signature.

Customs Rules about what you can carry into Britain are standard but ever-shifting, so get the latest restrictions from **HM Revenue & Customs** (www.hmrc.gov.uk). Your own government is responsible for telling you what you can bring back home.

Doctors Ask your hotel first. Then try the G.P. (General Practitioner) finder at **www.nhs.uk**. North American members of the **International Association for Medical Assistance to Travelers** (IAMAT; www.iamat.org; ✆ **716/754-4883** in the U.S., or 416/652-0137 in Canada) can consult that organization for lists of local approved doctors. ***Note:*** U.S. and Canadian visitors who become ill while they're in London are eligible only for free *emergency* care. For other treatment, including follow-up care, you'll pay £60 to £150 just to see a physician (Covid-19 testing excepted). Pharmacists are permitted to consult with you about most common ailments.

Drinking Laws Legal drinking age is 18. Children 15 and younger are allowed in pubs if accompanied by a parent or guardian. Drinking on London's **public transport network** is forbidden; on-the-spot fines are issued to transgressors.

Electricity The current in Britain is 240 volts AC. Plugs have three squared pins. Foreign appliances operating on lower voltage (those from the U.S., Canada, and Australia use 110–120 volts AC) will require an adapter and possibly a voltage converter, although the range of capability will usually be printed on the plug. Many modern phone chargers and laptops can handle the stronger current with only an adapter. A few hotels provide North American–style outlets for a non-heating appliance such as a shaver, but don't count on one.

If your devices use a small USB-C plug, bring an adapter that allow it to use the older, flat USB-A type plug, because many hotels have not upgraded yet.

Embassies & Consulates In 2017, the **U.S. Embassy** moved from Grosvenor Square to an elaborate 4.9-acre complex in West London's Wandsworth district (33 Nine Elms Lane, SW11; uk.usembassy.gov; ✆ **020/7499-9000;** Tube: Vauxhall). Standard hours are Monday to Friday 8:30am to 5:30pm. All visits require an appointment. You may bring mobile phones but not tablets or laptops. For passport information, call ✆ **877/487-2778** in the U.S.

The **High Commission of Canada** (1 Trafalgar Sq., London W1; www.international.gc.ca/country-pays/united_kingdom-royaume_uni/index.aspx; ✆ **020/7004-6000;** Tube: Charing Cross) handles passport and consular services for Canadians. Hours are Monday,

Wednesday, and Friday 8 to 10:30am.

The **Australian High Commission** is at Australia House, Strand, London WC2 (www.uk.embassy.gov.au; ✆ **020/7887-5776;** Tube: Temple). Hours are Monday to Friday 9am to 4:30pm.

The **New Zealand High Commission** is at New Zealand House, 1 Pall Mall East, London SW1 (www.mfat.govt.nz; ✆ **020/7930-8422;** Tube: Charing Cross or Piccadilly Circus). Hours are Monday to Friday 9am to 5pm.

The **Irish Embassy** is at 17 Grosvenor Place, London SW1 (www.dfa.ie/irish-embassy/great-britain; ✆ **020/7235-2171;** Tube: Hyde Park Corner). Hours are Monday to Friday 9:30am to 12:30pm and 2 to 4pm.

Emergencies The one-stop number for Britain is ✆ **999**—that's for fire, police, and ambulances. It's free from any phone, even mobiles. Less urgent? Call 111.

Family Travel Attractions cater to the family market. The kingly treatment starts, at many places, with the so-named **Family Ticket,** which grants a reduced price for parents and kids entering together. For any length of stay, you can rent baby equipment from **The London Baby Equipment Hire Company** (www.babyequipmenthirelondon.co.uk; ✆ **07807/932-206**). If you need babysitting, **Sitting Pretty Babysitters** (www.sittingprettybabysitters.com; ✆ **07971/083-207**) will come to your hotel for a minimum of 3 or 4 hours, depending on the time of week; rates are around £13–£14 an hour with a £7.50 booking fee and a £21.50 membership fee.

If you are a **divorced parent** traveling with your children, bring proof to the airport that you are entitled to take your kids out of the country.

Resources for family-specific travel tips include the **Family Travel Network** (www.familytravelnetwork.com). **The Family Travel Files** (www.thefamilytravelfiles.com) lists tour operators and packagers geared to families, but its suggestions aren't always the most economical or efficient. ***Time Out*** (www.timeout.com/london) includes a section on kids' activities.

When it comes to **baby supplies,** pacifiers are called "dummies," diapers are "nappies," a crib is a "cot," and Band-Aids are "plasters."

Fitness **PureGym** (www.puregym.com) offers contract-free passes for 1 day, 3 days, or a week for as little as £20; it has facilities open 24 hours in Piccadilly (Rex House, 4–12 Regent St., SW1; ✆ **345/013-3386;** Tube: Piccadilly Circus), Waterloo (11–15 Brad St., SE1; Tube: Waterloo), and Holborn (Lacon House, 84 Theobalds Rd., WC1; ✆ **345/013-3502;** Tube: Holborn). Additional locations are in Marylebone, St Paul's, and Farringdon, plus others.

Health Traveling to London doesn't pose specific health risks. Common drugs are generally available over the counter and in large supermarkets, although visitors should know the generic rather than brand names of any medicines they rely on. For example, the generic general-purpose painkiller known in North America as acetaminophen is called **paracetamol** in the U.K.

Pack **prescription medications** in carry-on luggage and in their original containers, with pharmacy labels—otherwise they may not pass airport security. Also bring copies of your prescriptions, just in case. If you require **syringes,** always carry a signed medical prescription. Don't forget an extra pair of contact lenses or prescription glasses.

If you need the advice of a doctor or a nurse, the national health care system operates a free, 24-hour hotline: **National Health Service Direct** (www.nhs.uk; ✆ **111**). Citizens of many European countries are entitled to free health care while in Britain (www.dh.gov.uk/travellers), but not everyone is. Non-EU citizens should carry health or travel insurance. Also see "Doctors," p. 377.

Health Insurance **U.K. nationals** receive free medical treatment countrywide; visitors from overseas qualify only for free **emergency** care. **U.S. visitors** should note that most domestic health plans (including Medicare and Medicaid) do not provide coverage, and the ones that do often require you to pay for services upfront and file for reimbursement after you return home. You might want to buy international medical coverage from companies such as **United Healthcare SafeTrip** (www.UHCsafetrip.com; ✆ **800/732-5309**) or **Travel Assistance International** (travelassistanceinternational.com; ✆ **410/987-6233**). **Canadians** should check with their provincial health plan offices or call **Health Canada/Santé Canada** (www.hc-sc.gc.ca; ✆ **613/957-2991**) to find out the extent of their coverage and what documentation and receipts to bring home if they are treated overseas. **E.U. nationals** (and nationals of E.E.A. countries and Switzerland) with a European Health Insurance Card (EHIC) from their home country can use it until it expires. If you don't have an EHIC or you can't obtain a Provisional Replacement Certificate (PRC) for it, you may be charged 150% the standard NHS rate for treatment. Norwegians are entitled to medically necessary health care in the U.K.

Hospitals In the U.K., the ER is usually called A&E, or Accident and Emergency. If your need is urgent, dial ✆ **999** (it's free no matter where your phone is registered) rather than risk going to a medical center that doesn't offer A&E. You can search **www.nhs.uk** for the nearest A&E, or go to the 24-hour, walk-in A&E departments at **University College Hospital,** 235 Euston Rd., London NW1 (www.uclh.nhs.uk; ✆ **020/3456-7890;** Tube: Warren Street) or **St Thomas's Hospital** (Westminster Bridge Road, entrance on Lambeth Palace Road, London, SE1; www.guysandstthomas.nhs.uk; ✆ **020/7188-7188;** Tube: Westminster or Waterloo). For less serious needs, visit **Soho NHS Walk-In Centre** (1 Frith St., W1; www.clch.nhs.uk; ✆ **020/7534-6500;** Tube: Tottenham Court Road), which is open Tuesday through Friday 8am to 6pm and Saturday to Sunday 10am to 6pm. You may need to call ahead for a referral.

Inoculations Unless you're arriving from an area known to be suffering from a current epidemic, Inoculations or vaccinations are not required for entry into the U.K., including for Covid-19. You also don't need to furnish a negative Covid-19 test upon entry unless emergency measures have returned.

Insurance You may want special coverage for **apartment stays,** especially if you've plunked down a deposit, and for any **valuables** you may bring with you; airlines are only required to pay up to $2,500 for lost luggage domestically, less for foreign travel. Compare policies at **InsureMyTrip.com** (✆ **800/487-4722**), or contact one of the following reputable companies: **Allianz** (www.allianztravelinsurance.com; ✆ **866/884-3556**); **Generali Global Assistance** (formerly CSA Travel Protection; www.generalitravelinsurance.com; ✆ **800/874-2442**); **Travel Guard** (www.travelguard.com; ✆ **800/826-5248**); or **Travelex** (www.travelexinsurance.com; ✆ **800/228-9792**). Note that most insurers require you to purchase plans soon after you buy your trip and *before* you leave home. If you seek Covid-19-related coverage, make sure it's included in the policy that you purchase, because some exclude it.

Internet Wi-Fi flows freely at pubs, cafes, museums, and nearly all hotels. Sometimes, you will have to fill in an email address to activate it, but often it's a data collection ploy and you can write dummy information. (See box on p. 370.)

Even when you use your own devices, the 2025 Online Safety Act requires age verification for certain content, including some perfectly tame LGBTQ social sites. The UK regulator in charge of verifying you, Ofcom (www.ofcom.org.uk) accomplishes it through methods such as credit card checks, contacting your bank, or scanning facial images to determine age. When a computer looks at your selfie and proclaims you old, that's fun. Privacy advocates have serious issues with the security of this system.

Laundry Launderettes are not easy to find in central London, and expensive hotels will only clean your garment for roughly as much money as it would take to simply buy a new one. Look into the app **Laundryheap** (www.laundryheap.co.uk), which will pick up and drop off to your hotel for free. Prices start at £18 per 6kg (13 lbs.) £1.95 per item for dry cleaning, and £1.45 per item for ironing.

Legal Aid If you find yourself in trouble abroad, contact your consulate or embassy (see "Embassies & Consulates," p. 377). It can advise you of your rights and provide a list of local attorneys (for which you'll have to pay if services are used), but they cannot interfere on your behalf in the English legal process. For questions about U.S. citizens who've been arrested abroad, telephone the **Citizens Emergency Center** of the Bureau of Consular Affairs in Washington, D.C. (✆ **202/501-4444,** or 888/407-4747).

LGBTQ Travelers Gay and lesbian people have equality and marriage rights in England. Public displays of affection are barely noticed in the center of the city, although in the outer suburbs couples should show more restraint. Gay bashings are rare enough to be newsworthy, but it's true that an element of society can, once full of ale or fuzzy political rage, become belligerent. Particularly in parks at night, be aware of your surroundings and give wide berth to gaggles of drunken lads. This advice holds irrespective of your sexuality.

For nightlife planning, a source for information is the free **QX International** (www.qxmagazine.com). Also see nightlife listings on p. 290.

The long-running LGBTQ help center **Switchboard** (switchboard.lgbt; ✆ **0800/0119-100**) exists to help people in crisis, not dish on where the big parties are.

Luggage Storage Useful if you're taking those cheap European flights with steep luggage fees, **Left Baggage** (www.left-baggage.co.uk; ✆ **0800/077-4530**) has locations at Heathrow, Gatwick, and the big railway stations: It costs £15 per item per 24 hours, but will store things longer for more. The apps **Bounce** (bounce.com) and **Luggage Hero** (luggagehero.com), and **Stasher** (stasher.com) arrange with local businesses to keep your bags during business hours for a small hourly fee.

Mail Costs for using the **Royal Mail** vary by size, weight, speed, and format; plug your specifics into the calculator at www.royalmail.com, which also has a branch finder function.

Mobile Phones Anytime you call a mobile phone in Britain, the fee will be higher than calling a landline, although there is no fee to *receive* a call or text.

Apart from renting a phone (not recommended to the casual visitor), many tourists simply enable their international **roaming** feature. North American carrier T-Mobile offers standard packages that include calls and texting for free, although data is limited and throttled unless you pay extra for a special add-on data plan. Depending on your contract, your allowance may be scanty and your provider may bleed you for extra data, so it's crucial to know what your subscription includes and what your limits are. If you don't know, put your phone on airplane mode before you land in the U.K. and only use free Wi-Fi signals.

The other solution, if you have an unlocked phone that uses the GSM system, is to pop into any mobile phone shop or newsstand and buy a cheap **pay-as-you-talk** phone number from a mobile phone store. This method is rapidly losing favor and is increasingly hard to manage, so it's not recommended. But if you must: You'll pay about £5 for a SIM card, which you stick in your phone, and then you buy vouchers to load your new U.K. phone number with as much money as you think you'll use up (no refunds). That will give you a British number, which you can e-mail to everyone back home, that charges local rates (10p–40p per minute). Just call your provider before you leave home to make sure your phone is "unlocked" (last-generation phones are more likely to allow this as a default), so that the British SIM card will function in it. That service is usually free. U.K. mobile providers with pay-as-you-talk deals, all comparable, include **Vodafone** (www.vodafone.com), **O$_2$** (www.o2.co.uk), **Lebara** (www.lebara.co.uk), and **EE** (www.ee.co.uk).

Money British pounds are divided into 100 pennies (p), the plural of which is called "pence." Coins come in 1p, 2p, 5p, 10p, 20p, 50p, £1, and £2 (the 2-pound coin is commonly called a "quid"). Notes come in £5, £10, £20, and £50. The government recently completed a redesign of its money. The current British pound (£1), a small, chunky, gold-colored coin with silver faces, looks round but is actually subtly 12-sided. The previous version, truly round and golden without shiny faces, was phased out in 2017 and is no longer valid. Paper notes were replaced with polymer versions in recent years, so if someone tries to pass you a paper bank note, *refuse it!* If you find yourself holding outdated money and a local bank refuses to exchange it, go to the Bank of England on Threadneedle Street (Tube: Bank) to try to exchange it, but queues are long. Now and then, you'll receive notes printed by the Bank of Scotland; they're valid, but an increase in forgeries means some shops refuse them, so we recommend you decline them as well. Banks will exchange them.

In late 2025, the exchange rate hovered in the vicinity of £1 = US$1.32 but the trials of modern times have thrown that rate into flux; consult a currency exchange website such as **www.oanda.com/currency-converter** or the Oanda or XE apps.

All prices (including at most B&Bs but not at upscale hotels) are listed including tax, so what you see is what you pay. No guesstimating required.

Every visitor should have several sources for money, but cash is still a fail-safe. The simple solution is to pull cash from an ATM upon arrival; rates are the cheapest there. Before leaving home, find out if you need to warn your bank and your credit card issuers that you intend to travel internationally so that they don't place a stop on your account. You may also need to adjust your PIN, because English banks require 4-digit codes. (If you know your PIN as a word, memorize the numerical equivalent.) Most banks hit you with fees of a few pounds each time you withdraw cash, and your own bank may toss in a small fee of its own; gauge for yourself how much you feel comfortable withdrawing at a time to offset that fee. Also ask your bank if it has reciprocal agreements for free withdrawals anywhere.

Paying with **a mobile wallet** such as Google Pay or Apple Pay is fast, but it may only be accepted for individual purchases, generally up to £100.

Traveler's checks are dead—most places reject them—but creditors have come up with **traveler's check cards,** also called **prepaid cards,** which are essentially debit cards loaded with however much money you choose to put on them. They work in ATMs, and should you lose one, you can get your cash back in a matter of hours. You can reload the card mid-trip by calling a number or visiting a website, although there may be fees of a few dollars for ATM transactions. Try **NetSpend** (www.netspend.com; ✆ **866/387-7363**). The cards are not capable of contactless payment, but they can connect to digital wallets on your smartphone that are.

Changing cash is also on the outs. Old-fashioned cambios/bureaux de change are few and far between, although you'll still find a few at the airport and around Leicester Square. If you must change money, better rates are offered by banks (open 9:30am–4pm).

Newspapers & Magazines London offers more publications than one would think a city of its size could support. The broadsheets, ordered from left to right, politically speaking, are the *Guardian*, the *Independent*, the *Daily Telegraph*, and the *Times*. The salmon-colored *Financial Times* covers business. The tabloids are fluffier and more salacious: They include the *Sun*, the *Mirror*, *Daily Star*, the *Daily Mail*, and *Daily Express*. *Time Out* publishes a free listing of events and entertainments, mostly online.

Other popular magazines include the *Big Issue* (written and sold by homeless and formerly homeless people), *Radio Times* (TV listings and celebrity interviews), and *Hello!* and *OK!* (fawning celebrity spreads planted by publicity agents).

Packing For your wallet's sake, pack sparingly! It's not as easy as it used to be to wink your way through the weigh-in. **British Airways,** for example, grants coach passengers a puny 23kg (51 lb.); if you exceed that, you will be smacked with a flat fee of £65/ $100 per flight. Bags over 32kg (71 lb.) will be rejected outright. Some airlines, such as **Virgin Atlantic,** can be ruthless about making sure even your *carry-on* baggage weighs no more than 10kg (22 lb.). If you're taking multiple airlines, stick to the tightest restrictions of the lot. Many airlines (even the no-frills) discount for booking baggage at least 24 hours early, and charge more at the airport.

Pare toiletries to essentials. You're not going to the jungle—you will find staples like toothpaste, contact lens solution, and deodorant everywhere. Women should bring a minimum of makeup; the British don't tend to use very much themselves. Brits are also more likely to wear trousers than blue jeans. If you plan to go clubbing, pack some fashionable duds—Londoners love to look natty. Shorts are usually worn in only the most extreme weather conditions.

You'll be most comfortable if you dress in clothing that layers well. Even in winter, London's air can be clammy, and dressing too warmly can become uncomfortable. No matter what the average temperature is (see weather chart on p. 371), the air can grow cool after the sun sets; plan for that. A compact umbrella is wise year-round, as is an outer coat that repels water, because you never know when you're going to find yourself in one of those misty rains that make the British Isles so lush and green.

Don't bring illegal drugs (duh) or medical marijuana (duh), and also leave the pepper spray and mace at home; they're banned in the U.K.

Passports To enter the United Kingdom, all U.S. citizens, Canadians, Australians, New Zealanders, and South Africans must have a passport valid through their length of stay. No visa is required. A passport will allow you to stay in the country for up to 6 months. The immigration officer may also want to see proof of your intention to return to your point of origin (usually a round-trip ticket) and of visible means of support while you're in Britain (credit cards work). If you're planning to fly from the U.S. or Canada to the U.K. and then on to a country that requires a visa (India, for example), secure that visa before you arrive in Britain.

Pharmacies Every police station keeps a list of pharmacies (chemists) that are open 24 hours. Also try **Zafash,** a rare chemist that is open until midnight (233–235 Old Brompton Rd., SW5; www.zafashpharmacy.co.uk; ✆ **020/7373-3506** or 020/7373-7755**;** daily 9am–10pm; Tube: Earl's Court). For non-emergency health advice, call the NHS at ✆ **111.**

Police Dial ✆ **999,** or 112 if the matter is serious. London has two official police forces: the City of London police (www.cityoflondon.police.uk), whose remit covers the "Square Mile" and its 8,600 residents; and the Metropolitan Police ("the Met"), which covers the rest of the capital. Opening hours for all the Met's local police stations are listed at www.met.police.uk. In a non-emergency, you can contact your local police station by dialing ✆ **101.** Losses, thefts, and other criminal matters should be reported at the nearest police station immediately. You will be given a crime number, which your travel insurer will request if you make a claim against any losses.

Safety Crossing the street is the most perilous thing you'll do. Always look down to see which way traffic is flowing—the street will be painted "Look right" or "Look left" so you'll know. Also, a steady-lit green man on the crosswalk signal means it's safe, but when the green man flashes, do not begin crossing—it means cars are about to gun it again.

Few places in London are unsafe. Neighborhoods that might be called sketchy are usually distant from the

Tube lines, and they only feel tense after dark, when shops close. Simply be sensitive to who's around you and you'll do fine.

Phone snatching rates have been skyrocketing since 2020. Each day, dozens of people on the sidewalks (here, called *pavements*) are so absorbed in their smartphones that they don't notice the moped-driving device snatchers zoom up, seize their phone, and speed off. Thieves will even trick you into taking out your phone by pretending to be friendly and ask you to take out your phone to add them on social media. Be protective about where you use your phone and, of course, where you put your cash and what you leave sitting in the open.

Pickpocketing, including slashed bags, is also on the rise, particularly near major tourist attractions (Buckingham Palace, Westminster Abbey) and on the Tube. Don't allow yourself to be distracted by any strangers, even if they look like innocent elderly folks. Stay alert even if someone merely asks the time—modern thieves operate in teams and your valuables might be wrapped up and slipped in a post box before you even have a chance to notice the loss.

London is always on the lookout for terrorists, and it has been since the days of IRA violence. It's why you won't find many rubbish bins in Tube stations. Don't leave bags unattended, even for seconds, or security may take it.

Guns are banned in London—even on most police officers—so you don't often see the kind of violence taken for granted in the United States. Londoners cite knife crime as a problem, but most victims are young men who themselves carry knives. Some male tourists have gotten fleeced at "hostess bars" in Soho. If you do suffer a lapse of judgment and accept the barker's invitation to go into one, understand that you might have cash exacted by lunkheaded yobs with tattooed fingers.

We advise against hiring **cycle pedicabs** that congregate in tourist districts at night because we have heard too many reports of passengers being ripped off or threatened in them. The city is reportedly figuring out how to regulate them, but they're also annoying and cause congestion.

Should you find yourself on the business end of the legal system, you can get advice and referrals to lawyers from **Legal Aid Agency** (www.gov.uk/legal-aid). Crime victims can receive volunteer legal guidance and emotional fortification from **Victim Support** (www.victimsupport.org.uk; ✆ **0808/168-9111**). In the event of a sexual assault, find help through the **Rape Crisis Federation** (www.rapecrisis.org.uk; ✆ **0808/902-9999;** some caseworkers will only assist females).

Senior Travel Don't hide your age! Seniors in England—usually classified as those age 60 and over—are privy to all kinds of price breaks, from lower admission prices at museums to a third off rail tickets (to apply for the **Senior Railcard,** go to www.senior-railcard.co.uk). You may hear seniors referred to as OAPs, which stands for Old Age Pensioners, although that acronym is falling out of use—perhaps because it's rare to find a solvent pension fund anymore. Don't be offended if you're referred to as a "geezer"—in England, it's a compliment, meaning a fun-loving (if sometimes rowdy) bloke.

If you're over 50, you can join **AARP** (601 E St. NW, Washington, DC, 20049; www.aarp.org; ✆ **202/434-3525**) to wrangle discounts on hotels, airfare, and car rentals. Elderhostel's well-respected **Road Scholar** (www.roadscholar.org; ✆ **800/454-5768**) runs many classes and programs in London designed to delve into literature, history, the arts, and music. Packages last from a week to a month and include airfare, lodging, and meals.

Smoking Smoking is prohibited by law in any enclosed workplace, including museums, pubs, public transportation, and restaurants. If in doubt, ask permission.

Student Travel Have ID on hand, and always mention you're a student—it'll save you cash. Attractions gladly offer discounts of around 25% for full-time students. However, your high school or university ID may not cut it where clerks haven't heard of your school: Before leaving home, obtain a recognized ID such as the **International Student Identity Card** (ISIC; www.isic.org). Those 25 and under who are not in school can obtain an **International Youth Travel Card,** also through ISIC, which performs many of the same tricks as a student discount card.

Taxes Prices of all goods in the U.K. are quoted inclusive of taxes. Since 2011 the national value-added tax (**VAT**) has stood at 20%. This is included in all hotel and restaurant bills, and in the price of most items you purchase.

Options for tourists to get some VAT refunded for certain shopping purchases have changed. Refunds are no longer possible at the airport. See p. 261 for details and see the latest information on www.gov.uk/tax-on-shopping/taxfree-shopping.

Telephones When dialing a number in this book from abroad, precede it with your country's international prefix (in the U.S. and Canada, it's 011), add the U.K.'s country code (44) and drop the first zero in the number.

To make an **international call** from Britain, dial the international access code (**00**), then the country code, then the area code, and finally the local number. When calling from a mobile phone, dial the full number including area code.

Directory assistance is at www.bt.com or ✆ **118-500.** Local calls start with 020.

The main **toll-free** ("freephone") prefixes are 0800, 0808, and 0500. Numbers starting with 07 are usually for mobile phones and will be charged at a higher rate. Numbers starting with 09 are premium-rate calls that will usually be very expensive (around £1.50/minute) and may not even work from abroad.

Many attractions, hotel companies, and services have changed their standard phone numbers to profit-generating ones that charge for every minute you call them. You often can't reach 0845, 0870, and 0871 numbers (charged at 10p a minute or less) from abroad, and when you can, you're charged more. Use the Web instead to get information.

The majority of London's **payphones** are gone or derelict. You can barely find a working one, let alone rely upon them.

Phonecards, though rarely used today, can be an economical method for both international and national calls. They are reusable until the total value has expired. Cards can be purchased from newsstands and post offices, and offer rates of a few pence per minute to most countries.

Hotels routinely add outrageous surcharges onto calls made from your room. Rather than dial directly using a hotel phone, use the Wi-Fi to make Internet calls.

Time London is generally 5 hours ahead of New York City and Toronto, 8 hours ahead of Los Angeles, 11 hours behind Auckland, and 9 hours behind Sydney. It is 1 hour behind western continental Europe. Greenwich Mean Time is London time.

Tipping **Waiters** should receive 10% to 15% of the bill unless service is already included—*always* check the menu or bill to see if service was already added. If a restaurant charges an "admin fee" or a cover, that is not a tip. At **pubs,** tipping isn't customary unless you receive waiter service (not food drop-off). Fine **hotels** may levy a service charge, but at the finest ones, grease the staff with a pound here and there. Staff at B&Bs and family-run hotels don't expect tips. **Bartenders** and **housekeepers** need not be tipped. There's no need to tip **taxicab drivers** but most people round up to the next £1, although a 10% to 15% tip is becoming increasingly standard.

Toilets London doesn't have enough of them. Washrooms can be found at any free museum in this guide, any department store, any pub or busy restaurant (though it's polite to buy something), and at Piccadilly Circus, Green Park and Bank Tube stations (find more at: content.tfl.gov.uk/toilets-map.pdf). Train stations may also have toilets; they're free at Charing Cross, Paddington, London Bridge, and Waterloo but may charge about 50p at Victoria. At Baker Street, they charge men but not women. On weekends, open-air *pissoirs* for men are placed throughout the West End.

VAT See "Taxes," above.

Visas No E.U. nationals require a visa to visit the U.K. Visas are also not required for travelers from Australia, Canada, New Zealand, or the U.S. To be sure that hasn't changed, search "visa" at **www.gov.uk** long before your travel dates. The usual permitted stay is 90 days or fewer for tourists, although some nationalities are granted stays of up to 6 months. If you plan to work or study, though, or if you're traveling on a passport from another country, you'll need to obtain the correct paperwork.

Although you may not need a visa, as of 2025 everyone does require an **Electronic Visa Authorisation (ETA),** which pre-screens visitors to assure the UK government that you don't truly need a visa. (The U.S. and EU do the same thing to tourists, too.) ETAs cost £16 and last for 2 years of multiple entries. Although some airlines will push you to use third-party partners that add extra fees, it can be handled without added fees in about 10 minutes through the free **UK ETA** app. Visitors 10 and older must scan their face, take a selfie, and have the passport they will be using for travel. If you can't use the apps, there's a webpage where it could take longer: apply-for-an-eta.homeoffice.gov.uk/apply/electronic-travel-authorisation/how-to-apply

Visitor Information Three official information units supported by British taxes are set up to help tourists, but only online: **Visit Britain** (www.visitbritain.com); **Visit England** (www.visitengland.com); and **Visit London** (www.visitlondon.com). The only official information bureau with a public office is across the road from St Paul's Cathedral north of Millennium Bridge: The **City of London Information Centre** (St Paul's Churchyard; www.thecityofldn.com/directory/city-of-london-information-centre; ✆ **020/7332-1456;** Mon–Sat 9:30am–5:30pm, Sun 10am–4pm) sells attraction tickets and Oyster cards, runs tours, and supplies brochures and counsel for day trips throughout the country. It publishes walking tours, a free City Visitor Trail audio walking tour (www.thecityofldn.com/article/city-visitor-trail), and children's discovery trail maps.

Excellent independent sources for things to learn and things to do include **Londonist.com, CultureCalling.com,** and **TimeOut.com/London**.

Women Travelers First and foremost, lone women should avoid riding in **unlicensed London taxicabs,** especially at night. Flag down a black cab, hail one via the apps **Gett** or **FreeNow** (set your app up with your credit card ahead of time), or call a minicab instead. **Addison Lee** (www.addisonlee.com; ✆ **020/7387-8888**) has a huge, efficient fleet, and will text you the registration plate of your cab for added security. Its free app is faster than the phone for arranging rides.

A club and not an agency, **Women Welcome Women Worldwide** (www.womenwelcomewomen.org.uk; ✆ **07716/922529**) connects travelers worldwide and costs £47 a year to join.

Index

See also Accommodations and Restaurant indexes, below.

General Index

A

B

C

Q

R

S

T

U

V

W

Y

Accommodations

Restaurants

Photo Credits

Front cover: Taljat David / Shutterstock; p. i: Tartezy / Shutterstock; p. iii: Pajor Pawel / Shutterstock; p. 2: Photo.eccles / Shutterstock; p. 3: Courtesy of Young V&A / Luke Hayes; p. 4: © Chapter of St Paul's / Graham Lacdao; p. 5: Courtesy of The Goring / BEN CARPENTER; p. 6: Courtesy of Andrew Edmunds; p. 7: Courtesy of 10 Greek Street; p. 8: Courtesy of Claridges / James McDonald; p. 9: Courtesy of The Hoxton Shoreditch; p. 10. Courtesy of Postal Museum & Mail Rail / Tommy Ga-Ken Wan; p. 11, top: Courtesy of Hidden London at London Transport Museum / Alick Cotterill; p. 11, bottom: Chris Seddon / Shutterstock; p. 12: Courtesy of The British Library / Sam Walton; p. 13: Alex Segre / Shutterstock; p. 14: Robert Mullan / Shutterstock; p. 18: © Historic Royal Palaces / Richard Lea-Hair; p. 19: © The Dean and Chapter of Westminster / David Lambert; p. 20: Melissa Baucom; p. 21: © Chapter of St Paul's / Graham Lacdao; p. 22: Ewelina W / Shutterstock; p. 23. Courtesy of Southbank Centre / India Roper-Evans; p. 24, top: Pat_Hastings / Shutterstock; p. 24, bottom: Courtesy of Coram's Fields; p. 26, top: Courtesy of Victoria and Albert Museum / David Parry; p. 26, bottom: Courtesy of Brixton Village; p. 29: Stefan Constantin 22 / Shutterstock; p. 31, top: Courtesy of Spitalfields Market / Brendan Bell; p. 31, bottom: William Barton / Shutterstock; p. 33, top: Songquan Deng / Shutterstock; p. 33, bottom: Eyesonmilan / Shutterstock; p. 40: Jason Cochran; p. 45: Courtesy of St. Pancras Renaissance / J Filipe Wiens; p. 47: Courtesy of The Great Northern Hotel; p. 51: Courtesy of The Haymarket Hotel / Simon Brown; p. 52: Courtesy of L'Oscar / La Réserve Genève; p. 54: Courtesy of The Henrietta Experimental Hotel / Patrick Locqueneux & Mr Tripper; p. 59: Courtesy of St. Ermin's Hotel; p. 60: Courtesy of Lime Tree Hotel; p. 62: Courtesy of The Beaumont / Antony Weller; p. 64: Courtesy of Montcalm Mayfair; p. 66: Courtesy of Inhabit Southwick; p. 69: Courtesy of Brown's Hotel / Janos Grapow; p. 70: Courtesy of Bankside / Peter Jackson; p. 73: Courtesy of Canopy by Hilton London City / John Athimaritis; p. 74: Courtesy of Lost Property / Viktor Kery; p. 78: Courtesy of The July London Victoria / Helen Cathcart; p. 86: Courtesy of Clipstone / Sam Harris; p. 88: Courtesy of Honey & Co. Bloomsbury; p. 91: Courtesy of The Ivy; p. 93: Courtesy of Brasserie Zedel; p. 95: Courtesy of Grodon's Wine Bar / Paul Marc Mitchell; p. 96, top: Courtesy of Mildreds / Hayley Kelsing; p. 96, bottom: Courtesy of Rasa Sayang; p. 97: Courtesy of Speedboat Bar; p. 98: Courtesy of J. Sheekey / Jean Cazals; p. 99: Courtesy of The Barbary / Mickaël A. Bandassak; p. 100: Courtesy of Flat Iron / Justin DeSouza; p. 101, top: Courtesy of Browns; p. 101, bottom: Courtesy of Bancone / Milly Fletcher; p. 103: Courtesy of 1 Hotel Mayfair / Jon Day; p. 107, top: Maggie Jones; p. 107, bottom: Courtesy of Restaurant Story; p. 112: Courtesy of The Clove Club / Anton Rodriguez; p. 114: Courtesy of Beigel Bake / © Blake Ezra Photography Ltd. 2022; p. 115: Courtesy of

Poppies / Haydon Perrior; p. 118, top: Courtesy of Eataly; p. 118, bottom: Courtesy of Maltby Street Market; p. 119: Courtesy of Guinness Open Gate Brewery / Rob Jones; p. 120: Courtesy of Spitalfields Market / Brendan Bel; p. 123, top: Courtesy of The Devonshire / Ashley Palmer-Watts; p. 123, bottom: David; p. 127, top: Courtesy of Green King; p. 127, bottom: Courtesy of Green King; p. 128: Courtesy of The Ten Bells; p. 131: Courtesy of The British Library; p. 136: Jeafish Ping / Shutterstock; p. 139: Courtesy of The Foundling Museum / Ed Lyon; p. 141: Courtesy of Petrie Museum / UCL / ©O.Siddons 2020; p. 144: Courtesy of The Courtauld Gallery London / Hufton+Crow; p. 146: Courtesy of London Transport Museum; p. 148: Ale Argentieri / Shutterstock; p. 151: Courtesy of The National Portrait Gallery / Jim Stephenson; p. 154: Courtesy of The Benjamin Franklin House; p. 157: Courtesy of Churchill War Rooms / Richard Ash; p. 157: Tomas Marek / Shutterstock; p. 160: Courtesy of Spencer House / © Jarrold Publishing; p. 162: © The Dean and Chapter of Westminster; p. 168: Jonathan Konrath; p. 170: Melissa Baucom; p. 173: Melissa Baucom; p. 174: Alice-photo / Shutterstock; p. 177: Ralu Spatareanu / Shutterstock; p. 182: Courtesy of Imperial War Museum London / Andrew Tunnard; p. 183: Courtesy of Old Operating Theatre Museum and Herb Garret; p. 185: Melissa Baucom; p. 187: Courtesy of HMS Belfast / Andrew Tunnard; p. 190: © Chapter of St Paul's. Photo by Graham Lacdao; p. 191: Cowardlion / Shutterstock; p. 192: Nature's Charm / Shutterstock; p. 197: Chris Lawrence Travel / Shutterstock; p. 199: Courtesy of St Magnus the Martyr; p. 202: Museum of Docklands / John Chase; p. 204: Courtesy of V&A Storehouse / Kemka Ajoku; p. 205: Nui7711 / Shutterstock; p. 206: © National Maritime Museum, Greenwich, London, 2022; p. 208: Courtesy of Chiswick House and Gardens / Andre Pattenden; p. 210: Courtesy of Dulwich Picture Gallery / Agnese Sanvito; p. 211: Goga18128 / Shutterstock; p. 214: Courtesy of Fuller's Brewery Tours / Kin Ho; p. 220: J Thomas Salas / Shutterstock; p. 222: chrisdorney / Shutterstock; p. 224, top: Courtesy of Open Air Theatre / Pamela Raith; p. 224, bottom: Andy Wasley / Shutterstock; p. 227: Courtesy of Brit Movie Tours; p. 228: Courtesy of Eating London Tours; p. 229: Courtesy of In the Footsteps of Mudlarks; p. 230: Courtesy of Look Up London; p. 231: Courtesy of City Cruises / Mark Hakansson; p. 237: Courtesy of Coal Drop Yards / John Sturrock; p. 239: Courtesy of Leadenhall Market; p. 240: Courtesy of Fortnum and Mason / Natasa Leoni; p. 242: BasPhoto / Shutterstock; p. 244, top: Courtesy of LASSCo / Danielle Dietrich; p. 244, bottom: Meghan Lamb; p. 246: Courtesy of Stanfords; p. 248: Alan Kean / Shutterstock; p. 249: Courtesy of John Smedley; p. 250: Courtesy of Luna & Curious; p. 252: Courtesy of Berry Bros. & Rudd / Krystian Krzewinski; p. 255: Courtesy of Labour and Wait; p. 256, top: Courtesy of Choosing Keeping / Hikaru Funnell; p. 256, bottom: Melissa Baucom; p. 258: Courtesy of Brixton Village; p. 259: I Wei Huang / Shutterstock; p. 260: Eduardo Dreizzen / Shutterstock; p. 261: Courtesy of Spitalfields Market / Brendan Bell; p. 265: Courtesy of ABBA Voyage / Johan Persson; p. 266: Courtesy of The Bush Theatre / Tristram Kenton; p. 267: Courtesy of Donmar Warehouse / Manuel Harlan; p. 268: Courtesy of Royal National Theatre / Brinkhoff-Moegenburg; p. 269: Courtesy of Southbank Centre / Morley von Sternberg; p. 271: Courtesy of Donald Strachan; p. 273: Courtesy of The King's Head; p. 275: Courtesy of Kings Place / Nick Rutter; p. 276: Courtesy of Royal Albert Hall / Andy Paradise; p. 278: Courtesy of Ain't Nothin' But / Osmaan Malik; p. 280: Courtesy of Jazz Café / Khris Cowley; p. 282: Courtesy of Scala / P Bourne; p. 284: Courtesy of O_2 / Luke Dyson; p. 286: Courtesy of Pleasance Theatre Islington; p. 288: Courtesy of The Electric Cinema / Tom Mannion; p. 291: Courtesy of Comptons; p. 294: Neil Bussey / Shutterstock; p. 297: S.Borisov / Shutterstock; p. 299: Bill Perry / Shutterstock; p. 300: William Barton / Shutterstock; p. 303: Premier Photo / Shutterstock; p. 304: ParrySuwanitch / Shutterstock; p. 308: chrisdorney / Shutterstock; p. 309: chrisdorney / Shutterstock; p. 311: © Chapter of St Paul's. Photo by Graham Lacdao; p. 312: Courtesy of London + Partners / Jon Reid; p. 313: Pres Panayotov / Shutterstock; p. 319: cktravels.com / Shutterstock; p. 322: William Barton / Shutterstock; p. 324: JJFarq / Shutterstock; p. 327: cktravels.com / Shutterstock; p. 329: Christo mitkov christov / Shutterstock; p. 330: © Visitlondon.com / Jon Reid; p. 333: Jack Pease Photography; p. 336: Alwye / Wiki; p. 337: Courtesy of Visit Bath; p. 338: Courtesy of Visit Bath; p. 339: Courtesy of Visit Bath / Charlotte Harris; 341: e X p o s e / Shutterstock; p. 342: Keith Barnes / Shutterstock; p. 343: ©Blenheim; p. 346: chrisdorney / Shutterstock; p. 347: Paul Hudson / Flickr; p. 348: polymathmo / Shutterstock; p. 350: Alexey Fedorenko / Shutterstock; p. 351: Courtesy of Salisbury Cathedral / Martin Cook; p. 353: Courtesy of Chapter of Canterbury Cathedral / Matt Wilson; back cover: Sven Hansche / Shutterstock.